The NEW Baseball Bible

Notes, Nuggets, Lists, and Legends from Our National Pastime

Dan Schlossberg

SPORTS PUBLISHING

Sports Publishing books may be purchased in bulk at special discounts for sales promotion, corporate gifts, fund-raising, or educational purposes. Special editions can also be created to specifications. For details, contact the Special Sales Department, Sports Publishing, 307 West 36th Street, 11th Floor, New York, NY 10018 or sportspubbooks@skyhorsepublishing.com.

Sports Publishing® is a registered trademark of Skyhorse Publishing, Inc.®, a Delaware corporation.

Visit our website at www.sportspubbooks.com.

10 9 8 7 6 5

Library of Congress Cataloging-in-Publication Data is available on file.

Interior photos courtesy of the author, unless otherwise indicated.

Cover design by Rain Saukas
Cover photo credits: Tom Seaver: Courtesy of Dan Schlossberg
    David Ortiz, Yankees, and Ken Griffey Jr.: AP Photos
    Cy Young and baseball trio: Library of Congress

Print ISBN: 978-1-61321-835-8
Ebook ISBN: 978-1-61321-836-5

Printed in China

To Jen, Ali, and Sam

The best JAS trio on the planet

In appreciation for all the love, laughter, and support

Through thick and thin.

Contents

Foreword

My fans may argue about whether baseball is actually a sport or really just a way for me to implement every known prank or joke I could play on my teammates. Whichever you decide, baseball has been my life and I was blessed with enough talent to hang around for 22 years.

I am probably the only guy revered or feared by managers in eight different cities. My baseball travels started in 1966 with the Angels; after that I played with the White Sox, the A's, the Phillies, the Yankees, the Padres, the Dodgers, the Cubs, and the Dodgers again. Somehow I managed to get four World Series rings and play on eight divisional title–winning teams. Even when I played on losing teams, I always managed to make the guys laugh and have a good time.

Rooming with Jimmy Piersall and lockering next to Dean Chance and Bo Belinsky as a rookie got me off on the wrong foot—or should I say "hotfoot?" Bill Rigney, my first manager, explained the Piersall matchup by saying he didn't want to screw up two rooms. How did he know?

Piersall was a guy who would slide into a base and then squirt the umpire with a water gun. He gained national attention by trotting around the bases backward on his 100th home run. Piersall once hid behind the monuments in Yankee Stadium's center field when our pitcher was getting shelled. Jimmy said he had nine children to feed and didn't want to get hurt.

Danny Ozark, my manager in Philadelphia, spent a lot of time looking for me too. All he had to do was look in his office: I was always on the phone making some kind of deal. Tommy Lasorda knew that better than anyone. In Dodgertown, I once strung a rope from his hotel room door handle to a palm tree, making him miss breakfast before a three-hour spring-training bus trip. For a man who never missed a meal, that was a real trauma.

I really believe laughter is good for the soul. Just ask Ron Cey—he'll tell you about how I cut his locker in half and made it into a doll-size locker, chair and all. I remember when Jerry Reuss and I dragged the infield at Dodger Stadium, Sparky Lyle sat on birthday cakes, Moe Drabowsky used the bullpen phone to call for takeout food, and Gaylord Perry drove hitters and umpires crazy by doctoring the ball so well nobody could catch him. And let's not forget Larry Bowa smashing the toilet in the Phillies' dugout after striking out, Lou Piniella kicking his shoe over the fence after making an out, and Billy Russell not talking to me for a week after he made three errors in a game. He came to the park early the next morning to find that I had sandbagged and roped off the area behind first base where the fans sit so that no one would get hurt by his throws!

When Dan Schlossberg asked me to write the Foreword for this book, I jumped at the chance. Outside of my own best-selling books, *Temporary Insanity*, *Over the Edge*, and *Some of My Best Friends Are Crazy*, I have not found another volume that captures the lighter side of the game so well. Enjoying a good laugh and putting smiles on my teammates' faces is important to me.

My cap's off to Dan Schlossberg, a prolific baseball writer who shares that approach. He knows his stuff and this book proves it. He has a great sense of humor and never takes himself too seriously while still managing to cover all the bases.

Beyond the section on "Baseball's Funny Men" and the zany quotes and anecdotes liberally sprinkled over almost 400 pages, my favorite section deals with the hot dog. It reminds me of when I used to stand in line for Dodger dogs during games.

So grab your favorite drink and a chair and prepare to immerse yourself in the pleasures of America's national pastime.

—Jay Johnstone
Pasadena, California

Preface

[**Editor's Note:** Much of the material found in this book first appeared in *The Baseball Catalog*, which has had nearly a dozen revisions and updates since its initial publication in 1980. Fellow author Alan Schwarz was one of its admirers.]

I became a baseball fan because of *The Baseball Catalog*.

It was July 1980, my 12th birthday. I had watched dozens of Yankees games on WPIX in New York, some NBC Games of the Week, some "This Week in Baseball" with Mel Allen. I'd bought my first packs of Topps baseball cards and begun to memorize the statistics on the back. But I still knew nothing about the history of this wonderful game. My father went to the bookstore, scanned the shelves, and swung. Boy, did he knock it out of the park!

The Baseball Catalog opened up a whole new world—well beyond the legends of Ty Cobb, Ted Williams, and the Boys of Summer Dodgers, but little anecdotes and factoids as delightful and downright weird as the game itself. Hank Aaron blasted a home run onto the roof of Sportsman's Park in St. Louis but was ruled out because his foot had been out of the batter's box? Cool! Edd Roush swung a 46-ounce bat? Are you kidding me? Then, some pages later, there it was—my first glimpse of Willie Mays's over-the-shoulder catch. Whoa! Saddled with glasses as thick as first base, I was particularly fond of the bit on George (Specs) Toporcer, who in 1921 became the first fielder to wear the tools of myopia.

There were the basics, of course, my Baseball Trivia 101: Johnny Vander Meer's consecutive no-hitters, Bill Wambsganss's unassisted triple play in the World Series, the rainout in Houston's very roofed Astrodome. But it went so much farther.

Even for today's media members, pickled in the game's 150 years of trivia, this book—now called *The New Baseball Bible*—should be required reading. When two balls somehow find themselves in play—which actually happens about once a year—they could refer to the 1914 afternoon when a Federal League batter hit a line drive right into a pile of fresh baseballs behind the mound, scattering them all over the infield while the batter circled the bases. And did you know that in 1952, the Pirates were allowed to return their starting catcher to a game after their backup catcher got hurt because the Cubs manager said it was OK? Guaranteed that not one baseball writer today, and probably no executives or even umpires, knows that one.

From riots and rule changes, stats to superstitions, these little tidbits cannot be found in any book other than Dan Schlossberg's masterpiece. And now it has been updated to include all that has taken place in recent decades. Joe Maddon ordering his pitcher to walk Josh Hamilton with the bases loaded. Lorenzo Cain hitting cross-handed in high school because he didn't know better. Ron Wright getting three at-bats in his entire career but making six outs—striking out, hitting into a double play, and hitting into a triple play.

I actually knew Ron Wright. I interviewed him as a young baseball writer while he was a prospect for the Class A Durham Bulls. I wound up covering baseball for two decades, writing two books and thousands of articles, always trying to share the joy of this glorious and goofy sport with readers. I learned to do that right here, soaking in this revision of *The Baseball Catalog*, my first and favorite baseball book of all time.

—Alan Schwarz
New York, NY
Author, *The Numbers Game*

Acknowledgments

Gathering the graphics for this book took years. Some of those who provided invaluable assistance have changed jobs, retired, or passed away. But their names remain on this list in grateful appreciation.

Artists: John Anderson, James Fiorentino, Ronnie Joyner, Bob Laughlin, Margie Lawrence, Charlie McGill, Lou Mercurio, Thomas Salomon, Bill Purdom and the other artists of Bill Goff's GoodSportsArt.com.

Baseball personalities: Bobby Cox, Moe Drabowsky, Ernie Harwell, Waite Hoyt, Billy Hunter, Monte Irvin, Ralph Kiner, Clyde King, and Frank Lane.

Collectors: Kevin Barnes, Barry Halper, Duke Hott, Jason Hyman, Bill Jacobowitz, John Kain, Clay Marston, Bill Mazeika, Michael Mercurio, Tom Reid, and A. Kent Sykes.

Cooperstown colleagues: Jim Gates, Brad Horn, John Horne, Jeff Idelson, Craig Muder, and Bruce Markusen of the National Baseball Hall of Fame and Museum.

Editors: Walter Anderson, *Parade*; Rick Cerrone, *Baseball Magazine*; Irwin Cohen, *The Baseball Bulletin*; Joyce Jack, *Vista/USA*; Tim McQuay, *USA Today Sports Weekly*; Murray Olderman, Newspaper Enterprise Association; Phil Patton, East/West Network; Milton Richman, United Press International; Linda Roberts, *Carte Blanche*; C. C. Johnson Spink, *The Sporting News*; and Burdette C. Stoddard, *The Detroit News*.

Photographers: Mel Bailey, Ray Boetel, Wanda Chirnside, Tom DiPace, Laura Gaynor, Allen Gross, Joe Licata, Bill Menzel, and Barbara Morgen.

Publicists and executives: Seth Abraham, Marty Appel, John Blundell, Steve Brener, Bob Brown, Larry Cancro, Bob Chandler, Larry Chiasson, Hal Childs, Pat Courtney, Bill Crowley, Blake Cullen, John Dittrich, Randy Donaldson, Katy Feeney, Bob Fishel, Mel Franks, Monique Giroux, Matt Gould, Rich Griffin, Bill Guilfoile, Brad Hainje, Tim Hamilton, Jay Horwitz, Monte Irvin, Tom Mee, Phyllis Merhige, Adrienne Midgley, Mickey Morabito, Sharon Pannozzo, Buck Peden, Arthur Richman, Jim Schultz, Glen Serra, Larry Shenk, Tom Skibosh, Jim Small, Ken Smith, Stu Smith, Howie Starkman, Andy Strasberg, Don Unferth, Dean Vogelaar, Chris Wheeler, Rick White, and Ethan Wilson.

Project partners: Jay Johnstone, who could pinch hit for me anytime, and longtime friend and professional colleague Bob Ibach, who often has.

SABR friends: Marc Appelman, Evelyn Begley, Bob Davids, Morris Eckhouse, Vince Gennaro, Cliff Kachline, Doug Lyons, Perry Barber, Howie Siegel, and John Thorn.

Skyhorse, parent company of Sports Publishing: acquisitions editor Julie Ganz and publicist Jake Klein.

Special thanks: Literary agent Rob Wilson and independent sports publicist Ira Silverman.

Super helpful: N.P. Allerup, Pabst Beer; Sy Berger, Phil Carter, Heather Greenberg, Clay Luraschi, and Alexis Melisi, The Topps Company; Judy Bradley, Rawlings Sporting Goods; Kathy Casper, PGA National Resort & Spa; Bennett Curry and P.J. Shelley, Hillerich & Bradsby Company; Bob Faller, The Otesaga Resort and Spa; Morgan Johnston and Sharon Jones, jetBlue; J.Y. Foster, Fair Play Scoreboards; James E. Holland and Debbie Mirandi, attorneys; Larry Horwitz and Heather Taylor, Historic Hotels of America; Jim Johnston, Descente Sporting Goods; Justin Kanoya, Upper Deck Card Company; Maggie Linton, Sirius XM Satellite Radio; Chris Lucas and Ed Lucas, authors; John Maclean, Sofia Hotel, San Diego; David Maurer and Bruce Campbell, Insty-Prints; Steve Trevor, All Star Vacation Homes; Mitch and Matt Palin, Minuteman Press; Robert D. Opie, publisher; Dr. Jim Parkes; Personalized First Day Covers; and Lynn Small, United Airlines.

Supporters: Phyllis Deutsch, Ali Nolan, Sophie Nolan, Jenny O'Rourke, Samantha Schlossberg.

Introduction

Woody Allen once produced a movie called *Everything You Wanted to Know About Sex but Were Afraid to Ask.*

That concept, coupled with the old-time graphics of *The Sporting News* and *The Old Farmer's Almanac*, were the driving forces behind this book.

First produced as *The Baseball Catalog* in 1980, when it was a Book of the Month Club alternate, it has had numerous revisions since. The most recent was a 2002 paperback called *The Baseball Almanac: Big Bodacious Book of Baseball.*

In the 15 years since, the baseball world has undergone cataclysmic changes. Each league now has three five-team divisions, unbalanced schedules, and daily interleague games. Ballparks have been built, records have fallen, and new stars have emerged.

But the game is basically the same one Alexander Cartwright created in 1846, three decades before the advent of the National League signaled the start of organized professional baseball.

Although it is physically impossible to produce a book covering everything that transpired on and off the field since Cartwright's day, this volume includes items never published previously—including many photographs, illustrations, and artifacts collected over decades of involvement in the game.

Suffice to say that *The New Baseball Bible* was not just written; it was assembled like a giant jigsaw puzzle.

This volume runs the gamut from the Cincinnati Red Stockings to the Arizona Diamondbacks. But it emphasizes the good old days before revenue-raising gimmicks threatened to compromise the integrity of America's national pastime.

During those glory years, there were two eight-team leagues, winners went straight to the World Series, and games were played on real grass illuminated by the sun. Night games on weekends or during the postseason were taboo and tickets were cheaper than today's ballpark franks.

You can't quite smell the hot dogs when you pick up this book, but you can come pretty darn close.

Beyond the exploits of the players, teams, and executives documented here are such off-the-field and off-the-wall characters as the goat owner who cursed the Cubs, the peanut vendor who made the longest Opening Day toss, the woman who struck out Babe Ruth, and the blind sportscaster who told the commissioner he had all the qualifications to be a major league umpire!

Hilda Chester, Schottzie, and Morganna are included too, along with the two Bob Millers of the 1962 Mets and the two Rick Ce(r)rones of the 1997 Yankees.

Putting this book together was a process that took years and involved talking to Ralph Kiner about being the biggest star on a bad ballclub, Monte Irvin about life in the Negro Leagues, and Clyde King about wartime spring training in the north. It also meant listening to Warren Spahn and Juan Marichal discuss their 16-inning duel—a 1963 marathon both refused to leave before Willie Mays settled the issue with a solo home run that represented the only run.

The idea here is to inspire older, more traditional fans but also to woo the younger generation back from its flirtation with the faster sports of basketball and hockey. As Bill Veeck once said, "Baseball is meant to be savored but not gulped."

Sport Shirt Bill was right on the mark.

When I became a baseball fan in 1957, Dwight D. Eisenhower was president of the United States and the Milwaukee Braves beat the New York Yankees in the World Series. They got there without designated hitters, interleague games, and endless rounds of playoffs.

I watched with my father, Ezra Schlossberg, who turned down the sound on our old black-and-white Zenith and explained the nuances of the game to a son who was eager to learn.

The lessons stuck, especially after he took me to Yankee Stadium a year later for my first game, with the Yankees hosting the Washington Senators.

I knew I wanted to write about baseball long before I enrolled in the Newhouse School of Public Communications at Syracuse University. What a kick it was when I discovered later that I could even earn money writing the backs of the same baseball cards I used to purchase!

My first baseball interview happened when I was a high school senior. As sports editor of *The Hilltop Star* at Passaic (NJ) High School, I arranged to meet Bobby Bragan, manager of the lame-duck 1965 Milwaukee Braves, at Shea Stadium. I still remember his gray road flannels adorned with red script numbers and letters and the white "M" on his red-and-blue cap.

Some memories never fade.

The New Baseball Bible is meant to be a book of memories. It celebrates the best, the worst, and the most unusual aspects of the game and the people who played it.

Pretty enough to reside on a coffee table, it is also practical enough to leave in a bathroom. Pick it up anywhere, flip the pages in any direction, and smiles will flow.

That's especially true in the brief Jay Johnstone foreword. He cultivated a reputation as an All-Star prankster, documented his adventures in three separate books of his own, and is still regarded as a legend in the art of practical jokes. The list of colorful characters also includes Chipper Jones, Puddin' Head Jones, Vinegar Bend Mizell, and hundreds of others whose monikers make sportswriting so much fun. Babe Ruth alone had a half-dozen.

Ruth could hit, pitch, and carouse with the best of all time, thereby earning plenty of exposure in the pages that follow. But his polar opposite, Hank Aaron, broke most of his baseball records even though he had the additional burdens of night ball, relief pitching, coast-to-coast travel, television publicity, and a torrent of threats and hate mail sparked by his race.

Ruth and Aaron are here but so is Francisco Cabrera, a third-string catcher whose two-run single won a pennant in the last inning of the last game before the 1992 World Series. Such

unexpected events help make baseball the great game it is.

As Joaquin Andujar, when asked for a one-word description of the game, said, "Youneverknow."

In addition to players, managers, and executives, this book pays homage to the presidents, movie stars, and other celebrities who contributed to the lore of the game. Baseball knows no party lines. It welcomes men like Ronald Reagan, who used the game as a springboard to the White House, and Jimmy Carter, a rabid Braves fan who always wore his Atlanta hat in the ballpark.

This volume even attemps to fix a few twisted facts from the films *Field of Dreams* and *42*.

Before the advent of the computer age, keeping facts straight was an uncertain science. But an organization called The Society for American Baseball Research [SABR] has done herculean work in repairing erroneous baseball records, espousing forgotten history, and providing a powerful online forum for nearly 7,000 rabid fans, writers, researchers, historians, and educators. My membership, which began more than 40 years ago, has been rewarding both personally and professionally.

Colleagues and SABRmetricians who thumb through these pages may disagree with names, dates, or records, especially pertaining to the game's early years when games were scored in pencil and reporting was more flowery than accurate. Constructive criticism is always welcome—especially with an eye toward future editions—but getting those early records straight is no easy task. My theory for this book was simple: when sources disagreed, a best-of-three rule settled the score.

For the most part, the illustrations, captions, and sidebars herein tell the story of the game well, covering as many bases as possible.

Because this volume could have been called *Baseball Information Please*, there's a detailed index designed for historians, researchers, and just plain fans.

Like me.

—Dan Schlossberg
Fair Lawn, NJ

Chapter 1

The early game was definitely different, with fielders above not even wearing gloves. Future Hall of Famers Cap Anson and Connie Mack are also in this illustration from the *Police Gazette*.

Beginnings of Baseball

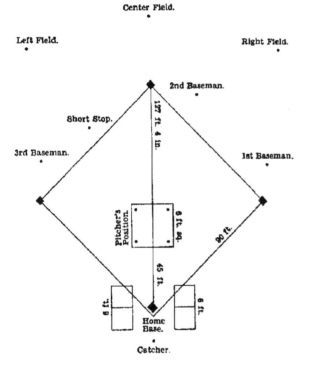

Base Ball at Hoboken

New York, July 6, 1853. Friend P. —The first friendly game of the season, between the Gotham and Knickerbocker Base Ball Clubs, was played on the grounds of the latter. The game was commenced on Friday the 1st, but owing to the storm had to be postponed, the Knickerbockers making nine aces to two of the Gotham.

British Origin of Baseball

In Spalding's *Base Ball Guide of 1903*, English-born editor Henry Chadwick traced the origin of the game to the British sports of rounders, town ball, and a third game called old cat.

"More than 70 years ago, when I was a schoolboy in England," he wrote, "my favorite field sport was the game of rounders. This was played with an ordinary ball and with stout, round sticks as bats.

"After school time, we boys would proceed to the nearest playing field, select a smooth portion of it, and lay out the ground for a contest. This was easily done by placing four stones, or posts, in position as base stations, and by digging a hole in the ground where the batsman had to stand.

"We then tossed for sides and innings and started the game. Custom made the rules of play, as there was no written code to govern the game."

In the 18th century, shortly before the American Revolution, a poem called "Base Ball" appeared in *A Little Pretty Pocket Book*. It was first published in Great Britain in 1744 and reprinted in Worcester, Massachusetts, in 1787. It read:

> *The ball once struck off,*
> *Away flies the boy*
> *To the next destined point,*
> *And then home with joy.*

These early accounts cast considerable doubt on the long-standing theory that Abner Doubleday "invented" baseball at the sleepy village of Cooperstown, New York, in 1839. Though a 1907 special commission lent credence to the Doubleday story—perhaps in an attempt to give America credit for the game's origin—later research indicates Doubleday was a plebe at West Point in 1839 and probably did not get to Cooperstown that year.

Alexander Cartwright: Father of Baseball

The Baseball Hall of Fame in Cooperstown gives Alexander Cartwright the title "Father of Modern Base Ball." That inscription decorates his plaque in the Hall of Fame's gallery.

Cartwright was a teller at the Union Bank of New York in 1845 when he organized the first regular team, the Knickerbockers, and wrote rules to govern the sport. A talented draftsman, he set bases 90 feet apart, established nine players on a side, three outs per inning, and an unchangeable batting order.

The loosely organized games played at the time consisted of teams with 11 to 20 players each. Bases were made of stakes, stones, or sand-filled sacks that could be kicked away by fielders. Runners were put out—literally—when fielders plunked them in the middle of the back with the baseball.

Cartwright developed the concept of a nine-inning game later. The first game played under his rules ended when the New York Nine scored its 21st run (then called an ace) in the fourth inning (called a hand). New York added two more, the Knickerbockers took their final turn at bat, and the game ended in a 23–1 defeat for the home team. The site was the Elysian Fields, Hoboken, New Jersey, on June 19, 1846.

A talented pitcher, Cartwright served as umpire in that first game. His goal was to make both sides understand the new rules, and he succeeded. Cartwright was fair but stern; he fined a New York Nine player named Davis six cents for swearing.

By 1849, the Knickerbockers had reached such a level of respectability that they wore uniforms for the first time. In 1857, the nine-inning format replaced the 21-run rule.

The First League

The National Association of Baseball Clubs, the first league, was organized in New York in 1857, and the Fashion Race Course in Jamaica, New York, was declared the site for all games. The season ran from July to October because the players felt it was too warm to play in May and June. Perhaps the weather pattern has changed, but the "dog days of August" have wilted pennant hopes of contenders throughout the modern era, which began in 1901.

In 1858 there was evidence that baseball was catching fire with the fans. Spectators paid 50 cents each to see Brooklyn and New York clash at the Fashion Race Course; attendance was 1,500.

Two years later, the Excelsiors of Brooklyn became the first team to go on tour. Twice during a five-game swing upstate, they scored more than 50 runs in a game, and they returned home undefeated.

Slim Pickins

Troy of the National League had a paid attendance of 12 for a game in 1882.

Good Start

Ross Barnes hit the first home run in National League history, for the Chicago White Stockings on May 2, 1876, but hit only one more for the rest of his career.

First Trade

The first trade in baseball history occurred on November 15, 1886 when the Cincinnati Red Stockings of the American Association sent catcher "Honest Jack" Boyle and $400 to the St. Louis Browns for Hugh Nicol, an outfielder who stood only 5'4" tall but had exceptional speed.

Fall Classic?

After the 1886 campaign, a 15-game exhibition series was staged between the St. Louis Browns of the American Association and Detroit Wolverines of the National League. Detroit won 10 of the games.

J. S. Thompson & Co.   Tyree Building, 56 Fifth Avenue, Chicago.

Library of Congress

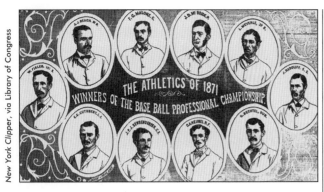

One of the best organized teams, the Athletic Baseball Club of Philadelphia, adopted a nickname that still survives today.

Lopsided Scores

Early handicaps on hurlers helped hitters immensely. Forest City, based in Cleveland, beat the Brooklyn Atlantics 132–1 in a five-inning game in 1870. In another game that year Forest City scored 90 runs in the first inning and had the bases loaded with nobody out when rain halted play at Utica, New York.

Spalding's Sensational Season

In 1875, one year before the formation of the National League (and several years before modern pitching rules were established), A. G. Spalding of Boston (National Association) posted a 57-7 record using only fastballs and curves.

A. G. Spalding helped found the National League in 1876.

The First Professional Team

Baseball fever boomed in 1860, when the Olympic Town Ball Club of Philadelphia, organized in 1833, decided to abandon the imported British sport of town ball and play baseball instead.

By 1869, Harry Wright, originally a cricket player, had gathered nine other top players to form the Cincinnati Red Stockings, the first professional team. Though the average player did not earn much more than $1,000 that season, the Red Stockings were more concerned with pride than price; they went undefeated in 69 games (there was one tie) and launched an amazing 130-game winning streak that did not end until June 14, 1870.

Only once did Cincinnati fail to score 16 or more runs in a game, and one of their decisions was a 103–8 triumph over the Buckeyes. The team was so popular that President Ulysses S. Grant received them in the White House.

The Red Stockings, named for their scarlet hose, kindled the establishment of the National Association of Professional Baseball Players in 1871, but the first pro league was riddled with constant franchise and player shifting, plus the influence of gamblers and other unsavory characters in the ballparks. Tinged with dishonesty, the league lost its fans and folded.

The National League

William A. Hulbert, owner of the Chicago National Association club, and Boston pitcher A. G. Spalding then laid the groundwork for the National League, with authority concentrated among the team owners and a strong constitution to protect the game's integrity.

A 70-game schedule was drawn up for the eight-club circuit, but the New York Mutuals and the Philadelphia Athletics were expelled before season's end for failing to take their final western road trips. Admission to games was 50 cents, or 10 cents to those who arrived after the third inning.

Well into the 1880s batters ordered their own pitches and runners interfered with fielders trying to make plays. Pitchers were obliged to throw underhand until 1881 and faced numerous other restrictions that remained in force until 1884. Their distance from batters was much closer until 1893, when the current standard of 60 feet, 6 inches was introduced—quite by accident.

Pitching distance had been 45 feet until 1881, then 50, then "60 feet, 0 inches." The surveyor misread the "0" as a "6" and the mistake was never corrected.

In the early days of the game, proximity to home plate allowed hurlers to work more and win more. Old Hoss Radbourn won 59 and lost 12 for Providence of the National League in 1884. In the modern era, it would take a star pitcher three seasons to win that many.

Early Problems in the Game

One of the National League's biggest problems was constant player movement between seasons. In 1879, the first reserve rule was invoked. Clubs were allowed to place five men "on reserve" so that other teams would not sign those players for the following year. The list gradually grew from five to fifteen and, finally, to the entire roster.

The best test of the reserve clause was the creation of a second major league, the American Association, in 1882. At first it competed for National League players, as did the Union Association (which lasted only for the 1884 season), but the AA eventually came to terms with the older NL.

National League president Abraham Mills was hailed as "the Bismarck of baseball" when he signed the first National Agreement with the American Association in 1883. The pact set up an 11-player reserve list, guaranteed territorial rights, set minimum salaries at $1,000, and even created a postseason series between league champions—the first "World Series."

Players deemed it an honor to be placed on reserve because those who weren't were not considered valuable by their teams. But the reserve clause allowed owners to deal out arbitrary salary cuts because it forbade free movement of players between teams.

Labor vs. Management

Player/owner friction, which reached an explosive climax with the demolition of the reserve clause in 1975, is almost as old as the game itself. Noting that owners were using the reserve clause to keep salaries of stars at low levels in the 1880s, law school graduate John Montgomery Ward, top star of the New York Giants, started a union called the Brotherhood of Professional Base Ball Players.

Among other things, Ward wanted each team to lift its arbitrary salary ceiling. Following the 1888 season, the owners agreed, and a delighted Ward set sail with Albert Spalding on a round-the-world baseball tour. When he returned in March of 1889, he found the players about to strike because the owners had reneged on their promises. Ward urged them to play that year with an eye out for investors in a new league.

In 1890 many of the game's stars drifted to the new Players League, which put teams in seven of eight National League cities. The exodus of players crippled the American Association and weakened the National, which coaxed many of its players to return the following year. Several Players League backers bought into the NL.

Because National League owners took an estimated $500,000 bath when the Players League drained it of top talent, economy became mandatory. Ed Delahanty's salary was slashed from $2,100 to $1,800 and left-handed catcher John Clements went from $3,000 to $1,800.

In 1896 New York Giants pitcher Amos Rusie sat out the entire season because the team attempted to deduct a $200 fine from his

Abe Lincoln Played Baseball

Abraham Lincoln was playing in a closely contested baseball game in 1860 when a message arrived for him. He told the messenger not to interrupt him during the game. Afterward, he found out he had been nominated for president by the Republican Party.

Old Hoss Was Warhorse

Old Hoss Radbourn, who won 309 games in 11 seasons, was the winning pitcher in the most lopsided shutout of all time—a 28–0 win for Providence over Philadelphia on August 21, 1883.

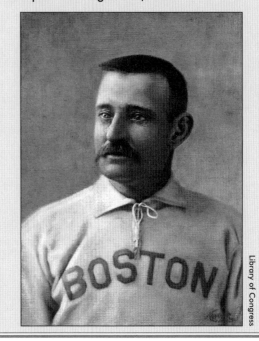

Library of Congress

Strong-Armed Pitcher

One-armed Cleveland pitcher Hugh Daily no-hit Philadelphia, 1–0, in 1883.

Red Stockings Were Nonchalant

The Cincinnati Red Stockings took winning so matter-of-factly that when pitcher Asa Brainard spotted a rabbit on the field during a game, he threw the ball at it as two runners scored.

Tim Keefe and Mickey Welch both won more than 300 games and found their way to the Baseball Hall of Fame.

Library of Congress

Disgruntled players formed the rival Players League in 1890.

contract. A series of lawsuits eventually persuaded the league to cough up the $3,000 he had demanded.

Teams were understood to have a per-player salary limit of $2,400 and a club ceiling of $30,000. They were not bound to pay injured or ill athletes, and the Baltimore Orioles were commended for a "humanitarian" gesture after they paid John McGraw $1,200 upon his return from a long bout with typhoid fever.

The collapse of the Players League and American Association left the National with an unwieldy 12-club structure dissimilar from that created by the second wave of expansion in 1969. The original 12-team format was not broken into divisions, thereby enabling a team to suffer the ignominy of a 12th-place finish. Four NL teams were dropped after the 1899 campaign, restoring the league to eight members.

CLEVELAND PLAIN DEALER

THE SEASON IS OPEN

Cleveland and Chicago Had the Day to Themselves

HOFFER'S WILDNESS LOST THE GAME

Philadelphia-Washington, rain
Baltimore-Boston, rain
Detroit-Milwaukee, rain
Chicago 8-Cleveland 2
Special to the Plain Dealer

CHICAGO, April 24—McAleer's men had two disastrous innings today, the first and second, then steadied down and played hard ball, but Comiskey's aggregation had turned into the home stretch and the game was won and lost. Hoffer could not control the ball in these two innings, apparently unable to get it far below the shoulder. He steadied wonderfully in the third and pitched good ball the remainder of the game. The season opening was a great success.

Resplendent in their new white suits and marching with proud steps to strains of music by the Rough Riders' Band, the champion White Stockings were led by Clark Griffith from their club house to the field, encircled it twice and assembled about the flagpole on the extreme northeast corner of the park, where the championship pennant, won by hard and consistent playing last year, was flung to the breeze.

When the ceremonies at the flagpole were concluded and the White Stockings had pulled the bit of white bunting to the top, the two teams—Comiskey's champions and McAleer's Clevelanders—marched abreast to the diamond. Robert E. Burke arose and delivered a short speech to the ball tossers, complimenting the local aggregation on their prowess of last year and wishing them the same good fortune for the season on 1901. He then tossed a new ball into the diamond. Umpire Connolly handed it to pitcher Patterson, who did the club honors for the White Sox, and at 3:35 o'clock the first game of the season was on.

The grandstand was decorated with flags and bunting, draped gracefully about the boxes and the entire front of the stand. Back of the decorations and filling the stand to the utmost, as well as the bleachers, 9,000 "fans" were assembled. With critical eyes, they marked the playing of last year's stars, as well as the new acquisitions from the National League—Mertes, Jones, Sullivan, Bradley and McCarthy. In practice just prior to the game, these men were greeted with rounds of applause.

The weather could not have been more ideal for a ball game. The bright sun dried the diamond and made the outfield hard and fast. It was warm and balmy and a light refreshing breeze blew across the park from the lake. Roy Patterson and "Boston" Sullivan were chosen by Manager Griffith as the battery to represent the champions in the opening game, while Hoffer and "Bob" Wood were the battery for the visitors.

Pickering was the first Clevelander up; and he caught the second ball Patterson pitched, sending a long fly to "Dummy" Hoy in center field. McCarthy, the ex-National Leaguer, was given a cane and umbrella and he answered by swatting a sizzling grounder to Hartman. The third baseman tried to get it, but it struck his foot and caromed off; Shugart finally picked it up, but McCarthy reached first. Then Genins sent an easy fly to Hoy, and LaChance went out on a grounder to Brain. Chicago, aided by Hoffer, started to win the game in the first inning. In this act he gave three men bases on balls and allowed Hartman to single, netting three runs.

Cy's Streak

Cy Young threw 23 straight hitless innings in 1904: two innings April 25, six innings April 30, a perfect game May 5, and six innings May 11.

Hitless Wonders

The Dead Ball Era was exactly that. The 1906 Chicago White Sox hit *seven* home runs in 154 games, earning their "Hitless Wonders" nickname, and none in the World Series against the crosstown Cubs. Neither team hit a home run in the six-game Series.

The American League

What was to become the American League surfaced for the first time in 1900 as the American Association. When this new circuit began, it announced goals of fostering honest competition without the reserve rule and supporting itself by luring big crowds with low ticket prices.

Created from the remains of the Western League, which Ban Johnson served as president, the American League took its present name on November 14, 1900, with a lineup that included Baltimore, Buffalo, Chicago, Cleveland, Detroit, Milwaukee, Philadelphia, and Washington.

Eight AL teams played a 140-game schedule with 14-man rosters in 1901. The Chicago White Sox recorded the best attendance—354,350—as the circuit drew a combined total of 1,683,584. Both Chicago and Boston drew more fans than National League rivals in those cities.

League players came primarily from National League teams. The prize was Napoleon Lajoie, who jumped crosstown from the Phils to the A's and hit .426, highest in league history. The star second baseman was later barred from playing in Philadelphia because of the intracity squabble over his services and was sold to Cleveland. When the Indians visited Philadelphia, Lajoie languished on the beach in nearby Atlantic City, New Jersey.

More than 110 of the American League's 185 players had National League experience, including Baltimore player/manager John McGraw. Early in the year, McGraw discovered a talented black second baseman, Charlie Grant, and attempted to circumvent the unwritten "color line" by informing rivals that Grant was a full-blooded Cherokee named Tokomoma. The ruse failed.

In a rough-and-tumble season, the AL's best-educated battery belonged to the Athletics: left-handed pitcher Eddie Plank, from Gettysburg College, and Dr. Mike Powers, a catcher from Notre Dame.

By January 1903, the AL achieved major status when a new National Agreement was drawn and ratified in Cincinnati. Two AL franchises had shifted—Baltimore to New York and Milwaukee to St. Louis—and Boston had replaced Buffalo. The National League of that year had Boston, Brooklyn, Chicago, Cincinnati, New York, Philadelphia, Pittsburgh, and St. Louis.

There were no further changes in the baseball map until 1953, when the Boston Braves shook the sports world by moving to Milwaukee. (The outlaw Federal League of 1914–1915 failed in its brief challenge to the majors.)

With the 1903 agreement between leagues, the reserve rule was tightened. It read, "Contracts with players must be respected under the penalties specified. The right and title of a major league club to its players shall be absolute, and can only be terminated by release or failure to reserve under the rules of the agreement by the club to which a player has been under contract."

Protection of the Minors

The agreement also guaranteed the independence of minor league teams and prohibited a big-league club from "farming" a player to the minors. Branch Rickey, a colorful and innovative executive, later reversed that concept.

The major/minor relationship in 1903 stipulated that big-league teams could purchase players from the minors (called the National Association) between August 15 and October 15 for the following prices: $750 from Class A (the highest minor league), $500 from Class B, $300 from Class C, and $200 from Class D.

Though those prices seem low from the perspective of the late 1990s—where the minimum league salary was $200,000—money was low in volume but high in value in the early days of the game. A little went a long way.

Consider this: the first National League franchises, in 1876, sold for $100 each. Five years earlier, National Association franchises went for just $10. Umpires worked gratis until 1883, then were paid $5 per game by the home team. In 1888, visiting clubs received 15 cents from each paid admission to the ballpark. And clubs deducted $30 per season from player salaries for uniform costs and 50 cents per day for meal money.

When the champion Boston club of the National Association made a season's profit of $2,261.07 in 1875, other team executives were startled. Baseball was not known as a profitable business.

Once the major leagues solidified, however, profits climbed as clubs in both circuits played constant schedules under practical rules that stabilized at the same time as the two leagues.

How the Schedule Changed

When the National League began operation in 1876, its eight members played schedules of 70 games each. As the league's size and membership varied, so did the schedule, finally climbing to 112 games in 1884 and 126 two years later.

By 1901, when the American League shattered the National's monopoly on big-league baseball, the two circuits were playing 140 games each. That increased to 154 games in 1904. Each club played its rivals 22 times—11 home and 11 away.

With expansion to 10-team leagues in 1961 and 1962 came extension of the schedule to 162 contests—9 home and 9 away for each team against each rival. The advent of divisional play in 1969 did not destroy the 162-game concept but did jettison the idea that each team should play a constant number of games against each rival.

With 12 teams in each league, intradivision clubs, such as the New York Mets and Philadelphia Phillies, played each other 18 times—9 home and 9 away—but faced interdivision clubs, such as the Los Angeles Dodgers, only 12 times—6 and 6.

All games counted in the standings, with a best-of-five championship series to determine the league's pennant-winner. The playoffs were expanded to a best-of-seven format in 1985.

Distaff Game

English baseball in the 19th century was played primarily by women.

Real Debut?

Even if Abner Doubleday did play baseball in Cooperstown in 1839, the first record of a game was made one year earlier. That contest was played in Canada: in Beachville, Ontario.

Flat Bats

From 1885 to 1893, National League hitters used flat bats. The idea—to boost sagging offense—worked, but so many bats splintered that the rule was abandoned.

Hot Stove Leagues

Early ballplayers kept in playing shape during the off-season by playing baseball in their hometowns—often keeping warm with hot stoves. The Hot Stove Leagues didn't last, but their name morphed into a metaphor for fans keeping warm during the winter by talking baseball rather than playing it.

A Towering Achievement

On August 25, 1894, Chicago NL catcher William Schriver became the first player to catch a ball thrown from the top of the Washington Monument.

BATTING RECORD
Of Clubs Members of the National League of Professional Base Ball Clubs, SEASON OF 1876.

NAME OF CLUB.	WHERE LOCATED.	No. of Gmes pl'yed.	No. of Games won.	BATTING.						
				Times at bat.	Runs scored.	Average per game.	Runs earned.	Average per game.	1st Bases.	Percentage of base hits per time at bat.
Chicago	Chicago, Ill........	66	52	2,818	624	9.45	267	4.03	926	.328
Hartford	Hartford, Conn.	69	47	2,703	429	6.22	154	2.23	711	.264
St. Louis	St. Louis, Mo..	64	45	2,536	386	6.03	109	1.70	642	.253
Boston..	Boston, Mass..	70	39	2,780	471	6.73	167	2.38	723	.260
Louisville	Louisville, Ky. ..	69	30	2,594	280	4.06	107	1.55	641	.247
Mutual	Brooklyn, N. Y..	57	21	2,202	260	4.55	72	1.26	494	.223
Athletic	Philadelphia, Pa.	60	14	2,414	378	6.30	145	2.41	646	.267
Cincinnati.....	Cincinnati, O.	65	9	2,413	238	3.66	77	1.18	555	.230
Total		520	257	2(,.60	3066	5.89	1098	2.11	5338	.261

Tie Games Played—LOUISVILLE, 3; ATHLETIC, 1; HARTFORD, 1

The first unbalanced 162-game schedule was created with AL expansion to 14 clubs in 1977. It lasted only two seasons.

In 1979, the league adopted a slate that called for each team in the two seven-team divisions to play each opponent 12 times—6 home and 6 away—for a total of 156 games. Clubs then played each intradivisional rival one additional game.

The NL adopted that format when it expanded to 14 teams in 1993.

Before the advent of divisional play in 1969, champions of the American and National Leagues were automatic World Series opponents. When divisional play made its debut, a best-of-five playoff called the Championship Series determined winners in each league. The LCS format changed to best-of-seven in 1985 after general managers insisted that was a better barometer of discovering the best teams.

The 1994 advent of a three-division format featuring a wild-card winner mandated an earlier round of playoffs, a best-of-five Division Series, to determine Championship Series opponents.

The introduction of interleague play in 1997 and further expansion in 1998 did not alter the 162-game schedule but did create an unbalanced schedule so that teams did not play the same number of games against each opponent—or even play the same opponents.

The addition of a second wild card in 2012 allowed 10 of the 30 teams into the postseason, mandated the need for a sudden-death wild-card game, and increased the odds that the best teams would not reach the World Series. A third-place finisher even had the potential to become a world champion (three teams from the NL Central reached the 2015 postseason, along with the divisional champions of the league's other two divisions). In 2014, for the first time in baseball history, a world champion (the San Francisco Giants) survived four playoff rounds.

Schedules were shortened by war (1918) and labor disputes (1972, 1981, 1994-95). In addition, the 9/11 terrorist attacks delayed the 2001 campaign for a week.

By shifting the Houston Astros, a 1962 National League expansion team, from the NL Central to the American League West, the two leagues had 15 teams each for the first time.

Under the current format, teams play 19 games against each of the four opponents in its division, six or seven games against 10 intraleague rivals, and 20 interleague contests.

Chapter 2

Bill Menzel

The designated hitter rule, introduced in 1973, was made for David Ortiz. The left-handed Dominican slugger hit more than 500 home runs, primarily for the Boston Red Sox, before retiring after the 2016 season.

How Some Rules Apply

Babe Ruth

John Anderson

Babe Ruth (above) and Hank Aaron (below) were the first men to top 700 home runs. Though the records list their career totals as 714 and 755, respectively, varying interpretations of the rules leave those figures open to debate.

Bud Skinner

Rules and Records

Baseball rules are constantly changing and, because of that fact, old records that are broken must be viewed in light of rule changes that have been made.

In 1879 a pitcher had to throw nine balls to give up a walk, and in 1887 it took four strikes to get a man out. At one time, the catcher stood 20 or more feet behind the batter and the pitcher got credit for a strike even when his pitch bounced before passing through the strike zone. The batter (called striker) received credit for a hit when he walked and the runner got a stolen base each time he advanced on a teammate's hit.

For a while, bases on balls counted as hits, inflating batting averages of early players.

Sudden-Death Home Runs

Rule changes had a great effect on home-run kings Babe Ruth and Hank Aaron. Did Ruth actually hit 714 lifetime home runs or 716? And did Aaron really have 714 to his credit when he broke Ruth's record on April 8, 1974?

On September 8, 1918, Ruth was a hard-hitting pitcher for the Boston Red Sox. With a man on first in the bottom of the ninth inning of a tie game, he came to bat against Cleveland and hit the ball over the fence. Under present-day rules that would be a home run—but it wasn't then.

A sudden-death rule was in effect in 1918. Once the winning run scored, the game was automatically over. So Ruth was given only a triple, since it took three bases to force home the decisive tally.

Little more than a year later, on September 20, an overflow crowd was standing behind a roped-off area in front of the bleachers at Boston's Fenway Park. The Red Sox and White Sox agreed before the game that any ball hit into the crowd would be a triple. Ruth hit a ball over the crowd and into the bleachers, but it struck something hard and bounced back into the crowd. The umpire couldn't tell whether the ball cleared the wall and incorrectly awarded three bases to Ruth—even though he had actually hit a home run.

Home Runs After 1954

By 1954, nearly 20 years after Ruth's retirement, rules governing home runs had changed in certain respects, some beneficial to Ruth and others to Hank Aaron, who started his career that season.

Balls that cleared the fence fair but landed foul were considered nothing more than long strikes for Ruth but counted as home runs for Aaron. Conversely, balls that bounced over the wall on one hop were homers for Ruth but ground-rule doubles for Aaron.

The new home-run king, who ended his career in 1976 with a career count of 755 home runs, missed a definite homer on August

19, 1965, when his clout onto the roof of Sportsman's Park, St. Louis, was ruled an out by umpire Chris Pelekoudas.

Aaron was particularly incensed because his victim was crafty left-hander Curt Simmons, a longtime nemesis. Pelekoudas made the call when Cardinal catcher Bob Uecker pointed out that Aaron's back foot was out of the batter's box when he took his stance.

A rule dictates that the batter must remain in the box until the pitcher delivers the ball—but Uecker wisely kept quiet about it until the appropriate moment. The umpire is not obligated to cite the batter for such an infraction unless the opposing team appeals.

There is no way to document how many home runs Ruth and Aaron hit without credit because of rained-out games (anything less than five innings, or four-and-a-half with the home team ahead). Baseball historians have settled on final figures of 755 for Aaron and 714 for Ruth.

These figures reflect only regular-season games, with All-Star and World Series totals excluded.

The Designated Hitter

The most radical baseball rule change of the 20th century was the introduction of the designated hitter by the American League in 1973. Though it was first suggested by National League president John A. Heydler in 1928, and formally presented to baseball's Rules Committee by Pacific Coast League President Dewey Soriano in 1961, the recommendation lay dormant until the International League adopted it as an experiment in 1969. AL owners finally adopted the DH as a three-year experiment late in 1972, after eight of the twelve league clubs lost money and nine failed to draw a million customers.

Bill Menzel

Ron Blomberg, here with author Dan Schlossberg, became the first designated hitter by accident. Listed as the No. 6 hitter for the Yankees for their April 6, 1973 opener at Fenway Park, Blomberg came to bat during a first-inning rally. The bat he used to make history later became the only one displayed by the Baseball Hall of Fame as the result of a walk.

The Designated Hitter

A hitter may be designated to bat for the starting pitcher and all subsequent pitchers in any game without otherwise affecting the status of the pitcher(s) in the game. A Designated Hitter for the pitcher must be selected prior to the game and must be included in the lineup cards presented to the Umpire-in-Chief.

It is not mandatory that a club designate a hitter for the pitcher, but failure to do so prior to the game precludes the use of a Designated Hitter for that game.

Pinch-hitters for a Designated Hitter may be used. Any substitute hitter for a Designated Hitter becomes the Designated Hitter. A replaced Designated Hitter shall not reenter the game in any capacity.

The Designated Hitter may be used defensively, continuing to bat in the same position in the batting order, but the pitcher must then bat in the place of the substituted defensive player, unless more than one substitution is made, and the manager then must designate their spots in the batting order.

A runner may be substituted for the Designated Hitter and the runner assumes the role of Designated Hitter. A Designated Hitter may not pinch run.

A Designated Hitter is "locked" into the batting order. No multiple substitutions may be made that will alter the batting rotation of the Designated Hitter.

Once the game pitcher is switched from the mound to a defensive position this move shall terminate the Designated Hitter role for the remainder of the game.

Once a pinch-hitter bats for any player in the batting order and then enters the game to pitch, this move shall terminate the Designated Hitter role for the remainder of the game.

Once the game pitcher bats for the Designated Hitter this move shall terminate the Designated Hitter role for the remainder of the game. (The game pitcher may only pinch hit for the Designated Hitter.)

Once a Designated Hitter assumes a defensive position this move shall terminate the Designated Hitter rule for the remainder of the game. A substitute for the Designated Hitter need not be announced until it is the Designated Hitter's turn to bat.

—Official Baseball Rules, 1978

Slugging Pitchers

Pitchers with 35 or more lifetime homers are Wes Ferrell (Indians, Red Sox), 38; Bob Lemon (Indians), 37; Red Ruffing (Yankees), 36; and Warren Spahn (Braves), 35.

Youngest Perfect Game Pitcher

Jim "Catfish" Hunter had just turned 22 when he pitched a perfect game against the Minnesota Twins for the Oakland A's in 1968. Hunter was the youngest man ever to pitch a perfect game.

The First DH

Ron Blomberg of the Yankees was the first designated hitter.

DH Didn't Hinder Holtzman

Though he did not bat during the season because of the American League's designated hitter rule, Oakland A's pitcher Ken Holtzman hit well during World Series play in 1973 and 1974. His pair of doubles in 1973 led to rallies that helped Oakland beat the Mets, while his double and home run contributed to another world title the following fall.

Power Pitchers

Between the 1973 advent of the designated hitter rule and the 1997 introduction of inter-league play, no American League pitcher hit a home run. Roric Harrison (Orioles) hit the last pre-DH homer in 1972, while Bobby Witt (Rangers) hit the first homer by an AL pitcher against National League pitching in 1997.

Sluggers "Escaped" DH

Four sluggers who reached the Hall of Fame might not have attained stardom had the designated hitter rule applied when they played. The four—Babe Ruth, George Sisler, Ted Williams, and Stan Musial—all began their careers as pitchers.

The rule allows a specified player to take the batting turn of the weakest hitter in the lineup (usually the pitcher) without entering the contest. The player who yields his batting spot to the DH does not have to leave the game—though a man who yields to a traditional pinch-hitter must.

What the Critics Say

Critics contend that the rule denies good-hitting pitchers the built-in edge they normally have over weak-hitting rival pitchers. They say it interferes with managerial strategy, such as whether to use a late-inning pinch-hitter for the pitcher, whom to choose, and what relief pitcher should be called into action.

Another anti-DH argument is that the rule extends the careers of "over-the-hill" stars and allows "incomplete" players (hitters who can't run or throw) to remain in the majors.

Supporters suggest the DH improves the offense and makes the game more exciting. When the International League tried the rule in 1969, the overall batting average of its top team climbed 17 points. Designated hitters batted .261 with 108 homers and 472 runs batted in. A year earlier, pitchers hit only .160 with 24 home runs and 204 runs batted in.

In 1975, both major leagues proved almost equal in overall batting average (.257 for the NL and .258 for the AL) though playing under different rules. Because of the DH, American League clubs outscored NL counterparts, averaging 4.30 runs per game against 4.13. AL hitters averaged .76 home runs per game, as opposed to .63 in the NL. The designated hitters produced 222 home runs and 962 runs batted in on a .254 batting average, while NL pitchers hit just .150 with 10 home runs and 283 RBIs.

In the first three years of the DH rule, the overall American League batting average was .258. In 1972, the last year pitchers hit in that league, it was .239.

Views of the League Presidents

Naturally, the two major league presidents had opposite viewpoints as to the value of the DH rule in 1973. National League chief executive Chub Feeney said, "Baseball is a game of teams which emphasizes individuals in competition. Use of the DH takes something away from the game. Baseball has always been the hardest game to play because any player must be a whole athlete—able to do everything."

Lee MacPhail of the American League said the rule restored balance to a game that had begun to overemphasize pitching and defense. He also noted that league attendance had jumped since its inception. "While it would be preferable if both leagues followed identical playing rules," he explained, "the situation in the National League with respect to offensive/defensive balance is dissimilar to ours because most of their parks have artificial turf—an innovation which has changed the game as much as the designated hitter rule."

Early Fouls

During the 19th century, a foul tip caught by the catcher was an automatic out—on any count.

Rain Checks

Fans in Detroit received the first rain checks in baseball history—in 1888. Ticket holders for a rained-out game were admitted free to the next contest.

No Walkoffs

Before 1920, walkoff home runs were a rarity. Since the game ended the minute the go-ahead run scored, a home run with the bases loaded in a tie game would count as a single. Only if the batter himself represented the winning run would a ball over the fence be considered a home run.

What DH?

Pitcher Red Ruffing hit two home runs as the Yankees beat the Browns, 7–6, in 10 innings on September 18, 1930. Twelve years later, Boston Braves pitcher Jim Tobin hit *three* home runs in one game.

Wildest Wild Pitch

The wildest wild pitch in baseball history didn't advance a runner. It was merely called a ball—not an unusual development when Phil Marchildon was on the mound for the Philadelphia Athletics. On August 1, 1948, he beat the Detroit Tigers, 4–2, but walked seven, hit a batter, and threw a pitch that traveled 10 rows up on the third base side before it made contact with the head of a fan. That spectator, Sam Wexler of Toledo, was leaning over to light a cigar when the ball hit him. Taken to the first aid room, he returned puffing and smiling. Wexler told the *Owosso Argus-Press*, "I didn't know what hit me. It's a little sore up there. That must have been the wildest wild pitch in history."

Long Wait

Phillies pitcher Jim Hearn lost a game two months after he retired. The starting pitcher against Pittsburgh on May 10, 1959, he left the game as pitcher of record on the losing side. The game was suspended, forcing it to be completed in July. When it was, Hearn was charged with the loss.

The DH in the World Series

Though the designated hitter rule was adopted in time for the 1973 season, agreement to use it in World Series games (or even meaningless spring-training games) was not reached for several years. The AL wanted it, the NL did not, and Commissioner Bowie Kuhn had to settle the stalemate. He ruled that the DH can be used in years that the World Series begins in the home park of the American League club. It was first used in 1976 but backfired on the AL Yankees when Dan Driessen, the first National League DH, helped the Cincinnati Reds to a four-game sweep.

Reaction to the DH

When the designated hitter rule was first enacted, several pitchers objected. Terry Forster, then with the Chicago White Sox, had the strongest argument after he hit .526 (10-for-19) in 1972, and knocked in the winning run as a pinch-hitter for third baseman Hank Allen in a late-season game.

Forster's .397 lifetime batting average is the best of any player to appear in at least 500 games.

In 1973 Oakland A's manager Dick Williams prepared for the World Series by using four pitchers as pinch-hitters in one game. Catfish Hunter singled, Ken Holtzman walked, Darold Knowles hit a sacrifice fly, and Vida Blue struck out.

The following season, Texas Rangers pitcher Ferguson Jenkins, the only pitcher to appear in an AL lineup as a hitter that year, singled in the sixth to break up a no-hitter and scored the first run as he beat Minnesota, 2–1, to win his 25th game.

The DH prolonged the careers of Orlando Cepeda, Tommy Davis, Billy Williams, Rico Carty, Harmon Killebrew, and even Hank Aaron, who hit his last home run in that role in 1976.

First Series DH

Cincinnati's Dan Driessen became the first DH in World Series history in 1976. He hit .350 as the Reds swept the Yankees.

One-Year Wonder

Eddie Murray of the 1977 Baltimore Orioles was the first DH voted AL Rookie of the Year. The 21-year-old switch-hitter had 27 home runs that season.

New York Yankees

Don Baylor, then with the California Angels, used the DH as a springboard to the 1979 Most Valuable Player award. The first MVP to play more than 50 games as a designated hitter, he hit .296 with 36 homers and led the American League with 120 runs scored and 139 runs batted in. Baylor, then 30, played 65 games as the DH, 97 in the outfield, and 1 at first base. Four years later, he became a fulltime DH after signing with the Yankees as a free agent.

Dynamic DH

Tony Oliva of the Minnesota Twins was the first DH to hit a home run. He did it on April 6, 1973.

Full-Time Job

The first DH to play in all 162 games was Rusty Staub of the 1978 Detroit Tigers.

The Balk Rule

The first balk rule was enacted in 1898 and refined two years later, ostensibly to provide protection for baserunners who were constant victims of deceiving motions by pitchers.

The basic balk is a motion to deliver the ball to home plate or first base that is not followed through. When it occurs, baserunners are entitled to move up one base. If a batter hits a ball delivered during a balk, play proceeds without penalty. Nor does the rule apply when bases are clear.

When he is ready to deliver the ball, the pitcher must have his back heel in contact with the rubber, a 24 by 6-inch slab imbedded in the pitcher's mound. A balk may be called if a pitcher touches the rubber when he does *not* have the ball.

In 1963 and 1978, National League umpires were ordered by the league to enforce the balk rule to the letter. Minor "balk wars" ensued as pitchers charged the arbiters were overstepping their bounds.

Variations between leagues in interpreting the balk rule caused a minor controversy prior to the 1975 World Series because Red Sox star Luis Tiant had developed a tricky pickoff move which, according to NL standards, seemed to be a balk. Tiant still won two of his club's three triumphs against the Reds that fall.

The Balk Rule

8.05 If there is a runner, or runners, it is a balk when—
(a) The pitcher, while touching his plate, makes any motion naturally associated with his pitch and fails to make such delivery;
(b) The pitcher, while touching his plate, feints a throw to first base and fails to complete the throw;
(c) The pitcher, while touching his plate, fails to step directly toward a base before throwing to that base;
(d) The pitcher, while touching his plate, throws, or feints a throw, to an unoccupied base, except for the purpose of making a play;
(e) The pitcher makes an illegal pitch;
(f) The pitcher delivers the ball to the batter while he is not facing the batter;
(g) The pitcher makes any motion naturally associated with his pitch while he is not touching the pitcher's plate;
(h) The pitcher unnecessarily delays the game;
(i) The pitcher, without having the ball, stands on or astride the pitcher's plate or while off the plate, he feints a pitch;
(j) The pitcher, after coming to a legal pitching position, removes one hand from the ball other than in an actual pitch, or in throwing to a base;
(k) The pitcher, while touching his plate, accidentally or intentionally drops the ball;
(l) The pitcher, while giving an intentional base on balls, pitches when the catcher is not in the catcher's box;
(m) The pitcher delivers the pitch from Set Position without coming to a stop.

—Official Baseball Rules, 1978

Boston Red Sox

A controversial pickoff move—which might have been considered a balk by some National League umpires—did not prevent Boston's Luis Tiant from winning two games in the 1975 World Series.

Tough K

Pittsburgh rookie Doe Boyland struck out while sitting on the bench. In his first major league at-bat, Boyland was lifted with a 1-2 count after the Mets made a pitching change. When replacement Rennie Stennett took a called third strike, Boyland was charged with the strikeout.

Series DH

Lou Piniella was the first designated hitter to bat in the World Series. He doubled to right in the second inning for the Yankees against the Reds on October 16, 1976. The next day, Cincinnati's Dan Driessen became the first DH to hit a home run in the Fall Classic.

In-Justice

When ex-Brave Zane Smith beat Atlanta, 1–0, for the Pittsburgh Pirates in the fifth game of the 1991 NL Championship Series, he had some unforeseen help from David Justice. In the fourth inning, the Braves right fielder crossed the plate but was called out for missing third.

Wagner Sought Changes

In 1904 Pittsburgh shortstop Honus Wagner asked for a ban on freak deliveries and suggested the standard pitching distance of 60 feet, 6 inches was too short.

Merkle's Boner Cost Mathewson Victory Crown

Because Christy Mathewson was deprived of a certain victory when Fred Merkle forgot to touch second base in a late-season Giants/Cubs contest in 1908, he ended his career with 373 victories, a total later equaled by longtime Phillies star Grover Cleveland Alexander. No NL pitcher ever won more. It's possible Mathewson would rank alone at the top if victory hadn't become a tie because of "Merkle's boner."

Rare calls of the balk rule occur when a pitcher drops the ball by accident. This happened to Red Sox reliever Sparky Lyle against the Yankees in 1969, and a run scored as a result. It also happened to Boston's Diego Segui, who balked home the winning run in May 1974 when hitter Jerry Terrell of Minnesota reached down to pick up some dirt and Segui stopped his motion.

Rules Violations

Violation of baseball rules often proves costly—to both team and individual. Under pennant pressure, mistakes happen and the most fundamental rules are not followed.

For example, it is illegal to pass preceding runners on the bases. Runners must touch all bases in order (or reverse order when forced to return, *except* on a home run or ground-rule "automatic," which requires the runner to start at his original route).

Runners may not return to missed bases if a following runner has scored. Runners must touch the next base safely when forced to advance. All plays must be completed.

The defensive team may appeal that a runner has missed a base and, if correct, the umpire will call the runner out when the defensive team tags the base while in possession of the ball.

"Merkle's Boner"

The most famous rules violation in baseball history was "Merkle's boner" on September 24, 1908. The New York Giants and the Chicago Cubs, fighting for the National League pennant, were locked in a 1–1 tie in the ninth inning at New York when the Giants put Moose McCormick on third and Fred Merkle on first with two outs.

Al Bridwell drilled a hit to center field and McCormick raced home with the apparent winning run. But Merkle, seeing him score, stopped short of touching second and headed for the clubhouse. Cubs first baseman Frank Chance saw what happened and screamed for the ball; he knew he could touch second and make Merkle the victim of a force play, thus ending the inning with the score still tied.

Giants' pitcher Joe "Iron Man" McGinnity heard Chance, sprang off the bench, and tackled him before he could reach second. Meanwhile, the fans—thinking the game was over—had spilled onto the field in a rush for the exits.

McGinnity grabbed the ball and threw it into the crowd. Chance appealed to umpire Hank O'Day, who ruled Merkle out because of interference from McGinnity. The game ended in a tie and had to be replayed when the two teams finished the season with identical 98-55 records.

The Cubs won the replay and the pennant, but 19-year-old Merkle, perpetrator of the costliest blunder in baseball history, actually received a raise from Giants' manager John McGraw and went on to become an excellent player.

Touching All Bases

Touching all bases is one of baseball's primary rules, but mishaps can occur on the base paths. Baserunning blunders are common.

In 1916 pitcher Ernie Koob of the St. Louis Browns was deprived of victory while "scoring" in the 15th inning; he had missed third base and was called out when the opposition appealed. The game was called for darkness two innings later, with the score 0–0.

Red Sox starter Howard Ehmke got a "gift" no-hitter against the Philadelphia A's near the end of the 1923 season when rival pitcher Slim Harriss failed to touch first on an apparent double off the right-field fence. He too was called out on an appeal play.

Yankee slugger Lou Gehrig, trotting around the bases after hitting the ball over the fence, lost the 1931 home-run crown when teammate Lyn Lary—on base at the time—proceeded from third base to the dugout rather than completing the circuit to home plate. Gehrig, who didn't see the play, was ruled out for passing Lary and was credited with a triple, as he had touched only three bases safely. That year, Gehrig and Babe Ruth each hit 46 home runs to share the home-run title.

Hank Aaron was involved in the strange ending of Harvey Haddix's 12-inning perfect game, which he pitched for Pittsburgh against Milwaukee in May 1959.

In the last of the 13th, Felix Mantilla was safe on an error by Don Hoak (ending the perfect game). Eddie Mathews sacrificed him to second and Aaron was intentionally walked to set up a potential inning-ending double play. But Joe Adcock foiled the strategy by slamming the ball over the fence, an apparent three-run homer and the only hit off hard-luck Haddix.

Mantilla scored but Aaron, rounding second, saw the ball disappear over the wall and was so stunned that he forgot to continue his circuit of the base paths. He headed directly for the dugout, and Adcock, making a grand home-run trot, was ruled out when he passed the spot where Aaron had made his departure. Instead of a 3–0 victory, the Braves wound up 1–0 winners—and Adcock had a double instead of a home run.

A strange footnote to the game was the pitching of Lew Burdette, who yielded 12 hits but no runs in 13 innings to win. Haddix gave up one and lost.

Baserunners must stay alert at all times. On August 15, 1926, Babe Herman tripled into a double play when he didn't.

In the seventh inning, with one out and the bases loaded, Herman slammed a pitch toward the right-field fence. The ball might have been caught—and the runners had to wait and see if it would be—but Herman put his head down and ran.

The Dodger runner scored from third, but pitcher Dazzy Vance, running from second, mysteriously slowed down as he rounded third on his way home. Chick Fewster, running from first, had caught up to Vance but knew he couldn't pass him on the base paths.

Herman, closing in on Fewster and Vance, looked like he would pass both runners. Coach Mickey O'Neil yelled "Back! Back!" to Herman, but Vance—not used to running the bases—answered the cry. He turned back toward third and slid in from the home-plate side. Herman slid in from the second-base side. Fewster stood stock still on the base and watched.

The 12-inning perfect game of Harvey Haddix in 1959 had an unexpected finish in the 13th when Hank Aaron failed to complete his circuit of the bases after Joe Adcock's homer. The final score was 1–0.

The Submarine Delivery

Carl Mays, Yankee ace in the 1920s, used a submarine (underarm) delivery. During his motion, he often scraped the ground as he delivered to the plate.

Umpires tend to keep a close watch on middle infielders attempting to turn the double play. Here Yankee shortstop Phil Rizzuto, a master in the field, gets the call he needed.

Slugger Catfish

Among pitchers who objected to the designated hitter rule was Jim "Catfish" Hunter, who once received a $5,000 bonus from Oakland A's owner Charley Finley for his hitting ability. The last pitcher to hit .300 and win 20 games in the same season, Hunter hit .350 while posting a 21–11 record in 1971.

Surprise Shot

The first home run by a Mariners pitcher was a grand slam. Because the DH rule does not apply to National League home games, Felix Hernandez hit the home run while batting against Mets ace Johan Santana at Shea Stadium on June 23, 2008. As a result, Seattle won, 5–2. It was the first slam by any AL pitcher since the advent of the designated hitter in 1973.

Bending the Rules

Free substitution is banned in baseball, but rules against it were bent during a Pirates/Cubs game in 1952. Pittsburgh catcher Clyde McCullough was forced out by an injury, and reserve receiver Ed Fitzgerald had already appeared as a pinch-hitter.

Cubs manager Phil Cavarretta said he did not mind if Fitzgerald reentered the game and the umpires permitted the unusual maneuver. The Pirate home crowd cheered the sportsmanlike decision of the visiting manager.

Third baseman Eddie Taylor grabbed the ball and tagged all three runners. The umpire ruled Vance entitled to the bag but called Fewster and Herman out, ending the inning.

Brooklyn manager Wilbert Robinson was beside himself. But it wasn't as bad as the time Herman stole second while runners were at second and third.

Gary Geiger of the Red Sox suffered an embarrassing moment in 1961 when he hit a run-scoring triple in the bottom of the 11th inning against the Los Angeles Angels. Thinking his hit had won the game, Geiger headed for the clubhouse. An Angel infielder tagged him for the first out of the inning. Geiger's hit had actually tied the game and he would have been on third with nobody out.

Throwing a Glove at the Ball

Fielders are penalized for throwing gloves, caps, or other parts of their uniform at balls in flight. Rule 7.05 (c) provides three bases for a hitter if a fielder throws his glove at and touches a fair ball.

In 1947 the same rule applied to foul balls as well. On July 27, Boston's Jake Jones got credit for a triple on a foul ball with two outs and the bases empty in the sixth inning against the St. Louis Browns. He hit a roller inside the third-base line that looked like it *might* go fair. Pitcher Fred Sanford, realizing Jones would have a certain infield hit if that happened, threw his glove to keep the ball foul. The glove and ball met and Jones immediately had an automatic triple.

In 1954 the rule was amended to apply only to fair balls.

Warm-Up Pitches

In 1911 the American League instituted a short-lived rule forbidding pitchers to take warm-up pitches between innings. Boston's Ed Karger was doing just that—and the outfielders

Warm-Up Pitches

8.03 When a pitcher takes his position at the beginning of each inning, or when he relieves another pitcher, he shall be permitted to pitch not to exceed eight preparatory pitches to his catcher during which play shall be suspended. A league by its own action may limit the number of preparatory pitches to less than eight preparatory pitches. Such preparatory pitches shall not consume more than one minute of time. If a sudden emergency causes a pitcher to be summoned into the game without any opportunity to warm up, the Umpire-in-Chief shall allow him as many pitches as the umpire deems necessary.

—Official Baseball Rules, 1978

were taking their time returning to the positions—when Stuffy McInnis, part of the Athletics' famed $100,000 infield, stepped into the batter's box and hit a warm-up pitch far over the fielders' heads. It was an easy home run, and the umpire said it was perfectly legal under prevailing rules.

Missed Third Strike

A strikeout is incomplete if the catcher does not catch the ball (Rule 10.17). The batter may advance to first base, provided there is no runner there before two are out. Should the catcher retrieve the ball and tag the batter, or throw the ball to first base before his arrival, the batter is out. A batter who bunts foul on the third strike is also a strikeout victim. In all cases, the pitcher is credited with a strikeout even if a defensive lapse by the catcher allows a runner to reach base.

There have been multiple instances of pitchers striking out four men in one inning because one of the strikeout victims reached base when the catcher missed the third strike. Only once, however, has a pitcher fanned *five* in one inning.

Joe Niekro of the Houston Astros, whose knuckleball was as difficult to catch as it was to hit, did it during a 1977 exhibition game. The ball twice eluded catcher Cliff Johnson on third strikes, allowing runners to reach base.

Two Balls in Play

Baseball rules stipulate that the game be played with one ball at a time. The ball is often changed—when it becomes discolored or roughed up—but never is a new ball entered by the umpire until the old one is removed.

On June 30, 1959, however, the Chicago Cubs threw two balls to second base simultaneously in a bid to erase baserunner Stan Musial of the St. Louis Cardinals.

Musial was at bat with a three-ball, one-strike count when Chicago pitcher Bob Anderson delivered a pitch that home-plate umpire Vic Delmore called ball four. But Cub catcher Sammy Taylor argued that the ball hit Musial's bat and was therefore foul, increasing the count to three balls and two strikes.

Taylor did not give chase as the ball bounced toward the backstop. Delmore contended the ball hit Taylor's glove, glanced off the umpire's arm, and rolled toward the screen.

When Musial reached first, he heard teammates yell, "Run! Run!" He took off for second. If Delmore's call was correct, the ball was still in play. Third baseman Alvin Dark raced in and threw to shortstop Ernie Banks. At the same instant, pitcher Anderson took a new ball—which the umpire absentmindedly gave him during the argument over the ball-four call—and threw to second.

Anderson's throw sailed into center and Musial, seeing the error, headed for third base. He had gone only a few steps when Banks, holding the original ball, tagged him out.

Umpire Bill Jackowski ruled Musial out because he was tagged with the original ball. The Cardinals protested the decision, then dropped their protest after winning, 4–1.

Was There a Difference Between Leagues?

When the leagues had separate umpiring staffs, many pitchers said the strike zone was 8–10 inches higher in the American League than in the National. They also said NL hitters were more aggressive—an opinion substantiated by the fact that they hit 184 more home runs and had a batting average nine points higher than AL counterparts in 1972, the last year before the American League adopted the designated hitter.

Baseball's Only Rain-In

The only rained-in game in baseball history occurred in Houston on June 15, 1976, when torrential rains flooded the city with up to 10 inches of water. The Houston Astros and the Pittsburgh Pirates managed to get to the rainproof Astrodome, but the umpires, fans, and most stadium personnel did not.

Stormy Weather

The 1997 Florida Marlins had rain delays in 14 of their first 70 games. Ten of the delays lasted more than an hour. A three-game interleague series vs. the New York Yankees had delays that consumed five hours and 29 minutes.

Crediting the Pitcher

A starting pitcher must go five innings in a game to be eligible for the victory—with one exception. Should a game be stopped after it has become an "official" game (five full innings, or four and a half with the home team ahead), but before it has gone six innings, the starter is eligible for victory after pitching four innings.

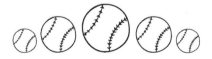

Why Phils Failed to Cheat the Curfew Law

On June 8, 1947, the Philadelphia Phillies lost an estimated $10,000 because an unthinking reserve catcher, just back from the minor leagues, failed to stall long enough to allow the Pennsylvania curfew to stop a game between the Pirates and Phils.

The game was tied 4–4 after eight complete innings in Philadelphia, but the Pirates took a 5–4 lead in the ninth on Ralph Kiner's home run. If the 6:59 P.M. Sunday curfew had stopped the game before the Phils had completed the home half of the ninth, it would have ended in a tie, since the score would have reverted back to the end of the previous completed inning. A tie would have forced a replay as a future doubleheader, guaranteed to bring out 10,000 more fans than a single game.

In the top of the ninth, Hank Greenberg of Pittsburgh allowed himself to be tagged on the base paths after he followed Kiner's two-out homer by getting hit with a pitch.

In the bottom of the inning, Phillies' manager Ben Chapman told his players to delay as much as possible. The first man popped out, but the second, Charley Gilbert, was a pinch-hitter who deliberately took excessive time to select a bat. He argued with the umpire, fouled off a series of pitches intentionally, but then struck out. One more out and the Phillies would lose the game and the additional $10,000 they would make if it ended in a tie.

Chapman called for catcher Hugh Poland, stationed 300 feet away in the bullpen. To the dismay of his teammates, Poland ran in. Had he walked in, he would have saved valuable time. Minutes remained on the clock. When he reached the batter's box, the delaying tactic suddenly dawned on Poland. He argued briefly with umpire Babe Pinelli, who hurried him back into the batter's box. Poland took two strikes, then lofted a lazy fly that Wally Westlake caught—just 52 seconds before curfew.

The Rain Rule

Because baseball rules do not mandate completion of all games, there have been 19 no-hitters of fewer than nine innings since 1900. There have also been "official" games shortened by rain, hail, fog, snow, gnats, darkness (before night baseball), and power failure (after the advent of night play).

For a variety of reasons—some of which will be explained here—the "rain rule" (which allows unfinished games to go into the record as if they were played to completion) is ridiculous.

Basically, the rule makes it legal for a game to be called after five complete innings, or after four and a half if the home team is ahead. If an inning is in progress and the game is called at any time after the fifth inning, the game is suspended if (1) the visitors have tied the score and the home team has not scored or (2) the visitors have taken the lead while an inning is in progress and the home team has not scored.

If a tie game is called after completion of an inning, all records count but the game must be replayed from the beginning.

One notable exception: if the home team ties the game at any time from the fifth inning onward and the game is called by the umpire at that time, the score does *not* revert to the previous completed inning. Instead, the game becomes a tie, all records count, but the game must be replayed from the beginning.

If a game is called *before* five innings are completed (four and a half with the home club leading), none of the records count. Roger Maris lost one home run to the rain in 1961, when he slammed 61 homers in 162 games and suffered the indignity of an asterisk (*) after his record because it was accomplished in an expanded schedule.

To illustrate the rain rule, suppose Pittsburgh is playing at Atlanta and leading, 4–2, when rain cancels the contest after four and a half innings. The game and its records would not count. If Atlanta led by the same score, they would.

This hypothetical example—and many real-life examples—underline the importance of playing all major league games to completion. Games stopped by curfew, prearranged time limits, light failure, and darkness (if law prevents turning on the lights) are considered suspended contests and must be completed from point of interruption. But some games stopped by weather are treated differently.

The Rain Rule

3.10 (c) The Umpire-in-Chief shall be the sole judge as to whether and when play shall be suspended during a game because of unsuitable weather conditions or the unfit condition of the playing field; as to whether and when play shall be resumed after each suspension; and as to whether and when a game shall be terminated after such suspension. He shall not call the game until at least 30 minutes after he has suspended play. He may continue the suspension as long as he believes there is any chance to resume play.

—Official Baseball Rules, 1978

Problems with the "Rain Rule"

Bill Terry, one-time slugger of the New York Giants, lost the 1931 batting crown by three-thousandths of a percentage point because he lost a base hit in a game canceled by darkness.

Playing a doubleheader in Brooklyn, Terry singled in his first at-bat of the second game. Confident he had won the batting title in a tight three-way race with Jim Bottomley and Chick Hafey, he retired from the lineup.

But Fresco Thompson of the Dodgers—the Giants' arch-rival—set fire to several scorecards as a signal that it was too dark to continue. Umpire Bill Klem spent considerable time looking for the culprit, then called the game. None of the records counted.

In the days when clubs depended on 10-hour train trips to travel around the league, it was often necessary to stop a game early to coincide with local railroad schedules. This was done by previous agreement between clubs—and such games were terminated at the appointed hour, rather than suspended.

In the early '50s, when Satchel Paige was the ace relief man for Bill Veeck's St. Louis Browns, the Browns were nursing a one-run lead late in the game and due to catch a train in less than an hour. Veeck told Paige to get the opposition out quickly for fear the game would revert to the previous inning and plunge the Browns into a tie.

Paige accomplished his mission by striking out the side with only 10 pitches. "The umpire missed one," he told Veeck as they boarded the train.

Stalling to Twist the Rules

Crafty Clark Griffith, manager of the New York Highlanders (later the Yankees) in 1907, was one of many big-league pilots who tried to twist the rain rule to their advantage by using stalling tactics.

White Sox hurler Ed Walsh had a 4–1 lead in the fifth inning as rain—and even hail—fell steadily. Griffith, hoping the game would be called and have to be replayed, inserted himself as a relief pitcher for New York and took his time warming up. When he pronounced himself ready, rain fell hard and play was held up.

To Griffith's dismay, play resumed 10 minutes later. Sox runners were at first and third when Griffith walked Billy Sullivan and then served an easy pitch to Walsh, who socked a two-run double. Chicago suddenly realized the situation and tried to end the inning quickly.

Sullivan waltzed home on Walsh's double, but allowed himself to be tagged out short of the plate. Ed Hahn hit a ground ball and waited out infielders who were in no mood to tag him out. Fielder Jones, White Sox manager, then tapped the ball to Griffith, but the pitcher let it go through his legs for a deliberate error.

Kid Elberfeld retrieved it and threw to first baseman Hal Chase, but Jones refused to touch first and Chase would not make the putout to end the inning.

Three Knotty Problems

Because the unexpected is expected in baseball, umpires must have thorough knowledge of baseball rules. Here are three problems that have happened before and may happen again.

1. An outfield fly strikes a bird in flight. The center fielder catches the ball and the right fielder catches the stunned bird. The correct ruling? The ball is in play because it is no longer "in flight" once it hits the bird. The batter may advance at his own risk.

2. Another touchy situation occurs when a baserunner attempts to score and anticipates a close play at home. He slides but misses the plate—while the catcher fails to tag him as he whizzes by. Since umpires are not bound to monitor missed bases for the defensive team, the right ruling is "safe" until an appeal is made. Then the call would change to "out."

3. Proper interpretation of the rules makes it possible for a team to get six hits in the same inning without scoring. For example, the first two batters hit singles. One is thrown out trying to steal third, the other is picked off. Three infield hits follow. The next hitter's grounder strikes the runner moving from first to second; the batter gets credit for a hit, but the runner is out for interference. No runs, six hits, no errors.

Rain Delay

Few pitchers steal bases, but Red Faber swiped three in an inning on July 14, 1915. With his White Sox holding a 4–2, fourth-inning lead and rain threatening, the A's tried to stall—hoping the game would be called before it became official. Trying to delay, Philadelphia's Joe Bush hit Faber with a pitch. But Faber, seeking to speed things up, took off for second, hoping to get thrown out attempting to steal. The A's ignored him, and also paid scant attention when the pitcher stole third and home—giving the Sox the run that proved decisive in an eventual 6–4 win.

When Rains Came

Rain erased seven home runs in one game on May 11, 2003. The St. Louis Cardinals were playing the Chicago Cubs at Wrigley Field and the wind was blowing out to right field at a 23-mph clip. Moises Alou homered in the first, Albert Pujols hit a grand slam in the second, followed by a Corey Patterson solo shot. Then Tino Martinez and Troy O'Leary connected in the third. Martinez homered again in the fourth, along with Alex Gonzalez. Then it rained in the top of the fifth, negating the 11–9 St. Louis lead and all player records from the game.

In Suspense

Determined not to let the elements interfere with the action, Major League Baseball allowed rain-delayed World Series games to be suspended rather than stopped. The new rule first applied on October 27, 2008, when Game 5 in Philadelphia was halted in the middle of the sixth inning in a 2–2 tie. Rather than requiring the game to be replayed from the beginning, it was resumed from the point of interruption two days later. The Phils won the game, 4–3, and the 5-game Series.

Frosty Forfeit

Snowball-throwing fans forced a forfeit of the 1907 New York Giants opener against the Philadelphia Phillies. The barrage began in the eighth inning but increased so quickly that play had to be halted.

Umpire John Sheridan finally ordered the Yankees to make the plays or face a forfeit. Griffith had no choice. The game continued until the last of the sixth, when the deluge broke and terminated play. Chicago won, 8–1, and Walsh was credited with a no-hitter—one of the two he threw in his career.

Fog-Outs and Other Unusual Postponements

On May 20, 1960, the Cubs and the Braves were victims of the first fog-out at Milwaukee County Stadium. Umpire Frank Dascoli, having trouble seeing the outfielders from home plate, took his three crew members and headed into the outfield, where the Cubs' three men were already stationed. Frank Thomas of the Cubs hit a fungo and none of the seven could see it. That clinched it. The game, 0–0 in the last of the fifth, was wiped out.

The only previous fog-out in National League records also involved the Cubs—at Brooklyn in 1956. The Cubs had previously lost a game to the elements when gnats descended on Ebbets Field in the sixth inning of a doubleheader nightcap on September 15, 1946. The sun was out, but the gnats so irritated the fans that they waved their white scorecards to shoo them away and created a hazard for players' vision. The Dodgers were awarded a 2–0 win since five innings had been completed.

Records of the Pacific Coast League, a Triple-A circuit, show (1) an Oakland game in the '40s called because mounted army troops had churned up the turf during maneuvers, (2) a seismic shock in Seattle that occurred during a game and forced cancellation, (3) a midday game in Ventura, California, called off because of a total eclipse, and (4) a 24-inning 1–1 tie in Sacramento, forced to stop because wind blew a neighbor's thick black smoke (from burning trash) over the playing field.

A 1921 Appalachian League game was postponed because of a homicide. After a girl's body was found at the Kingsport, Tennessee, ballpark, police closed the stadium to avoid confusing bloodhounds in their search for the killer. The game against Knoxville was called.

Forfeits

A team may forfeit a game to an opponent if it does not abide by an umpire's ruling, if it cannot control unruly fans, or if it knowingly violates the rules.

When a game is forfeited, it goes into the books as a 9–0 victory, but batting and pitching records count if the contest has survived the minimum five-inning standard for "official" games.

Stalling tactics by the Phillies robbed St. Louis slugger Joe Medwick of sole possession of the 1937 home-run crown. Medwick's homer had helped the Cards take a 3–0 lead in the third inning of the nightcap of a doubleheader, but the game began late because of a heavy shower that began just as the first game ended.

It would have been hard to squeeze in the required five innings before curfew curtailed the game, and Phillies manager Jimmy Wilson began a deliberate effort to delay when St. Louis jumped off to the early lead. He had failed to heed several warnings from umpire Bill Klem before Klem decided to award the game to the Cardinals by forfeit.

Since five frames had not passed, Medwick lost the home run and finished in a tie with Mel Ott of the Giants at 31 each.

Rowdy Fans Force Forfeits

Unruly crowds have contributed to many forfeits in baseball. As early as 1905, Brooklyn fans stormed the field with their team on the short side of a 16–0 score, and umpires handed victory by forfeit to the New York Giants.

Rowdy Philadelphia fans caused a forfeit of the Phillies' 1907 opener when they pelted umpire Bill Klem with snowballs. Detroit fans, angered when a Tiger was hit by a pitch, caused a disturbance that resulted in a forfeit to the Yankees in 1924.

The Philadelphia faithful were at the scene of the 1937 forfeit, caused by stalling, that robbed Cardinal Joe Medwick of the home-run crown; but one of the more famous forfeits in baseball annals occurred two years later in Boston.

With Sunday curfew approaching in the second game of a Sunday doubleheader between the Red Sox and the Yankees, New York tallied twice in the top of the eighth to take a 7–5 lead. Only 20 minutes remained before curfew would stop the game.

After looking at the clock, the Yankees began to make deliberate outs so that the top and the bottom of the inning could be completed. If the entire inning was not completed, the score would revert to the previous complete frame, leaving the game a 5–5 tie.

Seeing the farce, normally staid Boston fans showed their disgust by hurling straw hats, soda bottles, seat cushions, and other objects onto the field. Fenway Park was quickly covered with debris and therefore not in playing condition. Hence, the forfeit—and accompanying $1,000 fine for the Red Sox.

Boston was on the receiving end of a 1941 forfeit in Washington when the Senators' notoriously inept ground crew failed to cover the field on time during a rain delay in the top of the eighth. The umpires ruled their delay was deliberate since the Senators held a 6–3 lead at that time.

Stalling by manager Eddie Stanky caused the St. Louis Cards to forfeit to the Phils—following a brawl between the clubs—in 1954; but fans caused forfeits in the early '70s, at Washington in 1971 and Cleveland in 1974.

The Senators had been leading the Yankees in their final game in the capital before moving to Texas for the 1972 campaign, but souvenir-hungry fans couldn't wait for game's end to storm the field. The transplanted Senators, as Texas Rangers, recouped the '71 forfeit when they benefited from Cleveland's Beer Night Promotion three years later. Overindulgent fans made play impossible.

When Walks Were Hits

For one season—1887—walks were counted as hits. Tip O'Neill led the American Association with a .492 batting average. With the rule removed the following year, O'Neill again led the league. This time, he hit .332.

The Sacrifice Fly

Rules regarding the sacrifice fly have changed several times. In 1908, the present sacrifice fly rule was created: no time at bat is charged to a batter for a fly ball (with less than two outs) that enables a runner to score from third base. In 1926, the rule was expanded to award a sacrifice fly when any runners moved up a base. The sacrifice fly rule was abandoned in 1939, but the original (1908) version was restored in 1954.

Relievers Forced Change in ERA Rule

When baseball rule-makers realized the growing importance of relief pitching, they changed the qualifications governing the earned run average title. Before 1950 eligible pitchers had to throw at least 10 complete games. Under the revised rule, they had to work as many innings as their team played games (162). Hoyt Wilhelm became the first reliever to win the ERA crown in 1952, when he worked 159 innings under the 154-game schedule.

Utley Rule

After a Chase Utley slide injured Mets infielder Ruben Tejada in the 2015 NL Division Series, Major League Baseball enacted Rule 6.01(j), requiring runners to slide for the base rather than the infielder. On April 5, 2016, Tampa Bay second baseman Logan Forsythe threw wide to first while trying to complete a double play that would have ended the game. Instead, two runners scored to put Toronto up, 4–3. The Rays challenged and won, as the umpires ruled baserunner Jose Bautista deliberately interfered with Forsythe. Toronto lost its runs and the game, 3–2.

Across the Years with the Rule Book

Following is a list of the major rules additions and changes that occurred between the time the first set of rules was compiled in 1845 by Alexander Cartwright and the permanent adoption of the designated hitter rule in 1976.

In 1857 the game, previously decided when one side scored 21 aces, became a contest of nine-innings duration, regardless of the score.

In 1858 the pitcher could make a short run in his delivery and was relieved of the "called ball" penalty; called strikes were introduced; a batsman was out on a batted ball, fair or foul, if caught on the fly or first bounce, and the base runner was not required to touch each base in order.

In 1859 the catcher was first tried standing close behind the batter. Catchers complained that it hindered their powerful throws to second base.

In 1863 the bat was regulated in size; the pitcher's box was now 12 feet by 4 feet; no step was allowed in the pitcher's delivery and he had to pitch with both feet on the ground at the same time; home base and the pitcher's box were marked; no base could be made on a foul ball; base runners were required to return to base and could be put out in the same manner as the striker when running to first base.

In 1864 the "out on a fair bound" was removed and the "fly catch" of fair balls adopted. Then the rule was added that each base runner must touch each base in making the circuit, and Henry Chadwick introduced the first system of scoring.

In 1865 official averages were first introduced.

In 1867 the pitcher's box was made a six-foot square and the pitcher was permitted to move about as he wished; the batter was given the privilege of calling for a high or low ball, and the first curveball was introduced by Candy Cummings.

In 1872 the ball specifications as to size and weight were changed into what they are to this present day.

No further rules changes per se were introduced until the National League's first season of 1876.

The years and major changes follow in chronological order:

1877—Canvas bases 15 inches square were introduced, the same measurement as today; home plate was placed in the angle formed by the intersection of the first- and third-base lines, as today; the hitter was exempted from a time at-bat if he walked.

1879—Player reserve clause was for the first time put into a contract; the number of "called balls" became nine and all balls were either strikes, balls, or fouls; the pitcher had to face a batsman before pitching to him; a staff of umpires was first introduced.

1880—Base on balls was reduced to eight "called balls"; the base runner was out if hit by a batted ball; the catcher had to catch the pitch on the fly in order to register an out on a third strike.

1883—The "foul bound catch" was abolished; the pitcher could deliver a ball from above his waist.

1884—All restrictions on the delivery of a pitcher were removed; six "called balls" became a base on balls; championships were to be decided on a percentage basis, as today.

1885—One portion of a bat could be flat (one side); home base could be made of marble or whitened rubber; chest protectors worn by catchers and umpires came into use.

1887—The pitcher's box was reduced to four feet by 5 and a half feet; calling for high and low pitches was abolished; five balls became a base on balls; four "called strikes" were adopted for this season only; bases on balls were recorded as hits for this season only; the batter was awarded first base when hit by a pitch; home plate was to be made of rubber only (dropping the marble type) and was to be 12 inches square; coaches were recognized in the rules for the first time.

1888—Player reserve clause was written into the contracts of minor leaguers for the first time; the base on balls exemption from a time at-bat was restored; a batsman was credited with a base hit when a runner was hit by his batted ball.

1889—Four balls became a base on balls, as today; a sacrifice bunt was statistically recognized.

1891—Substitutions were permitted at any point in the game; large, padded mitts were allowed for catchers.

1893—Pitching distance increased from 50 feet to 60 feet, 6 inches, as today; the pitching box was eliminated and a rubber slab 12 inches by 4 inches was substituted; the pitcher was required to place his rear foot against the slab; the rule exempting a batter from a time at bat on a sacrifice was instituted; the rule allowing a flat side to a bat was

rescinded; the requirement that the bat be round and wholly of hard wood was substituted.

1894—Foul bunts were classified as strikes.

1895—Pitching slab was enlarged to 24 inches by 6 inches, as today; bats were permitted to be 2¾ inches in diameter and not to exceed 42 inches; infield-fly rule was adopted; a held foul-tip was classified as a strike.

1901—The American League became a major league and rules from this point on occasionally were instituted for one league only, as the foul-strike rule, used only in the National League; catchers, under protest, were compelled to remain continuously under the bat, but they complained that the base runner received too much of an advantage this way.

1903—Foul strike rule was adopted by the American League.

1904—Height of the mound was limited to 15 inches higher than the level of the base lines.

1908—Pitchers were prohibited from soiling a new ball; shinguards were reintroduced, this time by Roger Bresnahan; the sacrifice fly rule was adopted, exempting the batter from a time at bat when a runner scored after the catch.

1910—The cork center was added to the official baseball, the start of the new ball (which today can be cord, rubber, or similar material).

1917—Earned-run statistics and definitions were added to the rules.

1920—All freak deliveries, including the spitball, were outlawed, but registered spitballers were allowed to play out their string; the failure of a preceding runner to touch a base would not affect the status of a succeeding runner; the batter was given credit for a home run in the last of the ninth inning if the winning run was on base when the ball was hit out of the confines of the playing field; the number of runs batted in was to be included in the official score; frivolous "ninth-inning uncontested steals in one-sided games" were discarded.

1925—Pitcher was allowed to use a resin bag; the minimum home-run distance was set at 250 feet (existing parks with shorter fences were exempted).

1931—Sacrifice fly rule was brought back, this time with a man scoring after the catch only; defensive interference was changed from an offense solely by a catcher to one by a fielder as well; the quick-return pitch, squeeze play, and wild pitch were defined; players were to remove their gloves from the field when batting and no equipment was to show on the field at any time; no fielder could take a position in line with a batter's vision with the deliberate intent to in any way distract the batter; regulations referring to a batter contacting his own ball were clarified as was the area of bases awarded a batter and/or base runner when a defensive player threw his glove or other equipment at a batted or thrown ball or in the case of spectator interference.

1959—Regulations were set up for minimum boundaries for all new parks, 325-400-325 feet.

1968—The antispitball rule was rewritten and tightened up because of the wave of moistened pitches that floated plateward the prior season.

1969—The pitcher's mound was dropped five inches and the strike zone was shrunken to the area from the armpits to the top of the batter's knees to assist the hitters against the pitching dominance; the save rule was added to the official rules for the first time.

1971—All major league players were ordered to wear protective helmets at bat and all Class A and rookie league players were required to wear ear-flap type helmets at bat in the 1971 season.

1973—With the influx of so many new gloves and shapes and colors, the rule on glove size and color was minutely outlined for standardization; specific guidelines were set out to determine cumulative performance records; the American League began using designated hitters for pitchers on an experimental basis.

1974—The save rule was rewritten; minimum standards for individual championships were outlined.

1975—The ball, always covered with horsehide, was permitted to be covered with cowhide because of the shortage of horses and their hides; suspension for three days became mandatory if batter were to hit a fair ball with a filled, doctored, or flat-surfaced bat; the save rule again was changed.

1976—The American League's designated hitter experimental rule was put into the official rules on an optional basis.

—*The Sporting News*, June 5, 1976

Chapter 3

Lou Brock slides into second with another stolen base. Umpire Harry Wendelstedt signals his safe arrival.

Umpires

The First Umpires

Early umpires sat in rocking chairs 20 feet behind home plate.

Evans Enjoyed Himself

Umpire Billy Evans was behind the plate when Al Schacht was pitching a game for the Senators. "Have you thrown your fastball yet?" Evans asked. "Yes," Schacht replied, "about 10 times." Evans then pressed the button, letting the air out of his chest protector. "Good," he said, "I guess I won't need this."

Strike Zone Uniforms

Innovative owner Bob Howsam outfitted the minor-league Denver Bears in "strike zone uniforms" in 1952. The suits were white only between the knees and the chest.

Shrinkage

After watching National League scoring increase in 1962, the first year of expansion, baseball commissioner Ford Frick convinced owners to widen the strike zone to pre-1950 dimensions: top of the armpit to the bottom of the knee. The result was an increase in strikeouts, fewer walks, and the shrinkage of batting averages to their lowest since 1908.

Tough Job

Umpiring is a physically taxing profession. John McSherry suffered a fatal heart attack at age 51 while working home plate in Cincinnati on Opening Day of the 1996 season.

Father and Son

In 1998 Harry and Hunter Wendelstedt became the first father-and-son tandem to umpire the same major league game.

The Job of an Umpire

Umpires are paid by their leagues to officiate impartially at all games. Among other duties, they decide whether a field is in playable condition, call runners safe or out on the bases, and pass instant judgments on balls and strikes at home plate. Umpires are "the law" on the diamond and their decisions are final.

Umpiring was informal in the early days of baseball. When John Gaffney, unable to coax an apology from Giants manager John Montgomery Ward, refused to take the field for an 1886 contest, Pittsburgh pitcher Pud Galvin, sitting in the stands, replaced him.

Umps often risked life and limb—especially when the roughhousing Baltimore Orioles were in town. John Heydler, a pre-1900 umpire who later became National League president, said of the Orioles, "They were mean, vicious, and ready at any time to maim a rival player or umpire if it helped their cause." A little-enforced rule of 1881 empowered arbiters to fine pitchers for deliberately throwing at hitters, but the rule proved immensely unpopular and had to be dropped. It has since been reinstated.

The Strike Zone

The strike zone has always been the chief concern of the umpire. The calls of the home plate umpire make or break no-hitters, preserve or ruin shutouts, win or lose games, and even decide championships.

There have been several adjustments in the strike zone. In 1887 the strike zone was defined as the area from the top of the shoulders to the bottom of the knees, but was changed to "armpits to knee-tops" in 1950. From 1963 to 1968, however, the zone resumed its original definition and batting statistics fell in all categories.

A more recent standard, the same one in use from 1950 to 1962, was reinstituted in 1969. It defines the zone as halfway between the shoulders and the waist at the top and the knees at the bottom.

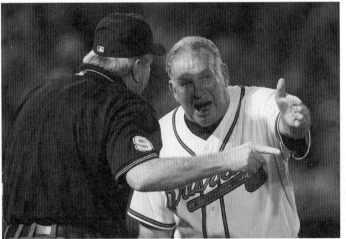

AP Photo/John Bazemore

Bobby Cox was ejected more often than any other manager. He was thrown out 158 times during the regular season and three times during the postseason.

Bill Klem:
Most Famous Man in Blue

Ten umpires have done their jobs so well that they are now enshrined in the Hall of Fame: Bill Klem, Jocko Conlan, Cal Hubbard, Billy Evans, Tommy Connolly, Bill McGowan, Al Barlick, Nestor Chylak, Hank O'Day, and Doug Harvey.

Klem, whose 35-year career as a field official began in 1905, ranks at the top of the list. He was the first arbiter to use exaggerated gestures to call balls and strikes. He developed the style while taking leisurely horseback rides in the quiet of the seashore pines near Lakewood, New Jersey.

Two Klem quotes sum up his legacy to the sport: "I never missed one in my heart," and "Baseball is more than a game to me—it's a religion."

Klem worked exclusively behind the plate for his first 16 seasons—even after the two-umpire system came into general use around 1920. He had an established reputation for excellence at calling balls and strikes and won a record number of World Series assignments (18 in all) as a result.

Umpiring crews were increased to three in the '30s, and later to the present-day four. World Series games had only two arbiters—one from each league—when the classic began in 1903. Regular-season games that year had only one umpire.

Umpire Feats

Emmett Ashford—first black umpire (1966)

Ted Barrett—first to work home plate in two perfect games

Jon Byrne—first Australian to umpire MLB game

Bill Dinneen—pitched one no-hitter, officiated in five

Bernice Gera—first female ump

Bill Haller—brother of catcher Tom Haller

Jim Joyce—botched call ruined perfect game

Bill Kunkel—pitched in MLB, son played in MLB, also NBA official

Ron Luciano—Syracuse football star who later wrote four books

Jerry Neudecker—last man to use outside chest protector, retiring in 1985

Jake O'Donnell—only man to officiate in both MLB and NBA All-Star Games

Pam Postema—first female umpire to work MLB exhibition game

Brian Runge—first and only third-generation ump after dad Paul and grandfather Ed

Charlie Williams—first black home-plate ump in World Series (1993)

Richard Baker

Bill Klem (center) was among the umpires working the 1915 World Series. He was so highly respected that he spent the last 18 years of his career working exclusively behind the plate.

Fan Attacks Umpire

The umpire accepts derision from men in uniform and jeers from fans as part of his profession. Sometimes he has to put up with more. In 1981 Mike Reilly was tackled from behind by an irate fan during the seventh inning of the American League East Division Series between the Milwaukee Brewers and the New York Yankees. The incident was witnessed by 54,000 fans at Yankee Stadium.

Wrist-Hitter

Umpire George Moriarty broke his wrist during a postgame fight under the stands with four members of the Chicago White Sox. They had accused him of deliberately making bad calls during the White Sox/Indians game.

St. Louis Cardinals

Tension shows on the faces of both infielder and umpire (Harry Wendelstedt) as Dal Maxvill sets to receive a throw at second base.

From Four to Six Umpires

In the Pittsburgh/Detroit series of 1909, four umpires were assigned, but worked in alternating pairs. Klem and Billy Evans of the American League sat in the stands for the opener, eating peanuts and keeping score, but a controversial hit by Max Carey of the Pirates stirred them to action.

The ball went into the stands, but a special ground rule set aside only a specified area as home-run territory. If the ball landed elsewhere, the hit would count as a double. Neither Klem nor Evans could tell where the ball hit, and the umpires on duty weren't sure either. All four umpires, accompanied by two bewildered managers, marched out to the stands and let the crowd convince them that the ball was actually a two-base hit.

Evans decided fans shouldn't be allowed to substitute for professional umpires and immediately wired American League president Ban Johnson. The next day, all four arbiters were working. The World Series crew was later increased to six—with two umpires monitoring the foul lines.

Both Klem and Evans, plus their countless colleagues in blue, were the traditional victims of abuse from both sides. Umpiring is such a thankless job that NL arbiter Dolly Stark curtailed his career with this remark: "I'm sick of being in a profession in which the greatest compliment I can receive is the silence of the crowd."

McGraw vs. Klem

Fiery umpire baiter John McGraw, longtime manager of the New York Giants, had a close relationship with Klem—fast friends off the field but arch-rivals when in uniform. One afternoon McGraw blew his top after a Klem call went against his team.

A Chicago batter hit the ball against the left-field scoreboard, but the sphere struck a section of board where the vertical line delineating foul territory from fair did not appear. McGraw sent a groundskeeper out to check for a dent in the scoreboard—only to learn Klem had made the right call.

In a game at Pittsburgh years later, bespectacled pitcher Danny MacFayden, incredulous that Klem had called his last pitch "ball four," raced home with glasses in hand, shouting to the umpire, "Here, you need these more than I do!" The pitcher was promptly ejected—over the protests of Pirates manager Frankie Frisch.

"I'm not ejecting him for questioning my eyesight," Klem said, "but for screaming so loudly that the crowd could hear him." At that, MacFayden replied, "The only reason I did that was I was afraid your ears might be as bad as your eyes!"

Anyone calling Klem "catfish" faced instant ejection. The remark was a personal affront because it reminded Klem of an argument he once had with Columbus manager Bill Clymer in the American Association. "Why you old catfish!" Clymer clamored after a close call went against him. "You can't talk, you can't smile, you can't do anything but move your gills!"

Klem, also quick with one-liners, put one over on Hack Wilson in 1930—the year Wilson set a National League standard with 56 home runs and a major league record of 191 runs batted in.

When the slugger questioned a strike call by saying, "You missed that one, Bill," the ump answered, "If I had your bat in my hands, I wouldn't have."

Earlier in his career, Klem gave the heave-ho to mild-mannered Pie Traynor. Inquisitive reporters asked about it after the game. "He wasn't feeling well," Klem explained. "He told me he was sick and tired of my stupid decisions."

The Hazards of Umping

Sometimes the life of an umpire is threatened with more than the traditional cry of "Kill the umpire!" On September 6, 1907, Billy Evans was struck on the head by a bottle thrown from the stands in St. Louis. He suffered a fractured skull and nearly died.

In 1921, at age 37, Evans had to rely on his boxing know-how when 35-year-old Ty Cobb—as great an agitator as he was a hitter—challenged him to a fight under the Griffith Stadium stands in Washington. The only precondition to the match,

which was ruled a draw by witnesses, was that league president Ban Johnson would not be informed of the proceedings.

There are many documented cases of illegal "umpire bumping" by players, brief on-field bouts, and a celebrated 1961 shin-kicking exchange between Dodger coach Leo Durocher and Jocko Conlan. The basic routine of an umpire continues to be an endless battle of words and wits, most of them involving challenges to the arbiter's eyesight.

After John McGraw referred to him as "a blind robber," umpire Robert Emslie showed up at Giants practice with a rifle. He marched out to second base, split a match, and inserted a dime. Then he walked to home plate, aimed, and fired, sending the dime spinning into the outfield with his first shot. McGraw argued with him again—but never challenged his eyesight.

PUTTING HIS FOOT IN IT, AGAIN

Leo Durocher was an umpire baiter as a player and a manager. His antics earned him several suspensions.

Mea Culpa

The umpire admitted he blew the call. The problem was that it robbed Armando Galarraga of a perfect game on June 2, 2009. After retiring the first 26 Cleveland Indians, the Detroit pitcher induced an infield grounder. Galarraga raced to cover first and took the feed in time from first baseman Miguel Cabrera. But umpire Jim Joyce called the runner safe. Because video replay challenges were not yet part of baseball rules, the call stood—even though the umpire later said he was wrong.

Machines Veto Homers

Josh Donaldson lost two home runs in one game to instant replay machines. It happened to the Toronto third baseman and future American League MVP on September 8, 2015.

Fan Ejection

Veteran umpire Bob Davidson, better known as Balk-a-Day Bob for his frequent balk calls, could have a new nickname soon. On August 2, 2016, he ejected a heckler from the stands in Philadelphia. It was actually the second time in six seasons that Davidson booted a fan from the stands; he also threw someone out in Milwaukee in 2010.

Long Tenures

Bill Klem umpired the most games (5,368), but Joe West served the most seasons (38 through 2016).

Umps Control Balls

Prior to 1906 the home team manager was in charge of supplying new baseballs. Charges were frequent that freshly introduced balls were "doctored" to help the home club and the leagues decided to place control of the balls with the umpires.

Umps to Remember

American League umpire uniform Nos. 2, 9, and 16 have been retired in memory of the late Nick Bremigan, Bill Kunkel, and Lou DiMuro, respectively. Nos. 1, 2, and 3 have been retired by the National League in honor of umpires Bill Klem, Jocko Conlan, and Al Barlick.

Smokefree Zone

American League umpire Frank Umont once ejected Baltimore manager Earl Weaver for smoking a cigarette in the dugout before the game started. The next day, Weaver brought out the lineup card with a candy cigarette dangling from his lips.

Umpires began raising their right arms to indicate strikes at the request of Dummy Hoy, an outfielder who played 14 seasons, mostly before the turn of the century. Hoy was a deaf-mute who could not hear the umpire call strikes at the plate.

Pitcher Babe Ruth challenged umpire Brick Owens so vehemently on a ball-four call to the first Washington hitter on June 23, 1917, that the umpire ejected him. Reliever Ernie Shore came on to retire 26 men in a row, plus the man Ruth walked, who was thrown out trying to steal second. Because of an umpire's decision, Shore managed to record the only perfect game that was not a complete game.

To ward off challenges to his vision, Southern Association umpire Harry "Steamboat" Johnson actually carried a card, signed by an eye doctor and certified by a notary public, stating that his vision was 20/20 in both eyes.

When Charlie Grimm was in one of his three terms as manager of the Chicago Cubs, umpire Charley Moran called a Cub out on a close play. Grimm led a protest posse out of the dugout. He put his hand on the umpire's head and said, "The first man to touch this blind old man is fined 50 bucks!"

Fresco Thompson of the Brooklyn Dodgers, with a rule book thrust in his face by an umpire seeking to silence his protest, came up with this gem: "How can I read that? If it's yours, it must be in braille."

On a day when the Cincinnati Reds were particularly rough on Al Barlick, he finally took action—giving the thumb to second baseman Johnny Temple. Infuriated, Temple asked how the bigger stars on the team can say the same thing without ejection. "I don't mind taking it from the lions and tigers," Barlick replied, "but I ain't about to take it from the gnits and gnats."

On occasion an entire bench sends a steady stream of insults in the umpire's direction. Unable to pinpoint the chief source, the arbiter may eject the entire dugout. That's exactly what Frank Dascoli did to the Brooklyn Dodgers on September 27, 1951, the last week of the Giant/Dodger pennant race that ended in Bobby Thomson's miracle home run for New York.

One of the 15 players Dascoli banished that day was rookie outfielder Bill Sharman, a minor leaguer added to the Dodger roster for the final days of the season. Sharman, who later achieved stardom in basketball, thus became one of the handful of players in the history of baseball to be a manager's whim away from playing, but never to get the call.

Instant Replay

Instant replay began in baseball on August 28, 2008. Six days later, an Alex Rodriguez home run was challenged by Tampa Bay manager Joe Maddon, who claimed it was foul. Crew chief Charlie Reliford agreed to the request but upheld the call after consulting with the video room of Major League Baseball. On September 19, the use of video replay gave Tampa first baseman Carlos Pena a home run that was originally ruled a ground-rule double because of fan interference. It was the first time instant replay resulted in a call being reversed.

Abusing the Umpire

Repartee between catcher and umpire generally centers on the same subject—though umpires report that almost all catchers have smaller strike zones when they're hitting than they do while catching. Not in the umpire's eyes, however.

When star Yankee receiver Yogi Berra was especially unhappy with Cal Hubbard's calls one day, the veteran arbiter stopped the game and said, "Look, there's no point in both of us umpiring. One of us has to go." Berra, agreeing to be quiet, answered, "Cal, don't you know when I'm kidding and when I'm being ferocious?"

Berra's successor, Elston Howard, complained about a ball-four call to Harmon Killebrew, who had homered, tripled, and doubled twice in four previous trips to the plate one evening. "You sure put him on that time," said Howard to the umpire. The reply was quick: "Yeah, but I held him to one base."

Unusual Plays and Decisions

Calling time and deciding plays not necessarily in the rule book are also duties within the province of an umpire.

Once while Frankie Frisch was running the Pirates in the early '40s, his club was one run behind the Phillies in the ninth, with Frankie Zak at second and Babe Russell the potential winning run at the plate.

Zak called time to tie his shoes and umpire Scotty Robb complied, waving his arms for temporary suspension of play. But the pitch was on its way and Russell hit a home run that would have won the game if time had not been called. The home run didn't count and Russell, given the chance to bat again, made an out to end the game. The next day, Zak appeared with zippers on his spikes instead of laces.

In an International League game in 1963, Rico Carty homered twice in the same at-bat because time had been called just before he hit the first one. When play resumed, Carty calmly proceeded to hit the next pitch out of the Toronto ballpark.

One of the most unusual plays in the annals of umpiring occurred during a Federal League game in 1914. One of the two umpires failed to appear, so the other stood behind the pitcher in order to see home plate and to be closer to all the bases. When the hitters started fouling off too many balls, the umpire, Bill Brennan, stacked a pile of fresh baseballs behind the pitcher's mound. (In those days, umpires did not carry a fresh supply in special coat pockets, as they do now.)

No sooner did Brennan set up his pile than batter Grover Lund lined a pitch into the stack, scattering the balls around the infield. Since no one knew what to do, Lund circled the bases while the infielders tagged him with every ball in sight.

No one could prove which was the batted ball, so Brennan ruled the 70-foot shot a home run—undoubtedly the shortest one ever hit.

Paul Richards vs. ump Hank Soar.

After pregame preliminaries, Perry Barber (above) wears her game-face. She was part of the all-female umpiring crew who worked a 2008 exhibition game between the University of Michigan and the New York Mets at Port St. Lucie, FL. From left are Barber, Mets manager Willie Randolph, Michigan coach Rich Maloney, Ila Valcarcel, Theresa Fairlady, and Mona Osborne.

Spittin' Image

After Baltimore's Robby Alomar spit in the face of umpire John Hirschbeck on September 27, 1996, baseball needed a court order to keep the umpires from boycotting postseason games. Alomar served a five-game suspension at the start of the 1997 campaign.

Spitball or Sinker?

Dodger first baseman Norm Larker complained to umpire Frank Secory that Milwaukee pitcher Lew Burdette was throwing spitballs in a game in the early '60s. Secory replied that they were sinkers. Larker responded, "Oh, yeah? One of them sinkers just splashed me in the right eye."

Bill Summers went against the script too—literally. The veteran umpire, working on a Hollywood movie set, got into his crouch, then called, "Strike One!" The director stopped the shooting and said, "Bill, that was supposed to be 'Ball one.'" The ump responded, "Tell the pitcher. I call them as I see them."

Strange Gripe

Umpires expect arguments on certain calls, but they never expect a pitcher to argue *against* a strike call. But, to prove anything can happen in baseball, St. Louis Browns' pitcher Jim Walkup did just that during the Rogers Hornsby regime of the mid-'30s.

Hornsby had warned his pitchers they would be subject to a $50 fine if they threw a pitch over the plate after having a no-ball, two-strike count on a hitter. (Hornsby followed the baseball theory that wise pitchers "waste" a pitch with a 0-2 count in the hope that the anxious batter will swing wildly and strike out.)

On the day Walkup had the prescribed 0-2 count, his third pitch just nipped the corner of the plate. The umpire yelled, "Strike three!" Walkup argued, but the umpire refused to reverse his call and the pitcher was out $50.

Umps Across the Years

1876—William McLean becomes first professional umpire
1878—National League tells home teams to pay umpires $5 per game
1882—American Association is first league to hire full-time umpire staff
1882—NL bars umpire Richard Higham for alleged collusion with gamblers
1885—Umps add chest protectors as regular equipment
1888—AA's John Gaff stays behind catcher for all calls except with runners on base, when he moves behind pitcher
1909—First year four umps work World Series
1911—Bill Dinneen is first former player to umpire in World Series
1921—First time umps apply rubbing mud to balls before games
1935—First umpire training school opens in Hot Springs, Arkansas
1946—Bill McKinley is first ump school graduate to reach majors
1947—First time six umps work World Series
1950—League presidents rather than umps decide fines
1952—Four-man umpire crews assigned to all games
1956—Ed Rommel and Frank Umont become first umps to wear glasses
1970—First umpires strike lasts one day during League Championship Series
1978—Amateurs officiate while umpires, seeking better benefits, strike for 13 days
1979—Umps strike again, forcing MLB to hire replacement umps
1984—Amateur umps work Game 1 of NLCS because of umpire strike
1991—AL ump Steve Palermo shot while trying to break up robbery in New York
1998—Harry and Hunter Wendelstedt become first father-and-son team to work same game
2006—Bruce Froemming works 5000th game
2008—Limited instant replay, for home run calls only, starts August 28
2009—First use of instant replay in World Series yields home run for Alex Rodriguez
2014—MLB expands instant replay with consent by players and umpires unions
2015—Outfield timers installed to speed up pace of game

Ronnie Joyner

How Managers View Umpires

Though they tend to argue loud and long, managers and players generally respect umpires.

Clyde King, one-time Brooklyn Dodgers' pitcher who saw Leo Durocher bait umpires, and later became a manager himself, conceded, "Overall, umpires do a good job. They are conscientious. Most umpires are human beings who make mistakes and know that. Ninety-five percent of the time, an umpire knows when he's missed a play. But there's a limit as to how long you can argue.

"Leo could argue louder and more vehemently than any manager I knew without getting thrown out. I really believe some of the umpires enjoyed having confrontations with Leo. Umpires respect good managers, others they don't respect.

"As a manager, I never went out to argue if I didn't think an umpire missed a play. There were a few instances where I've talked an umpire into changing his call because he asked another umpire. But most of them are too stubborn to do that.

"Consistency by an umpire is what managers look for—in handling the game, calling balls and strikes, and calling the bases. We should get the best umpires behind the plate every other day instead of every fourth day. That way they'll be sharper. It's just like the extra man on the bench who claims he can't get his hitting stroke because he doesn't play regularly."

The Umpire Today

The 68 umpires in MLB today earn from $120,000 to $400,000 per year, depending upon seniority. They also receive $340 per diem for lodging and food, four weeks' vacation, and first-class airfare when traveling. Those selected for All-Star or postseason games receive additional compensation. Their labor contract with Major League Baseball is negotiated by the World Umpires Association. Only a handful of the 225 minor-league umpires, whose top pay is about $3,000 per month, will reach the big leagues. An average of one per year will reach MLB to stay.

When working, umpires travel in four-man crews. Umpires make their own travel and hotel arrangements and handle their own equipment. They dress and shower at the ballpark in a special room far removed from the team dressing rooms. All these practices stem from innovations by Bill Klem early in the century.

Current equipment includes a mask, a uniform, and a padded chest protector, usually worn under clothing. The old balloon protector, which had to be adjusted before each pitch, gives more protection, but the chest protector pad is far more comfortable.

Because of the great variety of pitches and number of pitchers used per game, modern umpires like to know what each man has in his repertoire. They exchange information often.

That became easier in 2000 with the centralization of major league umpires into a single staff, rotated among all 30 ballparks.

Crowd Pleasers

During the early years of the game, umpires were picked from the crowd. Often prominent community members, they rested in chairs behind home plate and were treated with respect and courtesy by the players.

Kill the Umpire?

Fans twice took the cry "Kill the Umpire" literally. It happened during minor-league games in 1899 (Sam White in Alabama) and 1901 (Ora Jennings in Indiana).

An Ump to Remember

Bill Klem umpired in 18 World Series during his 37-year tenure and was so highly regarded that the New York Giants honored him with "Bill Klem Night" at the Polo Grounds.

Canine Caper

Umpire Brick Owens was bitten by a dog during a game in 1912. The dog, which belonged to Honus Wagner, dashed out of the dugout after Wagner was ejected for arguing with Owens.

Back from the Dead

The St. Louis Browns once scored six two-out runs in the ninth after the umpire called the game-ending out. It happened on May 20, 1922 when the Browns were playing the Yankees at the Polo Grounds. New York led 2–1 when the Browns exploded for a seven-run rally and won 8–2. The last six runs scored after a decision by first-base umpire Ollie Chill was reversed.

Sweatshirt Flap

A sweatshirt worn by Cleveland pitcher Johnny Allen caused a controversy at Fenway Park on June 7, 1938. When umpire Bill McGowan ordered Allen to trim the ragged edges of his sweatshirt, the pitcher refused and stormed off the mound. He explained later that he had trimmed the sleeves to allow a freer flow of air but the umpire ruled that the tattered sleeves distracted Boston batters.

Tough Boot

When umpire Drew Coble ejected soft-spoken slugger Cal Ripken Jr. from a 1989 game, he said he felt like he was ejecting God from Sunday school.

The umpire's ball-and-strike calls are vital to the success of every pitcher. Here, the ump is ready to signal a called third strike on Seattle's Phil Bradley, giving Red Sox right-hander Roger Clemens a record 20 strikeouts in a nine-inning game on April 29, 1986 (he did it again 10 years later). Clemens went on to play (and win) in the 1986 All-Star Game and also received the '86 Cy Young Award and the MVP trophy.

Umpires in Cooperstown

Umpires enshrined in the Baseball Hall of Fame are Al Barlick, Nestor Chylak, Jocko Conlan, Tommy Connolly, Billy Evans, Doug Harvey, Cal Hubbard, Bill Klem, Bill McGowan, and Hank O'Day.

Men in Blue?

Not always. When leagues controlled their own umpiring staffs, umpires wore blue suits and looked alike except for the fact that the American League umps used outside chest protectors. Such balloon protectors were banned in 1977 except for those using them at the time (Jerry Neudecker, who retired in 1985, was the last to use one). Umpire uniforms evolved, with such variations as gray slacks, red blazers, and even ties before the staffs were combined in 2000. A year later, all umps started wearing black blazers, gray slacks, and caps emblazoned with the MLB logo.

October Assignments

The advent of instant replay convinced Major League Baseball to add a seventh man to the six-man umpiring crews assigned to work the League Championship Series and World Series, beginning in 2014. The extra ump rotates between the replay booth and field for both events. Six-man crews continue to work the wild-card and Division Series games. At the start of the 2016 season, there were 76 full-time umpires divided among 19 crews, plus two slots for Triple-A umpires to be promoted when MLB umpires are on vacation or the disabled list.

Versatile Guys

Roderick Wallace and Big Ed Walsh are the only men who played, managed, and umpired in the major leagues.

Musical Umpire

Umpire Joe West, a country singer when he's not officiating, heard his tunes used as introductory music for Dodgers players as they were introduced during a home game on June 5, 2016. The tribute, suggested by infielder Chase Utley, expired after the first time around the Los Angeles lineup.

Female Arbiters

A half-dozen female umpires have worked in the minor leagues. Pam Postema lasted the longest, from 1977 to 1989, but retired after her 1991 sex discrimination lawsuit was settled without trial. The latest, Jen Pawol, was hired by the Gulf Coast League in 2016.

No Ump at Home

Part of a 2007 exhibition game between the Reds and Rays was played without a home plate umpire. After Marty Foster, who started the game there, was hit in the head with a pitch, the game continued with Derek Cooper calling balls and strikes from behind the pitcher's mound and Tom Hallion stationed on the third-base line. That arrangement continued until Chad Fairchild, who had been umpiring at first, found a chest protector and other equipment needed to work behind home plate. The Rays won the game, played in St. Petersburg, by a 15–1 score.

The Toughest Calls

Among the most difficult calls an ump faces every day is the call of interference. This would apply to the baserunner who aims for the infielder rather than the base in an attempt to break up a double play. To avoid approaching runners, fielders attempting to pivot at second and make a relay to first often throw the ball before touching the base or step off the base before getting the ball.

The "phantom double play" was accepted for years—only because the runner's slide at the fielder was accepted. The man with the glove was forced to cheat a little or risk amputation.

Previous to 1978, when American League umpires were ordered to enforce the rules strictly, such illegal tactics as the slide at the fielder and the phantom double play were overlooked with a knowing wink.

Beanballs—intentional pitches at batters' heads—were also an accepted, though scoffed upon, part of the game. Umpires were empowered to take strict measures against both pitchers and managers believed to be practicing this forbidden but traditional art.

Other tough calls are application of the rules governing postponements and suspensions of play (especially because of foul weather) and the batter's half-swing. Players' lightning-fast reflexes make it tough to tell whether a hitter has taken a swing or held back. Umpires watch the wrists; the batter must "break his wrists" to be charged with a swinging strike when the ball is out of the strike zone.

How Umpires Position Themselves

Umpires must be agile to make correct calls on fastballs that come in high on the outside corner of the strike zone. Before umps were consolidated under the umbrella of Major League Baseball in 2000, National League umpires worked on the right side of the catcher and looked over his right shoulder when a right-handed hitter was up. They went the opposite way for a left-handed hitter. American League umpires stood directly behind the receiver and looked over his head. NL umpires, with the inside protector, shielded their bare hands behind the catcher, while AL arbiters kept them grasped behind their backs to provide a better fit for their cumbersome balloon protectors, which fit tightly under the chin.

Each ump has his own stance and some, like National Leaguer Jerry Crawford and father Shag before him, actually touch the catcher. The Crawford style involved a hand placed between the catcher's hip and rib cage. Most players didn't object.

Recruiting of Umpires

Umpires are recruited from the high minors—and get jobs there after graduating from umpire schools. Veteran National League arbiter Ed Sudol, who lasted more than 30 seasons, began his career during the bitter winter of 1941, when he was a construction worker in Passaic, New Jersey.

Why Freak Pitches Were Banned

The spitball, emery ball, and other deliveries that involved doctoring of the ball were outlawed in 1920 as officials tried to "clean up" the game in the wake of the Black Sox scandal of 1919. Team and league executives thought heavier emphasis on offense would make fans forget the scandal quickly.

Lucky Break

Before he became a successful umpire, Nestor Chylak was blinded for 10 days by a German artillery shell.

Pressure Cooker

In the late innings of Don Larsen's 1956 perfect game in the World Series, home-plate umpire Babe Pinelli started sweating bullets. "What a spot to be in," he said later. "If I had to call a base on balls, it would go down as the Crime of the Century."

Electric Ump

Branch Rickey's Brooklyn Dodgers tested an electronic umpire during 1950 spring training. The machine, built by General Electric, used mirrors, lenses, and photoelectric cells designed to detect a strike. The short-lived experiment did have long-term results: it helped Duke Snider master the strike zone.

Toasted Twice

Earl Weaver was once tossed twice in one day by the same umpire. It happened on August 15, 1975 when Ron Luciano bounced the Baltimore manager in the opener of a doubleheader, then banned him again before the nightcap even started.

Ironman Ump

Bill McGowan was the Cal Ripken of umpiring. He went 16 years without missing an inning (2,541 consecutive games).

British Perspective

Tom Connolly, an American League umpire from 1901 to 1931 and the league's chief umpire through 1953, was an English native who never saw baseball before age 15. Born in 1870, he came to the United States as a teenager, became a minor-league ump, then moved to the National League in 1898. He umpired the first game in the new American League three years later and the first World Series in 1903.

The Umpires Weren't Thirsty

In 1957 Pittsburgh manager Bobby Bragan, while arguing with the umpires, tried to make peace by offering them a drink of orange juice. He was banished to the clubhouse and, shortly thereafter, replaced by Danny Murtaugh. Murtaugh had four terms with the Pirates and became one of the club's most successful managers.

Harvey's Credo

Longtime NL umpire Doug Harvey said of his semi-anonymous role, "When I am right, no one remembers. When I am wrong, no one forgets."

Critical Switch

Early in Game 7 of the 1992 NL Championship Series, home-plate umpire John McSherry took ill and was replaced by first-base ump Randy Marsh. According to Pittsburgh catcher Spanky Lavalliere, that altered the strike zone before the ninth inning, when Pirates pitchers were charged with two critical walks during Atlanta's pennant-winning rally.

Father Knows Best

In 1998, Harry and Hunter Wendelstedt became the first father-and-son combination to umpire the same game.

"One wintry night I got home, opened up *The Sporting News*, and it was like a divine inspiration," he recalled. "I opened right up to a full-page ad for Bill McGowan's Umpire School. There was a picture of a girl in a bikini leaning up against a palm tree and I decided that was for me. I answered the ad and went to the school in Daytona Beach, Florida. I met my wife there, started my career there, and that's where I live now."

When umps are scouted in the minors, major league officials look for knowledge of fundamentals, technique, mobility, and control of managers, players, and even themselves in pressure situations. Conditioning is also important, since umpires stay on the field until the game ends—even if it takes 25 innings, the length of one game Sudol handled.

Stop-action cameras showing "instant replay" have helped the profession, according to former American League supervisor of umpires Dick Butler, because the video invention gives umpires a 99 percent rating for accuracy. Scoreboards that show such replays seconds after the call are taboo, however; if the umpire's judgment is wrong, the replay could rile a crowd—which already dislikes the umpire simply because it's a baseball tradition.

An Error for the Umpire

Umpires do make occasional mistakes. In a pre-1900 National League game between Baltimore and Washington, umpire Jack Kerns kept the game going in fast-approaching darkness.

Oriole catcher Wilbert Robinson held a strategy conference with pitcher John Clarkson. During the meeting, Robinson slipped Clarkson a lemon and told him to throw it on his next pitch. Clarkson stuck the baseball into his back pocket and threw the lemon to the plate.

"Strike One!" roared the umpire. Robinson called time, then turned around to face the umpire. He opened his glove to reveal the lemon.

"When you can't tell the difference between a baseball and a lemon, it's time to stop," he said. The embarrassed umpire capitulated.

Wide Angle

Umpires' decisions have a direct bearing on the outcome of games and pennant races. After the Florida Marlins and the Atlanta Braves split the first four games of the 1997 National League Championship Series, portly umpire Eric Gregg suddenly created a new definition of the strike zone in Game 5 of the best-of-seven match. Many of his called strikes—including the one that caught Fred McGriff looking on in amazement to end the game—were clearly 12 to 18 inches off the plate.

As a result, Florida rookie Livan Hernandez beat Atlanta ace Greg Maddux, 2–1, and finished with 15 strikeouts, an NLCS record.

When National League umpire Randy Marsh enforced a more traditional strike zone in Game 5 of the World Series against Cleveland, Hernandez had eight walks and only two strikeouts in eight innings, instead of two walks and 15 strikeouts in nine innings.

Chapter 4

Mickey Mantle (top), Jackie Robinson (center), and Kirby Puckett (bottom) all advanced to Cooperstown because they knew how to play the game. Mantle hit a record 18 World Series homers, starting with this 1953 shot off Preacher Roe, while Robinson intimidated opponents on the bases. Puckett's leaping catch robbed Ron Gant in Game 6 of the 1991 World Series, which ended a day later in a 1–0, 10-inning thriller.

Playing the Game

A Strikeout to Remember

In his only major league appearance, Arlas Taylor of the A's yielded seven hits in two innings against the Indians on September 15, 1921. Taylor's only strikeout victim was Joe Sewell, the toughest batter to strike out in major league history! Sewell averaged only one strikeout per 63 at-bats in his long career. Sewell fanned just three times in 353 at-bats during the 1930 campaign, but two of the strikeouts occurred in the same game.

Deceptive Standings

Won/lost percentage is more important than games behind in determining team standings. Here is an actual example from early in the 1978 season:

National League East

	W	L	Pct.	GB
Phila.	5	3	.625	½
N.Y.	8	5	.615	–
Chi.	6	5	.545	½
Mont.	5	5	.500	1
St.L.	5	7	.417	2
Pitts.	3	7	.300	3

How to Prove a Box Score

A box score is in balance (or proved) when the total of the team's times at bat, bases on balls received, hit batters, sacrifice bunts, sacrifice flies, and batters awarded first base because of interference or obstruction equals the total of that team's runs, players left on base, and the opposing team's putouts.

A's Swindle Indians

On July 25, 1930, the Philadelphia Athletics twice executed rare triple steals against the Cleveland Indians. It was the only time the triple steal has been used twice in the same game.

Crafty Carey Was Capable Culprit

Pittsburgh's Max Carey was thrown out only twice in 53 steal attempts in 1922. That success ratio remains a major league record.

Statistics

Baseball's individual records are determined through the daily box scores. Keeping score is easy, but there are a variety of methods. In any system the objective is to keep a complete and accurate game record that can be read weeks—or even years—later.

Scorebooks come in two styles—with blank squares or with smaller squares within the squares. Fans prefer the first (and ballpark scorecards are made this way) because there's more room to write.

To guarantee uniformity in professional scoring, the *Official Playing Rules of Baseball* includes a section on scoring regulations. Under any system, it is essential to keep track of substitutes, position changes, and all pitching statistics. Unfortunately, the "streamlined" box score adopted by the major wire services in the early '70s dropped the practice of showing position changes, thereby making it impossible for the avid fan to follow the game as closely as he would like. Before detailed boxes were restored to the wires, *The Sporting News* was the sole source of boxes showing defensive movement of players during the game.

Modern records are "unofficial" in many cases because key statistics currently used in the game were not always recognized.

For example, the *Chicago Tribune* began reporting runs batted in during the 1880 season, but the idea received such a cool reception it was discontinued until 1891, when the National League and the American Association ordered their official scorers to keep track of RBIs. By June, NL scorekeepers abandoned the practice; the AA men obeyed their orders, but the league folded after that campaign.

Runs batted in returned in 1907 at the urging of *New York Press* sports editor Jim Price, but the American and National League did not give RBIs official recognition until 1920!

Batting averages were not used until 1871, when Boston and Cleveland of the National Association (forerunner to the National League) conceived the concept of dividing hits by times at bat. Up to that point, teams had kept records only of the most hits.

Won/lost records for pitchers gained semiofficial status only in 1887, when pioneer baseball writer Henry Chadwick began keeping such records. Previously, pitchers who worked the most innings in a winning game received the victory—even if they were out of action when the game was decided.

Records of complete games weren't kept until National League secretary (and later president) John Heydler began the practice in 1909, long before the American League followed suit. In 1912, Heydler also introduced the idea of ERA (earned run average).

Relief pitchers' saves began—unofficially—when *The Sporting News* created its Fireman of the Year Awards in 1960, but did not win official recognition by the majors until 1969.

Historians thumbing through old records have attempted to include all major leaguers, 1876 to the present, in the game's official register, but the process proved both tedious and difficult. Because pre-1900 rules were quite different, most historians consider true records to be those made in the 20th century.

When Pete Rose put together his 44-game hitting streak of 1978, he tied the National League mark of Wee Willie Keeler, who did it in 1897. But he surpassed the "modern" league record of Tommy Holmes, who hit in 37 straight games in 1945.

Learn to Score and Enjoy Baseball More

Much of the fun at a ballgame is keeping your own scorecard. Fans can enjoy baseball to its fullest extent by keeping score, as it allows you to trace the complete progress of the game and pinpoint those crucial plays that bring victory or defeat.

All you need is a basic knowledge of baseball's rules. Although there are countless scoring methods, experts use a simple code based on numbering players by position and tracing action through the use of symbols.

It's easy and fun. In fact, why not devise your own scoring system with the basic suggestions on this page? Part of the fun of scoring is improvising a system that you can decipher after the game is over.

One suggestion on player substitutions is to use a heavy or wavy line under or over a box to indicate a change, either of a pitcher or a batter. Another is if a batter flies to the right fielder, merely use the figure 9. If it is a foul fly—9F.

Just number the players as follows:

Pitcher	1
Catcher	2
First Baseman	3
Second Baseman	4
Third Baseman	5
Shortstop	6
Left Fielder	7
Center Fielder	8
Right Fielder	9
Designated Hitter	DH

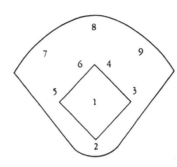

And use these simple symbols for plays:

Single	–
Double	=
Triple	≡
Home Run	≣
Error	E
Foul Fly	F
Double Play	DP
Fielder's Choice	FC
Hit by Pitch	HP
Wild Pitch	WP
Stolen Base	SB
Sacrifice Hit	SH
Sacrifice Fly	SF
Caught Stealing	CS
Passed Ball	PB
Balk	BK
Struck Out	K
Base on Balls	BB
Force Out	FO
Intentional Walk	IW

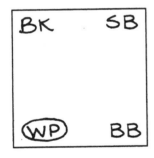

In this example, the hitter reached first base on a walk, stole second, advanced to third on pitcher's balk, scored on pitcher's wild pitch. Be sure to trace a player's complete progress around the bases. Indicate scoring plays by encircling or boxing symbol.

Team	Pos.	1	2
Right Fielder	9	4-6 W	
Second Baseman	4	3 FC	
First Baseman	3	=	
Center Fielder	8	SF8	
Designated Hitter	DH	K	
Left Fielder	7		4-6 –
Catcher	2		DP 6-3
Third Baseman	5		≣
Shortstop	6		7
Pitcher	1		
Totals R/H		1/1	1/2

Inning 1

Walked and was forced out at second (second baseman to shortstop).

Reached first on fielder's choice when runner was forced out, advanced to third on double by third-place hitter, scored on fourth-place hitter's sacrifice fly.

Doubled and did not advance further.

Flied out to center field scoring runner on third.

Struck out—end of inning.

Inning 2

Singled, later forced out at second (second baseman to shortstop in first half of double play).

Hit into double play, second baseman to shortstop to first baseman.

Hit home run.

Flied out to left fielder—end of inning.

Good Eye

Although players produced 50-homer seasons 23 times before 1998, only once has any of those sluggers had more home runs than strikeouts. It happened in 1947, when Johnny Mize of the New York Giants had 51 homers and 42 strikeouts.

Super Cy

Cy Young's records include 749 complete games in 815 starts, 511 wins, and 7,356 innings pitched. He had five 30-win seasons during a 22-year career that stretched from 1890 to 1911.

Reversal of Fortune

What a difference a day makes; Hub Leonard of the 1916 Red Sox pitched a no-hitter against the Browns a day after the same club had knocked him out in the first inning.

Why White Sox Warned Appling

Shortstop Luke Appling, a specialist at tiring a pitcher by hitting countless fouls, was warned by the White Sox to cease and desist because he was losing too many balls.

Home-Run Derby

Dale Long of the 1956 Pirates, Don Mattingly of the 1987 Yankees, and Ken Griffey Jr. of the 1993 Mariners homered in eight consecutive games. Frank Howard of the 1968 Senators hit 10 homers in six games while Stan Musial of the 1954 Cardinals and Nate Colbert of the 1972 Padres each hit five home runs in a doubleheader.

In the Squat

Ivan Rodriguez (2,427), Carlton Fisk (2,226), Bob Boone (2,225), Gary Carter (2,056), and Jason Kendall (2,025) are the only catchers to work at least 2,000 games behind home plate.

How to Figure Averages Like an Expert

Individual Batting—Divide the total number of times a player has been at bat into the total number of hits he has made. Example: Player White has 361 official times at bat and has been credited with 92 hits. Dividing 92 by 361 results in a batting average of .255.

To win a batting championship in the major leagues, a player must have a total of 502 appearances at the plate (at-bats, sacrifice flies, sacrifice hits, walks, and hit-by-pitch). The number 502 was set as the qualifying standard because it is the product of games scheduled (162) multiplied by 3.1 (the average number of times a player goes to bat during a game).

Slugging Average—Divide the total number of times a player has been at bat into the total number of bases he has accumulated. Example: Player Green has 534 official times at bat and is credited with a total of 382 bases (home run, four; triple, three; double, two; single, one). Dividing 534 into 382 gives a slugging percentage of .715.

Earned Run Average—The number of earned runs a pitcher has allowed is multiplied by nine, the number of innings in a game. The product is then divided by the number of innings he has pitched. Example: Pitcher Black has allowed 63 earned runs in 174 innings. The formula is 63 times 9, divided by 174. The result is an earned run average of 3.26.

A pitcher must hurl 162 innings in a season to qualify for the earned run average championship. The number was selected to represent one inning pitched for each game scheduled.

Fielding Average—The total number of putouts, assists, and errors on a player's record are added. Also add the number of putouts and assists he has. Then divide the first sum (putouts, assists, errors) into the second sum (putouts, assists). Example: Player Brown has 167 putouts, 67 assists, and 3 errors. The formula is 167 plus 67 plus 3, divided into 167 plus 67. That results in a fielding average of .987. A fielding champion must appear in 108 games at his position, except a catcher, who must appear in 81 games.

Won/lost percentage is reached by dividing the number of victories by the total games won and lost.

The **number of games behind the leader** in the standings is determined by comparing the leading team's record with the trailing team's figures on a minus-plus basis—12 victories and 4 losses, against 7 victories and 8 losses is a difference of 5 victories and 4 losses. The total of nine is then divided by two—indicating a difference of 4½ games.

To determine the "**magic number**" in a pennant race, compute the number of games yet to be played, add one, then subtract the number of games ahead in the loss column of the standings, from the closest opponent.

Running

Running the bases well presents an easy path to victory. Not only is speed important, but also instinct. A base stealer must get the best jump and make the best slide or he won't be successful. Proper slides can break up double plays, keep big innings alive, and avoid injuries for the baserunner.

"I practiced running as hard as I practiced anything," Ty Cobb conceded years after he had retired from the game. "When I was a kid, I bought all the 'How to Sprint' books advertised in *The Police Gazette*. I spent hours out in the field learning to pump my knees high and especially to break into a fast start.

"I would jog 10 steps, break into a sprint, slow down, and start all over. I spent many hours learning to run in a straight line at top speed with my head over my right shoulder, so that I could watch what the outfielders were doing with the ball.

"I didn't have a lot of natural speed on the bases, but I knew how to run."

Cobb's 1915 record of 96 stolen bases stood until 1962 when Maury Wills stole 104 times in the first year of the expanded 162-game schedule. Lou Brock topped both men when he swiped 118 bases in 1974. Brock also surpassed Cobb's lifetime total of 897 steals—a record once considered as safe as Babe Ruth's 714 home runs. Rickey Henderson now holds the records for stolen bases in a career and a single season (130 in 1982). He is the only man with more than 1,000 lifetime steals.

Mastery of bunt and slide techniques contributed greatly to Cobb's game. He compiled the all-time batting mark of .367 largely because he reached base often on bunts. Cobb taught himself pinpoint bunting control by putting a sweater down on the field and trying to make the ball come to a stop on the sleeve. As a sliding aid, he learned to "read" the eyes of the man covering second as the throw came in. He then aimed his slide away from the tag.

Even slow-footed runners can win games on the base paths. In close plays, they can knock the ball out of a fielder's mitt with a well-placed kick. "If you're coming home and the ball is going to beat you, your only shot is to knock the ball loose," conceded Bob Boone, a catcher who has been on the receiving end of many collisions.

Kicking helps in the infield too. During the 1951 World Series, Eddie Stanky of the New York Giants knocked the ball out of Phil Rizzuto's glove as the Yankee shortstop attempted a tag. After the game, Rizzuto told the media Stanky had made a smart play.

Straying from the base line is illegal, but officials generally look the other way when runners dump infielders trying to pivot during a double play.

"As soon as the second baseman or shortstop catches the ball, I'm out, so I disregard the base," admitted Hal McRae, an aggressive Kansas City Royal of the '70s. "The fielder becomes the base. And the best way to keep him from relaying the throw is to knock him down. He can't throw when he's on his back."

Smart infielders learn to jump as well as pivot.

Ty Cobb

Maury Wills

Stealing Home

Stealing home is one of the most difficult feats of baseball. Ty Cobb did it a record 54 times, and even 30 pitchers have done it since 1900. Maury Wills tried it once, but batter Frank Howard missed the sign and slammed a hard liner that just missed the startled runner. Lou Brock also disdained the idea. But Rod Carew liked it, and made it seven times in 1969. Pitcher Nolan Ryan—who once lost a game when Amos Otis stole home—called the play "humiliating."

Robbing Rickey

Branch Rickey's career as a catcher was short-circuited in a single game: on June 28, 1907, 13 Washington runners stole successfully against Rickey's Yankees in a 16–5 romp.

Allen Gross

Rickey Henderson's shoes preceded his plaque into the Hall of Fame. The fleet left fielder holds records for stolen bases in a season and a career.

Joe Medwick of St. Louis created a controversy with a hard slide into Detroit's Marv Owen during the 1934 World Series.

Better than Nothing

Herb Washington, a Michigan State track star, got into 105 major league games without ever throwing a pitch or coming to bat. Used strictly as a pinch runner by Charley Finley's world champion Oakland Athletics in 1974, Washington stole 31 bases in 48 attempts and scored 33 runs.

Record Robbers

The world champion Cincinnati Reds of 1975, led by Joe Morgan, were successful base stealers 82 percent of the time, a major league record.

Wild Bill Runs Wild

Detroit pitcher Wild Bill Donovan singled, then stole second, third, and home (on a double steal), in beating Cleveland, 8–3, on May 7, 1906. He also hit a triple in the game.

Stealing Bases

Before the lively ball era began in 1920, base stealing was an important part of baseball offense. One run often made the difference in a game when home runs were unlikely, and swift players could turn a walk, single, or error into a double by picking an opportune moment to steal.

Increased emphasis on the home run convinced most big-league managers to play for "the big inning," and to stack their batting orders with lumbering sluggers rather than speedy baserunners. The hit-and-run became a favorite tactic as the tendency toward stealing declined in direct proportion to the absence of fast, cunning runners.

Ty Cobb's old standard of 96 steals was achieved in 1915, but Babe Ruth's bat triggered an offensive boom five years later and base thievery declined. Even Cobb's game changed. In the 10 years he played after 1918, he never stole more than 28 bases and had 15 or fewer six times.

By 1938 the National League leader in stolen bases, Stan Hack of the Cubs, had only 16 to his credit. As late as 1950, Dom DiMaggio paced the American League with 15.

Gradually, things began to change. Players like Jackie Robinson and Willie Mays proved the value of speed plus power, and Luis Aparicio proved that teams could win with a combination of pitching, speed, and defense—even if they didn't have power.

Maury Wills, who reached the majors in 1959, showed that Herculean performances by a base stealer could be just as important as consistent production from a home-run hitter. In 1962 his exploits on the bases were almost enough to offset a late-season drive by the San Francisco Giants, who repeated their miracle finish of 1951.

Ironically, 1962 was also the year Lou Brock was playing his first full season in the National League. He stole 16 bases for the Cubs—and 24 the next season—but drew more recognition for a prodigious home-run clout into the distant center-field bleachers at New York's Polo Grounds.

Only the St. Louis Cardinals saw Brock's immense potential and, in 1964, they traded veteran starter Ernie Broglio and two other players to get him. At the time, the deal looked like a real "steal" for the Cubs, but it turned out to be just the opposite.

In his first 16 seasons (not counting an 11 at-bat trial with the 1961 Cubs), larcenous Lou stole 900 bases. It took Ty Cobb 24 seasons to reach his mark of 897.

"He had great speed and utilized it well," said Wills of Brock after the former had left the playing field for the broadcast booth. "He got a great jump despite the fact he didn't take a big lead."

Brock, who said he ran only when reasonably sure of making it, became baseball's second-best base stealer because he studied the pitchers. "The thing I looked for," he said, "was how they released the ball—quick, fast, moderate, or slow. That determined when I could go."

Joe Torre, a former catcher and Brock teammate who later became a manager, recalled his technique of stealing. "When Brock got on," said Torre, "the catcher tried to get the ball out of his glove before it even got to him. The game is all rhythm and when you don't have that, you end up watching people like Lou Brock steal bases. When he was on base, he made the infielders play out of position and messed up the pitcher's timing. The pitcher kept looking over his shoulder and trying to throw to the plate at the same time."

Ty Cobb took a long lead and used a hook slide, but Brock— with greater speed than Cobb or Wills—got away with a short lead and pop-up slide—almost no slide at all. That helped preserve his body from the painful "strawberries" that afflict so many base stealers.

Injury can cripple the team that depends on a one-man running show, but a collection of base thieves can often overcome the absence of a single individual. The 1976 Oakland A's finished 10th in batting with a .246 team average, but wound up second—just two and a half games from the top—because they established an American League record with 341 steals.

In finding success 73 percent of the time, the A's missed tying the major league mark of the 1911 New York Giants by six. But Oakland did become the first team in the modern era to have three players with 50 or more stolen bases: Don Baylor, Bill North, and Bert Campaneris.

"They throw some pressure on you—no doubt about that," said catcher Thurman Munson of the Yankees, American League champions that year. "Most of those guys are so good that if they get a jump, they're going to steal."

With the exception of the delayed steal—where the runner breaks after the relaxed catcher throws the ball back to the pitcher—most steals are achieved against the pitcher—especially a man who neglects to hold runners close to the bases.

A flaw in the pitcher's motion may alert runners about his intentions—is he throwing to first or pitching to the batter? Top runners can tell by watching the movement of the shoulder.

Base stealing is a more hazardous trade than hitting home runs because the runner risks injury every time he slides—which is often. Many of the most serious accidents of baseball history occurred during slides (especially when players changed their minds after committing themselves). One such accident, in March 1954, knocked Bobby Thomson out of the lineup and gave an obscure youngster named Hank Aaron the chance to play every day. Except for his own sliding fracture—suffered that fall—Aaron stayed in the lineup for 21 years, long enough to become baseball's new home-run king.

Fielding

Many baseball managers believe the best offense is a good defense.

Teams built around speed, defense, and pitching have won numerous championships, while power-laden clubs that were weak in defense often failed to play well.

Leo Durocher was criticized heavily when he traded several sluggers to secure such players as Alvin Dark and Eddie Stanky, who provided stability around second base that helped the New York Giants stage their 1951 "miracle."

The 1959 Chicago White Sox, led by the double-play team of Nellie Fox and Luis Aparicio, won the American League pennant for the first time in 40 years.

Championship teams are invariably strong "up the middle"— catcher, shortstop, second base, and center field. Hall of Famer

Joseph J. Licata

Atlanta's Gerald Perry tries to score on the front end of a double steal as Baltimore backstop Mickey Tettleton readies the tag.

When St. Vrain Ran the Wrong Way

Weak-hitting pitcher Jimmy St. Vrain of the 1902 Cubs, hitting left-handed for the first time, hit a grounder to Pittsburgh shortstop Honus Wagner and was so startled he made contact that he ran to third.

Lopes Catches Carey

Dave Lopes of the Dodgers stole safely 38 straight times in 1975 to erase Max Carey's 1922 record. Vince Coleman holds the current record of 50 consecutive steals in 1988.

Sun Field

It's debatable whether Brooklyn pitcher Billy Loes ever lost a ground ball in the sun, but it's a fact that the sun plays havoc with outfielders in search of fly balls. Fenway Park has always been especially rough in the fall. "In Boston," a verse goes, "the sun rises in the east and sets in the eyes of the right fielder."

Jose Canseco (above) became the first member of the 40/40 Club in 1988 when he hit 42 homers and stole 40 bases for the Oakland Athletics. Barry Bonds of the San Francisco Giants became the National League's first 40/40 man in 1996.

Multiple Miscues

The 1901 Detroit Tigers and the 1903 Chicago White Sox share the embarrassing record of most errors in one game: 12.

Timing Makes Good Hitters

Swinging a heavy bat does not guarantee home-run production. A man who swings a lighter bat but has good timing will get better distance on the ball than the player with a heavy bat but poor timing. The objective is to let bat meet ball at the moment of greatest power in the swing.

Frankie Frisch, a second baseman in his playing days, once said, "The muscle men who sweep the ball over the wall attract the attention, but the skillful artists who operate around the second base bag win the pennant. The voters should pick more infielders for the Hall of Fame."

Phil Rizzuto, a one-time American League Most Valuable Player who played shortstop for the Yankees before taking to the airwaves, is an excellent example of a highly-regarded infielder who had trouble entering the Hall. Rizzuto, instrumental in many New York championships, was a World Series hero in 1951. "They never would have done it without that little pest," said Herman Franks, coach of the losing Giants, in reference to Rizzuto.

Honus Wagner, also a shortstop, was the most sure-handed fielder of his era—and perhaps of all time. Wagner, one of five charter Hall of Famers elected in 1936, began an 18-year career with the Pittsburgh Pirates in 1900.

According to *Baseball Magazine* of August 1943, "Perhaps the greatest pair of hands baseball has ever seen dangled at the end of the long arms of Hans Wagner. They, indeed, were more like twin steam shovels than human hands, literally ploughing under National League infields. The Flying Dutchman of the Pirates never fielded the ball alone. He would blithely scoop a handful of dirt too and ball and dirt would go flying over to first base impartially. It left Old Honus hidden behind a smoke screen of his own raising."

Lou Boudreau, Cleveland shortstop at the time the Wagner article appeared, was not only a capable fielder but also a shrewd tactician who became the club's player/manager. In 1946 he devised the radical Ted Williams shift—designed to thwart the Boston pull hitter's amazing success against the Tribe.

After Williams had hit three homers—one with the bases loaded—to give the Red Sox an 11–10 victory in the opener of a doubleheader on July 14, Boudreau stationed six fielders on the right side of the diamond—where the left-handed Williams placed nearly all of his hits.

The left fielder, playing deep shortstop, was the only man on the left side of the infield.

Williams, a student of hitting, could have overcome the shift by bunting or slicing the ball to the opposite field, but such strategy would have reduced his power. Though other clubs copied the Ted Williams shift (though none so radically as the Indians), the slugger decided to overpower the defense. He said later that the

Derek Jeter . . . good glove at short.

shift probably deprived him of 20–30 points on his lifetime batting average, which was an excellent .344.

The Red Sox slugger did get even with Lou Boudreau on September 13, 1946. In the first inning at Cleveland, he belted the only inside-the-park home run of his career—a 400-foot drive to left-center that proved to be the only run of the game. The 1–0 win gave Boston the pennant.

Radical defenses had been tried before Ted Williams reached the majors. Branch Rickey, the great executive who managed the Cardinals in the early '20s, concocted a shift against Cy Williams, the Phillies' left-handed slugger who also hit to right field with consistency. Ken Williams of the Browns, who played at the same time, also was a left-handed pull hitter and also inspired opponents to shift to right.

Babe Ruth hit left-handed too, but a shift tried on him by Cleveland's Tris Speaker was unsuccessful. Later, Luke Appling—a right-handed hitter who hit to right—overcame a Yankee shift.

In 1937, the Chicago Cubs shifted to left against Wally Berger of the New York Giants. In a critical doubleheader in late summer, however, the value of the shift was questioned when Berger slammed a ball to Billy Herman, a second baseman playing in the shortstop's spot. Herman couldn't reach first, though strong-armed Billy Jurges—who might have made the play if not for the shift—stood only a foot away.

Herman's miscue opened the gates for the Giants, who reversed a 7–2 deficit and went on to sweep both games. They knocked the Cubs out of the race and went on to win the National League pennant.

Defensive Strategy

In the seventh game of the 1962 World Series at San Francisco, the New York Yankees loaded the bases with nobody out in the fifth inning of a scoreless game. Manager Alvin Dark of the Giants had two choices: (1) play the infield in to try to cut off a run at the plate if the batter hit a grounder, or (2) play the infield back to decrease the chance of the ball going through—possibly igniting a big inning—and hope for a double play on a ground ball. The

Pitcher Ted Lyons once said of Stan Musial (above) that his batting stance reminded him of a kid peeking around the corner to see if the cops were coming.

Stealers Can Slump

"Stealing is like hitting—you can go into slumps," said George Case, who swiped 61 bases for the 1943 Senators. "I remember being thrown out three or four times in a row. Clyde Milan was coaching for us and said, 'You're not taking your good lead, and you're too tensed up, too afraid of being picked off. Relax and it'll come back.'"

Ozzie the Run Saver

According to Whitey Herzog, Ozzie Smith regularly saved the St. Louis Cardinals 75 runs per year with his acrobatic shortstop play. He won 13 straight Gold Gloves (1980–1992) and set assorted defensive records, including fielding percentage, assists by a shortstop, and most years leading a league in chances and assists.

In one of several defensive gems that made him 1970 World Series MVP, Baltimore third baseman Brooks Robinson snares a Game 3 liner hit by Cincinnati's Johnny Bench.

Leo Durocher, best known as a manager, was also an excellent shortstop for the St. Louis Cardinals.

second choice involved conceding a run unless the DP was infield-to-home-to-first.

Dark, confident his team would get the run back quickly, selected the second choice and did get the desired double-play grounder. However, that was the only run of the game as the Yankees won the World Championship.

In the 1977 World Series against the Yankees, Dodger manager Tom Lasorda faced a similar situation: runners on second and third, one out, in a 3–3 game in the fourth inning of Game 3. With Mickey Rivers the batter, Lasorda's choices were: play the infield in, play it back, or walk Rivers in the hope that the next man would hit into an inning-ending double play.

Like Dark, Lasorda played the infield back, got the grounder, but gave up the run. He too was confident his team would score and he did not want to risk a big inning, which might have resulted from a two-run hit over a drawn-in infield.

Defensive decisions contribute just as much to a victory or defeat as insertion of the proper relief pitcher or pinch-hitter. The five-man infield can save a tie game for the visiting team after the home club loads the bases with less than two out.

Usually, the center fielder is brought into the infield between the second baseman and shortstop. The left and right fielders are brought closer together and drawn toward the plate, since a long fly will score the winning run anyway.

From their new position, the outfielders can throw home on short fly balls, keeping the runner at third base, or try to nail him at home if he attempts to score. The transplanted center fielder guards against balls going up the middle.

Such an alignment greatly increases the chances of a double-play grounder or a force play at the plate.

Not all infields are good defensive units, however. Zeke Bonura, with the White Sox in the '30s, once allowed four runs to score on a game-ending third out. With the bases loaded and two down, the batter grounded to Bonura. He picked it up, dropped it, repeated the routine, then kicked it some more. When he looked up, all three runners had scored and the batter was en route to third. Bonura threw the ball in that general direction, but it wound up in the dugout.

Slightly more than 20 years later, Dick Stuart proved so erratic at first base that he was called "Stonefingers" and other less-than-complimentary nicknames. When he took a wife, he beamed with pride and told a writer, "Behind every successful man there stands a good woman." The newsman responded, ". . . with a first baseman's glove?"

For on-the-field embarrassment, Houston's Norm Miller won't soon forget the day he tried to score on a passed cast. Atlanta catcher Bob Didier caught a low, outside fastball from sidearm reliever Cecil Upshaw. The ball knocked off a small, plastic cast Didier had been wearing on a sore finger, and the white plastic device went spinning toward the backstop. Houston's third-base coach, Salty Parker, mistook the cast for the ball and sent Miller home.

Halfway there, Miller looked up to see Didier waiting for him with the ball. "Talk about a look of total disbelief!" said Atlanta pitcher Gary Neibauer. "Miller's eyes got big as saucers and he just stood there as Didier tagged him out."

New York Daily News

Willie Was Wonderful

Former teammate Monte Irvin on Willie Mays: "I've talked to many players, black and white, who say that no one could play center field like Willie Mays. Not only was he so great going back to field the fly ball or catch a line drive, but he was terrific coming in too. He could catch the low liner like there was nothing to it. He saved many games for the Giants.

"There was a period where he could have been Most Valuable Player eight or nine years in a row; he was that valuable to the club. He could cut the ball off in left- or right-center and keep it to a single. He would always make the big catch in a crucial situation.

"One year in Pittsburgh, he went back on a ball hit directly over his head. By the time he got to where the ball was going to fall, the wind had carried it over to the right so he couldn't bring his glove across his body. So all he did was catch the ball in his bare hand on a dead run. He always got a great jump on the ball, had huge hands, and great reflexes."

Hank Aaron and Willie Mays, representing the cities (but not the teams) of their big-league births, enjoyed a nostalgic meeting at Hall of Fame Day in Cooperstown.

Bob Bartosz

Reprinted with permission, National Baseball Hall of Fame Library, Cooperstown, N.Y.

The Iron Horse

Lou Gehrig's consecutive-games streak stood for 56 years until Cal Ripken Jr. broke it in 1995.

Baseball's Iron Horse replaced Wally Pipp at first base on June 2, 1925, and played every Yankee game until May 2, 1939, when manager Joe McCarthy replaced the ailing Gehrig with Babe Dahlgren. Gehrig never played again. Sixteen years to the day after he replaced Pipp, Gehrig died of amyotrophic lateral sclerosis (ALS), a nervous system disorder.

Gehrig's streak actually started June 1, 1925, when manager Miller Huggins used him as a pinch-hitter for Pee-Wee Wanninger. It almost ended on July 12, 1934, however, when Gehrig left a game in the first inning with a severe case of lumbago. He returned for one at-bat the next day.

Freaks of Fielding

Anything can happen in baseball and usually does.

In 1905 Jack McCarthy of the Cubs threw out three Pittsburgh runners at the plate in a single game. No other player has performed that feat.

Twenty-two years later, an unassisted triple play—the most unusual defensive play in the game—occurred on successive days, May 30 and 31.

In 1945 second baseman Irvin Hall of the Athletics smashed a Dutch Leonard pitch back to the Washington moundsman. Leonard got his glove on the ball, but then lost it. A hasty search revealed that the ball had lodged inside the pitcher's pants!

A's shortstop Eddie Joost played the comedic role in 1948 when a grounder from Boston's Billy Goodman literally went up his sleeve, then dropped to the waist inside his uniform shirt. Ted Williams, the runner at third base, was so overcome with laughter he couldn't run home.

Philadelphia was victimized again when a Washington player socked a long ball to center in old Griffith Stadium. It rolled into the small doghouse-type box where the flag was stored. Socks Siebold poked his head and shoulders into the box in a vain search for the ball while the surprised Senator circled the bases with an inside-the-doghouse home run.

A real dog had the last bark during an American Association game in 1886. Chicken Wolf, batting for Louisville in the last of the 11th, hit a line drive to right for a base hit. Cincinnati's Abner Powell gave chase, but a dog—which had been sleeping near the fence when the action started—chased Powell and grabbed his leg just as he was about to throw the ball toward the infield. The dog let go just as Wolf crossed the plate with the winning run.

Fielding Facts

There are no left-handed catchers in baseball primarily because there are no left-handed catcher's mitts. In the early days of the game, almost all batters were right-handed (left-handed batters were converted) and it was easier for a right-handed catcher to whip a throw to first or second without a batter standing in his way.

A notable exception was John Clements, hard-hitting receiver for the Phillies and several other clubs shortly before the turn of the century. Joe Wall and John Donahue were left-handed catchers who played briefly in 1901 and 1902, and Dale Long of the Cubs caught several games in 1958. On one occasion, Long used a first baseman's mitt because the team had no left-handed catcher's mitt.

While first basemen may throw from either side, teams prefer to have a left-hander at that position—the mitt would be closer to the other infielders—while right-handers must be stationed elsewhere in the infield. The tough double-play pivot would be difficult for a southpaw, and a third baseman needs to have his glove hand facing into the infield.

Ironically, superstar third baseman Brooks Robinson, who retired in 1977 after more than 20 seasons with the Orioles, is a natural left-hander who was right-handed only when field-ing and batting. Eddie Mathews, Hall of Fame third baseman of the Braves, was a left-handed batter who threw from the right side.

Longevity by position, according to statistics computed over the years, ranks catchers first, pitchers second, outfielders third, and infielders last. Though catching is the most difficult position physically, the demand for capable catchers is the major reason receivers have the longest survival spans in the major leagues.

Hitting

Babe Ruth reached base 54 percent of the time he came to bat during the 1923 season. Reaching base safely 375 times in 697 appearances, the powerful Yankee outfielder hit .393 with 41 home runs, 151 runs scored, and 130 runs batted in. But the secret to his success was his patience at the plate; he walked 170 times. Ruth's .540 on-base per-centage was surpassed in 1941 when Ted Williams posted a .553 mark.

Baseball teams treasure batters who can get on base—whether they do it by hitting, walking, or being hit by pitches. Good contact hitters are also valued. A strikeout gains noth-ing, but a ground ball or timely fly ball may produce a run or move previous runners into scoring position.

Hitting a baseball is one of the most difficult jobs in sports. The ball takes only 5/10ths of a second to travel from pitcher to hitter—and the hitter has only 2/10ths of a second to move his bat from his shoulder to the contact zone. That leaves 3/10ths of a second for him to:

- pick up the ball visually
- determine what kind of pitch is coming

How to Hit Without a Bat

Hall of Famer Napoleon Lajoie singled twice in 1906 without holding a bat. He was able to rap hits over first base by tossing his bat at the ball.

Fast Fizzle

The first man to homer in his first two regular-season at-bats, outfielder Bob Nieman of the 1951 St. Louis Browns hit only 123 more hom-ers in the remaining 3,450 at-bats of his career. Keith McDonald homered in his first two at-bats in 2000 with the St. Louis Cardinals. He had 3 career hits—all home runs—in 7 AB.

Hot Start

Oakland outfielder Reggie Jackson had 37 homers at the 1969 All-Star break but hit only 10 more the rest of the way, finishing with a career-best 47.

Punchless Champ

Rod Carew won a batting title without hit-ting a home run in 1972.

Mr. Dependable

Only four men have hit safely in at least 135 games in a single season: Rogers Hornsby (1922), Chuck Klein (1930), Wade Boggs (1985), and Ichiro Suzuki (2001).

Four-Homer Games

No major-leaguer has hit five home runs in a game, though both Stan Musial and Nate Colbert had five in a day during doubleheaders. The following men hit four home runs in a game:

Date	Player & Club	Score
American League		
06-03-1932	Lou Gehrig, Yankees	NY 20, Philadelphia 13
07-18-1948	Pat Seerey, White Sox	Chicago 12, Philadelphia 11
06-10-1959	Rocky Colavito, Indians	Cleveland 11, Baltimore 8
05-02-2002	Mike Cameron, Mariners	Seattle 15, Chicago 4
09-25-2003	Carlos Delgado, Blue Jays	Toronto 10, Tampa Bay 8
05-08-2012	Josh Hamilton, Rangers	Texas 10, Baltimore 3
National League		
05-30-1894	Bobby Lowe, Braves	Boston 12, Cincinnati 11
07-13-1896	Ed Delahanty, Phillies	Chicago 9, Philadelphia 8
07-10-1936	Chuck Klein, Phillies	*Philadelphia 9, Pitts. 6
08-31-1950	Gil Hodges, Dodgers	Brooklyn 15, Boston 3
07-31-1954	Joe Adcock, Braves	Milwaukee 15, Brooklyn 7
04-30-1961	Willie Mays, Giants	San Francisco 14, Milw. 4
04-17-1976	Mike Schmidt, Phillies	*Philadelphia 18, Chic. 16
07-06-1986	Bob Horner, Braves	Montreal 11, Atlanta 8
09-07-1993	Mark Whiten, Cardinals	St. Louis 15, Cincinnati 2
05-23-2002	Shawn Green, Dodgers	Los Angeles 16, Milw. 3
06-06-2017	Scooter Gennett, Reds	Cincinnati 13, St. Louis 0
09-04-2017	J.D. Martinez, Diamondbacks	Arizona 13, Los Angeles 1

(*) 10 innings

KNOW THEM BY THEIR STANCE:

THEY TOSSED AWAY THE BOOK ON CORRECT HITTING...

HEINIE GROH, USED A "BOTTLE BAT"– STOOD WITH BOTH TOES FACING THE MOUND...

TY COBB, ONE OF THE GAME'S GREATEST HITTERS, USED A CROUCH, CHOKED HIS BAT... LED A.L. BATTERS 11 OUT OF 12 YEARS..., 1907 TO 1919

STAN LOPATA, HAS A "SQUAT" WHICH HAS UPPED HIS BATTING AVERAGE FROM .220 TO .290 FOR THE SEASON!

BABE RUTH... WITH THAT STAND-UP,- FEET-TOGETHER STANCE THAT SYMBOLIZED HIS GREAT HOME RUN POWER...

The Sporting News

- decide if it will be a ball or strike, and
- decide whether to swing or take the pitch.

It is simply amazing that Joe Sewell, playing a full schedule, struck out only four times in 1925 and tied that record in 1929. In 1930 Pat Caraway of the White Sox fanned Sewell twice on May 26. The Cleveland shortstop did not strike out again that season.

Nellie Fox of the 1958 White Sox went a record 98 games without a strikeout because he followed a simple philosophy at the plate: "Meet the ball," he said. "Keep your eye on the ball. A big swing has more arc, but doesn't follow the baseball."

Power hitters have a tendency to strike out because they swing hard. Babe Ruth held the lifetime strikeout record for years until Mickey Mantle passed him. Reggie Jackson tops the current list with 2,597, followed by Jim Thome (2,548), Adam Dunn (2,379), Sammy Sosa (2,306), and Alex Rodriguez (2,287).

Joe DiMaggio, who struck out only once per 18.48 at-bats and homered once per 18.89 at-bats, was a notable exception to the rule that long-ball hitters strike out often. Mantle, DiMaggio's successor in center field, went down on strikes once per 4.74 at-bats.

In one of Mantle's big years, however, he teamed with Roger Maris to give the Yankees the finest single-season 1-2 batting punch. With Maris hitting 61 homers and Mantle 54 in 1961, the Yankees hit 240, a record that has been topped several times since. The 1997 Seattle Mariners hold the current record for team home runs in a season (264).

The best lifetime home-run tandem consisted of Hank Aaron and Eddie Mathews, who belted 863 during their days as teammates with the Braves.

Aaron, who had an unorthodox cross-handed batting style as an amateur, was one of many successful hitters whose pose at the plate defied basic batting rules. Al Simmons, the Philadelphia A's star of the '30s, was another with a unique style. Simmons stood deep in the batting box with feet close together. When he swung, he took a long step with his left (front) foot—but toward third base rather than the pitcher. Though experts said he was hitting "with his foot in the bucket," Simmons did shift his hips and weight into the pitch and hit with authority—often to the opposite field.

Left-handed hitter Stan Musial, like Simmons a Hall of Fame outfielder, also stood deep in the box and often hit to the opposite field. In 1948 he missed the opportunity by one home run to lead the National League in batting, base hits, doubles, triples, homers, runs, runs batted in, and slugging.

With 230 hits, Musial hit .376 and had a slugging average of .702, based on 46 doubles, 18 triples, and 39 homers. He scored 135 runs and knocked in 131. Moreover, he fanned just 34 times in 611 at-bats.

Musial's corkscrew stance was marked by the position of his feet—close together, as in the style of Babe Ruth. The Yankee slugger stood taller in the box, however, and had a classic swing that made writers of the time suggest that he looked as good striking out as he did hitting a home run.

Ty Cobb crouched and choked up on the bat while batting, and induced Harry Heilmann to do the same with the Tigers. The latter kept his feet six inches apart and a foot from the plate. With his hands two inches up the bat handle, Heilmann bent over to get a good view of every pitch.

Babe Ruth's records weren't all positive. For years he held the mark for most strikeouts by a hitter.

Eddie Mathews teamed with Hank Aaron to produce the most home runs by teammates—863.

Lou Boudreau's "hunchback" stance also involved an obvious bend that was effective but dangerous; pitched balls came close to the Cleveland player/manager.

Rogers Hornsby stood far from the plate and stepped into the pitch. Joe DiMaggio kept his feet spread far apart. Heinie Groh kept his toes facing the mound and used a short "bottle bat" which helped him hit fastballs consistently.

Without question, the most unusual stance was Mel Ott's. The powerful left-handed slugger lifted his front foot several inches off the ground just before he unleashed his swing.

"I got my main power from my back foot," he explained. "With my right foot off the ground, I wouldn't be caught flat-footed. I had a better chance to wait on the pitch."

The patient Ott slammed 511 homers for the Giants.

Bunting

The bunt is an offensive maneuver with multiple purposes. It is most often used as a sacrifice, to move a runner into scoring position (second or third base). It may be used in a squeeze play to score a runner from third. Or it may be employed by a speedy batter hoping to reach first base—and gain an infield hit—before a play can be made on him.

Dickie Pearce, shortstop of the champion Brooklyn Atlantics, dropped the very first bunt in 1866—moving his hand along the bat, easing it back, and softening the impact of ball against wood. The ball rolled a short distance in fair territory and died, while Pearce raced to first base with an infield hit.

By 1910, a full decade before the dawn of the home-run era, the bunt was widely used. Napoleon Lajoie once beat out six bunts in a doubleheader. Ty Cobb and George Sisler helped themselves to .400 batting years by bunting often. When the infield played in, looking for the bunt, they swung away. With the defense back, they bunted—always trying to keep the ball away from the pitcher.

Hall of Fame pitcher Lefty Grove hated the bunt. "I don't have too much trouble with the guys who swing from their heels," he said. "The hitters who get under my skin are the pests who bunt and drag, or poke at the ball. They're hard to fool."

Heinie Manush, a heavy hitter of the late '20s and '30s, became a superb bunter who taught the technique to several other players. Johnny Pesky, Phil Rizzuto, Eddie Stanky, and Cookie Lavagetto mastered the bunt and helped their clubs win games with seemingly harmless infield dribblers.

In September 1951, Rizzuto and Joe DiMaggio, the runner at third, worked a perfect squeeze play for the Yankees against the Indians.

With the bases loaded and one out in the last of the ninth, Rizzuto batted against Cleveland ace Bob Lemon in a tie game. If Rizzuto had hit away, he might have grounded into an inning-ending double play. The first pitch was low, but the umpire called it a strike. Rizzuto staged a big argument on purpose, hoping to convince the Indian infield he wanted a better pitch because he would be swinging.

The trick worked because none of the infielders moved in. DiMaggio, an excellent runner, made the squeeze work by not breaking for home too soon—a runner who does may alert the pitcher in time for him to make a pitch-out that will allow the catcher to tag the runner coming home.

"Lemon had no idea Joe was coming until it was too late," Rizzuto recalled. "Suddenly, with the pitch on its way and Joe breaking for home, I dumped the ball down, and that was the ballgame."

When bunting for a hit, Rizzuto made a practice of laying the ball down almost after the pitch was past him. A right-handed batter, he was also capable of pushing the ball toward first base. This was the drag bunt, executed while the batter is in motion toward first base.

The suicide squeeze—the most difficult bunt play—can make the manager look like a genius or a goat. If the batter misses the ball, the runner coming home from third is certain to be tagged out by the catcher. If he bunts the ball, he must push it far enough from the plate so that the catcher can't reach it, yet out of reach of the pitcher or any infielder.

On the safety squeeze, the runner from third breaks for home only after the ball is bunted.

Pete Rose, longtime Cincinnati infielder, used the bunt to win the 1969 batting title from Roberto Clemente on the last day of the season and, nine years later, bunted for a base hit to keep his long hitting streak alive.

Strange Home Runs

The home run—the grandest achievement in baseball—is usually a mighty shot over a distant fence. But not always.

When Babe Ruth was with the Boston Red Sox in 1919, he was credited with a home run on an infield fly. "It must have been the highest pop-up ever hit," said Ruth's victim, pitcher Lefty Leifield of the St. Louis Browns. "The infielders were running around like chickens with their heads cut off, yelling that they couldn't see the ball.

"When that ball came down, Babe had already rounded third. There wasn't any chance to make a play on him and three runs scored."

On June 19, 1942, Dom DiMaggio of the Red Sox sliced the ball down the right-field line. White Sox outfielder Wally Moses watched it roll under the bullpen bench, where he parted the feet of the occupants in frantic search. By the time he found the sphere, DiMaggio had scored the only run of the game.

Earlier in the century, Cascade held a 1–0 lead over Buckhorn with two out in the last of the ninth when the Buckhorn batter sent

Phil Rizzuto was so adept at bunting that he coached young Yankees in the art for years after his retirement. During his playing days from 1941 through 1956, the diminutive shortstop hit .273 with 149 stolen bases but only 38 home runs. Rizzuto, a New Yorker by birth, was Most Valuable Player of the American League in 1950.

Packed Lineup

The 1931 New York Yankees had eight future Hall of Famers: Babe Ruth, Lou Gehrig, Earle Combs, Bill Dickey, Herb Pennock, Lefty Gomez, Red Ruffing, and Joe Sewell.

Joe DiMaggio's bat and glove were so outstanding that his excellent instincts on the bases were often overlooked.

Ted Williams had a much higher average at Fenway Park.

Rules Robbed Ted Williams

In 1954 Ted Williams lost the batting title because he fell 14 official at-bats shy of the required total of 400. Williams, a feared slugger who received 136 walks, hit .345, four points higher than spray hitter Bobby Avila, who walked only 59 times. But bases on balls are not counted as official at-bats. Qualifications for the batting crown subsequently were changed to count plate appearances rather than official trips.

How Williams Hit .406

Ted Williams, last man to hit .400, reached the figure by banging out six hits in eight trips during an end-of-season doubleheader between his Red Sox and the Philadelphia A's in 1941. He wound up with a .406 mark for the season. Going into the twin bill, Williams' average was .39955.

Friendly Field

Even though he was a left-handed power hitter in a park that favored righties, Ted Williams hit .361 in Fenway Park, his home field, but "only" .328 on the road.

the ball toward the left-field fence. Just as it got there, however, it broke in two. Half completed the journey into home-run territory, while the left fielder caught the other half. After a protracted argument, the umpire ruled the game over, with Cascade the victor by a score of 1–½.

Then there was the time Cleveland's Jimmy McAleer hit a ball into an empty tomato can at the base of the outfield wall. Hugh Duffy, unable to pry the ball loose, threw the whole can toward the infield, which relayed it home. Tagged with ball in glove, McAleer would have been out. But tagged with ball in can was something else. The umpire ruled him safe.

The longest home run was produced by a spontaneous combination of long ball and hopper. Joe Hauser, with Baltimore of the International League, deposited the ball in a passing coal car, which hauled it 32 miles.

Pitcher Wes Ferrell, an excellent hitter, homered in the eighth to tie and in the twelfth to win for the Red Sox, 3–2, over the White Sox on August 22, 1934.

Light-hitting Joe Niekro hit the first (and only) home run of his then-10-year career in 1976—a game-winning blow off brother Phil, a good hitter.

Hoyt Wilhelm, even a lighter hitter than Joe Niekro, homered in his first at-bat as a rookie with the 1952 Giants. But he never hit another home run or triple over the rest of his 21-year career as a relief specialist.

Pitcher/outfielder Johnny Cooney of the Boston Bees in the '30s hit his first homer after playing 15 years, then hit another the next day. He played five more years without hitting any more.

Many players have homered in their first at-bat, but Bob Nieman of the 1951 Browns was the first man to hit home runs in his first two plate appearances in the majors. Keith McDonald also did so, in 2000 with the St. Louis Cardinals.

Yankee teammates Babe Ruth (right) and Lou Gehrig homered in the same game 72 times—16 of them back-to-back.

Eight years later, a pinch-runner homered for the Red Sox. Gene Stephens, inserted as a runner for Ted Williams during a Boston uprising, was cut down in a force-play, but the rally continued and his batting turn came up again. Manager Billy Jurges let him bat and Stephens responded with a grand-slam homer. Boston won the contest from New York, 13–3.

Lefty-Righty Percentage

Left-handed hitters have an advantage over right-handed pitchers and an overall edge over right-handed batters. For these reasons, and because a majority of pitchers are right-handed, many natural right-handers become southpaw swingers or switch-hitters.

When a left-handed batter faces a right-handed pitcher, he has an excellent vantage point. The ball will be delivered in his direct line of sight and the curve will break toward him rather than away from him.

The lefty-lefty match is more difficult, but Ty Cobb believed it could be conquered. "What I did," explained Cobb, a left-handed batter who baffled pitchers of all types, "was stand as far back in the batter's box as I could. That gave me an extra split second to watch the ball and a chance to hit it after it had broken. I also tried to hit it in the direction it was breaking—often to left field (the opposite field) instead of pulling it to right."

Curveball pitchers pose particular problems for hitters, who must decide instantly whether the ball will curve or hit them in the head. Batters who bat from the opposite side than the

Gavvy Cravath, Early HR King

Dead-ball slugger Gavvy Cravath of the Phillies won six home-run titles by learning to hit to the opposite field in cozy Baker Bowl, with its 280-foot line in right. In 1915, he slammed 24 homers—more than 10 percent of the National League's total.

Two Sluggers in One Lineup

Probably the best seasons enjoyed by slugging teammates occurred in 1927 and 1932. Babe Ruth and Lou Gehrig powered the Yankees to the 1927 title—Ruth with 60 homers, 165 runs batted in, and a .356 average. Gehrig slugged 47, knocked in 173, and hit .373. Five years later, Al Simmons of the Athletics hit 35 homers, knocked in 151 runs, and batted .322 but was overshadowed by Jimmie Foxx, with 58 homers, 169 RBIs, and a .364 mark. The A's also won.

Youth Is Served

On August 20, 1945, Tommy Brown of the Brooklyn Dodgers became the youngest major leaguer to hit a home run. At 17 years, 8 months, and 14 days of age, he connected against Pittsburgh's Preacher Roe.

Early and Late

Rusty Staub, Ty Cobb, Alex Rodriguez, and Gary Sheffield were the only players to homer in the majors before their 20th and after their 40th birthdays.

Super Slammers

The following players hit two grand slams in one game:

American League

Tony Lazzeri, Yankees, May 24, 1936
Jim Tabor, Red Sox, July 4, 1939
Rudy York, Red Sox, July 27, 1946
Jim Gentile, Orioles, May 9, 1961
Jim Northrup, Tigers, June 24, 1968
Frank Robinson, Orioles, June 26, 1970
Robin Ventura, White Sox, September 4, 1995
Chris Hoiles, Orioles, August 14, 1998
Nomar Garciaparra, Red Sox, May 10, 1999
~Bill Mueller, Red Sox, July 29, 2003

National League

*Tony Cloninger, Braves, July 3, 1966
#Fernando Tatis, Cardinals, April 23, 1999
Josh Willingham, Nationals, July 27, 2009

(~) hit one right-handed, one left-handed
(*) only pitcher to perform this feat
(#) hit slams in same inning

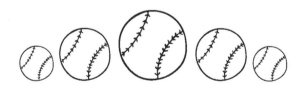

Ruth Fooled Defense in Final Flurry

Babe Ruth's last great home-run display—three in a game for the Boston Braves at Pittsburgh's Forbes Field on May 25, 1935—also featured a solid single through the shortstop hole. The Pirate shortstop had shifted to the right side of second in a common shift used against the aging left-handed pull hitter.

Talented Ted

Experts who insist that Ted Williams was the best hitter in baseball history have evidence to back them up: he was the only man to win more than two titles in each of the three top hitting categories—batting average, home runs, and runs batted in. Here is how the top hitters fared:

Name	Led in Batting	HRs	RBIs
Ted Williams	6	6	4
Ty Cobb	12	1	4
Babe Ruth	1	12	6
Rogers Hornsby	7	2	4
Jimmie Foxx	2	4	3
Joe DiMaggio	2	2	2
Mickey Mantle	2	4	1
Willie Mays	1	4	0
Honus Wagner	8	0	3
Hank Aaron	2	4	4
Stan Musial	7	0	2
Lou Gehrig	1	3	5
Miguel Cabrera	4	2	2

pitchers throw get a better viewpoint, but the rule doesn't apply to the screwball. A righty's screwball behaves like a lefty's curve and breaks away from the left-handed hitter. For that reason, switch-hitter Frankie Frisch batted left-handed against left-handed screwball pitcher Carl Hubbell.

Normally, the all-southpaw match is difficult. Even Stan Musial conceded, "You don't know when to pull the trigger against a southpaw. A right-hander may fool you and you still can hit the pitch. You're dead if you guess wrong against a southpaw."

The great Cardinal star, strictly a left-handed batter, never enjoyed the luxury of a perfect view at all times. Switch-hitters do. Robert Ferguson, second baseman/manager of the New York Mutuals (later Giants) in 1871, led the way, and Max Carey, Frisch, Mickey Mantle, Red Schoendienst, and Pete Rose perfected the practice.

Mantle, a natural right-hander converted to the left side by his right-handed-throwing grandfather, was the most powerful switch-hitter in baseball history. Ten times he hit a home run right-handed and a home run left-handed in the same game.

Frisch and Rose compiled the best batting marks for switch-hitters. Each had a .348 season.

The Los Angeles Dodgers of the '60s drove pitchers batty with an infield comprised entirely of switch-hitters: Wes Parker, Jim Lefebvre, Maury Wills, and Junior Gilliam from first to third.

Anyone batting from the left side has an advantage because he is several feet closer to first base and, when completing his swing, is directly facing the bag. A right-hander stands on the third-base side of the plate and must uncoil, turning himself halfway around, before he can begin his race to first.

In 1947 an enterprising sportswriter from *The New York Sun*—using 1946 statistics—calculated that left-handers enjoyed an 18-point advantage over right-handers at the plate. The figure wavers from year to year, but there's no doubt southpaw swingers have an edge on their right-handed counterparts.

Pinch-Hitting

Pinch-hitting is an art that several players have refined to a science. It involves coming off the bench in a crucial situation—invariably with no previous warm-ups except for batting practice—and making or breaking a team's fortunes.

Because pitchers are generally weak hitters, they often depart for pinch-hitters in the late innings of close games. The American League's introduction of a designated hitter in 1973 reduced the role of the pinch-hitter because the DH batted whenever the pitcher's batting turn came up.

Managers in both leagues who play percentage baseball frequently substitute left-handed pinch-hitters for right-handed batters (and vice versa) after the defensive team makes a pitching change. If a right-hander replaces a left-hander on the mound, a manager may yank a right-handed batter for one who swings from the left side.

Top stars are seldom removed for pinch-hitters unless they are hurt or the score is lopsided when their batting turn comes up.

After striking out twice and popping up against Lefty Grove on Opening Day of the 1927 season, Babe Ruth was removed for Ben Paschal, who stroked a run-scoring single to help the Yankees beat the A's, 8–3. That was the year Ruth hit 60 home runs.

Smoky Burgess, a rotund catcher of the '50s, was the most prolific pinch-hitter of baseball history until Manny Mota exceeded his record 144 pinch hits in 1979. Lenny Harris topped Mota's 150 in 2001. Jerry Lynch swatted 18 pinch-homers (a record later broken by Cliff Johnson), while Dave Hansen and Craig Wilson hit seven in a season. Frenchy Bordagaray, also with Brooklyn, hit .465 in emergency roles—a 1938 record that stood until Ed Kranepool of the New York Mets hit .486 as a pinch-hitter.

In 1976 third-string catcher Jose Morales of the Montreal Expos found his niche as a pinch-hitter. He set records for pinch hits (25), at-bats (78), and games (82) by an emergency batsman. John VanderWal of the Colorado Rockies superseded Morales in 1995 when he collected 28 pinch hits. Lenny Harris of the New York Mets now holds the records for pinch-hitter at-bats (83) and games (95), which he accomplished in 2001.

Early baseball rules discouraged the use of pinch-hitters. In fact, National League clubs could not make any substitutions before the fourth inning in 1876, that circuit's first season.

Dode Criss of the St. Louis Browns was the first heavy-duty pinch-hitter, when he registered 12 hits in 41 at-bats—twice the workload of any previous batting substitute—in 1908. The following year, John McGraw of the Giants began using Moose McCormick and Otis Crandall as pinch-hitters.

In 1911, the same year he earned the nickname "Doc" for saving "sick" ballgames as the first regular relief pitcher, Crandall was the hero of Game 5 of the World Series against the Athletics.

With two outs in the ninth and the Giants behind, 3–1, Crandall doubled home a run, scored the tying run himself, then pitched a scoreless tenth. The Giants scored a run to win, 4–3.

Two years later, Ham Hyatt of the Pirates made quite a splash by socking three pinch-hit homers with the dead ball then in use. A pitcher, Ray Caldwell of the Yankees, hit pinch-homers in consecutive games in June 1915.

Red Lucas, a pitcher with a strong bat, collected 114 hits in pinch-batting roles—fourth on the all-time list—and Wes Ferrell, Red Ruffing, Don Newcombe, Don Drysdale, and Ken Brett also proved adept at pinch-hitting, usually for their fellow pitchers.

Tommy Davis, two-time National League batting king for the Dodgers, became an excellent pinch-hitter in his later years. His lifetime emergency average was .320. Dave Philley (.299) once collected nine straight pinch hits for the Phillies.

Other outstanding pinch-hitters were Vic Davalillo, Tito Francona, Johnny Mize, Red Schoendienst, Enos Slaughter, and Elmer Valo.

Pitching

Before the 1997 Colorado Rockies and later the 2000 Houston Astros superseded them, the 1947 New York Giants and the 1956 Cincinnati Redlegs shared the National League record for most home runs by a team. None of those teams won a pennant, however, because their pitching wasn't up to championship caliber.

Slugging Switchers

Baseball history is filled with the exploits of switch-hitters. Mickey Mantle (536), Eddie Murray (504), and Chipper Jones (468) hit the most home runs, with Jones and Mark Teixeira the only ones to collect 40 home runs and 40 doubles in the same season. Players who homered from both sides of the plate in a game most often were Teixeira and Nick Swisher, who did it 14 times each. Carlos Baerga, Mark Bellhorn, and Kendrys Morales switch-hit home runs *in the same inning*, while Garry Templeton collected 100+ hits from both sides of the plate in the same season.

The Switch-Pitcher

Noted baseball executive and manager Paul Richards was a switch-pitcher in high school. As a pro at age 20 in 1928, Richards was playing third for Muskogee of the Western Association when he was inserted as a relief pitcher. Topeka sent switch-hitting Charlie Wilson to the plate. Richards, determined to throw from the same side as the batter, staged a standoff with the batter, who kept switching in the batter's box as Richard switched gloves on the mound. Finally, Richards let Wilson choose the side he preferred.

Didn't They Play?

Pinch-hitters received no credit for games played until 1907 in the American League and 1912 in the National.

Pitcher Pinches Rivals

Yankee pitcher Ray Caldwell hit pinch homers in consecutive games on June 10 and 11, 1915. He also hit a home run in the next game, on June 12th, a game he pitched.

Potent in the Pinch

Matt Stairs leads the career list in pinch-homers with 23, while Dave Hansen (2000) and Craig Wilson (2001) share the single-season mark of 7. Gordy Coleman had the best lifetime pinch-hitting average (.333) while Ed Kranepool (1974) had the best single-season average in the pinch (.486). John Vander-Waal had a record 28 pinch-hits in 1995, but Lenny Harris had the most in a career.

Robin Roberts not only had six straight 20-win seasons for the Phillies but once pitched 28 consecutive complete games. He was elected to the Baseball Hall of Fame in 1976.

Flawless Performances

The following men pitched perfect games, with 27 men up, 27 down:

American League

Cy Young, Red Sox, May 5, 1904
Addie Joss, Indians, October 2, 1908
Charlie Robertson, White Sox, April 30, 1922
*Don Larsen, Yankees, October 8, 1956
Catfish Hunter, Athletics, May 8, 1968
Len Barker, Indians, May 15, 1981
Mike Witt, Angels, September 30, 1984
Kenny Rogers, Rangers, July 28, 1994
David Wells, Yankees, May 17, 1998
David Cone, Yankees, July 18, 1999
Mark Buehrle, White Sox, July 23, 2009
Dallas Braden, Athletics, May 9, 2010
Philip Humber, White Sox, April 21, 2012
Felix Hernandez, Mariners, August 15, 2012

(*) World Series

National League

Lee Richmond, Worcester, June 12, 1880
Monte Ward, Providence, June 17, 1880
Jim Bunning, Phillies, June 21, 1964
Sandy Koufax, Dodgers, September 9, 1965
Tom Browning, Reds, September 16, 1988
Dennis Martinez, Expos, July 28, 1991
Randy Johnson, Diamondbacks, May 18, 2004
Roy Halladay, Phillies, May 29, 2010
Matt Cain, Giants, June 13, 2012

Many baseball insiders insist that pitching is 75 to 90 percent of the game. Light-hitting teams with good pitching, backed by good defense and often good speed, have won pennants many times. Heavy-hitting teams with weak pitching haven't.

In 1930 the Philadelphia Phillies had a team batting average of .315. Each of the eight regulars hit .300. Yet the club finished last because its pitchers allowed the opposition to score a record average of 6.71 earned runs per game!

"When you get consistently good pitching," said Walter Alston, longtime manager of the pitching-rich Dodgers, "you keep the score low and have a chance in every game. You can try to use all the ways there are to score a run, and benefit from any error or lucky break. You're never out of the game.

"But if your pitching gives up a lot of runs, there will be times when you're out of business early, where the only way to get back is with a lot of slugging of your own. So it's pretty hard to be lucky when your pitching is bad."

Good control and a variety of pitches are invariably hallmarks of baseball's best pitchers. Southpaw Carl Hubbell, who won a record 24 straight games for the Giants in 1936 and 1937, was always right around the plate. On July 2, 1933, he didn't walk one batter while pitching a six-hit, 1–0 victory over the Cardinals in a game that took 18 innings.

Cy Young, who would go on to post a record 511 lifetime victories, illustrated the importance of good control when he worked for the Red Sox in 1904, walking only 28 in 380 innings pitched.

Before the advent of the lively ball in 1920, pitchers worked more often, primarily because relief pitching was not widely practiced and also because they did not have to bear down as hard on the collection of slap hitters who then populated the majors. Many old-timers worked doubleheaders—Iron Man McGinnity winning three of them in August 1903 and Ed Reulbach tossing a double shutout five years later.

The four biggest winners of baseball history were Cy Young (511), Walter Johnson (414), and Christy Mathewson and Grover Cleveland Alexander (373 each). All were active at the same time, though Young had reached the end of the line when Alexander was a sophomore in 1912.

Speaking from a hitter's viewpoint, Casey Stengel, a 1912 rookie, later recalled his memories of that era. "Johnson was the most amazing pitcher in the American League and Alexander in the National," he said. "Alexander had to pitch in that little Philadelphia ballpark [Baker Bowl] with that big tin fence in right field and he pitched shutouts—which must mean he could do it. He had a fastball, curve, change of pace, and perfect control. With Johnson, you knew what was coming but you couldn't hit it. He had perfect control too."

Ty Cobb said Johnson might have been even more effective. "If he had been willing to throw a few dusters and keep the batters on edge worrying about that cannonball he threw," suggested Cobb, "nobody knows how many more games he might have won. But obviously he was afraid of his own speed and what he might do to the batter."

Warren Spahn, a left-hander who mastered the screwball after his fastball faded, won more games than any pitcher of the lively ball era: 363. Spahn, who retired in 1965, probably would have joined Johnson and Young at the 400 level had he not lost four

Warren Spahn (right) won 363 games, more than any left-hander in baseball history and all of them after World War II. Just ahead of him on the lifetime list were Grover Cleveland Alexander (above) and Christy Mathewson, with 373 each.

youthful years to wartime military service. Spahn was 26 when he won his first game for the Braves.

Pitching Feats

Pitchers with a high ratio of strikeouts to walks are usually successful, but high strikeout totals are not necessary for victory. In the '20s, Cleveland's Emil Levsen pitched a double-header victory over the Red Sox, 6–1 and 5–1, without a single strikeout.

By contrast, a total of 20 men from the same team have been fanned in a nine-inning game five times: Roger Clemens (1986 and 1996), Kerry Wood (1998), Randy Johnson (2001), and Max Scherzer (2016).

An obscure right-hander named Tom Cheney fanned 21 in a 16-inning, 2–1 triumph for Washington over Baltimore in 1962.

Johnny Vander Meer was not as overpowering as the 20-strike-out men but was the first man to work consecutive no-hitters. Others who threw two hitless games in the same campaign were Dean Chance, Jim Maloney, Allie Reynolds, Nolan Ryan, Max Scherzer, and Virgil Trucks, but none of them were back-to-back.

The Trucks feat was especially remarkable because his two 1–0 gems comprised 40 percent of his victory total in 1952. Without the no-hitters, Trucks would have had a 3-19 record for last-place Detroit!

When Reynolds threw his second no-hitter the previous September, catcher Yogi Berra threw a scare into the Yankee Stadium crowd when he dropped a foul pop that would have ended the game. That error gave the hitter—Ted Williams—another chance. But Reynolds made him pop to Berra again.

300 Wins Club

Pitcher	Wins	Date of 300th
Cy Young	511	07-03-1901
Walter Johnson	417	05-14-1920
Christy Mathewson	373	08-28-1912
Grover Cleveland Alexander	373	09-20-1924
Warren Spahn*	363	08-11-1961
Pud Galvin	361	07-07-1900
Greg Maddux	355	08-07-2004
Roger Clemens	354	06-13-2003
Tim Keefe	342	06-04-1890
Steve Carlton*	329	09-23-1983
John Clarkson	328	09-21-1892
Eddie Plank	326	09-11-1915
Nolan Ryan	324	07-31-1990
Don Sutton	324	06-18-1986
Phil Niekro	318	10-06-1985
Gaylord Perry	314	05-06-1982
Tom Seaver	311	08-04-1985
Old Hoss Radbourn	309	05-14-1891
Mickey Welch	307	08-11-1890
Tom Glavine*	305	08-05-2007
Randy Johnson*	303	06-04-2009
Lefty Grove*	300	07-25-1941
Early Wynn	300	07-13-1963

(*) threw left-handed

Types of Pitches Thrown to Baffle Batters

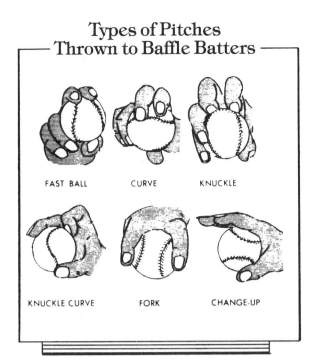

FAST BALL   CURVE   KNUCKLE

KNUCKLE CURVE   FORK   CHANGE-UP

Ryan, who fanned a record 383 batters in 1973, broke by one the old standard of Sandy Koufax and later surpassed Koufax's feat of hurling four no-hitters. In 1965, Sandy's last season, he pitched his only perfect game, blanking the Cubs. Chicago pitcher Bobby Hendley pitched a one-hitter himself.

The Koufax/Hendley duel might have been the best-pitched complete game to be played in the regulation nine innings, but a battle between Fred Toney of the Reds and Hippo Vaughn of the Cubs on May 2, 1917, was far more gripping. At the end of nine, both pitchers had pitched no-hitters! Vaughn yielded two hits in the 10th to lose, 1–0, while Toney kept his no-hitter intact.

Cincinnati's Doc Parker was guilty of the worst pitching performance in history on June 21, 1901, when he yielded 21 runs on 26 hits to Brooklyn. But the Philadelphia Athletics made an effort to corner the market on bad pitching.

In 1916 Bruno Haas walked 16 Tigers in his debut. In 1932 reliever Ed Rommel allowed 14 runs on 29 hits in a 17-inning relief job against Cleveland, but won, 18–17. Four years later, Hod Lisenbee yielded 26 hits in a 17–2 rout at the hands of the White Sox.

Lisenbee might have been better off walking a few hitters—but don't tell that to Milt Pappas. The Cubs right-hander missed a perfect game in 1972 when he walked Larry Stahl on a 3-2 pitch with two outs in the ninth.

Early Wynn won 300 games despite bouts of wildness, while Bill Fischer would be totally forgotten if not for his ability to throw strikes. Fischer, spot-starting with the Kansas City A's in 1962, pitched a record 84⅔ innings without yielding a walk. His record that year was only 4-12, however.

Many pitchers are effective even though they give up many hits and walks. Yankees Lefty Gomez, in 1941, and Mel Stottlemyre, in 1970, pitched 11-walk shutouts (Stottlemyre's was over 8.1 innings), and Larry Cheney of the Cubs stopped the Giants, 7–0, on a 14-hitter in the World War I period.

What Pitchers Throw

The repertoire of the major league pitcher consists of much more than fastball and curve. Only overpowering pitchers—Walter Johnson and Sandy Koufax, for example—could survive with such a limited assortment.

Legal deliveries currently in use include the fastball, curveball, slider, sinker, forkball, knuckleball, palmball, screwball, change-up, and knuckle curve. The spitter, emery ball, shine ball, grease ball, and sandpaper ball occasionally pop up too—despite the fact that such trick pitches were banned in 1920.

Though Candy Cummings threw the first curve in 1864, skeptics had to be convinced six years later that a ball would actually curve. The National Bureau of Standards has since decided that a baseball can curve no more than 17½ inches.

Curves pose problems for young pitchers because they place a strain on the elbow. Improperly thrown, they become "hanging curves" and often result in a home run or extra-base hit. Proper grip of the curve is up to the individual pitcher, but in all cases, the index finger guides the ball and the middle finger pulls.

Like the curve, the fastball is held across the seams. Wrist flexibility gives the ball movement as well as velocity, and the good fastball will, in effect, act as a mini-curve; it will tail to one side or the other, and may even rise—especially when thrown by a side-armer.

The slider approaches the plate like a fastball, but suddenly slides a few inches to the side. It may also break downward. A derivation of the slip pitch once taught by catcher-turned-manager Paul Richards, the slider came into widespread use in the early '60s. Whitey Ford didn't throw one until 1961. The pitch is popular among pitchers because it is easy to throw and hard for batters to identify.

Both the forkball and the sinker drop sharply when they reach the plate. The former is often called a "split-fingered" fastball because of the way it is usually held.

Like the slider, the palmball is a pitch that traces its origin to the slip pitch. It breaks down across the plate. It is gripped with the palm and pushed toward the plate.

The change-up can be any pitch that will balance a pitcher's primary delivery, usually his fastball. The change must look exactly like the other pitch when thrown, but must arrive at a different speed. The change, off a fastball, is thrown with a locked wrist.

The screwball, once known as the fadeaway, is a reverse curve. It helps make a left-handed pitcher effective against a right-handed batter and vice versa. The good screwball, like a slider, should look like a fastball en route to the plate. But, like the forkball and the knuckleball, it's a tough pitch to throw properly. It involves "turning the ball over" with a quick snap of the wrist.

Knuckleball pitchers place their nails or knuckles on the ball and throw it with a locked wrist. There's no rotation and the ball floats to the plate, riding the wind currents on the way.

The spitball, developed by Elmer Stricklett around the turn of the century, is thrown by wetting the first and second fingers and holding the ball so those fingers do not touch the seams. The ball slips from the fingers without any spin and floats to the plate with seams clearly visible. But the pitch will break very sharply at the last minute.

Carl Hubbell, longtime ace of the New York Giants, explained the overall theory of pitching: "The whole art is in the wrist. You use the body, the shoulder, and arms in getting power behind the throw but the twist of the wrist determines just what the ball will do."

Every unusual pitching delivery became the primary weapon for pitchers who found it easy to throw. Christy Mathewson, Carl Hubbell, and Warren Spahn were masters of the screwball—and relievers Mike Marshall and Tug McGraw found late-inning success with the same delivery.

Sparky Lyle, who joined Marshall as the only bullpen ace to win the coveted Cy Young Award for pitching excellence in its first 22 seasons, depended heavily on the slider.

Hoyt Wilhelm, the first relief pitcher to win the earned run average title (1952), was primarily a knuckleballer. So were Ed Rommel, Jesse (Pop) Haines, Freddie Fitzsimmons, Schoolboy Rowe, Wilbur Wood, and Phil Niekro.

Control Artist

Of all pitchers who worked at least 3,000 innings since 1900, Lew Burdette issued the fewest walks.

Dutch Master

Control artists—even those with great curveballs—tend to give up more than their fair share of home runs. Just ask Bert Blyleven, the only pitcher to yield 50 home runs in a season (1986).

Saving Headlines

Roger Clemens was the first pitcher to record his 4000th strikeout and 300th win in the same game.

Spitter or Sinker?

Gaylord Perry, often accused of using the banned spitball, once said of his victory total, "Three-hundred wins is nothing to spit at."

Control Master

Carl Hubbell of the Giants yielded six hits and no walks during a 1–0, 18-inning victory over the Cardinals in a doubleheader opener on July 2, 1933.

Record Streaker

Control artist Carl Hubbell, star left-hander of the New York Giants, won a record 24 games in a row over two seasons, 1936 and 1937. Rube Marquard, who pitched for the same club in 1912, holds the single-season mark with 19 straight.

One-Man Show

Rick Wise hit two home runs while pitching a no-hitter. He did it in 1971 as his Philadelphia Phillies defeated the Cincinnati Reds, 11–0.

Super Steve

Steve Carlton won 27 of Philadelphia's 59 victories in 1972 (45.8 percent) to win the first of his four Cy Young Awards.

Sandy Koufax became a star when he learned to throw his fastball more slowly. Second-string catcher Norm Sherry, later a manager, suggested he master the curve, shorten his stride, and conceal his intentions from batters and coaches.

ElRoy Face, who posted an 18-1 record for the 1959 Pirates and won 22 relief victories in a row over two seasons, called on the forkball, the same pitch that later helped Bruce Sutter of the Cubs.

Burt Hooton, an original Cub who later went to Los Angeles, was the creator of the knuckle curve, a spinning pitch that is easier to catch than the straight knuckleball.

According to his catcher, Sandy Koufax threw a curve that "collapsed at the plate like a folding chair."

Walter Johnson, Bob Feller, and Koufax were among the top fastball pitchers in baseball history.

Johnny Podres, Brooklyn World Series hero of 1955, had a clever change-up; Grover Cleveland Alexander and one-time Yankee reliever Wilcy Moore mastered the sinker; and Hall of Famer Eddie Plank threw the palmball.

Among successful spitballers before the pitch was outlawed were Jack Chesbro, Ed Walsh, and Burleigh Grimes.

Satchel Paige, whose pitching career spanned 40 years, threw a bee ball (snapping fastball), jump ball (a hopper that jumped 4–6 inches), and a hesitation pitch (slow curve), in addition to other pitches.

The hesitation pitch was so good it was banned by the American League. "Will Harridge, the president of the league, said I was tricking the batters and umpires," Paige reported. "He said I had the batters swinging at the ball when I still had it in my hand. And he said the umpires were calling strikes when the catcher thumped his empty glove."

Of all the pitches, the knuckler places the least strain on the arm. But catchers have as much trouble holding it as hitters do

Cleveland player/manager Lou Boudreau talks to the ump while rubber-armed reliever Satchel Paige waits. The 42-year-old rookie—marooned for years in the Negro Leagues—was a key man in his club's 1948 pennant drive. His pitching repertoire was extraordinary.

hitting it. In 1966 the Braves shipped Phil Niekro to the minors because they didn't have a catcher who could handle the pitch.

"There are two ways to catch a knuckleball," said Charlie Lau, a catcher-turned-coach. "Unfortunately, neither of them works."

The pitch is so slow when matched against the standard fastball that it fouls up the timing of the free-swinging sluggers. When Hoyt Wilhelm was in the American League, Minnesota manager Bill Rigney admitted, "I hate to see my guys bat against him. They swing three times before the first knuckleball is halfway to the plate."

As a rookie with the Giants, Wilhelm dared any of his teammates to catch three out of five knucklers. None—including Willie Mays—could do it. Relying strictly on the knuckleball, Wilhelm lasted in the majors until he was just shy of age 49. For five straight years, when he was already in his 40s, Wilhelm allowed fewer than two earned runs per game.

The Pickoff

Successful pitchers are often good hitters and excellent defensive players—men who can win their own games with bat or glove in crucial situations. Many have mastered the pickoff play.

"I depend on deceiving the runner," said Warren Spahn, the great left-hander for the Braves, at the height of his career. "The move to first must have coordination. I try to get the movement with my head and my right knee exactly as I do when throwing to the plate. The difference is that, at the last moment, I have to step toward the base instead of the plate.

"The runner is looking for the pitcher to tip his move, but I try hard to confuse him. I look at home plate, then to first base a couple of times. If the runner starts looking at my head, I know I've confused him. When I pick somebody off, it's the runner who has tipped *himself* off."

Sign Stealing

Baseball larceny is legal. Base stealing is an important aspect of offensive play, while sign stealing plays a lesser—though often important—role. The "miracle" New York Giants of 1951, for example, raced from last to first because of an elaborate spy network that gave advance warning on upcoming pitches to such hitters as Willie Mays.

There are no rules against stealing the signs of the opposing catcher (or coaches)—provided that no mechanical device is used in the process. Even that regulation is often overlooked.

"There's no excuse for anybody stealing signs if you work at it," suggested Ralph Kiner, a daily observer of baseball as player and announcer since 1946. "You can set up a system like a war and code your messages so nobody will pick them up. You can change your signs with every pitch. The fault is not with the people stealing the signs, but with the people giving them. You can code them so they can't be stolen."

Religious athletes frown on the practice of sign stealing, but it's been part of the game since the National League was born in 1876.

National League

Hoyt Wilhelm, the first reliever to win the ERA crown, was king of the knuckleballers. He floated his way to more than 1,000 career appearances—leaving the major leagues just short of his 49th birthday.

Longest Relief Stint

Zip Zabel of the Cubs worked 18⅓ innings of relief in beating the Brooklyn Dodgers, 4–3, in 19 innings on June 17, 1915. It was the longest relief stint in baseball history.

Four 20-Game Winners

The 1920 White Sox and the 1971 Orioles were the only teams to produce four 20-game winners in the same season.

Double No-Nos

Jim Bunning, Randy Johnson, Hideo Nomo, Nolan Ryan, and Cy Young pitched no-hitters in both leagues.

Pitchers Can Hit

Gene Stechschulte (Cardinals) and Jason Jennings (Rockies) proved in 2001 that pitchers can hit. The former became the first pitcher ever to hit a pinch-homer on the first pitch he saw, while the latter became the first player since 1900 to homer and pitch a shutout in his big-league debut.

That very first season, the Hartford club was accused of stealing signals. Not many years later, catcher Morgan Murphy of Philadelphia rigged an elaborate buzzer system from the clubhouse—where he studied enemy signs with binoculars—to third-base coach Bull Childs. One buzz signaled fastball, two buzzes a curve. Childs, feeling the vibrations under foot, then relayed the information to batters with a prearranged word code.

When the American League began play in 1901, the Philadelphia Athletics followed the lead of the Phillies. Dan Murphy, a club employee, stationed himself on a rooftop beyond the center-field wall and used high-powered field glasses to watch the rival catcher's fingers. He then twirled a weathervane to signal A's batters. One windy day, however, he was unable to control the vane and the club had to do without his help.

Pittsburgh's Chief Zimmer, a fine catcher who happened to be the head of the Ball Players' Association at the turn of the century, was caught red-handed when stealing signs from a large billboard at old Exposition Park. Several Cincinnati players noticed the sign moving while the Pirates batted. They rushed the spot and found Zimmer with binoculars tucked under his arm.

In New York, manager George Stallings of the Highlanders (later Yankees) of 1909 and 1910 rented an apartment overlooking right-center field and planted an agent there. He used field glasses and mirrors to "telegraph" instructions to the plate.

When the plot was discovered, Stallings put his man inside the "O" of a colorful whisky billboard on the rim of the outfield. The spy held out his hand as a signal—right for a fastball and left for a curve.

Determined to overcome the New York sign stealers, Washington catcher Gabby Street instructed ace pitcher Walter Johnson to work an entire game without signals. Street, not knowing what was coming at any time, kept himself braced for Johnson's powerful fastball. He made passed balls on several unexpected curves, but the Senators won, 3–2.

In 1912 fleet Eddie Collins of the A's twice stole six bases in a game in a period of 11 days. Chief Bender's ability to read the enemy catcher was the major factor in his success.

Not only do sign stealers watch the catcher to learn defensive signals of the opposition, they also watch the first- and third-base coaches, who flash such signals as "take the next pitch," "hit-and-run," "steal," or "suicide squeeze." The sign stealers can set their defense accordingly.

In 1957 *The Sporting News* polled a panel of experts in a search for the best dozen sign-stealers since World War I. This list was produced: Del Baker, Eddie Collins, Frank Crosetti, Charley Dressen, Leo Durocher, Freddie Fitzsimmons, Art Fletcher, Mike Gonzalez, Billy Herman, John McGraw, Merv Shea, and Rudy York.

Baker called nearly every pitch for Hank Greenberg, Detroit's star slugger of the '30s and '40s, but nearly got him killed when he signaled a curve and the pitcher threw a high, inside fastball. Greenberg listened for a code word from Baker. If the coach shouted, "Come on Hank, paste this one," the word "come" told Hank a fastball was coming. But if Baker yelled, "All right,

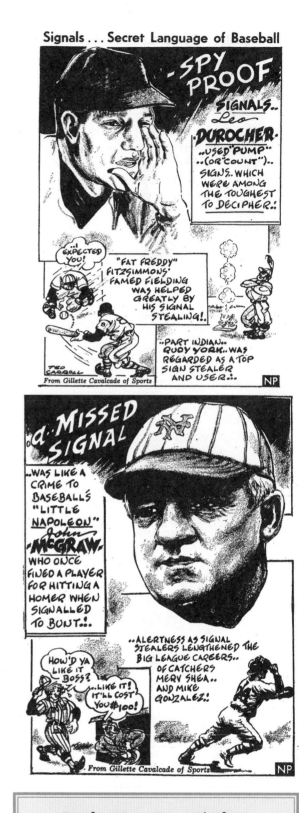

Signals . . . Secret Language of Baseball

Ruth Was Top Pitcher

Babe Ruth, pitching 44 games for the Boston Red Sox, led the American League with a 1.75 earned run average in 1916. One of his 23 victories was a 1–0 defeat of Walter Johnson in a 13-inning game at Fenway Park.

From Gillette Cavalcade of Sports

O'Doul Was Chased as Pitcher

A lifetime .349 hitter, Lefty O'Doul was a pitcher who became an outfielder. Pounded for 16 runs, including a record 13 in an inning (three of them earned), during a 27-3 loss to Cleveland on July 7, 1923, the Boston southpaw pitched just eight more times that year before a four-year exile to the minors.

Hank, get one now," the word "get" told him the pitch would be a curve.

Sign stealing backfired on one of the masters, Charlie Dressen, during the Brooklyn/New York World Series of 1953. Yankee infielder Billy Martin, later a manager himself, intercepted Dressen's sign for the squeeze bunt because the Dodger manager had carelessly used the same sign that he had used as Martin's manager in the Pacific Coast League several years before.

Dressen was so adept at sign stealing that he bragged about it. Managing the 1953 National League All-Stars, the manager held a pregame meeting. Asked what signals he would use, the Dodger pilot said, "Don't worry about it, men. I'll give each of you the signals used on your own team."

Though he could pick off enemy signs as well as hide his own, Dressen blew a 13½-game lead in the closing months of the 1951 season because Leo Durocher had also turned the art of sign stealing into a science. Coaches Fred Fitzsimmons and Herman Franks were also expert spies, but the key agent for the Giants was the man who watched the enemy from a peephole in the center-field clubhouse. A buzzer rang once for fastball and twice for curve, but several Giants disdained the advance signals. They were leery of being crossed up.

Among the game's great hitters, Hank Aaron, Joe DiMaggio, Rogers Hornsby, Stan Musial, Babe Ruth, and Al Simmons refused to heed sign stealers, while Greenberg and Willie Mays liked to have a sneak preview.

Ty Cobb had access to pitch-by-pitch tips but ignored them. Many of his Detroit teammates didn't. In an outfield billboard that read THE DETROIT NEWS, BEST NEWSPAPER IN THE WEST, a Tiger spotter opened the slots in the "B" to indicate what pitches were coming. With the top slot open, a fastball followed. If the bottom slot opened, the pitch would be a curve.

With sign stealing so rampant, did Bobby Thomson have advance knowledge of the high, inside pitch he hit for "the shot heard 'round the world" in 1951? No, said Thomson, teammate Monte Irvin, and manager Leo Durocher years later. The three-run blast in the home ninth, which erased a 4–2 Dodger lead to give the New York Giants a 5–4 victory and the pennant, was hit without help. Had Thomson known what Ralph Branca was throwing, Durocher insisted, he would have swung at the first pitch—a fastball down the middle. He had hit a Branca slider for a homer earlier in the series.

Some pitchers inadvertently "telegraph" their pitches through quirks in their deliveries, or by allowing hitters to see the way they grip the ball. Two notable examples were Walter Johnson and Sandy Koufax. The Tigers "read" Johnson and the Astros "read" Koufax, but both men were so overpowering that they managed to win anyway.

Legal Tricks

Shrewd players and managers employ a variety of trick plays to help win games.

Home-Run Ball Found Outfield Hole

The American League's first pinch-hit grand-slam home run was hit by Cleveland's Marty Kavanagh in a 5–3 victory over the Red Sox in 1916. The ball rolled through a hole in the outfield fence and could not be recovered in time to make a play.

NL Bid for DH Failed

In 1928 National League president John Heydler suggested the designated hitter idea to John McGraw of the Giants and Wilbert Robinson of the Dodgers. The managers liked it, but the concept failed when the American League showed no interest.

One-Dimension Wonders

Although the 1930 Phillies had a .315 team batting average, they finished dead last because of dreadful pitching and defense. The team's ERA was 6.71, the worst in baseball history, while the fielders made 239 errors in 154 games.

Scoreboard Deception

When Marty Marion managed the White Sox in the '50s, scoreboard spy Del Wilber told batters what was coming by moving the number 10 in the Chicago lineup. When the number moved slightly, the batter could expect a fastball. If it stood still, a curve was on the way.

How Complex Are Signals?

Signals must be simple enough for the slowest thinker on a team to remember them. But they must also be concealed in such a way that the sharpest thinker on the opposite bench cannot decipher them. Some clubs use different signs for each player. Many use a sequence of signals with only one serving as the key. The catcher and pitcher may agree to follow only the second sign flashed.

The best-known deception is the hidden-ball trick, the simple ruse of a fielder tagging an unsuspecting runner with a ball thought to be in the hands of the pitcher.

One-time Yankee shortstop Frank Crosetti was a master of the play, but he needed the full cooperation of the pitcher to make it work. While Crosetti concealed the ball in the back of his glove—exposing the bare palm to convince his victim that he didn't have it—the pitcher pretended that he did.

Lefty Gomez and Red Ruffing were expert at feigning possession while making sure not to step on the pitching rubber—a move that would blow the strategy and produce a balk call. Ruffing maintained a constant dead-pan expression, while Gomez manicured the mound as if getting ready to pitch.

Without wasting too much time—a delay would tip off the runner or, more likely, the third-base coach—Crosetti would talk to the nearest umpire in an effort to get his attention. The runner, thinking the pitcher was ready, would take a lead of several steps, giving Crosetti his cue. A lunge and a quick tag produced a most humiliating putout.

Lou Boudreau, shortstop/manager of the Indians in the '40s, told a radio interviewer one night that there was no excuse for any player to be caught by the hidden-ball trick. But the next day, the season's opener, Boudreau himself was the victim of White Sox third baseman Tony Cuccinello.

One of Cuccinello's predecessors in Chicago had been a specialist in setting hidden-ball traps. Willie Kamm, who played in the '20s and '30s, hid the ball under his armpit in a wrinkled sweatshirt that formed a perfect pocket. He could even flap his arms without losing it.

Two of the more embarrassing moments of hidden-ball history involved the Red Sox. In the late '30s, Crosetti caught shortstop/manager Joe Cronin—the man who taught the play to the Yankee infielder when both were in San Francisco.

Nearly 20 years later, the Red Sox had the tying run on second and the winning run on first with two outs in the ninth inning against Chicago. The White Sox led, 3–2, as shortstop Chico Carrasquel conferred with pitcher Sandy Consuegra. He returned to his position, slipped behind Sammy White, who had taken a short lead off second, and tagged him for the final out.

The hidden-ball trick is almost as old as the game itself. According to the late Arlie Latham, who began his pro career before the century changed, it was frequently used in the early days of the majors. It was even banned briefly because players hoping to pull it off took too much time trying to complete the trick play.

Since Ty Cobb was an outfielder, he wasn't involved in the defensive end of the hidden-ball trick—but he had plenty of other slick maneuvers.

Cobb, whose .367 lifetime average has not been surpassed, actually practiced limping. "It's a great help to stumble deliberately at first base and come up lame, or seem to be hurt by your slide," he once said. "If your act is good enough, the pitcher and catcher relax and it's no trick at all to steal second."

Because many managers follow "percentage baseball," which dictates that right-handed hitters perform better against left-handed pitchers (and vice versa), manager Bucky Harris of the Washington Senators succeeded in getting John McGraw of the

New York Giants to list a left-handed lineup for Game 7 of the 1924 World Series.

Harris had right-hander Curly Ogden warm up in plain sight and start the game, while star southpaw George Mogridge—winner of Game 4—cranked up in secret under the stands. In the first inning, Ogden walked one and fanned one before he was lifted in favor of Mogridge. Washington went on to win, 4–3.

Talking It Up and Bench-Jockeying

Talk is an important element of the game. Unsettling the opposition can force mistakes that will win games, and constant jabber on the field or on the bench helps keep all team members involved in the contest.

Former pitcher Moe Drabowsky said he was oblivious to comments from the stands or rival dugouts, but he remembered hearing the infielders of other clubs.

"Rocky Bridges was a great one for yelling, and it really helped our pitchers," said former Brooklyn reliever Clyde King. "You'd be surprised at some of the things that were said. The infield chatter was geared to keep our pitchers on their toes.

"Jackie Robinson was always yelling encouragement too. Once in awhile, you could hear one of the infielders' comments through the crowd noise and it would give you a little jack-up on the mound. Pee Wee Reese might come in halfway from shortstop to the mound and just give you a little clenched fist gesture. He was saying, 'Bear down, you can get this guy out.'

"One time, I came in to relieve against the Giants with the bases loaded. Eddie Stanky came over, took the ball, rubbed it up, and gave it back. Then he said, 'You're a college guy. You're supposed to be smart. Let's see how you get out of this.' Two pitches later, I got out of it."

The needle is invariably friendly among teammates, but hostile toward rivals. The Gashouse Gang Cardinals of Dizzy Dean, Pepper Martin, and Joe Medwick were masters at riling the opposition—as were John McGraw, Leo Durocher, and Billy Martin.

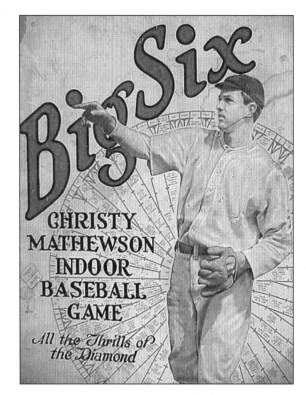

"Next to control, the whole secret of big-league pitching is mixing 'em up. It means inducing a batter to believe that another kind of ball is coming from the one that is really to be delivered, and thus preventing him from getting set to hit it."
—Christy Mathewson

Pepperpot Managers

The era of the mid '30s featured three player/managers who doubled as head cheerleaders for their teams: Joe Cronin (Red Sox), Mickey Cochrane (Tigers), and Gabby Hartnett (Cubs).

Water Made Mitt Crackle

In an attempt to intimidate enemy hitters, catcher Ossie Schreckengost soaked his mitt in water before catching fastballer Rube Waddell. When the ball hit the mitt, a loud CRACK! could be heard all over the park.

Oscar Melillo Had a Ball

Bill Rogell, Detroit infielder of the '30s, delivered milk in the Chicago area during the winter—an unexciting job except for one stop. Oscar Melillo, St. Louis Browns' infielder, was one of his customers. When Rogell arrived at his colleague's home—just as the sun was peeking over the horizon—he purposely rattled the bottles and bellowed, "Here's your milk, Melillo!"

The victim picked out a prime time for revenge. In a tie game the following spring, Rogell led off the 10th inning with a double. Confident he would soon score the go-ahead run, he took a three-step lead off second. That was Melillo's cue.

"Remember how you used to wake me up in the morning by shouting, 'Here's your milk?'" Oscar asked. Rogell broke into a wide grin. "Well," Melillo concluded, "here's the ball."

With a quick lunge, Rogell was tagged out—the victim of the oldest, and most humiliating, trick in the game.

Bench-jockeying from the Brooklyn bench helped pitchers (from left) Joe Black, Russ Meyer, Billy Loes, Carl Erskine, and Preacher Roe.

Durocher Dished It Out

Veteran manager Leo Durocher was one of the all-time great bench-jockeys. "He knew how to rile a guy," said Clyde King, a pitcher for Durocher in Brooklyn. "He wouldn't get personal; he'd always keep his remarks light and airy. But he could really get to you. He'd say some funny things to get your mind off whatever you were trying to do. He'd break your concentration whether you were at bat or in the field."

How Chatter Helps

"Noise helps you hustle," said Eddie Dyer, manager of the Cardinals in the '40s. "If you feel a little down and perhaps are inclined to loaf a little, the guy playing next to you can pep you up by making a lot of holler. You hear him and invariably and immediately snap out of it. I know, because it's happened to me. Cardinal clubs have been noisy clubs and the record shows they've been winning clubs."

Bench-jockeying began a slow death with the influx of college-educated players into the majors after the Second World War. Interleague trading was also a factor, since former roommates and teammates often populate enemy benches.

"The game is not as rough as it used to be," said Ralph Kiner, who played in the '40s and '50s before embarking on a long broadcast career in the '60s. "In the old days, it was common knowledge that everybody was thrown at. I don't think a pitcher has that right."

Beanballs, always a factor in baseball, were decreased by regulation in the '70s, but rule-makers can't do anything about boos.

This form of bench-jockeying by fans bothered Bob Elliott so much at Pittsburgh that he never became a good player there. The deluge of derision began after he booted a ball at third base. Once traded to the Boston Braves, Elliott blossomed into the Most Valuable Player.

"Most bench-jockeying is done in a kidding sort of way," said Clyde King. "I remember one time when we were having trouble beating Sal Maglie. Some of our guys were yelling at him. He hit one of them with the bases loaded one day and that was the only run we got. Finally, we decided, 'Hey, maybe we shouldn't be getting on this guy.'"

An agitated opponent may become a more difficult adversary, but Billy Martin didn't figure it that way. The veteran manager, once a scrappy infielder for some half-dozen clubs, subscribed to the theory that made players lose their cool—and their skills.

Leo Durocher agreed. "He was the best bench-jockey," said former manager Danny Ozark, who was cool, calm, and collected by contrast. "His voice carried—it was piercing. He even got on his own players—not just the other guys."

Once, when Durocher made the mistake of offending the gentle giant, Frank Howard, he found himself held by the neck several feet off the ground. Howard said, "Mr. Durocher, don't ever say that again."

Brooks Robinson, also of a gentle disposition, quieted the Oriole bench when the players overdid the razzing of an opposing pitcher. Robinson didn't want the man to be too agitated when his turn to bat came up.

Oriole pitcher Mike Cuellar was one of several stars who took a verbal pounding from Gene Mauch, fiery manager in several cities. Larry Bowa was Mauch's target when Gene was with Montreal.

Pete Rose, the longtime National League star, played an aggressive brand of ball that included constant chatter from the bench and from his position in the infield. Rose often visited opposing players before a game, then attacked the same "friends" after play began.

"The defense can't yield to pressure," said Maury Wills, explaining the purpose of infield talk. "It must do all the little things—and do them steadily. All defensive players must think, at all times, 'What will I do in the event the ball is hit to me?'"

Jabbering players seldom use invective—though this was once standard operating procedure in the game—and shy away from questioning ability. But the needle is always there. Bob Gibson gave it to rivals and teammates on the Cardinals, and Tim

Vicious bench-jockeying exploded into a fight between two contenders—the Braves and the Dodgers—in June 1957. Milwaukee shortstop Johnny Logan, a leading protagonist, takes aim at Brooklyn manager Walter Alston as Eddie Mathews (41) piles onto battlers behind them. At far right, Gil Hodges tries to quell the fray.

McCarver, longtime batterymate, learned from him. McCarver later established his own reputation.

Gil Hodges, the slugging Dodger first baseman who later managed the Mets and the Senators, never said much on the field. "He let his bat do the talking," said Clyde King.

Many other players followed suit, leaving the bench-jockey roles to players who seldom played and managers seeking to win at any cost.

Arranged Match

Boston's Smokey Joe Wood outdueled Washington's Walter Johnson, 1–0, in a specially arranged matchup on September 1, 1912. The game gave Wood, en route to a 34-win season, his 16th straight victory.

Mind Games

Bob Feller was the thinking man's pitcher. "The best thing to do to keep a hitter from getting his power behind the ball," he said, "is keep him apprehensive about what you're going to throw. Make the hitter start to think."

The Hit-and-Run

The hit-and-run play is a favorite weapon of managerial strategy, especially when a team does not have great speed on the bases. It is designed primarily to keep out of the double play but also to advance a runner from first to third if the batter hits safely. On the hit-and-run, the runner at first breaks with the pitch and the batter swings no matter where the pitch is. On the run-and-hit play, the runner breaks but the batter does not have to swing. Either play is worked best when the pitcher has good control (the ball figures to be near the plate) and the hitter has good bat control (he might hit it through the defensive hole created by the man who moved over to cover second).

No-Hit Debut

Bobo Holloman of the St. Louis Browns threw a no-hitter against the Philadelphia Athletics in his starting debut on May 6, 1953. He never pitched another complete game in the major leagues and was through before that season ended.

Reliever's Perfect Game

Baltimore Orioles reliever Dick Hall threw a "perfect game," retiring 28 batters over five straight appearances, in 1963.

Fast Start

On April 7, 1986, Boston's Dwight Evans became the first player to hit the season's first pitch for a home run (vs. Jack Morris of Detroit at Tiger Stadium).

First Meeting

The first big-league hit ever yielded by Walter Johnson was a bunt single by Ty Cobb on August 2, 1907.

Pitching Tandems

Lifetime (300 wins minimum)
(records indicate years pitchers were teammates)

San Francisco Giants

				WINS	TEAM	YEARS	PENNANTS
Mathewson	328-133	Wiltse	135-85	463	NY (N)	11	5
Plank	267-148	Bender	191-103	458	Phi (A)	12	5
Spahn	264-158	Burdette	179-120	443	Mil (N)	13	2
Ruffing	219-120	Gomez	189-101	408	NY (A)	13	7
Newhouser	200-147	Trout	161-153	361	Det (A)	14	2
Hubbell	204-121	Schumacher	154-117	358	NY (N)	12	3
Lemon	201-116	Feller	154-105	355	Cle (A)	11	2
Maddux	178-77	Glavine	171-60	349	Atl (N)	10	3
Drysdale	177-134	Koufax	163-185	340	LA (N)	11	5
Marichal	202-97	G. Perry	134-109	336	SF (N)	10	1
Walsh	189-123	White	143-105	332	Chi (A)	10	2
Grove	195-79	Walberg	130-106	325	Phi (A)	9	3
Mathewson	178-69	McGinnity	145-81	323	NY (N)	6	2
Friend	176-190	Law	141-124	317	Pit (N)	13	1
Lemon	166-92	Wynn	149-183	315	Cle (A)	8	1
Lemon	186-106	Garcia	126-82	312	Cle (A)	9	2
Roberts	205-165	Simmons	107-97	312	Phi (N)	11	1
Brown	171-70	Reulbach	135-62	306	Chi (N)	8	4
Leever	157-65	Phillippe	148-79	305	Pit (N)	10	4

Single Season

YEAR	TEAM						WINS
1904	NY (N)	McGinnity	35-8	Mathewson	33-12		68
1904	NY (A)	Chesbro	41-12	Powell	23-19		64
1903	NY (N)	McGinnity	31-20	Mathewson	30-13		61
1908	NY (N)	Mathewson	37-11	Wiltse	23-14		60
1908	Chi (A)	Walsh	40-15	White	19-13		59
1904	NY (N)	McGinnity	35-8	Taylor	21-15		56
1912	Was (A)	Johnson	32-12	Groom	24-13		56
1944	Det (A)	Newhouser	29-9	Trout	27-14		56
1916	Phi (N)	Alexander	33-12	Rixey	22-10		55
1920	Cle (A)	Bagby	31-12	S. Covaleski	24-14		55

Cleveland Indians

Right-handers Gaylord Perry (bottom right) and Juan Marichal (top left) formed a fearsome twosome as teammates in San Francisco before Perry was swapped to Cleveland.

Chapter 5

Allen Gross

As this Hall of Fame display suggests, baseball equipment has evolved over the years. Injuries and errors were common when equipment was primitive.

Equipment

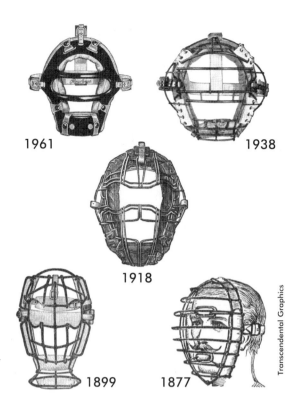

1961   1938

1918

1899   1877

The Outside Finger

Yogi Berra, Hall of Fame catcher for the New York Yankees, began the custom of leaving one finger (usually the forefinger) outside the mitt. He did it to reduce the wear-and-tear on his left hand by putting more padding between hand and ball. Many catchers copied his style, though fielders at other positions also borrowed it occasionally.

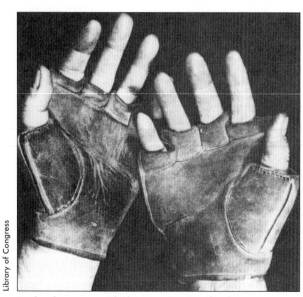

Early gloves provided no protection for fingers.

Much More than Bats and Balls

Though country ballplayers had little more than bats and balls as equipment, professional baseball requires not only a full wardrobe for athletes, but also catcher's and fielder's equipment, batting helmets, mechanical pitching machines, the omnipresent bats and balls, and much more.

Gloves were unknown in the game until Charles White, first baseman for champion Boston of the National Association, braved the jeers of rivals when he wore a thin, unpadded mitt in 1875. Other players picked up the idea, but it did not become universal until Providence shortstop Arthur Irwin broke a finger on his left hand in 1883.

Irwin protected his bandage with a buckskin driving glove several sizes too large and padded the insides. When John Montgomery Ward, a star of the era, copied the concept, manufacturers began mass production.

Catchers did not have adequate protection until 1908. Early mitts had little or no built-in padding, and Ossie Schreckengost of the A's stuffed his with goose feathers to cushion the blow of Rube Waddell's fastball early in the century. Other players used raw beefsteak to provide padding.

The first unpadded catcher's mitt was used in 1875, but the padded mitt did not appear until Buck Ewing of the Giants wore one 15 years later. The first chest protectors, primitive by modern standards, were worn by both catchers and umpires in 1885, 10 years after Harvard's Fred Thayer and a nameless Boston tinsmith coinvented the catcher's mask.

Thayer wanted his catcher to stand immediately behind the plate (a practice not adopted by the majors until 1893), but the reluctant Harvard receiver expressed concern for his facial features in the event of a foul tip or missed pitch. Thayer took a fencer's mask to the tin man to get eye holes cut in the wire mesh. The latter suggested replacing the mesh with wide-spaced iron bars—the first "bird-cage" mask.

With face, hand, and chest protectors, catchers still had exposed knees and legs. Roger Bresnahan of the Giants solved the problem when he invented shin guards in 1908. On September 24 of that year, *The New York Times* reported, "Roger Bresnahan makes an entrance, accompanied by a dresser who does him and undoes him in his natty mattress and knee pads."

Bresnahan also introduced the first helmet, which he designed after a serious beaning in 1907. The American League made helmets mandatory in 1957, but most players began to wear them after Ray Chapman of the Indians was killed by a fastball thrown by submarine pitcher Carl Mays of the Yankees in 1920.

Though Chapman was the only man killed in major league history, slugger Tony Conigliaro of the Red Sox narrowly missed a similar fate in 1967 when a pitch from Jack Hamilton of the Angels struck him just below the helmet, broke his left cheekbone, and caused blurry vision that shortened his career.

"I don't think there was anybody who was closer to death than I was the night I got hit," recalled Conigliaro, who managed comeback seasons in 1969 and 1970 before his eyes failed again. "I said a couple of prayers just to stay alive. I wasn't even thinking about my future in baseball."

The untimely end to the career of Conigliaro, who had hit 104 home runs by age 22 when the incident occurred, caused other clubs to extend the standard helmet downward to include earflaps.

Protection of players changed dramatically throughout baseball's first century, but the basic ingredients—bats, balls, and gloves—remained the same. Guidelines for each were specified in the *Official Baseball Rules*, published by the commissioner of baseball.

Uniforms: Colors and Style

For many years, baseball teams wore flannel uniforms with conservative markings—white at home and gray on the road. But new materials and styles of the '60s—especially public acceptance of men wearing bright colors—returned the baseball uniform to the rainbow days of the 19th century.

The first uniformed team, the New York Knickerbockers of 1849, wore long cricket-style pants, but the first professional team, the Cincinnati Red Stockings of 20 years later, began the tradition of wearing shorter pants and long colored stockings.

In the National League's first year, the Chicago White Stockings had a different colored hat for each player, including a red, white, and blue topping for pitcher/manager Al Spalding.

At its winter meeting of 1881, the league voted to have its clubs wear stockings of different colors: Cleveland dark blue, Providence light blue, Worcester brown, Buffalo gray, Troy green, Boston red, and Detroit yellow. Position players had to wear shirts, belts, and caps as follows: catchers scarlet, pitchers light blue, first basemen scarlet and white, second basemen orange and blue, third basemen blue and white, shortstops maroon, left fielders white, center fielders red and black, right fielders gray, and substitutes green and brown. Pants and ties were universally white and shoes were made of leather.

The plan caused too much confusion and was quickly dropped, but color remained part of the game. The Chicago White Stockings wore black uniforms and white neckties under Cap Anson in 1888 and had daily laundry service. The weekly *Sporting Life* complained that the pants were so tight they were "positively indecent."

The Chicago White Sox saluted American fighting men in World War I by incorporating patriotic colors into their uniform logo.

Allen Gross

Base Ball, BATS
-AND-
MASKS
CHAPIN'S
Celebrated League Mask, $2

We have a large line of Fishing Tackle, Croquet, Lawn Tennis, Roller Skates, Hammocks, Playing Cards, Pocket Cutlery, Foot Balls, Boxing Gloves, Fencing Foils and Kennel Supplies.

Obsolete Equipment

Early baseball equipment included sliding gloves and sliding pads for baserunners and knee pads for catchers. Turn-of-the-century receivers wore strips of felt under their stockings to protect their legs from foul tips or missed pitches. The sliding pads—worn to avoid strawberries—were welcomed by those who slid into a base with feet first, while sliding gloves were most appreciated by headfirst sliders. The sliding glove came all the way up to the elbow.

Baseball Hall of Fame

The Hall of Fame's uniform display contains 60 outfits, from heavy wool flannels to modern double knits. The exhibit includes uniforms from the St. Louis Browns, the Washington Senators, the Seattle Pilots, and other defunct teams, plus the green suits worn by the Cincinnati Reds on St. Patrick's Day, satin uniforms worn by the Boston Braves for better visibility at night, and short pants tried by the Chicago White Sox.

1960
Washington
Senators

1911
Detroit
Tigers

1969
New York
Mets

1957
Milwaukee
Braves

1934
New York
Giants

1932
Boston
Red Sox

1927
Pittsburgh
Pirates

Marc Okkonen

In 1889 Pittsburgh wore new road uniforms consisting of black pants and shirt with an orange lace cord, an orange belt, and orange-and-black striped stockings.

The St. Louis Browns, whose nickname changed to the Cardinals when their uniforms took on more red, wore shirts with vertical stripes of brown and white, complete with matching caps.

Pre-1900 styles dictated laced shirts with collars and ties, open breast pockets, and occasionally red bandana handkerchiefs as good-luck tokens. John McGraw, manager of the Giants, was the first baseball official to order uniform shirts without collars, and he also discarded the breast pockets, which sometimes served as a resting place for a batted ball.

The Giants and Phillies started the trend of wearing white at home and dark, solid colors on the road and, in 1911, the concept of whites and grays became mandatory—partly because it was sometimes hard to tell the home club from the visitors.

In an effort to lure fans to the ballpark, Charley Finley outfitted his Kansas City Athletics in green, gold, and white suits in the '60s and invited the scorn of the baseball world. Some of his own players expressed embarrassment at playing in "softball uniforms." Others likened the suits to pajamas.

But the Finley concept of color—which included mix-and-match combinations of caps, shirts, and pants—caught on quickly. In 1971 the Pittsburgh Pirates introduced form-fitting double knits, complete with pullover tops, and six years later designed three sets of uniforms—gold, black, and striped—that could be worn in nine different combinations.

"The players certainly look better," said one-time Pirate slugger Ralph Kiner. "When you see pictures of players from the '50s

Then and Now

When they filled the void created by the departure of New York's National League teams, the Mets adopted the color scheme of both, borrowing blue from the Brooklyn Dodgers and orange from the New York Giants. Uniforms are from (top to bottom): 1945, the last time "Brooklyn" ran across Dodger road grays; 1969, baseball's centennial season; and 1951, when NL teams wore a patch to celebrate the league's 75th anniversary. The "660" inscribed on the seat is the eventual career total of the rookie who wore that jersey, Willie Mays.

Colorful Orioles

The 1901 Baltimore Orioles wore pink caps, black shirts with a large yellow "O" on the left front, black baggy pants with yellow belts, yellow stockings, and double-breasted jackets with wide yellow collars and cuffs and two rows of pearl buttons. Glass and metal were not prohibited from the major league uniform until 1931.

Origin of Road Grays

Connie Mack instigated the practice of dressing his players in gray uniforms away from home. His A's played hard, aggressive baseball before the home fans but did not wish to spoil their clean uniforms away from home. Although players refused to slide and dirty their whites, Mack reasoned they wouldn't mind so much if road uniforms were gray.

Color War

The 1937 Brooklyn Dodgers switched from blue to green caps, socks, and shirtsleeves. On the road, they went from gray to tan uniforms. They still finished sixth in an eight-team league.

Patriotic Suits

The New York Giants wore red, white, and blue uniforms during World War II fund-raising exhibition games.

Can't Keep Track

The Chicago White Sox changed their uniform styles 57 times between 1901 and the early '90s.

Players Bought Uniforms

Major-leaguers bought their uniforms until 1912. Price: $30.

Flannels Caused Problems

Early baseball uniforms consisted of eight-ounce flannels that absorbed their weight in sweat and shrank after laundering. Players usually began the season with suits at least one size too large.

Fined for Play Without Spikes

Pittsburgh fined slugger Pete Browning for playing with spikeless shoes in 1891.

Ruth Wore White Mitt

Babe Ruth wore a white glove while playing the outfield for the Boston Red Sox.

Number Nine

Because the backstrap of the chest protector obscured his uniform number, longtime San Diego backstop Benito Santiago opted to wear 09 so that fans would recognize him.

Before and After

Cliff Mapes wore No. 3 after Babe Ruth and No. 7 before Mickey Mantle. A career .242 hitter with 13 homers, Mapes was wearing No. 3 when the Yankees officially retired it in 1948, the year Ruth died. Mapes switched to No. 13 and then to No. 7, which he was wearing when Mantle reached the majors in 1951. When Mapes was traded to the Browns that year, Mantle switched from No. 6, which he wore as a rookie, to No. 7.

Pitchers Last to Use Gloves

Pitchers, as a group, were the longest holdouts against wearing gloves during games. Catchers wore the first mitts, followed by outfielders and infielders.

St. Louis Birds

According to *The Sporting News*, the double-bird emblem used since 1921 by the St. Louis Cardinals originated when a member of the St. Louis County Presbyterian Church looked out the window and saw two redbirds in a tree. Mrs. Clarence L. Keaton, in charge of decorating the church for a Men's Fellowship meeting featuring Branch Rickey as speaker, used two red birds. Rickey liked the look and adopted it for his team.

in old baggy-looking pants, remember that was the style then. We wore wool flannels only because we never knew any better."

Numbers

With the experiment of different colors for different positions a decided dud, several farsighted executives discovered a different way to facilitate fan identification with players.

The 1888 Cincinnati Reds wore numbers on their sleeves, but players complained about being a number instead of a person, and the numerals came off.

The Cleveland Indians repeated the Cincinnati experiment on June 26, 1916, when they wore sleeve numbers against the White Sox, and the St. Louis Cardinals tried the idea for two years in 1924 and 1925, but the concept of numerals was not fully accepted until the New York Yankees donned large digits on uniform backs in 1929.

New York's original numbering system corresponded to the batting order. Since Babe Ruth hit third and Lou Gehrig fourth, Ruth received No. 3 and Gehrig No. 4.

Most players wear numerals between 1 and 50, but there have been many exceptions. Bill Voiselle, 21-game winner for the New York Giants in 1944, hailed from Ninety Six, South Carolina, and wore No. 96 at the end of his career. Willie Crawford wore No. 99 for the Oakland A's in 1977. Paul Dade asked the Indians to give him No. 00 that same year, and the team had to prepare a special uniform for him. Al Oliver, seeking "a new start" with the Texas Rangers in 1978 after nine years with the Pittsburgh Pirates, asked for and received No. 0.

Probably the most unusual number ever worn by a major league player was ⅛, the digits sewn on the back of Bill Veeck's midget, who walked for the 1951 St. Louis Browns in his only appearance.

Shoes

The first baseball teams wore canvas shoes with cleats, but the Harvard College nine launched a trend toward leather in 1877. Heels and toeplates were sold separately until 1890, when they were combined to improve traction.

Spikes came into general use in 1888 and it wasn't long before Cleveland Spiders manager Patsy Tebeau ordered his men to file them before a big game. "Give 'em steel," he ordered. The Spiders won the fear and respect of rivals with spikes-high slides, and their aggressive style of play was quickly copied.

To counter the Cleveland running game, Pittsburgh pilot William Chase Temple had his players line up on the field, in full view of the Spiders, with files in hand. The deterrent factor forced the Cleveland nine to use moderation.

In the minors, Omaha manager Billy Fox suggested rounding off the corners and cutting deep, square notches into the sharp edges of the spikes. Fox said this shaping of the shoe-bottom would bruise an opponent's shin without breaking it open.

The danger of being cut by flying spikes brought sanitary hose into the game. Players feared infection from the dye in their colored hose and began the practice of wearing white cotton stockings underneath.

The development of suitable spikes helped batters "dig in" at home plate and gain traction on the base paths. Old-style cleats contained five to seven ounces of steel, but modern spikes are much lighter, with each spike placed individually as opposed to the former single unit with protruding prongs.

Modern players own two pairs of shoes: one with metal cleats for standard fields and another with multiple cleats and soles made of heat-resistant polyurethane for artificial surfaces.

Shoe and spike design changed little through the years, though the advent of white shoes made from kangaroo leather (introduced by Adidas in 1967) brought color to the traditional black shoe.

Today's teams wear red, blue, brown, green, white, and other colors.

Spikes, providing extra traction, came into general use well before the turn of the century.

Glasses

In 1973 one of every seven big-leaguers wore glasses or contact lenses. Vision correction is an easy problem in the modern era, but old-time teams were reluctant to hire players with imperfect eyes.

William Henry White won 229 games as a bespectacled pitcher with three clubs from 1877 to 1886, but he was the lone major-leaguer to wear glasses until Specs Meadows joined the St. Louis Cardinals in 1915. Six years later, the Cards had the first fielder with glasses, George "Specs" Toporcer. He hit .279 in eight years as an all-position infielder.

St. Louis solidified its reputation as a home for four-eyed players when Clint "Scrap Iron" Courtney caught 119 games for the Browns in 1952. He was the first receiver to wear glasses and proved his durability by lasting 11 years in the majors.

Fred Clarke of the Pittsburgh Pirates was the first ballplayer to wear sunglasses, shortly after the century changed. Today, no outfielder would be caught without them on a sunny afternoon.

Though the sight of umpires is often questioned by fans and players, arbiters are allowed to wear vision correction. Wise men in blue prefer contacts because they are not as obvious as glasses, but retired National League ump Larry Goetz did wear regular spectacles near the end of his 22-year career.

Several top sluggers of the 1970s wore glasses. American Leaguers Dick Allen, Reggie Jackson, and Jeff Burroughs won consecutive Most Valuable Player awards in 1972, 1973, and 1974 that they probably would have lost without the aid of their glasses.

Special shoes worn on artificial turf are heat resistant and contain special spikes.

Glasses were no impediment to Hall of Fame slugger Reggie Jackson, a member of the 500 Home-Run Club. Reggie played for the Athletics, the Orioles, the Yankees, and the Angels during his long career.

Pepper Martin of the St. Louis Cardinals had a tight grip on the bat.

Bats

Hitters have always been choosy about their bats. Weight, length, grip, and even color is of concern, but the texture of the wood is most important.

Many players personally choose the wood for their bats. Ted Williams spent hours looking through timber stacks for a narrow grain, while Al Simmons looked for the widest grain. Both were slugging outfielders who made the Hall of Fame.

Simmons swung the longest bat—38 inches—and Wee Willie Keeler the shortest—30½—while Babe Ruth's 54-ounce club was by far the heaviest. Simmons needed the long bat to reach the ball because he batted with his "foot in the bucket," stepping away from the plate as he swung. Keeler was a place hitter who "hit 'em where they ain't" and wielded exceptional bat control. Ruth, who usually swung a 44-ouncer, used a wide variety of bats during his career as a home-run slugger.

Both Ruth and Hank Aaron used similar bats, with the sole exception being weight. Ruth's basic weapon was a half-inch longer than Aaron's 35-inch brand, with a normal taper from barrel to handle. Aaron was the biggest star who never paid a personal visit to his bat manufacturer, Hillerich & Bradsby, makers of the Louisville Slugger. At the plate, however, he made good use of their product. He turned the bat in his hands until it felt comfortable. He paid little attention to the trademark, though most hitters believe it should be on the topside because the bat is less likely to break if the ball hits a smooth surface. Once, when batting against the Dodgers, Aaron rotated the bat, then stepped in to hit with the trademark facing out. Catcher John Roseboro said, "Your bat is facing the wrong way!" Aaron delivered one of baseball's classic answers: "I didn't come up here to read!"

Because modern players prefer lighter bats to the "wagon tongues" used by earlier sluggers, most bats are now made from strands of straight ash from Pennsylvania, New York's Adirondack Mountains, or other woods in the northeast.

Angry Old Bats

When the Louisville Slugger Museum posted a highway billboard bragging of "more old bats than a needlepoint convention," the Embroiders Guild of America complained. The group, also located in Louisville, has 20,000 members, some of them as old as 100.

Barry's Bat

When Barry Bonds hit a record 73 home runs in 2001, his weapon of choice was a 34-inch, 32-ounce Rideau Crusher with a red handle and a black barrel. Made of maple, the Bonds bat was crafted by Canadian carpenter Sam Holman, who emblazoned it with "SAM Bat" and the logo of a flying bat.

Ash, known for its resiliency and driving power, has been a favorite wood for years, but hickory and "Cuban timber" have fallen into disuse because they are too dense to facilitate the process of bat-building.

As in the game's early days, wood scouts judge a tree's bark, height, and age, and also determine strength, durability, and grain quality.

Trunks of selected trees are cut into bolts 40 inches long, sawed into squares or split, and turned into rounds for storage. Then they are naturally dried for up to two years and stacked for seasoning. Exposure to heat or improper drying can affect resiliency.

Bud Hillerich was 18 years old when he turned a new bat for Pete Browning, star slugger for a Louisville nine known as The Eclipse, and the athlete showed immediate results with a 3-for-3 performance the next day. Word spread and the simple woodturning shop of J. F. Hillerich became a thriving bat-making plant.

Today, Hillerich & Bradsby makes its famed Louisville Sluggers at a new plant in "Slugger Park," a six-and-a-half-acre complex in Jeffersonville, Indiana, eight miles from Louisville. The basic process is still the same.

Billets are turned on a lathe and sanded, with deadwood knocked off the ends. Wood is inspected and flame-treated, a process that hardens the outer surface. The trademark, code number, and player's signature are embossed on the sealed wood and a lacquer finish is applied.

The process varies slightly in the Adirondack Company's plant, and that firm also caters to players who demand specific dimensions in their bats. The Adirondack "batmobile" visits spring-training camps and manufactures bats in 35 minutes—meeting players' specifications precisely.

Both Hillerich & Bradsby and Adirondack are kept busy throughout the year because each player uses a number of bats per season. Babe Ruth once used 170 in a season because he gave many away to adoring young fans, but Lou Gehrig managed to get through a season with only six. Another slugger, Bill Terry, was even more frugal—using two en route to the 1930 batting championship with a .401 mark.

Eddie Collins, a star in the early part of the 20th century, ordered a half-dozen bats in late summer, took them home, and "seasoned" them by hanging them out in the winter winds. Collins borrowed the idea from an earlier Chicago star, Cap Anson, who had more than 200 bats hanging like salamis in his basement.

More than three million Louisville Sluggers are carved each year—most by mass production, but those ordered for professional players are carved by hand. None are exactly alike; they differ in weight, balance, length, shape of barrel and handle, and taping.

To keep bats in prime condition, players treat the bats with tobacco juice, pine tar, oil, and special sprays. Some have attempted to smooth the surface by rubbing Coke bottles against the wood.

Aluminum bats, popular in softball, are held together by rubber plugs and are stronger than wooden bats for that game; but the plugs sometimes fail and send the barrel flying off at high speed. The expression "don't fly off the handle," comes from a poorly put-together baseball bat, which can become a lethal weapon.

How Cobb Cared for Bats

Ty Cobb treated bats with tobacco juice in an effort to keep dampness out of the wood. Using a chewing tobacco called Nerve navycut—an especially juicy brand—Cobb rubbed his bats for hours with the hollowed-out thigh of a steer. The bone was still chained to a table in the Detroit clubhouse years after Cobb retired.

Roush Swung 46-Ounce Club

Edd Roush swung a 46-ounce bat, one of the heaviest in baseball history. Asked why, he said he was used to hauling heavy objects as a country farm boy who rose every morning at 4:30.

Model Bats Housed in Vaults

Original copies of bats ordered by players are stored in fireproof vaults. When a player orders more bats, his model is used to carve duplicates.

Ted's Tip

Early in his career, Willie McCovey followed a tip from Ted Williams that he switch from a 38-ounce bat to a 34-ounce bat. McCovey finished with 521 home runs—exactly the same number hit by Williams.

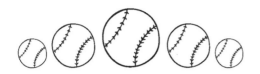

Balls

Baseballs have been dead and lively, white and colored, horsehide and cowhide. In 1883, five million of them were used in the United States, and the number has quadrupled since.

In 1872, four years before the founding of the National League, balls were standardized, though a cushioned cork center was not introduced until 1926. The "rabbit ball" earned its nickname because of its great hop. Hitters nudged it a little; it hopped a lot.

When cowhide replaced horsehide in 1974, teams complained during spring training that the new ball sometimes came apart at the seams. A new ball, with fewer but tighter stitches, was used a year later. Major league teams prepared an average of 65 baseballs and nine bases (not counting home plate) per game in 1997.

Since each ball's seams are hand-sewn, no two balls are alike. If a ball's seams are slightly raised, they will catch enough wind to make the curveball break more sharply.

Pitchers generally prefer to work with a lively ball because their teams will score more runs as a result.

The issue of live vs. dead ball usually doesn't faze the slugger. Babe Ruth hit 29 home runs (topping the Gavvy Cravath mark of 24) in 1919, when the dead ball was still in use and freak deliveries were legal (unusual pitches were banned in 1920).

Statistics before 1920 reflect the nature of the dead-ball era: stolen bases, hit-and-run plays, bunts, choked-up swings, spray hitters, and place hitters. Few, if any, went for the home run. The pennant-winning Chicago White Sox of 1906 hit seven for the season and two years later had only three. But "The Hitless Wonders" won games.

When Ruth began to crack home runs with regularity, and the game needed a boost after the staggering Black Sox scandal of 1919, a livelier ball came into play and the game changed. But not everyone was happy.

"When you monkey with the ball, you monkey with the game itself," said New York Giants manager John McGraw. "That's all right, of course, within reason. But you'd better make sure the ball is going to make the kind of game the fans want when you change it."

Ball Savers

On June 29, 1916, the Cincinnati Reds and the Chicago Cubs used only one ball in a nine-inning game.

Outfielders Played Deeper in 1920

With the introduction of the lively ball in 1920, major league outfielders learned to play further back. Two of the top center fielders of the day, Tris Speaker and Edd Roush, could no longer play shallow center and hope to reach hard-hit balls.

The Lively Ball

Washington pitcher Walter Masterson: "The ball has so much rabbit in it, you can hear the rabbit's heartbeat."

Ball Was Too Lively in 1930

The National League's souped-up baseball of 1930 had to be toned down after a season in which six of eight teams hit .300 and the other two topped .280. The pennant-winning Cardinals had 11 .300 hitters and the New York Giants hit a record .319. The Phils hit .315 but finished last—40 games from first—because their team earned run average was 6.71.

Colored Balls

Larry MacPhail introduced yellow baseballs in 1938 and Charley Finley tried orange balls 35 years later, but neither idea caught on.

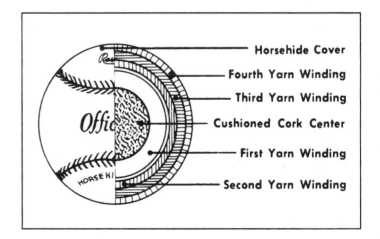

Horsehide Cover
Fourth Yarn Winding
Third Yarn Winding
Cushioned Cork Center
First Yarn Winding
Second Yarn Winding

The Ball

Starting with the 1977 season, the Official National League Baseball was manufactured by the Rawlings Sporting Goods Company. The ball, like every phase of National League Baseball, is subject to rigorous standards and specifications. Listed here are the specifications and the process involved in making an official National League baseball (AL ball is similar):

NATIONAL LEAGUE BASEBALL SPECIFICATIONS

The manufacturing of a National League baseball requires superior craftsmanship and quality materials to meet the rigorous standards and specifications set forth by the National League.

The following outlines these specifications and standards:

1. Cushion cork center consisting of composition cork sphere surrounded by one layer black and one layer red rubber ⅞ oz.

2. Approximately 121 yards 4/11 blue-grey woolen yarn to make circumference 7¾" and weight 2⅞ oz.

3. Approximately 45 yards 3/11 white woolen yarn to make circumference 8 3/16 and weight 3 1/16 oz.

4. Approximately 53 yards 3/11 blue-grey woolen yarn to make circumference 8¾" and weight 4¼ oz.

5. Approximately 150 yards 20/2 ply fine cotton yarn to make circumference 8⅞" and weight 4⅛ to 4⅜ oz.

6. Yarn used with exception of cotton finishing yarn to be 99% wool, 1% other fibers, and of the wool, 75% to be virgin wool and 24% reprocessed.

7. Apply coat special rubber cement.

8. Special alum tanned leather sewn with double stitch 10/5 red thread. Weight of cover ½ to 9/16 oz. Thickness of cover .045 to .055, the whole to make size 9 to 9¼" and weight 5 to 5¼ oz.

   The size of the ball shall be measured by a steel tape in graduations of 1/10th of an inch, with two pounds tension applied to the tape, measuring twice over two seams and once over four seams, and thereafter averaging three measurements, which shall establish the size of the ball.

9. When tested on an indoor driving machine (machine to be approved by the President of the National League) to determine and measure the resiliency of baseballs through the co-efficient of restitution with an initial velocity of 85 feet per second, the rebound of velocity shall be 54.6% of the initial velocity, with a tolerance of 3.2% plus or minus of said initial velocity.

NOTE: 85 feet per second is determined to be approximately equal to the velocity of a baseball which after being hit by a bat would carry 400 feet.

The Dead-Ball Era

The period before 1920 was known as the "dead-ball era." The ball had a different core than today's lively ball, moved more slowly, seldom took high bounces, and rarely reached the deepest part of the outfield.

Heavier bats were used to push, rather than drive, the ball, and pitchers took short strides, emphasizing control rather than strikeouts. They let batters hit the ball and hoped fielders would catch it. At the same time, they saved wear-and-tear on their arms and were able to work often.

Home runs were so rare that in 1902, National League leader Wee Tommy Leach failed to hit one out of the park. All six of his "homers" were inside-the-park jobs.

Brevity Best for Cubs

The late Phil Wrigley, owner of the Chicago Cubs, liked brevity on his team's jerseys.

"I always preferred CHICAGO rather than CHICAGO CUBS on the uniform," he said. "CUBS ends up on the stomach and that emphasizes it. Just CHICAGO across the chest makes them look huskier. CHICAGO CUBS looks like JOE'S GARAGE."

Substitute Balls

Because of the World War II rubber shortage, some of the baseballs used in big-league games during the '40s were made of balata, the material that constitutes the core of golf balls. The substitute ball, made by Spalding Sporting Goods, had a granulated cork center and a double shell of balata. The ball was a bust, however. It was 25 percent less resilient than the regular ball and was more dead than the ball of the dead-ball era. The leagues scrapped it and scurried to find enough prewar baseballs to replace the synthetic variety. Rubber manufacturing resumed in 1944.

League Balls Disappear

Before the 2000 campaign, both National and American League teams played with baseballs stamped with the signatures of their respective presidents. The consolidation of the two league offices, however, ended that tradition.

Newly designed Rawlings baseballs introduced for 2000 featured the silhouetted Major League Baseball batter logo and the blue stamped signature of then-Commissioner Allan H. "Bud" Selig.

A commemorative Millennium Opening Day baseball, also stamped with Selig's autograph, was used in the home openers of each team except the Chicago Cubs and the New York Mets, who used another specially marked ball for their historic two-game, season-opening series in Japan. It contained the number "2000" embellished in silver ink above the MLB logo.

Other balls, celebrating such special events as Independence Day, the All-Star Game, and the World Series, have also been used in major-league games. Starting in 2015, all MLB balls bore the stamped signature of new commissioner Rob Manfred.

The new all-purpose balls—available for retail purchase—confused collectors seeking signatures of Hall of Famers or other retired stars. Most indicated they would continue to use old league balls, rather than the MLB ball, for autographing purposes. Not surprisingly, the introduction of the MLB ball hiked prices of league balls, which went out of production.

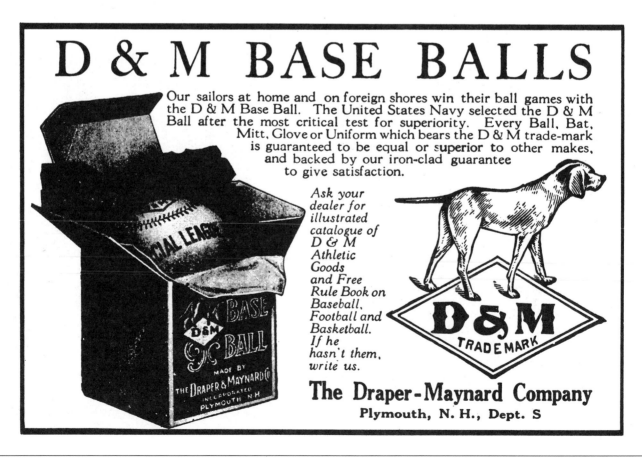

Wagner's Word

Honus Wagner was the first known pro athlete to endorse a retail product when he gave permission to have his autograph used on Louisville Slugger bats in 1905.

Yankees Logo

The intertwined NY logo of the New York Yankees, which became part of the team's uniform in 1909, was first used in a medal of honor given to the first New York City policeman shot in the line of duty. That medal was crafted by Tiffany & Co. in 1877.

First Pinstripes

The first team to wear pinstripes was the 1912 Yankees.

Who Knew?

A regulation baseball has 108 stitches.

Where Balls Begin

Balls used in the big leagues are hand-stitched in Costa Rica by artisans using American materials.

Nice Catches

The same San Francisco fan, Larry Ellison, caught the 660th and 661st home runs hit by Barry Bonds when he tied and passed Giants legend Willie Mays on the career home run list.

"Betsy Ann"

A bat used by Joe DiMaggio in the first 41 games of his 56-game hitting streak in 1941 went missing for four games until the slugger got it back before Game No. 46. The bat, which the slugger called Betsy Ann, cracked in the second inning of Game No. 54—before DiMaggio extended the streak. While active, Joe D. used it to produce hits in 49 of the 56 games.

Yankee No. 7s

Tony Lazzeri, Tommy Henrich, Bob Cerv, and Cliff Mapes all wore No. 7 for the Yankees before Mickey Mantle. Leo Durocher was the first to wear No. 7 for the Yankees.

Clever Concept

Minor-league outfielder John Neves wore a reverse 7 on his jersey in 1951. After all, he reasoned, Neves spelled backwards is seven!

Israel Tribute

The flag of Israel was featured on the uniform sleeve of the 2003 Houston Astros. The team wore a memorial patch that year after the space shuttle Columbia disintegrated upon re-entry, killing Israeli astronaut Ilan Ramon and everyone else on board. The astronauts had trained at the Johnson Space Center in Houston.

Broken Bat Problem

After studying the issue of broken bats in 2008, Major League Baseball made changes to bat composition that reduced breakage by nearly 50 percent.

Religious Number?

Although Jewish baseball players are rare, three of them wore the same number with the same team. Goody Rosen wore No. 32 for the Brooklyn Dodgers in 1937 and Cal Abrams wore it during the '50s before Sandy Koufax acquired it. The last man to wear the now-retired number was Bill Antonello in 1953.

Black Sox Again?

The Chicago White Sox trotted out black and silver uniforms when they moved into the new Comiskey Park, now called U.S. Cellular Field. The popularity of the color scheme prompted other teams to adopt it. They included the Marlins, Rockies, and Reds.

Pass the Cream

The San Francisco Giants switched to a cream scheme for their uniforms in 2000. Copycats included the Phillies, Indians, Mets, Twins, Braves, Cardinals, and Mariners.

Red in the Face

Red may be part of their nickname, but the Red Sox and Reds trail the Indians and Cardinals as purveyors of the color on their uniforms.

Deep Purple

The Colorado Rockies were the first team to introduce purple as a uniform color but not the last. The Arizona Diamondbacks and Tampa Bay Rays also flirted with the color for several seasons.

Holiday Colors

Teams used pink bats, matching their hats, sweatshirts, shoes, and armbands, on Mother's Day and baby blue hues on Father's Day during the 2016 campaign. Many also wore camouflage uniforms for Memorial Day.

Collins Saved Broken Bats

One-time Cardinal Rip Collins couldn't bear to throw away broken bats. He brought them home and converted them into a fence in front of his house.

Harry Walker Liked Two-Toned Bat

Harry "the Hat" Walker, 1947 NL batting king, was prowling the Louisville Slugger plant when he spotted a worker stirring stain with a bat. He liked the club, which had a brown barrel and white handle, and asked to buy it. Walker followed with a pinch-hit home run and placed the bat on permanent order.

Sandlot Bat Favored Fain

Ferris Fain, mired in a slump, watched a sandlot slugger hit several long drives in a game, then bought his bat for three times its value. He did well in a doubleheader the next day and sent the bat to Louisville, where he ordered a load of exact duplicates.

Umpires' Equipment

In addition to his uniform, including mask and chest protector, the umpire has various other pieces of equipment.

The ball-and-strike indicator keeps track of the count and allows the arbiter to correct the scoreboard, which occasionally deviates from the actual count. The official count is the one shown on the umpire's indicator.

The mound measuring stick, a little-known device, is used by umpires before each series between teams. The pitching mound must be sloped one inch per foot, and must be uniform with the warm-up mounds in the same ballpark. Mounds may be no more than 10 inches from ground level and no greater than 18 feet in diameter. Umpires must make sure the measurements are within the rules.

Umpires also use whisk brooms heavily. They are used not only to dust off home plate but also as outlets for the umpire's temper. When the arbiter gets into an argument, he can get out of it gracefully by whipping out the whisk broom, marching over to home plate, and dusting it off—whether it's needed or not.

The least-known equipment used by the umpire is the mud supply from a South Jersey creek. The unusually smooth silt, discovered by Philadelphia Athletics coach Lena Blackburne, was first applied to baseballs in 1937 after umpire Harry Geisel complained about the slickness of new balls.

The mud, with the texture of cold cream, did not scratch the ball or darken it noticeably. Geisel liked it and word spread so quickly that in 1938, American League president Will Harridge ordered all league umpires to apply it before games. The job, which took 20 minutes, put Blackburne in business, as the National League, International League, and American Association soon followed the AL's lead.

Chapter 6

AP Photo/Branimir Kvartuc

Dan Schlossberg

AP Photo/Richard Vogel

The Los Angeles Dodgers played at Los Angeles Memorial Coliseum (top) before Dodger Stadium opened in 1962. They renamed the street in front of the ballpark after Vin Scully announced the 2016 season would be his last as Voice of the Dodgers.

Ballparks

Turnstiles

Turnstiles were used for the first time in Providence in 1878. More than 6,000 fans crammed the ballpark—many of them arriving by two special trains from Boston—and 300 carriages ringed the outfield. Boston won, 1–0.

First Tarp

Frustrated by frequent washouts, baseball unveiled its first tarpaulin in 1884.

Oldest Franchise

The Braves are the oldest continuously-operating franchise in baseball. Four players from the Cincinnati Red Stockings, formed in 1869, relocated to Boston two years later and took the nickname with them. The Boston Red Stockings won National Association pennants from 1872-75 and joined the new National League in 1876. They have since played in Milwaukee and Atlanta as the Braves.

Early Ballparks

The first ballpark—Union Grounds in Brooklyn—existed seven years before the Cincinnati Red Stockings became the first professional team in 1869 and 15 years before the National League's first season in 1876. Admission was 10 cents.

Early stadiums were made of wood and had limited capacities. Often, there were no outfield fences, only a barrier at the end of the ballpark's property—a safeguard against freeloaders. Many parks had a special admission gate in this barrier for horse-drawn (and later horseless) carriages, which were allowed to park in the outfield. When fans exceeded a park's ability to seat them, they were also permitted to stand behind roped-off sections of the outfield—creating the need for special ground rules governing balls hit into the crowd.

In addition to uncomfortable seating on long, backless planks, wooden parks presented an obvious fire hazard. After a number of fires, concrete-and-steel stadiums began to replace wood ballparks. The last game in an old-style stadium was played at Robison Field, St. Louis, on June 6, 1920.

Another St. Louis stadium, Sportsman's Park (renamed Busch Stadium in 1953), enjoyed the longest lifespan of a major league field. First used by the Cardinals in the National League's initial 1876 season, it was reinforced with concrete and steel in 1908 and remained in regular service until May 8, 1966 (though it was unoccupied, 1878–1884, when the city had no big-league club).

Shibe Park, later renamed Connie Mack Stadium, attracted throngs of fans for the 1912 opener.

Library of Congress

Sites of Stadiums

Other than a 50-year span from 1903 to 1953, constant franchise shifting, expansion, and contraction changed the size, style, and location of major league ballparks.

Two modern clubs, the Brooklyn Dodgers and the Chicago White Sox, borrowed a pre-1900 concept of playing "home" games at a neutral site to hike attendance. The Dodgers played seven games in Jersey City's Roosevelt Stadium in both 1956 and 1957 before moving to Los Angeles, while the Chisox occupied deserted Milwaukee County Stadium for 9 games in 1968 and 11 in 1969.

A dozen championship games in 1902–1903 were played outside major league cities that then banned Sunday baseball. The Indians left Cleveland for contests in such cities as Canton, Columbus, and Dayton, Ohio, and played two games in Fort Wayne, Indiana. The Boston Braves played a "home" game in Providence, Rhode Island, and the Detroit Tigers visited Columbus and Toledo, Ohio, and Grand Rapids, Michigan.

Broadcast baseball, the home-run heroics of Babe Ruth, and the advent of night play mushroomed the popularity of the game and led to a building boom in stadiums after World War II. All but three of the thirty ballparks in the majors in 2001 were constructed after 1960.

The best illustration of the stadium-building boom was Sammy Sosa's ability to hit home runs in 45 different ballparks, a major league record.

Bucs' Bucks

Total construction price of Forbes Field, opened in 1909, was $1 million.

First PA System

The New York Giants installed baseball's first public-address system on August 25, 1929, in a game against Pittsburgh. Umpire Charles Rigler had a microphone inside his mask to broadcast ball-and-strike calls.

The Crosley Field Terrace

Most ballparks, past and present, have dirt "warning tracks" to tell outfielders in pursuit of long flies that they are approaching the outfield wall. Cincinnati's Crosley Field (1912–1970) had an incline, known as "the Terrace." Any outfielder running uphill knew he was running out of room.

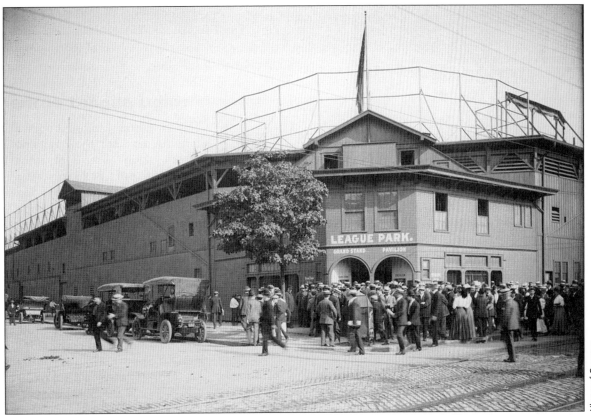

Library of Congress

The Cleveland Indians played in League Park before moving to the larger Municipal Stadium.

Brooklyn Attendance

Attendance at Ebbets Field ranged from a high of 1,807,526 in 1947 to a low of 83,831 in 1918. While Brooklyn was drawing 5.5 million total from 1953 to 1957, however, the Milwaukee Braves drew 10 million—causing the Dodgers to seek greener pastures.

Braves Borrowed Fenway

The Boston Braves played several home games in Fenway Park, home of the Boston Red Sox. Before the larger Braves Field was opened in 1916, the Braves used Fenway in 1913 to accommodate the crowd at a Memorial Day doubleheader, and late in their "miracle" season of 1914 (including the third and fourth games of the World Series). Fenway, with three times the capacity of the Braves' South End Grounds, was abandoned by the Braves in 1915, when Braves Field opened in August. In fact, the Red Sox played World Series games at the larger NL park in 1915 and 1916. The Braves borrowed Fenway again in 1946, after fans attending the Braves Field opener complained that the fresh paint on the seats hadn't dried. The incident became known as "the wearing of the green" in heavily Irish Beantown. The Braves paid more than $6,000 in cleaning bills and finished the opening series in Fenway Park.

Inviting Target

The short dimensions of Boston's Fenway Park helped 5'4" shortstop Freddie Patek hit three home runs and a double during a 20–2 win by the California Angels over the Red Sox on June 20, 1980.

Current Major League Parks

STADIUM	YEAR OPENED	CAPACITY
Fenway Park, Boston	1912	37,673
Wrigley Field, Chicago	1914	40,929
Dodger Stadium, Los Angeles	1962	56,000
Angel Stadium of Anaheim	1966	45,493
Oakland Alameda Coliseum	1966	35,067
Kauffman Stadium, Kansas City	1973	37,903
Rogers Centre, Toronto	1989	49,282
Tropicana Field, St. Petersburg	1990	31,042
Guaranteed Rate Field, Chicago	1991	40,615
Oriole Park at Camden Yards, Baltimore	1992	45,971
Progressive Field, Cleveland	1994	35,225
Globe Life Park in Arlington (TX)	1994	48,114
Coors Field, Denver	1995	50,480
Chase Field, Phoenix	1998	48,519
Safeco Field, Seattle	1999	47,943
AT&T Park, San Francisco	2000	41,915
Comerica Park, Detroit	2000	41,297
Minute Maid Park, Houston	2000	41,676
Miller Park, Milwaukee	2001	41,900
PNC Park, Pittsburgh	2001	38,362
Great American Ball Park, Cincinnati	2003	42,319
Citizens Bank Park, Philadelphia	2004	43,651
Petco Park, San Diego	2004	40,162
Busch Stadium, St. Louis	2006	45,538
Nationals Park, Washington	2008	41,313
Citi Field, Flushing, NY	2009	41,922
Yankee Stadium, Bronx, NY	2009	49,469
Target Field, Minneapolis	2010	38,871
Marlins Park, Miami	2012	37,422
SunTrust Park, Atlanta	2017	41,500

Home-Run Distances

Without established standards, teams built parks to suit their own needs.

With left-handed power hitter Babe Ruth as their main batting threat, the New York Yankees built Yankee Stadium with a short right-field porch—just 296 feet from home plate.

The park had long dimensions from home to center and left-center field, but was called "The House That Ruth Built" with good reason. He hit most of his shots to right—as did Roger Maris in 1961, when he broke Ruth's one-season record by hitting 61 home runs.

Baseball rules established a minimum distance of 325 feet from home plate to the nearest fence, and 400 feet from home to center, as of June 1, 1958. The rules also barred clubs from remodeling existing fences to bring them closer to home than the minimum distance, but allowed fields with shorter fences to retain them.

An earlier fence rule, passed by the National League in 1884, set a minimum distance of 210 feet and ordered that balls hit over closer fences would be ground-rule doubles rather than home runs. The Chicago White Stockings, forerunners of the Cubs, then had a fence just 196 feet from the plate.

Failure by the major leagues to set standard dimensions for all parks has triggered endless controversy among fans and players alike. Advocates of standard fences argued that, without them, it was unfair to compare player records. Opponents said different dimensions in each park made the game more interesting.

Right-handed hitters benefit from a short left-field fence, and left-handed hitters like a short right field.

The right-handed hitting Joe DiMaggio had great power to left, but played home games in Yankee Stadium, with its short right field. Meanwhile, left-handed batter Ted Williams, a dead pull hitter of the same era, had to cope with a long right field in Boston's Fenway Park—famous for its short left-field wall, nicknamed "The Green Monster" by pitchers.

Had DiMaggio and Williams exchanged places, they probably would have rewritten the record books.

Many ballparks got into the record book with their unusual dimensions. The Polo Grounds was just 258 feet to right field and 280 feet to left—easy pickings for Bobby Thomson's pennant-winning "shot heard 'round the world" in 1951.

Brooklyn's Ebbets Field, tailor-made for such southpaw sluggers as Duke Snider, was only 297 feet to right, but 348 to left. Playing the carom off the right-field wall at Ebbets Field was a challenge: there were nearly 300 different angles. The bottom of the barrier was concrete, the scoreboard was metal, and the screen was made of wire. The distance from home plate to the right-center corner was gradually shortened from the original 500 feet to 403.

Duke Snider always denied that he was the chief beneficiary of Brooklyn's short right-field dimensions. The 296-foot distance from home to the right-field foul line was negated by the erection of a scoreboard that towered 40 feet above the field. Snider said the height of the wall took away as many homers as the short distance provided. But he still hit 55 percent of his career home runs at home.

The Dodgers' first home in Los Angeles, the football-designed Coliseum, was just 251 feet to the left-field foul line and 320 feet to the left-center power alley, but 385 to right-center.

Baker Bowl's 280-foot right-field line benefited left-hand batter Chuck Klein of the Phillies—but helped visiting sluggers even more. In 1930, when the Phils hit .315 as a team, Klein hit 40 homers, knocked in 170 runs, and batted .386. But the team won only 52 times because its pitchers allowed rivals an average of 6.71 earned runs per game.

The average foul lines of parks built after World War II stretch 330 feet from home to the foul poles. Most modern stadiums are symmetrical, avoiding such shapes as the old Polo Grounds horseshoe. All—including the remodeled Yankee Stadium, opened in

Shibe Park

Shibe Park, later called Connie Mack Stadium, had an original seating capacity of 23,000 and was one of the first ballparks outfitted with a second deck when it opened in 1909. Construction cost was under $200,000.

No Miracle

Although the 1914 Miracle Braves went from last in July to World Champions in October, they were outdrawn by the crosstown Red Sox, 481,358 to 382,913.

Braves Field

Braves Field was so big that no ball cleared its left-field barrier in its first 11 seasons. The nation's largest ballpark when it opened in 1915, the Boston stadium stood one mile from Fenway Park and held 40,000 fans—many of whom rode the streetcar right into the stadium. In both 1915 and 1916, the Red Sox played their home World Series games at Braves Field because it held more fans than Fenway.

Boston Marathon

Braves Field was so cavernous that the New York Giants once had four inside-the-park home runs in the same game against the Boston Braves. It happened on April 29, 1922.

Pesky's Pole

Although he hit only six home runs in Fenway Park during his entire career, Johnny Pesky left a legacy when writers began referring to the ballpark's right-field marker as "Pesky's Pole." Popular as a player, coach, and manager, Pesky never showed much power but personified the player who achieved a lot with a little. That, coupled with the alliteration, produced a moniker whose origin remains shrouded in mystery.

The Red Seat

The Red Sox have a red seat in their ballpark. It marks the spot where a Ted Williams drive hit a fan's head on June 9, 1946. Still reputed to be the longest home run in Fenway Park history, the ball actually tore through the top of the straw hat worn by the 56-year-old fan, Joseph Boucher. The seat, painted red to mark the landing spot of the 502-foot homer, is in Section 42, Row 37, Seat 21.

Playing the Angles

Ebbets Field presented challenges to right fielders; there were nearly 300 different angles. The bottom of the barrier was concrete, the scoreboard was metal, and the screen was made of wire.

Brooklyn Farewell

The last game at Ebbets Field drew just 6,700 fans.

1976—maintain fences at least 300 feet from home. Yankee Stadium's right field now stands at 310 feet.

First and Last

The first home run hit over the right field roof at Pittsburgh's Forbes Field was also the final home run of Babe Ruth's career. Ruth, then playing for the Boston Braves, hit the homer—his 714th—against Guy Bush on May 25, 1935.

Muscular Mel

Mel Ott, lefty-hitting star of the New York Giants, hammered 63 percent of his 511 home runs in his home park, the Polo Grounds.

First Atlanta Homer

Home-run king Hank Aaron hit the most famous home run in Atlanta Stadium—the one that pushed him beyond Babe Ruth's career mark of 714—but not the first one. In a 1965 exhibition game against the Detroit Tigers, Tommie Aaron, Hank's younger brother, hit the first homer in the brand-new, circular ballpark. Hank hit 755 home runs in his career, Tommie 13.

Long Home Runs

Stadiums with difficult dimensions for home-run hitters cause considerable excitement when a slugger defies the odds with a long home run. Insiders refer to long-distance shots as "tape-measure homers."

By far, the "longest" home run in major league history was hit by Cincinnati catcher Ernie Lombardi in the '30s. His blast over the 387-foot center-field fence in Crosley Field landed in a truck that carried it 30 miles.

The tape measure had to come out on successive nights at the Polo Grounds in 1963 when Lou Brock, then with the Cubs, and Hank Aaron of the Braves became only the second and third hitters ever to reach the center-field bleachers in the Polo Grounds.

The ancient New York ballpark tantalized batters with short distances to the right- and left-field seats, and agonizingly long distances to center. Joe Adcock of the Braves was the first man to reach the bleachers with a 475-foot shot in 1953, but no one duplicated the feat until Brock—with only seven career home runs at the time—found the range. Aaron did it with the bases loaded.

Hank Aaron hits his 715th home run on April 8, 1974, against the Los Angeles Dodgers.

While Mickey Mantle's 565-foot shot off Chuck Stobbs in 1956 at Washington's old Griffith Stadium was probably the most famous tape-measure home run, it is not regarded as the longest. Babe Ruth (twice), Frank Howard, and Norm Cash are considered to be authors of longer home runs—though no official records are kept on the subject.

One thing is known: Shawn Green of the Los Angeles Dodgers staged the mightiest power display by a hitter in a single game. He collected a record 19 total bases in a game against the Milwaukee Brewers on May 23, 2002. With four home runs, a double, and a single, he topped Joe Adcock, who had four homers and a double for the Milwaukee Braves against the Brooklyn Dodgers on August 1, 1954.

Memories of Old Parks

Before 1900 major league stadiums shifted as frequently as the franchises. The Chicago White Stockings of 1884 were forced to open the season on the road because the Illinois Central Railroad had purchased Lakefront Park and announced plans to build a new depot there. Legal hassles followed and the team finally persuaded the railroad to allow play in Lakefront Park that year on the condition that the team would find new quarters for 1885.

In 1887 the Philadelphia Quakers opened their new Baker Bowl on April 30, when 14,500 fans watched the team beat New York, 15–9. Construction cost for the park was $80,000, the average major league player's salary in 1978.

Two years later, the New York Giants' Polo Grounds closed because of the extension of 111th Street, forcing the team to open the season on borrowed ground in Jersey City. Some home games were played on Staten Island before the "new" Polo Grounds, at 155th Street and 8th Avenue, was dedicated on July 8, 1889.

In 1890, however, the Players League put a franchise in New York and it built a park so close to the 155th Street Polo Grounds that Mike Tiernan of the Giants hit a home run from one park into the other! When the Players League collapsed, the Giants

Copyright 1994 by Andy Jurinko. Reprinted with permission, Bill Goff, Inc./GoodSportsArt.com.

The Polo Grounds had an unusual horseshoe shape and close right-field barrier.

Greenberg Gardens

The Pittsburgh Pirates, a bad ballclub in need of a gate attraction, shortened their home-run distances when Hank Greenberg joined the team in 1947. Left field was reduced from 365 feet from home to 335 feet, and left-center was cut by nearly 20 feet. The new section created behind the wall was called Greenberg Gardens, then changed to Kiner's Korner when Ralph Kiner became the club's top slugger. When Kiner was traded in midseason 1953, Branch Rickey wanted to tear down the short barrier at once because the Pirates had no other slugger who could reach the wall. But a league rule prevented him from restoring the original distances in midyear.

"Polo Grounds Swing"

The unusual dimensions of the Polo Grounds, longtime home of the New York Giants, perplexed pitchers and batters alike. Dusty Rhodes learned to cope by pulling the ball. "In the Polo Grounds," he said, "you either pulled the ball 260 feet and got a home run or you hit it 490 feet straightaway for an out."

Rhodes went 3-for-3 as a pinch-hitter in the 1954 World Series. Two of the hits were singles, the other a three-run homer off Cleveland's Bob Lemon in the 10th inning of the opener. The ball drifted into the close right-field stands, 260 feet from home. The disgusted pitcher threw his glove—and Rhodes said later he threw it farther than the ball was hit.

Two Wrigley Fields

The Los Angeles Angels, a 1961 expansion team, played their games at Wrigley Field, a compact California ballpark best known as the filming site for *Home Run Derby*. A combination of cozy dimensions and weak pitching at the park yielded 248 home runs, a major league mark that stood for 38 years.

Sun Delay

The setting sun sometimes delayed games at Parc Jarry, the first home of the Montreal Expos. At a certain angle, the sight of the sun shining through a narrow crack in the left-field corner blinded the first baseman to some of the throws from his infielders.

moved into their horseshoe-shaped park and remained there until leaving for San Francisco in 1958. The park had two more years of major league service as home of the expansionist New York Mets in 1962–1963.

When Ben Shibe and Connie Mack paid $150,000 for a brickyard, where they built Shibe Park (later Connie Mack Stadium) in 1909, they thought they might have ventured too far from downtown Philadelphia. But the city caught up with the park and virtually overran it, forcing the Phillies to build Veterans Stadium in time for the 1971 season.

The Phils were Baker Bowl tenants until 1938, while the Athletics played at Shibe Park. Shibe's right-field fence was originally 10 feet high, allowing tenants of apartments facing the park to have an unobstructed view. Fans in Shibe Park weren't so lucky; they often found themselves in seats behind steel support pillars.

During the Depression, the team added 40 feet to the height of the right-field fence, ending the tradition of freebies for ballpark neighbors and "guests" who paid to share the rooftop view. The A's, in need of revenue, finally allowed the Phillies to escape rusting Baker Bowl and share the costs of running Shibe Park.

Boston also had two teams until the Braves left for Milwaukee in 1953. In 1914, when the "miracle" Braves won the National League pennant, they played their two home World Series games in Fenway Park, the two-year-old Red Sox home, which had a larger capacity than the Braves' South End Grounds. But in 1915 and 1916, when the Red Sox won the American League flag and the Braves failed to repeat, the Bosox opted for the new Braves Field—with 4,300 extra seats—as their "home" park and won all three home games from NL opposition, including Babe Ruth's 14-inning, 2–1 triumph over the Dodgers in October 1916.

In St. Louis the Browns and the Cardinals switched their tenant/landlord relationship when Anheuser-Busch bought the Cards in 1953. The Cardinals bought the ballpark from the Browns and immediately began a $400,000 facelift. The National Leaguers had been renting the stadium for $35,000 plus approximate annual maintenance costs of $100,000 (half the maintenance). Under the new deal, the Browns rented for $175,000 per year, with maintenance costs included.

Lights had become part of baseball (except in Chicago's Wrigley Field) by the '50s, but they didn't always work properly. In Washington, Detroit's George Kell remembered what happened when the arc lights failed.

"There was a 2–2 count and the pitcher was in his windup when all the lights suddenly went out," he said. "I quickly hit the dirt. I must have stayed down there a good minute when I began to feel foolish and started to get up. Just as I did, the lights came on again. It was quite a sight. Every outfielder and infielder, even the catcher, was flat on the ground. The only guy standing was the pitcher. He *knew* where the ball was."

Crosley Field, Cincinnati, hosted the first night game in the majors in 1935, but the Reds did little to improve their lighting system after that. Still, major league lighting was far superior to that found in minor league ballparks.

"When I played in the minor leagues," said Ralph Kiner, "it seemed to me like kerosene lamps could have done as good a job."

Modern Baseball Stadiums

The major changes in baseball stadiums of today and those of the Babe Ruth era, some 70 years ago, are the introductions of lights, artificial turf, electronic scoreboards, and domes.

Night ball began in 1935 and played tricks on the eyes of batters for years—especially in its first 20 years, when teams played more often by day than by night. On June 15, 1938, Johnny Vander Meer of the Reds became the only man to pitch back-to-back no-hitters, but he was helped considerably in the second effort by the dim lights of Brooklyn's Ebbets Field. It was the park's first night game.

Artificial turf, a necessity caused by the creation of the first covered park, the Houston Astrodome, made its debut during an exhibition game between the Astros and the New York Yankees on April 9, 1965. President Lyndon Johnson, a Texan, watched Mickey Mantle's homer lead the Yankees to a 2–1 victory in the $31.6 million ballpark.

In 1998 10 fields had artificial surfaces and five had covers. The Toronto Blue Jays drew so well after opening their futuristic SkyDome in 1989 that they became the first team to draw four million fans in a season. But the Colorado Rockies, playing their first two years in 80,000-seat Mile High Stadium, set new marks for both game (80,227 on April 9, 1993) and season (4,483,350 in 1993).

Both artificial turf and domed ballparks caused problems—just as the advent of lights did years earlier. Light failure became such a factor in the game that contingencies regarding it were written into baseball rules. Turf failure and dome failure had to be handled by individual clubs that opted for such features.

The Chicago White Sox, on orders from President Bill Veeck, replaced their artificial infield with natural grass. Veeck was one of many baseball insiders who felt that the true bounces and aesthetic appearance of plastic grass did not counterbalance the wear-and-tear on athletes of the hard, hot surface. Nor did he like the turf's tendency to rocket balls through the infield and tilt the traditional balance between hitter and pitcher.

Ruth Pulled Perfect Fake

Babe Ruth was a good defensive outfielder. When Detroit's Tiger Stadium was called Navin Field in the late '20s, there was a board fence in left instead of double-decked stands. With one out left and Charlie Gehringer of the Tigers on second, the batter hit a long fly ball to Ruth in left. Ruth knew he could catch the ball, but pretended it had cleared the wall. Watching the dejected Ruth, Gehringer left for home. The minute he left the base, Ruth came to life, caught the ball, and fired to second for the inning-ending double play.

Long Dimensions

The outfield dimensions of Forbes Field were so deep that light towers were erected inside the playing field and the batting cage was stored in left-center.

Reds Dyed Grass Green

In 1937 the Cincinnati Reds became the first club to artificially color its diamond. The team dyed sun-burned grass green with a product recommended by the United States Greens Association.

There is a remarkable contrast between the old and new homes of the Dodgers in Los Angeles. Memorial Coliseum, used before Dodger Stadium opened in 1962, was built for football.

Dodger Stadium

Los Angeles Dodgers

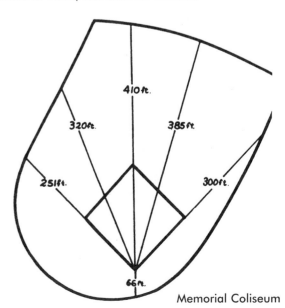

Memorial Coliseum

Big Parks, Short Fences

The Los Angeles Coliseum, originally built for football, had the largest capacity and most unusual dimensions in baseball during its brief tenure as home of the Dodgers, 1958–1961. It held 93,600 for baseball—and nearly reached that figure three times during the 1959 World Series against the White Sox. The park's left-field screen stood just 251 feet from home, and the left-center power alley was only 320 feet away. In right field, the distance down the line was 300 feet, but the right-center power alley was 385.

In the Astrodome, an active park from 1965 to 1999, the 4,500 plastic skylights caused a glare that resulted in fielders "losing the ball" in the roof. After conditions deteriorated to a point where outfielders wore helmets for day games, the team painted the skylights and reduced the day lighting by 25 to 40 percent. Since that time, electric lighting has been used for all games, day or night.

In a story on the Seattle Kingdome in 1977, columnist Mike Schuman of *The Baseball Bulletin* listed player complaints about the coloring of the dome, the proximity of bullpen mounds to the playing field, and high seams in the artificial turf near second base, where dirt meets carpet.

Olympic Stadium, which costs Montreal taxpayers an estimated $15,000 per day for maintenance, once had a "technical ring" with a central opening that measured 600 feet by 300 feet. Snowouts were a problem before the roof was completed in 1987.

The stadium had other problems. A game was postponed when explosions caused a fire in the tower, a windstorm later tore holes in the roof, and a 50-ton slab of concrete fell to the promenade—forcing the Expos to play their final 26 games of 1991 on the road.

Houston's switch from the cavernous Astrodome (above) to compact Enron Field, now called Minute Maid Park (below) proved so nightmarish for pitchers that *Sports Illustrated* profiled the new park under the headline, "Field of Screams." The downtown park, which opened in 2000, features skyline views, a retractable roof, and a working steam engine that hoots and whistles after a home run by the Astros.

Top image copyright 1999 William Feldman. Bottom image copyright 2000 Bill Purdom. Reprinted with permission, Bill Goff, Inc./GoodSportsArt.com.

Baseball executives who like intimate ballparks with unusual dimensions insist that such symmetrical parks as Riverfront and Three Rivers Stadium, both opened in 1970, destroy the color of the game. They frown on horizontal yellow "home-run lines" painted on the outfield wall, dislike artificial turf, and warn that fans who cannot see the game well enough to identify the players will quickly lose interest.

The two oldest ballparks currently in use, Fenway Park in Boston and Wrigley Field in Chicago, house healthy crowds consistently. Fenway opened in 1912 while Wrigley opened as Weeghman Field, then used by the Federal League, two years later. It assumed its present name in 1916 after the Feds folded and the local National League team took over the fledgling facility.

Although Fenway had a major facelift in 1934, Yankee Stadium stood unchanged from 1923 to 1974. That's when the city launched a two-year rebuild, originally projected at $24 million, that would end up with a $160 million price tag—more than triple the cost of building Royals Stadium, a particularly handsome baseball park that opened in Kansas City in 1973.

Remodeling Yankee Stadium was the only option open to New York City in 1972 when it appeared the team would join the football Giants in a baseball/football facility in The New Jersey Meadowlands, less than five miles from Manhattan but far more accessible than Yankee Stadium.

The bitter irony of the project was the total bill. The team could have built two parks from the ground up for the price of its two-year overhaul of a 50-year-old field.

Dimensions were changed slightly in the "new" stadium: 312 feet to left, 310 to right, and 417 to dead center field. Formerly, it was 301 feet to left, 296 to right, and 461 to center.

Obstructing pillars were removed and aisles—and seats—widened, reducing capacity from 65,010 to 57,545. Blue paint was used in liberal doses and the famous ballpark looked years younger. Only the dismal Bronx neighborhood remained the same.

During construction, the Yankees played home games at Shea Stadium, home of the National League Mets, giving Bill Virdon

Both New York teams opened new ballparks across from their old ones in 2009. The new Yankee Stadium (above) hosted the 2009 World Series but Citi Field, home of the Mets in Flushing, Queens, got more plaudits for its aesthetics as a ballpark. Construction cost of the new Yankee Stadium was $1.02 billion, making it the most expensive ballpark in history.

Flood in Pittsburgh's Park

With water knee-deep in Pittsburgh's Exposition Park on July 4, 1902, a special ground rule was created: any ball hit into the water (called Lake Dreyfuss after the Pirates owner) would be an automatic double.

Novel Approach

Longtime Sportsman's Park groundskeeper Bill Stockstick used a goat to help him trim the outfield grass for the St. Louis Cardinals. The goat was grazing in the outfield the morning after Frankie Frisch became the team's manager in 1933.

An Answer to Veeck

When the Yankees played at Chicago in 1960, the year Bill Veeck installed his exploding scoreboard, manager Casey Stengel and Yogi Berra, joined by other players, brought sparklers to the ballpark. When Mickey Mantle homered—and the partisan Veeck board was silent—the Yankees lit the sparklers and jumped up and down in the dugout.

Two for Shea

Shea Stadium was the only 20th century ballpark to host two regular-season games involving four different teams on the same day. On April 15, 1998, the Yankees hosted the Angels in the afternoon game, followed by a nightcap that featured a Mets home game against the visiting Cubs. The Yankees played at Shea because of emergency repair work at Yankee Stadium.

Double Bill

The Yankees and Mets played a doubleheader that used both New York ballparks on July 8, 2000. The Yankees won both games by 4–2 scores, taking the afternoon game at Shea and the nightcap in the Bronx, but the media obsessed over the beaning of Mets slugger Mike Piazza by Roger Clemens. The catcher had to be hospitalized with a concussion.

At 5,176 feet above sea level, Denver's Coors Field has thinner air—and less friction to slow down a speeding baseball—than ballparks at lower altitudes. With 15 percent fewer air molecules in the Mile High City, Coors Field has become a hitters' paradise. Down-the-line dimensions at Coors are 347 feet to left and 350 feet to right—largest in the National League except for Wrigley Field. But a ball hit in the Mile High City will travel 9 percent farther than a ball hit at sea level.

Sicks Stadium

Sicks Stadium, in Seattle, held 25,400 fans—more than adequate for Pacific Coast League play but below major league standards. Bad weather, bad financing, and the unavailability of a better facility forced the expansion Seattle Pilots of 1969 to abandon the stadium the following year. The Pilots became the Milwaukee Brewers.

Mistake on the Lake

During its tenure as home of the Cleveland Indians, cavernous Municipal Stadium was often called "Mistake on the Lake." When it was demolished after the 1996 season, remnants of the old park finally served a useful purpose: as an artificial reef in Lake Erie.

the unique distinction of being the only Yankee manager since the Babe Ruth era never to manage a game in Yankee Stadium.

Scoreboards

The baseball scoreboard, originally designed to tell spectators the score of the game, has become as much an attraction as the ballgame itself.

Old-style boards were manually operated, with run-markers put up by hand. When Dizzy Dean was pitching for Houston, then in the minor leagues, he hit a rare home run. Immediately afterward, he lost his control and walked three consecutive batters.

Taken from the game, Dean ran to the scoreboard and plucked the numeral "1" that represented his home run. The pitcher took the painted wooden square into the clubhouse, prompting a visit from the manager. "If I can't pitch," he said, "you can't have my run."

The St. Louis Cardinals, where Dean reached stardom, maintained an ancient scoreboard until 1938, when a $40,000 replacement, 136 feet long and 40 feet high, brought electricity into the picture. Inning-by-inning scores of out-of-town games were still posted by hand, but balls, strikes, hits, errors, numbers of players at bat, and other information was flashed in lights.

Multimillion-dollar boards broke into baseball with the wave of new stadium construction in the '70s, but Bill Veeck gave birth to the idea of using the scoreboard as an attraction to lure customers. In 1960 his exploding scoreboard delighted White

Sox players and fans but irritated the opposition so much that Cleveland center fielder Jimmy Piersall once threw a ball at the noisy monolith.

Veeck's board shot off multicolored rockets and gyrated wildly when a Chicago player homered, or when the Sox won a game, and other clubs parroted the creative concept by using lights instead of fireworks.

Wrigley Field, home of the tradition-minded Cubs, retained a board that displayed inning-by-inning scores of all games. The team also refused to follow the mass stampede to night baseball. The park remained lightless until 1988.

Tradition also bent at Fenway Park, where an animated board was added to the compact, ancient stadium, and in Yankee Stadium, which received a new board during the 1974–1975 refurbishing.

Modern boards feature "home-run spectaculars," animated cheerleaders, and even advertising—which helps defray massive maintenance costs. The major victim, in many cases, is the listing of other scores. They are flashed only occasionally and sometimes—if the team has too many birthdays to post or promotions to announce—not at all. Since not everyone at the ballpark is a fan of the two teams on the field, the absence of scores annoys numerous patrons.

Probably the best new board appeared at Veterans Stadium, Philadelphia, in 1971. Three staffers worked the board and coordinated activities with a public-address announcer who shared their booth. The organist sat in another booth, separated by glass, but worked closely with the scoreboard crew.

In Atlanta, the $1.5 million Fulton County Stadium scoreboard came equipped with a TV capability that included "instant replay." The Braves nearly forfeited a game when umpires walked off the field after the board showed "instant replay" of a close call.

During rain delays the board showed baseball movies, and flamboyant club owner Ted Turner joked that he could even hold baseball's first "Adult Night" and show X-rated films at the stadium.

The major gripe of baseball insiders against the new boards is their propensity to unnerve visiting teams by flashing giant "GO" or "CHARGE" signs, accompanied by blasts from the organ, in the middle of an inning. Leo Durocher, as Cubs' manager in the late '60s, raised the cry against Houston scoreboard chief Bill Giles, who later owned the Phillies.

In the absence of directives from either league office, the idea spread. When Durocher became Houston manager in 1972, he found himself enjoying one of the game's most creative home-run spectaculars.

"Fixing the Field" for the Home Team

Each major league club maintains its home field with meticulous care and a bag of tricks designed to help the home team and slow the opposition.

Groundskeepers may water the base paths or slope the foul lines to thwart a bunt-and-steal team, or freeze baseballs to help a weak-hitting, good-fielding home club.

Fabian Spent 50 Years as Groundskeeper

Henry Fabian was a groundskeeper for more than 50 years—half of them with the New York Giants. In 1914 ace Giant pitcher Christy Mathewson showed Fabian the value of a flat mound. The star pointed out that the average pitcher jerks his head back and fouls up his follow-through when working off a high mound. Fabian kept the Polo Grounds mounds low to the ground (a nine-inch slope), much to the delight of a later Giants' star, Carl Hubbell.

The Tarpaulin

The tarpaulin is used to cover infields when it rains. The old, heavy tarp absorbed moisture and required drying after the rain, thereby complicating the life of the ground crew. A lightweight spunglass tarp that weighed half as much, did not absorb water, and did not need drying was introduced by Cleveland's Emil Bossard in the '40s. By 1960 most tarps were similar to the 1,110-pound plastic-coated nylon cover used by the St. Louis Cardinals. Rolling and unrolling the tarp took nine men.

Before the Tarpaulin

Before canvas field covers were used to protect dirt infields from rain, groundskeepers resorted to other means of protection. Bill Stockstick, in St. Louis, poured gasoline over the field and burned it. If the field had excessive mud, he covered it with sawdust first, then poured on the gasoline and lit a match. Players complained of the fumes, and the method was rarely successful.

Both images copyright 1994-1995 by Bill Purdom. Reprinted with permission, Bill Goff, Inc./GoodSportsArt.com.

New York ballparks had personalities all their own. Mickey Mantle (No. 7, above) was only 24 on May 30, 1956, when he hit this Pedro Ramos pitch off the facade, 18 inches short of being the first ball hit out of Yankee Stadium. Across the Harlem River, the dimensions of the horseshoe-shaped Polo Grounds presented a more difficult target for Willie Mays. His first homer, shown below, came on May 28, 1951, in a Monday night game against Warren Spahn of the Boston Braves.

It was once common practice to place the visitors' dugout in line with the hot afternoon sun, but the prevalence of night baseball (except in Chicago's Wrigley Field) has diminished the value of that tactic. Many home dugouts—but not visiting dugouts—have heat and air-conditioning, and home clubhouses are invariably superior to those given the visitors. Bullpen lighting is generally better for the home team too.

Both Ty Cobb and Connie Mack were masters at freezing balls before slugging clubs came to town. Mack frightened visiting hitters by ordering his groundskeepers to build a 20-inch mound for ace pitchers Lefty Grove, George Earnshaw, Chief Bender, and Eddie Plank. Early Washington manager Joe Cantillion, taking the opposite approach, trained his pitchers to work on a flat mound; rival pitchers hated to pitch in the Senators' park.

The Yankees reached into their bag of tricks by raising or lowering a huge green curtain in center field of Yankee Stadium. If a power pitcher worked for New York, the curtain was up so that enemy batters had trouble picking up the ball against a sea of white shirts. If an ordinary pitcher was on the mound, the curtain was down to help the Yankee batters.

The Yankee Stadium ground crew had a reputation for speed in spreading the infield tarpaulin, but they prolonged the 10-minute job whenever New York was ahead in a game that had passed the minimum four-and-a-half innings. By moving slowly, the field could absorb enough water to make further play impossible. If the Yankees trailed, the crew worked as quickly as possible to keep the field dry and hope play would resume.

Groundskeepers sometimes work 16-hour days, paying special attention to the batter's box, pitcher's mound, and often the base lines. Hitters usually like smooth, flat ground and dislike holes

Cubs' Groundskeeper Caught Babe Ruth

Bobby Dorr, Chicago Cubs' groundskeeper for more than 30 seasons, was Babe Ruth's first warm-up catcher with the Baltimore Orioles of the International League. Dorr later created the concept of keeping fresh baseballs in a wooden box buried near home plate. Previously, new balls were thrown out from the bench or rolled down the screen behind the plate.

Ground Crew Chief Lived in Ballpark

Matty Schwab borrowed a minor-league custom when he persuaded Horace Stoneham, owner of the New York Giants, to build him a house under the Polo Grounds stands. The three-room cottage, under Section 31 of the left-field grandstand, was the Schwabs' summer home for many years.

"The Friendly Confines of Wrigley Field"

Hall of Fame slugger Ernie Banks, who spent his entire career with the Cubs, always lauded his home park, which he called "the friendly confines of Wrigley Field." The Wrigley family, which owned the team, spent several million dollars on beautification but refused to install lights. They maintained that the green vines on the outfield wall looked more attractive by day, when people would equate a trip to the ballpark with a picnic. "We're aiming at people not interested in baseball," Phil Wrigley once said.

that can break their stride and force them to swing under the ball. Pitchers have their own preferences as to height and texture of the dirt on the mound.

Washington's Camilo Pascual spent considerable time manicuring the mound whenever he pitched, earning the nickname "the Rake," and Catfish Hunter's well-known preference for a soft mound prompted Kansas City groundskeeper George Toma to pack the mound hard when Hunter came to town as a visitor with Oakland or New York.

"I made it as uncomfortable as the rules permitted," he said. "He relied a great deal on the shape and condition of the mound. I did my best to help him when he was here and later I did whatever I could to hinder him."

During Ty Cobb's day as a great base stealer, rival clubs trimmed their infield grass before Detroit came to town so that Cobb's bunts would reach fielders more quickly. When Maury Wills was en route to breaking Cobb's one-season record in 1962,

No Ads, Please

During their 61-year tenure at Forbes Field, the Pittsburgh Pirates refused to permit advertising billboards. The exception was a World War II recruiting sign featuring a marine sergeant.

Koufax on AstroTurf

Hall of Fame pitcher Sandy Koufax on the St. Louis AstroTurf: "I know one thing. I was one of those guys who pitched without a cup. I wouldn't do it on this stuff."

It's October 5, 1956, Game 2 of the World Series, the Yankees vs. the Dodgers at the venerable Ebbets Field.

Cost Increase

Turner Field, built for the 1996 Atlanta Olympics but occupied by the Braves a year later, cost $235 million—more than 10 times the cost of Atlanta Fulton County Stadium. Before it became Turner Field, Atlanta's ballpark was called Centennial Olympic Stadium.

The Ebbets Field Bullpen

The bullpen in Brooklyn's Ebbets Field (1913–1957) was a hazardous place to work. Squeezed between the left-field foul line and the stands, pitchers were pelted with assorted debris from the stands. Another problem was line drives from hitters; pitchers warmed up in a tiny space facing the plate, with left-handers on the outside and right-handers on the inside. An extra player stood behind bullpen catchers (who had their backs to home) to field balls hit in the pen's vicinity.

Signs Paid Bills

Advertising signs at Ebbets Field produced an average of $42,000 per season—enough to pay Dodger star Jackie Robinson.

Record Attendance

The 1991 Toronto Blue Jays were the first team in any sport to top 4 million in attendance, but the Colorado Rockies, playing in a football facility called Mile High Stadium, topped them two years later. The Rox drew nearly 4.5 million fans in 1993, their first season. No club has ever done better.

Jurassic Park?

The reason the Colorado Rockies have a dinosaur as a mascot is that dinosaur fossils were found throughout the grounds during the excavation and construction of Coors Field. Before the local brewery bought naming rights, the field was almost named "Jurassic Park." Instead, the team applied the dinosaur idea to its mascot, which it named "Dinger."

Curing Coors

Three years after teams combined for a record 303 home runs at Colorado's Coors Field, the Rockies introduced an enormous humidor to store baseballs before they were used in games. The 2002 addition, made after scientists decided that dry air and thin air were factors in home run frequency, reduced the subsequent home run totals to more reasonable levels.

Neutral No-hitter

Carlos Zambrano carved his niche in baseball history by pitching the only no-hitter at a neutral site. It happened on September 14, 2008 when the Cubs blanked the Astros, 5–0, at Milwaukee's Miller Park. The first of two Astros "home games" was moved from Houston because of Hurricane Ike.

Short Hop

Chicago's ballparks are closer together than any other big-league facilities. U.S. Cellular Field and Wrigley Field, linked by the Red Line subway, are separated by only 9.81 miles, just short of the 10.04 miles separating Yankee Stadium and Citi Field in New York.

the Giants tried to thwart the Dodger star by sanding the base paths. The Dodgers tried a similar tactic against the bunt-and-steal Phillies during the 1977 National League Championship Series, but NL President Chub Feeney made them remove the excess dirt.

The Senators helped slow-footed third baseman Harmon Killebrew, their top slugger, by letting the infield grass grow enough to slow balls hit his way. Earlier, the Indians watered down third-base territory—making it "the warm corner"—after slugger Al Rosen broke his nose nine times on hard-hit balls.

Richie Ashburn of the Phillies won the 1955 NL batting crown partly because his bunts down the third-base line never rolled foul; they coasted to a stop in fair territory because of "Ashburn's Ridge," an inclined foul line raised slightly above the rest of the infield level. St. Louis manager Eddie Stanky tried to thwart the Philadelphia tactic by stamping down the ridge with his spikes before the game.

The "Go-Go" White Sox, a hit-and-run team that singled opponents to death en route to the 1959 AL pennant, were also accused of harboring a raised third-base foul line. The Sox, and the pennant-winning Pirates of 1960, thrived on rock-hard infields in their home parks because line drives by their hitters got by enemy infielders quickly.

Fairchild Aerial Surveys

Fenway Park has always been a nightmare for pitchers—especially left-handers, whose best pitches frequently bounce off "the Green Monster," the huge left-field wall 315 feet from home. In 1950 the Sox beat the Browns 20–4 and 29–4 in consecutive games. They scored 17 runs in an inning against Detroit in 1953, winning, 23–3; beat the Senators, 24–4, in 1940; and lost to the Yankees by the same score in 1923.

Charges of partisan groundskeeping were hurled at the Houston Astros when they moved into the air-conditioned Astrodome in 1966. Ed Kranepool of the Mets noticed that the air-conditioning was blowing out when Houston hitters took their swings, but that the breeze stopped when visitors came to bat. He made the deduction by watching the flag in the outfield.

Though most groundskeepers will swear that their only duty is to maintain their field in good condition, they make the remark with tongue in cheek. It's not really legal to fix the home field in favor of one club, but it's an accepted part of the game.

Chapter 7

The Yankees toast pitcher David Cone after his perfect game against the Montreal Expos at Yankee Stadium on July 18, 1999. The 36-year-old right-hander needed only 88 pitches in baseball's 16th perfect game.

The Game

American League

Light towers in Arlington, Texas.

American League Lights

The Cleveland Indians and the Philadelphia Athletics were the first American League teams to install lights, and the Detroit Tigers, in 1948, the last. When Tigers owner Walter O. Briggs decided to light his park, he tested several lighting systems to avoid any that might be unflattering to female fans.

MacPhail Lit Two New York Parks

Night ball pioneer Larry MacPhail installed lights when he became an executive with the Brooklyn Dodgers (1938) and the New York Yankees (1946).

Sunday Ball

In the early years of pro ball, Sunday was literally a day of rest. At one time, Sunday games counted only as exhibitions and most cities banned them completely.

In 1878 the National League decided to expel clubs or those players who played on Sunday. Two years later the rule was used to throw Cincinnati out of the circuit. The early Reds had made $4,000 by leasing their park to a nonleague club—and selling beer during games—on Sundays.

Cincinnati—restored to good graces—beat St. Louis, 5–1, in the league's first recognized Sunday game on April 17, 1892. But Sunday restrictions continued for years, forcing several clubs to play in such neutral cities as Columbus, Ohio. Cleveland's Addie Joss beat Clark Griffith of the Yankees in Columbus, 9–2.

Sunday ball began in New York in January 1917, when Charles Ebbets of the Brooklyn Dodgers staged a benefit concert preceding a National League game against the Phillies. He claimed tickets were being sold only to the concert, but he and manager Wilbert Robinson were arrested and fined $250 each.

The New York Giants used the guise of a military benefit to play a Sunday game the following year, and managers John McGraw of the Giants and Christy Mathewson of the Reds were arrested. Magistrate Francis X. McQuade, named a club official when Charles Stoneham purchased the franchise in 1919, laughed off the charges and blasted the police.

Mathewson's arrest was ironic because he and Branch Rickey, among others, had steadfastly refused to participate in Sunday baseball, even when it was permitted.

By the mid-1930s, Sunday ball was universal and baseball was concerned with a new development—night games.

Night Baseball

On May 24, 1935, the Cincinnati Reds defeated the Philadelphia Phillies, 2–1, in the first night game played in the major leagues. President Franklin D. Roosevelt, sitting in the White House, threw a special switch that turned on the power in the new light towers above Crosley Field, where 20,422 spectators watched.

Baseball executives and writers panned the advent of night play, which they dubbed "MacPhail's Madness" after pioneering Cincinnati general manager Larry MacPhail.

"There is no chance of night baseball ever becoming popular in the bigger cities," said Washington owner Clark Griffith. "People there are educated to see the best there is and will only stand for the best. High-class baseball cannot be played under artificial light."

Cincinnati's $50,000 lights were not the first in organized ball. In fact, MacPhail had installed lights at Columbus, Ohio, when he owned that American Association club several years earlier. Des Moines of the Western Association had announced its intention to install lights prior to the 1930 season, but Independence, Kansas, of the same circuit got the jump on Des Moines by rigging a primitive illumination system and losing pro ball's first night game to Muskogee, 13–3.

Des Moines made its arc-light debut May 2 that same year with a 13–6 win over Wichita. The fan response was so enthusiastic that team president E. Lee Keyser announced that the teams would play another night game the following day. He added that night ball would be the salvation of the minor leagues because it attracted families and working people who could not attend day games.

The first night game on record was played between two amateur teams at Nantasket Beach, Massachusetts, in 1880, and another was played three years later when the Quincy Pros met the M. E. Collegians at Fort Wayne, Indiana. The power failed twice, much to the satisfaction of skeptics.

Quincy won, 19–11, in a seven-inning game marked by sloppy fielding. But *Sporting Life* reported, "Not the least difficulty was found at the bat. With between 25 and 39 lights, there is no question but what electric light ballplaying is an assured success." Only 17 lamps were used at Fort Wayne.

Night ball wasn't an idea that popped into somebody's head. Its origin was traced to a General Electric brochure advertising new lights at Boston Common. The State of Massachusetts had asked the company to provide lights with the power of daylight. The brochure, which showed children playing baseball on Boston Common, came to the attention of Lee Keyser at Des Moines.

GE employees at Lynn, Massachusetts, played ball under the lights in 1923—12 years before Larry MacPhail introduced the idea in the majors. MacPhail's original intent was to use night ball as a novelty; he urged baseball to restrict night games to seven per year. At first, this was done, but the number later doubled and eventually took over more than 50 percent of the schedule. Fan reaction was enormous.

What had been branded "madness under moonlight" and "a passing fad" became an integral part of baseball.

Weather

Bad weather often cancels or delays games. Sometimes it threatens the lives of the athletes.

Ray Caldwell of Cleveland carried a 2–1 lead against the Athletics into the ninth inning on August 24, 1919, and retired two batters. A bolt of lightning hit him, knocking him down. He recovered and—not wishing a repeat performance—made quick work of the last hitter.

First baseman Harold Jensen of Urbana, Ohio, in the Miami Valley League was struck and killed on August 7, 1949. Three other players and two umpires were knocked off their feet and all five were treated at a nearby hospital.

Five years earlier, 4 persons were critically injured and 26 others less seriously when the east roof of the Milwaukee Brewers' grandstand collapsed during a sudden windstorm. Neighboring cars and houses were also damaged. Needless to say, the game against Columbus was blown away. It went down as a seven-inning 5–5 tie.

Early in the century, Washington was proving the slogan, "First in war, first in peace, and last in the American League." Trailing Detroit 1–0 early in the game, manager Joe Cantillon was ecstatic as the Senators broke through for five runs. Seeing the end of an 18-game losing streak, Cantillon celebrated prematurely. A fierce

Bad Forecast

The 1909 Phillies were rained out for 10 straight days, a major league record.

Lightning KOd Big Leaguer

New York Giants' outfielder Red Murray was knocked unconscious by lightning just as he caught a game-ending fly in the 21st inning of a 3–1 win over Pittsburgh, July 17, 1914. Murray was otherwise uninjured.

Last to Light

The Chicago Cubs became the last team to introduce night home games. Scheduled for 8-8-88 so that fans would remember the date, the game was postponed one night by rain.

Quickie

Quick work: the St. Louis Browns beat the Yankees 6–1 and 6–2 in a 1926 doubleheader that took two hours and seven minutes. The first game took 55 minutes.

True Night Debut

The first night game at Wrigley Field was supposed to be played on 8-8-88. It rained that night, forcing a one-day postponement, but history suggests the true date of the first night game was July 1, 1943. That's when the All-American Girls Professional Baseball League played under portable lights that were removed right after their use. They did it again a year later—even though a wartime brownout was in effect for the length of the Lake Michigan shoreline.

Red Sox Squeezed Cleveland's Lemon

Cleveland's Bob Lemon led the American League with 23 wins in 1950, but missed a chance for number 24 when he blew a 10–0 lead against the Red Sox at Fenway Park on August 28. The Sox won, 15–14.

Coors Field Factor

Colorado's first game at Coors Field, on April 26, 1995, set the tone for many slugfests to follow. The Rockies won, 11–9, on a three-run, 14th-inning homer by Dante Bichette.

Ted Williams Beaned Pitcher

Ted Williams, known as a dead pull hitter, crossed up the defense one day and slammed a shot off an aluminum plate in the leg of wounded war hero Lou Brissie. The ball resounded with a loud clang, but the pitcher was not injured.

Big Innings

Wholesale collapse of a pitching staff can result in big innings for the opposition. In 1952 the Brooklyn Dodgers scored 15 runs in the first inning against Cincinnati (final score, 19–1). A year later, the Boston Red Sox tallied 17 times in the seventh en route to a 23–3 win over Detroit.

Ebbets Field scoreboard shows 15-run first inning, a major league record, which the Brooklyn Dodgers scored against the Cincinnati Reds in 1952.

storm broke, washing out the potential victory, and the uniformed players raced for their horse-drawn bus.

As the last man boarded, a lightning bolt struck and killed the two horses. Cantillon looked at his players, raised his hands skyward, and said, "What kind of justice is there in heaven that strikes those poor creatures dead and leaves these miserable vegetables sitting in here alive?"

Around the same period, lightning converted a single into a home run (or maybe a run home) during a semipro game in Cincinnati. The batter singled to right, lightning struck the ball, and the outfielder turned and ran. It was the only run of the game.

Lightning helped one-time home-run king Gavvy Cravath hit one over the fence. The Phillies and Giants were still playing as a thunderstorm, preceded by strong wind, approached from the west. Visibility was poor. With the aid of a bright lightning flash, Cravath hit a Red Ames pitch deep into the outfield. Dark silence followed, then everyone in the park heard the ball rattle the wooden bleachers. It too was the only run of the game.

Willie Tasby, outfielder for the Orioles in the '60s, actually played center field barefoot in approaching storms. Apparently, he didn't like the idea of standing in puddles while wearing metal spikes.

Phil Rizzuto, who played several years before Tasby broke in, was another who was especially wary of electric storms.

Montreal encountered another problem when it entered the majors in 1969: early and late-season snows canceled games. When six inches fell on May 6, 1970, Rusty Staub became the first man to homer into a snowbank. The ball cleared the right-field fence and sank into the snow.

Baseball Marathons

The longest game in major league history (26 innings) was a 1–1 tie between the Brooklyn Robins and the Boston Braves on May 1, 1920. The New York Mets played 25 innings in 1974, 24 in 1968, and 23 in 1964; the American League high was a 25-inning game between the Milwaukee Brewers and Chicago White Sox that spanned May 8-9, 1984.

Because baseball mandates completion of games if the teams are deadlocked after nine innings, marathon games are not uncommon. But consider this: those Robins of 1920 got no decision in their 26-inning contest against Boston. They lost to the Phillies in 13 innings the next day. Then the Braves beat them in 19 innings.

The Mets, whose early struggles recalled Brooklyn Dodger teams in lean years, could sympathize. They spent 10½ hours losing a doubleheader to the Giants in 1964, came up on the wrong side of a 1–0 score in the 24-inning game at Houston, and saw 50 players and 15 dozen balls used in the 25-inning match with St. Louis. The 23-inning game—the nightcap (literally) of a twin bill against the Giants on May 31, 1964—consumed seven hours and 23 minutes, a record for a major league game.

Marathons were in vogue before the Mets were born in 1962. In 1951, the Cardinals played two different teams on the same day. They narrowly avoided playing the first tripleheader since 1920.

The Cards and Giants played a doubleheader on Tuesday, September 11, with the first of those games a previous rainout transferred from New York. A single game slated for September 12 was rained out, but the Cardinals were scheduled to play the Boston Braves on September 13.

Because the Giants were in contention for the pennant, the game had to be played. But there were no other meetings planned between the two clubs. St. Louis owner Fred Saigh suggested a doubleheader—an afternoon game against the Giants and the regular night game against Boston.

Horace Stoneham, Saigh's counterpart, balked. He said the Giants "owned" the date and would exercise priority for the night game if rain prevented the afternoon contest. He added that should the sun prevail, a night game with Boston on the same date would hurt the afternoon game.

Meanwhile, a suspended Braves/Cards game of August 2 was scheduled to be completed before the start of the September 13 night game against Boston. Keeping that date, and adding the Giants' afternoon game, would create a "tripleheader." Commissioner Ford Frick was asked for assistance. He ordered the Giants to play the Cards in the afternoon and switched the completion of the suspended game to the following day.

History repeated itself on September 25, 2000, when the Cleveland Indians hosted two different teams at Jacobs Field, beating the Chicago White Sox, 9–2, before losing to the Minnesota Twins, 4–3.

Legitimate tripleheaders have been staged several times, all in the National League. On September 1, 1890, Pittsburgh swept Brooklyn, 10–9, 3–2, and 8–4. Six years later, Baltimore swept Louisville, 4–3, 9–1, and 12–1. On October 2, 1920, Cincinnati beat Pittsburgh, 13–4 and 7–3 before losing 6–0.

Brooklyn's 1890 tripleheader, featuring a midmorning opener, was the only one to include three nine-inning games. The last inning of the third game was lost to darkness in Baltimore and the last three of the finale were blacked out in Pittsburgh.

Late-Inning Explosions

The most overworked cliché in baseball concerns the uncertain nature of the sport: "The game isn't over until you get the last out."

Countless cases of ninth-inning lightning fill the record books. Bucky Walters of the Reds lost a game of brinksmanship against the New York Giants in 1940. Pitching in the Polo Grounds, Walters had a 3–0 lead in the ninth with two men out and a 3–2 count on Bob Seeds.

Walters walked Seeds, then went 3–2 on Burgess Whitehead. He hit a home run, cutting the lead to 3–2. Walters went 3–2 on Mel Ott, but walked him. Then, the pitcher got two quick strikes on Harry Danning. The next pitch left the park—a game-winning homer. Walters had missed four separate occasions to get the third strike across.

On July 16, 1920, Pittsburgh's Earl Hamilton suffered an even more agonizing defeat. He worked 16 scoreless innings against the Giants—then fell victim to a seven-run outburst in the 17th to lose, 7–0. A year earlier, the Reds ruined a string of 12 scoreless innings by Al Mamaux to blast Brooklyn, 10–0.

Most Runs in a Game

When the Chicago Cubs beat the Phillies, 26–23, on August 25, 1922, the two teams produced the most runs for a single game. Chicago took a 25–6 lead after four innings, then had to hang on for the win. In 1976 the Cubs led the Phils, 13–2, but Philadelphia came back for an 18–16 win in 10 innings.

Home and Home

The New York Mets and the New York Yankees played a day/night doubleheader in different ballparks on the same day in 2000. The Mets lost both the July 8 day game at Shea Stadium and the makeup night game at Yankee Stadium, five miles away, by identical 4–2 scores.

Reversing a Lost Cause

The 2001 Cleveland Indians, the 1925 Philadelphia Athletics, and the 1911 Chicago White Sox are the only teams to win games after facing a 12-run deficit. The Indians trailed the Seattle Mariners, 12–0 and 14–2, at Jacobs Field on August 5, 2001, before rebounding to win, 15–14, in 11 innings.

High-Scoring Clubs

Teams that scored at least 25 runs in a game since 1900:

Runs	Team and Opponent	Date
American League		
30	Texas vs. Baltimore	August 22, 2007
29	Boston vs. St. Louis	June 8, 1950
29	Chicago vs. Kansas City	April 23, 1955
27	Cleveland vs. Boston	July 7, 1923
26	Cleveland vs. St. Louis	August 12, 1948
26	Texas vs. Baltimore	April 19, 1996
26	Kansas City vs. Detroit	September 9, 2004
25	Cleveland vs. Philadelphia	May 11, 1930
25	New York vs. Philadelphia	May 24, 1936
25	Boston vs. Florida	June 27, 2003
National League		
28	St. Louis vs. Philadelphia	July 6, 1929
26	Cincinnati vs. Boston	June 4, 1911
26	Chicago vs. Philadelphia	August 25, 1922
26	New York Giants vs. Brooklyn	April 30, 1944
26	Philadelphia vs. New York Mets	June 11, 1985
26	Chicago vs. Colorado	August 18, 1995
25	New York Giants vs. Cincinnati	June 9, 1901
25	Brooklyn vs. Cincinnati	September 23, 1901

First AL Draftee Killed

Gene Stack of the White Sox, first American League draftee of World War II, was killed in action.

Ike Arranged Baseball Broadcasts

General Dwight D. Eisenhower arranged for broadcasts to the troops of the 1943 World Series between the New York Yankees and the St. Louis Cardinals. He said baseball boosted morale.

Matching Numbers

Warren Spahn, the only major leaguer to receive a battlefield commission during World War II, returned to win 363 games, most by any left-hander, and collect a matching 363 base hits.

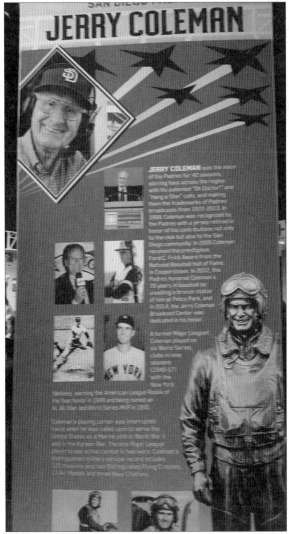

The American League twice featured nine-run rallies in the ninth with one out to go—both times in 1901. Cleveland trailed Washington, 13–5, on May 23, with two out and none on base when the hit parade started. Less than two weeks later, Boston did the same to Milwaukee, adding to a meager 4–2 lead.

Nine runs with an out to play represents the major league record, and the AL also has had eight-run explosions in that situation. The 1937 Yankees erased a 6–1 Boston lead at Yankee Stadium that way (the final three scored on a Lou Gehrig homer) and the 1961 Red Sox surprised Washington by overcoming a 12–5 deficit in the final frame.

The Yankees yielded a two-out, nine-run ninth to the Indians late in 1929 and blew another game by letting the St. Louis Browns score seven times with an out to go in 1922.

The National League record for last-ditch heroics stands at seven runs—a total achieved by the 1952 Cubs against the Reds. It began with the bases empty and the Reds coasting on the front end of an 8–2 score.

The War Years

Baseball wasn't the same in wartime. Though the game maintained a full schedule and played the World Series throughout World War II, the 1945 All-Star Game was skipped. In 1918 the All-Star Game had not yet been established, but the nation's war needs did supersede the interests of baseball teams. The final month was cut from the schedule.

During World War I, teams set aside one week per month as Red Cross Week and sent a percentage of the profits to the Red Cross for European War Relief. In 1918 baseball also sent some of its biggest names to the war.

Ty Cobb, Herb Pennock, Tris Speaker, George Sisler, Eddie Collins, and Christy Mathewson went overseas along with dozens of other players. The White Sox and the Indians sent 19 players each into the military.

Cobb was a captain in the chemical warfare division, while Mathewson was the only manager to serve in the First World War. Then running the Reds, Mathewson endured poison gas attacks in France during a training exercise and never regained his health; he died prematurely in 1925.

Longtime catcher Hank Gowdy had the unusual distinction of serving in both world wars, while Ted Williams served in World War II and the Korean Conflict.

The influence of the Second World War on baseball was far more obvious than the influence of the first war because its long duration and multiple battle theaters demanded more men.

Before they shortened the 1918 season to a September 1 finish, owners had debated playing out the schedule using players who were above or below draft age, but decided against it. In World War II, they were forced to use that policy or shut the game down.

Jerry Coleman (left) and Ted Williams were the only major-leaguers called to active military service in both World War II and the Korean Conflict. Coleman's efforts were saluted in a special exhibit at 2016 All-Star FanFest in San Diego, where he worked as a Padres announcer.

Joe DiMaggio was among the major-leaguers whose salaries fell when they were called to serve in the Armed Forces during World War II.

Fans Returned Balls

Fans returned the balls hit into the stands during the wars. These were given to servicemen.

Cards Searched for Players

The St. Louis Cardinals advertised for players in 1943. The St. Louis organization lost more than 200 athletes to the military.

Three's Company

One of baseball's strangest games was played as a wartime fund-raiser on June 26, 1944. The New York Yankees, the New York Giants, and the Brooklyn Dodgers met in a three-way, six-inning contest before a standing-room-only crowd at the Polo Grounds. Each team played successive innings against the other two, then sat out an inning. Final score: Dodgers 5, Yankees 1, Giants 0.

More than 500 players helped the Allies against the Axis, starting with Phillies pitcher Hugh Mulcahy—the first draftee.

Cleveland's Bob Feller, who won 25 games and saved two others in 1941, began the exodus of top stars when he enlisted in the navy shortly after the bombing of Pearl Harbor. Feller, Warren Spahn, and Ted Williams were three outstanding players whose records would have been even better had the war not intervened.

Ballplayers in service frequently got to play for military teams. When Ted Lyons of the White Sox pitched for his navy team on Guam, his first game was against an army squad starring Joe DiMaggio. "I left the country to get away from DiMaggio," Lyons quipped, "and here he is!"

An army/navy game in Cleveland, shortly before the 1942 All-Star Game, drew 62,094 fans—primarily because Feller was pitching for Mickey Cochrane's Great Lakes Naval Training Station team. The Cochrane crew won 63 games, including four over major league opposition.

Players and managers who stayed behind in the States often volunteered to visit the battle fronts under the auspices of the USO. Baseball shows featured films, autographs, amusing anecdotes, and bull sessions. When Yankee pitcher Hank Borowy returned

U.S. Treasury Department

Star pitcher Bob Feller missed a certain shot at 300 wins by serving in the U.S. Navy during the Second World War. The Cleveland fireballer won eight battle stars for his actions on the USS *Alabama*.

Ted Williams, Air Ace

Marine Corps Captain Ted Williams flew 39 combat missions during the Korean War.

No Night Games in 1943

Night games were banned in 1943 because of blackout restrictions.

Hank Greenberg retained his batting eye in the service, enabling him to be ready to play when his stint ended. His last-day grand slam in the ninth inning enabled the Tigers to win the 1945 American League pennant.

from a trip to Alaska's Aleutian Islands with Frankie Frisch and Dixie Walker, he said, "We did some 200 shows there and they didn't want to let us go. I never realized there was so much heart felt, deep-down interest in baseball. After 12 hours on the jump from camp to camp, we'd get back to our shack dog-tired to find a delegation of men waiting to talk to us until two or three o'clock in the morning."

Five units of stars stumped military bases in the 1944–1945 off-season. They went to Europe, the Mediterranean, the Middle East, the Far East (China, Burma, and India), and the Pacific.

At home, baseball had deteriorated—understandably—into a comedy of errors. After receiving a "green light letter" from President Franklin D. Roosevelt in January 1942, baseball brass was determined to provide the morale-boosting entertainment that the chief executive sought. "Sports kept people occupied and helped them not to think of the war all the time," said pitcher Hal Newhouser. "Baseball had to continue."

More than 200 draft-board rejects translated their 4-F classifications into major league jobs. More than a dozen of them played for the pennant-winning St. Louis Browns of 1944, but the most famous played for the same team the following year.

One-armed outfielder Pete Gray, 28, was purchased by the Browns after hitting .333 with five home runs and 68 stolen bases for Memphis, where he was voted Most Valuable Player in the Southern Association.

Originally right-handed, Gray lost that limb in a truck accident. As a left-handed hitter with the 1945 Browns, he hit .218 in 77 games. His fielding was below par for a normal player, but sensational for a man who had to catch and throw with the same arm.

Not to be outdone, a pitcher with a wooden leg—Bert Shepard—pitched five innings for the Washington Senators that season.

The quality of play was so poor that the players who finished second and third in the American League batting race—Tony Cuccinello and John Dickshot of the Chicago White Sox—were released after the season, even though they had hit .308 and .302, respectively. Batting king George "Snuffy" Stirnweiss of the New York Yankees hit .309 with 10 homers—then hit .246 with 10 homers over the next seven seasons!

Washington's 40-year-old catcher, Rick Ferrell, had the unenviable task of handling four knuckleball pitchers. Yankee outfielder Johnny Lindell spiked teammate Herschel Martin in the nose when the pair collided in pursuit of a fly ball. The leagues averaged about 1,500 errors more than usual.

Many clubs dumped their scouts because most able-bodied athletes were overseas, but the Dodgers didn't and began building toward their future "Boys of Summer" champions. Brooklyn also followed a pattern adopted by other clubs—activating old stars to fill out the roster. Babe Herman, out of the league since 1936, came back at age 42. Yankee pitcher Paul Schreiber, the same age, had been out since 1923 but stayed in shape by pitching batting practice.

The minor leagues were stripped bare. Thirty-two teams suspended operations. Those who continued—like Nashville of the Southern Association—turned to old-timers or teenagers. Ex-pitcher Red Lucas, always a good hitter, became a pinch hitter at Nashville and hit .421 at age 43.

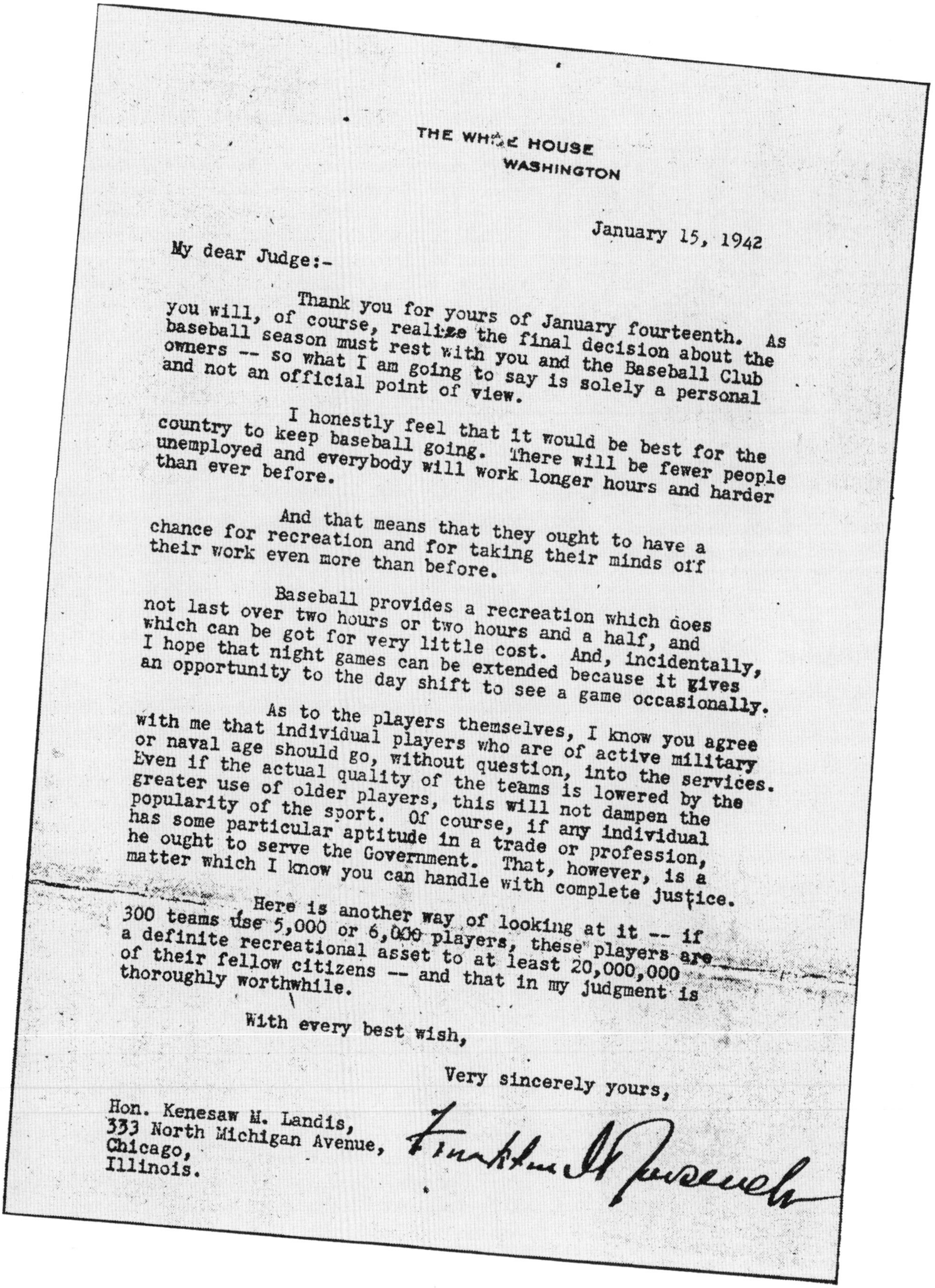

THE WHITE HOUSE
WASHINGTON

January 15, 1942

My dear Judge:-

Thank you for yours of January fourteenth. As you will, of course, realize the final decision about the baseball season must rest with you and the Baseball Club owners -- so what I am going to say is solely a personal and not an official point of view.

I honestly feel that it would be best for the country to keep baseball going. There will be fewer people unemployed and everybody will work longer hours and harder than ever before.

And that means that they ought to have a chance for recreation and for taking their minds off their work even more than before.

Baseball provides a recreation which does not last over two hours or two hours and a half, and which can be got for very little cost. And, incidentally, I hope that night games can be extended because it gives an opportunity to the day shift to see a game occasionally.

As to the players themselves, I know you agree with me that individual players who are of active military or naval age should go, without question, into the services. Even if the actual quality of the teams is lowered by the greater use of older players, this will not dampen the popularity of the sport. Of course, if any individual has some particular aptitude in a trade or profession, he ought to serve the Government. That, however, is a matter which I know you can handle with complete justice.

Here is another way of looking at it -- if 300 teams use 5,000 or 6,000 players, these players are a definite recreational asset to at least 20,000,000 of their fellow citizens -- and that in my judgment is thoroughly worthwhile.

With every best wish,

Very sincerely yours,

Franklin D. Roosevelt

Hon. Kenesaw M. Landis,
333 North Michigan Avenue,
Chicago,
Illinois.

This letter from President Roosevelt to Commissioner Landis tells the story; the president wanted baseball to continue during the war as a morale booster.

The 1946 Newark Eagles, loaded with talent of major league caliber, beat the Kansas City Monarchs for the championship of the Negro Leagues. Organized ball did not drop its color line until 1947.

Klan Threatened Dodgers

The Ku Klux Klan blasted the announcement that the integrated Dodgers of Brooklyn would play three April 1949 exhibitions against the Atlanta Crackers of the Southern Association. Owner Earl Mann, backed by Atlanta's press and the police, staged the game without a hitch.

Spring Segregation Persisted

Though blacks were well established in baseball by the early '60s, segregation still divided several major league clubs during spring training.

When the 1945 All-Star Game was scrubbed, the move was made not only because of travel restrictions (a good excuse) but also because there were no stars to represent the leagues. A two-day series of exhibition games was staged to raise money for war relief.

The stars began to return after the war ended in Europe, and later, in the Pacific. They had to play themselves back into shape—a task that is always difficult—but had maintained good condition in the military. Timing was the missing ingredient, but by season's end, Hank Greenberg had it. His last-day grand slam in the ninth inning gave the Tigers the American League pennant.

The Color Line

Adrian "Cap" Anson was the greatest star of the National League's first quarter-century. A standout hitter and manager, he was also an excellent promoter. He had one flaw: he was prejudiced against blacks.

Though two brothers, Moses and Welday Walker, had already played in the majors at Toledo of the American Association, Anson slammed the door on any other blacks considering the profession. He is the man who drew the infamous "color line" that kept blacks out of organized ball until Jack Roosevelt Robinson signed with the Brooklyn Dodgers at the tail-end of the 1945 season.

There were 20 blacks in baseball in 1882. (One of them, George Stovey, struck out 22 Bridgeport batters in a single game for Newark, New Jersey, five years later.)

By opening its doors to black talent, the Brooklyn Dodgers developed a dynasty in the '50s. Among the team's stars were Duke Snider, Jackie Robinson, Roy Campanella, Pee Wee Reese, and Gil Hodges.

Neither Walker was a good ballplayer and they drifted out of the American Association to several minor-league teams and eventually out of baseball. None of the blacks were made to feel welcome, and soon the game was devoid of nonwhite players. Anson and other executives determined to keep it that way, and the tradition of segregation persisted.

Unrest over the color line was muted, to a degree, by the formation of professional Negro Leagues, but black players showed they could hold their own during exhibitions with big leaguers and a drive to admit them began.

The Los Angeles Angels of the Pacific Coast League invited three blacks for a tryout, then withdrew their invitation without explanation. Bill Veeck, owner of the Milwaukee franchise in the American Association, bid for the Philadelphia Phillies, with the intention of signing several black stars for the struggling club, but his purchase was not completed.

Also in 1944, the Red Sox gave a short Fenway Park tryout to three black stars—after two city councilmen threatened to strip the Sox and the Braves of exemptions from Sunday blue laws. One of the three was Jackie Robinson of the Kansas City Monarchs, a powerful Negro League team.

All three did well, and Boston manager Joe Cronin said he was impressed, but the men were informed that signing players after short tryouts violated Red Sox policy. They suffered the indignity of filling out applications—a step most athletes never take—and were given the standard line: "Don't call us, we'll call you." Not only did they never hear from the Sox, but Boston was the last team in the majors to integrate. Pumpsie Green finally broke the Boston barrier in 1959.

A year after the escapade in Boston, Branch Rickey was telling Jackie Robinson what problems he would face as the first black

Given a chance, black players blossomed into some of baseball's brightest stars. Among those who had Hall of Fame careers were (top to bottom) Roy Campanella, Ferguson Jenkins, Ernie Banks, Frank Robinson, and Hank Aaron.

Jackie Had Power When Needed

Jackie Robinson wasn't primarily a power hitter—he twice hit 19 homers for his one-season high—but he produced when it counted. On the last day of the 1951 season the Dodgers and the Giants were tied for the top. The Giants knocked off the Braves and the Dodgers had to beat Philadelphia to force a playoff. Brooklyn was behind, 6–1, when word came out of the Giant win. The Dodgers tied it, 8–8, but almost lost it in the 12th. With two outs and the bases loaded, the batter hit a low-liner to the right of second base. Jackie Robinson dove and speared it just above the ground, then crashed heavily on his shoulder. In the 14th, he found a fastball he liked and deposited it over the left-field wall to win the game, 9–8.

The Races Mix

Bobby Grich, white infielder, and Don Baylor, black outfielder, were among the first interracial roommates in the game.

player in the major leagues. He also warned him that he wanted a ballplayer "with guts enough not to fight back."

Robinson, a gifted but outspoken athlete, wasn't sure he was the right man, but finally accepted Rickey's offer, reporting to the Dodgers' top farm team at Montreal in 1946. "I had to do it for so many reasons," Robinson said later. "For black youth, for my mother, for Rachel [his wife], and for myself. I even felt I had to do it for Branch Rickey."

Rickey, who had spent considerable time and money recruiting baseball's first black player of the modern era, was correct in anticipating trouble. Several Dodgers circulated a petition protesting Robinson's presence. The Cardinals and Phillies threatened strikes—stopped only when Commissioner Happy Chandler threatened lifetime suspensions. Hotels were always segregated during spring training but sometimes during the regular season too.

Incendiary taunts, including vicious name-calling, were hurled from every enemy dugout. But Robinson kept his word and his cool. He convinced the Dodgers—and their opponents—with a winning style of play that included aggressive baserunning, fine fielding, and steady contributions with the bat. He was an outstanding curveball hitter—a rarity for a rookie.

Robinson had been a second baseman but moved to first during his first Dodger season. He returned to second on a full-time basis in 1949 and was named to the All-Star Major League Team by *The Sporting News* for four successive seasons.

He was an All-Star other years too, but played a variety of positions, including first, second, third, and the outfield. In 10 seasons he hit .311, twice led the National League in stolen bases (he stole home 19 times), and won the batting title with a .342 mark in 1949.

Jackie Robinson was the recipient of baseball's first Rookie of the Year Award in 1947. He was named Most Valuable Player in the National League two years later.

"My main ambition," Robinson said, "was to get along well enough with whomever I was playing so they would realize there wasn't any friction because I was colored and they were white. I wanted them to know we *could* play together. It wasn't so important that *I* go to the major leagues, it was just important that *somebody* go."

Robinson's entry immediately opened the door for others. Larry Doby, one of 14 blacks signed by Bill Veeck's Cleveland

Leo Durocher and Willie Mays.

Indians in those early years of integration, became the first black American League player late in 1947. Other early blacks in the majors were Satchel Paige, Roy Campanella, Don Newcombe, and Monte Irvin.

Frank Robinson became the first black manager with Cleveland in 1975, and the first black manager to be fired in 1977. Larry Doby, who followed Jackie Robinson as the second black player, followed Frank Robinson as the second black manager. Bill Veeck hired him with the White Sox in 1978.

The end of the color line was hailed by some historians as the real beginning of major league baseball. Contributions by black players have been numerous. Hank Aaron became the new home-run king. Maury Wills and then Lou Brock and Rickey Henderson set single-season stolen-base records. Brock and Henderson surpassed Ty Cobb as career leaders.

Though his career was shrouded in controversy, Barry Bonds hit seven more home runs than Aaron and more than 100 more than Willie Mays, a legendary talent many historians considered the best player of the modern era. Bob Gibson and Ferguson Jenkins were brilliant pitchers for years. Ernie Banks won consecutive MVP awards while Frank Robinson won a Triple Crown and joined a bevy of black stars in the 500 Home Run Club. Reggie Jackson even hit three home runs in a World Series game and five in one Fall Classic.

The list of accomplishments is endless.

The Trials and Travails of Travel

Baseball teams have traveled by rail, bus, subway, automobile, trolley, airplane, and assorted other conveyances.

But the pioneering Cincinnati Red Stockings of 1877 came up with a new idea after three straight days of rain prevented their home opener. They obtained a barge and floated to Louisville, where it was dry enough to play.

Not long after, the same club reached the Arizona territory via rail and stagecoach.

In the early days of the American League, shortly after the turn of the century, teams made the Detroit/Cleveland run by overnight steamer on Lake Michigan. Indian third baseman Bill Bradley, assigned to a stateroom with a cocky rookie, was about to turn in one night when he hit upon an idea that would knock the first-year player down a peg.

He put on his nightshirt, then strapped a life preserver on top of it and lay down in the bottom bunk. The rookie, not knowing what to do, decided he would follow the older man's example.

As soon as the lights were out, Bradley quietly unzipped himself and went to sleep, while the rookie squirmed all night in an effort to make himself comfortable.

Neither man said a word until the return trip, when the freshman blurted, "Nix on those life preservers. I'd rather drown."

Teams once traveled extensively by train.

Dan Schlossberg

Sox Pick Wrong Car

Red Sox players Oscar Melillo and Eric McNair accidentally went to sleep on a train taking the Philadelphia Athletics out of Boston on July 4, 1937. Their teammates were on another train that left at the same time.

The 1912 Boston Red Sox board a train for a road trip.

Library of Congress

Cards kept players occupied on the road. New York Giants Clyde Castleman, Mark Koenig, and Harry Danning were frequent players.

Fans Catered Dodger Train

Dodgers Hugh Casey and Curt Davis called ahead when they found out where the team train would stop en route to their next game. In one town, fans brought barbecued ribs to the train. The players looked forward to that midnight feast.

On the Road

What do players do on the road? Clyde King, a pitcher in the '40s and '50s and a manager in the '70s, had an answer: "They play cards a lot in their rooms. We used to go to movies a lot. We looked forward to playing in Chicago, where they had only day games and we could go to movies at night. I went to two double features many times in Chicago. Nowadays, players have business connections in so many towns. They also make more appearances on the road than they used to."

Train Trips

Baseball travel in the majors was primarily by rail until the early '50s. Though train trips consumed more time, players found them more relaxing. Forced to spend so much time together, teammates got to know one another very well and unity resulted.

"Some players thought the trains had rough wheels and it was a rough ride," recalled ex-Brooklyn pitcher Clyde King, "but we enjoyed it. We'd have a Sunday afternoon game at Ebbets Field, then go down to the station. They'd have a dining car all set up for us, we'd go in and sit down to a nice meal. Then we'd play cards—I played bridge a lot. Usually, we'd have Monday off and, if we were going to St. Louis, we'd travel all day Monday. We played bridge and talked baseball."

Waite Hoyt remembered trains of the Babe Ruth era, 20 years before King played in the majors. "We made a railroad trip from Washington to St. Louis wearing just our underwear," he said. "You opened the windows when you were in the Pullman berth at night and in the morning you'd be covered with coal dust."

Star players had lower berths, average players the uppers. When the train reached the team's destination in the early hours of the morning, the baseball cars were uncoupled and shunted onto a siding. Players later hauled their own luggage down the tracks to the station, hailed cabs for the team hotel, and went back to sleep once they got there. Few players caught much sleep on trains.

Since writers, team executives, and sometimes even umpires shared the trains with athletes, impromptu interviews flowed during the course of a trip. The bar car was as thick with quotable stories as it was with smoke.

Only one player—Ed Delahanty in 1903—was killed in train travel, but there were several close calls.

Delahanty, the lone casualty, lost his life on July 2, 1903, when he fell from the International Bridge at Buffalo, New York, after his ejection from a train because of drunkenness. The train, from Detroit, had almost reached its destination: the Buffalo terminal.

During the Second World War, the Brooklyn Dodgers were en route from St. Louis to Chicago when a gasoline truck, loaded with an extra tank, was struck at a Joliet, Illinois, grade crossing at 4:00 in the morning. It exploded, sending gas and flames all over the train and igniting a coal yard nearby.

The Dodgers had been sitting up—or sleeping on the floor—because train frequency and accommodations were limited in wartime. No one got burned because the train's momentum carried it through the burning remains of the truck, but the engineer and fireman lost their lives. The automatic brake stopped the train.

Clyde King, who was there, remembered the incident vividly. He described how the intense heat from the blast melted the train's thick double windows, and recalled the startled Luis Olmo—awakened from his position on the floor—running through the aisles, stepping on people, in the panic.

Despite that experience, the Dodgers made their preference for rail travel known several years later, after the team started to make some trips by air.

Air Travel

The Cincinnati Reds became the first big-league team to fly on June 7, 1934. Two players, Mark Koenig and Jim Bottomley, refused to board the flight and took a train instead.

On July 30, 1936, the Boston Red Sox became the first team to fly to their next game. But group air travel was far from established. In 1938 a hurricane battered New England, leaving flood waters in its wake. The St. Louis Cardinals, stranded in Boston, had to get to Chicago to meet their schedule.

An enterprising club official chartered a mail plane, jammed 21 players inside, and took off for the Windy City. The official had wired Cardinal owner Sam Breadon for permission, but storm-snarled communications lines delayed the message. By the time Breadon answered WAIT FOR OTHER MEANS, the team was in flight.

The same hurricane, incidentally, washed out normal shore routes between New York and Boston, causing the New York Giants—the next opponent of the Boston Braves—to reach the city via overnight steamboat!

With the flight of the Cardinals, air travel began its long route to predominance over other means of transportation. It wasn't easy, however. Planes of the period were primitive by modern standards and flights were invariably long and bumpy.

The Dodgers flew for the first time in 1940, but Babe Phelps sometimes opted for the train instead. As late as 1947, pitcher Kirby Higbe was a bundle of nerves in the air. Pee Wee Reese tried to calm him. "If your number's up, you'll go," Reese said. That didn't satisfy Higbe. "Suppose I'm up here with some pilot and my number ain't up, but *his* is!"

The war returned ballclubs to the rails, but with victory in sight late in 1945, 11 major league teams signed "volume travel plan" contracts with United Air Lines. In 1946 the New York Yankees became the first team to travel extensively by air. But Red Ruffing—who had bitter memories of his days in the Army Air Force—was one of several players who declined to fly. Manager Joe McCarthy said he would leave the choice of transportation up to each player, but said he expected every man to attend every game.

After several particularly rough flights (the team used a four-engine C-54 transport), the majority of Yankee players balked at flying in 1947. They gradually became accustomed to the idea, and other clubs followed a pattern of mixing rail with air travel rather than switching suddenly.

As rail travel declined and air service improved, flying became widely accepted among players. Don Newcombe and Preacher Roe of the Dodgers and Jackie Jensen of the Red Sox never liked it, however.

After the Dodger plane was forced to land during an especially rough flight home from spring training in 1951, Roe got out, rented a car, and drove the rest of the way.

The 1957 world champion Milwaukee Braves used air travel extensively. The club posed for this picture before departure. Note superstars Warren Spahn (top of ramp), Hank Aaron (third from top), and Eddie Mathews (fourth from top).

First Club to Fly

The Hollywood Stars of the Pacific Coast League became the first professional team to fly in 1928.

Jet Lag

Coast-to-coast air travel crosses four time zones and creates the problem of "jet lag"—especially for anyone headed east to west. Roberto Clemente was one of many players who suffered, according to former Pirate coach Clyde King. "It's not as bad as you think it is," he said. "Most players can rise to the occasion."

Long Trip

One year after they played the first major league games in Mexico, the 1997 San Diego Padres hosted the St. Louis Cardinals for three games in Honolulu—the first big-league games ever played in Hawaii.

Players Paid for Rooms

Early major leaguers were charged 50 cents per game for rooms when on the road.

Giants Rode Barouches to Park

The 1905 world champion New York Giants, following the custom of their day, rode from their hotel to the ballpark in uniform. The players sat in handsome barouches—open carriages—drawn by horses wearing black and yellow blankets. The Giants were hated intensely by other teams because of an overaggressive style of play, and fans outside of New York sometimes stoned the carriages.

Reds Lost Frey in '40

The Cincinnati Reds lost second baseman Lonny Frey for the 1940 World Series when the heavy lid to the dugout water cooler fell and landed on his foot, breaking a bone, during a late-season game.

Loud Laughs Injured Player

As Red Sox roommates Dom DiMaggio and Sam Mele went to bed in May 1947, the former's bed collapsed. Mele laughed so loudly he aggravated an old sacroiliac condition. He ached so badly that he was forced to leave the next day's game in the third inning.

Several times in 1961, Jensen refused to accompany the Red Sox on plane hops. In June he drove 850 miles from Boston to Detroit and played the following day. Two months later, after beating Washington with a 10th-inning home run, he lost $750 in salary when he would not board an airplane to Los Angeles.

Fear of Flying was more than a best-selling book—it was a problem facing men of enormous strength and flexibility.

Roommates

Except for top stars, baseball players usually have roommates on the road. Sometimes the matched pairs have trouble adjusting.

Early in the century, Philadelphia Athletics pitcher Rube Waddell actually signed a contract forbidding roommate Ossie Schreckengost from eating Animal Crackers in bed. The pact became known as "The Animal Crackers Contract."

Burly Ernie Lombardi, hard-hitting Cincinnati catcher of the '30s, kept roommate Chick Hafey awake with his snoring. Hafey tried to solve the problem by tying Lombardi's big toe to the bed.

The expansion Los Angeles Angels of 1961 paired 5'5", 140-pound Albie Pearson and 5'8", 170-pound Rocky Bridges in one room and 250-pound Steve Bilko with 245-pound Ted Kluszewski in another. In one hotel, they were across the hall from each other. Bridges phoned the traveling secretary and suggested he switch assignments. "If you don't, the hotel will tilt!" he said.

Fun-loving Babe Ruth liked to share his zest for high living. Whenever he ordered food from room service, he insisted roommate Jimmie Reese eat with him. "He'd order six eggs and I'd have two," Reese said, years later.

Many clubs like to put highly rated rookies with experienced veterans, often matching pitchers with other pitchers, or sometimes pitchers with catchers. Players of similar temperaments or positions are grouped wherever possible.

When he first joined the Philadelphia Athletics, Mickey Cochrane was matched with incumbent catcher Cy Perkins. The latter's pointers paid off so well that Cochrane took his job.

Brash freshman Ted Williams was placed in the same room with soft-spoken veteran Charlie Wagner by Red Sox manager Joe Cronin and the duet proved a perfect match. Williams calmed down and developed into a superstar.

Young Curt Simmons roomed with experienced Dutch Leonard, another Phillies pitcher, and Eddie Stanky was placed with double-play partner Alvin Dark by the Boston Braves. Simmons became an outstanding major league pitcher, while the Stanky/Dark tandem helped the Braves win the 1948 pennant.

Boston's Dom DiMaggio earned the nickname "the Little Professor" because of the influence of roommate Moe Berg, a capable but light-hitting catcher who spoke seven languages and held almost as many college degrees.

Brothers on the same team were not necessarily roommates. The Deans of St. Louis, Dizzy and Daffy, were separated. Dizzy lived with Pepper Martin, "the Wild Horse of the Osage," and the Cardinal cutups frequently visited their teammates with midnight serenades on the guitar.

Luke Sewell and Joe Sewell of the Indians also slept in separate quarters.

Certain pairs were inseparable: pitching aces Lew Burdette and Warren Spahn of the Braves, drinking buddies Mickey Mantle and Whitey Ford of the Yankees, and longtime leaders Stan Musial and Red Schoendienst of the Cardinals. Starting in the '20s, Joe Judge and Sam Rice set a roommate record by sharing hotel rooms for 18 consecutive seasons with the Washington Senators.

It was an accident of fate that paired Yogi Berra and Bobby Brown of the Yankees. Brown, using his baseball salary to pay his way through medical school, was deep into a textbook one night when he suddenly slammed the cover shut. Berra, watching him, piped up, "How did it come out?"

Fines, Fights, and Feuds

Fines are baseball's primary way of punishing fighters. The game is supposed to consist of nine innings—not 15 rounds—but tempers grow short when the heat of the pennant race begins to match the air temperature of midsummer.

The game's best-known fighters were Ty Cobb, John McGraw, Leo Durocher, Clint Courtney, and Billy Martin, but almost every player in major league history has witnessed bench-clearing brawls.

Fights often begin over beanballs—deliberate brush-back pitches designed to keep a batter from "digging in" at home plate. A pitcher has a decided edge when the hitter is unable to relax at the plate.

Beanballs are serious business. Ray Chapman of Cleveland was killed by a pitch in 1920, Mickey Cochrane suffered a career-ending skull fracture when struck in 1937, and Tony Conigliaro's career ended prematurely when his vision failed as the result of a beaning.

Current baseball rules mandate an automatic $50 fine when an umpire warns a pitcher about throwing too close to batters. A second warning means ejection from the game. Umpires are even empowered to warn both teams about beanballs before a game begins, if circumstances warrant.

Home-plate collisions, severe bench-jockeying, spikings of fielders by runners, and hard tags of runners by fielders have also contributed to the game's history of fights and fines.

Umpires are often involved, and occasionally even fans. Ty Cobb received an indefinite suspension from the American League on May 15, 1912, after attacking a heckler in the stands at New York. His Tiger teammates wired the league office from Philadelphia the next day that they would strike until Cobb was reinstated. On May 18, Cobb took the field with his teammates and was ordered off by the umpires. All the Detroit players went with him.

Manager Hugh Jennings activated two coaches, recruited some semipros headed by pitcher Al Travers—later a priest—and lost to the A's, 24–2. Travers earned $25 for his one-day stand in the majors. He had batted fourth and pitched the whole game.

Two days later, American League executives held a special meeting to discuss the Cobb case. Detroit's players were ordered to return or face expulsion from the game. Each was fined $100— twice what Cobb paid when he was reinstated on May 25.

Billy Martin's volatile temper, coupled with his small size and penchant for drinking, resulted in several memorable brawls during his tenure as a player and manager. His fight card ranged from New York's Copacabana Club to battles with Jim Brewer, Dave Boswell, and even a marshmallow salesman.

Why Teams Fight

Why do ballplayers engage in fisticuffs on the field? Longtime Pirates' manager Danny Murtaugh had an answer: "During the season, a lot of things happen. The players are bound to get on each other. I've seen guys have it out in our clubhouse—and we were winning. It's just part of our game. It can happen whether you're winning or losing."

Belle's Sour Note

Albert Belle was fined $50,000 by Major League Baseball for the verbal tirade he directed at NBC-TV reporter Hannah Storm prior to Game 3 of the 1995 World Series at Cleveland. Belle, then with the Indians, unleashed a string of obscenities at Storm on the dugout steps after she requested an interview. The temperamental outfielder, who later played for the White Sox and the Orioles, incurred other fines and suspensions during a career that ended in 2000.

Baseball Fights

Ebbets Field fans were stunned after a 1940 contest when a fan attacked home-plate umpire George Magerkurth.

Though bench-clearing brawls represent the typical baseball fight, one-on-one encounters occasionally occur under the stands, in airplanes, or in hotel rooms.

It's hard to envision Casey Stengel in such a situation, but the fact is that the youthful Stengel, as manager of the Brooklyn Dodgers in the '30s, delivered a right hook that bloodied the lip of Leo Durocher, then St. Louis Cardinals shortstop, under the Ebbets Field grandstand.

Umpire George Moriarty battled several White Sox at Cleveland after a doubleheader defeat on Memorial Day 1932. Pitcher Milt Gaston, who started the melee beneath the stands, and Chicago manager Lew Fonseca were fined $500 each, catcher Charley Berry (later an umpire) $250, and catcher Frank Grube $100.

John McGraw, razzing rookie Phillies' third baseman Paul Sentell from his third-base coaching box during a 1906 game at Baker Bowl, precipitated a free-for-all that caused both to be ejected. They proceeded under the stands to continue their fight.

Boston player/manager Joe Cronin and the Yankees' Jake Powell clashed under the stands after an earlier go-round on the field in the '30s. Rico Carty and Hank Aaron battled on the Atlanta airplane in 1967. And Billy Martin, then managing Minnesota, KOd pitcher Dave Boswell in a Detroit bar two years after breaking up a battle between Boswell and teammate Bob Allison.

Ty Cobb won unanimous decisions over umpire Billy Evans under the stands and Buck Herzog of the Giants in a Dallas hotel. "I got beat," Herzog said, "but I knocked the bum down and he'll never forget a little guy like me having him on the floor."

On the field, Hall of Fame catcher Bill Dickey of the Yankees broke the jaw of Washington outfielder Carl Reynolds with a hard right after a rough collision at home plate on July 4, 1932. Reynolds was out six weeks and Dickey four; he was slapped with a 30-day suspension and $1,000 fine.

Cardinal catcher Mickey Owen attacked Leo Durocher, player/manager of the Dodgers, after a force-out at second base in an Ebbets Field game in 1940, and bad feelings between the two contenders were smoothed only after Brooklyn general manager Larry MacPhail entered the St. Louis clubhouse to speak to the Cardinal players.

The Red Sox/Yankee feud was too strong for such diplomacy after the Second World War. In 1952 Boston's Jim Piersall scrapped with Yankee infielder Billy Martin, who was manager at New York when Red Sox pitcher Bill Lee was injured in a fight with slugger Graig Nettles in 1976.

Martin was also involved in a giant free-for-all between the Yankees and the St. Louis Browns in June 1953. The chief culprit was St. Louis catcher Clint Courtney, called "Scrap Iron" for his aggressive approach to the game. Courtney and Martin had tangled the previous year, and both were among the fighters after the catcher spiked popular Yankee shortstop Phil Rizzuto in 1953.

Courtney paid a $250 fine and Martin $150, as the league assessed $850 in penalties.

Martin was at it again in 1960, when he broke the jaw of Cubs pitcher Jim Brewer during his brief tenure as an infielder for the Reds. Brewer sued for $1,000,000 but eventually settled for $10,000. A beanball had precipitated that fight.

A beanball-in-reverse prompted Giant pitcher Juan Marichal to rap Dodger catcher John Roseboro with his bat in 1965. The pitcher insisted Roseboro's return throw to Sandy Koufax was deliberately close to his head.

Other brawls of note:

• 1902: John McGraw, then player/manager of the Baltimore Orioles (today's Yankees), was spiked at third base by Detroit's Larry Harley. In the ensuing fight, McGraw suffered a knee injury that ended his playing career.

• 1906: After McGraw's Giants brawled with the Phils on the field, irate Philadelphia fans hurled debris at New York's departing barouches. Roger Bresnahan stood, lost his balance, and fell into the crowd. He ran for his life, barricaded himself in a corner store, and waited to be freed by police.

• 1909: Ty Cobb spiked Frank "Home Run" Baker of the Philadelphia A's during a hot pennant race between the A's and Tigers. The fans were so angry at the incident that Cobb's life was threatened and he had to be escorted to and from the ballpark.

• 1924: Bert Cole (Tigers) hit Yankee Bob Meusel in the back with a ninth-inning pitch at Detroit, with New York leading 10–6. In the 30-minute fight that followed, fans ripped out seats and threw them into the fray. Umpire Billy Evans forfeited the game to the Yankees and Meusel and Cole were suspended 10 days each. Meusel paid a $100 fine and Cole and Babe Ruth $50 each.

• 1932: When fleet Ben Chapman of the Yankees slid hard into second, Washington second baseman Buddy Myer gave him

Two Fabled Feuds

Because of geographic proximity and location in the same leagues, the Dodgers and the Giants of the National League and the Red Sox and the Yankees of the American League have always been intense rivals.

Though Brooklyn is one of New York's five boroughs, it always felt inferior to Manhattan—a complex that infected the baseball teams as well. After Arthur Devlin of the Giants punched a Washington Park spectator in 1906, Dodger president Charles Ebbets asked the National League to "protect my customers against rowdy New York players."

In 1914, Giants coach Wilbert Robinson became Dodgers manager—a move so popular that sportswriters dubbed the team "Robins" in his honor. Leo Durocher took the reverse route in 1948, when he jumped from manager of the Dodgers to manage the Giants in midseason. Throughout the '50s, both teams were perennial pennant contenders.

Since the rivalry resulted in turnstile revenue for both teams, Dodgers owner Walter O'Malley asked Horace Stoneham, his Giants counterpart, to move west with him after the 1957 season and keep the competition going.

Before the Dodgers and Giants left, they contended with the Yankees for tabloid headlines. Except in October, when one of them faced the Bronx Bombers in the World Series, the Yankees were preoccupied with the Red Sox, who competed with them for fame and fortune. Boston fans hated the Yankees since owner Harry Frazee sold Babe Ruth and other top stars in the early '20s.

Robert D. Opie

The rocky relationship between Yankee slugger Babe Ruth and GM Ed Barrow is hinted at here by Barrow's clenched left fist, which accompanied this icy handshake. Ruth's list of fines and suspensions was almost as long as the list of his records on the baseball field.

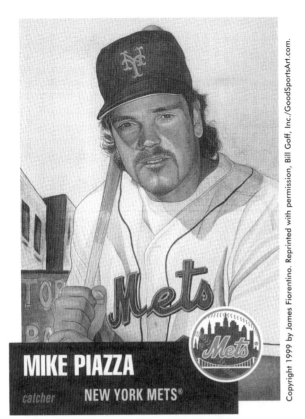

MIKE PIAZZA

catcher　　**NEW YORK METS**®

Mild-mannered Mike Piazza missed the 2000 All-Star Game with a concussion after a Roger Clemens pitch hit him in the head in the first inning of the July 8 night game at Yankee Stadium. The next time they faced each other, in the first inning of World Series Game 2 on October 22, the catcher shattered his bat on a foul ball. Thinking the ball was fair, Piazza ran toward first as Clemens tossed the jagged barrel of the bat in his general direction. The stars stared at each other and exchanged words as both benches emptied, but the only casualty was Clemens' wallet. He was slapped with a $50,000 fine.

Angry Outbursts

Inability to control explosive tempers sometimes interferes with big-league careers. On April 11, 1991, Cincinnati reliever Rob Dibble received a three-day suspension and a $1,000 fine from the National League after his pitch behind Eric Yelding's back ignited a bench-clearing brawl with Houston. Seventeen days later, Dibble drew a four-day suspension and a $2,000 fine for heaving a ball at a heckler and striking teacher Meg Porter on the elbow. Cleveland outfielder Albert Belle, who also drilled a heckler with a ball in 1991, drew a six-game suspension from the American League and was ordered to donate a week's salary to the charity of his choice.

a friendly kick in the rear as he was leaving. Washington's Earl Whitehill made a sarcastic remark to Chapman, who was on his way to the clubhouse, and a battle began. Fans fought among themselves. Only Babe Ruth and Lou Gehrig remained aloof—not wishing to injure their hands.

• 1937: Cardinal Dizzy Dean collided with baserunner Jim Ripple (Giants) at Sportsman's Park, St. Louis. A free-for-all followed.

• 1941: The White Sox and Browns fought after Elden Auker hit the head of Joe Kuhel of Chicago with a pitch.

• 1943: Catchers Mickey Owen of the Dodgers and Walker Cooper of the Cardinals were among combatants in a brawl that erupted when Brooklyn's Les Webber threw some close pitches to Stan Musial.

• 1945: The White Sox and Browns battled again when Chicago's sharp-tongued pitcher Karl Scheel got under the skin of rival George Caster. In retaliation, Caster threw the ball at Scheel in the dugout.

• 1953: Brooklyn's Carl Furillo suffered a broken finger in the fight that followed his confrontation with Giants manager Leo Durocher. Furillo had been hit by a pitch.

• 1954: Milwaukee slugger Joe Adcock chased diminutive Giants' pitcher Ruben Gomez 500 feet to the clubhouse in dead center field after a beanball. Gomez went inside, grabbed a knife, and warned the lumbering first baseman not to come any closer.

Fines

Before free agency ushered in the age of the spoiled millionaire, the highest fine in baseball history was leveled against Lenny Randle, infielder of the Texas Rangers, during spring training of 1977. Randle, upset with his failure to win a regular job, punched manager Frank Lucchesi several times in full view of players and fans at the Pompano Beach, Florida, ballpark.

Randle was immediately suspended and fined $10,000. He never played for the Rangers again. Dealt to the New York Mets, he enjoyed his finest major league season that year, hitting .304 and stealing 33 bases, then a club record.

Babe Ruth and Ted Williams drew $5,000 fines—Ruth for "breaking training rules" and Williams for spitting and making obscene gestures at fans.

Ruth was slapped with the penalty in 1925—the same year he sat out the first month with a giant stomachache suffered en route home from spring training. Neither he nor the club had been doing well, but Ruth was up to his usual playboy antics during a midwestern swing. Manager Miller Huggins hired a detective to trail him and delivered a complete report to owner Jacob Ruppert, who backed him all the way. The owner sided with the manager when Ruth delivered a him-or-me ultimatum.

Three years earlier, Babe Ruth had lost his appointment as Yankee captain after a heated argument with umpire Tommy Connolly. American League president Ban Johnson slapped a $100 fine on Ruth, suspended him for five days, and took away his captain's job.

Among other stiff fines in the game's history was a $1,000 assessment against Giant pilot John McGraw early in the century. McGraw also drew a five-day suspension for knocking down umpire Bill Byron during a fight in Cincinnati.

Bill Klem, another umpire of the McGraw period, continued an on-field argument with Tiger outfielder Goose Goslin in a Detroit elevator and was fined $50 for foul language by Commissioner Kenesaw Mountain Landis.

Arguing with umpire Tom Dunn cost Leo Durocher $25 during his term with the Dodgers, and fans considered it such an injustice that they collected 2,500 pennies to pay it.

A fight between umpire George Magerkurth and the Giants' Billy Jurges cost each man $150 in 1939. They contested the call of a home run by Cincinnati's Harry Craft.

In the '30s, Cleveland pitcher Johnny Allen persisted in wearing a tattered sweatshirt that made it difficult for batters to see the ball. The league issued a cease-and-desist order. Lack of action led to a $200 fine.

When the Cardinals' Dean brothers missed an exhibition game in Detroit in 1934, manager Frankie Frisch charged the elder Dizzy $100 and Paul $50. The players contested the fines and took the case to the commissioner, where they lost easily. The Boston Braves once slapped $300 fines on Al Javery and Tom Nelson for missing a train, and the New York Yankees slapped minor levies on stars who skipped a "Welcome Home, Yankees" luncheon before the 1978 season opener.

Managers of all clubs are frequent targets for fines because it is their responsibility to argue loudest and longest. Even pilots with gentle temperaments run into trouble on occasion.

While Leo Durocher, Eddie Stanky, and Gene Mauch were noted for the "politics of confrontation," one of the champion umpire baiters in baseball history had to be Earl Weaver. He was

---

2014—Michael Pineda (Yankees) banned 10 games for using pine tar during a game
2015—Brook Jacoby (Blue Jays coach) barred for 14 games for postgame conduct toward umpires
2016—Aroldis Chapman (Yankees) suspended 30 games for violating MLB's domestic violence policy

---

Suspension Sampler

These were some of the more memorable suspensions not involving gambling or drug abuse:

1932—Bill Dickey (Yankees) suspended 30 days and fined $1000 for punching Carl Reynolds (Senators)
1977—Lenny Randle (Rangers) suspended 30 days for punching manager Frank Lucchesi
1980—Bill Madlock (Pirates) suspended 15 days and fined $5000 for shoving his glove in the face of umpire Gerry Crawford
2000—John Rocker (Braves) suspended 28 games (reduced to 14 upon appeal) for controversial statements about fans
2000—Carl Everett (Red Sox) got 10 games and $5000 fine for bumping and beaking umpire Ronald Kulpa after arguing over his foot placement in the batter's box. Everett dropped his appeal because he had to rest the hand he injured when hitting a bat rack and water cooler after his outburst.
2004—Frank Francisco (Rangers) banned 15 games for tossing a chair at a fan in a lower box
2005—Kenny Rogers (Rangers) suspended 20 games (reduced to 13) and fined $50,000 for attacking a TV cameraman who had to be hospitalized
2006—Michael Barrett (Cubs) got 10-game ban for punching A.J. Pierzynski (White Sox) and sparking a brawl
2013—Ian Kennedy (Diamondbacks) banned 10 games for his part in brawl vs. Dodgers

---

Mouth of the South

Longtime Atlanta Braves general manager John Schuerholz said John Rocker had "a million-dollar arm and a 10-cent head." The 6'4" left-handed closer, who could hit triple digits on his pitches, Rocker reached the majors in 1998 and saved 38 games for the pennant-winning Braves a year later. But his published offseason comments about New Yorkers to *Sports Illustrated* writer Jeff Pearlman resulted in a fine and suspension, reduced on appeal to 14 games at the start of the 2000 season. Teammates gave him the cold shoulder when he returned. Even meetings with Hank Aaron and Andrew Young didn't dissuade Rocker, whose diatribes continued. The image-conscious Braves, frustrated they couldn't repair the damage, traded the controversial closer to Cleveland in 2001. Rocker, who also pitched for Texas, later added fuel to the fire by admitting he used steroids. His career went down in flames after five seasons.

Shoving Match

While protesting a called third strike on September 1, 1992, Vince Coleman of the New York Mets became embroiled in a heated argument with the home plate umpire. Frustrated over what he perceived as a quick ejection, Coleman then turned his fury on manager Jeff Torborg, who had come out to help him. The two got into a shoving match in full view of the Shea Stadium stands and the argument continued after the manager followed the player into the clubhouse. The Mets hit Coleman with a two-day suspension that cost him more than $32,000 in salary.

Bob Gibson, a star right-hander, was idled several months with a broken leg.

10-Year Rule
Waived for Joss

To be eligible for the Hall of Fame, a player must have performed in 10 major league seasons. The requirement was waived for Addie Joss, who was one game short when stricken by tubercular meningitis just as he was to pitch the first game of the 1911 season for Cleveland. Joss, who died a week later at age 31, had 160 victories and a 1.88 lifetime ERA, second only to Ed Walsh's 1.82. The wily right hander had an uncanny ability to predict the score ahead of time. Before his perfect game against Walsh and the White Sox on October 2, 1908, he announced, "They ain't gonna score." They didn't.

Before arthritis forced him to retire in 1966, Sandy Koufax pitched four no-hitters, including this perfect game against the Cubs on September 9, 1965.

ejected 90 times in his 17 years as a big-time pilot. Many times, those ejections were accompanied by fines.

Injuries

Injuries shape baseball's pennant races and change the course of history. Hank Aaron, free of major injuries after a leg fracture at the end of his rookie year, managed to break Babe Ruth's lifetime home-run record by playing often, as well as consistently. Sandy Koufax failed to achieve many pitching milestones because his career was halted by arthritis at 30. Lou Gehrig, once known as "the Iron Horse" for his durability, was forced to retire at age 36 by amyotrophic lateral sclerosis, the neuromuscular disease that took his life in 1941.

Ray Chapman, Cleveland shortstop, was the only man ever killed on the field when a Carl Mays pitch struck him in 1920, but dozens of players have been severely injured. Mickey Cochrane's triple skull fracture, also caused by a pitched ball, ended his playing career in 1937, the same season a line drive from Earl Averill's bat fractured Dizzy Dean's toe in the All-Star Game and forced the pitcher into an unorthodox style that ended his career prematurely.

Dodger outfielder Pete Reiser, unmindful of outfield walls even after padding and warning tracks were added, suffered two broken ankles, torn cartilage in his left knee, a broken bone in his right elbow, ripped muscles in his left leg, and countless concussions, contusions, and abrasions. As a rookie, he won the National League batting crown with a .343 mark in 1941 and was running away with another in 1942, with a .381 mark in July. Then he hit the outfield wall in St. Louis. His final mark was .310.

Like Reiser, Ted Williams was hurt when he crashed into a wall. The Red Sox slugger broke his elbow trying to catch a drive by Ralph Kiner in the 1950 All-Star Game.

Cal Ripken Jr. was the victim of a freak injury at the All-Star Game. Posing for the 1996 AL team picture, he was standing next to Roberto Hernandez when the closer lost his balance and started to fall. Hernandez flung his arm wildly, catching Ripken squarely in the nose and breaking it.

Cancer curtailed several sluggers in successive seasons, including Eric Davis (1997), Darryl Strawberry (1998), and Andres Galarraga (1999).

Car crashes caused physical problems for several players. Roy Campanella, star catcher of the Brooklyn Dodgers, was paralyzed after his car skidded into a tree on an ice-slicked highway. Casey Stengel broke a leg when struck by a driver on a fog-shrouded street in Boston. Art Houtteman's car was struck by a truck during spring training in Lakeland, Florida, and the pitcher was given last rites. He recuperated and resumed his career, but his child was killed and his wife injured in a second car crash.

Dizzy Dean once fell out of a car when driver Glen Russell stopped short, but Dean—who fell on his head—was not injured badly. Bobo Newsom, the longtime pitcher, broke both legs in a crash, then had another accident the day his casts were removed; at a South Carolina mule auction, one of the animals kicked him and broke his leg again.

Bob Gibson missed several months of pitching with a fractured leg and Wilbur Wood, hit by a line drive, suffered a shattered kneecap. Hank Greenberg twice beaned pitchers with scorching liners; one of them fractured Jim Wilson's skull and threatened his career. After another line drive broke his leg, Wilson rebounded to throw a no-hitter for the Braves against the Phillies in 1954.

Pitcher Jim Lonborg, whose surprise 22–9 season helped the miracle Red Sox win the wild American League race of 1967, was injured off the field. A ski accident that winter broke his leg, limiting his activities as a pitcher the following season. He was never again the same pitcher that he was in 1967.

Another pitcher, Lou Brissie, narrowly escaped amputation of his left leg when a Nazi shell exploded at his feet during World War II. After 23 operations, he returned to the big leagues— wearing a catcher's shin guard under his uniform.

Gene Bearden, Cleveland's top starter in the pennant year of 1948, also survived war injuries. He was on the deck of the light cruiser *Helena* when Japanese torpedos struck in 1943. Bearden, with a crushed knee and damaged skull, spent the rest of the war as a patient in naval hospitals.

Bruce Campbell was even more fortunate; he survived spinal meningitis to return to the Cleveland Indians after a year's absence in the '30s. So did Max Alvis, another Indian, in 1964.

Two Braves, Red Schoendienst and Rico Carty, missed seasons nine years apart with tuberculosis. Schoendienst's absence in 1959 cost the team its third consecutive National League pennant, as Felix Mantilla (.215), Casey Wise (.171), and Mel Roach (.097) could not replace the .310 mark Red had compiled in 1957 before the illness struck late in 1958.

The Braves were victims of a no-hitter by Brooklyn's Ed Head in 1946. What made the feat unusual was the arm Head

Career Stoppers

The following players are among those whose careers have been interrupted or halted by illness or injury:

1905—Napoleon Lajoie missed two months after he developed blood poisoning from the dye in his stockings after being spiked.

1920—Joe Leonard, sent home after playing one game, died of a ruptured appendix on May 1.

1922—Austin McHenry died of a brain tumor after the season.

1924—Jake Daubert died of complications from appendix and gallstone surgery.

1938—Satchel Paige missed a season after breaking his arm while throwing a curve.

1947—Negro League star Josh Gibson died of a brain tumor.

1964—Jim Umbricht died of cancer at age 33.

1965—Dick Brown, diagnosed with a brain tumor, retired, then died five years later.

1972—Roberto Clemente died in New Year's Eve plane crash while flying relief supplies to victims of Nicaragua earthquake.

1978—Lyman Bostock was murdered in Gary, IN case of mistaken identity.

1979—Novice pilot Thurman Munson died in August crash of plane he was flying in Ohio.

1988—Dave Dravecky developed cancer in his pitching shoulder, returned briefly, but later had the arm amputated.

1989—Dave Winfield missed the season after back surgery.

1989—John Olerud, then a junior at Washington State, had surgery to repair an aneurysm at the base of the brain but returned to play two months later.

1991—Roberto Hernandez needed an eight-and-a-half-hour operation to remove blood clots from his right forearm but was saved from amputation by the transplant of a vein from his right leg.

1995—Eric Davis missed a season with a herniated disc in his neck.

1996—David Cone missed several months after circulatory problems and surgery to repair a small aneurysm in his pitching arm.

2016—Marlins ace Jose Fernandez died in September boat crash near Miami Beach.

Big-League Handicaps

Several handicapped players played in the majors. In addition to one-armed Pete Gray, who played with the wartime Browns of 1945, Hugh Daily of the 19th century had one arm, Tom Sunkel was blind in one eye, and Dummy Taylor and Dummy Hoy were deaf mutes. Urban Shocker had heart disease, Sandy Koufax had a circulatory ailment and arthritis, and Catfish Hunter diabetes. Pitcher Jim Abbott, who jumped from the University of Michigan to the majors in 1989, was born without a right hand.

Long Layoff

Marty Marion, star shortstop for the St. Louis Cardinals, did not walk for a year after he fell off a cliff as a youngster.

The Other Yount

Unlike brother Robin, who reached the Hall of Fame, Larry Yount never got his career off the ground. A 1971 rookie reliever with the Houston Astros, he hurt his right shoulder on his first warm-up pitch and never pitched another game in the majors. Official baseball records show he had one game played but no batters faced.

Mark the Bird

After taking the world by storm in 1976, when he won 19 games and started the All-Star Game as a rookie with the Detroit Tigers, Mark (the Bird) Fidrych hurt his knee while shagging fly balls in spring training. He returned May 27 and won six of ten decisions before his arm gave out. Although he tried to return, Fidrych won only four games over the next three seasons and retired.

Miscarriage of Justice

Slugging outfielder David Justice separated his shoulder with a swing-and-miss in what would turn out to be his last at-bat for the Braves. The season-ending mishap occurred in May 1996, ten months before Justice was traded to Cleveland.

Killed in Action

Mike Coolbaugh was killed by a line drive after he retired. A former third baseman in the major leagues, he was coaching first base for the Double-A Tulsa Drillers when he was struck in the head by a line drive in the ninth inning of a game at Little Rock on July 23, 2007. He was 35 years old.

Star Minnesota outfielder Kirby Puckett, a 10-time All-Star who led the Twins to two world championships, missed the end of the 1995 season after a pitch from Cleveland's Dennis Martinez broke his jaw. During 1996 spring training, vision problems unrelated to the beaning forced his permanent but premature retirement.

Minnesota Twins

used—his right. A natural left-hander, he was severely injured in a school bus crash as a youngster. He was determined to play ball anyway and learned how to throw right-handed.

Mordecai Brown's farming machine mishap cost him two fingers but enabled his ball to take a strange hop when thrown. "Three-Finger" Brown won 239 games and a place in the Hall of Fame.

Red Ruffing pitched although he was missing the big toe on one foot; Monty Stratton was successful in the minors on one leg; and Elden Auker led American League pitchers with a .720 winning percentage (18-7) because batters were baffled by his underhand delivery. Auker had thrown normally before an old football injury forced him to make adjustments.

The list of pitchers with serious injuries is almost endless. Every season, tendinitis, sore arms, and elbow bone chips take their toll on talented players. One of the most impressive comeback stories was fashioned by Tommy John of the Los Angeles Dodgers in 1976, two years after he had ruptured a ligament in his left elbow. John's injury required complete reconstruction of the arm—a first in medical science.

On July 17, 1974, with a club-leading 13–3 record, John suffered the injury at home against Montreal. A tendon from his right forearm was placed in his left elbow by Dr. Frank Jobe. Recovery was probable, pitching again was doubtful. The southpaw threw out the first ball at the All-Star Game—right-handed.

John missed all of 1975. In 1976 he split 20 decisions, then went 20–7 in 1977. "Tommy John surgery" has since been used successfully on many others.

Player Size and Sex

Fred Patek, 5'4" shortstop of the Kansas City Royals, started the 1978 All-Star Game for the American League. Patek and one-time American League MVP Phil Rizzuto, a shortstop who stood 5'6", proved size was no obstacle to success in baseball.

If it were possible, an All-Star team of short players could be placed on the field. Here's how it might look:

Pos.	Player	Yrs.	Hgt	Wgt	Avg
C	Ray Schalk (1912–1929)	18	5:07	155	.253
1B	Joe Judge (1915–1933)	19	5:09	155	.297
2B	Jose Altuve (2011–present)		5:06	170	.311#
SS	Rabbit Maranville (1912–1935)	23	5:05	155	.259
3B	Sparky Adams (1922–1934)	13	5:04½	151	.286
OF	Wee Willie Keeler (1892–1910)	19	5:04½	140	.345
OF	Harry Leibold (1913–1925)	13	5:06½	157	.267
OF	Hack Wilson (1923–1934)	12	5:06	190	.307
P	Bobby Shantz (1949–1964)	16	5:06	139	W119 L99

(#) through 2016 season

Tiny Miller Huggins, who managed such musclemen as Babe Ruth, stood just 5'4" and weighed less than 150 pounds. But he lasted 13 seasons as a player and was a well-respected manager.

Although the All-American Girls Professional Baseball League lasted nearly 10 years after its wartime launch in the '40s, no woman made the all-male minors until 1997. That's when former Southern California College star Ila Borders, the first woman ever to receive a college baseball scholarship, served as a left-handed relief pitcher for two teams in the independent Northern League.

On July 9, 1998, the 23-year-old Borders became the first female pitcher to start a regular-season professional game. She worked five innings for the Duluth-Superior Dukes against the Sioux Falls Canaries in the independent Northern League.

One year earlier, the Colorado Silver Bullets, an all-female professional touring team, posted their first winning record (23-22) after three losing seasons.

Borders and the Bullets weren't the first distaff ballplayers to make an impact on the male-dominated pro ranks.

Shortstop Eleanor Engle signed with the Harrisburg Senators in July 1952 but the Class B Interstate League voided her contract. When Fort Lauderdale's Class B club offered a contract to first baseman Dorothy Kamenshek, the All-American Girls Professional Baseball League refused to let her leave.

Seattle Mariners

Flamethrowing southpaw Randy Johnson stands 6'10", making him the tallest member of the Baseball Hall of Fame. Seattle's first 20-game winner, he threw no-hitters in both leagues en route to five Cy Young Awards.

Liner Struck Score

On May 7, 1957, Gil McDougald of the New York Yankees—the second batter in the first inning—hit pitcher Herb Score in the eye with a line drive. Score, a 20-game winner the previous year, suffered a broken bone and eye damage and was never again the same pitcher. McDougald, hounded by fans after the accident, retired in 1960 at age 32. Score was 29 when he finally gave it up in 1962.

Fatal Crash

Cleveland pitchers Steve Olin and Tim Crews were killed and pitcher Bob Ojeda seriously hurt in a spring-training boating accident near Orlando, Florida, on March 22, 1993.

Don't Copy Me

Although his team took NL Central division titles in each of his first three seasons, Houston manager Larry Dierker had trouble staying off the disabled list. In 1997, his first year, he twisted his knee while rollerblading from Wrigley Field to his team's downtown Chicago hotel. Two years later, he missed 27 games after suffering a grand mal seizure that required brain surgery.

Early Wynn was one of several players to play in four decades (1939–1963). He won a total of 300 games.

Baseball Graybeards

Two-dozen players performed in the major leagues after their 45th birthdays. They are pitchers Satchel Paige (59) and Jack Quinn (50); Jamie Moyer and Hoyt Wilhelm (49); Phil Niekro and Nick Altrock (48); Nolan Ryan, Jesse Orosco, Charlie Hough, Tommy John, Randy Johnson, and Hod Lisenbee (46); and position players Charley O'Leary (58); Minnie Minoso (56); Jim O'Rourke (54); Julio Franco, Arlie Latham, and Hughie Jennings (49); Gabby Street, Deacon McGuire, and Johnny Evers (48); and Jimmy Austin, Sam Thompson, and Dan Brouthers (46).

Player Longevity

Pitcher Nick Altrock, infielder Julio Franco, and outfielder Minnie Minoso played baseball in five different decades. Two-dozen players, including several Hall of Famers, have played in four different decades. Nolan Ryan's tenure reached 27 years, a major league record, in 1993.

One woman who did play was Jackie Mitchell, a pitcher used in exhibition games by the Chattanooga Lookouts of the Southern Association in 1932. In one game she fanned Babe Ruth, Lou Gehrig, and Tony Lazzeri.

For more on Women in Baseball, see Chapter 18.

Prolonged Careers

Baseball has always been known as a game for young or old, tall or short, lean or brawny. Many of the game's best players maintained excellent year-round physical condition and managed to play past the age of 35. Some even made it to 40.

In 1897 Cap Anson hit .285 in 114 games for Chicago of the National League. At age 46½, he ended his career on October 3 of that year with two home runs against St. Louis. No other nonpitcher played regularly at such an advanced age.

Sam Thompson, 46, played eight games for the 1906 Tigers and collected several hits—including a triple—when Ty Cobb and others were idled by injuries. Thompson had played in the majors 20 years earlier.

In 1912, when the Tiger players struck in protest of Ty Cobb's suspension (he had hit an abusive fan), manager Hugh Jennings, 43, quickly gathered a team of collegians, semipros, and former players, including himself, 41-year-old Joe Sugden, and 48-year-old Jim McGuire. Sugden and McGuire both singled and scored the only two Tiger runs in a 24–2 defeat by the Philadelphia Athletics. By playing in that game, McGuire established the record for most years played at 26 (later tied by Eddie Collins and Tommy John and broken by Nolan Ryan). Jennings, who pinch hit, did so again six years later at age 49.

Spitballer Jack Quinn, 48, won a game for the Dodgers in August 1932 and pitched for the Reds just before his 49th birthday on July 5, 1933. In 1972 knuckleballer Hoyt Wilhelm also just missed spending his 49th birthday in the big leagues; the Dodgers cut him with less than a week to go. Wilhelm managed to keep his ERA below the 2.00 mark for five consecutive seasons after his 40th birthday.

Satchel Paige was past 50 when he pitched three scoreless innings for the Kansas City A's against Boston as a publicity stunt on September 25, 1965, but he might have been that old—records are uncertain—when he out-dueled Detroit's Virgil Trucks, 1–0 in 12 innings on August 6, 1952.

Paige, then with the Browns, led the American League in relief victories and innings pitched that same season. He was 42 when he broke into the majors with the Cleveland Indians in 1948.

Reliever Don McMahon, winding up with the San Francisco Giants in 1974, was still firing his fastball at age 44, but Warren Spahn prolonged his career by switching from power to finesse.

With pinpoint control and a sharp-breaking screwball, Spahn won 20 or more games in a season 13 different times, pitched his only two no-hitters at ages 39 and 40, and posted a remarkable 23-7 record—with seven shutouts and a 2.60 ERA—as a 42-year-old mound marvel in 1963.

Spahn said he conceded the middle 13 inches of home plate to the batter, but claimed the two inches on either side for himself. He aimed his pitches for those spots.

UNLIKE A PIECE OF MACHINERY WHICH WEARS OUT SOONER IF IT GETS HARD USAGE...THE HARDEST WORKERS IN BASEBALL, **THE CATCHERS**, LAST LONGER ON AN AVERAGE, THAN PLAYERS IN OTHER POSITIONS........

RANKING 3RD IN PLAYING LIFE, **OUTFIELDERS** AS A GROUP, ARE QUITE FAR BEHIND BATTERY MEN IN LENGTH OF SERVICE... ...MEL OTT's 17 SEASONS MAKES HIM A STANDOUT........

Bill DICKEY......
WITH 15 SEASONS BEHIND THE YANKEES' PLATE, IS NOT THROUGH YET

I CAN STILL GET DOWN OKAY...NOW IF I HAD A DERRICK TO PULL ME UP I COULD GO ON AN' ON!

Gabby HARTNETT.....
COMPLETED HIS 20TH YEAR AS A NATIONAL LEAGUE RECEIVER.....

???
DOESN'T LOOK LIKE A FEROCIOUS MAN-KILLER!

3rd BASE

THE HOT-CORNER HAS FIVE 10-YEAR MEN TO BOAST ABOUT...

Charley GEHRINGER.....
THE TIGERS' MECHANICAL MAN, PUT IN A TERM OF 16 SUMMERS......

..but...
I KNEW I'D CRACK EARLY! GUESS I WAS JUST TOO DELICATE FOR TH' GAME!

SQUEEE-E-E
CREAK

Eddie COLLINS'....
QUARTER OF A CENTURY IN THE BIG SHOW IS THE EXCEPTION PROVING THE RULE THAT INFIELDERS HAVE THE SHORTEST CAREERS...

PITCHERS
RATE NEXT TO CATCHERS IN DURABILITY.... FOR INSTANCE: **LEFTY GROVE**.... WON HIS 300TH GAME IN 1941...HIS 17TH YEAR OF MAJOR LEAGUE HURLING..

Jim Berryman

Beanballs

Eight beanballs that made a major impact:

1920—Carl Mays of the Yankees hits Cleveland's Ray Chapman, who dies of his injuries a day later.

1937—Detroit player/manager Mickey Cochrane, his skull fractured, lies unconscious for 10 days and never plays again.

1956—Cincinnati's Hal Jeffcoat breaks Don Zimmer's cheekbone, idling the Brooklyn infielder for the season.

1963—After a Bob Gibson pitch breaks his collarbone, San Francisco slugger Jim Ray Hart is never the same.

1966—Jack Fisher's pitch breaks Ron Santo's cheekbone, and prompts introduction of helmet earflap.

1967—Vision problems plague young Boston slugger Tony Conigliaro after Jack Hamilton hits his head with a pitch.

1970—After he's struck in the left eye by a Ken Tatum pitch, breaking his nose, Paul Blair can't recapture his confidence.

1997—San Francisco's J. T. Snow fractures his eye socket when Seattle fireballer Randy Johnson hits him in the face during an exhibition game.

The Moyer Miracle

Reliance on control rather than velocity allowed Jamie Moyer to pitch past his 49th birthday. In 2012, the last of his 25 seasons, the left-handed junkballer became the oldest pitcher to win a game and the oldest player to knock in a run. Two years earlier, he had become the oldest to pitch a shutout—making him the only man to blank opponents in four different decades. Moyer yielded a record 522 home runs while pitching for eight different teams.

Why McGraw Fined Injured Pitcher

Giants manager John McGraw fined pitcher Zeke Barnes $100 after the pitcher reported with a bad ankle and injured wrist—suffered in a bathtub fall. The pitcher profited from the incident when a concern that manufactured bathtub mats gave him $200 to endorse its product.

A Difficult Putout

Al Schacht, the noted baseball clown, was pitching in a 1928 benefit game for Eddie Plank when he got the first two men out in an inning. He then called in all the fielders but the catcher as batting practice pitcher Ike Powers came to the plate. Powers connected with the ball and unleashed a drive deep to right field. As he circled the bases, Schacht retrieved the ball, fired it home, and nipped Powers by an eyelash.

Another ancient pitcher, 41-year-old Ted Lyons, recorded a fine season at an advanced age in 1942. Working only on Sundays, the White Sox star posted a 14-6 record and 2.10 ERA for a poor ballclub and completed all 20 of his starts.

Sentiment doesn't last forever and some of the athletes who prospered in their 40s took hard falls. A notable example was Spahn, who suddenly lost his magic overnight and never again had a winning season after his 23-7 record of 1963.

Stunts

In addition to strange goings-on before, after, or even during a ballgame, fun-loving players have never been averse to attempting Herculean feats off the field.

Hall of Fame pitcher Walter Johnson, whose 417 victories rank second only to Cy Young's 511, owned a powerful right arm. It was so strong, in fact, that Johnson duplicated George Washington's feat of throwing a silver dollar across the Rappahannock River.

Johnson's catcher, Gabby Street, became one of few men brave enough to catch a ball dropped from the top of the Washington Monument in August of 1908. Drama critic Pres Gibson, a close friend of Street's and a loyal supporter of his outstanding defensive ability, arranged the stunt to prove a bet. Street did not wish to embarrass Gibson, but he also wanted to impress Washington fans and writers.

Gibson took 13 balls to the top of the monument, 500 feet in the air, while a crowd gathered to watch Street at the base. Gibson began to throw, but the wind played tricks with the ball. Several hit the side of the structure and bounced away, others were out of reach. Only after Gibson moved to the other side of the monument, away from the wind, did Street have a real chance. He missed several close balls, then grabbed one—the last ball Gibson had.

Eight years later, Brooklyn Dodgers' manager Wilbert Robinson, an old catcher himself, decided to top Street's feat. He arranged to have aviatrix Ruth Law and Dodger trainer Frank Kelly drop a ball from an airplane. The plane was up to about 400 feet when Kelly made his drop—but he didn't throw a baseball. Instead, he dropped a red grapefruit.

Unable to distinguish the falling object, Robinson assumed it was a baseball and waited patiently for it to fall into his glove. When the grapefruit hit, it splattered red juice in all directions. "Oh my God!" screamed Robinson. "It broke me open! I'm covered with blood!"

Benefits

Baseball players are as quick to help others as they are to provide laughs. On July 24, 1911, a group of American League stars played the Cleveland Indians in a special game for the benefit of the Addie Joss family. Joss, Cleveland's star pitcher, died suddenly in April from an attack of spinal meningitis. He had been scheduled to pitch the opening game. Had he pitched even

part of that game, he would have entered his 10th big-league season and won Hall of Fame eligibility. Despite his spectacular record, Joss was barred from consideration for many years until the 10-year rule was lifted for his exceptional case. He was admitted to the Hall in 1978.

The exhibition game in his honor was won by the All-Stars, 5–3. Players included such greats as Ty Cobb, Eddie Collins, Tris Speaker, and Walter Johnson. Among the Indians in action were Cy Young, Joe Jackson, and Napoleon Lajoie.

On June 14, 1937, four major league teams played an exhibition doubleheader at Charleston, West Virginia, to raise funds for the Kanawha Valley Children's Tuberculosis Hospital. The Reds played the Athletics and the Senators played the Phillies, raising $17,000 for the hospital fund. On August 16, the St. Louis Cardinals battled Columbus (American Association) in an exhibition before a Charleston-Zanesville (Middle Atlantic) game, adding $10,000 to the hospital fund.

Throughout the history of the game, clubs and individuals have done considerable charity work. In 1977, for example, several clubs made large contributions to the Jackie Robinson Foundation and National League All-Stars Greg Luzinski and Dave Winfield spent thousands of dollars from their own pockets to purchase game tickets for disadvantaged children.

Such actions usually receive no public exposure.

Off the Field

Most baseball people have special hobbies or occupations in the off-season. Many who come from rural backgrounds are wintertime farmers. College-educated players often go into teaching, especially when their classroom assignment coincides with coaching a schoolboy team.

The Game's Remarkable Influence

Eleven-year-old John D. Sylvester of Essex Fells, New Jersey, was given 30 minutes to live by doctors after a severe attack of blood poisoning in October 1926. Young John spent his remaining time listening to the World Series. That was the day Babe Ruth hit three home runs in one game. Amazingly, John began to recover. *The New York Times* reported that Horace Sylvester Jr., the boy's father, and the physicians attributed the recovery to messages of encouragement received from Ruth and other stars. When Ruth hit his three home runs, the boy's fever began to break and his recovery began.

Youngest Player

Left-handed pitcher Joe Nuxhall of the Cincinnati Reds was the youngest player to appear in the majors. He made his debut on June 10, 1944, at the age of 15 years and 10 months. He pitched two-thirds of an inning in an 18–0 loss to the Cardinals.

Lone Senator Homer

Power production was off sharply in the war-stripped majors of 1945. The Washington Senators hit only 27 home runs as a team—only one in their home park, Griffith Stadium. It was an inside-the-park job by Joe Kuhel.

Double Dribble

Before throwing a pitch for the Brewers, to whom he had been traded by the Royals, Zack Greinke cracked a rib playing basketball—forcing him to start the 2011 season on the disabled list. Two years earlier, Greinke had asked Aaron Boone how he had recovered from an off-season basketball injury that sidelined him for the entire season.

Members of the New York Hilltoppers (later the Yankees) in 1905 didn't have to worry about injury on August 4, when the club's winning battery consisted of two doctors—pitcher Jim Newton and catcher Mike Powers.

The Yankees produced two other doctors in infielder Bobby Brown (a lifetime .439 batter in the World Series) and pitcher George "Doc" Medich, who performed in the '70s.

"Baseball gave me the financial opportunity to put myself through medical school," said Brown, a Fort Worth cardiologist who also served as American League president. "The experience of playing with those truly great Yankee teams [early in the '50s] was a tremendous influence, enabling me to adapt to all types of crises. The atmosphere of total dedication on those teams will last with me forever."

Record-breaking reliever Mike Marshall, who won the National League's Cy Young Award after working 106 times in 1974, spent his off-season teaching kinesiology—the science of muscle movement in relation to body tissue—to students at Michigan State University.

Juan Marichal, a spectacular Giants starter of a decade before, became an accomplished skin-diver and once was hired to photograph sharks off the coast of his native Dominican Republic.

In the '40s, Washington's fleet George Case ran a Trenton, New Jersey, sporting goods store and coached the Rutgers University team. Rip Sewell worked for a California motor oil concern. And veteran managers Billy Southworth and Joe McCarthy retired to quiet farm living.

Before Curt Flood challenged baseball's reserve clause in 1969, he had become such an accomplished painter that St. Louis owner Gussie Busch commissioned the outfielder to do a family portrait. Rawly Eastwick, who gained his freedom in the second wave of big-name free agents, also showed talent with a paintbrush.

Jim Bouton, a Flood contemporary, confined his talents to the typewriter and stirred waves of resentment when he penned the inside baseball book *Ball Four* in 1970. He used the book as a springboard to mushroom his career as writer, sportscaster, and television personality.

Yogi Berra and Phil Rizzuto opened a successful bowling alley in Clifton, New Jersey; Red Schoendienst cultivated his interest in a retirement home; and Warren Spahn pitched hay instead of baseballs to the cattle on his ranch near Hartshorne, Oklahoma.

Many Latin players switch uniforms to perform in winter leagues in their native countries. Darrell Evans devoted more time to his relaxing hobby: collecting postage stamps of animals. Garrulous Joe Garagiola escaped the sportscaster stereotype and tackled other broadcast assignments. Mike Marshall played chess. Maury Wills played his banjo in nightclubs. Denny McLain appeared at the organ.

Big leaguers plan investments—and watch their weight. Golf, tennis, racquetball, and swimming are popular ways to maintain condition for the coming season.

Some baseball insiders simply relax. They are able to live off their baseball salary, plus money from endorsements and investments.

"I never made a dollar outside of baseball," said longtime coach and manager Charley Dressen. Many others could say the same.

Chapter 8

Dan Schlossberg

Hank Aaron (44) and Eddie Mathews (41) hit a record 863 home runs as teammates. They homered in the same game 75 times en route to membership in the 500 Home Run Club. Aaron was the lifetime leader for 33 years before Barry Bonds passed his total of 755.

Famous Faces

As a black man chasing a white man's record in the Deep South, Hank Aaron withstood a torrent of hate mail to become the career home run champion. This Hall of Fame exhibit highlights his journey.

Aaron Failed in First Game

Hank Aaron went 0-for-5 in his first major league game—as left fielder for the Milwaukee Braves against the Cincinnati Reds on April 13, 1954. Though he spent his minor-league career in the infield, and most of his major league career in right field, Aaron ended his stay with the Braves as a left fielder in 1974.

Ruth Left for Pinch-Hitter in Debut

In Babe Ruth's major league debut on July 11, 1914, he pitched the Boston Red Sox to a 4–3 win over Cleveland, but was lifted for pinch-hitter Duffy Lewis in the seventh inning. A single by Lewis led to the winning run.

Hank Aaron vs. Babe Ruth

Baseball has always been a game of comparisons. Ted Williams vs. Joe DiMaggio. Willie Mays vs. Mickey Mantle. Christy Mathewson vs. Grover Cleveland Alexander. Ty Cobb vs. Lou Brock.

Perhaps the biggest argument of all erupted when Hank Aaron approached the mightiest record in all of sport—Babe Ruth's career total of 714 home runs.

Aaron took on more than a record; he took on a legend. "There has always been a magic about that gross, ugly, coarse, gargantuan figure of a man and everything he did," wrote Paul Gallico of Ruth.

The contrast between the two men was as remarkable as the contrast between the game of baseball that Ruth played and the game of Aaron's day (he broke Ruth's record 39 years after Ruth's retirement).

Aaron and Ruth were born one day apart—the former on February 5, 1934, and the latter on February 6, 1895, making both men Aquarians. Aaron was a black man from Mobile, Alabama; Ruth was a white man from Baltimore, Maryland.

Both came into great wealth in baseball after emerging from poverty, both spent little time in the minors, and both spent most of their careers as right fielders. In addition, both were paid as well as the presidents who saw them play.

Babe Ruth began his big-league career as a left-handed pitcher for the Boston Red Sox but hit so well that he soon became an outfielder. He joined the New York Yankees in 1920 and quickly became the premier slugger in the major leagues.

Ruth missed the tiring cross-country plane trips required of modern players; St. Louis was the western outpost of the American League when he played.

Because modern managers parade an endless stream of relievers with unorthodox deliveries and unusual pitches, Aaron faced an additional obstacle. Not only did Ruth avoid the phenomenon of relief pitching, but he also played all his games in daylight; the first night game was played in 1935, the same year Ruth retired.

Overall pitching improvement, the advent of night ball, and widespread use of relievers caused the overall major league batting average to fall from .282 in Ruth's heyday to .252 in Aaron's. For that reason, Aaron's National League average of .310 can be favorably compared with Ruth's .342 when the 30-point differential is considered. (In two years as an American League designated hitter, Aaron lost five points off his lifetime average.)

Though Ruth twice stole 17 bases, he never topped the 20 mark, which Aaron did six times. Both men played on teams laden with power. Lou Gehrig batted behind Ruth, forcing pitchers to give Ruth pitches around the plate. A walk might mean a two-run homer by Gehrig.

Aaron also was followed by power hitters—Eddie Mathews, Joe Adcock, Rico Carty, Orlando Cepeda, and others.

The two men became the home-run kings of the game with vastly different batting stances. Aaron generated his power with

Early Home-Run Kings

When Babe Ruth hit 29 home runs in 1919, he broke Gavvy Cravath's single-season record of 24, set in 1915. Ruth replaced Roger Connor as the all-time home-run king when he socked number 139 in 1921.

Ruth Won $10 for No. 60

Babe Ruth won a $10 bet from teammate Tony Lazzeri when he hit his 60th home run in 1927.

Ruth Broke into NL with Bang

Babe Ruth had two hits—including a home run—in four at-bats against Carl Hubbell in his National League debut in 1935.

New Record

Before Babe Ruth, no American Leaguer had ever hit more than 16 home runs in a season.

Babe vs the AL

In 1920, his first year with the Yankees, Babe Ruth out-homered all seven opposing teams in the American League. In fact, the only NL team to top Ruth was the Philadelphia Phillies, with 64. Ruth had 54 all by himself.

The First 60

Babe Ruth actually hit 60 homers six years before he set the official record in 1927. In 1921, he lost a sure home run when he hit a ball to right at the Polo Grounds, where the Yankees played home games at the time. Umpires Tommy Connolly and Ollie Chill ruled the hit a double after a fan reached out to grab it. Ruth finished that season with 59 home runs.

Golf Star Too

Babe Ruth was a star off the diamond too. He won more awards playing golf than baseball.

Lefty Catcher?

Before he took up pitching, Babe Ruth played schoolboy baseball as a left-handed catcher. Since his reform school had no left-handed catcher's mitt, he caught the ball with his left hand, then removed the right-handed mitt to throw it with his left arm.

quick, powerful wrists, while Ruth relied on massive shoulders and forearms for strength that moved from arms to bat.

Hall of Famer Eddie Mathews, who formed a devastating 1–2 power punch with Aaron, remembered his style at the plate. "He wasn't a classic hitter and young players shouldn't copy him," said Mathews of Aaron, who batted right-handed—the opposite of Ruth. "He hit off the front foot—a flat-footed stance in any batting textbook. It sounds wrong to say the man who broke Babe Ruth's home-run record had a fundamental batting flaw. Let's just say that Hank Aaron hit differently than anybody else."

Both Aaron and Ruth were students of hitting. Ruth had an extra insight because he broke into the majors as a pitcher with the 1914 Boston Red Sox. He won 94, lost 46, and compiled a fine 2.28 lifetime earned run average in six seasons as a pitcher, and for 43 years held the record for most consecutive scoreless innings pitched in the World Series.

Aaron never pitched but, like Ruth, broke into the lineup after conversion from his original post as an infielder. He filled in at second base numerous times in his career.

The greatest Aaron/Ruth controversy stems from the fact that Ruth collected his 714 home runs in 8,399 times at bat, nearly 3,000 fewer than Aaron. Ruth ranks first in the number of home runs per 100 times at-bat with 8.5.

A pro-Ruth fan calculated that the Yankee star would have hit an additional 231 home runs with 2,800 more times at bat—for a career total of 945! But the same fan suggested that record-keepers deduct 5 percent of that total because of the home-run advantage accorded left-handed hitters. He came out with a revised total of 898 home runs.

The advantage for a lefty is that there are far more right-handed than left-handed pitchers in the game, and a lefty has a statistical batting edge against a right-hander.

Ruth definitely benefited by batting left-handed. After joining the Yankees in 1920, he had the good fortune to play in the old Polo Grounds because Yankee Stadium had not yet been built.

Babe Ruth connects for his 60th home run on September 30, 1927. The Bambino held the single-season and career home-run records for 34 years.

NATION MOURNS RUTH

Game's Most Famous Star Dies at 53

Babe's Last Bow in Yankee Uniform

His Homers Created New Era in Play

Bam's Big Earnings Also Helped Raise Pay Level for All Players

Started Life as Waif on Waterfront

Placed in Industrial School at Age of 7, Remained There Until 19

By FREDERICK G. LIEB

NEW YORK, N. Y.

Baseball's most renowned of all stars, the inimitable George Herman (Babe) Ruth, the idol of millions, is dead. During his magnificent career, pitchers frequently struck out the great Bambino, but he quickly struck back with his prodigious wallops. But, when the Grim Reaper struck Babe out at New York's Memorial Hospital, Monday, August 16, there was no home run to hit in reprisal. The once power-

lieved he was a year older than he actually was. It wasn't until 1934, when he needed a passport for a baseball trip to the Orient with a team of American stars, that he learned his correct age. A Baltimore birth certificate then revealed he was born on February 6, 1895. Up to that time, the Babe thought he was born "in February, 1894."

Like his fellow star on later-day Yankee world's champion teams, Lou Gehrig, Ruth was of German descent on both sides. The writer once was told by a former baseball official that Ruth's first contract in the Interna-

developed a headstrong will, and was difficult to handle. Some neighbors, feeling that the saloon was no place in which to bring up a child, had him committed to St. Mary's Industrial School, a Roman Catholic semi-reform school.

Put Into St. Mary's at 7

Some parts of Ruth's early life have been grossly exaggerated, especially the story that he was such a bad boy he had to be put away. This obviously is incorrect, as Ruth was committed to St. Mary's before he was 7 years old. It also is not true that Ruth was a motherless waif when he was sent to St. Mary's. His mother died some years after he entered the institution, and he was permitted to attend her funeral. His father lived until Ruth became a big leaguer, and shared to some degree George's early success as a pitcher with the Red Sox. But, with the exception of a few times when Babe was out on permission, St. Mary's was the only home he knew from the time he was 7 until he reached the age of 19, when he went south with the late Jack Dunn's Baltimore International League Orioles.

Three brothers of St. Mary's—Brother Paul, head of the school; Brother Albert, in charge of athletics and recreation, and Brother Matthias, the Babe's patron saint—were chiefly responsible for molding George Herman's early character. Babe always retained his love and loyalty for the school and the Catholic brothers, who paved the way for his life of useful citizenry. He helped repeatedly in raising funds for the school; the St. Mary's band frequently played at Yankee Stadium, and in the Baltimore industrial school George Ruth was held up as a shining example of what a St. Mary's boy can do in the outside world.

At St. Mary's, they realize they can't count on all of their boys becoming great baseball stars, and the youngsters are taught trades so that they can support themselves in the outside world. And the particular trade they

something personal emanated from him which made everyone feel akin to the magnetic Babe.

By a curious turn of the wheel of fate, Ruth's death followed by less than a month the release of the motion picture on his life, "The Babe Ruth Story." Accompanied by his wife, Claire, he attended the premiere at the Astor Theatre, July 26. Physicians at Memorial Hospital had permitted him to visit the theater and see the picture, because "it might do him good." A cordon of police protected him from the crowd which wanted to slap him on the back in the old way, but he was under a terrific strain. He and his family remained only 20 minutes.

To those who were close enough to hear his husky voice, Babe said it was a "good picture," and he enjoyed seeing himself on the screen. What really went through his mind as he watched Bill Bendix portray Hollywood's version of his legendary career and exploits will never be known.

* * *

Lived on Borrowed Time

Friends and some of Babe's old intimates had known for some time that he was waging a losing battle. He rallied bravely from his severe illness of the winter of 1946-47, but physicians knew that his days were numbered.

In a way, his passing was much like the going of his former teammate in baseball's foremost "one-two punch," Lou Gehrig.

While Lou held on gamely to the end in 1941, Babe hoped "the docs," as he called them, would find some remedy for his condition.

The writer, who knew Ruth intimately and traveled with the Yankees when Babe was at the height of his vigor, talked to him at his Riverside Drive apartment not long before he went to Memorial Hospital for what again was to have been a check-up. And Babe commented: "Sure, when a fellow has been very sick, he gives some thought to leaving here. But I still have much to live for.

"You know I always loved life; I

GEORGE HERMAN RUTH . . . February 6, 1895 — August 16, 1948

the motion picture on Babe's life is a good illustration of the legends which have sprung and will spring from this fabulous character. Yet no player ever has left as great an impression on America's national game as this man, who changed baseball from the stolen base, play-for-one-run game to the home run circuses of today.

Drawing a salary greater than the President of the United States in his lush years, Ruth opened the eyes of all players to their earning possibilities. Once when some players from

a rival bench were riding Ruth, Waite Hoyt, then an ace Yankee pitcher, remarked: "They're a fine bunch of guys to be riding Babe. Why, they can thank him for half of the salary that they draw."

The Babe will stand out in history more prominently than any other American athlete. No matter whether a person knew anything about baseball, he knew Babe Ruth. And in a sense, that was true all over the world. In Japan, he was known almost as intimately as in the United

States, and once when his death was reported in 1925, a London newspaper printed a two-column obituary.

In the 1920s, his name appeared in print more often than any American other than the President of the United States. Yet, in the middle '90s, it would have taken a daring soothsayer to predict such a career for a waif born in a Baltimore (Md.) waterfront saloon.

So obscure was Ruth's birth and so humble his origin that for the greater part of his playing career, he be-

Babe Died Without Learning Cause of His Fatal Illness

The right-field fence—just 254 feet away—was an easy mark for the Babe, who smashed 54 home runs that season, 25 more than he had hit in 1919.

He hit 59 the next year but slipped to 35 in 1922 when he spent a third of the season under suspension. In 1923 Yankee Stadium opened and instantly won the nickname, "The House That Ruth Built." Its right-field fence was 296 feet away—still one of the easiest targets in the game. From 1926 to 1932, Ruth never hit less than .323 or had fewer than 41 homers in a season.

While Aaron played in Milwaukee and Atlanta ballparks that were also conducive to the long ball, he aimed at fences 330 feet from home.

Aaron faced other problems not encountered by Ruth—the pressure of breaking another man's record, constant media exposure, and the need to maintain prime condition and consistency (Aaron's one-season high was 47 homers, but Ruth hit 54 or more four times).

"In my mind," said Aaron, "a hitter is always able to hit, but first he must be fit and able to get on the field to play."

The six-foot, 180-pound Aaron was always in shape, but Ruth wasn't. His record reflected the fact that he was out of shape. After hitting 41 homers at age 37 in 1932, he slipped to 34, then 22, and finally just 6 in 1935 at age 40. The rotund Yankee slugger was felled by his own insatiable appetite for life's pleasures.

In 1925, when he was just 30, Ruth guzzled countless hot dogs, sodas, and beers during spring training and triggered a gastric revolt in his overworked digestive tract. Teammate Waite Hoyt once joked that if someone sawed Ruth in two, half the concessions of Yankee Stadium would fall out.

Ruth partied late into the night—and sometimes all night. Once before a big game, Washington's Goose Goslin tried to tire Ruth out by keeping him up 'til sunrise. Goslin limped back to his hotel room to recuperate, but Ruth went to Walter Reed Army Hospital to autograph balls. Later that day Ruth socked two homers while Goslin went 0-for-5.

"He had to be the greatest power hitter, the greatest player," said Stan Musial of Ruth. "He was good enough to pitch and bat fourth, like the star of a high school team."

When a young fan asked Babe Ruth if he could hit .400 by concentrating on hits instead of homers, he answered, "Four hundred? Hell, I could hit *five* hundred!"

The young Hank Aaron didn't pay much attention to the Babe Ruth legend. "Why should I have read about a man playing a game I couldn't get into at the time?" Aaron explained.

Aaron certainly did not copy Ruth's home-run swing. Ruth's blasts followed great, sweeping curves en route to the outfield seats, while Aaron specialized in line-drive shots. "The Sultan of Swat," for Babe Ruth, and "the Hammer," for Hank Aaron, were fitting nicknames.

Ruth wore a camel-hair coat, dangled a cigar, smiled broadly and easily, and tooled around in a snappy roadster. Hank Aaron, almost an introvert by contrast, drove a Chevrolet Caprice and never drew the attention of the media until he approached Ruth's record. Ruth had charisma; Aaron didn't. But the fans—except for a tiny minority that scribbled racial hate letters—backed the challenger when he neared the mark.

44 for 44

When Hank Aaron broke Babe Ruth's lifetime record for home runs on April 8, 1974, he did it on the fourth pitch of the fourth game of the fourth month against a pitcher wearing his own No. 44. The four-time home run king matched his uniform number with four 44-homer seasons, including one in which he tied for league lead with fellow No. 44 Willie McCovey.

Tough Tandem

Hank Aaron and Eddie Mathews homered in the same game 75 times, more than any other teammates.

Inside the Parker

Hank Aaron hit his only inside-the-park home run against a future U.S. senator. The future home run king, then an outfielder for the Atlanta Braves, did it on May 10, 1967, against Jim Bunning of the Philadelphia Phillies.

Another Hank Mark

Hank Aaron is the lifetime leader in total bases with 6,856. Stan Musial is second with 6,134.

Six Degrees

The opposing right fielder when Hank Aaron hit his last career home run on July 20, 1976 was Bobby Bonds, father of the man who eventually broke Aaron's record of 755 home runs. Aaron, playing for the Brewers at Milwaukee County Stadium, hit his farewell homer against Dick Drago of the California Angels.

53 for 53

Barry Bonds hit his 53rd home run on the 53rd anniversary of the death of Babe Ruth, who died at age 53. It was also the 53rd multi-homer game of Bonds's career. The final score, not surprisingly, was 5–3.

Barry's Bonanza

Barry Bonds became the National League home run king in 2006. That was the year he topped Henry Aaron's total of 733 in the NL. Aaron hit 22 more as a designated hitter for the Milwaukee Brewers, then in the American League.

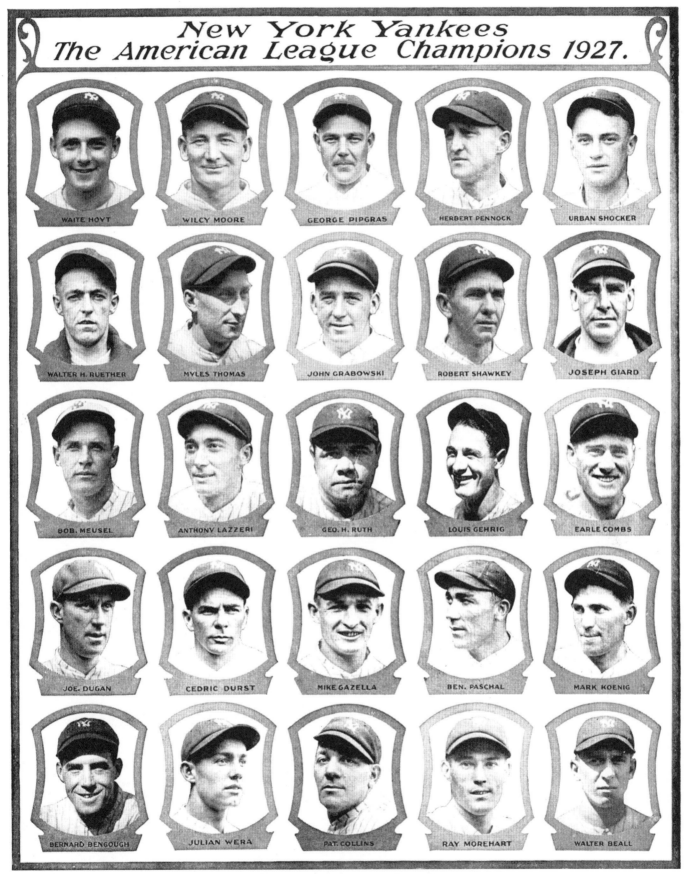

New York Yankees
The American League Champions 1927.

WAITE HOYT — WILCY MOORE — GEORGE PIPGRAS — HERBERT PENNOCK — URBAN SHOCKER

WALTER H. RUETHER — MYLES THOMAS — JOHN GRABOWSKI — ROBERT SHAWKEY — JOSEPH GIARD

BOB. MEUSEL — ANTHONY LAZZERI — GEO. H. RUTH — LOUIS GEHRIG — EARLE COMBS

JOE. DUGAN — CEDRIC DURST — MIKE GAZELLA — BEN. PASCHAL — MARK KOENIG

BERNARD BENGOUGH — JULIAN WERA — PAT. COLLINS — RAY MOREHART — WALTER BEALL

Greatest Team Ever?

The 1927 New York Yankees had Babe Ruth, Lou Gehrig, and a host of other heroes. When the team took batting practice before playing the Pittsburgh Pirates in the World Series, Pittsburgh's hitters looked on in amazement.

"I didn't always think 'home run' when I came to the plate," Aaron conceded after the record had fallen. "I was concentrating on getting a hit, trying to win the game. If a home run was needed, then I thought it was my duty to try and get it. First you play baseball, then you play to win, and then you go for home runs. The understanding of the fans is important."

A contemporary of Aaron's, switch-hitting infielder Pete Rose, set many batting records of his own. But he looked at Aaron with admiration.

"I felt like I knew Babe Ruth," he said. "And he was so great. But so was Henry Aaron."

Awards

Baseball honors its best players with a series of awards at the end of each season. Members of the media vote for the Most Valuable Player in each league, as well as the Rookie of the Year, Cy Young Award winner, Manager of the Year, and Comeback Player of the Year.

Several publications make their own awards. *The Sporting News* polls the players to pick All-Star lineups based on the entire season, a better perspective than the actual starting teams that clash in the annual midsummer classic. *Baseball Weekly* All-Stars and awards are based on the consensus of its staff.

Award winners invariably come from contending clubs, but there are exceptions. Ernie Banks twice won MVP honors when the Chicago Cubs finished fifth and Andre Dawson of the 1987 Cubs became the first Most Valuable Player whose team finished last.

League leaders in batting and pitching frequently win the writers' attention when ballots are taken. But there are exceptions there too.

Maury Wills was Most Valuable Player of the National League when he broke Ty Cobb's single-season record with 104 stolen bases in 1962, but Lou Brock failed to win the award when he stole 118 times in 1974. Both Wills and Brock played for clubs that narrowly missed the pennant during their big years, but the voters of 1974 handed the award to the leader of the championship club, Steve Garvey.

Willie Stargell, whose Pirates finished two and a half games behind in 1973, was equally deprived when writers named batting champion Pete Rose as the league's MVP. Stargell had hit 44 homers, driven home 119 runs, and recorded a .646 slugging average, while Rose had only 5 homers and 64 RBIs to go with his .338 average. But Cincinnati was a winner.

No one had a more justified complaint than Ted Williams, however. The Boston Red Sox slugger twice won the rare Triple Crown of batting—league leadership in batting average, home runs, and RBIs—but failed to win the American League's MVP trophy.

Williams did win the MVP in 1946, when the Red Sox finished first, and in 1949, when they missed by a game, but his 1942 and 1947 Triple Crowns were bypassed by writers who selected Yankees Joe Gordon and Joe DiMaggio, respectively.

Oddly, Lou Gehrig also missed the award in a Triple Crown season. Detroit's catcher/manager Mickey Cochrane hit .320 with only two homers and 76 runs batted in for the 1934 season but brought his club home first. In New York, Gehrig led the league with a .363 average, 49 homers, and 165 runs batted in. His slugging percentage was a resounding .796. But the New York Yankees finished second, seven games behind.

Babe Ruth leaves for spring training in 1930.

Photo Finish

Had either of the two Seattle voters placed him on their 1996 AL Most Valuable Player ballots, Seattle shortstop Alex Rodriguez would have beaten out Texas outfielder Juan Gonzalez. But Bob Finnigan and Jim Street placed Rodriguez third and fourth, respectively, allowing Gonzalez to win, 290–287, tying the three-point margin of Roger Maris over Mickey Mantle in 1960. The only closer vote had come in 1947, when Joe DiMaggio beat Ted Williams, 202–201.

Lonesome Sluggers

Since the advent of the MVP Award in 1931, more than a dozen players have had 50-homer seasons without winning the trophy that year. They include Mark McGwire (four times), Sammy Sosa (three times), Ralph Kiner (twice), Hank Greenberg, Mickey Mantle, Johnny Mize, Willie Mays, Cecil Fielder, Prince Fielder, Alex Rodriguez, Luis Gonzalez, Brady Anderson, Greg Vaughn, Andruw Jones, and Ken Griffey, Jr.

Triple Threats

To win a Triple Crown, a batter must lead his league in hitting, home runs, and runs batted in. It's a rare feat but not impossible, as these records show:

Year	Player & Club	AVG	HR	RBI
American League				
1901	Napoleon Lajoie, Athletics	.426	14	125
1909	Ty Cobb, Tigers	.377	9	107
1933	Jimmie Foxx, Athletics	.356	48	163
1934	Lou Gehrig, Yankees	.363	49	166
1942	Ted Williams, Red Sox	.356	36	137
1947	Ted Williams, Red Sox	.343	32	114
1956	Mickey Mantle, Yankees	.353	52	130
1966	Frank Robinson, Orioles	.316	49	122
1967	Carl Yastrzemski, Red Sox	.326	44	121
2012	Miguel Cabrera, Tigers	.330	44	139
National League				
1878	Paul Hines, Providence	.358	4	50
1894	Hugh Duffy, Boston	.438	18	145
1922	Rogers Hornsby, Cardinals	.401	42	152
1925	Rogers Hornsby, Cardinals	.403	39	143
1933	Chuck Klein, Phillies	.368	28	120
1937	Joe Medwick, Cardinals	.374	31	154

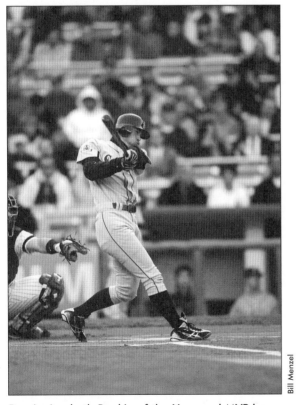

Bill Menzel

By winning both Rookie of the Year and MVP honors in 2001, Seattle's Ichiro Suzuki joined Fred Lynn of the 1975 Red Sox as the only men to take both awards in the same season. Ichiro, who uses only his first name, won after becoming the first player since Jackie Robinson in 1949 to lead the majors in batting (.350) and stolen bases (56).

The first MVPs were World Series opponents Lefty Grove, pitcher of the Philadelphia Athletics, and Frankie Frisch, second baseman of the St. Louis Cardinals. Their selection set a precedent of picking players from championship clubs.

Prior to 1931, when the Baseball Writers Association of America created the Most Valuable Player Award, each league occasionally rewarded its outstanding player on an annual basis. League awards were given from 1922 to 1929 and, prior to that, Chalmers Awards (automobiles) from 1911 to 1914. Neither had the prestige that the baseball writers gave to the MVP.

Since rookies were not considered bona fide candidates for MVP honors the writers launched a separate award for freshmen in 1947. The first Rookie of the Year was Jackie Robinson, who not only broke the color line, but made a successful conversion from second to first, led the league with 29 steals, and hit .297 to help the Dodgers win the pennant.

Frank Robinson and Orlando Cepeda were the only unanimous Rookies of the Year who later became unanimous MVPs. Robinson was also the only man to be MVP in both leagues.

Like the rookie award, which was given to one player in each league in 1949, the Cy Young Memorial Award for pitching excellence began as a single citation. Don Newcombe, who had been Rookie of the Year in 1949, was the initial winner in 1956, while another Dodger—southpaw Sandy Koufax—was the first unanimous choice seven years later.

Koufax was also a unanimous choice in 1965 and 1966, the last year of his career and also the last year of the single Cy Young Award. In the second year of separate honors, Denny McLain of the Detroit Tigers and Bob Gibson of the St. Louis Cardinals staged the only sweep of Cy Young and MVP honors. McLain, with a 31-6 record for the champion Tigers, was a unanimous choice for both—the only time that has happened.

The McLain/Gibson victory represented the only example of two pitchers winning MVP Awards in the same season.

Only four relief men—Jim Konstanty of the 1950 Phillies, Rollie Fingers of the 1981 Brewers, Willie Hernandez of the 1984 Tigers, and Dennis Eckersley of the 1992 Athletics—have won the MVP, and only eight—Sparky Lyle, Mike Marshall, Bruce Sutter, Steve Bedrosian, Fingers, Hernandez, Mark Davis, and Eckersley—have won the Cy Young Award.

Before Barry Bonds became the first four-time MVP in 2001, the only National Leaguers to win as many as three were Roy Campanella, Stan Musial, and Mike Schmidt. Joe DiMaggio, Mickey Mantle, Yogi Berra, and Jimmie Foxx won three each in the American League. Roger Clemens earned seven Cy Youngs Randy Johnson earned five, and Steve Carlton and Greg Maddux four each (including a record four straight for Maddux from 1992 to 1995). Gaylord Perry was the first to win the Cy Young in both leagues, a feat later duplicated by Randy Johnson, Pedro Martinez, Roger Clemens, Roy Halladay, and Max Scherzer.

MVP Anywhere

Robin Yount of the Milwaukee Brewers won the American League's MVP award as a shortstop in 1982 and as a center fielder in 1989.

Single-Season Stars

BATTING—Napoleon Lajoie, Phila. AL (1901), .426; Rogers Hornsby, St. L. NL (1924), .424; George Sisler, St. L. AL (1922), and Ty Cobb, Detr. AL (1911), .420.

HOME RUNS—Barry Bonds, S.F. NL (2001), 73; Mark McGwire, St. L. NL (1998), 70; Sammy Sosa, Chic. NL (1998), 66; McGwire (1999), 65; Sosa (2001), 64; Sosa (1999), 63; Roger Maris, N.Y. AL (1961), 61; Babe Ruth, N.Y. AL (1927), 60; Ruth (1921), Giancarlo Stanton, Miami (2017), 59; Jimmie Foxx, Phila. AL (1932), Hank Greenberg, Detr. (1938), McGwire, Oak.-St. L. (1997), and Ryan Howard, Phila. NL (2006), 58; Luis Gonzalez, Ariz. (2001), and Alex Rodriguez, Texas (2002) 57; Hack Wilson, Chic. NL (1930) and Ken Griffey Jr., Sea. (1997 and 1998), 56.

RUNS BATTED IN—Hack Wilson, Chic. NL (1930), 191; Lou Gehrig, N.Y. AL (1931), 185; Hank Greenberg, Detr. AL (1937), 184; Gehrig (1927) and Jimmie Foxx, Bost. AL (1938), 175; Gehrig (1930), 173.

RUNS SCORED—Ruth (1921), 177; Gehrig (1936), 167; Ruth (1928) and Gehrig (1931), 163; Ruth (1920 and 1927) and Chuck Klein, Phila. NL (1930), 158; Rogers Hornsby, Chic. NL (1929), 156.

STOLEN BASES—Rickey Henderson, Oak. AL (1982), 130; Lou Brock, St. L. NL (1974), 118; Vince Coleman, St. L. NL (1985), 110; Coleman (1987), 109; Henderson (1983), 108; Coleman (1986), 107; Maury Wills, L.A. NL (1962), 104; Henderson (1980), 100.

PITCHING VICTORIES—Jack Chesbro, N.Y. AL (1904), 41; Ed Walsh, Chic. AL (1908), 40; Christy Mathewson, N.Y. NL (1908), 37; Walter Johnson, Wash. AL (1913), 36; Joe McGinnity, N.Y. NL (1904), 35.

EARNED RUN AVERAGE—Dutch Leonard, Bost. AL (1914), .096; Mordecai Brown, Chic. NL (1906), 1.04; Bob Gibson, St. L. NL (1968), 1.12; Mathewson (1909) and Johnson (1913), 1.14.

GAMES PITCHED—Mike Marshall, L.A. NL (1974), 106; Kent Tekulve, Pitt. NL (1979), and Salomón Torres, Pitt. NL (2006), 94; Marshall, Mont. NL (1973), and Pedro Feliciano, N.Y. NL (2010) 92; Tekulve (1978), 91; Marshall, Minn. AL (1979), Tekulve, Phil. NL (1987), and Wayne Granger, Cinn. (1969), 90.

GAMES SAVED IN RELIEF—Francisco Rodriguez, Anaheim (2008), 62; Bobby Thigpen, Chic. AL (1990), 57; John Smoltz, Atl. (2002) and Eric Gagne, L.A. NL (2003), 55 each; Trevor Hoffman, S.D. (1998) and Randy Myers, Chi. NL (1993), and Mariano Rivera, N.Y. AL (2004), 53 each; Gagne, L.A. (2002), 52; Dennis Eckersley, Oak. (1992), Rod Beck, S.F. (2008), Jim Johnson, Balt. (2012), Mark Melancon, Pitt. (2015), and Jeurys Familia, N.Y. NL (2016), 51 each; Rivera, N.Y. AL (2001), Johnson, Balt. (2015), and Craig Kimbrel, Atl. (2013), 50 each.

STRIKEOUTS—Nolan Ryan, Calif. AL (1973), 383; Sandy Koufax, L.A. NL (1965), 382; Randy Johnson, Ariz. NL (2001), 372; Ryan (1974), 367; Johnson (1999), 364; Johnson (2000), 347; Rube Waddell, Phila. AL (1904), 349; Bob Feller, Cleve. (1946), 348; Ryan (1977), 341.

WINNING PERCENTAGE (15 wins minimum)—ElRoy Face, Pitt. (1959), .947; Johnny Allen, Cleve. AL (1937), .938; Greg Maddux, Atl. (1995), .905; Randy Johnson, Sea. (1995),

Believe It or Not

Stan Musial never won a home-run crown and Willie Mays never led in runs batted in.

Wedding Date

Even his wedding couldn't interrupt Lou Gehrig's streak of 2,130 consecutive games; he played on the day he was married.

Famous Fan

Wally Pipp was in the stands when Lou Gehrig stopped his streak on May 2, 1939. Only 11,379 fans were in Briggs Stadium, Detroit, when the Yankees captain took himself out of the lineup. He had played in a Kansas City exhibition game on June 12, the day the Hall of Fame opened. He checked into the Mayo Clinic the next day and received his fateful diagnosis.

Ted over Ty

Although Ty Cobb took more batting titles (12), Ted Williams led his league in on-base percentage more often (12 times).

Terrific Ted

Ted Williams had a lifetime on-base percentage of .482. That's no typo, folks.

Trophy Trifecta

Willie Stargell was the only player to be MVP of the regular season, the League Championship Series, and the World Series in the same season (1979).

Twin MVPs

The National League had a pair of Most Valuable Players in 1979, when Keith Hernandez (Cardinals) and Willie Stargell (Pirates) deadlocked for first place in the annual voting. It was the only tie in the history of the award, given since 1931.

With pitchers and hitters recognized through various awards, sure-handed fielders—who contribute handsomely but anonymously to many championships—were given an award of their own. In 1957, the Rawlings Sporting Goods Company, in conjunction with *The Sporting News*, created the annual Gold Glove Awards. Voting procedure changed several times to include the media, the players, and the managers. One team was selected in 1957, but separate teams for each league were chosen thereafter. Winners receive a Gold Glove trophy, presented before a game at their home stadium the following year; repeat winners get an additional gold crest.

Strong Start

Grover Cleveland Alexander won 28 games for the Phillies as a rookie in 1911, 37 years before the creation of the Rookie of the Year Award.

Marichal Shut Out

With six 20-win seasons and 243 victories during a Hall of Fame career that stretched from 1960 to 1975, Juan Marichal should have been an annual contender for the Cy Young Award. But he never received a vote because of stiff competition. Here's why:

		W	L	ERA
1963	Marichal	25	8	2.41
	Sandy Koufax	25	5	1.88
1964	Marichal	21	8	2.48
	Dean Chance	25	5	1.88
1965	Marichal	22	13	2.13
	Sandy Koufax	26	8	2.04
1966	Marichal	25	6	2.23
	Sandy Koufax	27	9	1.73
1968	Marichal	26	9	2.43
	Bob Gibson	22	9	1.12
1969	Marichal	21	11	2.10
	Tom Seaver	25	7	2.21

.900; Ron Guidry, N.Y. AL (1978), .893; Fred Fitzsimmons, Brooklyn (1940), .889; Lefty Grove, Phila. AL (1931), .886.

Lifetime Leaders

BATTING—Ty Cobb, .367; Rogers Hornsby, .358; Shoeless Joe Jackson, .356; Ted Williams and Tris Speaker, .344 each; Babe Ruth and Harry Heilmann, .342 each; Bill Terry, .341; George Sisler and Lou Gehrig, .340 each.

HOME RUNS—Barry Bonds, 762; Hank Aaron, 755; Babe Ruth, 714; Alex Rodriguez, 696; Willie Mays, 660; Ken Griffey Jr., 630; Albert Pujols, 614; Jim Thome, 612; Sammy Sosa, 609; Frank Robinson, 586; Mark McGwire, 583; Harmon Killebrew, 573; Rafael Palmeiro, 569; Reggie Jackson, 563; Manny Ramirez, 555; Mike Schmidt, 548; David Ortiz, 541; Mickey Mantle, 536; Jimmie Foxx, 534; Willie McCovey, Ted Williams, and Frank Thomas, 521; Ernie Banks and Eddie Mathews, 512; Mel Ott, 511; Gary Sheffield, 509; Eddie Murray, 504.

RUNS BATTED IN—Hank Aaron, 2297; Babe Ruth, 2214; Alex Rodriguez, 2086; Cap Anson, 2075; Barry Bonds 1996; Lou Gehrig, 1995; Stan Musial, 1951; Ty Cobb, 1933; Jimmie Foxx, 1922; Eddie Murray, 1917; Willie Mays, 1903; Mel Ott, 1860; Carl Yastrzemski, 1844; Ted Williams, 1839; Ken Griffey, Jr., 1836.

RUNS SCORED— Rickey Henderson, 2295; Ty Cobb, 2244; Barry Bonds, 2227; Hank Aaron and Babe Ruth, 2174 each; Pete Rose, 2165; Willie Mays, 2062; Alex Rodriguez, 2021; Cap Anson, 1999; Stan Musial, 1949.

STOLEN BASES—Rickey Henderson, 1406; Lou Brock, 938; Ty Cobb, 897; Tim Raines, 808; Vince Coleman, 752; Eddie Collins, 741; Max Carey, 738; Honus Wagner, 723; Joe Morgan, 689; Willie Wilson, 668; Bert Campaneris, 649.

PITCHING VICTORIES—Cy Young, 511; Walter Johnson, 417; Grover Cleveland Alexander and Christy Mathewson,

Warren Spahn (left) holding his 1957 Cy Young Award and Hank Aaron (right) holding his MVP award.

Milwaukee Journal

373 each; Warren Spahn, 363; Greg Maddux, 355; Roger Clemens, 354; Steve Carlton, 329; Eddie Plank, 326; Don Sutton and Nolan Ryan, 324; Phil Niekro, 318; Gaylord Perry, 314.

EARNED RUN AVERAGE (minimum 1,500 innings)—Ed Walsh, 1.82; Addie Joss, 1.88; Smokey Joe Wood, 2.03; Three Finger Brown, 2.06; Christy Mathewson, 2.13; Rube Waddell, 2.16; Walter Johnson, 2.17.

GAMES PITCHED—Jesse Orosco, 1252; Mike Stanton, 1178; John Franco, 1119; Mariano Rivera, 1115; Dennis Eckersley, 1071; Hoyt Wilhelm, 1070; Dan Plesac, 1064; Mike Timlin, 1058; Kent Tekulve, 1050; LaTroy Hawkins, 1042; Trevor Hoffman, 1035; Lee Smith and Jose Mesa, 1022 each; Roberto Hernandez, 1010; Mike Jackson, 1005; Goose Gossage, 1002.

GAMES SAVED IN RELIEF—Mariano Rivera, 652; Trevor Hoffman, 601; Lee Smith, 478; Francisco Rodriguez, 430; John Franco, 424; Billy Wagner, 422; Dennis Eckersley, 390; Joe Nathan, 377; Jonathan Papelbon, 368; Jeff Reardon, 367; Troy Percival, 358; Randy Myers, 347; Rollie Fingers, 341; John Wetteland, 330; Francisco Cordero, 329; Roberto Hernandez, 326; Jose Mesa, 321; Huston Street, 324; Jose Mesa, 321; Todd Jones, 319; Rick Aguilera, 318; Robb Nen, 314.

STRIKEOUTS—Nolan Ryan, 5714; Randy Johnson, 4875; Roger Clemens, 4672; Steve Carlton, 4136; Bert Blyleven, 3701; Tom Seaver, 3640; Don Sutton, 3574; Gaylord .Perry, 3534; Walter Johnson, 3509; Greg Maddux, 3371; Phil Niekro, 3342; Ferguson Jenkins, 3192; Pedro Martinez, 3154; Bob Gibson, 3117; Curt Schilling, 3116; and John Smoltz, 3084.

WINNING PERCENTAGE (100 wins minimum)—Spud Chandler, .717; Clayton Kershaw, .692; Whitey Ford, .690; Pedro Martinez, .687; Don Gullett, .686; Mike Mussina, .682; Lefty Grove, .680; Babe Ruth and Joe Wood, .671; Vic Raschi, .667; Christy Mathewson, .665; Roy Halladay, .659; Roger Clemens, .658; Sal Maglie, .657; Sandy Koufax, .655; Johnny Allen, .654; Max Scherzer, .653; Ron Guidry, David Price, and Stephen Strasburg, all .651; Lefty Gomez, .649.

* Records through 2017 season (modern era only, 1900–present)

Future Hall of Famers Al Simmons, Lou Gehrig, Babe Ruth, and Jimmie Foxx gave the American League enormous firepower in the 1933 All-Star Game, the first ever played.

400 Total Bases, Season

Babe Ruth, Yankees, 1921	457
Rogers Hornsby, Cardinals, 1922	450
Lou Gehrig, Yankees, 1927	447
Chuck Klein, Phillies, 1930	445
Jimmie Foxx, Athletics, 1932	438
Stan Musial, Cardinals, 1948	429
Sammy Sosa, Cubs, 2001	425
Hack Wilson, Cubs, 1930	423
Chuck Klein, Phillies, 1932	420
Lou Gehrig, Yankees, 1930	419
Luis Gonzalez, Diamondbacks, 2001	419
Joe DiMaggio, Yankees, 1937	418
Babe Ruth, Yankees, 1927	417
Babe Herman, Dodgers, 1930	416
Sammy Sosa, Cubs, 1998	416
Barry Bonds, Giants, 2001	411
Lou Gehrig, Yankees, 1931	410
Lou Gehrig, Yankees, 1934	409
Rogers Hornsby, Cubs, 1929	409
Larry Walker, Rockies, 1997	409
Joe Medwick, Cardinals, 1937	406
Jim Rice, Red Sox, 1978	406
Todd Helton, Rockies, 2000	405
Chuck Klein, Phillies, 1929	405
Hal Trosky, Indians, 1936	405
Jimmie Foxx, Athletics, 1933	403
Lou Gehrig, Yankees, 1936	403
Todd Helton, Rockies, 2001	402
Hank Aaron, Braves, 1959	400

Firm Farewell

Sandy Koufax was the only man to win a Cy Young Award in his last season. He went 27-9 with 27 complete games, 317 strikeouts, and a 1.73 ERA in 1966 before arthritis forced him to retire at age 30. In his final five years, the Dodger lefty went 111-34, won five straight ERA crowns and pitched four no-hitters.

MVP Controversy

Though Pedro Martinez won All-Star MVP honors and the AL's Cy Young Award for 1999, he lost the MVP race because two writers refused to list him among their Top 10 choices. Had either George King of *The New York Post* or La Velle E. Neal III of the *Minneapolis Star* cast a first-place vote for the Red Sox star, or even placed him fourth or higher, Martinez would have won. Though he had more first-place votes than winner Ivan Rodriguez, Martinez missed becoming the fourth AL starter to win both the MVP and Cy Young in the same season.

Rogers Hornsby compiled the best lifetime batting average of any National League player. His .358 mark ranked second to Ty Cobb of the American (.367).

Ruth's Records

Babe Ruth may have lost the single-season and lifetime home run records but still owns major league marks for most seasons leading a league in slugging (13), homers (12), and runs (8). He also had the most 40-homer seasons (11) and the most consecutive ones (7) plus the most home run crowns (12) and was the only man to lead his league in three different decades.

Pete Rose, who spent most of his career with the Cincinnati Reds, collected more hits than any man in baseball history. Andy Warhol finished this portrait in 1985.

Bat Master

Three-time .400 hitter Rogers Hornsby, whose .424 in 1924 remains the top mark of the modern era, let nothing irk him at bat. Boston Braves' catcher Al Spohrer—a former Hornsby teammate—knew he liked a good steak almost as much as he liked a base hit.

Spohrer started talking food as soon as Hornsby came to the plate. As the Chicago pitcher whizzed across two strikes, the catcher told Hornsby that his wife had discovered a Boston butcher who provided excellent cuts. He also said his wife had become an excellent cook. He closed with a suggestion that Hornsby stop in for dinner the next time the Cubs came to Boston.

Just as Spohrer made his last remark, Hornsby, who took a big stride from the closed stance, stepped into a pitch and hit it far over the left-field wall at Wrigley Field. As he reached home, he spotted the frustrated catcher and said, "What night shall we make it, Al?"

Famous Families

Baseball has always been a family game—for players as well as spectators.

For more than a dozen seasons, the Pittsburgh Pirates pounded rivals with two left-handed-hitting outfielders—brothers named Paul and Lloyd Waner. The Waners were in the majors from 1927 to 1945—long enough to hit well over .300 and earn separate plaques in the Hall of Fame. When they hit consecutive homers in 1938, they became the only brothers to do it.

The three DiMaggios never played together; the three Alous and the three Cruz brothers also spent most of their careers with opposing clubs. Paul Reuschel did spend some time with brother Rick of the Cubs, and the two produced the only combined shutout ever thrown by brothers.

Joe Niekro was also teamed with Phil for a spell in Atlanta, but wilted in the bullpen and found himself only after returning to a starter's role elsewhere. Pitcher Ken Brett, who once homered in four consecutive starts, gave younger brother George, a third baseman, various hitting tips, and George won three batting titles with the Kansas City Royals. Lee May and Carlos May were also strong-hitting brothers in the '70s.

Fraternal third basemen were Ken Boyer of the Cardinals and Clete Boyer, who played for the Yankees and the Braves. A third brother, Cloyd, pitched for the Cards before Ken came up in 1955. St. Louis also signed a pair of hot pitching prospects in the McDaniels—Lindy and Von—but the latter was curtailed by a sore arm early in his career. Lindy became one of the top bullpen aces in baseball history.

Joe and Luke Sewell, shortstop and catcher, formed an earlier brother combination, teaming their talents for the Indians of the '20s, while New York clubs in opposite leagues owned the

Good Genes

In 2008, Aaron Boone became the fourth member of his family with 1,000 hits, joining grandfather Ray, father Bob, and brother Bret.

Wolf's Lair

When Philadelphia southpaw Randy Wolf started the nightcap of an April 18, 2001, twin bill, brother Jim was the third-base umpire—a National League first.

No Wizard of Ozzie

Being the identical twin brother of a baseball superstar doesn't always help. Ozzie Canseco, brother of Jose, never hit a home run during a major league career that lasted only 24 games.

Humble Start

Calvin Griffith was a batboy for the 1924–1925 Washington Senators, the team owned by his uncle and adoptive father Clark Griffith.

Pittsburgh Pirates

Because baseballs were costly, brothers Lloyd and Paul Waner—Pittsburgh's "Big Poison" and "Little Poison"—played corncob baseball as youths on an Oklahoma farm. "The constant practice of hitting the strange curves of the corncob did more than anything else to build up my batting," Paul explained. "You had to keep your eye on the cob because it would blind you if it hit you in the eye or hurt if it hit your head. There were more curves in those corncob games than I have ever seen in a real baseball game."

Multiple Brothers

Hall of Famer Ed Delahanty, who played at the turn of the century, had four brothers in the majors, and veteran manager Steve O'Neill, Cleveland catcher of the World War I era, had three. There were never more than three Delahantys or two O'Neills in the majors at the same time.

Why Tigers Kept Quiet

The Detroit Tigers kept arguments to a minimum on July 14, 1972. The brother of catcher Tom Haller was plate umpire Bill Haller.

Hill of Benes

Brothers pitched for the same team in the same postseason game for the first time in 1996, when Andy and Alan Benes worked for the St. Louis Cardinals vs. the Atlanta Braves in Game 4 of the NLCS.

Twins Tangle

When Mark Mimbs beat brother Mike, 6–5, for Norfolk against Columbus in an International League game on April 29, 1998, it was the first time twin pitchers had opposed each other in professional baseball.

Hank (No. 44) and Tommie Aaron, teammates with the Braves in the '60s, hold the record for home runs by brothers. Hank hit 755 and Tommie 13.

Joe and Dom DiMaggio were part of a three-brother tandem that played in the majors at the same time. Joe was with the Yankees, Dom with the Red Sox, and Vince with the Pirates.

Meusels—Irish with the Giants and Bob with the Yankees. Both Meusels played the outfield and hit with authority; Irish ended at .310, Bob at .309.

Tony and Billy Conigliaro, outfielders both, played together briefly with the Red Sox in the '60s, but Joe Torre, a catcher/first baseman, joined the Braves just as brother Frank left.

The brothers Dean proved to be dynamite as pitchers or talkers. Jay Hanna had acquired the nickname "Dizzy" before Paul joined him with the Gashouse Gang Cardinals of 1934. Dizzy was less than successful in hanging the nickname "Daffy" on his younger brother, but he made good his preseason promise that they would combine for 45 victories.

Dizzy won 30 games and Paul 19—plus two apiece in the winning World Series against Detroit—and engineered a double shutout against Brooklyn that included a nightcap no-hitter by rookie Paul. "Why didn't you tell me you wuz gonna throw a no-hitter?" asked Dizzy, who allowed three hits in his game. "I woulda throwed one too."

Although the Deans might have been the most famous pitching brothers, they were not the most successful. Phil and Joe Niekro won 539 games, 10 more than Gaylord and Jim Perry. The Niekros pitched more innings than any other brother tandem, while the Perrys recorded more strikeouts.

The Perrys combined for 38 wins in their only season as teammates (with the 1974 Indians) and, six years later, were the only brothers to pitch against each other in the same All-Star Game. They are also the only brothers to win Cy Young Awards.

The two Aarons out-homered all other brothers—including several trios—but the three Alous played the most games. The Waners had the most hits, while the DiMaggios had the most runs batted in.

There have been 15 brother batteries and five fraternal double-play combinations, including Cal and Bill Ripken (1987–1992). The best pitcher/catcher tandems were Mort and Walker Cooper and Wes and Rick Ferrell.

In 1941 Joe and Dom DiMaggio became the first brothers to appear as teammates on an All-Star team, while Carlos and Lee May were the first brothers to play on opposite sides in 1969.

Roberto and Sandy Alomar Jr. were All-Star rivals in 1990 but teammates a year later.

Nearly 350 fraternal pairs have played in the majors, but the first father and son to play at the same time were the Griffeys (Ken Sr. and Jr.), on different teams in 1989 and together in 1990. They are also the only father and son to win MVP honors in the All-Star Game (12 years apart).

In 2001 Tim Raines Jr. played in the same outfield with his father after the Orioles obtained Senior late in the season.

Baseball history lists more than 120 other father-and-son pairs. Some of those fathers even managed their own sons but Cal Ripken Sr. was the only man who managed two sons simultaneously.

In 1992, the Boones became baseball's first three-generation family when Bret, son of Bob and grandson of Ray, made his debut. The Bells became the second three years later when David, son of Buddy and grandson of Gus, reached the majors.

Six 1997 All-Stars were sons of former All-Stars: Roberto and Sandy Alomar (sons of Sandy Sr.); Moises Alou (Felipe); Barry Bonds (Bobby); Ken Griffey Jr. (Ken Sr.); and Todd Hundley (Randy).

KEN GRIFFEY JR.
outfielder   SEATTLE MARINERS™

Ken Griffey Jr., then with the Seattle Mariners, got an unprecedented opportunity in August 1990 when the Mariners acquired his father, Ken Griffey Sr. The Griffeys, who one year earlier had become the first father and son to play in the majors simultaneously, thus became the first father and son to play for the same team at the same time. Senior and Junior batted second and third while playing left and center field, respectively. They even hit consecutive home runs against the California Angels on September 14.

When Dizzy Dean predicted, during 1934 spring training, that he and brother Paul would combine for 45 wins, skeptics laughed. Paul had yet to pitch a big league inning. But Dizzy was prophetic: the Deans won 49—30 for Dizzy and 19 for Paul. One of Paul's wins was the only no-hitter by a member of the Dean family.

My Turn

On July 5, 1935, Tony Cuccinello of the Brooklyn Dodgers and brother Al of the New York Giants became the first brothers on opposing teams to homer in the same game. Brooklyn won 14–4.

Niekro Brothers Battle

When Phil Niekro (Braves) beat Joe Niekro (Cubs), 8-3, on July 4, 1967, it was the first time brothers had opposed each other since Jesse Barnes (Robins) beat Virgil Barnes (Giants), 7-6, on May 3, 1927. The Niekros met six other times—one of them a 1–0 win for Joe with the expansion San Diego Padres of 1969.

Olympic track star Jim Thorpe (right) who teamed briefly with Chief Meyer as a New York Giant, hit .252 in seven seasons. His biggest hit scored the run that ended the 1917 double no-hitter between Fred Toney and Hippo Vaughn. Thorpe also played pro football.

Century Club

Mel and Todd Stottlemyre are the only father-and-son pitching tandem to both reach triple digits in victories.

30/30 Family

Bobby and Barry Bonds, both slugging outfielders, are the only father-and-son tandem to hit 30 home runs and steal 30 bases in the same season. Barry tied Bobby's record when he did it for the fifth time in 1997. Barry and Bobby Bonds joined the same team for the first time in 1993 when the San Francisco Giants signed the son as a player and his dad as a batting coach.

Remember the Alomar

The San Diego Padres traded brothers Sandy Alomar Jr. and Roberto Alomar to American League teams in separate winter meetings trades in 1989 and 1990, respectively. In 1991 the Alomars became the first brothers to start the All-Star Game since Joe and Dom DiMaggio started for the American League in 1949.

Two-Sport Stars

Overlapping seasons make it difficult for baseball players to tackle another professional sport, but quite a few have tried and succeeded.

Long before Bo Jackson and Deion Sanders balanced baseball and football careers, baseball players Christy Mathewson, Charlie Dressen, Rube Waddell, and Jim Thorpe also played pro football. George "Pop" Halas, who gained fame as coach of the Chicago Bears of the National Football League, hit .091 in his sole season in the majors—as the last Yankee right fielder before Babe Ruth. Greasy Neale, who led the Philadelphia Eagles to the NFL title in 1949, hit .259 in seven full seasons as an outfielder, 1916–1922.

Baseball/basketball switchers included Ron Reed, Steve Hamilton, Dick Groat, Chuck Connors, Dave DeBusschere, and Gene Conley.

DeBusschere had a 3-4 career record with the White Sox in the '60s, but the 6'6", 220-pound athlete thrived in basketball and eventually became commissioner of the American Basketball Association. In his first year as a pro, he tried to balance a two-year, $25,000 contract from the Detroit Pistons with a $70,000 signing bonus from the White Sox. Gene Conley, center for several NBA clubs, was also a successful pitcher—and an example for DeBusschere.

"I like all sports," he said. "When it's basketball season, I like basketball, and when it's baseball season, I like baseball."

Had pro football, basketball, or hockey offered the financial promise of baseball before World War II, several key baseball figures might have opted for other sports.

Boston Red Sox slugger Jackie Jensen, American League Most Valuable Player in 1958, was an All-American football player who managed to play in both the Rose Bowl and the World Series. Chuck Essegian, who hit two pinch-homers in the Series for the 1959 Dodgers, was the only man to play in the Rose Bowl and hit a home run in the World Series.

In addition to Jensen and Essegian, college football stars who chose baseball as a career included Frankie Frisch, Mickey Cochrane, Jackie Robinson, and Dave Winfield. Frisch was captain of Fordham's baseball, basketball, and football teams, and Winfield starred in the same three sports at Minnesota. Cochrane topped them all; he was a five-way star at Boston University—baseball, football, basketball, track, and boxing.

Baseball's Funny Men

Joe Garagiola was right when he said baseball is a funny game. Baseball history is filled with practical jokes, hard-to-believe anecdotes, and one-liners that could keep a comic in business for months.

It's possible to pick an All-Star team of funny men: C-Yogi Berra; 1B-Catfish Metkovich; 2B-Germany Schaefer; SS-Rabbit Maranville; 3B-Doug Rader; OF-Babe Herman, Jim Piersall, and Ping Bodie; P-Rube Waddell, Dizzy Dean, and Lefty Gomez, starters, and Sparky Lyle, Moe Drabowsky, and Billy

Loes, relievers; MGR-Casey Stengel (American) and Charlie Grimm (National).

Berra, a Hall of Fame catcher who was one of five men to manage championship teams in both leagues, has always been the subject of kidding because of his short, squat appearance and long nose. When the New York Mets persuaded him to come out of retirement and serve as Warren Spahn's catcher in 1965 (when Berra was 40 and Spahn was 44), he was asked if he could remember any older battery. "I don't know if we'll be the oldest, but we'll certainly be the ugliest," Yogi replied.

He always came up with the right comment at the right time. As a youth, someone asked how he liked school. "Closed," Berra responded. When hometown fans honored him during his rookie year of 1947 at St. Louis' Sportsman's Park, he blurted into the mike, "I want to thank everyone for making this night necessary." Twenty-five years later, when presented with a $25 check for a radio interview with longtime announcer Jack Buck, he said, "You've known me all these years and you can't spell my name?" The check was made out to "the Bearer."

In the days of train travel, the Yankees often played "Twenty Questions." On his 19th question, Berra asked, "Is the subject living?" Told that he was, Berra then asked, "Is the subject living *now*?"

In the clubhouse, Yogi once received a message from his wife that she wouldn't be home after the game because she was going to see *Dr. Zhivago*. The catcher wondered aloud, "What's wrong with her now?"

Relaxing before a game, Yogi wandered up to longtime coach Frank Crosetti. "Remember the first time you saw me?" he asked.

The Forsch Brothers

When Ken Forsch (Astros) pitched a no-hitter against Atlanta in April 1979, the Forsch family became the first to boast two brothers who had both pitched no-hitters. Brother Bob (Cardinals) had pitched a no-hit game in 1978.

Thanks, Bro

Joe Niekro hit his only major league homer against brother Phil, beating him in a 1976 game. Together, the Niekros won more games (538) than any other pair of pitching brothers.

Three of a Kind

As a 1963 game progressed in New York, the San Francisco Giants found themselves with a major league first—an outfield manned entirely by brothers. Matty, Jesus, and Felipe Alou contributed another first when they batted back-to-back-to-back in the eighth inning. All three hit groundouts.

Ray Boetel

Max Patkin (right), clowning here with look-alike Rusty Riley of the West Palm Beach Braves, never missed a show in a 40-year career that brought him into 4,000 ballparks. Once a Class A pitcher, Patkin began his series of one-night stands in 1951, and has traveled more than three million miles since. He gained fame for an uncanny ability to twist his body into many odd positions.

Stengel Gave
Brooklyn the Bird

Traded to Pittsburgh in 1918 after six years in Brooklyn, Casey Stengel was booed his first time up. In the outfield, he noticed a sparrow had caught itself on the fence. Seizing the opportunity, he tucked the bird under his cap. When he came up again, the crowd again booed— as expected. Stengel called time, stepped back, and gave a sweeping bow, allowing the bird to escape.

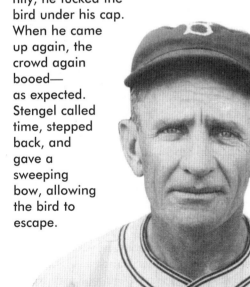

National League

Crosetti responded, "Sure, you were just coming out of the navy and were wearing a sailor suit."

"I bet you didn't think I looked like a ballplayer," said Berra.

"You didn't even look like a sailor," the coach answered.

In the game, Berra often applied his wit, but he was an alert, aggressive player. One day he questioned an umpire's call. "Turn around or I'll bite your head off," the ump stormed. "In that case," said Berra, "You'll have more brains in your stomach than you have in your head!"

When he was beaned and X-rayed in Detroit, a writer seized the opportunity to write, "X-Rays of Berra's head showed nothing."

But Berra's proclivity to use the wrong word or say the wrong thing at times did not diminish his stature among opponents or teammates. Stengel once said of him, "Yogi is the smartest baseball man on my club. He can bat against a pitcher once and know more about him than the pitcher's mother."

Babe Herman, who compiled a .324 lifetime average in 13 seasons, had some Yogi Berra in him—plus a lot more. "I'm a serious fellow," he told Brooklyn writers. "I even read books." A reporter was ready. "What did you think of the Napoleonic Era?" he asked. "I think it should have been scored a hit," Herman replied.

The Dodger outfielder, who had a tendency to cause foul-ups on the base paths, disdained the clown image and told the writers to get off his case. Satisfied, Herman whipped a cigar from his pocket and a writer offered to light it. "Never mind, it's already lit," said Herman, who took a puff to prove the point.

On a steamy summer day in St. Louis, he arrived at the ballpark in a pure white suit. "My, how cool you look!" said a well-dressed, well-built young woman. Herman surveyed her carefully. "You don't look too hot yourself," he replied.

Lefty Gomez, a contemporary of Herman's in the '30s, was not only a great pitcher but also a great talker. One night he argued with Jimmie Dykes about how to pitch to a hitter with two men on base. They decided to have Mike Kelly settle the argument, but Kelly—asleep in his room—told them, "Go away. Wait until tomorrow." At that point, Gomez said, "What? And leave two men on base??"

Pitching to slugger Jimmie Foxx was easy, according to the Yankee star. "I give him my best pitch and then run to back up third."

In 1934 Gomez dominated American League pitchers but maintained a weight of only 165 pounds. A club executive told him, "Put on 10 pounds and you'll make them forget Jack Chesbro (an earlier Yankee who won 41 games in 1904)." After Gomez listened, but sank to an 11-15 record, he told the official, "Forget Chesbro? Hell, I almost made them forget Gomez."

El Goofy—a nickname he acquired for obvious reasons—went out with a bang. Traded to the lowly Boston Braves, he said, "I'm throwing twice as hard but the ball is only going half as fast."

Pitchers, as a group, seem to have a zany streak. En route to a 25-win season in 1904, Rube Waddell of the Athletics took a 1–0 lead into the ninth against Cleveland. Before anyone was out, the bases were loaded. Waddell waved in his outfielders, instructing them to sit on the fringes of the infield, while he proceeded to strike out the side.

Waddell once ran out the side exit of the ballpark in pursuit of a fire engine. The incident occurred between innings of a game he was pitching. When the sides changed, the A's had no pitcher.

Another time Rube woke up in a hospital bed with a monstrous hangover and numerous bandages. Asked how he got there, playful catcher Ossie Schreckengost reconstructed the situation. "You said you could fly so you opened the window and jumped," he said. He would have stopped him, said the catcher, if not for the $100 he bet that he could do it.

Dizzy Dean once told his catcher to drop a foul pop. He had bet a friend that he would strike out Vince DiMaggio (Joe's brother) four consecutive times. He was working on number four when DiMaggio popped up. The catcher obliged—while manager Frankie Frisch grew frantic in the dugout—and Dean completed the strikeout, winning a grand total of $80.

Manager Charley Dressen of the Dodgers wondered about one of his pitchers—Billy Loes—before the 1952 World Series against the Yankees. "The paper says you picked the Yankees to beat us in seven games," shouted the irate manager. "I was misquoted," Loes stammered. "I picked them in six games!"

Bill Lee, Red Sox southpaw of the '70s, wore No. 37 but admitted he would have preferred No. 337. "If you turn that upside down, it spells LEE," he said. "Then I could stand upside down and people would know me right away."

Yankee reliever Sparky Lyle sat on birthday cakes, sawed up chairs, and pulled myriad other practical jokes, but his best involved rookie pitcher Rick Sawyer. For a week, Lyle watched Sawyer's shower routine. Then he "borrowed" his towel and smeared the underside with black shoe polish. He returned it to the rack exactly the way Sawyer had left it. Finished with his shower, Sawyer first dried his hands, then his face. It took him awhile to figure out why he was suddenly turning black.

Moe Drabowsky, an even more active prankster than Lyle, said he had a definite need for enjoying the lighter side. "If you think about how you're going to pitch to Roberto Clemente with the bases loaded," he said, "you'll go crazy. You have to find humor in the game."

A great imitator, Drabowsky learned the phone numbers of all the bullpens in the league and ordered opposing relievers to warm up at unusual times. He also became a specialist at giving hot-foots.

"We'd put a book of matches down by a guy's shoes, take a can of lighter fluid, and run a trail 35 feet long, around corners," he said. "All of a sudden, you'd see this flame, like a snake, approaching the guy's shoes and then a big puff of smoke. We burned the cuffs on a few pairs of pants that way."

Drabowsky—who once called Hong Kong from the bullpen and ordered takeout food for 40—has many favorite stories. The best involved star shortstop Luis Aparicio, who had a fear of crawling things.

"One day, I put a couple of small snakes into Aparicio's uniform pants pocket before he got to the clubhouse," said Drabowsky. "He put his uniform on and, as he buckled his pants, he felt something squirm in his hip pocket. I think he set an all-time record for getting undressed."

Years earlier, Leo Durocher was a victim twice—the first time as a Cardinal baserunner put out by the hidden ball trick. That

Streaker Madness

Yogi Berra was playing left field when a streaker ran across the outfield. The game was held up several minutes while the offending fan was corralled. After the game, a writer asked Yogi whether the streaker was a man or a woman. "How should I know?" he said. "He had a bag over his head."

Bob and Cy

Bob Feller attended Cy Young's funeral but never won a Cy Young Award. The pitching trophy was created in 1956—the year Feller retired—because writers felt pitchers were overlooked in the voting for Most Valuable Player.

Nothing for Nolan

Roger Clemens, Greg Maddux, and Steve Carlton won a combined 15 Cy Young awards without a no-hitter while Nolan Ryan had seven no-hitters without a Cy Young.

Timely Hit

Pete Rose became the career hit leader, passing Ty Cobb, on the 57th anniversary of Cobb's last game in the majors.

Fielders were Hitters

The only father-and-son tandem in the 50 Home Run Club is the Fielders. Cecil hit 51 for the 1990 Detroit Tigers while Prince hit a league-leading 50 for the 2007 Milwaukee Brewers. At age 23, he was the youngest man to hit 50 home runs in a season. The Fielders finished their careers with 319 home runs apiece.

Name That Pitch

After yielding a game-winning homer to Cincinnati's Barry Larkin, Cub pitcher Bob Patterson said, "It was a cross between a screwball and a change-up. It was a screwup."

Towel Tricks Help Runners

In many old parks, bullpen occupants had better perspectives than outfielders on certain plays. The Brooklyn Dodgers assigned the man sitting closest to home on the bullpen bench to signal runners with a white towel when it was safe to advance. The Dodgers picked up many extra bases as a result.

Perfect Record for Dropout

John Paciorek of the 1963 Houston Colts played only one game in the major leagues. He went 3-for-3 with two walks and scored four runs as Houston beat the Mets, 13–4. His brother, Tom, later played for several clubs.

Hitless Wonders

Who are the most frustrated batters of all time?

Willie Stargell is a candidate. In 1978 he broke Mickey Mantle's record of 1,710 lifetime strikeouts. Adam Dunn, who fanned 222 times for the White Sox in 2012, and Mark Reynolds, with 223 for the 2009 Diamondbacks, hold single-season "honors" in the American and National Leagues, respectively.

A strikeout represents only a single out—a double play means two. In 1984 Boston's Jim Rice set a one-year standard by grounding into 36 twin-killings. Miguel Tejada of the 2008 Astros did it 32 times for the NL record.

The worst performance on a single day is no contest: Charles T. Pick of the Boston Braves, 0-for-11, on May 1, 1920.

Bullpen prankster Sparky Lyle specialized in sawing off chairs.

night he dined with the manager of the St. Louis hotel where he was living. Knowing Leo liked chocolate ice cream, his host had two huge portions brought to the table. The delighted Durocher dug in with enthusiasm—until his spoon struck a solid object: a hidden baseball.

Another Cardinal, Joe Medwick, once toured Europe with a group of entertainers. Granted an audience with the Pope, each visitor revealed his occupation: "I'm a singer," "I'm a dancer," and so forth. When Medwick's turn came, he said, "I'm a Cardinal."

Catfish Metkovich, who came up to the majors when Medwick was near the end of his career, also produced a one-liner of note. Returning to the Pirate bench after a strikeout at the hands of Boston's Max Surkont, Catfish complained of the "radio ball." His teammates were incredulous. "Radio ball?" they asked. "Yeah," said Metkovich. "You could hear it but you couldn't see it."

A later Pirate, good-hitting but weak-fielding Dick Stuart, was in the lineup at first base when the stadium announcer blared, "Anyone who interferes with the ball in play will be ejected from the ballpark." Pittsburgh manager Danny Murtaugh said, "I hope Stuart doesn't think that means him."

Fans have a sense of humor too. The Pirates once got a note that read: "I'm enclosing a check for two tickets for myself and my wife. The little woman has been working hard and deserves a rest. However, I'd like one ticket behind first base and one ticket behind third base. After all, I need a rest too."

Chapter 9

Ronnie Joyner

By the time his 29-year managerial career was over, Bobby Cox ranked fourth on the career victory list. In two stints with the Atlanta Braves and one with the Toronto Blue Jays, he won five pennants and one world championship. His Braves finished first for 14 straight seasons, a professional sports record that is the team equivalent of Cal Ripken, Jr.'s consecutive games playing streak.

Managers

Manager's Nightmare

Most Consecutive Losses Since 1900

American League

Year	Club	Lost	Home	Road
1988	Baltimore	21	8	13
1906	Boston	20	19	1
1916	Philadelphia	20	1	19
1943	Philadelphia	20	3	17
1975	Detroit	19	9	10
1920	Philadelphia	18	0	18
1948	Washington	18	8	10
1959	Washington	18	3	15
1926	Boston	17	14	3
1907	Boston (2 ties)	16	9	7
1927	Boston	15	10	5
1937	Philadelphia	15	10	5
1972	Texas	15	5	10

National League

Year	Club	Lost	Home	Road
1961	Philadelphia	23	6	17
1969	Montreal	20	12	8
1906	Boston	19	3	16
1914	Cincinnati	19	6	13
1962	New York	17	7	10
1977	Atlanta	17	3	14
1911	Boston	16	8	8
1944	Brooklyn	16	0	16
1909	Boston	15	0	15
1909	St. Louis	15	11	4
1927	Boston	15	0	15
1935	Boston	15	0	15
1963	New York	15	8	7

The Hazards of Managing

A major league manager is not known for his longevity. When his team fails to win the pennant—or fails to win the World Series—the disappointment of the owner and the fans is invariably vented on the manager. The only other alternative of a vengeful ownership is the outright release of the 25 players.

Managers are hired to be fired. It is the foremost baseball cliché, but also the most accurate one. The most noteworthy exception, Connie Mack, spent 50 seasons at the helm of the Philadelphia Athletics, but he also owned the team and certainly would not fire himself.

Not counting Mack, 15 men managed in the majors for at least 20 years: John McGraw and Tony LaRussa (33 each); Bucky Harris, Bobby Cox, and Joe Torre (29); Gene Mauch and Sparky Anderson (26); Casey Stengel and Bill McKechnie (25); Joe McCarthy and Leo Durocher (24); Walter Alston and Lou Piniella (23); Bruce Bochy and Lim Leyland (22); Jimmie Dykes, Dick Williams, Tommy Lasorda, and Dusty Baker (21); and Cap Anson, Clark Griffith, and Ralph Houk (20).

Since teams look for experience in selecting a manager, many men have run more than one club. Frank Bancroft managed seven different teams and three others—Jimmie Dykes, Dick Williams, and John McNamara—had six each. Dykes was even traded for another manager when Detroit sent him to Cleveland for Joe Gordon in 1960. He failed to win a single pennant and his managerial career ended when Cleveland cut him loose in 1961. The trade of managers had hurt both sides.

More than 40 managers have run three teams each since the turn of the century, and Bucky Harris actually had eight terms as a pilot, including three with Washington and two with Detroit.

In six separate seasons of baseball's century, clubs operated with more than one manager. Early in 1943 Casey Stengel was struck by a car on a rainy night in Boston's Kenmore Square. Idled by a broken leg, Stengel yielded the reins temporarily to comanagers George Kelly and Robert Coleman.

The Chicago Cubs tried a rotating college of coaches for five seasons, starting in 1961, but junked the idea when players complained they were getting conflicting advice from the rotating head coaches. In the last season before owner Phil Wrigley installed the no-manager system, Charlie Grimm began his third term at the helm but switched places with broadcaster Lou Boudreau in midseason.

colorized by Don Stokes

Ty Cobb tried his hand as a manager late in his career. Cantankerous and combative early in his career, Cobb had to curb his temper in dealing with young players on his own team. This picture was taken in 1924.

When Wrigley unveiled the coaching plan, he explained that the Cubs had tried every type of manager imaginable, from inspirational leader to slave driver. Since 1945, when the easygoing Grimm won a pennant in his second tour of duty in Chicago, none had succeeded.

The incredible lack of job security facing the big-league manager is underlined by the fact that three pennant-winning pilots were fired after their teams lost the World Series. Bill McKechnie, an outstanding handler of pitchers, was dropped by the Cardinals in 1928, Casey Stengel by the New York Yankees in 1960, and Yogi Berra by the Yankees in 1964.

Stengel had won 10 pennants in 12 years as manager of the Yankees but was ostensibly dismissed because of his old age (70). Never mind that Connie Mack was 88 when he resigned as the active manager of the A's in 1950. Stengel sat out a year, then took over the expansion New York Mets of the National League for their first four seasons. Eight years after Stengel retired, Yogi Berra—who followed him from the Bronx to Queens—became one of seven managers to win pennants in both leagues (Joe McCarthy, Alvin Dark, Sparky Anderson, Dick Williams, Jim Leyland, and Tony La Russa were the others).

Common reasons for a manager's dismissal include inability to win, failure to communicate with or control the players, availability of a better man, or less-than-cordial relations with ownership.

Failure to perform a manager's duties can also quicken the end. A successful pilot must establish cordial relations with the local press, keep 25 players happy even though only 9 of them play at the same time, and argue with such haste and diplomacy that neither manager nor players are ejected from the game.

Frankie Frisch seemed to take unusual risks in arguing when his teams played in New York or Brooklyn, and umpires always thought the antics were deliberate so that, following ejection, he could visit his New Rochelle home, 30 minutes away.

Champion umpire baiter Leo Durocher argued loud and long, but was prepared in advance for an early exit. He had prearranged signs with sportswriter Barney Kremenko, who always sat in the same seat in the press box. Once thrown out of a game, Durocher would arrive in the press box and take a seat behind Kremenko. Durocher whispered, Kremenko touched his ear, and Bobby Thomson stole second. One day, with Durocher seated behind him, Kremenko innocently adjusted his glasses. The manager blew up. "You've just given the steal sign!"

Durocher lasted 24 seasons because he was a fiery, resourceful manager who always managed to out-think his opponent. One of his toughest rivals was Charley Dressen, manager of the Dodgers in the early '50s. Dressen was successful with the veteran Dodgers but—like many before him—struggled when he ran the Washington Senators.

One day the Senators trailed, 22–1, with two out and nobody on base in the ninth. Pitcher Mickey McDermott suddenly announced, "Don't worry, gang. Charley will think of something!"

It was once said of Dressen, not unkindly, that he talked so much he would finish two games ahead of his club by the time

Uncle Robbie Had a Flair

Hall of Famer Dazzy Vance recalled the era of Wilbert Robinson—Uncle Robbie to his players—in Brooklyn: "Robbie was not the smartest baseball man, but he was the best psychologist. His aim was to get his players in the right frame of mind and keep them that way. Before games, he held a relaxation period. He chatted and told stories and poked fun at himself and others until everyone felt at ease."

McGraw Fined Homer Hitter

John McGraw of the Giants once fined Sammy Strang $25 for hitting a home run with two men on base. Strang had been ordered to bunt.

How Mack Quieted Angry Grove

Longtime Philadelphia Athletics' manager Connie Mack did not swear—one reason he was not ejected from a game in a career that spanned more than 50 years. In 1929, when star pitcher Lefty Grove got ruffled after consecutive errors by Max Bishop and Jimmie Dykes, Mack decided to remove him from the game. "That will be all for you today, Robert," he said while the A's were batting. Grove, halfway down the bench replied, "To hell with you, Mr. Mack." With that, the soft-spoken pilot stood up, walked over to Grove, and pointed. "And the hell with you too, Robert," he said. The whole bench—even Grove—laughed. The pitcher departed peacefully, laughing all the way to the clubhouse.

McKechnie Served Boudreau Well

When Cleveland's young player/manager, Lou Boudreau, signed veteran pilot Bill McKechnie as pitching coach, he made a master stroke. McKechnie joined the Indians in 1946 for the record coaching salary of $20,000 and all but a written affidavit that he would concentrate on pitching and refuse any future managerial offers.

Stengel Guessed Wrong

"You can't say I don't miss 'em when I miss 'em." That's how Casey Stengel recalled his early appraisal of left-handed pitcher Warren Spahn, when both were Boston Braves in the '40s. When Spahn refused to brush back a hitter, Stengel admonished him. "Young man," he said, "You have no guts."

Century Mark

Sparky Anderson and Whitey Herzog are the only managers to guide teams to 100-win seasons in both leagues.

Worth the Price

Cap Anson signed the longest contract ever given to a manager. After winning five NL pennants with the Chicago White Stockings from 1880 to 1886, Anson inked a 10-year deal to keep the job. During a baseball career that started in 1871, Anson played for 27 seasons and managed for 19, creating such concepts as the pitching rotation, platooning, signals, and hit-and-run plays.

Frank Robinson's Debut

Player/manager Frank Robinson—the first black manager hired and later the first fired—slammed a home run in his first at-bat in the double role. The home run, on April 7, 1975, helped the Cleveland Indians defeat the New York Yankees, 5–3.

the season ended. But, despite his propensity to jabber endlessly, Dressen managed five different teams. Talent is appreciated.

Player/Managers

In the early years of baseball, most managers were also active players. Some were also full or part-owners of their teams, and many handled such general manager functions as trade-making and contract negotiations.

Adrian "Cap" Anson, player/manager of the Chicago National League club from 1879 to 1897, was the game's first great showman. In an effort to attract an audience, he devised unusual uniforms, including colorful Navajo bathrobes, dark blue bloomers, form-fitting pants, and even dress suits for one game. Anson also started the practice of having players parade to the park in open barouches. An early advocate of spring training, he took his charges south in 1886. He also had more than 3,000 hits in his career.

In 1898 Brooklyn owner Charles Ebbets said he did not believe in a bench manager. He preferred a man who could lead by example—and many pilots did just that until the practice faded after the Second World War.

Connie Mack, John McGraw, Miller Huggins, and Bucky Harris were among the great all-time managers who took command while still on the active list. Managers Frank Chance of the first-place Cubs and Fred Clarke of the third-place Pirates hit .319 and .309, respectively, as regular players for their teams in 1906.

Cleveland's Tris Speaker hit .388 and won the World Series in 1920.

Rogers Hornsby hit .317 as second baseman and manager of the world championship Cardinals of 1926 and, one year earlier, hit .403 with 39 homers and 143 runs batted in after replacing Branch Rickey as manager early in the campaign.

Ty Cobb managed the Tigers for six seasons without much success, but continued to hit the ball hard. In one of those years, 1922, he hit .401—the high mark for a player/manager in the American League.

Other player/managers whose active careers did not diminish immediately after they assumed their double roles included Bill Terry, Gabby Hartnett, and Frankie Frisch in the National League and Joe Cronin and Mickey Cochrane in the American League.

Terry, John McGraw's successor with the New York Giants, zoomed from seventh to first in 1933, his first full season as pilot, and kept the team in contention with his strategy as well as batting heroics for two more seasons.

He retired as a player in 1936, however, because of bad knees. When the team sank in the standings, 10½ games from the top in mid-July, Terry disobeyed a doctor's order and went back on the active list. He tripled home the winning run that day—launching a 15-game winning streak—as the Giants went on to win the pennant.

Probably the best example of a player/manager was Lou Boudreau, who took on the Cleveland job at the tender age of 24 in 1942. He'd only been in the majors three seasons, but thought he could translate his enthusiasm and instincts on the field into leadership his teammates would respect. In 1948 his club won the World Championship after copping the American League pennant in a one-game playoff with the Red Sox. In that game, Boudreau slammed two home runs and two singles to spark the 8–3 victory.

Boudreau was the last great player/manager. By the time Cleveland hired Frank Robinson in 1975, he was 39 years old and far off his Triple Crown form of 1966. Phil Cavaretta, with the Cubs of the early '50s; Solly Hemus, who played less than 20 games for the Cardinals in 1959; Joe Torre, who played even less for the Mets after replacing Joe Frazier in 1977; Don Kessinger, manager of the White Sox in 1979; and Pete Rose, who took over the Reds in 1984, were the only player/managers since Boudreau.

Modern baseball has become so personalized and so complex that owners expect managers to devote full attention to the game without having to worry about their own batting averages.

Great Managers

When the Brooklyn Dodgers elevated Walter Alston, the manager of their Triple-A farm at Montreal, to the major league job in November 1953, he explained his philosophy of managing to the press.

An off-season biology and industrial arts teacher in his native Ohio, Alston said: "Teaching students is very much like managing baseball players. You've got to encourage some, you've got to drive others, if you are going to get the best out of every individual."

Player/Managers Faced Extra Problem

In addition to the usual job risk faced by any major league manager, player/pilots knew they could be traded at any time. Rogers Hornsby was one of several who lost their managing jobs when they were traded. Hornsby led the St. Louis Cardinals to the World Championship in 1926, but was traded to the New York Giants after the season ended.

Suit Over Uni

The reason Connie Mack preferred a business suit to a baseball uniform was his penchant for screaming at players after games. By letting players shower and dress alone, the longtime manager imposed a personal cooling-off period.

Counting Pitches?

Connie Mack didn't believe in pitch counts. On August 26, 1916, Joe Bush threw a no-hitter for the A's the day after throwing three bad innings against the Indians.

Reprinted with permission, National Baseball Hall of Fame Library, Cooperstown, N.Y.

One of the best player/managers, Lou Boudreau of the Cleveland Indians, led his club's 1948 pennant drive.

Alston's technique worked with a variety of Dodger teams. In 23 seasons he won seven pennants and four World Championships—some with good-hitting clubs, others with teams molded around speed, pitching, and defense. His ability to change as the team changed made him a great manager.

The same can be said for John McGraw, Casey Stengel, Connie Mack, and Joe McCarthy—the only managers to win more often than Alston. McGraw and Stengel won ten pennants each, Mack and McCarthy nine. McCarthy and Stengel were World Champions seven times each and Mack five times.

"McGraw, Mack, and McCarthy were the best managers I ever saw," said sportswriter Grantland Rice, a journalistic star of the Babe Ruth era. "Miller Huggins is up there too. You must also include Billy Southworth, Bucky Harris, and Casey Stengel. McGraw was as colorful as any manager in baseball. There were few dull moments at the Polo Grounds when he was leading the Giants. 'Little Napoleon' was a fitting nickname."

Huggins ran the Yankees from 1918 until his death in 1929, and was more referee than manager. The ballclub was populated by talented but independent ballplayers who often disobeyed training rules and directives from management. Babe Ruth was a prime offender.

The 5'6", 140-pound Huggins was no physical match for any of his players—especially the 6'2", 215-pound Ruth. But the manager slapped his star with an indefinite suspension and a $5,000 fine for a series of infractions in 1925.

Ruth rebelled. "People have been asking me what the trouble is with this team," he said. "I haven't wanted to say it before, but I will now. The trouble with the team is Huggins. I think we have the best team in the league this year and look where we are."

Yankee management backed the field pilot—even after Ruth unleashed a him-or-me ultimatum. "Huggins will be the manager as long as he wants to be," said Col. Jacob Ruppert, the team's owner. "You can see where we stand and where Ruth stands."

The team finished seventh that season, but Huggins rallied the troops to win three consecutive pennants. Swirling controversy took its toll on the fragile pilot, however, and he died at age 50 shortly before the end of the 1929 campaign.

Huggins and other successful managers incorporated ideas first advanced by John McGraw with the Giants. The fiery third baseman with a .334 lifetime average ran the team for 30 years—1902 to 1932—and preached an aggressive approach, in attitude as well as technique.

His teams used the bunt and hit-and-run, developed defenses on rival hitters, and employed the first pinch-hitters and relief pitchers. A fighter who stuck up for his players but exercised absolute authority over them, McGraw actually developed a hatred of his opponents on the field—though he was friendly with many of them away from the ballpark.

Heroic Huggins

At 5'6" tall, Miller Huggins was smaller than any of his Yankees players. But he had a highly successful tenure as a manager from 1918 until his death in 1929. Although his ballclub was populated by talented but cantankerous players who often disregarded training rules and directives from management, Huggins held his own with the support of ownership. When he slapped Babe Ruth with a $5,000 fine and indefinite suspension for several infractions in 1925, the star rebelled and the team dropped to seventh in an eight-team league. Huggins rallied the troops to win three straight pennants.

John McGraw was called "Little Napoleon" by contemporaries who respected and feared him.

Frisch Got Pay Cut for Two Jobs

Frankie Frisch made $18,500 as player/manager of the 1934 St. Louis Cardinals—double the salary of any other player—but considerably below his peak pay of $28,000, which he earned strictly as a player.

The Vitt Rebellion

Dissension causes problems for any ballclub, and teams have lost pennants because players and manager could not get along. "Failure to communicate" is often the rationale for dismissing a manager.

In 1940 Cleveland Indians manager Oscar Vitt was so disliked that a band of players asked club owner Alva Bradley to release him. He refused and the team lost the pennant on the last weekend of the season. The following year, with Vitt replaced by Roger Peckinpaugh, the club dropped from a strong second to a weak fourth.

Dark Philosophy

Alvin Dark, one of a handful of managers to win pennants in both leagues, said he always relied on a P word while managing: power in San Francisco, pitching in Oakland, and prayer in Cleveland.

High Praise for Lou Boudreau

Fellow player/pilot Frankie Frisch on Lou Boudreau, who led the 1948 Cleveland Indians to the World Championship: "In the World Series, he directed his outfielders, had to think of his bullpen, and I often wondered whether he was giving signs to his catcher. When I think of Boudreau, I must say he was one of the great shortstops and also a great leader—an inspiration to a club and a fellow to set an example."

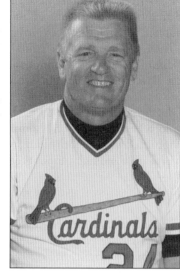

One of 37 pilots to produce more than 1,000 victories, Whitey Herzog guided five division winners and one World Champion. UPI named him Executive of the Year in both 1981 and 1982, when he doubled as manager and general manager of the Cardinals.

Volatile Billy Martin had a habit of winning with new teams, then wearing out his welcome in a hurry. He had a record five different stints as manager of the Yankees.

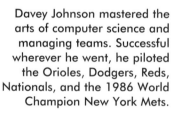

Davey Johnson mastered the arts of computer science and managing teams. Successful wherever he went, he piloted the Orioles, Dodgers, Reds, Nationals, and the 1986 World Champion New York Mets.

AP Photo/Ralph Freso

Jimmie Reese spent nearly 80 years in professional baseball as player, coach, scout, and minor-league manager. Born James Herman Soloman, he changed his name because of rampant anti-Semitism when he started his pro career in 1917. He later roomed with Babe Ruth. Reese remained active as a coach with the Angels past his 90th birthday.

McGraw's driving spirit produced 10 pennants and 10 second-place finishes. He won 2,583 games, more than any National League manager (and 2,763 in total). Connie Mack, eschewing McGraw's stormy technique, led the majors with 3,731 victories in his 53 seasons. That may be the safest record in sports.

"Talent comprises 75 percent of managing," said Mack. "Strategy is 12½ percent and the other 12½ percent is comprised of what a manager can get out of his team."

Mack, one of few managers who wore street clothes in the dugout (he preferred high starch collars), thought the gentlemanly approach would produce the best results. Many of his players regarded him as a father figure—especially during the 18 seasons he managed after the age of 70.

Though he was occasionally sarcastic, he rarely uttered a foul word or even a negative comment about anyone else. The soft-spoken manager called on a computer-like memory and sixth sense of baseball wisdom to win games.

Joe McCarthy won one pennant with the Cubs and eight with the Yankees. He had two near-misses with the Boston Red Sox in 1948 and 1949, ending his career just as Casey Stengel was winning his first of a record five consecutive World Series with the Yankees.

Overloaded with talent on the Yankees, Jimmie Dykes called McCarthy a "push-button manager," implying that anyone could do the job and suggesting that the team probably could win without a manager.

But McCarthy, who never played in the majors, preferred a low-key image and developed it to perfection. Controversy was at a minimum under his administration, but winning was at a maximum. Clubhouse disputes were settled quietly, but players who didn't show enough interest in the game were moved quickly.

"Guys who rush in and out of the clubhouse rush in and out of the big leagues," he said.

McCarthy couldn't afford to move Babe Ruth's big bat, but he was often tempted. Ruth resented McCarthy because the slugger coveted the Yankee managing job for himself.

Ted Williams, the great Red Sox star, played three seasons for McCarthy and liked the businesslike pilot. "He was the best manager I ever saw," said Williams, later a manager himself (and winner of the Manager of the Year Award at Washington in 1969). "McCarthy was always on top of the game and knew the limits and abilities of all his players." McCarthy's .614 winning percentage underscores that point.

No manager has ever done better.

Bucky Harris

Bucky Harris was a 27-year-old second baseman in his fourth major league season when he was appointed manager of the Washington Senators in 1924. When he proceeded to win the pennant and the World Series, the press referred to him as "the boy wonder" and the name remained with him through 29 seasons as a big-league manager.

The 5'9", 155-pound Harris was credited with keeping the Griffith family in baseball because of his heroics as a rookie

From College to the Majors

Though the minors is the traditional training ground of major league managers, several big-time pilots were recruited from the college ranks. Branch Rickey, coach at the University of Michigan, was named to manage the St. Louis Browns in 1913. Jack Slattery, fresh off the Boston College campus, began the 1928 campaign as Boston Braves manager. Bobby Winkles left Arizona State for the California Angels in 1973. And Eddie Stanky, a former major league manager, left the University of South Alabama to take the Texas Rangers' managing job in 1977. He got homesick, however, and resigned after one day on the job.

Dykes Shoved Mack

Jimmy Dykes, who became manager of the Philadelphia Athletics in 1951 after Connie Mack ended a tenure that began in 1903, once pushed his predecessor into a pile of bats.

It happened during the 10-run explosion of the A's in the seventh inning of the fourth game in the 1929 World Series against the Cubs. Chicago led, 8–0, before the outburst.

As the eighth run crossed for Philadelphia, the excited Dykes screamed, "We're tied; we're tied!" He pounded the man next to him so hard that he fell off the bench and into a pile of bats. Only his legs were visible.

Dykes, then a 32-year-old utility infielder, suddenly realized who he had pushed. "I pulled him out and said—very apologetically—'Gosh, Mr. Mack, I'm awfully sorry,'" Dykes recalled. "He said, 'Don't worry, Jimmy. Right now anything goes.'"

Clyde's the Guy

Jackie Robinson's first major league manager was Clyde Sukeforth, a coach appointed on an interim basis after the suspension of regular Brooklyn pilot Leo Durocher for the entire 1947 campaign. After two games, scout Burt Shotton took over, leading the Dodgers the rest of the way.

Mack's Marks

Although Connie Mack had more wins (3,731) than any other manager, he also had more losses (3,948). His 50-year tenure as manager of the Philadelphia Athletics outlasted two world wars, a depression, and six Roosevelt administrations.

Mack Tribute

New York City honored Connie Mack's 50 years as a major league manager before his 50th year. Mack was 86 and near retirement when he received a "Salute to Connie Mack" parade in 1949, his 49th year as a manager. He managed the Philadelphia Athletics again the following season.

Bucky Harris, who once worked in a coal mine, managed for 29 years but lost more often than he won.

pilot. Washington attendance jumped from 357,046 in 1923 to 584,310 in 1924 and enabled Clark Griffith, the owner (and manager through 1920), to purchase a $125,000 home—an enormous price. Harris got a $30,000 contract—a vast improvement over the 16 cents per hour he once earned as car-coupler in a coal mine.

He won a second consecutive flag in 1925, but lost a seven-game World Series when he allowed star pitcher Walter Johnson to absorb a 15-hit beating in the finale. Johnson, then 37, was pitching against Pittsburgh on a dark, rainy day but had a 6–4 lead going into the last of the seventh. The Pirates scored twice to tie, but Washington forged ahead, 7–6, in the eighth. In the home half, with the tired Johnson remaining on the mound, Pittsburgh scored three more to win, 9–7.

American League president Ban Johnson wired Harris that he should have replaced the veteran pitcher. The manager responded, "I went down with my best." The line has become a baseball classic.

Harris won another World Championship with the 1947 Yankees, and finished third, 2½ games behind, with the same club the following year, but new ownership replaced him with Casey Stengel, a two-time National League failure. Almost immediately, Harris returned to Washington for his third stint with that club. He had five other terms elsewhere, including two with Detroit.

"I was no genius," he always said. "If you don't have the players, you can't win." Harris' career winning percentage was .493.

Casey Stengel

Stengel sacrificed a potential career as a left-handed dentist from Kansas City (the "KC" initials inspired his nickname) to become one of the best managers in baseball history.

A disciple of the Giants' John McGraw, his manager in the '20s, Stengel earned a well-deserved reputation as a strategist as well as a showman. He employed McGraw's win-at-all-costs tactics and proved the platoon system practical as manager of the talent-rich Yankees from 1949 to 1960, but relied on his clowning instincts to keep fans happy when he ran bad ballclubs with the Brooklyn Dodgers, the Boston Braves, and the New York Mets.

Stengel played for five National League clubs, starting with the 1912 Dodgers and ending with the 1925 Braves, and launched his major league managerial career with Brooklyn in 1934. He managed for seven minor-league seasons before reaching the majors and returned to the minors for five more years in the '40s before landing the Yankee job in 1949.

Just as Stengel was influenced by McGraw, several modern managers—notably Billy Martin, Ralph Houk, and Whitey Herzog—were influenced by Stengel. That influence stems from Stengel's Yankee years, when he won 10 pennants and finished second once and third once.

Under his platoon system, Stengel's daily lineup was unpredictable. A few players—like Joe DiMaggio and later Mickey Mantle—played every day, but most of the others moved up and down the lineup and played a variety of positions. When he had the league's best catchers, Yogi Berra and Elston Howard, Stengel kept both bats in the lineup by using one of them at first base or in the outfield. Hank Bauer batted anywhere from first to eighth but swung a big bat, and Gil McDougald was an infield regular who starred at three different positions.

Though platooned players disliked the concept, many admitted years later that Stengel's maneuvering was wise. The veteran manager had an excellent memory, a mental book on all rival players, and exceptional baseball instincts. He knew when to play percentage baseball—inserting a left-handed pinch-hitter against a right-handed reliever, for example—and also when to go against "the book." In 1958 Stengel's Yankees became one of the few teams in baseball history to overcome a 3–1 deficit and win the World Series.

Stengel's fractured English, which he poured out in endless interviews with a delighted press corps, coupled with his genius to earn him the nickname, "the Old Perfessor." But he was adept at making himself perfectly clear in the clubhouse.

Far from the buffoon image he projected, Casey was a fighter—a quality inherited from the McGraw years. As Brooklyn manager in the '30s, he battled Leo Durocher, St. Louis shortstop and later a manager himself, after a fierce argument on the field. Stengel said he won by using his "famous punch to the kneecap."

Once, riding the trolley home from Ebbets Field, he saw a Dodger player disciplining one of his children on the sidewalk. The child had swiped some fruit from an open stand, but all Stengel knew was that the player had gone hitless that afternoon. Casey leaned out and yelled, "You go 0-for-4 and take it out on the kid, huh?"

Brooklyn was also the place where Stengel slid into second with a man already there. He was fined $50 (big bucks at the time) and censured by Brooklyn president Charles Ebbets, who said, "Stengel is the world's greatest ballplayer—from the neck down!"

As a minor-league outfielder, Casey entertained fans by sliding into his defensive position in center field. An insane asylum was located right behind the ballpark and, after one inning, his manager pointed to the building and said, "It's only a matter of time, Stengel."

It was also in the minors that Stengel encountered a manhole in right field. During one boring game, he climbed in. Almost immediately, the batter hit a high fly to right. Stengel lifted the cover with his bare hand and caught the ball in his glove.

Though Stengel and McGraw formed a mutual admiration society, the dictatorial Giants manager did not share Casey's penchant for clowning. But Stengel, who compiled a .284 batting average in 14 seasons, was a solid player. After he hit two key home runs in the 1923 World Series, Casey announced, "The Series stands two games for the Yankees and two for Stengel. What happened to the Giants?"

Fun-loving Stengel spent his nights on the town with Irish Meusel, but the pair deliberately went their separate ways when they discovered McGraw had put a tail on them. Stengel told the manager he would have to hire separate detectives. "I ain't gonna save this ballclub no more money by doubling up," he said.

Hugh Jennings Defended Young Cobb

When young, outspoken Ty Cobb had a hard time with veterans on the Tigers, manager Hugh Jennings—a champion in his first three seasons (1907–1909)—ended the discussion. "Cobb is going to be a great player," he said, "and he is not going to be driven off this club if I have to fire everybody but him and start over!"

Old Age?

Casey Stengel was 70 when the Yankees fired him after the team lost the 1960 World Series to the Pittsburgh Pirates. During 12 years with the team, Stengel won 10 pennants and seven World Championships. "I'll never make the mistake of being 70 again," he told reporters at his farewell conference.

Mickey Mantle's batting feats had much to do with Casey Stengel's success as manager of the Yankees. He won 10 pennants in 12 years.

A Hug at Third Hurt Brooklyn

Uncle Wilbert Robinson was managing the Brooklyn Dodgers in the early '20s. One day, with the team in a ninth-inning tie, Zack Taylor hit the ball over the center fielder's head. As he rounded third, Robinson, coaching there, grabbed him in a big congratulatory bear-hug. The throw came to the base and Taylor was tagged out.

Fine Performance

Joe McCarthy was the first manager to win pennants in both leagues when the Yankees beat the Cleveland Indians, 9–3, on September 13, 1932. He had won previously with the 1929 Chicago Cubs.

Kansas City Chief

The only man to manage two different teams in the same AL city was Joe Gordon, who ran both the Kansas City Athletics and Kansas City Royals.

Computer Manager

Davey Johnson believed his facility with computers gave him an extra edge. While playing for the Orioles, he used an IBM System/360 to write a lineup simulation that suggested he should bat second for Baltimore. Although manager Earl Weaver wasn't persuaded, Johnson relied on computer-generated information as manager of the Mets, Reds, Orioles, Dodgers, and Nationals. He won Manager of the Year honors in both leagues but not in 1986, when his Mets won the World Series.

Shortest Tenure

Wally Backman spent just four days as manager of the Arizona Diamondbacks in 2004. Four days after his November hiring, the *New York Times* revealed that he not only had financial problems but had been arrested twice. Thoroughly embarrassed, team officials said they had not done a criminal investigation on their new hire. Bob Melvin replaced him.

In later years Casey proved an engaging after-dinner speaker, constantly in demand on the winter banquet tour. He recalled thousands of incidents in detail and hardly needed to exaggerate; his run-on sentences and twisted grammar, known as Stengelese, were entertaining in their own right.

When it came to winning, however, Casey Stengel was all business. Upset with an umpire in Boston, he took off his uniform shirt and thrust it forward. "Wear this and play on our team for a while," he told the startled official.

In Boston and Brooklyn, Stengel twice finished fifth in the eight-team league. (Miraculously, he never finished last.) In New York, he was a roaring success—with the Yankees, who had an excellent farm system and veteran nucleus, and with the Mets, who relied on entertainment and nostalgia in their early years.

Leo Durocher

Leo Durocher's 24-year managerial career began with the 1939 Brooklyn Dodgers and ended with the 1973 Houston Astros. In between he managed the New York Giants and the Chicago Cubs.

A fiery competitor who compiled a .247 lifetime average over 15 full seasons, Durocher established an early reputation as a fighter when he shoved Babe Ruth into a locker before Ruth could make good on a threat to punch him. This incident occurred when both were with Brooklyn—Durocher finishing his playing career and Ruth serving as a symbolic coach who didn't flash signs.

As a manager, Durocher's name was always in headlines. He was the pilot of the "miracle" New York Giants, who made the most dramatic comeback in the game's history to win the 1951 pennant, and was credited with the development of Willie Mays.

A champion umpire baiter and friend of many celebrities, the erudite and controversial pilot was suspended for the entire 1947 season by Commissioner Happy Chandler for reasons that were never specified. He returned to his job as Brooklyn manager in 1948 but shocked the world in mid-July when he suddenly resigned to become manager of his arch-rival, the New York Giants.

In New York he engineered one of the most stunning upsets in World Series history—a four-game sweep of the Cleveland Indians in 1954.

Durocher transformed the Giants from a collection of slow-footed sluggers to a team with championship defense, adequate speed, and strong pitching to accompany the big bats. The Giants hit 179 home runs in 1951—opposed to 221 in 1947—but won 17 more games.

After an 11-year hiatus from the field, Durocher became the first manager of the Chicago Cubs after a five-year experiment with the coaching college ended after the 1965 season, and jacked the club into contender status after finishing last in 1966.

Chicago seemed to have the National League East championship locked up by August 1969, but the team wilted in the summer heat (the Cubs played only day games at home) and finished sec-

FRACTURED PERFESSER

One must assess

and peruse the talent astutely

from out fount of experience

we should contrive to assemble an aggregate of proven aptitude, and that's no euphemism

we'll imbue spirit

and insist on utmost effort

and I say, un-equivocally, we will finish

'ER-R-R, WOULD YOU MIND REPEATING THAT?'

MURRAY OLDERMAN

ond, eight lengths behind the miracle Mets. They were closer in 1970—five games behind Pittsburgh.

Durocher didn't have the personnel to win at Houston, where he transferred immediately after leaving the Cubs in midseason of 1972, and retired the following year with a parting shot at the high-priced modern player.

"When I played," he said, "the manager said 'Sit down, shut up, and listen.' Today, the players look you right in the eye and say, 'How dare you talk to me that way? I make $100,000.'"

Durocher, hardly one to be intimidated by his employees, did not like the new breed. He played and managed with military precision, battling opponents as if they were using bullets instead of baseballs.

Once, referring to Mel Ott, the man he later succeeded as Giants manager, Durocher said, "See Ott? He's a nice guy. And nice guys finish last."

The phrase became baseball's most famous quote, as well as the title of Durocher's book. It is now found in the pages of *Bartlett's Familiar Quotations*.

Durocher was intelligent, articulate, even suave, but could never have been accused of being a nice guy on the field.

Trade Mandates Signal Change

Teams must change their signals—or risk having them stolen—after every trade they make. Many clubs have individual signals for each player. Some use a count sign; the player may receive his signal on the third movement. Others use an indicator signal that something big is coming, while others simply use a key signal followed by the actual signal.

Stengel's Quick Quip

When Tug McGraw was hit hard by the opposition while working for the Mets, manager Casey Stengel came out to the mound. Pointing to the hitter, McGraw said, "I struck out this guy the last time I faced him. Let me stay in." Stengel responded, "I know you struck him out. But it was in this same inning!"

Quick Hook

Managers fired during spring training:

1954—Phil Cavaretta, Cubs—told reporters his team wouldn't make the first division
1978—Alvin Dark, Padres—had trouble communicating with players
1999—Tim Johnson, Blue Jays—lied about Vietnam service, lost credibility with team
2002—Joe Kerrigan, Red Sox—former pitching coach fell out of favor with new owners

Durocher, a teammate of Babe Ruth's with the Yankees, pushed the slugger into a locker after both had moved to Brooklyn.

Leo Durocher rebuilt the Cubs after the team junked its five-year experiment with a board of rotating head coaches.

Umpires expected to do battle with him—though occasionally his encounters were designed for showmanship rather than argument.

"A lot of times," remembered former Brooklyn pitcher Clyde King, "he'd run out, make a lot of motion with his hands, kick the ground, and run back. He felt it would help the club. He wanted to make the umpire bear down. Maybe he was arguing for the *next* close play.

"Leo would do anything to win. I admired him as a manager—he was a good manager—and he was great to me as a young player.

"One day when I was pitching, I was sitting near Durocher and his coaches when there was a close play at first base. I said, 'Hey, Skip, I thought he was safe.' Durocher looked at me and said, 'I thought he was out.'

"That indicated to me that Leo did not argue unless he really thought he was right."

Al Lopez

While Casey Stengel was managing the Yankees to 10 pennants in 12 seasons, 1949 to 1960, the only manager who beat him was Al Lopez—first with the 1954 Cleveland Indians, later with the 1959 Chicago White Sox.

A former catcher who was a tremendous handler of pitchers, Lopez patterned himself after Bill McKechnie, his manager with the Boston Braves in the '30s.

"Bill taught me the secret of success is earning the respect of your men," said Lopez, who advocated quiet, stable leadership. "Respect and good pitching. Bill never overworked a pitcher. Whenever a pitcher's turn came up to start, he was well rested and as ready to work as a man could be.

"McKechnie knew the capabilities of his bullpen better than any manager I ever saw. He knew his relievers so well that he always had the right man ready for the right spot. And the man's arm was always fresh and strong. Bill also had amazing patience. 'A hasty decision,' he used to say, 'is usually a mistake.'"

Lopez made a career of finishing second—he did it 10 times—because his teams had pitching that was equal to or better than what the Yankees had. But superior hitting and, occasionally, better defense, allowed New York to prevail.

Like McKechnie, Lopez was a sharp judge of talent who maintained a rapid shuttle between majors and minors. He got good mileage out of old arms by telling his pitchers to forget earned run averages and pace themselves. The '59 White Sox featured 39-year-old Early Wynn (22-10) as the top starter and NL rejects Gerry Staley, 38, and Turk Lown, 35, as the top relievers. A Punch-and-Judy attack led by Nellie Fox and Luis Aparicio paced the offense.

Wynn was 34 and Bob Feller 35 when the Indians rolled up an AL record 111 victories in 1954, but Mike Garcia, 30, and Bob Lemon, 33, were at the top of their game. This foursome—together seven years—was probably the best starting quartet in the history of baseball.

In their seven seasons together, Lemon won 20 five times, Wynn three times, Garcia twice, and Feller once. Lopez was their manager in five of those seasons, 1951 to 1955.

The son of a Spanish immigrant who made cigars in Tampa, Lopez said he could not compare his pennant-winning clubs—except in spirit. Lopez had both spirit and pride. He actually declined an offer to manage the talent-rich Yankees in 1961 because he would not succeed his friend, Casey Stengel. Beating him was one thing; taking his job was something else.

Paul Richards

Like Al Lopez, Paul Richards was a catcher with a reputation for getting the most out of his pitchers.

He inherited a sixth-place club in Chicago when he accepted his first job as manager with the 1951 White Sox, and immediately cut the team's "games behind" column from 38 games to 17. Richards moved the Sox up another notch in 1952 for the first of three consecutive third-place finishes.

Richards was so impressive that the Baltimore Orioles, one year removed from St. Louis, gave him the dual job of manager and general manager before the 1955 season opened. He nurtured the team's young, inexperienced players and developed several stars, including Brooks Robinson, an 18-year-old third baseman who broke in with the O's during Richards' first season there.

"If any man knows more about pitching than Paul Richards, he's in hiding," said White Sox general manager Frank Lane, who gave Richards his first managing job.

When the Orioles emerged as full-fledged contenders in 1960, they did it with a starting rotation whose leader, Chuck Estrada, was 22 years old. Other members of the Big Four were Milt Pappas, Jack Fisher, and Steve Barber, all 21.

Richards taught his "Kiddie Korps" how to pace themselves, how to hold runners on base, and how to throw various pitches. His pet project was the slip pitch, though he knew the ins and outs of the knuckleball too. Veteran Hoyt Wilhelm was 36 when the Orioles finished second in 1960, eight games behind the Yankees, and catcher Gus Triandos reduced his league-leading number of passed balls by using an oversized mitt Richards had helped develop just for the knuckler.

Several years earlier, when Richards asked Wilhelm to start, the veteran relief pitcher responded with a 1958 no-hitter against the Yankees and a league-leading 2.19 ERA the following summer.

Richards left the Orioles late in the 1961 campaign to try a new challenge with the Houston Astros, a National League expansion club. He later moved from Houston's front office to Atlanta's but had problems with veteran stars Joe Torre, whom he traded, and Clete Boyer, whom he released.

When Bill Veeck, an old admirer, purchased the White Sox in 1976, Richards joined the syndicate and agreed to serve as field manager that season before returning to the front office.

Mild-mannered Al Lopez (right) finished second 10 times with the help of players like Herb Score (left) and Ralph Kiner. Lopez went all the way with the 1954 Indians and the 1959 White Sox.

McGraw Beat Giants in Debut as Pilot

John McGraw, 26, beat the New York Giants, 5–3, on April 18, 1899, in his debut as manager of the National League's Baltimore Orioles.

Frankie Frisch on John McGraw

Frankie Frisch, captain of the New York Giants and later a three-time manager of other clubs, said John McGraw was a great influence on him. "We swashbuckled, baited umps, roared, roasted, and rattled our own players and almost everyone else," Frisch recalled. "We swore. Everyone in baseball swore then. McGraw himself was the world's greatest user of four-letter words. When he ran out of the shopworn kind, he invented a few of his own."

Recycling Rajah

When Bill Veeck hired Rogers Hornsby to manage the St. Louis Browns a generation after his father had fired him as Chicago Cubs manager, his mother sent him a telegram that said, "What makes you think you're smarter than your daddy?"

Paul Richards, who had two terms as manager of the White Sox, was expert at handling pitchers.

10 Commandments for Success in the Majors

By Joe McCarthy

1. Nobody ever became a ballplayer by walking after a ball.
2. You will never become a .300 hitter unless you take the bat off your shoulder.
3. An outfielder who throws back of a runner is locking the barn after the horse is stolen.
4. Keep your head up and you may not have to keep it down.
5. When you start to slide, slide. He who changes his mind may have to change a good leg for a bad one.
6. Do not alibi on bad hops. Anybody can field the good ones.
7. Always run them out. You never can tell.
8. Do not quit.
9. Do not fight too much with the umpires. You cannot expect them to be as perfect as you are.
10. A pitcher who hasn't control hasn't anything.

Walter Alston

Only Connie Mack (Athletics) and John McGraw (Giants) managed one club longer than Walter Alston, who guided the Dodgers for 23 years from 1954 to 1976.

Alston won the Associated Press Manager of the Year Award six times, was the winning manager in a record seven All-Star Games, and finished first or second in 15 seasons.

Known as "The Quiet Man," Alston believed in treating his youthful players like men. He scolded when he had to—never publicly—and kept aloof from his athletes.

Alston batted only once in the majors—he struck out with the St. Louis Cardinals in 1936—but was adept at handling other major leaguers, including "The Boys of Summer" who played for the Brooklyn teams of the '50s. When he became Dodger manager, the New York press asked—in print—"WALTER WHO?"

Charley Dressen preceded Alston as Brooklyn pilot—and won consecutive pennants after the agonizing last-ditch defeat of the 1951 playoffs—but lost his job by insisting on a multiyear contract. Alston held onto his by signing 23 consecutive one-year contracts and surviving even when his coaching staff included former Dodger pilot Leo Durocher.

When the Dodgers finished seventh in 1958, their first Los Angeles season, and eighth in 1967, after the retirement of Sandy Koufax and the trades of Maury Wills and Tommy Davis, the media screamed for Alston's scalp. Calmer—and apparently wiser—heads prevailed.

Alston made the most of his talent, which varied greatly from year to year. He paraded nearly 50 third basemen before discovering Ron Cey and frequently resorted to left-right platoons. "When I had Gil Hodges, Jackie Robinson, and Duke Snider in Brooklyn," he said, "I didn't have to platoon. Give me a lineup like that and I won't."

Alston's outer calm didn't fool his players. The veteran manager commanded respect and performance. Those who didn't do the job were traded, sent to the minors, or even challenged to fistfights under the stands.

Walter Alston provided such stability that the Dodger organization won a reputation as being the best in baseball. Rivals longed to play in Los Angeles and coaches used their Dodger credentials to jump to vacant managing slots elsewhere.

Among Alston coaches who became major league managers were Preston Gomez, Danny Ozark, and Tommy Lasorda.

Modern Managers

"Today's manager must be a psychiatrist as well as baseball strategist. Many games have been won by figuring out what a player is thinking and how a pat on the back is much better than a kick in the rear. Maybe the old-time managers could give an inflexible order, but today's players don't roll over that easily. A manager must think of his player as an individual with completely different problems from any other player."

The words were spoken by Dick Williams, then manager of the Montreal Expos and former boss of the Boston Red Sox, the

Oakland A's, and the California Angels. Once a strict disciplinarian, Williams mellowed in his approach to his players, but not in his approach to winning ballgames.

"I was a no-good horse's tail at Boston," he conceded. "I had to be. Hell, I'd been one of them as a player there in '63 and '64. I'd been caught for curfew myself. I didn't win any friends, but nobody turned down the World Series checks."

Williams won again with the Oakland A's of 1972 and 1973—and took those clubs to the World Championship. On national television, 1973 MVP Reggie Jackson indicated Williams and said, "The man on my left taught me to win. He didn't give me pep talks but he taught me to win in the last two years and two days."

The talented manager was always sarcastic and outspoken, as well as fiercely independent. He resigned the Oakland job because of constant interference from owner Charles O. Finley, who doubled as general manager.

Another veteran pilot, Gene Mauch, began his managing career at Philadelphia in 1960.

Mauch and Williams were similar types. Both were accused of "overmanaging," but both disputed the suggestion. Their moves were unpredictable and they wanted to keep that reputation, since it put the opposition on the defensive. Williams said a bad manager could cost a team up to two dozen ballgames.

While Williams used a four-man platoon at second base, a stream of pinch-hitters, pinch-runners, and relief pitchers, and assorted trick plays, Mauch called on a vast storebank of baseball knowledge. Called "the Little General" when he preceded Williams in Montreal, Mauch was reputed to know the rule book better than most umpires.

"When the game starts, you throw away the book and make your decisions according to the situation," he said in 1973. "There's no cut-and-dried strategy. It varies from game to game and situation to situation."

Mauch kept constant tabs on rivals by reviewing box scores and digesting histories, including such statistics as weather information, trends, and other data. He was a walking computer, in addition to being a keen student of the game.

"Ask him to recall any situation in a game years ago and he'll tell you the count, where the pitch was, what it was, and who hit it," said Montreal executive Jim Fanning after Mauch left for Minnesota. "He'll not only do it, but he'll use all of that to beat you."

An admiring rival, three-time manager Dave Bristol, once coached for Mauch. "You have to start managing against him when your plane lands in town," Bristol said.

Mauch, like Williams, was a utility infielder for several clubs. Both sat and observed the men calling the shots.

The late Billy Martin was another infielder-turned-manager. A volatile disposition and tendency to cross the front office cost Martin jobs in Detroit, Minnesota, and Texas before he won two consecutive pennants with his old team, the Yankees, in 1976 and 1977.

Martin won divisional championships with the Twins, the Tigers, and the Athletics, and brought the Rangers home as surprise runners-up, thereby establishing an unchallenged reputation as a winning manager. Martin, like Tom Lasorda of the Los Angeles Dodgers, got closer to his players than many of his contemporaries.

Walter Alston was almost unknown when he became Dodger manager in 1954, but he lasted 23 seasons in the job.

Ozzie's Tantrum

White Sox manager Ozzie Guillen was suspended and fined by Major League Baseball for commenting about an ejection on Twitter.

Strange Strategy

Tampa Bay manager Joe Maddon once ordered Texas slugger Josh Hamilton walked intentionally in the ninth inning. The only problem was the bases were loaded at the time. The Rays still won, 7–4, even though the unorthodox Maddon put the potential winning run on base.

Last Expos Boss

Frank Robinson was the last manager of the Montreal Expos and first manager of the Washington Nationals. He came with the club when it relocated for the 2005 campaign.

The Jennings Experiment

Dan Jennings had never managed in a 32-year baseball career before the Marlins moved him from general manager to manager on May 17, 2015. He did not last in either role.

Joe McCarthy on Managing

Longtime manager Joe McCarthy, who left the game in 1949, usually enjoyed his job. "Sometimes I think I'm in the greatest business in the world," he said. "Then I lose four straight and want to change places with a farmer."

Dick Williams was the only manager to guide the Montreal Expos to a first-place finish. The team won the NL East flag during the second half of the 1981 split season (player strike) but lost to Los Angeles in the ninth inning of the last NLCS game. Williams won pennants with the Boston Red Sox (1967) and San Diego Padres (1984) and World Series with the Oakland A's (1972 and 1973). He was elected to the Baseball Hall of Fame in 2007.

Irwin Cohen

Helped by career hit king Pete Rose (right), Sparky Anderson won four pennants in nine years with Cincinnati's Big Red Machine in the '70s before embarking on a longer tenure with the Tigers. He was the first manager to win World Championships in both leagues.

"Billy Martin was a man's manager," said Jeff Burroughs, who won the Most Valuable Player Award when Martin managed him at Texas in 1974. "He treated you like a man, stuck up for you on and off the field, and taught you how to win. He was a little peppery second baseman who didn't have all the natural athletic tools to become a superstar, but he worked hard and learned all the little things about the game to help the team win."

Frank Quilici, who managed the Twins briefly, also admired Martin. "Billy was the type of guy who just got enraptured with the ballgame," said Quilici, who played for Martin when the Twins won the AL Western flag in 1969. "He was a very smart baseball man, he was very intense, and he was a perfectionist. That's what he tried to get out of his players."

Earl Weaver, who became manager of the Baltimore Orioles in July 1968, was another manager who accomplished major miracles—sometimes with minor talent. When the Orioles lost regulars Bobby Grich and Reggie Jackson plus 20-game winner Wayne Garland after the 1976 season, the media predicted Weaver's wonders would cease. But the Birds finished second, tied with Boston at 2½ games out of first.

Weaver finished third once—in 1972—in his first 10 seasons. In 5 of those 10 he won a divisional title. Three times, 1969, 1970, and 1971, Baltimore advanced to the World Series. Weaver won the World Championship in 1970.

"People often talk about how many games a manager can win, but what wins games is how the players perform," Weaver insisted. "When the manager makes out a lineup card, chooses a pinch-hitter, or makes a pitching change, he's playing a part in the game.

"Knowing when to get a guy out of the lineup is probably one of the most important, and toughest, parts of managing. If a guy goes hitless in four or five games and you take him out, did you make a mistake only the last time you played him, or every time? Did you make a mistake because he might be ready to break loose? Getting a guy out of the lineup at the right time is important, but it's just as important to have him in at the right time."

Weaver realized the Orioles were changing, and he changed to meet the revised roster of players, almost reliving his days as a successful minor-league pilot in a productive farm system. A major success, in 1977, was pitcher Mike Flanagan, who lost 8 of his first 10 decisions. Weaver kept him in the rotation and watched him win 12 of his next 14, and become an All-Star pitcher in 1978.

"I just had to have faith," he said. When the Orioles' holdover veterans and half-dozen rookies meshed in 1977, the team surprised all observers and generated two pleasant surprises for Weaver: a three-year contract and the Manager of the Year Award.

Sparky Anderson, like Weaver, became an instant success after taking command of the Cincinnati Reds in 1970. Anderson was one of 20 managers to win a pennant in his first season. He won five divisional titles (four pennants and two World Series) in his first eight years and twice finished second. His Reds averaged 96 wins per year in that span. Bobby Cox, Joe Torre, and Tony LaRussa all managed in both leagues during careers that culminated in their simultaneous 2014 enshrinement in the Baseball

Hall of Fame. All won world championships during their dugout tenures.

Managerial Strategy

There are various aspects to managerial strategy. First the manager must field a team of alert, aggressive players. To keep his athletes that way, curfew rules have become universal in baseball.

John McGraw's early Giants adhered to an 11:30 P.M. curfew on the road and a midnight curfew at home—in season, of course.

Rogers Hornsby devised an ingenious way to catch violators. One night he handed the only elevator operator a brand-new ball at the stroke of midnight. He bribed the man to get the signature of every player he saw that night—and then hand in the ball the next morning.

Gil Hodges told his players on the Washington Senators that anyone out after curfew the previous evening was to put $100 in the empty cigar box in his office. He said he could name four offenders. When he looked in the box later, he counted $700.

In addition to keeping his team in prime physical condition, a good manager must (1) know the capabilities—as well as the potential—of each man; (2) provide strong, but not overbearing, leadership; (3) have thorough understanding of the rules and how they can be used to best advantage; (4) communicate well with his players—particularly the pitchers; (5) know the weaknesses of rivals; (6) be able to deal with his own front office; and (7) maintain smooth relations with the media.

It is difficult to keep bench warmers happy because every player thinks he should play every day. But the manager who can convince an athlete he's more valuable in a reserve role will be better off.

Art Shamsky of the Cincinnati Reds was a prime example of a productive reserve. A left-handed-hitting outfielder, Shamsky came off the bench on August 12, 1966, to pinch hit a home run in the eighth. He stayed in the game and homered again in the tenth and eleventh.

Shamsky didn't play the following day because the opposition started a left-handed pitcher, but he was back in action a day later, with a right-hander working. The slugging substitute connected in his first time up for his fourth consecutive home run, tying a major league record.

Mother's Day

With the Pirates one game from elimination in the 1979 World Series against the Orioles, Pittsburgh manager Chuck Tanner heard his mother had died. Choosing to stay with the team, he said, "My mother was a great Pirates fan. She knew we're in trouble so she went upstairs to get some help." Apparently, the manager was right: Pittsburgh won the last three games and the world championship.

Though his record for futility was unmatched among managers (no pennants in 26 years), Gene Mauch was considered a walking computer by dugout rivals.

Earl Weaver, who retired as Baltimore Orioles manager after the 1986 season, recorded a .583 winning percentage during 17 seasons on the job.

Manager Ted Williams

Former Red Sox slugger Ted Williams was named Manager of the Year in the American League in 1969, his first year as a pilot, when he improved the Washington Senators' winning percentage from .404 to .531. It was the best of his four seasons with the team, including one in Dallas/Fort Worth after the Washington Senators became the Texas Rangers.

Interim Zim

After serving as Joe Torre's bench coach in 1998, Don Zimmer knew the Yankees well enough to manage the team himself. He got his chance at the start of the '99 season, when Torre was sidelined by prostate cancer surgery. Despite a spat between the interim manager and owner George Steinbrenner, the team went 14-7 with Zimmer at the helm. The owner, miffed at Japanese import Hideki Irabu, called him "a fat toad" but ordered the manager to give him a start. Zimmer balked, causing an icy silence between the veteran pilot and the mercurial owner.

Bucking the Odds

Risky business: Arizona manager Buck Showalter ordered an intentional walk to Barry Bonds even though the bases were loaded in the bottom of the ninth inning at San Francisco. The unorthodox maneuver worked, as the D'backs beat the Giants, 8–7.

Wrong Team

Although he grew up rooting for the San Francisco Giants and idolized Willie Mays, Ned Yost rooted against them in the 2014 World Series—when he managed the American League team trying to beat the Giants. Yost's Kansas City Royals lost in seven games.

Maddon's Magic

Convinced that Joe Maddon's magic would end the tenure of the Cubs in the NL Central cellar, Chicago gave him a five-year, $25 million contract after the 2014 season. The Cubs had not won a playoff game in 12 years, a pennant in 70 years, or a World Series in 107 years.

Platooning has been part of baseball since George Stallings once worked the left-right percentage to his advantage with the World Champion Boston Braves of 1914. Tris Speaker won a world title for Cleveland by platooning at first base and in two outfield spots. And Casey Stengel perfected the art with the Yankees.

Basically, percentages favor a left-handed batter against a right-handed pitcher, and vice versa. Should the opposition send up a right-handed pinch-hitter for a left-handed batter, the wise manager would employ a right-handed pitcher to stop him.

On May 15, 1951, rookie White Sox manager Paul Richards used a loophole in the rules to play percentages in the eighth inning of a game against the Red Sox. He moved right-handed pitcher Harry Dorish to third base and brought in star left-hander Billy Pierce to pitch to left-handed batter Ted Williams. After Williams popped up, Richards brought Dorish back, and he went on to win the game.

Billy Meyer, managing Pittsburgh at the same time, had his own favorite play. With the bases loaded and a 3-1 or 3-2 count on the batter, the runner on third broke for home. He deliberately started slowly so that the pitcher would forget the count and think he had an easy out at the plate. Meyer's idea was to induce the pitcher to lob an outside toss to the catcher for the tag—but the throw would actually be ball four and force a run home.

In the 1972 World Series, Dick Williams used a trick play to strike out Cincinnati slugger Johnny Bench. With the count 3-2,

Connie Mack was called "The Tall Tactician" because of his managing skills with the Philadelphia Athletics. He wore a business suit in the dugout as a restraint against his temper, figuring that he'd be able to cool off after a tough loss if he didn't meet the players in the showers.

he told catcher Gene Tenace to hold out his hand, the traditional sign for the intentional walk. Tenace would then return to normal position just as reliever Rollie Fingers was set to deliver. Williams conducted his conference on the mound and gestured toward first base as Fingers nodded in agreement. The pitcher would throw a breaking ball rather than a fastball to camouflage the ruse further.

Bench assumed his stance and the Oakland players did their part in the field. The surprised catcher was called out on strikes.

"Bench was completely fooled," Williams recalled. "The pitch was an excellent one. It caught, maybe, the outside corner of the plate. We got the next man too and saved a run because there was one out with a man on third before Bench came up."

As a rule, managers play to win on the road and to tie at home. Since baseball has a built-in advantage for the home club, the theory is based around the fact that familiar surroundings, partisan fans, and the sudden-death advantage of the home ninth—or subsequent innings—will enable the home team to break the tie and go on to victory.

Another adage for contending clubs is: play .500 against the top teams and murder the tail-enders. A championship cannot be forged without a high winning percentage, and few clubs can maintain a high ratio of wins to losses against top-flight opposition.

Skilled managers gamble by sending runners for extra bases, utilizing the stolen base (and the double-steal), employing the suicide squeeze play and the hit-and-run. In any of these situations, the manager will look bad if the players fail to execute.

Buck Showalter of the Arizona Diamondbacks tested the theory in 1998, when he ordered his pitcher to walk San Francisco's Barry Bonds with the bases loaded and the D'backs leading, 8–6. The next hitter worked the count to 3-2 before lining out to end the game. Showalter's strategy had not been used for 54 years, since Giants manager Mel Ott ordered a bases-filled intentional pass for Cubs slugger Bill Nicholson.

Managers and Pitchers

Handling the pitching staff is generally considered to be the most difficult aspect of managing. A rotation must be established, relief corps assembled, and a special coach chosen to monitor all pitchers.

Cardinals' Series Strategy Paid Off

The St. Louis Cardinals walked Babe Ruth 12 times in the 1926 World Series (he still hit four home runs). Ruth, frustrated when Grover Cleveland Alexander walked him with two outs in the ninth inning of Game 7 and the Yankees behind, 3–2, tried to surprise St. Louis by stealing second. He was thrown out easily—ending the World Series—in what baseball experts say was the only stupid play of his career.

Charley Dressen Used His Head

Charley Dressen, longtime major league manager, was a bundle of excitement during a game. Once, when Gil Hodges was at bat for his Dodgers, Dressen watched the count run to 1-2. The next pitch was high and outside—so far that the catcher missed it—but the umpire called strike three. When Hodges, assuming the pitch to be ball three, failed to run toward first, Dressen yelled, "Run! Run!" but the first baseman failed to hear him. The screaming manager, jumping up and down in the dugout, banged his head on the ceiling and collapsed. Hodges finally got the idea and made it to first—but for days afterward he avoided Dressen whenever he saw the manager rubbing the sore spot on his head.

Picking the right relief pitcher is an aspect of strategy that drives managers crazy. But Oakland's Dennis Eckersley was almost a sure thing in 1988 with 45 saves, a 2.35 ERA, and only 11 walks in 73 innings pitched. After saving all four ALCS wins against Boston, he entered the ninth inning of the World Series opener in Los Angeles with a 4–3 lead and retired the first two men. But a rare walk to Mike Davis, a .196 hitter during the season, set the stage for Kirk Gibson, whose hamstring and knee injuries were so severe that he could only hobble. On a 3-2 pitch, Gibson hit a game-winning homer. His only World Series at-bat produced a 5–4 win that sparked the underdog Dodgers to the world title.

Copyright 1992 Bill Purdom. Reprinted with permission, Bill Goff, Inc./GoodSportsArt.com.

Sleepless Nights

Bad ballclubs turn managers prematurely gray, create ulcers, and cause many sleepless nights for field bosses.

Burt Shotton, who later found success with the Brooklyn Dodgers, suffered through the nightmare of the 1930 Phillies, a team with eight .300 hitters and a .315 team batting average but a leaky defense and inept pitching staff. The club made 239 errors in 154 games (the 1962 Mets made 210 in 162) and posted a 6.71 team earned run average. Opponents scored 19 runs in a game against the Phils four times!

Tough Decision

Preston Gomez, baseball's first Latino manager, twice pinch-hit for pitchers who had completed eight no-hit innings in a game. In both cases, succeeding relief pitchers blew the no-hitters in the ninth. The luckless starters were Clay Kirby of San Diego and Don Wilson of Houston.

Waste of Time

Veteran pitching coach Johnny Sain says the only purpose of a meeting on the mound with catcher, pitcher, and manager is to stall while a reliever warms up in the bullpen. "If a microphone were placed out there, all you'd hear would be a lot of grunts," he noted.

A little-known aspect of the game is the conference on the mound. What does the manager really say?

When Paul Richards was running the Orioles, he approached Connie Johnson after three hits had loaded the bases. "Connie, it's about time you were getting someone out," Richards offered. "You know," Johnson replied, "I was just thinking about that myself."

Moe Drabowsky remembers an encounter with Fred Hutchinson, the Reds pilot who once pitched himself. "The bases were loaded—I had just walked a couple of guys—and the score was tied," he related. "All of a sudden I went to 2-0 and with every pitch, I heard a strange noise from the dug-out: 'Hmphfff!'

"Throw another pitch and 'Hmphfff!' It was Hutch. When it was a ball, it would upset him so much. Finally, I looked out of the corner of my eye and saw him charging out of the dugout. When he arrived, he said, 'Look around you, what do you see?' I didn't know what he was referring to. He said, 'The bases are loaded now. You better get this next guy.' Then he turned around and went back to the dugout. Fortunately, I got the next guy."

A manager may tell a joke or argue with an umpire to relax a pitcher in a pressure situation, but Clyde King said no one ever asked him where he was going to dinner or what movie he was going to see that night. "I played for Charley Dressen, Leo Durocher, Walter Alston, and Burt Shotton, and those guys were all business," he said.

When King became a manager, he had a club rule that no pitcher could argue about leaving the game.

"I learned you can't depend on the catcher to tell you whether the pitcher is losing his stuff," King reported, "because he might be the roommate or a close friend of the pitcher and it would put him on the spot. As a big-league manager, I believed that if I had to rely on someone else to tell me when a pitcher was losing it, I might not be qualified to be a manager."

Coaches

Each major league club carries three or four coaches during the season. Two flash signs to hitters and direct baserunners from coaching boxes behind first and third base when their team bats; another supervises the bullpen; any others share the dugout bench with the manager.

Forlorn Babe Ruth, rebuffed in his bid to become a major league manager, spent some time as first-base coach for the Brooklyn Dodgers in the late '30s.

Early baseball managers, including John McGraw, preferred to handle all aspects of running their teams. Substitute players manned the coaching boxes, and nonplaying managers frequently filled one of the boxes themselves.

There's always a hitting coach and a pitching coach, though the latter sometimes is a former catcher rather than a former pitcher.

Many of the coaches are former managers seeking to find new jobs as pilots or just-retired players hoping to move into managerial slots without following the traditional route up from the minors.

Coaches use six basic signs: bunt, take, hit-and-run, squeeze, steal, and forget-previous-sign. The third-base coach is particularly important because his decisions help—or hurt—the team in scoring runs. Often he must gamble, and always decisions must be instantaneous.

In the '20s, KiKi Cuyler of the Cubs threw out Travis Jackson of the Giants at home plate. Jackson had been trying to score from second on a single and had received a green light from third-base coach Pancho Snyder. Chicago's bench-jockeys taunted Snyder for letting Jackson go through against Cuyler's powerful arm.

"Never again in a million years," the coach replied.

Later in the game, Cuyler threw out another Giant at home. "Hey, Pancho," the Chicago bench screamed, "time sure flies!"

The good third-base coach is automatically the heir apparent to the incumbent manager. When an incumbent goes, and ownership decides not to look outside the organization, the third-base coach rates the slight edge over the team's Triple-A manager for the big-league job.

Pitching coach Johnny Sain, unlike many other coaches, was never a drinking buddy of the manager's. Nor was he a candidate to become a manager and hire an unemployed former boss to coach for him.

Sain concerned himself only with pitching and developed more than a dozen 20-game winners in the '60s and '70s. In both Minnesota and Chicago, he helped Jim Kaat blossom into a top winner.

Like Sain, Art Fletcher, Frankie Crosetti, and Eddie Yost gained reputations as competent, satisfied coaches who did not desire the manager's chair.

The irony of coaching history is that men fired as managers by a certain club frequently return as coaches—and indirect threats to their successors.

Charley Dressen and Leo Durocher both returned to the Dodgers, Johnny Pesky to the Red Sox, and Yogi Berra to the Yankees, among others. All were considered excellent aides.

Billy Hunter spent 14 years as third-base coach on the Baltimore Orioles and entertained several managerial offers before joining the Texas Rangers in 1977.

"The third-base coach probably can control the game on offense more than the manager can," he said. "He has everything right in his hands. He can hold the runner up or send him in, and it is his judgment that will determine whether a runner is out or safe.

"If you can't be a player, be a third-base coach: he's in the game as much as anyone. He has to know not only every outfielder's arm, but every infielder's arm too. When there's a

Baseball-Football Tie

Hugo Bezdek, who managed the Pirates before 1920, is the only man who managed in the majors and coached in the National Football League—but never played in either.

Four Coaches at First

The Washington Senators used four coaches at first base in one game in 1968. Nellie Fox, the normal first-base coach, was ejected in the ninth inning and replaced by utility infielder Bernie Allen. Allen, needed as a pinch-hitter later, was replaced by Cap Peterson, but Peterson had been previously announced as a pinch-hitter and was technically out of the game. The Senators replaced him with pitcher Camilo Pascual. P.S. Washington won in 12 innings.

Charley Dressen, veteran coach and manager, finds time for a spring training stroll with a young Yogi Berra on February 29, 1948, in St. Petersburg, Florida. Dressen was then a Yankee coach under Bucky Harris.

Dressen a Top Coach

Charley Dressen coached for several clubs, including the Yankees and the Dodgers, and was highly regarded for his vast storehouse of baseball knowledge. He was an excellent judge of his own pitchers and the enemy's and was particularly adept at stealing signs from other clubs.

Grammas Explains Signals

Third-base coach Alex Grammas, one of the best at his trade, explained how signals are flashed: "A coach usually goes through 8 or 10 motions, but only 1 or 2 mean anything. Each guy has his own individual style. When I was coaching at Cincinnati, I'd go to my cap, my arm, my leg, and back to my arm. I used to use my nose and ears a lot."

cutoff play, that comes into account. Many times the shortstop is a very good relay man but the second baseman is not. If the first baseman has the ball, he may not throw too well. The left fielder is usually the worst arm in the outfield.

"A good third-base coach will watch infield practice, will watch the outfielders throw, and if somebody's not throwing too well, he might give him a little test during the ballgame."

Hunter coached during the heyday of Frank and Brooks Robinson and Boog Powell—heavy hitters who helped the Orioles become the most successful team of their time. Many Baltimore runners were thrown out because Hunter gambled on their chances of scoring.

"My theory at third," he explained, "was that if you had a 50-50 chance of making it, I sent the runner. You can only do that with a contending club because of the risk involved. I felt that if we made the other team throw, they made more mistakes. When you're cautious, a lot of times you might not score any runs, but when you gamble, you might get two or three."

Doubling as third-base coach, a frenetic Leo Durocher, managing the New York Giants, whoops up a storm as Willie Mays heads for home.

Chapter 10

Baseball's leaders often occupy front-row seats at games. Enjoying a 1989 spring training exhibition game are baseball commissioner Bart Giamatti (center) and Presidents Bobby Brown (left) of the American League and Bill White of the National League.

The Brass

Landis Hugged 1931 Series Star

Commissioner Landis embraced 1931 World Series star Pepper Martin and told him he'd like to trade places with him. Martin, earning $4,500, replied, "Well, that'll be fine, Judge, if we can swap salaries too!" The baseball czar was then earning $65,000.

The Black Sox

Chick Gandil, one of eight Chicago players banned for life by Judge Landis in the Black Sox scandal of 1919, apparently instigated the plot by contacting gamblers in Boston three weeks before the World Series. Buck Weaver, also in the group, backed out of the plot and played to win but was thrown out of the game because he didn't reveal the conspiracy.

Meanwhile, Cincinnati's Edd Roush said gamblers who knew the Sox were going to lose deliberately tried to bribe a Reds player with $5,000 to dump a game in favor of Chicago and twist the plot. He informed manager Pat Moran, who verified the attempted bribery.

A ninth major leaguer was banned in the Black Sox scandal: second baseman Joe Gedeon of the St. Louis Browns was handed a lifetime suspension by American League president Ban Johnson for betting on the Reds after learning that the World Series was fixed.

The Government of Baseball

Since January 12, 1921, organized baseball has been headed by a commissioner hired by the major league club owners.

He is in the unusual position of wielding power over his employers because he has total authority to protect "the best interests of baseball" by (1) investigating and punishing acts detrimental to the game, (2) resolving interleague disputes, (3) handling serious labor/management problems, and (4) enforcing the five documents governing the game: the Major League Agreement, the Major League Rules, the Major-Minor League Agreement, the Major-Minor League Rules, and the National Association Rules.

Judge Kenesaw Mountain Landis, earning $7,500 on the federal bench in Illinois, agreed to become the first commissioner only after he was granted the autocratic powers needed to restore the integrity of the game after the 1919 Black Sox scandal.

Landis, who served until his death in 1944, wasted no time in using his powers. Within months he handed permanent suspensions to the eight White Sox players accused but acquitted of throwing the 1919 World Series to the Reds, and impounded Babe Ruth's World Series share—and suspended him for 40 days—for illegal postseason barnstorming.

A. B. "Happy" Chandler, Ford Frick, General William D. Eckert, Bowie K. Kuhn, Peter Ueberroth, Bart Giamatti, Fay Vincent, Bud Selig, and Rob Manfred followed Landis as commissioner, but none ruled with the iron hand of the game's first czar.

Like the stock market, the commissioner's authority has risen and fallen during the 80-year existence of the office.

The World Series *Enquirer* page of October 10, 1919.

While Judge Landis had near-total power to clean up the game in the wake of the Black Sox scandal, browbeaten owners tied the hands of later commissioners, creating chaotic conditions within the game's structure.

That situation changed when owners agreed to abolish the league offices and consolidate power under Bud Selig as the game entered the 21st century. The last league presidents, Leonard Coleman of the National League and Gene Budig of the American, had been reduced to little more than figurehead status anyway.

Under previous commissioners, league presidents were able to approve player contracts, fine players or managers, arbitrate intraleague disputes, hire and fire umpires, and review protested games, among other functions.

All those functions have been absorbed by the commissioner, who previously settled disputes involving owners and leagues, made major decisions on baseball matters, and intervened in issues deemed too important to be settled by the individual leagues.

All-Star and World Series gate receipts help pay operating expenses for the commissioner's office.

Before the advent of the commissioner, league presidents acted arbitrarily in their own selfish interests—as opposed to the best interests of the game. Each was the highest executive in baseball and answered only to the club owners of his own league. As a result, battles between leagues were frequent. In the 19th century, battles raged with more intensity off the field than on.

Colonel A. G. Mills, an early National League president, managed to create a calm in the storm when he hammered out a mutually satisfactory arrangement between the National and the new American Association in 1882. This first National Agreement gave the AA official status as a major circuit and protected players and owners in both leagues. For his diplomatic success, Mills won the nickname "the Bismarck of baseball."

A later National League leader, Nick Young, was unsuccessful when he took a kindly, rather than aggressive, stance toward the owners. His umpires were scorned and roughhousing teams dominated timid opponents—often without regard to rules and invariably beyond the bounds of good sportsmanship.

The new American League had a tight rein on its umpires and club owners when it launched life as a major league in 1901. President Ban Johnson sought peace and recognition from the National but when he didn't get it, a two-year war broke out between leagues.

The war, accented by frequent player raids across league lines, ended early in 1903 when Cincinnati Reds President Garry Herrmann helped establish a three-man National Commission to rule the game.

Johnson and National League president Harry Pulliam—both former baseball writers—took two seats, while Herrmann was awarded the third for laying the groundwork.

In effect, Herrmann took the role of an early "commissioner" because the two leagues often took opposite sides in disputes.

Ironically, one of those disputes later involved Herrmann's position on the commission. John Heydler, a former umpire who had succeeded Pulliam as National League chief, succumbed to internal pressure and voted against Herrmann's retention on the commission. But he and Johnson deadlocked on the choice of a successor and the swing seat remained empty in 1920—the same season news of the Black Sox scandal broke.

Shoeless Joe: Black Sox Superstar

Shoeless Joe Jackson was the biggest star banned from baseball in the Black Sox scandal. "He was the finest natural hitter in the history of the game," said Ty Cobb. "He never figured anything out or studied anything with the scientific approach I used—he just swung." Babe Ruth admitted he copied Jackson's batting style. Tris Speaker said Jackson never slumped. Shoeless Joe couldn't read or write, but he could hit. His lifetime average was .356.

Ruppert Played Sandlot Ball

Colonel Jacob Ruppert, beer baron owner of the Yankees during Babe Ruth's heyday, was a sandlot pitcher from New York's East Side who liked to work out with his Yankees in spring training.

Landis Held AL Together

The American League was faced with the threat of secession when Judge Landis was merely a candidate for commissioner. Boston's Carl Mays, a pitcher under suspension for insubordination, was sold to the Yankees for $50,000 in July 1919, but American League president Ban Johnson canceled the deal and increased the suspension from 10 days to indefinitely. The Yankees won a court injunction against Johnson, and the Red Sox, the Yankees, and the sympathetic White Sox actually threatened to quit the league with a fourth club and increase the National to a 12-team circuit. Using the threat as a wedge, the rebel clubs forced the other American League owners to subscribe to the Lasker Plan, which made Landis commissioner. He quieted the various factions as soon as he assumed office early in 1921.

Judge Kenesaw Mountain Landis had a tough job as baseball's first commissioner: erasing the memory of the 1919 Black Sox scandal.

Staggered by the exposure of the scandal in September, club owners of both leagues realized the importance of hiring a powerful commissioner to protect the game.

Chicago advertising executive Albert Lasker, who held stock in the Cubs, conceived "the Lasker Plan," which was translated into legal language by White Sox attorney Alfred Austin and introduced by Sox owner Charles Comiskey. Lasker, Austin, and National League owners Barney Dreyfuss and William Baker discussed the job with Landis after other candidates—including former president William Howard Taft and Generals John Pershing and Leonard Wood—were rejected.

Though offered $50,000—a huge increase over his jurist's salary—Landis agreed only to consider the job. With teams anxious to prevent further scandals in the game, 11 club owners visited the Landis courtroom en masse while the judge was trying a bootlegging case. He recognized them when they entered but refused to be interrupted. "There will be less noise in the courtroom or it will be cleared," he announced.

The stunned owners liked the outspoken approach and agreed to grant Landis a contract with the precise wording he specified. The pact granted him absolute power to act "in the best interests of baseball" and has since been applied to every commissioner.

The Commissioners

Judge Kenesaw Mountain Landis

Kenesaw Mountain Landis was an ideal choice as the first commissioner of baseball. The game needed a strong man and his court record proved him to be just that. In baseball, he was even more authoritarian—actually a benevolent dictator.

Twice the intended victim of bombers in Chicago, Landis won national headlines in 1907 when he fined the Standard Oil Company $29 million in a freight rebate case. He came to the attention of baseball by withholding opinion on an antitrust suit resulting from the collapse of the Federal League in 1915. Seven years later, the case reached the United States Supreme Court, which granted an antitrust exemption to the game.

Landis was remembered by owners for his summary statement: "Both sides may understand that any blows at this thing called baseball would be regarded by this court as a blow at a national institution."

The judge guarded the game zealously after taking the commissioner's chair. When he was appointed at age 54, Landis was handed a seven-year contract for $50,000, but he accepted only $42,500 because he retained his judgeship for more than a year. The salary was lifted to $65,000 later, but Landis voluntarily sliced his pay to $40,000 during the Depression.

Landis conceded he knew little about baseball when he took the job, but he was well aware of the Black Sox scandal. Throughout his administration, Landis issued stiff suspensions or lifetime bans to anyone having even the slightest connection with disreputable characters. Among those he banned was Phillies owner Bill Cox, who bet on his own club.

"Baseball will continue on trial in America as long as baseball is played," Landis announced in his first public appearance as commissioner. "It is not enough to say that baseball must be as good as any other business. Baseball has got to be better in its morality than any other business."

Landis' first, and most difficult, task was to erase the memory of the Black Sox. He did this with lifetime bans that precluded eight players—five of them regulars—from even buying a ticket at any park of the majors or minors. In addition, their records—including the .356 lifetime batting average of out-fielder Shoeless Joe Jackson—were expunged from the official record books.

The commissioner acted after initial indictments were dropped and the athletes were acquitted of conspiracy charges in a second trial. The Grand Jury records that led to the original indictments were stolen during a change in the state attorney's office in Cook County.

"Regardless of the verdict of juries," Landis said, "no player who throws a ball game, no player that undertakes or promises to throw a ball game, no player that sits in a conference with a bunch of crooked players and gamblers where the ways and means of throwing games are planned and discussed and does not promptly tell his club about it will ever play professional baseball."

The suspension of the Black Sox was clear evidence that Landis would be a strict and active commissioner. He seldom had the patience to rely on his executive committee and was criticized for making decisions without them, but scuttled opposition by walking into major league meetings, contract in hand, and threatening to tear it up. The vast majority of owners so respected him—and feared the public reaction if he resigned—that they insisted he stay in office.

Even Babe Ruth, who had no patience for rules or those who tried to enforce them, remained on the good side of the commissioner when he was suspended for the first 40 days of the 1922 season after joining Bob Meusel and another Yankee teammate on an illegal barnstorming tour after the previous fall's World Series. The players' $3,000 Series shares were impounded until the suspensions ran out.

Landis had his hand in every aspect of the game. In 1922 he disagreed when umpire George Hildebrand called a World Series game for darkness with the sun still shining and issued an edict that future postponements would have to be cleared with the commissioner. Twelve years later, he removed Joe Medwick from the Cardinal lineup in the finale of the 1934 World Series at Detroit when Tiger fans showered the left fielder with debris after a controversy on the base paths. St. Louis led, 11–0, and Landis removed Medwick to keep the peace; a forfeit to the Cardinals could have started a full-fledged riot.

The white-maned executive handed yearlong suspensions to five players who jumped their contracts to play with independent clubs, banned for life four players in addition to the Black Sox eight, and cleared Ty Cobb and Tris Speaker of "fix" charges filed by Dutch Leonard. He ordered clubs to train close to home during World War II to cooperate with wartime travel restrictions, and even had Dizzy Dean removed as broadcaster for the St. Louis World Series of 1944 because he feared Dean's clowning and syntax were too undignified for a national audience.

But Landis was regarded as the players' friend. When he took charge of the game, a new form of player's contract was adopted.

How Landis Got His Name

Judge Kenesaw Mountain Landis was born in Millville, Ohio, on November 20, 1866, little more than a year after the end of the Civil War. His father, Dr. Abraham Landis, was a Union Army surgeon who suffered a leg wound at the Battle of Kennesaw Mountain, Georgia, on June 27, 1864. The doctor prayed that if his leg could be spared, he would name his son for that beautiful spot. The leg healed and the doctor kept his word—though he dropped an n in the boy's first name.

Respect for Landis Blocked Cub Farms

Out of respect for Commissioner Landis, who equated the farm system with slavery, the Chicago Cubs did not develop a minor-league chain during his tenure. Instead, the Cubs concentrated on buying players from independent minor-league operators.

Sox "Losers" of 1919 Got Winning Shares

When the Black Sox scandal of 1919 became public knowledge, Chicago White Sox owner Charles Comiskey fired the seven players accused and gave the remaining athletes on his team bonus checks that represented the difference between winners' and losers' shares in the World Series.

Finley Fired Player During Series

Charley Finley attempted to disqualify second baseman Mike Andrews when he made two damaging errors in the 12th inning of Game 2 in the 1973 World Series. The Oakland owner charged Andrews was injured and sought to replace him with young Manny Trillo. Commissioner Bowie Kuhn objected and Andrews was reinstated. The Andrews case angered the Oakland players.

The Commissioner's Powers

Baseball law gives the commissioner absolute power to regulate disputes "in the best interests of the game."

The late Dodger owner Walter O'Malley once gave this capsule summary: "All the owners are voluntary parties to an agreement stating that the commissioner has very broad powers and that if he takes jurisdiction in a matter that he deems not to be in the best interests of baseball, holds a hearing for all involved, including lawyers, then his decision is final and binding. We owners have a contract with each other that whatever his decision is, we will not have recourse in the courts."

Schedule Makers

Baseball schedules are drawn up by league executives. They plan all day games, then send copies to team traveling secretaries for individual adjustments. These officials, who know plane schedules by heart, plan night games, doubleheaders, and games starting at unusual times. The process takes 90 days.

Spring-training schedules are drawn up at a meeting of traveling secretaries. The job is done in one day.

Breadon Helped Hornsby

Sentimental St. Louis owner Sam Breadon, who sold controversial player/manager Rogers Hornsby from the Cardinals to the Giants after the World Championship season of 1926, rescued Hornsby when the slugger seemed headed out of the majors. Breadon signed Hornsby as a player for the Cards, arranged for him to take the managing job with the St. Louis Browns, and expedited his unconditional release so arrangements could be completed.

It gave the athletes the right—for the first time—to appeal any grievances against their club owner. Landis sat in on many cases and handed out rulings as if he were still wearing the black robes of the federal bench.

Two Cincinnati players, accused of collusion with gamblers by a Chicago racing publication, were cleared, and a number of veterans—along with dozens of minor-leaguers—became free agents under the Landis reign.

Though he maintained a stern exterior that literally made men quake in their boots when he confronted them, Judge Landis also had a lighter side. He entertained friends by impersonating the baseball people at his hearings. His vivid memory for dialogue and dialect made his character acting that much more memorable.

Happy Chandler

After Judge Landis died in office on November 25, 1944, the job of commissioner was inherited by his longtime assistant, Leslie O'Connor, while baseball brass searched for a suitable successor.

Landis had been such an unusual man that no one could fill his shoes. A man was needed who would grow into the job. U.S. Senator A. B. "Happy" Chandler of Kentucky tried but was voted out of office before his seven-year pact expired in 1952.

Chandler did make history, however, and some baseball insiders suggest he should be enshrined in the Hall of Fame, as were his predecessor, Judge Landis, and his successor, Ford Frick.

Chandler's most noteworthy contribution was throwing the weight of the commissioner's office behind Branch Rickey's efforts to integrate baseball. All 15 of Rickey's contemporaries in the majors voted against allowing Jackie Robinson—or any other African American—to play, but Chandler helped make it possible.

"Rickey came to me and said he couldn't bring in Robinson without my support," Chandler said, "and I told him he had all of my backing and all the backing of my office. The Jackie Robinson decision changed everything about sports. Baseball was first, and the others followed."

Robinson played under Burt Shotton in 1947 because Dodger manager Leo Durocher was under a one-year suspension from Chandler for unspecified conduct considered detrimental to the game. The issue came to a boil when he and Rickey advised the commissioner that Yankee executive Larry MacPhail had gamblers in his box at an exhibition game. MacPhail filed countercharges. After investigating, Chandler fined each club $2,000, suspended Yankee coach Charley Dressen 30 days, banned Durocher for a year, and even slapped a $500 fine on Brooklyn road secretary Harold Parrott, who had ghostwritten an "objectionable" Durocher column in the *Brooklyn Eagle*.

Since Chandler ordered all parties involved silenced on the case, the true cause for Durocher's suspension has never been specified.

The Kentucky commissioner was lenient with Durocher in comparison to the way he treated players who jumped to the outlaw Mexican League a year earlier. Sal Maglie, Mickey Owen, and others faced five-year bans, but Chandler pardoned the players involved after three.

He also was responsible for launching the players' excellent pension plan and signing baseball's first network television contract.

Ford Frick

Ford Frick became commissioner of baseball in September 1951—just before Bobby Thomson hit the most dramatic home run in history—but became known as "the asterisk commissioner" because of another slugger's performance.

In his 10th anniversary in the job, Frick decided to put an asterisk after all baseball records achieved under the new 162-game schedule. Since Babe Ruth had hit his 60 home runs in 154 games, Frick reasoned, Roger Maris did not really surpass him by hitting 61 in 162.

The decision set off a storm of controversy that grew the following fall after Maury Wills stole 104 bases in 162 games, surpassing Ty Cobb's one-season figure of 96. Cobb had stolen 94 bases after 154 games in 1915, but his Tigers had to replay two ties, giving him two extra chances to add to his total. Since Wills swiped 95 in his first 154 games, he actually created a new mark, using Frick's rationale in reverse. After 156 games, Wills had 97—still one more than Cobb over the same period.

Critics contended Frick's asterisk theory arose from his one-time friendship with Babe Ruth. Frick, a New York sportswriter and broadcaster, played golf and bridge with Ruth and ghosted several magazine articles under the slugger's byline.

Frick had moved into the busy world of the New York media from Colorado, where he taught journalism and wrote sports in Colorado Springs. Visiting Hearst editor Arthur Brisbane saw his work and brought him east.

Frick became National League public relations director in 1934 and league president a year later. His first notable achievement as an executive was finding funds to bail several clubs out of near-bankruptcy during those Depression days.

A contender for the vacant commissioner's job after the death of Judge Landis in 1944, Frick had considerable support, but not enough to overcome a late move by Happy Chandler. He remained National League president and took the strongest stance of his career when he blasted clubs, owners, and players who threatened to boycott games that included black players. He sent an especially sharp message to St. Louis Cardinals owner Sam Breadon, warning that prejudice would be met with lifetime suspensions—even if it hurt the league for five or ten seasons.

With Frick and Commissioner Chandler behind him, Branch Rickey was able to overcome almost unanimous opposition and bring Jackie Robinson into the game in 1947. Robinson won the Rookie of the Year Award that fall.

When he moved into the job of commissioner, Frick presided over an era of franchise shifts, expansion, and general growth of the game. Though he preferred to be a passive chieftain, Frick did take a major role in seeing that baseball secured good contracts in the young field of television.

Because he had failed to antagonize the club owners in his first seven-year term, Frick won reelection easily. He retired in 1965.

President's Half-Brother Owned Phils

Charles P. Taft, half-brother of President William Howard Taft, owned the Phillies for a brief period early in the century.

Cardinal Boss Suited Up

St. Louis Cardinals' owner Sam Breadon worked out in uniform with his team during spring training.

National League

Ford Frick was a key man in ending baseball's color line.

Families Kept Control of Clubs

Many teams have been owned by families who passed the chief executive's job from generation to generation. Clark Griffith passed the role to his adopted nephew, Calvin, with the Washington Senators (later the Minnesota Twins). Father/son chains have included William, Philip, and William Wrigley (Cubs); Charles, Lou, and Charles Comiskey (White Sox); Charles and Horace Stoneham (Giants); Walter and Peter O'Malley (Dodgers); and Bob and Ruly Carpenter (Phillies).

Bowie Kuhn tried to keep peace during the free-agent revolution, but often found himself the center of controversy.

Former Yale president Bart Giamatti (above) served only five months as commissioner before suffering a fatal heart attack that left deputy Fay Vincent in charge. Owners unhappy with his controversial decisions accepted his resignation in 1992.

Bowie K. Kuhn

Air Force Gen. William D. "Spike" Eckert, who earned his nickname playing basketball, was not on the original list of 156 candidates to succeed Frick. He was a compromise choice after the owners couldn't agree on any of the other 156 possibilities. Eckert should never have gotten the job and his performance proved it.

Eckert's replacement was tall, articulate Wall Street lawyer Bowie Kuhn, who had been associated with baseball's legal problems for 19 years when he became commissioner in 1969. Kuhn projected an image of authority. His dress was all-business and his attitude matched.

Kuhn's decisions were as controversial as any executive rulings in baseball history, but his keen interest in keeping peace in turbulent times proved ideal for management, labor, and fans.

Labor/owner disputes marred Kuhn's administration, but the commissioner succeeded in bringing major league baseball's three prime offices into the same city for the first time. The National and American Leagues, as well as the commissioner's office, began operating in the same building in midtown New York.

Kuhn was liberal in handing out suspensions—two years to Yankee owner George Steinbrenner for illegal political contributions, a year to Atlanta Braves' owner Ted Turner for tampering with another team's player, and separate three-month and three-week bans to Tiger pitcher Denny McLain in 1970 for association with gamblers and carrying a pistol.

One-time star outfielder Curt Flood, upset by his trade from the Cardinals to the Phillies in 1969, sued the commissioner in a test of the reserve clause, but his appeal was denied by the U.S. Supreme Court in 1972.

Three years later, however, pitchers Andy Messersmith and Dave McNally became the first players to test the option clause in their contracts. Contending that the clause bound them to their teams for only one year after the expiration of their contracts, the pair deliberately did not sign for 1975 and were ruled free agents by arbitrator Peter Seitz that winter.

The Messersmith decision, twice appealed unsuccessfully by the owners, toppled the traditional reserve system and forced labor and management to reach new understandings regarding player rights and contractual law.

The Kuhn administration created the Major League Baseball Promotion Corporation, engineered the creation of computerized All-Star ballots to return voting to fans in 1970, and produced a flood of news releases and publications designed to give the game greater exposure.

A very positive step in this direction was the syndication of a weekly highlights show for television, *This Week in Baseball*.

Aside from the labor/management situation, the biggest controversy Kuhn faced was his continuing war with the enigmatic owner of the Oakland A's, Charley Finley. Kuhn canceled sales of star A's Rollie Fingers and Joe Rudi in 1976, then watched the players exercise their newly won rights as free agents and sell themselves for more money than Finley could have received for them.

Peter V. Ueberroth

When Peter Ueberroth became commissioner of baseball in 1984, 21 of the 26 teams were losing money. Ueberroth reversed that trend by preaching "fiscal responsibility" among club owners, adding corporate sponsors, expanding licensing operations, and negotiating lucrative television contracts. Thanks to the increased promotion, total attendance zoomed to a record 56,331,213 in 1988.

"I'm pleased that the game has gone from a financial disaster to something that is financially viable," he said near the end of his term. "And I'm pleased that it went from an immoral, drug-ridden disaster to one of the best slices of society."

During the Ueberroth years, suspensions were issued to more than a dozen stars implicated in drug abuse; efforts were made to visibly increase minority hiring; night baseball became universal in the majors; and cable TV became an official partner of the game for the first time.

Ueberroth's crowning achievements were negotiations of a four-year, $1 billion network television contract with CBS, effective in 1990, and quick settlement of a potentially devastating 1985 player strike. The two days of games canceled by the August dispute were made up. Baseball club owners had to pay damages of $112.7 million after arbitrators ruled they had colluded to restrict the movement and salaries of veteran free agents following the 1986, 1987, and 1988 seasons.

Bart and Fay

Ueberroth's successor, National League president A. Bartlett Giamatti, spent only five months as commissioner before suffering a fatal heart attack at age 51 on September 1, 1989. His entire term was consumed by a legal tug-of-war with Pete Rose, baseball's lifetime leader in hits and the holder of 18 other major league records.

On August 24, 1989, Giamatti handed Rose a lifetime suspension for violations of Major League Rule 21. The decision ended a series of investigations and court rulings regarding allegations that Rose had bet on baseball games. The final agreement, however, did not contain a Rose admission that he had bet on baseball.

Fay Vincent, deputy commissioner under Giamatti, succeeded his boss. But he did not complete his term either.

On September 7, 1992, Vincent resigned in the wake of a no-confidence vote from team owners. He was temporarily replaced by a 10-man executive council consisting of eight owners plus the league presidents.

The owners had been troubled by Vincent's history of making executive decisions without consulting them first. He intervened to end the 32-day lockout that delayed the start of the 1990 season, leaving many owners upset at the terms of the settlement.

Vincent later made controversial rulings on expansion money and National League realignment, handed lifetime suspensions to owner George Steinbrenner and pitcher Steve Howe of the Yankees, and criticized TV superstations—the chief revenue source of several powerful owners.

He also became involved in the sale of the Seattle Mariners to Japanese interests and the attempted sale and transfer of the San Francisco Giants to Tampa/St. Petersburg, Florida.

Major League Baseball

Peter V. Ueberroth, organizer of the 1984 Los Angeles Olympics, followed that success with a five-year term as commissioner of baseball.

A Man of Letters

A. Bartlett Giamatti, 51, took office as the seventh commissioner of baseball on April 1, 1989. An Italian Renaissance scholar who was a professor of English and comparative literature before becoming president of Yale University, Giamatti was known to walk around campus with a Red Sox cap and transistor radio. "Men of letters have always gravitated toward sport," he explained. "I've always loved baseball. I wanted to be Bobby Doerr more than anything."

Who's Overpaid?

In 1997 Milwaukee Brewers owner Bud Selig made seven times more money moonlighting as acting commissioner than Bill Clinton made as president of the United States.

For more than five years, there was no commissioner of baseball. The game was run by an executive council of owners headed by Allan H. "Bud" Selig, chief executive of the Milwaukee Brewers. Unable to settle the 1994 player strike, Selig had the job of canceling the World Series.

Attorney Rob Manfred, a cum laude graduate of Harvard Law School, became the 10th commissioner on January 25, 2015. As lead negotiator for the owners in dealing with the Players Association, Manfred had managed to keep labor peace since the 232-day strike of 1994-95.

Removing Vincent from forthcoming talks on new labor and TV agreements and reducing the powers of the commissioner to make arbitrary decisions "in the best interests of baseball" became top priority for a majority of owners.

Bud Selig

After Vincent's 1992 ouster, the commissioner's office stood vacant more than five years—longer than the terms of previous occupants Giamatti (five months), Eckert (three years), and Ueberroth (four and a half years). Milwaukee Brewers owner Bud Selig served as acting commissioner.

Though Selig's watch was marred by a devastating 232-day player strike that erased the 1994 postseason, the remaining 29 club owners persuaded him to become full-time commissioner of baseball on July 9, 1998. He was approved by unanimous vote.

The only owner who became commissioner, Bud Selig eliminated league presidents—who had disciplinary power for more than a century—while consolidating operations under his authority. He introduced innovations that infuriated traditionalists but delighted teams whose treasuries profited. Interleague play and expanded playoffs, including one and then two wild-card clubs, were Selig brainstorms. He also engineered expansion to four new cities and the transfer of the Milwaukee Brewers franchise, which his family owned, across league lines from the American to the National League.

Selig also agreed to give home-field advantage in the World Series to the league that wins the All-Star Game. The rulebook strike zone was also restored under his watch. Before his reign ended, Selig was earning an estimated $14.5 million per year—much more than the sale price of the New York Yankees when George Steinbrenner bought the ballclub from CBS in 1973.

Rob Manfred

Rob Manfred, a cum laude graduate of Harvard Law School, was 56 when he became the 10th commissioner on January 25, 2015. An attorney who worked on collusion cases and collective bargaining, he was the chief negotiator for the owners in dealing with the players association. Manfred not only avoided any work stoppages but also convinced the union to expand revenue sharing and strengthen agreements regarding substance abuse and domestic violence.

The point man on the Biogenesis investigation that resulted in the suspension of Alex Rodriguez, he helped resolve the bankruptcy of the Los Angeles Dodgers, negotiate new agreements with the umpires union, instigate new rules regarding collisions on the base paths, and expand the use of instant replay. He grew up in Rome, New York, an hour from Cooperstown.

Team Executives

Major league teams are owned by groups or individuals who, as a rule, have made money in other businesses.

Many owners are activists who insist on negotiating their own trades, dealing with players directly, and hiring and firing managers. Others employ general managers to oversee their baseball operations. A business manager may run club finances, while the GM spends his time solely on improving the team and working with big-league players. A farm director runs the minor-league network for each big-time club.

Owners have been their own general managers and, at times, even field managers. Chris Von Der Ahe managed the St. Louis Browns (later Cardinals) in 1892 and parts of other years, and Charles Ebbets was in the dugout for the Brooklyn Dodgers when the 1898 season ended.

Horace Fogel ran the New York Giants for 42 games when he was part-owner of that club in 1902, and 10 years later—as full owner of the Phillies—became the first owner thrown out of the game (he had made wild charges that the 1912 National League race was rigged in favor of the Giants).

Judge Emil Fuchs, New York City magistrate and avid fan who liked to work out in uniform with his Boston Braves, placed himself in the dugout for the 1929 season, relieving Rogers Hornsby, but took a temporary leave in May to try a case in court. Fuchs returned and finished last. Bill McKechnie took over as manager in 1930.

In 1977 Ted Turner of the Atlanta Braves made himself manager after the team had lost 16 games in a row. He lost, 2–1, and had to give up his dual role as owner/manager one day later when National League president Chub Feeney invoked Rule 20 (e): a manager may not have financial interest in his team without special permission from the commissioner. Connie Mack, John McGraw, and Clark Griffith, among others, had been full-time owner/managers for years before baseball brass found any reason to question the idea of one man doing both jobs. But in 1926, Rogers Hornsby, player, manager, and part-owner of the World Champion St. Louis Cardinals, was traded to the New York Giants.

Since Hornsby owned more than $60,000 worth of Cardinal stock, how could he play for the Giants? The National League ruled that he had to sell it before he could don his new uniform.

A dispute arose as to the value of the stock, and a settlement was reached only after other teams pitched in to help the Cards pay Hornsby his asking price for divestiture.

Mack continued as owner/manager of the Athletics until 1950, but he, like Griffith and McGraw, was a player and manager who gained interest in ownership later. A nonplaying owner who goes the other way—like Fuchs in 1929 or Turner in 1977—can be accused of harming the game, the league, and the club because of inexperience at the job.

Early Owners

Early baseball brass consisted of men like Henry Lucas, who owned the St. Louis Maroons (early Cardinals) in 1885. He had three blacklisted players and decided to raise money for them. Field events, a ballgame, and even a fox chase netted enough revenue to garner $400 a man.

Cubs' Owner Got the Boot

Former sportswriter Charles Murphy won four flags in five years as owner of the Chicago Cubs, 1906 to 1910, but tore apart his team in anger when it failed to keep up the pace. He fired and traded stars and managers, berated the uniformed personnel, and angered Chicago fans so much that the National League booted him out after the 1913 season.

The Wrigleys of Chicago

The Wrigley family's association with the Cubs began in 1916, when William Wrigley Jr. bought stock in the club. His son, Phil, bought a large chunk of club stock in 1926, joined the board of directors three years later, inherited his father's shares in 1932, and became team president in 1934. "I became president because I got all the blame anyway," he said.

Owner Answers Letters

Phil Wrigley, owner of the Chicago Cubs, missed the first three games of the 1945 World Series against Detroit because he was answering letters from fans who couldn't get tickets.

Gabe Paul on Phil Wrigley

Veteran executive Gabe Paul on the late Cubs owner Phil Wrigley: "He's the only owner I ever knew who would vote against his own best interests if he thought it was good for baseball."

Fair Trade?

Phil Wrigley, owner of the Chicago Cubs, once gave the Brooklyn Dodgers minor-league outfielder Eddie Haas and the territorial rights to Los Angeles for $2 and the territorial rights to Fort Worth. The Dodgers made millions after moving to California while Haas failed as both a player and a manager.

Tom Yawkey's generosity made him popular with players of the Boston Red Sox.

Red Sox All-Stars Honored Owner Yawkey

Nine Red Sox stars who played under owner Tom Yawkey helped him mark his 21st anniversary with the team at a special Boston dinner on April 15, 1954. More than 700 people, including many big names of baseball, saw Yawkey receive an engraved 15-inch silver platter for "high principles and achievements" in sports.

"Steamshovels" Bought Braves

In the early '40s, a syndicate of Boston businessmen bought the Braves from Charles Adams.

Construction magnates Lou Perini, Guido Rugo, and Joseph Maney, who headed the syndicate, were better known as "the Three Little Steamshovels."

Two Yawkeys Owned Teams

Longtime Red Sox owner Tom Yawkey, who purchased the club at age 30 in 1933, was the son of former Tiger owner William Yawkey.

Lucas looked for his players on Saturday nights and handed them impromptu bonuses when they needed spending money. In return, he asked them to come to the park sober and ready to play.

After the Players League rebellion of 1890, ownership could not afford generosity. Nor were the owners in the mood to be kind to players who threatened the existence of the National League.

Rosters were reduced from 15 to 13 men in 1892 and salaries cut 30 to 40 percent. Cincinnati pitcher Tony Mullane, a 21-game winner, was asked to sign for $3,500 after earning $4,200 the year before. He refused and joined Butte of the Montana State League. The next spring he signed with Cincy for $2,100.

In 1898 the Robison family owned both the Cleveland and St. Louis clubs of the National League. The following year the family shifted many of Cleveland's top stars to St. Louis, strengthening the Cardinals but so weakening the Spiders that they finished with a record of 20 wins and 134 losses for a sickly .130 percentage. They had to play most of their games out of Cleveland because they were afraid of their own fans.

Shortly after the turn of the century, 32-year-old Helene Britton became Cardinals club president through inheritance. An early woman's rights advocate, she attended all National League meetings and sought to increase female attendance at games. She succeeded by hiring an attractive male singer to perform between innings.

Many of the early owners relied on top executives to make trades, sign players, and run their clubs. Colonel Jacob Ruppert, the beer baron who ran the Yankees in the Babe Ruth era, worked well with longtime baseball man Ed Barrow, while St. Louis Cardinals' owner Sam Breadon depended on the studious Branch Rickey. Tom Yawkey did well with Eddie Collins after the Boston sportsman became Red Sox owner at age 30 in 1933.

Perhaps the most respected old-time owner was Detroit's Frank Navin. When he died at age 64 in 1935, H. G. Salsinger of the *Detroit News* delivered this eulogy:

"More problems were settled in the back room of the Detroit club's headquarters, above the entrance of Navin Field, at

How DeWitt Started

Bill DeWitt, who won notoriety for trading managers with Frank Lane in 1960, was involved with the ownership of several clubs, including the Reds, the Tigers, the Browns, and the White Sox. A classic case of a man who worked his way up, DeWitt launched his baseball career by selling soda at Sportsman's Park in St. Louis.

Michigan and Trumbull Avenues, than at any other spot in the country. Mr. Navin generally sat there from late morning until late afternoon, and not a day passed but came long-distance calls from baseball men. Kenesaw Mountain Landis leaned heavily on Mr. Navin for advice and guidance.

"He was one of the few owners of major league clubs who knew the playing end of the game as well as the business end. Few of his players ever matched him in technical knowledge.

"He knew more about pitching than most of his pitchers will ever know, and more about batting. No man has ever made as thorough a study of a game as Mr. Navin did of baseball.

"Ballplayers liked to play for him. With all his technical knowledge, he was the most lenient of employers. Because he knew baseball, he understood how breaks figured in decisions; understood how certain happenings over which the player has no control can bring defeat.

"Like the late John Joseph McGraw, he criticized only laziness and stupidity in a player; he never held one responsible for an error."

Famous Team Executives

Branch Rickey

He that will not reason is a bigot
He that cannot reason is a fool
And he that dares not reason is a slave

Those words appeared on a sign that hung over Branch Rickey's desk in four different team offices: the St. Louis Browns, the St. Louis Cardinals, the Brooklyn Dodgers, and the Pittsburgh Pirates.

Rickey was regarded by many baseball men as the greatest executive in the game's history. He created the concept of the farm system, broke the baseball color line against tremendous odds, and developed sliding pits and complex pickoff plays.

Stories about Rickey's dealings at the contract table are almost legendary. "Negotiating with Rickey is like being in on the signing of the Declaration of Independence while taking a course in human relations," said former catcher Joe Garagiola.

Chuck Connors remembered, "It was easy to figure out Rickey's thinking on contracts. He had both players and money and didn't like to see the two of them mix."

Rickey's miserly reputation stemmed from his early days with the Cardinals, when the team was so strapped for finances that it held spring training in St. Louis one year. Rickey once distributed his own salary to help meet the payroll and the team was forced to wear its home uniforms on the road; it couldn't afford to buy a separate set.

Because the Cards couldn't afford to compete with other major league teams for the purchase of top players from the minors, Rickey suggested St. Louis develop its own talent. By 1940, his chain-gang farm system consisted of 32 minor-league teams and eight working agreements with clubs not owned outright. At one point he controlled the entire player supply of the Nebraska State and Arkansas-Missouri Leagues. (Commissioner Landis later limited working agreements to one per league.)

Connie's Start

The advent of the American League gave Connie Mack a great opportunity. He convinced Ben Shibe, a Philadelphia sporting goods producer, to buy a franchise, took a 25 percent ownership stake, and became both manager and treasurer. By 1912, he had acquired another 25 percent, making him half-owner. Mack later became full owner of the club.

Mighty MacPhails

Long-time baseball executives Larry and Lee MacPhail are the only father-and-son tandem in the Baseball Hall of Fame. The former was elected in 1978 and the latter 20 years later. Lee's son Andy MacPhail, current president of the Philadelphia Phillies, continues the family tradition of front-office service.

Rickey Rested on Sunday

Branch Rickey, Christy Mathewson, and several other players and managers early in the century did not play ball on Sunday.

The Genius of Rickey

"Rickey's genius was organizational— training, scouting, finding, teaching, developing, always with excellent on-field judgement."
—Leonard Koppett in *The Sporting News*

Busch Liked Horses, Baseball

Young Gussie Busch, later owner of the Cardinals, rode horses with humorist Will Rogers in Wyoming and watched the St. Louis Browns play baseball. George Sisler was a favorite.

Bobby and John

Before they became partners in the record 14-year title run of the Atlanta Braves, John Schuerholz and Bobby Cox made three trades as general managers. The most significant of those swaps sent southpaw starter Charlie Liebrandt to Atlanta for first baseman Gerald Perry.

No Laughing Matter

When Braves executive Terry McGuirk confided to baseball commissioner Fay Vincent that the Braves were pursuing John Schuerholz as general manager, Vincent laughed and insisted Schuerholz would never leave Kansas City.

Frantic Frank Lane

White Sox general manager Frank Lane—often called Frantic Frank because of his tendency for nonstop talk and rapid-fire trades—was seated in the upper right field stands one day in full view of fans and players. Red Sox right fielder Jimmy Piersall heard Lane scream at his own second baseman, Nellie Fox, for some minor infraction. Piersall waited for quiet, then yelled to Lane, "Why don't you jump and get it over with?"

Beer Baron Busch Struck Out on Dark

Beer baron August "Gussie" Busch, owner of the St. Louis Cardinals since 1953, once tried to hire Alvin Dark as manager. Dark, a prohibitionist, said he could not work for the team, which was affiliated with Anheuser-Busch breweries.

How Clubs Make Money

Major league teams make money from ticket sales, broadcasting contracts, and advertisements purchased by yearbook and scoreboard sponsors. Many also get income from parking and concessions receipts. World Series money is divided among the clubs, leagues, and the commissioner's office only when the World Series lasts more than four games. Proceeds from the first four contests go to the players.

Youth in the Capital

Washington Nationals owner Ted Lerner, born and raised in the capital, sat in 25-cent bleacher seats at Griffith Stadium while attending Senators games with his father. He was also a high school classmate of future baseball commissioner Bowie Kuhn.

Evil Empire

Red Sox executive Larry Lucchino first called the Yankees "the Evil Empire" while talking to sportswriter Murray Chass in 2003.

Rickey, who served the Cardinals 25 years as president, general manager, and even manager on occasion, moved to the Brooklyn Dodgers' GM post in 1942 and, five years later, brought Jackie Robinson into the majors as the first black player of the modern era.

He earned a reputation for being an astute judge of raw talent, as well as a shrewd trader who peddled veteran players just before their value declined. "It's better to trade one year too early than one year too late," he insisted.

Once, a University of California professor wrote Rickey about a pitcher on his squad. The rookie was invited to camp and promptly hit three 450-foot drives into the center-field palm trees. Over the objections of the Cardinal manager, Rickey moved the boy to the outfield. The player—Chick Hafey—turned out to be the National League's batting champion with a .349 average in 1931.

Several years after Hafey's title, Rickey insisted the team keep 18-year-old outfielder Enos Slaughter. Several coaches and scouts objected, saying he couldn't hit. Slaughter went on to compile a lifetime .300 average over 19 seasons. He was the World Series hero of 1946 for the Cards.

Rickey had a bad ballclub with the Pirates of the early '50s, but he laid the groundwork for great Pirate teams to come.

Stubborn, outspoken, shrewd, and exceptionally intelligent, Rickey's last hurrah in baseball was restoring National League baseball in New York.

When he became president of the Continental League—a proposed new major—he so frightened executives of the existing majors that they absorbed several of his cities through expansion. Rickey agreed to abandon plans for the new circuit only after the National League agreed to return to New York, which had been without a National League club since the Dodgers and Giants fled to the West Coast after the 1957 season. In 1962, the New York Mets were born.

Larry MacPhail

Larry MacPhail's impact on baseball was so strong that his candidacy for the Hall of Fame was fought 30 years after he left the game.

MacPhail finally won election in 1978—40 years after he kept Babe Ruth in baseball by making him a coach with the Brooklyn Dodgers.

A dynamic but often abrasive executive, MacPhail broke into baseball when he purchased Columbus of the American Association in 1931. Three years later, he seized the reins at Cincinnati, one of several National League cities hard-hit by the Depression. He took over Brooklyn in 1937 and the New York Yankees in 1945.

At all three stops, MacPhail built a reputation as a financial wizard, ingenious promoter, and superb talent scout, but he was accused by critics of enjoying a martini as much as a home run. He battled with commissioners, owners, managers, and players—sometimes firing anyone in sight and rehiring them after he cooled off.

MacPhail is best remembered for bringing night baseball to the major leagues in 1935. When he announced that the Reds would play the first night game, opposition was almost universal, but fan reaction was so good that MacPhail also installed lights in Ebbets Field and Yankee Stadium when he arrived there. All other clubs, with the prolonged exception of the Chicago Cubs, eventually followed suit.

Night ball was intended strictly as a novelty—one of many MacPhail promotions—and the outspoken executive wanted baseball under lights limited to seven games per season. He lived to see clubs adopt schedules calling for more than 60 percent of their games after dark.

MacPhail was not only adept at promoting but also at building winning teams. Those twin talents rescued the Reds and the Dodgers from the brink of bankruptcy and restored the New York Yankee dynasty.

He acquired the players who jelled into the Cincinnati champions of 1939–1940, then guided the Dodgers to the 1941 flag—their first in more than 20 years. The MacPhail Yankees won the World Championship in 1947, but he left the game on doctor's advice after the season.

MacPhail promoted fashion shows, Old Timers' games, and televised baseball. When he came to Brooklyn from Cincinnati, he brought broadcaster Red Barber with him. He spent $200,000 to refurbish Ebbets Field when the Dodgers were in debt for more than twice that amount; he hired usherettes to attract male fans; and he was the first magnate to have his team travel extensively by air (the Yankees in 1946).

The Stadium Club—another MacPhail innovation—and an announced desire to "make every day Sunday" at the ballpark helped bring crowds to watch MacPhail's clubs. He pioneered the pension plan for executives and helped carve the initial pension plan for players. He also gave longtime executive E. J. "Buzzie" Bavasi his first job in baseball—as an assistant in the office of the Brooklyn Dodgers in 1939.

MacPhail's temper exploded in 1941 when the Dodgers' special train from Boston failed to pick him up at the 125th Street station en route to a team victory party. He blamed manager Leo Durocher—whose career as pilot was launched by MacPhail—and fired him that night. As usual, Durocher was rehired the next morning.

"He and Leo were so much alike there were always fireworks," recalled MacPhail's son, Lee, former general manager for the Orioles and the Yankees who became American League president.

MacPhail did fine Joe DiMaggio for missing a Yankee promotion and even accused Commissioner Happy Chandler of slander. His temperament was best reflected in a series of phone calls with his son, then running the Yankee farm at Columbus. When Lee hesitated in following Larry's order to hire Burleigh Grimes as manager, the elder MacPhail threatened him. "If

Ruppert Lost His Shirt

Yankee owner Jacob Ruppert literally lost his shirt during his club's World Series victory party on a train headed home from St. Louis in 1928. The players had begun to tear off each other's shirts, and team leaders Babe Ruth and Lou Gehrig—batting stars of the Series—broke into Ruppert's drawing room and ripped off his. Between them, Gehrig and Ruth got 16 hits, seven home runs, and 13 runs batted in during the four-game sweep of the Cardinals.

Bill Veeck was only 32 when he became president of the Cleveland Indians in 1946. Within two years, he had integrated the American League.

Grimes isn't there by noon tomorrow, clean out your desk," he warned.

MacPhail's arrival in New York was the result of a three-way purchase that also involved Dan Topping and Del Webb. The trio bought the club, the stadium, and the farm system for the ridiculously low price of $2.8 million, $100,000 less than the Yankees gave Reggie Jackson in a multiyear contract that began in 1977.

Topping and Webb purchased MacPhail's holdings for $1.75 million following a tumultuous World Series victory party. He'd been ordered by doctors to leave the game, but MacPhail was also uppity because arch-rival Branch Rickey, chief executive of the Dodgers, had turned his back when MacPhail offered his hand in peace. That confrontation, which occurred just prior to Game 7, soured the taste of victory for MacPhail.

"I'm through!" he screamed at the party. He fired everyone—including himself—but his was the only exit that was for real. No one knew what the doctors had told him. They found out later that a great showman was staging his last act.

Bill Veeck

The most unorthodox and creative owner in the game after World War II was Bill Veeck, son of a baseball writer who became president of the Chicago Cubs in 1919.

Sometimes called "Sportshirt Bill" because of an aversion to ties, Veeck read four books a week, peg-legged his way around the grandstand to talk to fans, and jotted down hundreds of ideas in a bulging card file that his wife said had a value of more than $3 million.

Veeck integrated the American League by bringing Larry Doby and Satchel Paige to Cleveland and introduced the first "home-run spectacular"—a scoreboard that shot flares, Roman candles, and other crowd-pleasing fireworks.

Long known as "the P. T. Barnum of Baseball," Veeck was only 32 when he bought the Cleveland Indians in 1946. He later bought three other clubs—including the Chicago White Sox twice.

Veeck's antics—which began during his four-year term as president of the Milwaukee Brewers in the American Association—generated such fan response that he was credited with saving the sagging White Sox franchise for Chicago in 1976. The team had been on the verge of moving to Seattle—filling an American League obligation there—and being replaced by the Oakland A's of Charley Finley, a Chicago insurance man.

In 1953, two years after he allowed a midget to bat in a regulation game, Veeck's conservative contemporaries translated their dislike of him into a no-vote on his request to move the floundering St. Louis Browns. Faced with losing more money in St. Louis or selling the team, Veeck sold.

He scouted for Cleveland—the team he once owned—in 1955 and, two years later, headed a Cleveland publicity agency that did promotions for the Indians. Attempts to buy the Senators, the Tigers, and the Pirates failed before Veeck and Hank Greenberg, his close friend, landed the White Sox from the Comiskey family in 1959. The team immediately won its first pennant in 40 years.

Ill health knocked Veeck out of the game in 1961, but he returned as White Sox owner in 1976, bringing along veteran baseball man Paul Richards as manager and putting Rudie Schaffer back into his job as business manager. Shrewd trades and endless promotion enabled the team to finish a surprising third in 1977 and draw a record Sox attendance of 1,657,135.

Though he lost a leg to a World War II injury suffered at Bougainville, Veeck drew on endless energy to achieve success.

His natural sense of humor, expressed so well in his book *Veeck as in Wreck*, made him a sought-after banquet speaker.

Once, when he accepted back-to-back engagements for a Springfield, Illinois, dinner and a St. Louis luncheon, he drove all night in a blizzard to keep the lunch date. An hour-and-a-half from the Chase Hotel, he could go no further by car and took to his feet. He was minus coat or hat and restricted to crutches because of recurring leg problems, but he hobbled through the raging storm to reach the hotel exactly at noon. No one was there.

"I had been so intent on making my appointment that it never occurred to me in all that time that nobody else was going to be crazy enough to come out in a blizzard to listen to me talk," he said.

Bill Veeck started in the game as a Wrigley Field vendor, selling peanuts, scorecards, and soft drinks. He became a Cubs office boy and worked his way up in the organization, becoming treasurer in 1940. A year later, at age 27, Veeck and veteran manager Charlie Grimm bought the Milwaukee Brewers (then a Triple-A club).

"Promotion plus a winning team breaks attendance records" said Veeck. He proved the idea at Cleveland, which drew an American League record 2,620,627 fans during the World Championship season of 1948.

"I can't afford to lose a single fan," Veeck said on several occasions. Often, his ballpark gimmicks were unannounced. Sometimes, the secret was essential—the league might have stopped some stunts before they started.

Walter O'Malley

Had Walter O'Malley convinced New York City politicians to build a domed stadium near Brooklyn's Long Island Railroad depot, both the Brooklyn Dodgers and the New York Giants would have stayed in the east.

When city fathers rejected the ideas of O'Malley in 1956, the engineer/attorney/owner sold Ebbets Field and kept the Dodgers there as renters. He even played eight games at Jersey City's Roosevelt Stadium that year—and seven more in 1957—as a "warning" that he was serious about securing better facilities for the Dodgers and their fans.

"I got worried about the location, the vandalism to automobiles, and the molesting of women," he said. A Queens site—now the location of the Mets' Shea Stadium—was suggested but rejected. "If I move from Brooklyn to Queens, I might as well move to the West Coast because we won't be the Brooklyn Dodgers in Queens."

Saving San Diego

An 11th-hour offer by McDonald's founder Ray Kroc prevented the San Diego Padres from becoming the third edition of the Washington Senators early in 1974. As a kid, Kroc had been a bleacher bum in Chicago's Wrigley Field.

Open for Business

During the 1975 winter meetings at the Diplomat Hotel in Hollywood, Florida, White Sox owner Bill Veeck instructed general manager Roland Hemond to set up a lobby desk with a phone and a "FOR SALE" sign. To make sure the gimmick got attention, Veeck told Sox publicity chief Buck Peden to call every half-hour. Seeing that activity convinced other club GMs to do deals with the Sox themselves.

Tony's Sponsor

Roland Hemond was the wise executive who recommended Tony La Russa to Bill Veeck. The 34-year-old manager later managed the A's and Cardinals during his Hall of Fame career.

Wrigley Was Riled by Writer

Chicago Cubs owner Phil Wrigley exploded with anger when *Chicago Daily News* sports editor Lloyd Lewis ran a mid-season box asking Cub fans to vote for a new manager. He had to be restrained from running a Cub-sponsored ad asking for readers to choose a new sports editor.

Women Owned Teams

Men do not have a monopoly on ownership of big-league ballclubs. Among women who have served as owners are Helene Britton (Cardinals), Joan Whitney Payson (Mets), Jean Yawkey (Red Sox), Grace Comiskey (White Sox), Joan Kroc (Padres), and Marge Schott (Reds). All but Payson and Schott inherited teams from their husbands.

Oakland owner Charley Finley sold players for cash when rising salaries and failing attendance curtailed his cash flow.

Los Angeles produced a huge baseball market, and the Dodgers set several attendance records.

O'Malley joined the Dodgers when Wendell Willkie, the 1940 Republican candidate for president, resigned as Dodger attorney. John F. Kennedy might have replaced O'Malley, but Ambassador Joseph P. Kennedy was rebuffed in efforts to buy into the club.

Club president by 1950, O'Malley owned 75 percent of the team when he went west after the 1957 campaign. He designed Dodger Stadium after finding flaws in other recent parks. O'Malley even scouted the Chavez Ravine site, originally a garbage dump. He used his engineering skills to estimate—accurately—that eight million tons of earth would have to be moved during construction.

Because of his numerous professional skills, demonstrated baseball expertise, and businesslike approach to the game, O'Malley was frequently called on as advisor during the game's biggest controversies. Several jealous contemporaries had the audacity to charge that O'Malley was the real commissioner of baseball.

Under O'Malley and such veteran executives as Buzzie Bavasi, the Dodgers maintained a strong major league club and a productive farm system.

Charley Finley

The most controversial executive of the postwar era—and perhaps in the game's history—was Charley Finley. In the tradition of Larry MacPhail, Finley was a showman, a first-rate talent scout, and a thorn in the side of many others—mostly his own employees.

After several unsuccessful efforts to buy a franchise, Finley purchased the Kansas City Athletics in 1961. Ten years later, as the Oakland A's, the club won the first of five consecutive divisional championships in the American League West. Sandwiched into the middle of that streak were three straight World Series victories.

Finley was an enigma from the start. An absentee owner who ran a Chicago insurance business, he spent hours on the telephone in daily conferences with his manager and was the busiest trader in the game—even when his club was the best in baseball.

He was scorned by contemporaries for many innovations that became standard: colorful uniforms, white shoes, scheduling the World Series on weekend days and weekday nights.

Though he tried working with a general manager in his early days as owner, Finley found—through bitter experience with Frank Lane—that he worked better alone. He also saved money by handling the job, and ran his front office with only a skeleton crew that included several relatives.

Attempts to move the Kansas City franchise to Louisville and the Oakland franchise to Denver did not endear him to the fans of either city, and Finley had to rely on his players to bring spectators to his park. Constant managerial changes and trades kept newspapers and magazines filled with stories about the A's—and such promotions as "Mustache Day" helped. Finley renewed the fashion of mustaches for ballplayers—and even manager Dick

Williams went along when Finley offered his uniformed employees a bonus for growing them.

During the lean years in Kansas City, he put bulls in the bullpen, rode mascot mule Charley O around the diamond, and built a "pennant porch" to imitate the short right-field fence of Yankee Stadium. The fence violated a rule about minimum distance to the plate and had to be modified.

The major gripe against Finley came from his managers. They said he interfered with their running of the ballclub. Dick Williams, who lasted longer and was more successful than any other manager under Finley, resigned in 1973 after winning three straight divisional flags—two of them resulting in World Championships.

Ted Turner

Youthful television magnate Ted Turner, also one of the world's top yachtsmen, bought the Atlanta Braves in 1976 and spent most of the following season under suspension for allegedly tampering with outfielder Gary Matthews, who then belonged to the Giants.

Matthews and pioneer free agent Andy Messersmith, once a top pitcher, were among the big names Turner brought to the Braves in an effort to thrust the team into contention, but the effort failed and Turner tried to unload his high-salaried players almost as quickly as he had signed them.

Turner knew little about baseball until his TV station began carrying the Braves games in 1975. After his purchase, he became such a prominent fan that President-elect Jimmy Carter, former governor of Georgia, said, "I need to talk to you, Ted, and learn how to become well known."

The trim, energetic Turner not only attended Atlanta games but stamped himself as the most uninhibited owner in baseball. He jumped fences to greet home-run hitters, collapsed on the dugout in a deathlike pose after defeats, threw himself into a collegiate mattress-stuffing contest, finished second in a race of motorized bathtubs, joined a pregame ostrich race, helped ballgirls sweep the bases between innings, played poker with players, hosted an end-of-season champagne party for fans, and painted THE ENEMY on the roof of the visitors' dugout.

After firing Bobby Cox as manager and bringing him back as general manager four years later, Turner decided to let his baseball men run the team. His gambit paid off when the revamped team launched a 14-year title run unequaled in any professional sport. Not long after the 1995 world championship, Turner turned his attention to CNN and other ventures, merging Turner Broadcasting with AOL Time Warner in a deal that ended his colorful baseball ownership.

George Steinbrenner

The minute he purchased the New York Yankees for $10 million in 1973, Cleveland shipbuilder George M. Steinbrenner III replaced Charley Finley as the game's most controversial and

Schott in the Dark

Marge Schott served more than seven years as principal owner of the Cincinnati Reds before her outspoken style prompted fellow owners to impose a one-year suspension and $25,000 fine on February 3, 1993. Schott, the only woman among the 30 club owners, was banned for allegedly making racial and ethnic slurs. The ruling did not involve team mascot Schottzie 02, a St. Bernard accustomed to walking on the field before games at Riverfront Stadium. The penurial Mrs. Schott was later forced to sell her majority interest in the Reds.

Musical Chairs

Baseball owners gave the children's game of "Musical Chairs" a new twist just before 2002 spring training. After a group headed by Marlins owner John Henry and former Padres owner Tom Werner bought the Boston Red Sox for a record $660 million, Henry sold the Marlins to Expos owner Jeffrey Loria, who was accompanied in his move from Montreal to Florida by his general manager, field manager, and most of his front-office staff. Major League Baseball assumed a one-year role as caretaker in Montreal, a franchise saddled with a bad ballpark and sagging attendance. Washington supermarket magnate Ted Lerner purchased the club, ending the 34-year drought of major league baseball in the nation's capital.

outspoken owner. In his first 17½ seasons, Steinbrenner changed managers 19 times and pitching coaches two dozen times—often rehiring men he had fired before (including Billy Martin a record five times).

Steinbrenner showed similar impulsiveness in collecting players, especially high-priced veteran free agents. He signed, among others, Catfish Hunter, Goose Gossage, Tommy John, Reggie Jackson, Don Baylor, Ken Griffey, Dave Winfield, Jack Clark, Mike Mussina, and Jason Giambi.

The team won five divisional crowns, four pennants, and two World Championships from 1976 to 1981 but was never free of controversy.

The stormiest season occurred in 1978, when the beleaguered Martin, caught in a crossfire between Jackson and Steinbrenner, said, "The two of them deserve each other—one's a born liar, the other's convicted." The reference to Steinbrenner's conviction for making illegal campaign contributions to Richard Nixon cost Martin his job.

Steinbrenner's ego often interfered with his judgment. Desperate to compete with the crosstown Mets for headlines in the New York tabloids, he had verbal battles with Jackson and Winfield in addition to Martin.

The owner's tempestuous tenure seemed over on August 20, 1990, when Commissioner Fay Vincent ruled Steinbrenner had violated "the best interests of baseball" by associating with gambler Howard Spira. Vincent said two days of testimony from Steinbrenner revealed "a pattern of behavior that borders on the bizarre."

Refusing Vincent's offer of a two-year suspension followed by a three-year probation, Steinbrenner received a lifetime ban instead. His title was changed from general partner to limited partner, leaving his family in control of the majority of team stock but prohibiting him from participating in personnel decisions. Fans disenchanted with the turmoil that had plunged the once-proud franchise into last place greeted the news with jubilation.

But their joy was short-lived: in one of his last acts before resigning himself in 1992, Vincent revoked the owner's suspension, effective March 1, 1993. Fortified by an unprecedented cable TV contract, Steinbrenner rebuilt the team into a juggernaut that won five pennants and four World Series from 1996 to 2001.

Owners to Remember

With the notable exception of Ted Turner, who named himself manager of the Braves for a night before Bowie Kuhn scuttled the move, owners don't wear uniforms. But, like players, they are often honored by their teams.

Fenway Park's Green Monster bears the initials of former Red Sox owners Tom and Jean Yawkey, painted white in Morse Code—a tribute to the *Titanic* sinking that occurred on the same day the Boston ballpark opened.

Walter A. Haas Jr. kept the A's in Oakland after buying the club from Charley Finley in 1980 and has an honorary jersey in right field with an Old English "A" instead of a number.

George Steinbrenner's constant meddling with manager Billy Martin's moves convinced Yankees players Thurman Munson and Lou Piniella to visit the owner in his Milwaukee hotel room. They talked for two hours, basically telling The Boss to fire his manager or leave him alone. Martin, asleep in a nearby room, heard their voices and knocked on the door himself. The players dove into the shower and closed the curtain, but Martin discovered them anyway.

A statue of the late George Steinbrenner stands outside the Yankees spring training park, a miniature Yankee Stadium originally called Legends Field but now known as George M. Steinbrenner Stadium.

The Mets saluted William Shea, the lawyer who brought National League baseball back to New York, with a "Shea" logo on the left-field fence in 2008, the final year the team played in Shea Stadium before moving to Citi Field. It appeared next to the team's retired player numbers.

The gold RK on the San Diego press box refers to Ray Kroc, the McDonald's founder whose 11th-hour rescue kept the club from moving to Washington. His name also appears in white lettering.

Even the Montreal Expos lasted long enough to honor their owner. Charles Bronfman was not only the first member of the team's Hall of Fame in 1993 but the honoree of retired uniform No. 83, selected to match his age, on the right-field wall of Olympic Stadium. The words FONDATEUR/FOUNDER were contained in the circular patch honoring the brewery magnate.

Strange Transition

Ruben Amaro, Jr. went from Phillies GM one year (2015) to Red Sox first base coach the next (2016).

Fehr's Fortune

During the tenure of Donald Fehr as executive director of the Players Association, the average player salary rose from $289,000 in 1983 to $3.24 million in 2009.

Dan Schlossberg

Cleveland shipbuilder George M. Steinbrenner bought the New York Yankees from CBS in 1973 for $10 million—a sum that pales in comparisons to the lavish player salaries he paid later. Known as The Boss because of his hands-on ownership style, he changed players and managers often before hiring Joe Torre—and basking in the rare air of stability—in 1996. His statue stands in front of George M. Steinbrenner Stadium in Tampa, where the Yankees hold spring training.

Chapter 11

Ronnie Joyner

The Cleveland Indians upset their fans when trade-happy general manager Frank Lane traded a home run king for a batting champ on the eve of the 1960 season. Rocky Colavito, a handsome matinée idol who had hit 42 home runs for the Tribe in 1959, was peddled to the Detroit Tigers for Harvey Kuenn, who had hit .353 the year before but had only nine home runs. Colavito contributed 35 home runs to the 1960 Tigers while Kuenn hit nine home runs again, this time for Cleveland.

Trades

Bobo Newsom's Travelog

To say Bobo Newsom was a well-traveled pitcher is an understatement. From 1935 to 1952 he played for, in order, the Browns, the Senators, the Red Sox, the Browns, the Tigers, the Senators, the Dodgers, the Browns, the Senators, the A's, the Senators, the Yankees, the Giants, the Senators, and the A's. He won 211 games and lost 222.

New Suitcase Simpson

Although Harry Simpson was known as "Suitcase" because he switched teams so often, Octavio Dotel, a pitcher whose career spanned 1999-2013, played for more different teams (13) than anyone in baseball history.

Medwick's Return

Slugger Joe Medwick, who first joined the Cardinals in 1932, was treated as an "enemy" after his trade to the Dodgers in 1940, but received a hero's welcome when he rejoined St. Louis seven years later. He received his unconditional release from the Yankees in 1947, but the Cards wanted a right-handed pinch-hitter and signed him. He wasn't recognized in pregame practice because he wore No. 21 instead of his familiar No. 7, but his name brought wild cheers when it was announced in the late innings with the team behind, 2-0. He smashed a long double in a pinch-hitting role—retiring for a pinch-runner—and, at 35, enjoyed two productive seasons before ending his career.

Joe D

The Yankees spent only $50,000 to purchase Joe DiMaggio from the San Francisco Seals of the Pacific Coast League on November 21, 1934.

Clever Catfish

Catfish Hunter signed his seven-figure Yankees contract in 1974 with a 15-cent pen.

Hefty Contract

Tom Hicks, owner of the Texas Rangers, paid the same amount for the entire ballclub in 1998 as he did to sign free agent Alex Rodriguez two years later ($252 million).

The Art of Trading

Teams trade players—and even managers—more often than kids trade baseball cards.

Revised reserve rules sometimes force executives to secure permission from players before completing deals, but the ritual of constant dealing continues as an integral part of the game.

During baseball's winter meetings, an annual weeklong convention, trades once happened so frequently that fans had trouble keeping track. The news from those conventions, reflecting the game's continuing position as America's national pastime, invariably dominates other sports news of the week.

"Trading is hoping," according to Maury Wills, who was sold or traded three times in his career. "General managers trade for what they hope will happen. There's never been a general manager who's so brilliant he can guarantee a sure-shot trade. Show me a general manager with a reputation as a shrewd trader and I'll show you a man who's been lucky."

Dealing for pitchers is especially risky, Wills said, because an arm can go bad overnight.

No player is immune from trades. Brooks Robinson spent his entire career with the Baltimore Orioles, 1955 to 1977, but he was a rarity. Such superstars as Babe Ruth, Rogers Hornsby, Jimmie Foxx, Hank Greenberg, Warren Spahn, and Hank Aaron experienced at least one trade.

"Being traded is like celebrating your 100th birthday," said NBC commentator Joe Garagiola, a former player. "It might not be the happiest occasion in the world, but consider the alternatives."

Big Deals

Four times in baseball history, four teams were involved in a trade (1953, 1977, 2002, and 2004). There were numerous three-way trades, one "conventional" deal that involved two teams but 17 players, and countless big-money transactions. There might have been a complete roster swap between Kansas City and Baltimore in 1958 if Orioles general manager Paul Richards hadn't decided to retain Brooks Robinson.

The most recent four-way deal took place in 2004 and involved two-time batting champion Nomar Garciaparra and two other veteran shortstops. The Red Sox sent the five-time All-Star shortstop to the Cubs and acquired shortstop Orlando Cabrera from the Expos and first baseman Doug Mientkiewicz from the Twins. Montreal got shortstop Alex Gonzalez from the Chicago, who also sent minor-league pitcher Justin Jones to Minnesota.

Some of the game's most stunning trades occurred after the advent of the free-agent era in the '70s, when executives were forced to rebuild clubs whose stars left voluntarily or to deal players involved in salary haggles. The former case was best illustrated early in 1978, when the Oakland A's sent star southpaw Vida Blue to the San Francisco Giants for seven players and cash. The latter example was shown on the trade deadline of June 15, 1977, when the New York Mets dumped disgruntled pitcher Tom Seaver on the Cincinnati Reds for four players—three of whom became immediate regulars.

Perhaps the most significant "forced trade" occurred on February 9, 1979, when the Minnesota Twins sent seven-time American League batting champion Rod Carew to the California Angels for four young players. The 33-year-old first baseman, who had threatened to become a free agent—leaving the Twins with no compensation—quickly parlayed his .334 lifetime batting average into a five-year, $4 million contract.

Minnesota had received better offers for Carew, but the player exercised veto power provided by the five-and-ten rule—giving ten-year major leaguers who have been with one club for the past five years the right to say no.

Ron Santo of the Chicago Cubs was the first to use that right, on December 4, 1973, but later accepted a deal that sent him to the crosstown White Sox.

A no-trade clause, inserted into many players' contracts, has had nebulous significance, just as the five-and-ten rule has done little to discourage trading activity. Generally, when a player finds out his club wants to trade him, he goes. Slugger Jeff Burroughs, dealt from the Rangers to the Braves for five players and $250,000 before the 1977 season, said he had a no-trade clause but did not wish to stay where he wasn't wanted.

Increased player freedom complicates the lives of executives who previously needed to reach agreement only with their counterparts—without talking to players, agents, and lawyers. But new rules did not prevent the Braves, the Pirates, the Mets, and the Rangers from engineering an 11-man swap on December 8, 1977.

"It was a trade that didn't happen in minutes or hours," said Pittsburgh manager Chuck Tanner. "It took a lot of days and a lot of conferences to get it done."

The swap sent first baseman Willie Montanez from Atlanta to Texas for pitchers Adrian Devine and Tommy Boggs, plus outfielder Eddie Miller. The Rangers, in turn, shipped Montanez and outfielders Tom Grieve and Ken Henderson to the New York Mets for pitcher Jon Matlack, and pitcher Bert Blyleven to the Pirates for outfielder Al Oliver and shortstop Nelson Norman. As part of the deal, the Mets also sent first baseman/outfielder John Milner to Pittsburgh.

In a previous four-team deal, on February 17, 1953, the Philadelphia Phillies sent pitcher Russ Meyer and cash to the Boston Braves for first baseman Earl Torgeson. The Braves sent Meyer to

The 1977 trade of Tom Seaver to the Cincinnati Reds by Mets GM M. Donald Grant was sparked by a salary dispute. Seaver had won three Cy Young Awards, the first during the Miracle Mets season of 1969, and was so valuable to the team that his nickname was "The Franchise."

Joe Torre, Ray Sadecki, and Orlando Cepeda

In 1966 the San Francisco Giants traded first baseman Orlando Cepeda to the St. Louis Cardinals for pitcher Ray Sadecki. Three years later the Cardinals traded Cepeda to the Atlanta Braves for catcher/first baseman Joe Torre. In 1974 they sent Torre to the New York Mets for Ray Sadecki. Cepeda and Torre won MVP Awards for St. Louis in 1967 and 1971.

Rickey Henderson, the single-season and career leader in stolen bases, was traded several times during his long career. He stole most of his bases during four stints with the Oakland Athletics but also played for the Yankees, the Blue Jays, the Padres, the Angels, and the Mets.

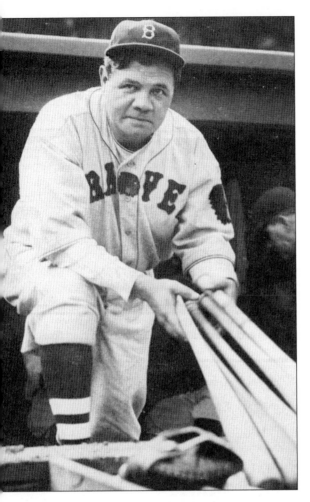

Babe Ruth was sold to the Yankees by the Red Sox for $125,000 on January 3, 1920, then returned to Boston with the National League Braves at the end of his career.

Ruth's First Sale Was a Bargain

Babe Ruth reached the majors in 1914 when Jack Dunn, owner of Baltimore (International), sold him to the Boston Red Sox with Ernie Shore and Ben Egan. The price for the trio was $25,000. The Philadelphia A's had declined to purchase Ruth earlier.

McGraw Sent Marquard to Brooklyn

Pressed for cash, John McGraw's last-place New York Giants of 1915 sold pitcher Rube Marquard to the arch-rival Brooklyn Dodgers for $7,500.

the Brooklyn Dodgers for infielder Rocky Bridges and outfielder Jim Pendleton. Then the Braves sent Bridges and a player to be named later to the Reds for first baseman Joe Adcock.

Trades are made for all kinds of reasons. Sometimes a bad team will deal in the hope that new faces will bring new customers. Salary disagreements and personality clashes force many trades. A player's wish to be closer to home or a team's desire to hire a new manager are other factors.

Dodger general manager Al Campanis (then farm director) sent his son, Jimmy, to the Kansas City Royals in 1968 because he thought that expansion team would let him catch regularly.

Washington owner Clark Griffith, another man with a baseball family, once acquired his son-in-law from the Cleveland Indians, but made a more successful trade when he sold another son-in-law, shortstop/manager Joe Cronin, to the Boston Red Sox in 1934. He'd been overwhelmed by Tom Yawkey's offer of $250,000—a staggering sum in Depression days—plus Lyn Lary, who would replace Cronin at short.

Player sales were more common in the early part of the century. Trading players for other players became such common practice that huge sales were frowned on by the commissioner of baseball.

When Bowie Kuhn canceled the sale of Oakland pitcher Vida Blue to the Reds for $1.75 million and a minor-league slugger, he announced, "Public confidence and the integrity of the game could be questioned if a team as strong as the Cincinnati Reds were allowed to buy a pitcher the quality of Blue, with the Oakland club being further weakened. I am sympathetic to the operating problems of Charley Finley, but there are other ways for him to improve his situation rather than the selling of talent. Player-for-player deals can strengthen a club and help it rapidly to rebuild."

Though Kuhn set an arbitrary ceiling of $400,000 as the maximum amount of cash that may be included in a single transaction, the old practice of selling stars brought financially strapped Connie Mack some $900,000 in the early '30s. Figuring in the inflationary spiral over 40-plus years, that money would have amounted to $4.5 million by modern standards.

The Sale of Babe Ruth

The first five-figure sale in baseball history occurred before the turn of the century. Mike "King" Kelly, a skilled but zany performer who had helped Chicago win five National League pennants in seven seasons, was sold to Boston for $10,000. That started a trend.

After losing the 1914 World Series to the "miracle" Braves, Athletics owner/manager Connie Mack began to break up his team in an effort to keep his stars in the American League rather than the rival Federal League.

Second baseman Eddie Collins, one of those who departed, brought $50,000 into Mack's treasury. Jack Barry and Frank (Home Run) Baker—two other members of the famed $100,000 infield—also went in the supermarket sweep.

The World Champion Boston Red Sox of 1918 followed Mack's lead the following year and began peeling off stars for bank notes. It seems owner Harry Frazee needed funds to underwrite his theater productions, and was willing to sacrifice athletes for dramatics. With the Yankee office two doors from Frazee's New York headquarters, he had a short walk and an eager customer. By 1923, 11 of his stars were Yankees. The biggest was Babe Ruth.

At age 24 in 1919, Ruth hit .322 with 29 home runs and 113 runs batted in, and compiled an 8-5 pitching record for the Red Sox, with one save and a 2.97 era. The power production staggered the baseball world as much as the purchase price of $125,000. The deal was announced on January 3, 1920. Nine months later, Ruth had compiled 54 home runs and the following year enjoyed perhaps the most remarkable season by any player: 59 homers, 168 runs batted in, a .378 batting average, and a 2-0 pitching record.

Harry Frazee lived to see Ruth hit 60 home runs in 1927. The man who got more money but less value in a trade than any of his contemporaries died in 1929.

Rogers Hornsby for Frankie Frisch

Rogers Hornsby, who had won six batting crowns by age 30, was player/manager of the World Champion St. Louis Cardinals in 1926. It was his first season as manager and he felt he should be rewarded, but his demands for a three-year, $150,000 contract angered owner Sam Breadon so much that he was dealt from the Cards.

The New York Giants had a well-entrenched incumbent manager in John McGraw, but welcomed the chance to get a hitter of Hornsby's caliber. He was only two seasons removed from his record .424 campaign.

McGraw had to give up local hero Frankie Frisch, who had earned the nickname of "Fordham Flash" as a college star, but eagerly made the sacrifice. He also threw in pitcher Jim Ring, who had won 11 games.

Frisch began his long managing career with the Cardinals in 1933 and, while Hornsby never managed the Giants, he did resume directing clubs from the field later. He had two terms with the Browns and one with the Reds.

When the Hornsby-for-Frisch trade was announced, fans were literally stunned. The player/manager of the World Champions was coming to New York, but a hometown favorite had to be sacrificed to get him. The deal made even more headlines than the Yankees' purchase of Babe Ruth six years earlier.

The Second Selling of the A's

Connie Mack's Philadelphia A's gradually recovered from the economic troubles of the World War I era and slowly returned to contender status. Mack finally found money to make some significant purchases—notably left-hander Bob "Lefty" Grove of the Baltimore Orioles in the International League.

Collins OKd Sale by A's

Second baseman Eddie Collins, one of several star players sold by the Philadelphia Athletics during the Federal League raids of 1914–1915, accepted his assignment to the Chicago White Sox only after owner Charles Comiskey offered him a five-year contract for $15,000 per season—big money at that time.

Sox Bought Doerr, DiMag from Minors

In addition to Ted Williams, the Boston Red Sox also acquired Bobby Doerr and Dom DiMaggio by direct purchase from minor-league teams.

Six-time NL batting champ Rogers Hornsby was a fan favorite in St. Louis, where he served as player-manager of the 1926 World Champions, but not in the Cardinals front office. Hornsby's demands for a three-year contract caused a rift that resulted in his trade to the New York Giants.

Baseball's Craziest Swaps

By Ernie Harwell in *Parade* magazine
February 26, 1956

colorized by
Don Stokes

When Depression-era realities caught up with Connie Mack, the owner-manager of the Philadelphia A's sold or traded a half-dozen top stars, including, left to right, Mickey Cochrane (to Detroit) and Jimmie Foxx (to Boston).

Grove's purchase price was $100,600. He was worth it, as he helped the Athletics jell into one of the most powerful teams in baseball history in 1929, when they won the first of two World Championships and three pennants.

But hard times set in again and Mack was forced to run another fire sale. On December 12, 1933, Grove, Max Bishop, and Rube Walberg were traded to the Boston Red Sox for Harold Warstler, Bob Kline, and $125,000.

Al Simmons, Jimmie Dykes, and Mule Haas had already been sent to the White Sox for $150,000 and Jimmie Foxx arrived in Boston two years later in a $150,000 swap disguised as a four-player trade. Detroit got Mickey Cochrane for $100,000. Pitcher George Earnshaw also wound up with the White Sox.

There were other sales too, bringing Mack a grand total of $900,000. But the deals knocked the A's out of contention and into a long period of snoozing in the basement of the American League. Only after they moved to Oakland (from Kansas City) in 1968 did the A's revive.

Under the sun's hot glare down south this week, major league ball players begin the painful routine of shedding winter fat and limbering up stiffened muscles. Throughout the spring-training grind they'll be lashed on by baseball's ever-present threat: look sharp or be traded. For most of them, the buyer would have to shell out thousands of dollars or other ball players. In baseball's poorer days, however, players were traded for whatever a hard-pressed club owner might need—and he could need almost anything.

Take Joe Engel, the president of the Chattanooga Lookouts. During the 1931 season he decided to stage a turkey dinner, but lacked the turkey. He quickly got together with Felix Hayman, who owned the Charlotte, North Carolina, team and—more important—a butcher shop. The result was a deal that sent Chattanooga shortstop Johnny Jones to Charlotte in return for one of Hayman's chunkier turkeys.

Some famous names were pawns in those weird trades. Denton T. "Cy" Young, for instance, won more games (511) than any pitcher in baseball history, but was so lightly regarded as a rookie that the Canton, Ohio, team, peddled him to Cleveland for a suit of clothes.

Baseball's greatest star, Babe Ruth, came to the New York Yankees in a deal almost as odd. A top pitcher and outfielder with the Boston Red Sox, Ruth was traded in 1919 by the impoverished Sox for $100,000 and a personal loan of $350,000 to the Sox owner, Harry Frazee (security for the loan: Boston's Fenway Park).

Players and plots of land often were tied in during baseball's early days. In the spring of 1913 the St. Louis Browns (now the Baltimore Orioles) trained on the field of the local team in Montgomery, Alabama. When time came to break camp, the Browns found they didn't have enough money to pay the rent for the field. After some dickering, they handed over rookie Clyde "Buzzy" Wares to the Montgomery team. (Wares spent a year in Montgomery, but later came up to the big leagues for keeps.)

The Browns may have picked up that method of paying rent from the Detroit Tigers. In 1905 Detroit trained in Augusta, Georgia, paying on rent day with pitcher Eddie Cicotte (later a star with the Chicago Black Sox).

Another great hurler, Robert Moses "Lefty" Grove, got started toward the majors by being exchanged for a center-field fence. Grove was toiling for the Martinsburg, West Virginia, club when Jack Dunn, owner of the Baltimore Orioles (then in the International League) spotted him. Dunn, learning that Martinsburg owed money for the erection of an outfield fence, offered to pay the bill in exchange for Grove. Martinsburg agreed and Grove went off to star at Baltimore, then moved up to the American League and eventually the Hall of Fame.

The strangest trades, though, have stemmed from somebody's being hungry. The Wichita Falls, Texas, team once traded Euel Moore for a plate of beans. Dallas sent Joe Martina to New Orleans for two barrels of oysters, thereby pinning the lifetime nickname of "Oyster Joe" on the pitcher. San Francisco shipped first baseman Jack Fenton to Memphis for a box of prunes. But when president Homer Hammond of San Antonio agreed to trade infielder Mike Dondero to Dallas for a dozen doughnuts, he managed to keep Dondero and have his doughnuts too; before signing the agreement, he ate them all up.

The hobbies of club owners also have figured in outlandish trades. Barney Burch of Omaha once gave up two players for an airplane and Nashville's Larry Gilbert traded a set of golf clubs to land Charlie "Greek" George.

At least one owner had to trade a player to get out of a personal jam. After a convention of baseball men, a club president found himself stone broke, unable to pay even his hotel bill. He promptly went down to the lobby, which was full of club owners, and sold one of his pitchers for cash, pocketing enough to pay his bill and train fare home.

But no baseball executive ever traded more cleverly than part-player, part-owner Willis Hudlin. After pitching with Cleveland for 14 years, Hudlin became part owner and pitcher for the Little Rock Travelers. Midway through 1944, owner Hudlin traded pitcher Hudlin to the St. Louis Browns. He pitched only two innings all season long and lost the game, but the Browns won the pennant and Hudlin got a slice of the World Series money. That winter, owner Hudlin bought back pitcher Hudlin from the Browns—and kept the change.

The Purchase of Ted Williams

During the heyday of the independent minor-league operator, the majors and minors dealt freely on an open market. Clubs were just learning the nuances of the farm system in the late '30s. Since Commissioner Kenesaw Mountain Landis disliked the concept, several clubs were slow in developing players on their own farms. They relied on dealing—whether for players or cash.

In December 1937 Eddie Collins was considering a deal with the San Diego Padres of the Pacific Coast League. They owned a strong left-handed-batting outfielder named Ted Williams. Williams, then 19, had hit .291 that year.

San Diego saw vast potential in Williams and made heavy demands on the Red Sox general manager, asking for five players and $25,000. Collins got over his initial hesitation and agreed to the purchase.

In a career starting in 1939 and ending in 1960, Ted Williams compiled a lifetime average of .344 and slammed 521 home runs. His .406 mark of 1941 has not been surpassed since.

Cubs Paid Huge Price for Dizzy Dean

Though he was only a shadow of his old self, Dizzy Dean commanded a huge sum when the St. Louis Cardinals put him on the market after the 1937 season.

The Chicago Cubs, seeking to make up the three-game deficit between first and second place that fall, put together an overwhelming package to land Dean the following April.

On April 16 Chicago sent pitchers Curt Davis and Clyde Shoun and outfielder Tuck Stainback, plus $185,000, to the Cardinals for the 27-year-old Dean.

"We knew his arm was questionable," Cub owner Phil Wrigley said years later, "but I thought it was a pretty good deal. We won the pennant and set an attendance record. Dean had a psychological effect on the team, and that's what we wanted him for.

ED. NOTE: Author Harwell left out of this article a trade that he himself was a part of—a trade almost as odd as any that he mentions. In 1948 Harwell was broadcasting the Atlanta Crackers' games. Branch Rickey, then with Brooklyn, heard Harwell and asked Earl Mann, owner of the Crackers, if he would release Harwell from his contract.

"I'll give him to you," replied Mann, "if you give me catcher Cliff Dapper on your Montreal farm. I want him for manager next year."

Rickey agreed, swapping a catcher for a broadcaster, and Harwell went to Brooklyn.

Two Teams, One Day

In 1922 Max Flack of the Cubs was traded for Cliff Heathcote of the Cardinals between games of a morning-afternoon doubleheader on Memorial Day. They were the first two major leaguers to play for two different teams on the same day.

Braves Got Burdette for Sain

The Braves made a successful waiver deal with the pennant-hungry Yankees in 1951 when they sent Johnny Sain, 33, to New York for Lew Burdette, 24, and $50,000. Burdette went on to win 179 games for the Braves and teamed with southpaw Warren Spahn to give the team an even more formidable left-right punch than the old Spahn-Sain tandem.

"Player to Be Named Later"

Some baseball deals involve a "player to be named later." In 1964 and again in 1970, players were traded for themselves. Vic Power was dealt to the contending Phillies by the Angels during the stretch drive in 1964, but was given back after the season. Hoyt Wilhelm went from the Braves to the contending Cubs late in 1970 and also was returned.

El Duque's Journey

Omar Minaya obtained Orlando Hernandez twice within three seasons. As general manager of the Montreal Expos, he landed the pitcher from the Chicago White Sox in 2003. Three years later, as general manager of the New York Mets, he brought El Duque back to New York from the Arizona Diamondbacks.

"We'd announce Dizzy Dean was going to pitch and we'd put on extra ticket sellers. People wanted to see whether his arm was good or bad. Baseball is a very controversial game. Take the controversy out and you'd kill it."

Dean posted a 7-1 record and 1.80 ERA for the Cubs—the difference between first and fourth place, as Chicago led the Pirates by two games, the Giants by five, and the Reds by six at season's end.

A 30-game winner for the Gashouse Gang Cardinals of 1934, Dean was never the same after Earl Averill broke his toe with a line drive during the 1937 All-Star Game. But, for that one season, he helped pitch the Cubs to a pennant.

Greenberg Goes to Pittsburgh

In 1946 Hank Greenberg led the American League with 44 home runs and 127 runs batted in. After the season he was sold to the Pittsburgh Pirates for $75,000 on waivers.

Waivers are necessary to overcome normal restrictions on trading. Interleague trading did not exist until the first interleague trading period opened for three weeks, starting November 21, 1959, and moving of players across league lines had to be accomplished by "waiving a player out of the league."

When all clubs express disinterest in a player who is about to be traded within one league, he can be sold or traded outside the league. Waiver deals have always been easily arranged because owners know who the two dealing parties are and often look the other way when a talented player finds his way onto the waiver list.

The theory is that if one owner helps another make his trade, the favor will be repaid when the second owner wants to trade.

Ralph Kiner, who played with Greenberg in Pittsburgh, recalled the deal well. "I guess he was making too much money in Detroit and they decided to go for a youth movement," he said.

Greenberg, 35 when the deal was made, teamed with Kiner to give the Pirates a solid one-two power punch, but the club finished last anyway. Kiner led the league with 51 home runs and Greenberg hit 25 in 1947, their first year together.

How Veeck Landed Vernon and Wynn

Bill Veeck knew Early Wynn and Mickey Vernon could help his Cleveland Indians win the 1948 American League pennant.

But Wynn and Vernon played for Washington under Clark

Griffith, who disapproved of Veeck's endless stream of gimmicks and outspoken comments about the game.

Griffith's son-in-law, Joe Haynes, was a sore-armed White Sox pitcher and definitely available. Veeck knew Griffith wouldn't relish the idea of his son-in-law playing in Cleveland, so he sent catcher Joe Tipton to Chicago for Haynes. Griffith sent his adopted nephew, Calvin, to negotiate.

The deal sent Haynes, Eddie Robinson, and reliever Ed Klieman to the Senators for Vernon and Wynn. Veeck also agreed to pay for Haynes' surgery. Veeck announced the trade at 4:45 A.M. because, he said, he didn't want to give Griffith time to change his mind.

While Haynes won 10 games in four years for Washington, Wynn won 163 over the course of nine years in Cleveland (1949 to 1957), and one more there in 1963. Wynn also notched 64 wins for Chicago, including 22 in 1959, when newly named owner Bill Veeck helped the Sox win their first flag in 40 years.

The man Veeck yielded for Joe Haynes never amounted to much in the majors. But enterprising White Sox general manager Frank Lane pulled a major coup by sending him to the Philadelphia Athletics for second baseman Nellie Fox. Fox, in turn, became the sparkplug of the 1959 White Sox and was voted the American League's Most Valuable Player. Wynn won the Cy Young Award for pitching excellence.

It all started because of Joe Tipton.

Braves Deals Won Flags for Giants

The Braves helped the Giants win their only pennants of the '50s by sending them three stars in two separate transactions. On December 14, 1949, they sent their talented double-play combination—shortstop Alvin Dark and second baseman Eddie Stanky—to New York for third baseman Sid Gordon, outfielder Willard Marshall, infielder Buddy Kerr, and pitcher Sam Webb.

Because the Giants had added speed and defense, and unloaded several slow-footed sluggers, they staged the most dramatic stretch drive in history to win the 1951 National League pennant.

The hero of that season was Bobby Thomson, whose last-of- the-ninth homer erased a Dodger lead and gave victory to the Giants. The Braves, seeking power, made several bids for him and finally succeeded on the eve of the 1954 season.

They sent left-handed pitchers Johnny Antonelli and Don Liddle, catcher Ebba St. Claire, infielder Billy Klaus and $50,000 to New York for Thomson and catcher Sam Calderone.

Cronin Sale Forced Manager Swap

When player/manager Joe Cronin was sold from the Washington Senators to the Boston Red Sox after the 1934 season, the transaction not only included a $250,000 payoff from Tom Yawkey to Clark Griffith, but also a five-year, $30,000 pact for Cronin as Boston's player/manager. Incumbent Red Sox pilot Bucky Harris took the vacant manager's job in Washington.

Casey Stengel Traded Himself

When Casey Stengel was president and player/manager of the Boston Braves farm team at Worcester, Massachusetts, he sold himself to the New York Giants farm club at Toledo, Ohio.

The Right Time

According to Fred McGriff, traded from San Diego to Atlanta on July 18, 1995, a midseason deal is tougher to take. "When you get traded in the middle of the year," he said, "you walk into a situation where you know some of the guys. But it's better to get traded in the off-season because you have all of spring training to get to know your teammates, going out to dinner or whatever. When you get traded during the year, you have to get right in there and start playing. I was lucky to play first base because I had a chance to meet people every night."

Whopping Commission

Agent Scott Boras got a $12.6 million commission when Alex Rodriguez signed with the Texas Rangers as a free agent in 2000.

What Pitcher Cost

The $101 million the Red Sox spent on Japanese star Daisuke Matsuzaka (between the posting fee and contract) before the 2007 season was nearly 100 times more than Warner Brothers paid to make *Casablanca*. They were aware of it too, since the grandfather and great uncle of Red Sox general manager Theo Epstein wrote the Humphrey Bogart classic.

Antonelli, 24, immediately blossomed into the ace of the Giants' staff, posting a 21-7 record and a league-leading 2.30 ERA. He went all the way in Game 2 of New York's four-game World Series sweep over the favored Cleveland Indians.

Thomson never even made it past spring training. He suffered a broken leg while sliding into a base and was replaced by an unknown 20-year-old rookie named Hank Aaron.

Roger Maris: From KC to NY

The man who broke Babe Ruth's single-season home-run record was, like Ruth, acquired in trade.

Roger Maris, also like Ruth, was a strong left-handed hitter who had the advantage of Yankee Stadium's short right-field porch, only 296 feet from the plate.

He began to notice the fence almost immediately after joining the club, producing 39 home runs and 112 runs batted in to win the American League's Most Valuable Player Award for 1960.

Maris became a Yankee on December 11, 1959, when the club sent outfielders Hank Bauer and Norm Siebern, first baseman Marv Throneberry, and pitcher Don Larsen to the Kansas City Athletics for Maris and two infield substitutes: shortstop Joe DeMaestri and first baseman Kent Hadley.

In 1961, with American League pitching universally weakened by expansion (and Maris having the luxury of not facing the strongest staff in the league), the Yankee right fielder connected 61 times. It was the only time in his major league career that Roger Maris reached the 40 mark in home runs.

Five years later, at age 31, he hit .233 with 13 home runs as the Yankees dropped to last place in the 10-team American League. After the season, he was traded to St. Louis for little-known third baseman Charley Smith. The one-time superstar of the World Champions enjoyed his last hurrah in the big leagues when he paced the Cardinals to the 1967 World Championship with a club-leading seven runs batted in. In two years with St. Louis, Roger Maris hit a grand total of 14 home runs.

17-Player Trade

General managers Paul Richards of the Orioles and George Weiss of the Yankees engineered the largest two-club deal in the game's history late in the 1954 season.

The Yankees received pitchers Don Larsen, Bob Turley, and Mike Blyzka; catcher Darrell Johnson; first baseman Dick Kryhoski; shortstop Billy Hunter; and outfielders Ted del Guercio and Tim Fridley.

Baltimore acquired nine players—pitchers Harry Byrd, Jim McDonald, and Bill Miller; catchers Gus Triandos and Hal Smith; second baseman Don Leppert; third baseman Kal Segrist; shortstop Willy Miranda; and outfielder Gene Woodling.

Larsen, 26, and Turley, 25, proved of immense value to the Yankees. Two years after the trade, Larsen pitched the only perfect game in World Series history and Turley won 21 regular-season games in 1958.

Triandos, Woodling, and Miranda became Orioles regulars, making solid contributions as Richards gradually built a strong young club around them.

Roger Maris, acquired from the Kansas City A's, first donned Yankee pinstripes in 1960, then hit 61 homers a year later.

Interleague Trading

Waiver-free interleague trading was permitted for the first time after the 1959 season. An interleague trading period was established from November 21 to December 15. Later, these dates were modified to extend the period from five days after the end of the World Series to midnight on the final day of the winter baseball meetings. A spring trading period was added in 1977.

Since the regular trade deadline remained June 15 for years, several observers suggested the spring period should be fixed for May 15 to June 15, thereby allowing teams to turn their talent searches to the other league before all trading ends.

Establishment of the spring period from February 15 to March 15 was ineffective for several reasons—primarily because managers did not have ample time to evaluate their squads in spring camp that soon, but also because any deal that could have been made then could have also been made the previous fall.

An early spring trading period discouraged trading in the winter and reduced the flow of baseball news when it was needed most—in the off-season, when teams are selling season tickets.

The first trades completed under the new interleague trading period in 1959 were far from earth-shaking. The Cubs sent first baseman/outfielder Jim Marshall and pitcher Dave Hillman to the Red Sox for first baseman Dick Gernert, and the Reds dealt pitcher Tom Acker to the A's for catcher Frank House.

Dozens of major deals have been made. Jim Bunning went from the Tigers to the Phillies and became the first man to pitch no-hitters in both leagues. Dave Johnson went from the Orioles to the Braves and, in his first season, slammed 43 home runs, a record for a second baseman. Felix Mantilla left the Mets to hit 30 home runs for the Red Sox. Dick Stuart, going to Boston from Pittsburgh, hit 42.

Juan Pizarro, 24-year-old left-hander, became ace of the White Sox staff in 1961 after a three-way deal involving the Reds and the Braves gave him his first opportunity to pitch regularly. The same deal sent another little-used Brave, Joey Jay, to the Reds, where he blossomed into a 21-game winner on a pennant-winning staff.

Slugger Frank Howard thrived with Washington after arriving from Los Angeles in a swap for pitcher Claude Osteen. That was clearly a deal that helped both clubs. A one-sided swap across league lines gave the Orioles outfielder Ken Singleton and pitcher Mike Torrez of the Expos in return for pitcher Dave McNally, outfielder Rich Coggins, and a minor-leaguer. All three Montreal additions were washouts.

Slugger David Justice was one of three marquee names involved in a blockbuster interleague trade at the end of 1997 spring training. The Atlanta Braves sent Justice, whose solo homer had won the 1995 World Series finale, and fellow outfielder Marquis Grissom to the Cleveland Indians for Kenny Lofton, who had led the American League in stolen bases in each of his first five seasons, and relief pitcher Alan Embree. Braves GM John Schuerholz said the swap freed up the money he needed to stop star pitchers Greg Maddux and Tom Glavine from becoming free agents.

Greenberg Laughed at Veeck's Pitch

During his tenure as boss of the Browns, Bill Veeck always needed money for basic expenses. He tried to convince Cleveland's Hank Greenberg, a close friend, to buy first baseman Hank Arft, but the Indians already had Luke Easter at the position. In his final plea, Veeck's teletype jammed and printed **ARFARFARFARFARF**. Greenberg wired back, **I CAN'T STOP LAUGHING. KEEP THAT DOG IN ST. LOUIS.**

Fans Reacted to Kiner Trade

New York Mets broadcaster Ralph Kiner, who witnessed the angry backlash of fans upset with the Mets for dealing Tom Seaver in 1977, recalled a similar reaction by Pirate fans when Branch Rickey traded him to the Cubs in 1953. Kiner, Joe Garagiola, and two others became Cubs in exchange for six players and $150,000.

After entertaining offers for slugger Mark McGwire, eligible for free agency after the 1997 season, Oakland sent him to St. Louis for three pitchers just prior to the July 31 trading deadline. Reunited with former manager Tony La Russa, McGwire not only re-signed with the Cards but finished the season with 58 home runs—34 in the AL and 24 in the NL.

How Mathews Heard

Third baseman Eddie Mathews, the only man to play for the Braves in Boston, Milwaukee, and Atlanta, was told of his 1966 trade to Houston by a sportswriter. A subsequent letter of apology from the team was addressed to Edward—rather than Edwin—Mathews.

Six Who Signed

During their 14-year title run, the Braves relied on developing their own players more than signing veteran free agents. But they did sign six who helped immensely: Terry Pendleton and Sid Bream arrived in 1991, Greg Maddux in 1993, Andres Galarraga and Walt Weiss in 1998, and Brian Jordan in 1999.

Tommy John, a quality left-handed starter, prospered after joining the Dodgers from the White Sox—even though he missed a year and a half with an arm injury. Ken Holtzman, also a southpaw, did well for the Oakland A's after Charley Finley sent center fielder Rick Monday to the Cubs to get him.

After the 1974 season the Milwaukee Brewers acquired Hank Aaron for a two-year swing around the American League as designated hitter. Aaron was 41 before the 1975 campaign opened, but he welcomed the opportunity to close his career in the city where it began. Milwaukee was the home of the National League Braves during Aaron's rookie year in 1954. The Braves got journeyman outfielder Dave May and young pitcher Roger Alexander in the ho-hum deal for their longtime superstar.

Aaron retired in the fall of 1976 and rejoined the Braves as an executive just as the team was landing its first bona fide slugger since his heyday: Jeff Burroughs. The price—five major league players and $250,000—paid off immediately as Burroughs slammed 41 home runs and knocked in 114 runs in his first Atlanta season.

Other sluggers also moved during the interleague trading period—notably Bobby Murcer and Bobby Bonds, who switched uniforms in a blockbuster trade between the Yankees and the Giants after the 1974 season. The Baltimore Orioles, who landed consistent Lee May from Houston for light-hitting rookie infielder Rob Andrews, scored several times in the interleague market, landing left-handed pitchers Ross Grimsley from the Reds and Mike Cuellar from the Astros, plus right-hander Pat Dobson from the San Diego Padres.

The three worst interleague trades were engineered by the Mets, the Giants, and the Reds—the first two within a two-week span. Seeking a third baseman, the Mets opted for longtime California Angels shortstop Jim Fregosi, a 29-year-old power hitter who had been held to a .233 average in 1971.

To get him, New York sent four players to the Angels, including outfielder Lee Stanton, who became a home-run hitter as a regular, and hard-throwing but erratic pitcher Nolan Ryan.

Fregosi, a failure, was gone within two seasons, but Ryan became the Angels' ace in his first season, with 19 wins, 329 whiffs, and a 2.28 ERA.

On November 19, 1971, the San Francisco Giants shipped Gaylord Perry to the Cleveland Indians for Sam McDowell in a trade of pitchers. Perry, 32, was four years older than "Sudden" Sam when the deal was made, but had much more life left in his arm.

The Giants later pulled another rock by sending slugging outfielder George Foster to Cincinnati for shortstop Frank Duffy and pitcher Vern Geishert. Foster was National League MVP in 1977, when he became the league's first 50-homer man since 1965.

Two other sluggers, Joe Carter and Fred McGriff, were involved in an interleague blockbuster during the 1990 winter meetings. In a trade of four All-Stars, the San Diego Padres sent Carter and Roberto Alomar to the Toronto Blue Jays for McGriff and Tony Fernandez.

Unable to afford him three years later, San Diego sent McGriff to Atlanta in a midseason swap that enabled the Braves to overtake the Giants in the last pre–wild-card divisional title chase.

How the Orioles Got Frank Robinson

In 1965 the Cincinnati Reds finished fourth in the National League, eight games behind the Los Angeles Dodgers. Their big star was 30-year-old outfielder Frank Robinson, who that year hit .296 with 33 home runs and 113 runs batted in.

During the winter meetings several Cincinnati executives approached Baltimore's major league scout, Jim Russo, and handed him a slip of paper with Robinson's name on one side and the names of three Orioles on the other side. Those names were Milt Pappas, Jack Baldschun, and Rookie of the Year Curt Blefary.

"I told our people, 'We've got to acquire Frank Robinson in a way that won't cost us Blefary,'" Russo recalled. "I felt we could replace the 13 games Pappas had won with Jim Palmer, who was 19 years old then. Our manager, Hank Bauer, was a little reluctant to give him up.

"We went back to the Cincinnati people and said we can't make the deal if Blefary is involved, but the day before that we had made a deal for Dick Simpson, and the Reds liked him. They said they had good reports on him from their Triple-A manager in San Diego, Dave Bristol."

That clinched the deal. Bill DeWitt, then the Reds general manager, sent Robinson away with bitter feelings when he called him "an old 30," and the slugger made up his mind to respond with his most spectacular season. He did just that, winning the Triple Crown of batting with a .316 average, 49 homers, and 122 runs batted in. He homered twice during the four-game World Series sweep over the Los Angeles Dodgers.

Robinson played six seasons in Baltimore and was so brilliant that the team retired his No. 20 after he was traded to the Dodgers for four prospects in the winter of 1971. The Orioles won four pennants in the six Frank Robinson years.

Deals of Recent Vintage

Growing demands by players precipitated an era of "spite trades" in the late '60s and early '70s.

Ken Harrelson was hitting .305, and averaging one RBI every two games when he got into a haggle with Kansas City Athletics owner Charley Finley. When manager Alvin Dark was fired in the turmoil, Harrelson called Finley "a menace to baseball" and was summarily fired.

The Boston Red Sox, suddenly in pennant contention after years of lurking near the league basement, jumped at the chance to sign the 25-year-old Harrelson, whose right-handed power was ideally suited to Fenway Park. His signing bonus and salary more than covered his contribution: three home runs and 14 runs batted in during the final weeks of a race the Sox won by one game.

That same season, Maury Wills was playing third base for Pittsburgh instead of shortstop for Los Angeles because of a falling-out with management the previous fall. After the Dodgers won their

Feeling the Draft

There are no guarantees about the annual amateur draft. Launched in 1965 to give bad teams a chance to compete with contenders for players, the draft was not always fruitful. The New York Mets, for example, drafted Steve Chilcott ahead of Reggie Jackson, while the Chicago Cubs chose Brooks Kieschnick ahead of Billy Wagner, Torii Hunter, and Jason Varitek.

Future slugger Barry Bonds was the *sixth* overall pick in the 1985 amateur draft.

Ron Blomberg was billed as "the next Mickey Mantle" when the New York Yankees drafted him first in the nation in 1967 but never amounted to more than the first designated hitter—an accident of history. A later Yankee first-rounder, pitcher Brien Taylor, got into a fight and ruined his career before it started.

On the other hand, the Washington Nationals got lucky: consecutive first choices in 2010 and 2011 netted All-Stars Stephen Strasburg and Bryce Harper.

The Rule 4 draft can last 40 or more rounds, a sharp deviation from the two-round NBA draft and seven-round NHL draft. Teams draft to the reverse order of the previous year's standings. A player who does not sign may be chosen again in a future draft.

Stardom is no certainty for the nation's top pick. In fact, no No. 1 choice reached the Baseball Hall of Fame before Ken Griffey Jr. was inducted in 2016. That same summer, the Hall's doors also opened for Mike Piazza, drafted in the 62nd round mainly because his father Vince was a longtime friend of Dodgers manager Tommy Lasorda in their hometown of Norristown, Pennsylvania.

At Lasorda's suggestion, Piazza became a catcher, learned on the job, and wound up hitting more home runs than anyone else who played his position.

When elected to Cooperstown in 2016, he was the highest draft choice ever enshrined.

Deadline Dealing

Two deadline deals enabled the Toronto Blue Jays to end a 22-year playoff drought in 2015. The team obtained slugging shortstop Troy Tulowitzki from the Colorado Rockies and veteran left-handed starter David Price from the Detroit Tigers.

New Home for Hamels

The Texas Rangers landed a bona fide stud in 2015 when they acquired left-handed starter Cole Hamels, along with fellow lefty Jake Diekman and $9.5 million, from the Philadelphia Phillies for Jorge Alfaro, Alec Asher, Jerad Eickhoff, Matt Harrison, Jack Thompson, and Nick Williams. Hamels was an American League All-Star for the first time in 2016.

Refusing a 1974 trade to the Atlanta Braves because he felt uncomfortable playing in the South, Dick Allen eventually wound up where he started: in Philadelphia.

After hitting 398 home runs and winning four home-run titles in his first 11 seasons, all with the Seattle Mariners, Ken Griffey Jr. was traded to the Cincinnati Reds in a five-player deal on February 10, 2000. The trade reunited the 10-time AL All-Star with his father, a former Reds player and current coach. Spurning a Seattle offer worth $40 million more, the 30-year-old Griffey signed a nine-year, $116.5 million contract with Cincinnati. Only four other players had ever been traded immediately after hitting 40 home runs in a season.

second straight pennant, Wills declined to complete a postseason trip to Japan; he left the team in Tokyo, causing owner Walter O'Malley to apologize to the Japanese premier. "A higher degree of devotion was expected," he said of Wills, who called in sick with a knee injury.

The St. Louis Cardinals lost two quality left-handers when salary talks came to an impasse. Steve Carlton, 26, won 20 games in 1971 and Jerry Reuss, 22, won 14 the same season, but both were gone in 1972. Carlton, dealt to Philadelphia for Rick Wise, immediately led the league with 27 victories and a 1.97 ERA. The team won only 59 games.

Gabe Paul, longtime executive with the Reds, the Astros, and the Indians (twice), deserves much of the credit for restoring the Yankee dynasty through shrewd trades that brought first baseman Chris Chambliss from Cleveland, second baseman Willie Randolph from Pittsburgh, center fielder Mickey Rivers and pitcher Ed Figueroa from California, and shortstop Bucky Dent from Chicago.

The Randolph deal was particularly impressive because he was the unknown factor in a deal that brought veteran pitchers Dock Ellis and Ken Brett to New York in exchange for veteran Yankee starter George "Doc" Medich, who went to Pittsburgh. Randolph had excellent minor-league credentials but could not budge incumbent second baseman Rennie Stennett.

Charley Finley, another shrewd dealer, took advantage of entrenched Pirate veterans when he obtained outfielder Mitchell Page, second baseman Mike Edwards, and pitcher Doug Bair (later dealt for first baseman Dave Revering). Seven former Giants arrived in 1978 for veteran Vida Blue; shortstop Mario Guerrero and pitchers John Henry Johnson and Dave Heaverlo were immediately impressive.

Finley even managed to land a quality player for a nonplaying manager in 1976, when he sent Chuck Tanner to the Pirates for veteran receiver Manny Sanguillen plus cash. Little more than a year later, he returned Sanguillen to Pittsburgh for several prospects.

Finley wasn't the first to trade active players for bench managers. After the 1967 season the New York Mets sent pitcher Bill Denehy and $100,000 to the Washington Senators for manager Gil Hodges, a former New York player, and more than 50 years before that, the old New York Giants sent superstar pitcher Christy Mathewson to the Cincinnati Reds as their new manager. The date of that five-player trade—which also made Reds of Edd Roush and Bill McKechnie—was July 21, 1916.

Probably the most lopsided trade of the post–World War II period was made on June 15, 1964, on the eve of the trading deadline.

The St. Louis Cardinals sent 28-year-old right-hander Ernie Broglio, an 18-game winner the year before, plus veteran reliever

Bobby Shantz and reserve outfielder Doug Clemens to the Chicago Cubs for an erratic but speedy outfielder with a tendency to strike out too often.

Lou Brock went on to become the greatest base stealer in the long history of the game. He established both single-season and lifetime records (both later broken by Rickey Henderson).

Many players moved on their own via free agency. Among those who helped their new teams most were future Hall of Famers Catfish Hunter (1975), Reggie Jackson (1977), Goose Gossage (1978), Nolan Ryan (1980), Carlton Fisk (1981), Andre Dawson (1987), Greg Maddux (1993), and Randy Johnson (1999). Other major players who rode free agency to greener pastures were Pete Rose (1979), Jack Morris (1991 and 1992), Barry Bonds (1993), Manny Ramirez (2001), David Ortiz (2003), and Vladimir Guerrero (2004).

The 2009 New York Yankees, apparently awash in cash, lavished $161 million on CC Sabathia and $180 million on Mark Teixeira. But the Arizona Diamondbacks left those figures in the dust when they convinced Dodgers pitcher Zack Greinke to use an "out" clause in his contract to sign a deal that paid him an average annual salary of $34 million—roughly a million dollars per start.

Dynamite Deals

With most restrictions removed, baseball trading can and does occur at any time. The busiest times are just before the July 31 deadline on deals that don't require waivers and the December winter meetings, when owners, general managers, and player agents congregate in the same hotel.

These are some of the 21st century swaps that changed baseball history:

* Los Angeles Dodgers trade Mike Piazza and Todd Zeile to the Florida Marlins for Manuel Barrios, Bobby Bonilla, Jim Eisenreich, Charles Johnson and Gary Sheffield, May 14, 1998
* Florida Marlins trade Mike Piazza to the New York Mets for Geoff Goetz, Preston Wilson and Ed Yarnall, May 22, 1998
* Oakland trades Josh Donaldson to Toronto for Brett Lawrie, Sean Nolin, Kendall Graveman, and Franklin Barreto, November 28, 2014
* Miami trades Jose Reyes, Mark Buehrle, Josh Johnson, John Buck, and Emilio Bonifacio to Toronto for Yunel Escobar, Henderson Alvarez, Jeff Mathis, Adeiny Hechavarria, Jake Marisnick, Justin Nicolino, and Anthony DeSclafani, November 19, 2012
* Florida sends Miguel Cabrera and Dontrelle Willis to Detroit for Cameron Maybin, Andrew Miller, Mike Rabelo, Eulogio de la Cruz, Burke Badenhop, and Dallas Trahern, December 4, 2007
* Atlanta deals Elvis Andrus, Neftali Feliz, Matt Harrison, Jarrod Saltalamacchia, and a player to be named later to Texas for Mark Teixeira and Ron Mahay, July 31, 2007
* Philadelphia trades J.A. Happ, Anthony Gose, and Jonathan Villar to Houston for Roy Oswalt, July 29, 2010
* Montreal swaps Cliff Lee, Brandon Phillips, and Grady Sizemore to Cleveland for Bartolo Colon
* Detroit deals Yoenis Cespedes to New York Mets for Michael Fullmer and Luis Cessa, July 31, 2015
* Detroit sends Prince Fielder to Texas for Ian Kinsler, November 20, 2013
* New York Mets move R.A. Dickey, Josh Thole, and Mike Nickeas to Toronto for Noah Syndergaard, Travis d'Arnaud, Wuilmer Becerra, and John Buck, December 17, 2012
* Detroit trades Curtis Granderson to New York Yankees and Edwin Jackson to Arizona; New York sends Austin Jackson and Phil Coke to Detroit and Ian Kennedy to Arizona; Arizona sends Max Scherzer and Daniel Schlereth to Detroit, December 8, 2009
* Colorado trades Matt Holliday to Oakland for Carlos Gonzalez, Greg Smith, and Huston Street, November 12, 2008
* Florida jettisons Josh Beckett, Mike Lowell, and Guillermo Mota to Boston for Hanley Ramirez, Anibal Sanchez, Jesus Delgado, and Harvey Garcia, November 24, 2005
* Boston trades Adrian Gonzalez, Carl Crawford, Josh Beckett, Nick Punto, and cash to Los Angeles Dodgers for James Loney, Ivan de Jesus, Allen Webster, Jerry Sands, and Rubby de la Rosa, August 25, 2012

Chapter 12

Dan Schlossberg

The Supporting Cast

Bob Sheppard joined the Yankees as public-address announcer in 1949 and quickly won a reputation as the team's poet laureate.

Sheppard's Day

When the Yankees gave PA man Bob Sheppard a day in 2000, he was introduced by Walter Cronkite and given a plaque in Monument Park. Sheppard, who announced 4500 regular-season games and 121 post-season games over a 58-year span, also threw out the first pitch of the game. Sheppard was also the public address announcer of the New York football Giants and a speech professor at St. John's University.

Long Tenure

Bob Sheppard spent more than half-a-century as PA announcer for the Yankees. Since his debut on April 17, 1951, he announced the lineups for more than 4,000 baseball games, including nearly 100 postseason contests. "Most men go to work," he said, "but I go to a game."

Megaphone Man

When Yankee Stadium opened in 1923, public address announcer Jack Lenz used a giant megaphone to shout batting orders, batteries, and substitutions. Known as "the little fellow with the big voice," the mild-mannered Lenz was the Lou Gehrig of announcers, handling more than 2,000 consecutive games for both the Yankees and Giants (who first hired him in 1915).

Stadium Announcers

Before the advent of sophisticated public-address systems, teams employed field announcers, megaphone men who announced lineups to the fans and served as liaison for both press box and scoreboard personnel.

The most famous field announcer was Chicago's Pat Pieper, an announcer at lightless Wrigley Field by day and a waiter at night. Long after electronic systems sent megaphones the route of the buffalo nickel and stadium announcers to press box locations, Pieper remained on the field. He was known for his drawn-out cry of "Play Ball!" which he delivered immediately after giving the lineups. Pieper was to Cub fans what Ed McMahon was to Johnny Carson.

Field announcers weren't paid much, and Brooklyn's Tex Rickards earned just $5 a game for many years. He made up in popularity what he missed in cash. Dodger fans even gave him a "night" at Ebbets Field.

Rickards was one of the best, but he wasn't flawless. One day coats were hung along the left-field railing and the umpire suggested they might interfere with play. Rickards boomed, "Attention please! Will the fans along the left-field railing please remove their clothing?"

A close relative of the early megaphone man was the downtown hawker. In the '20s, a San Franciscan proved so good at this job that he won the nickname "Foghorn" Murphy. He paraded up and down Market Street, urging fans to see the San Francisco Seals in action. When the team moved into Recreation Park, with its field-level bar in full operation, he didn't have to work as hard.

The coming of the PA system allowed fans in all corners of the park to hear each announcement. Bob Sheppard, the subtle and classical voice of Yankee Stadium, announced many of the game's greatest names through continuous World Series action. But Sheppard's contribution was more than oral; he developed into the team's poet laureate and, in 1961, penned this poem for Roger Maris just after his 61st home run:

They've been pitching me low and wide and tight
I've been tense and nervous, drawn and pallid
But my prayers are full of joy tonight
Thank you, God, for Tracy Stallard.

Organists

Gladys Goodding, the organist at Ebbets Field, Brooklyn, probably was the best-known musician in baseball history. She won her spurs the second day on the job—May 9, 1942—when she played "Three Blind Mice" as umpires Bill Stewart, Ziggy Sears, and Tom Dunn walked onto the field. The fans roared.

Goodding, who also played for boxing matches at St. Nicholas Arena and for hockey, basketball, and fights at Madison Square Garden, knew Stewart because the umpire was a hockey referee in winter. Stewart knew she had taken the organist's job at Ebbets Field and had just finished telling his umpire partners that she was his friend. At that instant, she broke into "Three Blind Mice."

Sears and Dunn looked at Stewart. "I thought you said she was a friend of yours!" they declared.

The talented organist, who began her professional career by playing background music for silent movies, first attracted the attention of sports fans in the winter of 1936–1937, when she worked Sunday afternoon hockey at the Garden. A fan suggested she should be working at Ebbets Field and, some time later, Gladys contacted Larry MacPhail. She finally made her debut in 1942, after MacPhail overcame fears that acoustics in the park were not conducive to the organ. Thus, Goodding became the only person to *play* for the Knicks, the Rangers, and the Dodgers.

Running the Scoreboard

Field announcers and organists worked in concert with scoreboard operators. Scoreboards originally were painted wooden billboards with slots where numerals would be placed by hand to indicate runs per inning. The age of electronics, coupled with animation, converted them into complex matrix operations run by skilled technicians.

The $1.5 million board unveiled at Atlanta-Fulton County Stadium in 1977 was operated by three people.

Animation involved some 900 separate computer steps, and the job involved much more than pushing buttons. Up-to-date statistics were programmed into the computer, lengthy start-up and shut-down procedures were followed, and the chief operator had to know how to handle the system's quirks.

First Organ

The Chicago Cubs were the first team to install an organ, in 1941.

Playing His Organ

Organist Eddie Layton was the only man to play for the New York Yankees, New York Rangers, and New York Knickerbockers. A Yankee Stadium staple since Mike Burke inaugurated organ music there in 1967, Layton was also a composer/performer whose 26 albums sold more than three million copies.

Fan Favorite

Wendy Stoeker, born without arms, became a fan favorite as an usherette for the Cedar Rapids Giants of the Class A Midwest League in 1976. She also proved valuable to the front office, typing letters and contracts with her toes and answering the telephone.

First Female Voice

Sherry Davis of the San Francisco Giants became the first full-time female public-address announcer in 1993.

A 1961 scoreless tie between the Yankees and the Red Sox was about to end with a historic home run. Roger Maris ripped Tracy Stallard's 2–0 pitch for his 61st home run, making him the new single-season home-run king.

The First Concessionaire

Though Harry M. Stevens was the first big-time ballpark vendor, he was not the first to try selling concessions at a ballpark. Joe Gerhardt, second baseman of Louisville's major league American Association club in 1883, had part of the bar concession, and five years later, third baseman Harry Raymond of the same team had a special arrangement to get extra money tacked onto his salary from scorecard sales.

The Hamburger

Like its close relative, the frankfurter, the hamburger is a meat product developed in Germany and named for its city of origin, Hamburg. The Germans actually imported the idea from the Baltic countries, but refined it, cooking and serving it as a "chopped steak."

Dr. J. H. Salisbury popularized the food after its introduction to the United States in 1884 and a variation developed with the name of "salisbury steak." By 1912, hamburgers, like hot dogs, were used as fast-food treats in buns and were introduced to ballparks.

When and Why Fans Eat

Joe McKeller, who ran food operations for ARA at Atlanta Stadium, said, "If the team is winning, they're in a good mood, and more apt to spend money. But if it's losing badly early in the game, people leave. I've never sold a hot dog to an empty seat.

"A game that goes into extra innings or a doubleheader is worth 40–60 percent more than a single game. A loose game compared to a tight game is better for me. A loose score is 10–9 instead of 1–0. In a tight game, people are so interested in the game, they won't leave their seats."

A Plaque for Toots

Baseball people have favorite watering holes in every major league city, but none could match Toots Shor's in New York. Its owner became famous for making newcomers feel comfortable.

Toots Shor's was so popular among sportsmen that its original site, 51 West 51st Street, was marked with a plaque in 1977.

Cashman's Start

Yankees general manager Brian Cashman got his start in baseball as a bat boy for the Dodgers.

Big Tipper

Generous superstar Ted Williams of the Red Sox gave his 1946 World Series check to the clubhouse boy as a tip.

Equipment Managers

While the scoreboard is the largest piece of equipment owned by a team (excepting those who own their ballparks), smaller items—like bats and uniforms—are carted around by the equipment manager. Longtime Minnesota Twins equipment man Ray Crump first joined the team as batboy in 1949, when the Twins were still the Washington Senators.

Because Crump was charged with ordering form-fitting uniforms, complete with players' surnames sewn on the back, anxious athletes flocked to him every spring to learn whether they had made the team. As a result, he and his wife never stayed at the same apartment complex as the ballplayers. Since she did the sewing, she also knew of pending trades or roster cuts before they were officially announced.

Once the veteran equipment manager disobeyed a request from management not to order a uniform for a player at the end of spring training. Crump's judgment proved correct. "After you've been around, you get to know these things," he said. "You can come close to picking the team."

Pete Sheehy spent so many seasons handling the equipment and running the clubhouse for the New York Yankees that the team named the clubhouse of the new Yankee Stadium in his honor after the refurbished ballpark opened in 1976. That was also Sheehy's 50th year with the club.

Many "characters" ran big-league clubhouses, including one personally scouted by Casey Stengel when his Boston Braves trained in Wallingford, Connecticut, during World War II. The rotund but capable Shorty Davis became part of the Boston scene in deed and phrase. He spouted even more fractured English than Stengel.

Watching threatening clouds gather above Bradenton, Florida, one spring, he blurted, "Looks like a toronto's coming up." He referred to the fishing paradise of South Florida as "the Evergladiators."

The Batboys

Baseball batboys hope their proximity to the stars will bloom into full-time jobs too. Sometimes they do, but more often they don't—leaving the batboy with memories he can cherish for life.

Generally, the batboy is little more than a uniformed mascot who depends on tips and possible World Series shares to make up for the paltry pay he receives from his team. In 1955, for example, the New York Giants gave Bobby Weinstein $3.75 for a day game, $4.50 for a night game, and $6 for a doubleheader.

Fordham University sophomore Joe Carrieri made only $2.50 per game from the Yankees that season, but had collected more than $1,200 in World Series shares, plus royalties from his book *Yankee Batboy* to help pay his tuition.

Carrieri, later a successful lawyer, said that at the time he would have favored a batboys' union. Like others in his position, he not only handled bats for players but also shined shoes, answered mail, ran errands, and fetched coffee, Cokes, or hot dogs for hungry athletes.

Batboys specialize in working with bats—smoothing out rough edges, sorting bats by batting order or uniform number in special dugout bat racks, and picking up bats dropped by players after they hit the ball.

In addition to bats, they supply sticky substances like pine tar, which enable players to grip bats firmly while swinging.

A number of major league executives began in baseball as batboys. Gabe Paul, president of several teams, was once a batboy in Rochester. Joe McDonald, once general manager of the New York Mets, was a substitute batboy in Brooklyn. And Donald Davidson, longtime front office man for the Braves and Astros, began as batboy for both Boston clubs at age 14 in 1939.

Batting Practice Pitchers

Many teams employ batting practice pitchers whose sole function is to warm up hitters before the game. They do not count on the roster and never appear in an actual game.

It's one thing to sharpen the eye and the swing against a friendly pitcher who throws what a hitter requests and quite another to face an enemy pitcher whose mission is the opposite.

The Yankees, first team to carry a batting practice pitcher, hired Paul Schreiber for that job in 1937, but the one-time Brooklyn Dodger hardly anticipated his activation at age 42 in the war year of 1945.

In the first of two appearances, he came on with two outs in the sixth and slammed the door on the Detroit Tigers—allowing just two walks in three and one-third innings. He had last pitched in the majors 22 years earlier!

Wives

Baseball wives must be patient, understanding, and self-sufficient. At home games, they sit together in the stands, rooting for their team and their husbands to do well. When the team is away, most wives stay home, tending to family obligations.

Wives know their husbands will be on the road for half the regular season—a total of nearly three months per year. In spring training, families usually accompany their husbands, but not always.

The family of Fred Stanley, a reserve shortstop for the Yankee World Championship team of 1977, moved 43 times in their first nine years of marriage. Others moved even more often.

After a tough defeat and/or a bad game for a player, his wife must avoid criticizing him or the team. Bad press also hurts. In season, wives share in the joy and the despair that naturally accompanies the game.

Veteran New York writer Dan Daniel, writing in *Baseball Magazine* of January 1937, pointed out other facts of life for the baseball wife:

"Managers fear wives of players. They fear grandstand gossip, they are afraid of cabals.

"During the game in the home city, many wives gather in a certain spot in the grandstand. They are sweet, all smiles, when

Most Valuable Mascot

By Ernie Harwell in *The Baseball Bulletin*

Here's a story about a strange character who had a short career in baseball, but stuck around several seasons with the old New York Giants simply because he was a good-luck charm.

The man's name was Faust—Vic Faust. One of the books says he was tall and lanky. Another says he was a midget. Maybe he was somewhere in-between. Anyway, he came along to the manager of the Giants, John McGraw, during the 1911 season. While the team was taking batting practice, Faust told McGraw that a fortune-teller had told him that if he pitched for the Giants, they would win the pennant.

McGraw had heard some ridiculous stories in his hard-bitten lifetime, but this one was the topper. It sounded even crazier after McGraw watched the would-be pitcher work out. Mr. Faust was no good. In fact, he was awful. But for some strange reason, McGraw took him in as mascot. The only possible explanation could be that, like many old-time baseball men, McGraw was superstitious. Or as the man once said, "I'm not superstitious, I just don't want anything unlucky to happen to me."

Anyway, for the rest of the season—home or away—Faust would warm up in his Giant uniform before each game and then take a seat in the dugout. His teammates took a liking to him and began to make him the butt of their many pranks. They would load Faust's suitcase with bricks. They sent him out for a can of striped paint or for the key to the pitcher's box. But he stuck around and he was a good-luck charm. That first season of Charles Victor Faust, the Giants won the pennant. And toward the end of the year, when the pennant was clinched, McGraw put him into two games. He's in the record book . . . two appearances, no wins and no losses.

The next season—1912—Faust was back again, warming up every day on the sidelines. And again the Giants won the pennant. In 1913 he was with the team again. By now he was famous in his own off-beat way, and he signed for a vaudeville tour. Faust left the team for four games and the Giants lost all four. So, he came back and the Giants again went on to win the title.

But Faust didn't last much longer. He never returned for the season of 1914. Instead, he spent the season in a mental institution, and in 1914 the Giants did not win the pennant.

That was Charles Victor Faust, who appeared officially in only two games, but hung around for three full seasons, because he was lucky. Well, he was lucky for the Giants, but not really lucky for Charles Victor Faust.

Leo Durocher, wife Laraine Day, and their two children, Michelle, ten, and Chris, eight, are headed for California and relaxation. This photo was taken after the New York Giants swept the Cleveland Indians in the 1954 World Series.

Unusual Variety of Food

The most unusual variety of baseball food was served to fans of the Triple-A Hawaii Islanders, who played in Honolulu's Aloha Stadium. They could purchase saimin, manapua, and crack seed in addition to the traditional hot dog or hamburger.

Saimin is a Japanese noodle cooked in shrimp broth and topped with slices of Chinese barbequed pork and green onions. It is served in a cardboard bowl and eaten with chopsticks. Manapua is steamed yeast dough stuffed with sweet pork and onions and eaten hamburger-style. Crack seed ranges from Li Hing Mui (salted plum seeds) to sweet-sour cherry seeds or spiced lemon peels.

Fair or Foul?

Although the odds are 300,000 to 1 against a fan being hit by a ball, according to Ripley's Believe It Or Not, Baltimore outfielder Jay Gibbons injured his own wife with a foul ball in 2006. Before the incident, Gibbons had been asking team management to provide better protection for women and children in the family section of Camden Yards.

Baby Ruth

Baseball's long association with confectioners includes candy bars named for players. The Curtiss Candy Company introduced the Baby Ruth bar in 1921 at the height of Babe Ruth's popularity but insisted it was named after baby Ruth, the late daughter of former president Grover Cleveland.

they meet. But once the game gets under way, it is every wife for herself.

"If the pitcher goes along hurling a three-hitter, and the shortstop boots one to lose the game, Mrs. Pitcher may say things unsweet. Mrs. Shortstop may retort about the games in which Mr. Shortstop helped Mr. Pitcher with hits and plays—games in which Mr. Pitcher wasn't so hot. These little exchanges sometimes grow into conflagrations, and these little debates sometimes kill pennant chances.

"Mrs. Pitcher goes home and inflames Mr. Pitcher against Mr. Shortstop, and vice versa, and when you get two or three of these things going at the same time, along about September 1, Mr. Manager is tearing his hair and hollering for a rule against marriage in baseball.

"In some cases, managers try to urge and foster marriages. But in most cases, the pilots discourage marriage and try to fight it off as long as they can, on one pretext or another."

Things are different when team officials are involved. Kay O'Malley, whose husband Walter owned the Dodgers, read all 14 New York newspapers (before 11 of them failed) and redlined anything about the team. She placed them on Walter's desk.

Mrs. O'Malley scored every game for many years and maintained friendships with the wives of such celebrities as General Douglas MacArthur. She developed a reputation as a very gracious woman.

Mary Frances Veeck always worked closely with husband Bill in his baseball affairs. The Veecks operated a partnership ever since their 1950 marriage and each referred to that arrangement by saying "we" owned the White Sox. Mary Frances conceived the idea of building an apartment in the ballpark when they ran the St. Louis Browns and visualized the day nursery in the ballpark and the "Brownie baby" promotion. The latter involved mailing of specially drawn contracts to parents of newborn sons, inviting them for a Browns tryout at age 18.

The Concessionaires

Fans and food have mixed at baseball games since the early days of the game in the late 19th century. But the staple of concessions operators—the hot dog—came along two years before ballplayers turned professional for the first time in 1869.

Coney Island pie vendor Charles Feltman, staggering from the competition of boardwalk restaurants that offered both pies and hot sandwiches, devised a charcoal stove and conceived the idea of putting hot sausages in fresh rolls.

The frankfurter at that point was just 12 years old; German butchers in Frankfurt first produced it in 1852. Feltman put franks in rolls and Harry M. Stevens, veteran ballpark vendor, sent employees with frank-loaded hot-water tanks trudging around stadiums hawking their wares. Cartoonist Tad Dorgan supplied the name "hot dog" to Stevens' 1902 experiment.

Stevens was an active baseball vendor for years before he started the tradition of serving hot dogs to customers. In Columbus, Ohio, he developed an improved scorecard and hired hawkers to yell: "You can't tell the players without a scorecard!" The quote has become as much a baseball classic as the hot dog.

In 1894 Stevens was handling concessions for the Giants at the Polo Grounds, but it took seven years for the "tube steak" to make its mark. The brochure of the modern Harry M. Stevens Company explains what happened:

"One cold spring day at the old Polo Grounds, around 1901, ice cream wasn't selling. Harry M. Stevens went out for sausages, boiled them, slipped them lengthwise into rolls, and sent his hawkers through the stands shouting, 'Get 'em while they're hot!'"

Though the term *hot dog* caught on, some sections of the country called them wieners or red hots. Detroit's Tiger Stadium—built in 1912—had RED HOTS signs above concessions stands.

On May 29, 1930, *The St. Louis Star* described Sportsman's Park hot dogs as "tender as a mother's kiss." The price was still 10 cents six years later, when average concessions prices listed scorecards at a nickel; ice cream, soda, or draught beer at a dime; and bottled beer at 20 cents.

Nearly a half-century has elapsed since *The Star* saluted the hot dog in Sportsman's Park; neither newspaper nor ballpark exist today, but the hot dog remains vitally important to the success of pro sports franchises.

All-Star Vendors

Myron O'Brisky earned a spot in the imaginary Hawkers' Hall of Fame in a half-century on the job in Pittsburgh. He estimated that he sold 15 million hot dogs, 20 million soft drinks, and 10 million bags of peanuts to 30 million Pirate fans and another 17 million Pitt and Steeler football fans.

Dodger Stadium peanut vendor Roger Owens became a celebrity because of his ability to make long, accurate throws to patrons. Owens began as a soda vendor when the team moved from Brooklyn to Los Angeles in 1958, then moved up to ice cream and finally peanuts. He met his wife over a bag of peanuts.

Owens claimed an accuracy range of 65 rows with a bag of peanuts weighing one and a half ounces, but he was "benched" for more than a month in 1976 after an ice cream vendor—hoping to emulate his style—hit a woman in the forehead with an ice cream sandwich. All vendors were barred from throwing items after the incident, but a "peanut boycott" ensued as fans refused to buy peanuts without the additional treat of watching Owens uncork his usual variety of trick throws.

After fans flooded the Dodger office with petitions and letters, Owens was reactivated. The Dodgers officially recognized his appeal by letting him throw out the first ball of the 1977 season—from the second-level (loge) section where he worked. It was not only the first time a peanut vendor was so honored, but also the longest opening pitch in baseball history.

Owens' one-game peak in sales—1,500 bags—helped financially, as he worked strictly on commission.

During an appearance on *The Tonight Show*, Owens invited Johnny Carson to test his throwing skill.

"I can't," said Carson, "I haven't had the training. I'd have to go to Florida for a couple of months for spring peanut training."

Keeping Braves fans happy is the mission of longtime Atlanta usher Walter Banks (right), who has provided personalized service to everyone from Ted Turner and Jimmy Carter to the author, pictured here.

Singing Usher

Pitcher Trevor Hoffman's dad Ed, a successful singer before settling in Anaheim, was known as "the singing usher" during his days as an Anaheim Stadium employee. He carried a tuner in his pocket and often filled in for National Anthem performers who failed to show up on time.

Moving Up the Ladder

Earl Mann, who owned the minor-league Atlanta Crackers for more than 25 years, began in baseball as a peanut vendor.

Many years later, also in Atlanta, usher Bob Hope became vice president and director of public relations for the major league Atlanta Braves.

Pitcher Practices Medicine

Ron Taylor, a relief pitcher for the 1969 World Champion Mets, later served as team physician for the Toronto Blue Jays.

Tommy John Surgery

Fortunately for Tommy John, the team physician of the Los Angeles Dodgers in 1974 was Dr. Frank Jobe. The veteran left-hander had posted a 13-3 record when he felt something pop in his elbow on July 17. Although he told the pitcher that odds against him were 100-to-1, Dr. Jobe offered him experimental ligament transplant surgery, replacing the torn ligament in the elbow with a healthy one from the leg. John's ability to recover, and to produce three 20-win seasons in five years after returning, led to the procedure's nickname. More than 40 years after the first ligament transplant surgery was performed on Tommy John, former Dodgers trainer Stan Conte blamed fatigue for the rash of recent Tommy John surgeries. He said young pitchers who throw hard are most susceptible.

Doc Gets a Save

Texas pitcher George "Doc" Medich, then a medical student, saved the life of a 61-year-old Baltimore fan struck by a heart attack on July 17, 1978. Medich administered heart massage until paramedics arrived.

Trainer Was Ejected

Milwaukee Braves trainer Joe Taylor recorded a "first" in 1957 when he was ejected from a game after joining a free-for-all on the field.

The Medical Men

Baseball medicine is a highly complex, intricate business with countless unknown factors. Each athlete must be considered as an individual patient, with individual rehabilitation programs to be planned in the event of injury.

When star left-hander Tommy John of the Los Angeles Dodgers tore the inner ligament that supports the elbow (the ligament stressed most by a pitcher), he missed half the 1974 season and all of 1975 before returning in 1976 at less than his usual form.

Thanks to the efforts of Los Angeles surgeon Dr. Frank Jobe, who has treated many ballplayers, John was able to regain his former abilities in 1977. His 20-victory season enabled the Dodgers to win the National League pennant.

Pitcher is the most chronically taxing position because of the constant throwing involved, insisted Dr. Jim Parkes, former team physician of the New York Mets, while catcher is most dangerous because of constant collisions with baserunners. First base, where many aging hitters end their careers, is easiest because of minimal movement and throwing. Emotions must be considered in sports medicine.

"In sports," said Dr. Parkes, "one day you're a hero and the next day you're a bum, and that's hard to take. If somebody had thrown me into an amphitheater with the president of the United States to operate on when I was an intern, I think I might have been a little uptight."

One way to cut the injury toll, the doctor said, is to maintain condition and teach players proper flexibility of the key joints. Team doctors work closely with trainers—especially when the team is on the road. If an injury occurs, the trainer describes it to the team physician by phone and the doctor gives his recommendations. If the mishap is serious, the home club's doctor provides necessary treatment; he calls the team doctor for further consultation if surgery is needed. Often a player will return home for an operation.

During trade talks, the physical condition of players involved is of prime importance. "If a team that is going to make a trade for a player requests medical information on him, it is entitled to know," said Dr. Parkes.

"Our club had the policy that if a trading club requested information, I had the green light to be absolutely objective. My own feeling is that if I were the club requesting information and it was refused, I wouldn't make the trade."

The Major League Physicians Association holds several meetings each year and broaches such subjects as acupuncture, acupressure, and kinesiology—advocated by relief pitcher Mike

Alternative Remedies

In their continuing effort to keep players healthy, major league teams have tried such medical alternatives as acupuncture and magnetic therapy. The former helped the back problems of San Diego general manager Kevin Towers in 1997 and sped the healing of Quilvio Veras' hamstring.

Also in 1997, Yankee rookie Hideki Irabu revealed that he pitched with magnets taped to his body. He said the magnetic field attracted and repelled charged particles in the blood, creating movement and heat, causing the blood vessels to dilate, increasing circulation and accelerating healing. The slight electrical charge created by the magnetic field also stimulated the nervous system, blocking pain.

Marshall—in relation to baseball medicine. Artificial turf is also a subject of controversy.

"When athletes come off AstroTurf, they're like arthritics," said Dr. Parkes.

"Their ankles hurt, their shins hurt, their backs hurt. AstroTurf is like concrete; there's no give.

"I am absolutely sure AstroTurf shortens players' careers. I see very good players coming off artificial surfaces in their home parks and I know their backs, knees, and feet suffer."

Vision, essential to success in the game, can be corrected by glasses. Hitters with two-tenths of a second to react to a 90-mile-an-hour fastball can find lenses to help them keep a sharp eye on the ball.

In 1979 bespectacled players in baseball included home-run sluggers Reggie Jackson and Jeff Burroughs. The Chicago Cubs chief power man, Dave Kingman, was one of 50 major leaguers who wore soft contact lenses, according to The Council on Sports Vision, based in Rochester, New York. The Council reported that 20 percent of all athletes wore some form of vision correction—more than half of those soft contact lenses.

The role of the baseball doctor, said Dr. Jim Parkes, is to give correct advice to a willing patient. "If you have a player or patient who gets good results, 90 percent of the credit goes to him," he said. "You must have a dedicated, responsible individual carry through in the treatment you give him."

Superscouts

It's common knowledge that scouts sign players for teams, but not many fans realize that special assignment scouts prepare advance reports and compile information for future trades on the major league level.

Connie Mack, owner/manager of the Philadelphia Athletics, actually pioneered the idea of the superscout (the widely used term for major league scout) in 1929, when he sent sore-armed pitcher Howard Ehmke on a scouting mission to follow the Cubs. When the World Series opened between the clubs, Ehmke—not Lefty Grove—opened for the A's and won handily.

The Dodgers were one of precious few clubs that embellished on Mack's idea. Clubs went into the World Series cold, hoping for the best, and gambled with every trade they made. Suddenly, baseball became a big business and owners wanted to protect their investments more carefully. The age of the superscout had dawned.

Jim Russo of the Orioles, Frank Malzone of the Red Sox, Howie Haak of the Pirates, Clyde King of the Yankees, and Ray Shore of the Reds were among those who established excellent reputations in the field. Shore traveled one city ahead of the Reds, watching their next opponent and reporting his findings to the team's manager.

He filed a report on each player's throwing ability, running speed, and hitting, and included suggestions on how to pitch to each hitter. He also monitored enemy pitchers.

"In advance scouting, the best information is current information," he said. "You might catch a hitter in a slump and pitch him differently or you might run into a strong-throwing outfielder with a sore arm and be able to take an extra base on him.

Short Report

When the Mets had ornery Rogers Hornsby scout all 18 teams during the 1961 season, his most complimentary report on any player said, "Looks like a major-leaguer." It was for Mickey Mantle.

Catcher Scout

Instead of relying on his regular advance scouts, innovative Baltimore Orioles manager Buck Showalter sent injured catcher Matt Wieters to scout the Tigers at Comerica Park during the last two games of the 2014 season. His advice helped the Orioles not only to beat the favored Tigers but to sweep them in a three-game American League Division Series.

Senator Scouted Senator

A United States senator scouted the top slugger in the history of the Washington Senators. The legislator, Herman Welker of Idaho, watched young Harmon Killebrew hit in his hometown of Payette, then notified Washington club owner Calvin Griffith about the prospect. Killebrew collected more than 500 home runs.

Baltimore Orioles superscout Jim Russo recommended trades for Frank Robinson, Mike Cuellar, Pat Dobson, Ken Singleton, Lee May, and others. Robinson won the Triple Crown in 1966, his first year with the club, and the Orioles won the World Series in four straight games from the Los Angeles Dodgers.

Team ticket managers play a key role behind the scenes. Among their chores is distribution of postseason ducats that may never be used. When pennant races are close, several clubs print playoff and World Series tickets. These, issued by the 1964 Chicago White Sox, are now souvenirs of a good team that didn't win.

"When I was watching Atlanta in Houston, Hank Aaron had a collision with the catcher and hurt his arm, but still continued to play. Aaron didn't have an outstanding arm, but it was accurate and he made the throw when necessary. I noticed in the next couple of games they were running on him—and scoring when they wouldn't ordinarily. We capitalized on it in running the bases against the Braves."

Reports are kept simple deliberately; Shore said he believed in being precise and to the point. He followed the same approach in scouting the American League for possible trade material.

"It helps when the manager and superscout have a close relationship and the manager will use the reports," Yankee scout Clyde King reported. "Most managers know the league, but they definitely need help in the opposite league. If there's some particular hitter who's giving the Yankees trouble, our manager will ask me to pay special attention to him and see if there's anything I can detect that will help us get him out."

Russo joined the Oriole organization when it was still operating out of St. Louis as the Browns. Russo recommended a pitcher and catcher from the semipro team he managed and the pair signed with the Browns.

One of his amateur discoveries was Johnny Bench. "We were exchanging information with Cincinnati that year, and I told them about Bench. They had not known about him," Russo revealed.

The Orioles bypassed Russo's recommendation and drafted another player, but the Reds—who by then had seen Bench—waited until the second round of the draft to name him. They gambled on the fact that Bench had played only eight high school games and might sneak by other scouts too. They were right.

Advancing to superscout from his regional assignment in the southwest, Russo prepared the reports that enabled the Orioles to sweep the 1966 World Series over the Dodgers. His analyses of rival clubs helped the Birds to three more pennants (and one world title) from 1969 to 1971.

The 1966 sweep was based, in part, on Russo's discovery that Sandy Koufax tended to throw rising fastballs that sailed out of the strike zone—but fooled hitters into swinging. Baltimore batters were told to wait on Koufax and the advice worked; he fanned only two men in six innings of Game 2 and was the losing pitcher.

Russo, who signed Oriole ace Jim Palmer and many other regulars, recommended trades that brought National Leaguers Mike Cuellar, Pat Dobson, Mike Torrez, Ken Singleton, and Lee May.

"My first recommendation in covering the major leagues was that we acquire Frank Robinson," Russo said, beaming with pride. "He was one of the greatest players I've ever seen."

Robinson won the Triple Crown in his first season in Baltimore.

On the amateur level, scouting is no longer a cutthroat proposition. The amateur free-agent draft binds each selection to one club. If he chooses not to sign, he goes through the draft six months later.

Scouting, too, has changed. A central scouting bureau serves most teams, though several have refused to join. Scouts of member teams turn their reports in to the bureau rather than to their own club. All members share such information.

Chapter 13

Old pros with California connections, Vin Scully (left) and Ronald Reagan discuss how baseball broadcasting has changed. Before he entered politics, Reagan did Cubs games for WHO Des Moines, while Scully started with the 1950 Brooklyn Dodgers and followed the team to Los Angeles.

The Media

"Father" Henry Chadwick

English-born Henry Chadwick, who took on the nickname "Father" for his many pioneer efforts in the game, is the only baseball writer enshrined in the Hall of Fame.

He wrote the first rule book in 1858, invented the box score, introduced many rules changes, and wrote baseball for 50 years, starting just before the Civil War.

Executives Were Writers

Hall of Fame baseball executives Ford Frick and Ban Johnson began as baseball writers.

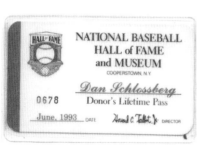
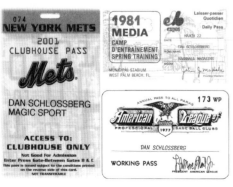

The Writers

Baseball writers, unlike broadcasters, are usually distant from the public eye. Newspapers and magazines devote ample space to the game, but readers often fail to remember bylines.

Most writers are known only by their contemporaries and the people they cover, though players who pick up a pen—like Christy Mathewson, Jim Brosnan, and Jim Bouton—do receive recognition.

Because New York is the nation's media center, top members of the city's press corps occasionally do become public figures. At least their names are known: Jimmy Breslin and James "Scotty" Reston, who advanced from sports to politics, and such baseball "lifers" as Maury Allen, Jimmy Cannon, Arthur Daley, John Drebinger, John Kieran, Tom Meany, Sid Mercer, Milt Richman, and Dick Young.

Many writers remained connected with the game after leaving the daily beat. Ken Smith moved to the Hall of Fame, Arthur Richman (Milton's brother) to the New York Mets, Clyde Hirt to editing magazines, and Carl Lundquist to public relations counselor, promoting products through baseball.

The best-known baseball correspondent in the city never got to a game. He existed only on television, as Oscar Madison, sports editor of *The New York Herald* and co-star of Neil Simon's long-running play and television series, *The Odd Couple*. Jack Klugman played the TV role with an omnipresent New York Mets hat, worn backward.

Early Baseball Writing

Early baseball writing reflected the journalism of the times. The following flowery account of a National League game appeared in the *Indianapolis Daily Sentinel* on Thursday, May 2, 1878:

"The opening game of the season between the Chicagos and Blues was witnessed by about 2,500 people, and resulted in a disastrous defeat to the Blues by a score of 5 to 4. This defeat may be attributed to the poor playing of Williamson on third, in consequence of which the Chicago boys scored three runs in the ninth inning. The managers of the home club would have made the nine much stronger by leaving Warner on third, who played so excellently in that position last season.

"The runs were made in the first, fifth, and ninth innings. Each side made their runs in the first inning on errors. In the fifth, the Chicagos scored a run in the first inning on errors. In the fifth, the Chicagos scored a run on base hits of Ferguson and Harbridge and slow fielding. In the sixth the Blues made two runs on hits by Flint and Croft and a two baser by Shaffer. In the ninth the Blues made another run, Shaffer taking the first on balls, stole second and came home on Nolan's two base hit. The Chicagos got in their work in this inning also. Start made a base hit, taking second on Anson's hit. Each then advanced a base on a muffled ball by Williamson. Start then came home on another fumbler by Williamson and Anson and Ferguson came home on a hit by a Harbridge.

"With the exception of Williamson the home club's fielding was all that could be desired. The Chicagos did not do near as well in the field and Harbridge, especially, showing his weakness in throwing to second. The batting was good on both sides, but the Blues carried off the honors, the Chicagos only hitting Nolan in the ninth inning after he had weakened on account of the turn of affairs.

"With the exceptions mentioned the game was well played and intensely interesting, each individual player trying his best to win for his club.

"Shaffer and Nolan deserve special mention for their batting, and before the season is over they will cause all the league pitchers to tremble when they step up to face them."

Ring Lardner

Damon Runyon and Grantland Rice became the nation's top chroniclers of baseball in the Babe Ruth era, but it was Ring Lardner who set the stage for writers seeking to employ realism instead of romanticism.

Lardner, out of Chicago, spent a half-dozen years traveling with the Cubs and the White Sox of the pre-Ruth, dead-ball period, then began writing short stories for the old *Saturday Evening Post* in 1914.

His "Alibi Ike" concerns a player who could hit, but couldn't field, follow instructions, or get along with other people.

Grantland Rice Meets Ty Cobb

Grantland Rice had many diamond adventures, but listed as his favorite his first encounter with Ty Cobb in 1903. Rice was working for the *Atlanta Journal* when he began to get unsigned letters urging him to watch a young ballplayer named Ty Cobb, then with the Anniston, Alabama, team.

Rice saw Cobb in Augusta, Georgia, Tris Speaker in Little Rock, Arkansas, and Shoeless Joe Jackson in New Orleans—when all were in their teens shortly after the turn of the century. Years later Rice said they were the three greatest players he had seen.

The writer also revealed that he had discovered the source of those unsigned letters in Atlanta—Ty Cobb himself.

As a player himself, Rice faced Rube Waddell, the zany pitcher who later made the Hall of Fame. "I first saw Waddell in 1898 when he pitched against me at Vanderbilt University," Rice recalled. "I believe the Rube had a greater combination of speed and curves than any pitcher who ever lived. He was almost as fast as Walter Johnson and had a back-breaking curve. Connie Mack agreed with this estimate."

Casey's Canine

Writers often develop strong friendships with men in the game. One example was Ed Rumill, who recounted this tale in the May 1977 issue of *The Baseball Bulletin*:

"My wife and I were invited to spend a day with Casey and Edna Stengel at their home in Glendale, California. Edna had suggested we come for lunch. All through a delicious shrimp salad, Edna's cute little cocker spaniel puppy sat beside my chair, looking up at me with big brown eyes, its tail wagging constantly.

"When the dessert course came, I said to our hosts, 'I'm not sure, but I think we may have a problem. Your little dog seems to have fallen in love with me. When we leave, we may have to take her with us.'

"'It's not that,' Casey replied. 'It's just that you're eating out of her dish.'"

Who's on First

Abbott and Costello are not in the Hall of Fame but their "Who's on First?" routine is often shown there. First performed for Kate Smith's radio audience in 1938, it became so popular that it was made into a solid gold record—also in the museum. The original version was one of 50 sound recordings selected for a new Library of Congress registry in 2003.

Kahn's Comment

Roger Kahn, celebrated author of *The Boys of Summer*, says three things about baseball have not changed in 100 years: "No manager ever thought he had enough pitching, no player ever thought the umpire was right, and no owner ever admitted to making money."

Plimpton's Pride

Writer George Plimpton once retired Willie Mays on a pop-up. It happened during a 1958 publicity stunt that preceded a New York exhibition game between stars of both leagues. With $1,000 to be awarded to the team that hit him hardest, Plimpton also got Ernie Banks on a fly ball but tired after facing six more National League hitters. His book *Out of My League* detailed the experience.

Grantland Rice launched his legendary journalism career in Atlanta during Ty Cobb's heyday but rose to the top of his profession during the Babe Ruth era. Rice also deployed his vast knowledge of the game as a pioneer in the art of baseball broadcasting.

Ed Sullivan Wrote Sports

Famous television host Ed Sullivan was sports editor of *The New York Graphic* in the '20s.

From Ballboy to Typewriter

New York Mirror sportswriter Ken Smith, later an executive at the Baseball Hall of Fame, once served as ballboy for the minor-league club in his hometown of Danbury, Connecticut.

Ty Cobb's 4,000th hit was almost ignored in the media.

Hugh Fullerton Halts World Series

One of the best early writers, Hugh Fullerton, actually stopped a World Series game in 1911. The Giants/Athletics classic had been delayed five days by rain, but the rains stopped in New York on the night that Game 4 was scheduled in Philadelphia.

Hoping the rain was still falling in Philly so he could keep a dinner date in New York, Fullerton headed for the New York hotel where American League president Ban Johnson was staying. If Johnson was gone, the game was on, Fullerton decided.

When the writer arrived at the president's door, it was open but the room was empty. Discouraged, Fullerton began to leave when the phone rang. "Hello?" said Fullerton. Robby McCoy, Johnson's personal secretary, mistook Fullerton for Johnson, but Fullerton recognized McCoy's voice at once.

The secretary reported no rain in Philadelphia but suggested the grounds might be too wet to play. He asked "Johnson" if he should call the game. Seizing the opportunity, Fullerton did his best Ban Johnson imitation: "Call it off, Robby, call it off!"

Leaving the room, Fullerton met the real Johnson. The writer coolly informed him that he had canceled the game—but he didn't reveal his personal interest. Johnson agreed, saying *he* wanted to keep a dinner date that night in New York anyhow!

Press Reaction to Record Breakers

In 1927 Ty Cobb achieved an unprecedented level of excellence (exceeded by Pete Rose 60 years later) when he smashed his 4,000th hit. But the press never noticed.

Neither the *Detroit Free Press* nor the *Detroit News* paid any attention to the hit—other than a passing reference in the "game notes" column of the former and a small headline in the latter.

H. G. Salinger of the *News* devoted his regular column to boxing and only mentioned Cobb's hit in passing, failing to point out its significance.

Babe Ruth's 714th home run, his last, received little attention in the media, but the number 700 seemed so insurmountable at the time that *The New York Times* of July 14, 1934, printed this headline: "Ruth's Record of 700 Home Runs Likely to Stand for All Time in Major Leagues."

When Hank Aaron approached and finally broke the record 40 years later, hundreds of media representatives were on hand. The Braves clubhouse was sealed off and a special interview room set up to accommodate both Aaron and the press corps he attracted. Aaron's followers included foreign as well as American reporters, males as well as females.

Women Writers

Jeane Hofmann, sportswriter for the *New York Journal-American* in the '40s, was a pioneer who found the press box as closed to her as the players' dressing rooms.

Signs read NO DOGS OR WOMEN in many places and male colleagues plagued Hofmann with endless pranks. A male writer told her Cincinnati outfielders warmed up by carrying sacks of cement on their shoulders so their bats wouldn't feel heavy by contrast.

As a general rule, Hofmann and females who followed her pioneer footsteps got along well with male contemporaries, but requests by "liberated" women to gain admittance to clubhouses ran into numerous roadblocks in the '70s.

Women of the typewriter charged they missed many big stories by not being in locker rooms, while males who were allowed inside received an unfair advantage. A stalemate developed between players seeking privacy and female writers seeking access, but disintegrated in 1979 when Commissioner Bowie Kuhn issued a directive that clubhouses be open to legitimate media representatives—regardless of gender.

Changing Styles in Covering the Game

Writers have made various changes in the baseball box score through the years. At one time, box scores revealed when each pinch-hitter or pinch-runner was used, how he did, who played more than one position, who participated in double plays, who the umpires were, and how long pitchers lasted when they pitched an inning in which they failed to retire a batter.

By 1979 the traditional box score had deteriorated substantially, so that fans or writers had to be mind-readers to decipher managerial strategy. Position changes were eliminated, so the last position an athlete played was the one that showed in the box score.

Pinch-hitters were listed only if they did not enter the game defensively; if they did, they were listed by the last position played. Nowhere was there an indication of how substitutes did. Umpires and names of participants in double plays were eliminated.

Only *The Sporting News* continued to print more detailed boxes (showing position changes), but that weekly discontinued publication of minor-league box scores when it transferred a huge chunk of its baseball space to other sports. Thousands of readers, who had referred to the tabloid as "the Bible of Baseball," objected.

The Sporting News, operated by the Spink family of St. Louis since 1886, had been known for carrying as much gossip and hearsay information about baseball as actual news. When coverage of other sports began in the '60s, space limitations forced an end to that tradition.

Fred Lieb's Long Tenure

Fred Lieb covered baseball for more than 65 years, beginning at age 21 with the 1911 *New York Press*. Lieb, who saw his first major league games in 1904, worked for several newspapers, including *The Sporting News*, before "retiring" to St. Petersburg, Florida, in 1948. Lieb wrote more than a dozen baseball books, including *Baseball as I Have Known It*, a review of his long sportswriting career.

The Secret Scorer

In 1911 American League president Ban Johnson suggested the identity of scorers be kept secret so they could not be influenced by players to change their decisions.

Chicago of the National League employed a mysterious "E. G. Green" as scorer from 1882 to 1891. Only team president A. G. Spalding knew that Mrs. Elisa Green Williams, mother of team treasurer C. G. Williams, was scoring the games.

Official Scorers

Writers usually serve as official scorers. The job is not easy. On August 29, 1973, a scorer's decision deprived Nolan Ryan of the California Angels of a no-hitter. The New York Yankees made just one hit that day—a pop fly that dropped between two infielders.

Both called for it, then both backed away, fearing collision.

Red Foley's Legacy

Red Foley of the *New York Daily News* served as official scorer in a record 10 World Series. A mid-Manhattan baseball bar, Foley's, adopted its name in his honor.

Los Angeles	AB	R	H	PO	A	E
Lopes,2b	4	0	1	0	4	0
Russell,ss	3	0	0	1	4	0
Smith,rf	4	2	1	1	0	0
Cey,3b	3	1	1	0	1	0
Garvey,1b	4	1	2	13	0	0
Baker,lf	4	0	1	2	0	0
Monday,cf	4	0	1	3	0	0
Yeager,c	3	0	1	4	2	0
bDavalillo	1	0	1	0	0	0
Hooton,p	2	0	0	0	0	0
Sosa,p	0	0	0	0	0	0
Rau,p	0	0	0	0	0	0
aGoodson	1	0	0	0	0	0
Hough,p	0	0	0	0	0	0
cLacy	1	0	0	0	0	0
Totals	34	4	9	24	11	0
New York	AB	R	H	PO	A	E
Rivers,cf	4	0	2	1	0	0
Randolph,2b	4	1	0	2	3	0
Munson,c	4	1	1	6	0	0
Jackson,rf	3	4	3	5	0	0
Chambliss,1b	4	2	2	9	1	0
Nettles,3b	4	0	0	0	0	0
Piniella,lf	3	0	0	2	1	0
Dent,ss	2	0	0	1	4	1
Torrez,p	3	0	0	1	2	0
Totals	31	8	8	27	11	1

```
Los Angeles ............2 0 1  0 0 0  0 0 1—4
New York .................0 2 0  3 2 0  0 1 x—8
```

a Struck out for Rau in seventh.
b Bunted safely for Yeager in ninth.
c Popped out for Hough in ninth.

Runs batted in: Garvey 2, Smith, Davalillo, Chambliss 2, Jackson 5, Piniella.
Double: Chambliss.
Triple: Garvey.
Home runs: Chambliss, Smith, Jackson 3.
Sacrifice fly: Piniella.
Double plays: Dent, Randolph and Chambliss; Dent and Chambliss.
Passed ball: Munson.
Left on bases: New York 5, Los Angeles 2.

Los Angeles	IP	H	R	ER	BB	SO
Hooton (L)	3	3	4	4	1	1
Sosa	1⅔	3	3	3	1	0
Rau	1⅓	0	0	0	0	1
Hough	2	2	1	1	0	3
New York	IP	H	R	ER	BB	SO
Torrez (W)	9	9	4	2	2	6

Hooton pitched to three batters in fourth.

Umpires: McSherry, Chylak, Sudol, McCoy, Dale, Evans.
Time: 2:18. **Attendance:** 56,407.

The box score is the result of scorekeeping decisions as well as game action.

Mikeman Must Score

Keeping score is part of the broadcaster's job. Since there are many different scoring systems, not all members of broadcast teams can read their partners' scorecards. Ex-player Ralph Kiner did not know how to score when he began in the booth. Fellow announcer Bob Prince taught him.

By the '90s, *Baseball America*, issued twice per month, developed a niche with extensive coverage of the minors and college baseball, while *USA Today Baseball Weekly* filled the void created when *The Sporting News* reduced its baseball coverage. The tabloid began publication in 1991.

Mr. Baseball: J. G. Taylor Spink

Without question, the single most influential journalist in baseball history was J. G. Taylor Spink, who ran *The Sporting News* for more than 45 years.

"No man has ever done so much in so many ways for the sport than has Mr. Spink," wrote Hugh Bradley of the *New York Journal-American* in 1961. "If he had not existed, organized baseball would have been forced to invent him."

Spink, who was called the game's best salesman, its best ambassador, and even "Mr. Baseball," was a dynamo of publishing prowess and baseball ideas who editorialized weekly on the strong and weak points of the game.

He drove his staff hard and often called contributors with new ideas in the dead of night, but solidified his paper's reputation as "the Bible of Baseball." Only after his death were other sports given any space in *The Sporting News*. Under the J. G. Taylor Spink regime, minor-league baseball was much more important than major league football, basketball, or hockey.

Spink ran up $30,000 annual phone bills and spent unlimited sums to improve the paper, which evolved into a tabloid during the '40s.

J. G. Taylor Spink was not often wrong, nor was he quick to admit his mistakes. One of his biggest occurred in 1948, when Cleveland Indians owner Bill Veeck purchased Satchel Paige, age 42 (at least), from the Negro Leagues. Spink charged repeatedly that Veeck had made a travesty of the game. Veeck answered with wires after each Paige performance.

Veeck's typical telegram read: NINE INNINGS. FOUR HITS. FIVE STRIKEOUTS. WINNING PITCHER PAIGE. DEFINITELY IN LINE FOR THE SPORTING NEWS AWARD AS ROOKIE OF THE YEAR.

Finally, Spink replied: "*The Sporting News* will make no change in its original editorial, except to express its admiration for any pitcher—white or colored—who at Paige's age can gain credit for five victories over a period of six weeks in any league, major or minor. But it cannot express any admiration for the present-day standard of minor-league ball that makes such a showing possible."

The Publicists

Increased competition for the public's entertainment dollar after World War II placed increased emphasis on the role of the baseball public relations man. Because publicity sells tickets, teams consider a good PR staff as vital as a solid infield defense.

Many of the best publicists in baseball culled their files for photos and background information used in preparing this book; they are listed on the Acknowledgments page.

Donald Davidson, who became a full-time Braves' employee during the pennant year of 1948, served as clubhouse boy, publicity director, traveling secretary, and special assistant to the president—sticking with the Braves through transfers to Milwaukee and Atlanta before running afoul of turbulent Ted Turner in 1976. He quickly hooked on with the Astros.

Though he never grew more than four feet tall, the result of a childhood disease, Davidson was always as demanding and decisive as he was efficient. Such traits, combined with his size, made him the target of thousands of pranks. He wrote about some of them in his hilarious book *Caught Short*.

One of the best involved his chief tormentors, star pitchers Warren Spahn and Lew Burdette. They arrived early at training camp one spring and warned the new gate attendant to watch out for a midget claiming to be a Braves executive. When Davidson arrived, the guard refused to admit him.

His patience exhausted, Davidson kicked the guard in the shins. He was about to retaliate when the pranksters, watching from concealed locations, arrived in time to save the executive's life.

On another occasion, with the team staying in a new hotel in Philadelphia, everyone was booked on the fifth floor. Someone came up with the bright idea to change Davidson's room to the 28th floor and bribed the unknowing hotel clerk to do it. Davidson got into the elevator, surrounded by several six-foot Braves who left at the fifth floor without a word. Unable to reach the button for the 28th, Davidson rode up and down several times before someone came to his rescue.

The best-known and best-liked public relations executive, Bob Fishel, spent many years with the Yankees before joining the American League's New York office.

In his assorted assignments in the game, he handled such PR duties as writing news releases, compiling statistics, running promotions, editing yearbooks, keeping photo files updated, answering media requests for photos, information, or credentials, and—perhaps most important—keeping mum about breaking news stories until they were announced by team officials at news conferences he arranged.

Fishel's connection with baseball began in 1946, after Bill Veeck had purchased the Cleveland Indians. Veeck had heard of Fishel's advertising and promotion prowess and wanted him to handle a huge campaign called, "We're giving the Indians Back to the Fans."

Broadcasting was a key ingredient of the program and, in 1947 and 1948, Fishel put together a strong Cleveland radio/TV network. He later worked for Veeck with the St. Louis Browns before moving to the Yankees.

Broadcasting

Baseball broadcasting did not begin until 1921 on radio and 1939 on television. Electronic communications were so well received by fans that the men behind the mike, like the players they described, soon became celebrities.

Mel Allen, Red Barber, Harry Caray, Bob Prince, and Vin

Radio in Two-Team Cities

Baseball's two-team cities had unwritten agreements about radio broadcasting, and most of them lasted until shortly after World War II.

A key rule stated that the team on the road would broadcast only when the home team wasn't playing. The idea was to convince residents to visit the ballpark of the team in town rather than sit home with an ear tuned to the radio.

Most clubs broadcast all or most home games in a promotional venture. When Sam Breadon, Cardinal owner, banned home radio during the Gashouse Gang's top year of 1934, attendance dipped alarmingly. With radio back in 1935, with the Depression still a factor, the count went to 517,805 from 334,863. France Laux was the key radio voice in town that year.

Russ Hodges carved his niche in broadcast lore on October 3, 1951. He was on the radio when Bobby Thomson hit a three-run, pennant-winning homer that turned a 4–2 deficit into a 5–4 win for the New York Giants over the Brooklyn Dodgers. He yelled, "The Giants win the pennant!" nine times.

Detroit Tigers

Ernie Harwell's career as a big-league broadcaster began in 1948 after the minor-league Atlanta Crackers traded him to the Brooklyn Dodgers for catcher Cliff Dapper.

Topps Baseball Trading Cards used courtesy of The Topps Company, Inc.

Pitcher Waite Hoyt, a former Babe Ruth teammate, told so many stories on the air that he cut a record called *Best of Waite Hoyt in the Rain*. He excelled at re-creating games, using only a teletype and sound effects.

Scully did not play big-league baseball, but became as well-known as fiery manager Leo Durocher or home-run king Hank Aaron. The vast audience provided by television allowed many announcers to achieve higher recognition factors than stars who wound up in the Hall of Fame.

Before radio, fans followed the game through newspaper reports. Inning-by-inning scores were posted in the windows of promotion-minded papers and telegraph offices. With competition high, labor costs low, and newsprint plentiful, papers printed multiple editions, including "baseball editions" with partial line scores appearing on the back (or even the front) page.

Radio, and later television, gave fans another outlet—and more immediate results of both the local game and other contests.

Firsts

Harold Arlin announced the first broadcast baseball game, a Phillies/Pirates contest, on Pittsburgh radio station KDKA, August 5, 1921.

Arlin, a Westinghouse foreman by day and announcer by night, was in the right place at the right time. After KDKA became the first operating radio station in 1920, he delivered broadcast "firsts" in football and tennis, and introduced by radio the voices of Will Rogers, Herbert Hoover, William Jennings Bryan, and Babe Ruth.

Ruth struck out on radio, however. In town for a Yankee/Pirate exhibition game, Ruth was supposed to read a speech prepared by Arlin, but he developed mike fright and couldn't speak. Arlin took his place and the station later got letters praising the quality of "Ruth's" voice.

The novelty of broadcast baseball spread when KDKA linked with two other Westinghouse affiliates, WJZ (in New Jersey) and WBZ (then in Springfield, Massachusetts, now in Boston), to carry the 1921 World Series between the New York Giants and the Yankees. Sportswriter Grantland Rice handled the mike and returned the following fall with another writer, Bill McGheehan, when the same clubs met.

In 1923 New York's WEAF, forerunner of WNBC, introduced a voice that would later make many broadcasting milestones—Graham McNamee. The following year WMAQ of Chicago became the first station to undertake regular local broadcasts when it aired all home games of the White Sox and the Cubs.

The Early Years of Broadcast Baseball

When radio first became available to ballclubs, some owners argued that broadcast games would reduce home attendance. If fans could hear a play-by-play report, they reasoned, why should they come to the ballpark? The same argument surfaced again years later, when television gave fans the opportunity to hear *and see*.

By 1936 radio broadcasting was universal everywhere in baseball but New York, where the Giants, the Dodgers, and the Yankees refused to accept it as a valuable promotional tool. The clubs maintained a united boycott until the close of the 1938 season, when the Giants sold exclusive air rights for $150,000 and the Dodgers got a contract for $77,000.

The idea of selling exclusive rights did not take hold until the '30s, more than ten years after the advent of baseball broadcasting. Detroit's WWJ actually refused to sell advertising time for seven years after Ty Tyson began announcing Tiger games in 1927. Even the World Series had no sponsor until Henry Ford signed a four-year, $400,000 pact in 1934.

At first stations competed with each other not for exclusive rights but for listeners. Several stations in each city broadcast the games of the home clubs.

After WMAQ's initial entry in Chicago in 1924, other stations noticed the enthusiastic reaction of the fans and launched rival broadcasts. Among the many voices to announce Chicago games were Joe E. Brown, the film comedian whose son spent many years as general manager of the Pirates, and Ronald "Dutch" Reagan, future actor and politician who "re-created" telegraphed game reports with special sound effects.

Others who earned their broadcast spurs as Chicago pioneers were Bob Elson, who launched a 30-year run as a baseball voice in 1931; Jimmy Dudley, a WIND employee whose work earned him a long stay as the main mikeman in Cleveland; and Russ Hodges, a one-time Dudley partner whose 1951 shouts of "The Giants win the pennant! The Giants win the pennant!" rank as the most memorable words ever spoken behind a baseball microphone.

The Re-created Play-by-Play

Jack Graney, who became the first ex-player to broadcast when he jumped from left field to the Cleveland microphone in 1932, was especially adept at re-creating away games. The practice was common in the majors until teams started bringing their announcers on road trips after World War II.

Another former player, Waite Hoyt, and garrulous Les Kieter continued to handle re-creations into the late '50s, when the practice ended on the major league level.

Re-creating a game was difficult, at best. The announcer worked with a "canned" sound track of cheering fans, which he would raise or lower in volume to indicate their level of excitement. He also had a hollow block of wood, which he would hit with a pencil or stick to represent the sound of bat hitting ball.

The play-by-play came in by teletype: MAYS. B1. S1. B2. ALOU STEALS SECOND. S2. FOUL POP. ERROR CATCHER. TRIPLE. RUN SCORES.

In Cincinnati, Waite Hoyt entertained listeners with a low-key style, frequent use of understatement, and the unusual habit of watching the action and *then* telling his audience what happened in the past tense!

Hoyt, a fabled storyteller who played with Babe Ruth on the Yankees, was such a master at filling time during games held up

Young Mel Allen was at the mike for the Yankees in 1950.

Radios at the Stadium

Dodger fans brought radios to the cavernous Los Angeles Coliseum because they were seated far from the field and had trouble seeing the action. They continued the tradition after the team moved to Dodger Stadium in 1962. Announcer Vin Scully tested the number of radios by asking fans to shout "Happy Birthday Frank" to umpire Frank Secory.

Plane Facts

To aid in the first telecast of a World Series, a B-29 bomber fitted with primitive TV equipment flew up and down western Pennsylvania at an altitude of 20,000 feet and sent signals to the ground. Although the link to the 1948 Braves-Indians games was not always reliable, it paved the way for the first coast-to-coast telecast three years later.

Phil Rizzuto was at the radio mike for Roger Maris' 61st homer.

Prince of the Pirates

Bob Prince joined the Pirates as a $50-a-week assistant to Rosey Rowswell in 1948 and soon won widespread recognition for his slow, nasal twang, coupled with his knowledge and passion for the game.

Prince, equally colorful off-mike, won bets by (1) diving from his third-floor window into the pool of the Hotel Chase in St. Louis, (2) keeping quiet for a solid hour on an airplane trip, and (3) parading in Bermuda shorts from the center-field clubhouse of the Polo Grounds to home plate, where Giant manager Leo Durocher kissed him on both cheeks.

by rain that a record was cut with the title *Best of Waite Hoyt in the Rain*. The album contained stories Hoyt told during a 25-year career as announcer for the Cincinnati Reds.

Ballplayers in the Booth

Like Waite Hoyt, former players who became broadcasters relied on their baseball experiences to provide insights and balance when working with professional announcers who were primarily reporters or narrators. Ralph Kiner, a charter member of the New York Mets air team, had excellent training.

"I heard a lot of Vin Scully when I was in Southern California and liked his style," Kiner recalled. "He's a narrator and storyteller and that's very good. The first year I was broadcasting, my partner was Bob Elson with the Chicago White Sox. He was excellent and probably the best interviewer I ever heard.

"In my early days, I listened to my own and other broadcasters' tapes, trying to figure out what direction to go in. I feel being natural is the answer. I don't listen to my old tapes now because I've developed my own style and don't want to change it.

"One of the secrets of broadcasting is not saying too much. My first broadcast, I said everything I knew in the first two innings and had nothing left."

Pregame preparation is part of Kiner's daily routine. He talks to home and visiting players and writers and reads a variety of publications, especially *The Sporting News* and *Baseball Weekly*.

"It's easy to find out about Hank Aaron or any other star," he said, "but it's difficult to find out anything interesting about any newcomer—other than where he's played before. Spring training is the place you can pick up a lot of background information."

When the visiting San Francisco Giants were without an announcer one late-summer day in 1977, Kiner took over the chores for KSFO radio. "I had to put the game in perspective for Giants fans," he said. "It was like being tossed into the water to learn how to swim. I had to make my own way, but I had done my homework ahead of time and it was interesting."

Bloopers on the Air

Even with preparation, no announcer is immune to bloopers. Sooner or later they strike every broadcast booth. Earl Gillespie of the Milwaukee Braves once said, "Al Deck is in the on-dark circle." And Herb Carneal, with the Springfield Cubs of the International League, contributed this gem: "Syracuse is threatening and, for the Cubs, Tony Jacobs is throwing up in the bullpen."

Early in his career behind the mike, former Yankee shortstop Phil Rizzuto announced, "There's the pitch. Yogi Berra swings and hits a high foul behind the plate. It's coming down . . . and Yogi Berra makes the catch!"

Even Mel Allen, the polished performer who began in 1938 and later won world acclaim as the No. 1 announcer for the Yankees, made broadcast boo-boos. In one game Allen assumed Les Moss was catching for the St. Louis Browns—until Moss appeared as a pinch-hitter in the ninth inning!

Famous Home-Run Calls

Though Mel Allen's southern drawl, coupled with the Yankees' home-run power, popularized the call, "Going, going, gone," the phrase was first used by Cincinnati's Harry Hartman in 1929.

Vin Scully's usual call is a simple, "Forget it," while Ralph Kiner says, "Kiss it good-bye," as the ball disappears over the fence. Russ Hodges said, "Bye, bye, baby," and many broadcasters refer to the home run as a ball that was "hit downtown."

By far the most original call was created by Rosey Rowswell in Pittsburgh, before the advent of television. When Kiner was cracking home runs for the Pirates, Rowswell imagined a little old lady with an apartment window facing Forbes Field. He yelled, "Open the window, Aunt Minnie, here it comes!" and then smashed a light bulb near the microphone when the ball left the park.

Descriptions of home runs that shattered Babe Ruth's one-season and lifetime records were broadcast by Phil Rizzuto of the Yankees on October 1, 1961, and Milo Hamilton, then with the Braves, on April 8, 1974. Both events occurred in the players' home parks.

Rizzuto's reaction:

"Here comes Roger Maris. They're standing up, waiting to see if Roger is going to hit No. 61! Here's the windup . . . the pitch to Roger . . . WAY OUTSIDE, ball one. (Boos) The fans are starting to boo . . . Low, ball two. That one was in the dirt. And the boos get louder. Two balls, no strikes, on Roger Maris. Here's the windup . . . fastball HIT DEEP TO RIGHT, THIS COULD BE IT! WAY BACK THERE! *HOLY COW, HE DID IT!!* 61 HOME RUNS!! They're fighting for that ball out there. Holy cow . . . another standing ovation for Roger Maris!"

Here's how Hamilton handled it:

"Now here's Henry Aaron. This crowd is up all around. The pitch to him . . . bounced it up there, ball one. (Loud round of boos) Henry Aaron in the second inning walked and scored. He's sitting on 714. Here's the pitch by Downing . . . Swinging . . . There's a drive into left-center field. That ball is gonna beee . . . OUTA HERE! IT'S GONE! IT'S 715! There's a new home-run champion of all time! And it's Henry Aaron! The fireworks are going! Henry Aaron is coming around third! His teammates are at home plate. Listen to this crowd . . . (thunderous sustained applause and cheers)."

AP Photo/David J. Phillip, File

Milo Hamilton broadcast games for the Browns, Cardinals, Cubs, White Sox, Braves, Pirates, and Astros. His call of Hank Aaron's 715th home run on Atlanta radio station WSB is often paired with the video of the 1974 milestone.

Harry Caray captivated fans with his broadcast work in both St. Louis and Chicago.

The Caray Way

Harry Caray became an announcer for the St. Louis Cardinals by writing the radio station manager that he could do a better job than the incumbent. Caray and partner Gabby Street won exclusive air rights over several rivals in 1947 and, after the team was purchased by Anheuser-Busch, went to Bavaria to research beer commercials.

Always anxious to find a new perspective on the game, he was broadcasting from the bleachers (and sitting with the fans) when he provided a graphic description of Curt Flood's "spectacular catch" at the base of the center-field wall. Caray could not actually see the play because it was out of his line of vision.

Skip's Start

With broadcast legend Mel Allen unable to broadcast the Braves/Astros game for Atlanta's WSB-TV on May 30, 1965, Skip Caray served as an emergency replacement. The Milwaukee Braves had already announced their intention to move to Atlanta in 1966, but Caray did not join their team full time until 1976.

First Family of the Booth

In 1992 announcers Harry Caray of the Cubs and Skip and Chip Caray of the Braves made baseball history when they became the first three-generation family of broadcasters to announce the same game.

The Age of Television

When Larry MacPhail transferred his talents from the Reds to the Dodgers in 1939, he brought broadcaster Red Barber with him. Later that year, on August 26, Barber was the announcer when newborn television station W2XBS aired a doubleheader between the Reds and the Dodgers from Ebbets Field. This pioneer baseball telecast reached only a handful of sets in existence then, but paved the way for a new trend in communications. In 1961 the technique became even more sophisticated when two minutes of a Cubs/Phillies game were beamed to Europe via the new Tel-Star satellite.

Early television was often trying. When WGN-TV of Chicago put baseball onto the little screen in 1948, announcer Jack Brickhouse kept one eye on the field and the other on the monitor. "Viewers don't like you describing things unless they can see what you're describing," he recalled. "At one point, the batter hit a tremendous fly. I described the flight of the ball and the fielder chasing it and was sure I saw him catch the ball as it came down inside the park. On my monitor, the ball was still in flight. The camera followed it over the wall, over housetops, and on until the cameraman realized he was not following the baseball but had picked up a bird in flight."

Announcers making the transition from radio to television had as much trouble as actors switching from silents to talkies. They didn't know whether to talk more or less, and realized their mistakes would become painfully obvious to fans who could see as well as hear.

They couldn't describe infield pops as long outfield drives. Television personalized the game not only because vision was provided but also because announcers, with less to say about action on the field, began to reveal personal insights about the players.

Network Coverage

The National Broadcasting Company pioneered network television coverage of the World Series in 1947 and of the All-Star Game in 1950. The network's New York affiliate handled the first big-league broadcast, in 1939, as well as the first sporting event ever televised—a Princeton/Columbia baseball game announced by Bill Stern that same year. The college game drew an estimated audience of 5,000 while the 1975 World Series colorcast between the Cincinnati Reds and the Boston Red Sox had more than 75 million viewers for the decisive seventh game.

The Columbia Broadcasting System won radio rights to the All-Star Game, Championship Series of the two leagues, and the World Series in 1976. Those rights extended to 267 affiliates, plus stations in Canada, Puerto Rico, the Dominican Republic, Venezuela, Panama, and other Latin American countries.

Actually, CBS, NBC, and Mutual had all worked All-Star and World Series games on radio as far back as the 1930s, but the rapid growth of the industry in the television era, plus expansion and restructuring of major league baseball, created the modern format, which allowed the three major networks to share coverage and provide massive doses of publicity for the game.

Baseball on the air has advanced a long way from Harold Arlin's lonely experimental mike at KDKA.

Mikemen Honored Too

Because broadcasters usually stay with teams longer than players, they often become icons in the minds of fans. Many teams have honored announcers with long tenure by naming broadcast booths after them. Others have raised flags, built statues, or painted memorials on outfield walls.

The late Ernie Harwell, longtime voice of the Detroit Tigers, has all three. His name hangs along with retired Tiger numbers on the Comerica Park wall in left-center field, while his statue stands at the stadium's front entrance. A Harwell portrait is there too.

A statue showing Harry Caray leading Wrigley Field fans in "Take Me Out to the Ballgame" resides near the ballpark's bleacher entrance and a Caray caricature adorns the WGN-TV booth. Previous Cubs announcer Jack Brickhouse is remembered not only with a statue but with the words "Hey, hey" on both foul poles.

There's a microphone painted on the wall of Busch Memorial Stadium, honoring Jack Buck, next to the Cardinals retired numbers.

The Mets named their radio booth after Bob Murphy and their television booth after Ralph Kiner. During the 2014-15 seasons, they also displayed a Kiner memorial logo that contained his name, a microphone, and the years 1922–2014, marking his lifespan. A microphone in a circle that hangs near retired Mets numbers bears Kiner's name.

Unlike Kiner, Tom Cheek never wore a jersey but did announce a record 4,306 games—the broadcast equivalent of Cal Ripken's consecutive games playing streak. A banner that flies on the "Level of Excellence" at Rogers Centre shows his name and the number 4,306.

San Diego's Jerry Coleman saluted a great play by saying "You can hang a star on that one!" A gold star, along with Coleman's name, adorns the front of the Petco Park press box, which was named for him after his demise in 2014.

The street fronting Houston's Minute Maid Park has been renamed Milo Hamilton Way. The Astros radio booth has also been named for the famous announcer, who preceded Pete van Wieren in Atlanta. The Braves have named their own booth in van Wieren's memory.

The Los Angeles Dodgers changed their address without changing their location. "Vin Scully Avenue" was created in 2016, the last year the longtime Voice of the Dodgers remained on the air. The Dodger Stadium press box has had his name since 2001.

Bob Uecker's name and the words "Fifty Years in Baseball" share the Miller Park wall with retired Brewers numbers.

And the Washington Nationals, who disowned the four numbers retired for Montreal Expos players before that team relocated to the nation's capital in 2005, did find room to remember two Washington Senators mikemen: Arch McDonald and Bob Wolff. Both names are on the Ring of Honor at Nationals Park.

Ed Lucas celebrates his 60th consecutive Yankee Stadium opener with baseball writer Dan Schlossberg. Blind since age 12, Lucas wrote a 2015 autobiography called *Seeing Home*.

Mouth that Roared

When baseball press boxes were open and broadcasters could be heard by the writers, one New York scribe told another, "I don't know which game we went to—the one we saw or the one we heard Graham McNamee broadcast."

Before Soundproof Booths

Early radio men broadcast right from the press box, without the soundproofing provided by booths. During the 10-run uprising by the Philadelphia Athletics in Game 4 of the 1929 World Series against the Cubs, Graham McNamee was at the mike when a writer accidentally played his foil: "McNamee, will you please pipe down?"

The Power of Video

After TBS television cameras beamed footage of fans waving foam-rubber tomahawks during games, viewers responded by sending tomahawks of all sizes and descriptions to Braves players and broadcasters. Tom Glavine and Steve Avery had them in the dugout one night and chopped along with the fans.

Perfect Head

The morning after Don Larsen's perfect game in the 1956 World Series, a *Daily News* headline read, "The imperfect man pitched the perfect game."

Musical Mind

Sixty-six songs by baseball broadcaster Ernie Harwell have been recorded by various artists.

Broadcast Highlights

1921—Grantland Rice provides World Series play-by-play via telephone for a three-station radio hookup involving KDKA Pittsburgh, WBZ Boston, and WJZ Newark.

1947—NBC's first World Series telecast is carried in New York, Philadelphia, Washington, and Schenectady.

1951—First nationwide telecast of World Series features Russ Hodges and Jim Britt.

1976—NBC and ABC begin alternate years of Fall Classic coverage.

1990—World Series shifts to CBS.

1994—Baseball Network awarded postseason rights, but strike cancels all games.

1995—First shared coverage of Series, with ABC and NBC both participating.

1996—FOX Sports has even years, NBC odd years of Series telecasts.

2000—FOX signs six-year deal to air all postseason games.

2005—MLB Network Radio, formerly MLB Home Plate, begins on XM Satellite Radio, adding Sirius Satellite Radio three years later.

2006—New deal gives FOX exclusives on All-Star and World Series while showing ALCS and NLCS in alternating years. TBS and ESPN are also involved.

2009—MLB Network, based in Secaucus, New Jersey, launches with original programming, expert analysis, and both regular-season and postseason games

2012—FOX signs extension to show World Series and All-Star Game through 2021 plus two Division Series and one League Championship Series per year.

Kiner's Question

During the difficult first year of the expansion Mets in 1962, Ralph Kiner struggled to find a star of the game for his postgame Kiner's Korner television show. In desperation, he invited Choo-Choo Coleman, a catcher who couldn't hit, field, or run. "What's your wife's name and what's she like?" Kiner said. Coleman thought for a minute and said, "Her name is Mrs. Coleman and she likes me."

Empty Park

Red Barber could not convince his cameraman to pan the Yankee Stadium crowd on September 22, 1966. The last-place Yankees, playing a makeup game against the Chicago White Sox on a dreary day, drew only 413 fans to the cavernous ballpark. Barber's candor in reporting that fact led to his dismissal shortly thereafter.

Frick Firsts

Mel Allen and Red Barber, longtime New York radio voices, were the first recipients of the Ford C. Frick Award for broadcast excellence.

First On The Fan

Yankees radio voice Suzyn Waldman spoke the first words on WFAN when the New York sports talk station went on the air on July 1, 1987.

Bad Timing

It was the shout not heard around the world when Barry Bonds hit his 715th home run to pass Babe Ruth on the lifetime list. Giants radio voice Dave Fleming discovered his mic went dead just before the historic clout. "I thought I made a good call but I got over it," he said.

Harry the K

Beloved Phillies broadcaster Harry Kalas died of a heart attack in the visiting broadcast booth in Washington on April 13, 2009.

Pricey Package

MLB has an eight-year, $12.4 billion national television package that brings revenue from FOX, ESPN, and TBS.

Chapter 14

AP photo, reprinted with permission, National Baseball Hall of Fame Library, Cooperstown, N.Y.

Jubilant Giants greet Bobby Thomson at the plate after his pennant-winning home run of 1951.

Big Moments

Unassisted Triple Play

Cleveland Indians second baseman Bill Wambsganss made an unassisted triple play to help his team defeat the Brooklyn Robins in the 1920 World Series.

Why the Giants Won

The 1951 New York Giants engineered the greatest comeback in a single season because of key player moves by manager Leo Durocher. On May 21 Whitey Lockman took over first base. On May 25 Willie Mays came up from Minneapolis to play center field. On July 20 Bobby Thomson went to third base and Don Mueller began playing right field every day.

Triple-Digit Wins

Since the 1969 advent of divisional play, two teams from the same division have won 100 games three times. They are the Yankees (103) and the Orioles (100) of the 1980 AL East; the Braves (104) and the Giants (103) of the 1993 NL West; and the Mariners (116) and the A's (102) of the 2001 AL West.

The Game's Most Memorable Moments

During the 1975 All-Star Game in Milwaukee, Major League Baseball began a nationwide campaign to choose its most memorable moments and personalities.

The search ended when Hank Aaron's 715th home run, on April 8, 1974, was voted Most Memorable Moment (MMM) and Babe Ruth, whose record Aaron broke, was named Most Memorable Personality.

The winners, selected by the media and key baseball officials, were honored at the 1976 All-Star luncheon in Philadelphia. Ms. Julia Ruth Stevens of Conway, New Hampshire, accepted the personality award in memory of her father, who died in 1948.

Winners of the three other Most Memorable Moment categories, revealed at a New York news conference, were: Don Larsen's perfect game in the 1956 World Series; Joe DiMaggio's 56-game hitting streak; and, as the National League's top moment, Aaron's 715th.

The Aaron home run was selected from a list of 72 nominees. As in other categories, the choice could come from a single play, game, series of events, or entire career.

Aaron's historic homer, produced in his home park at Atlanta Stadium, narrowly defeated Bobby Thomson's "shot heard 'round the world" in the competition. The Aaron blow received 485 votes among 2,391 cast in the overall category, while Thomson's pennant-winning home run of 1951 received 419.

Hank Aaron's 715th home run was voted Most Memorable Moment of baseball history in a poll completed in 1976, the year of the U.S. bicentennial celebration.

Larsen's perfect game ranked third with 313, followed by Ruth's "called shot" World Series homer of 1932 and DiMaggio's hitting streak.

Ruth was a runaway winner as Most Memorable Personality with 1,176 votes, against 370 for runner-up Casey Stengel. Dizzy Dean had 65. Aaron and Mickey Mantle tied for sixth with 61 each. Forty personalities were nominated.

Here are the top five finishers and vote totals in the World Series/All-Star, American League and National League MMM categories:

World Series/All-Star Votes

1. Don Larsen's perfect game in 1956 World Series   1,037
2. Bill Mazeroski's Series-winning homer in 1960   332
3. Babe Ruth's "called shot" home run in 1932   214
4. Carlton Fisk's game-winning homer in Game 6 of 1975 Series   127
5. Mets' miracle Series championship in 1969   114

Leading Finishes by All-Star Moments
7. Carl Hubbell's five consecutive strikeouts in 1934   72
13. Pete Rose's race home with winning run in 1970   23

American League

1. Joe DiMaggio's 56-game hitting streak in 1941   1,021
2. Roger Maris' 61st home run in 1961   394
3. Lou Gehrig's 2,130 consecutive-games playing streak   320
4. Ted Williams' six hits on final day of 1941 season to hit .400   126
5. Ted Williams' homer in final career at-bat in 1960   112

National League

1. Hank Aaron's 715th home run in 1974   785
2. Bobby Thomson's playoff-winning home run in 1951   781
3. Johnny Vander Meer's back-to-back no-hitters in 1938   271
4. Jackie Robinson's major league debut in 1947   130
5. Harvey Haddix's 12-inning perfect game in 1959   69

The club winners were revealed in December 1976. A special panel representing the media and baseball rounded out the final list of nominees in the national competition to make sure events and personalities on clubs no longer in operation were fairly represented.

Joe DiMaggio's 56-game hitting streak was Most Memorable Moment in American League voting.

Hondo's Heroics

Frank Howard, a 6'8" giant who weighed nearly 270 pounds, terrorized pitchers with his bat as well as his size. He remains the only man to hit eight homers over a five-game span twice, both during his 1968 tenure with the Washington Senators.

Pay Attention

George Brett celebrated his 3000th hit in 1992 by getting picked off. Tom Fortugno of the Angels caught the Kansas City slugger sleeping.

Marathon Man

Jim Palmer was the only pitcher to win World Series games in three different decades.

Super Sammy

Sammy Sosa (Cubs) compiled a record 1,621 total bases over a four-year span that started in 1998. That erased Chuck Klein's 69-year-old mark of 1,616.

Star slugger Harmon Killebrew delivered the Most Memorable Moment of the Minnesota Twins with a game-winning, ninth-inning home run, keeping the team in first place in July 1965.

Minnesota Twins

Most Memorable Moment Nominees

Regular Season
(In Chronological Order)

American League

1. Ty Cobb's 6-for-6 including three home runs—May 5, 1925
2. Lefty Grove's 1–0 loss after 16 straight wins—1931
3. Lou Gehrig's 2,130 consecutive-games playing streak—June 1, 1925, to April 30, 1939
4. Bob Feller no-hits White Sox on opening day—April 16, 1940
5. Joe DiMaggio's 56-game hitting streak—May 15–July 16, 1941
6. Ted Williams' six hits on final day of 1941 season (September 28) puts him over .400
7. Joe Cronin becomes first player to clout a pinch-hit homer in each game of a doubleheader—June 17, 1943
8. St. Louis Browns clinch only pennant—October 1, 1944
9. Lou Boudreau ties major league record and sets AL standard for most long hits in a game (five) with four doubles and home run—July 14, 1946
10. Satchel Paige's shutout against Chicago in his first complete major league game—August 10, 1948
11. Cleveland beats Boston to win only AL playoff—October 4, 1948
12. Allie Reynolds' second no-hitter of 1951—September 28
13. *White Sox win first pennant in 40 years—1959
14. Ted Williams homers in final career at-bat—September 26, 1960
15. Roger Maris' 61st home run—October 1, 1961
16. *Harmon Killebrew's ninth-inning homer beats Yankees and keeps Minnesota in first place—July 11, 1965
17. *Red Sox win 1967 pennant in final game
18. *Jim Hunter (A's) hurls perfect game vs. Twins—May 8, 1968
19. Denny McLain becomes baseball's first 30-game winner since 1934—September 14, 1968
20. *Baseball returns to Milwaukee—1970
21. *Steve Busby (Royals) hurls his first no-hitter—April 27, 1973
22. *David Clyde (Rangers), 18, wins major league debut—June 27, 1973
23. *Frank Robinson's (Indians) managerial debut, highlighted by his own home run—April 8, 1975
24. *Nolan Ryan (Angels) ties major league record with fourth no-hitter—June 1, 1975

National League

25. Boston Braves' miracle finish in 1914
26. Baseball's longest game, the Brooklyn/Boston 26-inning, 1–1 tie—May 1, 1920

*Designates most memorable moments for each club

Rickey and Ryan

Future Hall of Famers Rickey Henderson and Nolan Ryan competed for sports page headlines on May 1, 1991. Henderson notched his 939th career steal, passing Lou Brock as the lifetime leader, while Ryan pitched his seventh no-hitter and fanned 16.

Braves Blew 1959 Playoff Game

In 1959 the Milwaukee Braves took a 5–2 lead into the ninth inning of Playoff Game 2 but could not hold on. The Los Angeles Dodgers tied it in the ninth and won, 6–5, when Felix Mantilla made a throwing error in the twelfth.

27. First major league night game played in Cincinnati—May 24, 1935
28. Babe Ruth's final three homers, hit for the Boston Braves—May 25, 1935
29. *Johnny Vander Meer's (Reds) consecutive no-hitters—June 11 and 15, 1938
30. Gabby Hartnett's "Homer in the Gloamin'" gives Cubs NL lead—September 28, 1938
31. Jackie Robinson's major league debut—April 15, 1947
32. Dick Sisler's 10th-inning homer wins pennant for Phils—October 1, 1950
33. Bobby Thomson's ninth-inning playoff homer wins NL championship for Giants—October 3, 1951
34. Stan Musial slugs five home runs in doubleheader—May 2, 1954
35. Henry Aaron's home run gives Milwaukee first pennant—September 23, 1957
36. Roy Campanella's testimonial game lures 93,103 in Los Angeles—May 7, 1959
37. Harvey Haddix hurls 12 perfect innings for Pirates, loses in 13th—May 26, 1959
38. *Giants' 1962 playoff victory
39. *Jim Bunning's (Phillies) perfect game—June 21, 1964
40. *Astrodome inaugural—April 9, 1965
41. *Sandy Koufax (Dodgers) throws perfect game—September 9, 1965
42. Don Drysdale pitches record 58⅔ consecutive scoreless innings—May 14–June 8, 1968
43. *Expos' debut in Montreal, first major league game outside of United States—April 14, 1969
44. Tom Seaver's record 10 consecutive strikeouts vs. San Diego—April 22, 1970
45. *Ernie Banks' (Cubs) 500th home run—May 12, 1970
46. *Nate Colbert's five-homer, 13-RBI doubleheader—August 1, 1972
47. *Henry Aaron's (Braves) record 715th homer—April 8, 1974
48. *Lou Brock's (Cardinals) 105th stolen base—September 10, 1974

World Series/All-Star Game

49. Christy Mathewson's three shutouts vs. Athletics in 1905 Series—October 9, 12, 14
50. Bill Wambsganss makes only unassisted triple play in Series—October 10, 1920
51. Walter Johnson's first Series victory at age of 36—October 10, 1924
52. Grover Alexander saves 1926 Series with bases-loaded strikeout of Tony Lazzeri—October 10
53. Athletics overcome 8–0 deficit with 10-run seventh to beat Cubs—October 12, 1929
54. Babe Ruth's "called shot" homer in 1932 Series—October 1
55. Carl Hubbell's five consecutive strikeouts in 1934 A.S. game—July 10
56. Ted Williams' three-run game-winning A.S. home run in 1941—July 8

Nolan Ryan carved his niche in baseball history after throwing his fourth no-hitter for the California Angels.

Babe Ruth and Lou Gehrig of the Yankees hit two homers each to lead the Yankees to a 7–5 victory in Game 3 of the 1932 World Series against the Chicago Cubs. One of Ruth's home runs was his controversial "called shot" against Charlie Root.

Most Memorable Personalities

(In Alphabetical Order)

Hank Aaron
Yogi Berra
Roy Campanella
Roberto Clemente
Ty Cobb
Dizzy Dean
Joe DiMaggio
Leo Durocher
Bob Feller
Jimmie Foxx
Frankie Frisch
Lou Gehrig
Lefty Gomez
Lefty Grove
Babe Herman
Rogers Hornsby
Walter Johnson
Al Kaline
Sandy Koufax
Judge K. M. Landis

Connie Mack
Larry MacPhail
Mickey Mantle
Pepper Martin
Christy Mathewson
Willie Mays
John McGraw
Stan Musial
Mel Ott
Satchel Paige
Branch Rickey
Frank Robinson
Babe Ruth
Tris Speaker
Casey Stengel
Rube Waddell
Honus Wagner
Ted Williams
Cy Young

Yogi Berra

Lou Gehrig
National Baseball Hall of Fame Library, Cooperstown, N.Y.

Satchel Paige

National Baseball Hall of Fame Library, Cooperstown, N.Y.

Mel Ott

National Baseball Hall of Fame Library, Cooperstown, N.Y.

Rookie Cost Browns 1922 Flag

Connie Mack, manager of the Philadelphia Athletics, was so impressed by semi-pro pitcher Otto Rettig that he signed him to a major league contract. Rettig beat the St. Louis Browns the day he reported for his only major league victory. It was the margin of failure for the Browns, who finished one game behind the Yankees that season.

Playoff Records Counted

Under the old playoff rules, individual statistics compiled in league playoffs were considered part of the regular season's averages. The rule allowed Milwaukee Braves third baseman Eddie Mathews to win the NL home-run crown when he hit No. 46 against the Dodgers in 1959 and broke a tie with Ernie Banks.

---

57. Mickey Owen's muff of third strike that opened door to winning Yankee rally in 1941 Series—October 5
58. Cookie Lavagetto's double ruins Bill Bevens' no-hit bid in 1947 Series—October 3
59. Al Gionfriddo's catch robs Joe DiMaggio in 1947 Series—October 5
60. Willie Mays' back-to-the-plate catch off Vic Wertz in 1954 Series—September 29
61. Sandy Amoros' catch off Yogi Berra saves Dodgers in 1955 Series—October 4
62. *Don Larsen's perfect game in 1956 Series—October 8
63. Lew Burdette beats Yankees three times in 1957 Series—October 3, 7, 10
64. *Bill Mazeroski's climactic Game 7 homer in 1960 Series—October 13
65. Tony Perez wins longest A.S. game for NL with 15th-inning home run—July 11, 1967
66. Bob Gibson sets Series record with 17-strikeout game—October 2, 1968
67. *Mickey Lolich's three Series victories in 1968—October 3, 7, 10
68. *New York Mets' Series triumph in 1969
69. Pete Rose's dash to the plate in 12th wins 1970 A.S. game for NL—July 14
70. *Brooks Robinson leads Orioles to 1970 Series triumph
71. Roberto Clemente's all-around brilliance in 1971 Series

*Designates most memorable moments for each club

72. Carlton Fisk's 12th-inning game-winning home run in Game 6 of 1975 Series—October 21

Pennant Races

The most exciting aspect of major league baseball is the pennant race. Until 1969, when the American and National Leagues adopted divisional play, there were two races—one in each league—and a World Series between the winners. With split leagues, the number of races doubled, though actual league pennants are awarded only to the winner of the intraleague Championship Series.

Pennant races are often hotly contested and occasionally end in a tie. Before the creation of East and West divisions in the majors, National League races ended in a dead heat four times—in 1946, 1951, 1959, and 1962—and the American League season ended unresolved once—in 1948. An unusual makeup game decided the National's pennant chase in 1908, but it did not fall into the playoff category.

To advance to the World Series, a best-of-seven affair, today's teams must survive a best-of-five Division Series and a best-of-seven Championship Series. Before 1969 National League ties were settled in a best-of-three playoff, while AL deadlocks were resolved in a single, sudden-death contest. The sudden-death format was used for the first time in divisional play when the Yankees and the Red Sox tied for first place in the AL East race of 1978. New York won the Playoff, the Championship Series, and the World Series.

Predicting the pennant winners is a Herculean task—even for writers who have been following the game for years. Too many unknown factors are involved to make preseason prognostications reliable. Trades, injuries, unknown rookies, faded veterans, unpopular owners or managers, and countless other possibilities influence each team's chances.

Both the 1967 Boston Red Sox and the 1969 New York Mets won the pennant after finishing ninth in a 10-team league the year before. The 1945 Chicago Cubs won, but the same team was 30 games behind in 1944. The New York Giants were 35 games behind in 1953, but won the National League pennant of 1954—and swept the favored Cleveland Indians in a four-game World Series.

Should a tie occur under the present divisional format, an extra playoff would be necessary to dissolve the divisional deadlock.

In 1973 five of the six teams in the National League East were in contention with four days to go in the regular season.

There was even a remote chance that all five could wind up tied with identical records of 80–82. The standings at that point:

	W.	L.	Pct.	G.B.	Left
New York	80	78	.506	—	4
Pittsburgh	79	79	.500	1	4
St. Louis	78	81	.491	2½	3
Montreal	77	82	.484	3½	3
Chicago	76	82	.481	4	4

Good Timing

The only inside-the-park home run of Ted Williams' career clinched the 1946 AL pennant in Cleveland.

Musial Switch Won Flag for Cards

Stan Musial's switch from the outfield to first base in June 1946 plugged the only void in the lineup of the St. Louis Cardinals and enabled the team to win the National League pennant.

Giants Repeated Miracle of 1951

With star southpaw Sandy Koufax idled by a circulatory ailment in his fingers, the Los Angeles Dodgers were unable to hold the lead in the 1962 National League race. The San Francisco Giants, repeating their miracle finish of 1951, cut the lead to three games with eight to play and finally caught the Dodgers to force a playoff. In the last 13 games, the Giants were 7-6 but the Dodgers 3-10. San Francisco won the best-of-three playoff to win the right to face the Yankees in the World Series.

Seattle SuperSonics

En route to an AL-record 116 wins in 2001, the Seattle Mariners won 20 games in April, topping the 1997 Atlanta Braves by 1.

So What?

The 2001 Atlanta Braves were the only team to reach the postseason with a losing home record (40-41).

Distant Second

The Cardinals (11) and the Athletics (9) have won more world championships than any team but the Yankees (27).

First Divisional Champs

In 1969 the New York Mets and the Baltimore Orioles became the first pennant winners to be chosen through the Championship Series format. The Mets, champions of the NL East, swept the Atlanta Braves, champions of the West, despite three home runs from Atlanta slugger Hank Aaron. Baltimore swept three straight from Minnesota in the American League.

Trophy, Not Title

One year after Mike Scott (Astros) became the first man from a losing team to win MVP honors in the NL Championship Series, Jeffrey Leonard (Giants) repeated the rare feat, first performed by Fred Lynn of the 1982 Angels in the American League.

Clutch Comeback

The 1996 Atlanta Braves, trailing St. Louis three games to one in the best-of-seven NLCS, posted successive 14–0, 3–1, and 15–0 wins to advance to their fourth World Series of the decade.

Atlanta Braves

After getting only 10 at-bats during the regular season, Francisco Cabrera became an Atlanta folk hero with a two-out, two-run pinch-single in the ninth inning of 1992 NLCS Game 7, giving Atlanta a 3–2 win over Pittsburgh and the National League pennant.

Remaining Games

NEW YORK (4)—Away Chicago, Sept. 28, 29 (2), 30.
PITTSBURGH (4)—Home Montreal, Sept. 28, 29, 30. Oct. 1 makeup game against San Diego if necessary.
ST. LOUIS (3)—Home Philadelphia, Sept. 28, 29, 30.
CHICAGO (4)—Home New York, Sept. 28, 29 (2), 30.
MONTREAL (3)—Away Pittsburgh, Sept. 28, 29, 30.

The need for an intradivisional playoff never developed; the New York Mets, rebounding from a 12-game deficit and last-place standing on July 8, finished on top with an 82-79 record and .509 percentage—lowest ever recorded by a championship team. Moreover, the Mets beat the powerful Cincinnati Reds in the Championship Series and carried the Oakland A's a full seven games before losing the World Series.

The Shot Heard 'Round the World

The drama of the 1951 National League playoff between the Brooklyn Dodgers and the New York Giants outmatched all similar battles, including Dodger defeats by the Cardinals in 1946 and the Giants in 1962, and a Dodger victory over the Braves in 1959.

Cleveland's 8–3 playoff victory over the Red Sox in 1948—which snuffed out hopes of an all-Boston World Series—also could not compare with the 1951 match between New York's arch-rivals.

The Giants had finished third, five games behind Philadelphia, in 1950, but couldn't get on track in 1951. After winning their opener they lost 11 straight, prompting longtime fan Tallulah Bankhead to tell Groucho Marx, "Don't worry about the Giants. Don't forget: Leo Durocher is leading them." Marx twisted his cigar, thought a moment, and snapped, "Yes—but so is everybody else in the National League."

By August 11 the Giants were 13½ games behind the Dodgers. Brooklyn manager Charley Dressen had already pronounced them dead. After the Dodgers swept three straight from New York in early July, he said, "We knocked them out. They'll never bother us again."

While Dressen knew the Giants had a better club than their record showed, he let himself and his players be convinced that they could never be caught. The Giants had other ideas. They posted a 39-8 record down the stretch, while the Dodgers plodded along at .500, and Brooklyn actually had to win its final game or lose the pennant outright.

A bases-loaded catch by Jackie Robinson in the 12th and his home run in the 14th gave the Dodgers a 9–8 win over the Phillies and forced a playoff. The Giants won the opener, 3–1, but the Dodgers took the second, 10–0. The winner of the third game would win the pennant.

Brooklyn pitcher Don Newcombe held a commanding 4–1 lead going into the last of the ninth in the deciding game. Alvin Dark led off with an infield hit and Don Mueller followed with a solid single. When Monte Irvin popped out, Giants' fans in the Polo Grounds let out a collective groan. A double-play ball would end the game—and the season.

Jack Clark's three-run homer vs. Tom Niedenfuer gave the Cardinals a 7–5 win over the Dodgers in the decisive Game 6 of the 1985 NLCS. With first base open, Dodger pilot Tom Lasorda could have ordered an intentional walk for Clark, the only slugger in the St. Louis lineup.

Whitey Lockman, the next hitter, kept New York hopes alive with a solid double to left, scoring Dark to make the score 4–2, but Mueller was hurt sliding into third. He left on a stretcher as Dressen took advantage of the delay to rush Ralph Branca in from the bullpen.

Bobby Thomson—who had hit a home run against Branca in the opening game of the playoffs—was the scheduled hitter, with rookie Willie Mays to follow. Thomson had 30 home runs, more than any other Giant, but Branca elected to pitch to him.

The first pitch was a high, inside fastball, the type of pitch Thomson could hit for a home run. Catcher Rube Walker—filling in for the injured Roy Campanella—and Branca decided that Thomson would be looking for something low and away, or anything other than the same pitch he had just taken. They were mistaken.

Thomson's three-run home run, known as "the shot heard 'round the world," capped the Giants' pennant drive, called "the Little Miracle of Coogan's Bluff."

"No one ever expected it to happen," recalled Monte Irvin. "When Bobby hit the ball, we were kind of leaning, pulling, trying to *make* the ball go into the left-field stands. When it did, we didn't have an instant reaction. We kind of looked at each other and all of a sudden realized we were the champions. Then all bedlam broke loose."

As a footnote to history, Irvin pointed out that Jackie Robinson made sure Thomson touched every base during his trip to home plate. "He was a competitor right to the end," said the Hall of Fame outfielder.

Baseball's Greatest Races

Baseball history is filled with exciting pennant races—stories of hope and despair, ecstasy and dejection. The "miracle" Giants

Cubs Showed Way to Win in 1935

The pennant-winning Chicago Cubs of 1935 won 23 in a row, and 23 of 26 (an .885 percentage) in the month of September.

Presuming Pirates Left Hanging

When Pittsburgh built an eight-game lead over the Chicago Cubs by August 20, 1938, the Pirates anticipated participation in the World Series. The team built a new press box in Forbes Field to accommodate the expected hordes of writers. But the Cubs won 30 of their last 42 as Pittsburgh posted a 20-24 mark, and Chicago capped its drive with a September sweep of the Pirates. The highlight of that sweep—the famous "Homer in the Gloamin'" by Cub player/manager Gabby Hartnett—brought victory to Chicago just before darkness would have halted play.

Rookie Topped Feller for Flag

The Detroit Tigers won the 1940 American League pennant by one game over the Cleveland Indians. Rookie Floyd Giebell pitched the decisive game—a 2–0 victory over Indian superstar Bob Feller at Cleveland. Giebell won only two other games in his major league career.

Tigers Roar

En route to a World Championship, the 1984 Detroit Tigers won 35 of their first 40 games.

Wonderful Will

Will Clark won MVP honors in the 1989 NL Championship Series after hitting .650 (13-for-20) with eight RBIs, a 1.200 slugging percentage, and 24 total bases (an NLCS record)—helping the Giants beat the Cubs in five games.

Pitcher Jack Chesbro compiled a record number of victories for a single season in 1904 but made a fatal wild pitch.

Potent Pitching

One day after Baltimore's Mike Mussina set a Championship Series record with 15 strikeouts vs. Cleveland in 1997, Florida's Livan Hernandez duplicated the feat vs. Atlanta in the National League.

Picture This

Years after Bucky Dent's home run beat Don Zimmer's Boston Red Sox in a one-game divisional title playoff, Zimmer was hired by the Yankees and needed a nearby place to live. He rented Dent's New Jersey home—not knowing he would find a picture gallery of Dent's home run. Zimmer told reporters he couldn't stand it and turned every picture around.

Stranded

Ted Turner and Jane Fonda were among 14 people stuck in a Fulton County Stadium elevator for 10 minutes before Game 5 of the 1991 League Championship Series.

of 1951 overcame the greatest deficit in a single season, but the "miracle" tag was first applied to the Boston Braves of 1914, 11½ games behind in July but winners by 10 games at season's end. The Braves started 6-19 but went 68-19 the rest of the way.

Early leads often crumble under the pennant pressure of September. Joe Gordon, star second baseman and manager, described the feeling: "It's impossible to take the last few weeks in stride when you know that one bad bounce or wrong guess can send the entire season down the drain. Contenders crack from mental fatigue, not physical weariness. Experience only makes you more jittery, because you realize how many unexpected things can murder you."

In 1904 the Yankees (then called the Highlanders) missed a chance to win their first pennant because pitching ace Jack Chesbro, seeking his record 42nd victory of the season, uncorked a two-out wild pitch in the ninth inning against the first-place Red Sox in an end-of-season doubleheader. A New York sweep would have won the pennant. Instead, Boston won, 3–2, and the second game was unnecessary.

A wild pitch hurt the Chicago White Sox in a heated race four years later. On October 2, 1908, with the Sox fighting Cleveland and Detroit for the pennant, 40-game winner Ed Walsh pitched a four-hitter and struck out 15, but his two-strike, two-out spitball in the third broke off the glove of catcher Ossie Schreckengost and allowed a runner to score. Cleveland's Addie Joss pitched a perfect game to win, 1–0, in a contest experts considered the best-pitched pressure game in history. Detroit eventually won the pennant.

Like the American League, the National League featured a three-team chase, involving the Cubs, the Pirates, and the Giants.

Fred Merkle's baserunning boner (described in Chapter 2) had deprived the Giants of an apparent 3–2 victory over Chicago, and the league decided the game would be replayed if necessary when the season ended. Had the Pirates defeated the Cubs on the last day of scheduled play, Pittsburgh would have won the flag. But the Cubs won, forcing a tie with New York, and beat the Giants in the makeup game, 4–2. Mordecai "Three-Finger" Brown was the winning pitcher for Chicago in both victories—the first as a starter and the second as an early reliever.

In 1911 the American League's defending champions, the Philadelphia A's, were mired in the cellar in May, looking up at the Detroit Tigers, who had won 21 of their first 23. A's owner Connie Mack (also the club's manager) entertained his Detroit counterpart, Frank Navin, at dinner and said, "It's too bad you're so far out in front, Frank, you're ruining the race." Navin felt the sting of Mack's gentle needle on July 4, when the A's tied for the top, and again in early August, when Philadelphia zoomed past Detroit en route to a pennant margin of 13½ games.

Three years later, the "miracle" Braves, a fifth-place entry that finished 31½ games off the pace the year before, began a pennant march from the National League basement July 18 and knocked off the Athletics in four straight World Series games.

The Yankees started their domination of the American League in the '20s, winning 27 pennants in 42 years from 1923 to 1964, not only because they had great individual stars but also because the collection of talent helped each individual. "When you have great ballplayers playing alongside you, it makes you play so much harder," explained Phil Rizzuto, AL Most Valuable Player in 1950.

Like the Yankees, the Giants had a dynasty of sorts in the National League. Fiery John McGraw had won 10 pennants during his long tenure, and Bill Terry was smug from victory in 1933 when he let his pennant chances stall on a roll of the tongue.

Asked what he thought of the Dodgers, then an also-ran entry, Terry replied, "Oh, is Brooklyn still in the National League?" A group of gathered writers laughed, but the Dodgers laughed last. Brooklyn played the role of spoiler, ruining New York's chance to catch the Cardinals, who finished in front by two games. The Dodgers beat the Giants in the season's finale, 8–5 in 10 innings.

By 1942 the Dodgers were strong. Defending the 1941 crown, Brooklyn led St. Louis by 9½ games on August 15, and won 25 of its remaining 42 games, including the final eight. But the Cardinals closed with a 43-9 mark to finish first by two games—just as they had in 1934.

There was an all–St. Louis series in 1944, when the Browns won their only American League pennant by one game over Detroit and six over New York. The Browns finished strong, winning four straight from the Yankees, but went into the final day tied with Detroit. Last-place Washington defeated Dizzy Trout (27–14) as the Browns wrapped up the Yankee series and the pennant.

Detroit got its revenge the following year when Hank Greenberg, just back from a four-year military tour, cracked a ninth-inning grand slam in the opener of a doubleheader against the Browns to clinch the pennant. Had the Tigers dropped both games, they would have had a one-game playoff against Washington.

"My attitude was different from the other players," said Greenberg. "They had lost the pennant on the last day the previous year and were worried they would kick it away again. I was so glad to be back that baseball was just a picnic to me."

In 1948 the Red Sox eliminated the Yankees on the next-to-last day of the season and earned a playoff berth when Cleveland lost its final game to Detroit while Boston beat New York again. The pitching of rookie Gene Bearden and two home runs by player/ manager Lou Boudreau quashed Boston's hopes.

Red Sox fans were also disappointed in 1949, when the Yankees avenged their setback of the previous fall. Boston led by one with two to play against New York, but the Yankees won both games and the championship. Part of the blame was pinned on Red Sox catcher Birdie Tebbetts, who needled Yankee players about the pending pennant party in the Boston clubhouse. Stirred by his remarks, the New Yorkers overcame a 4–0 deficit to win, 5–4. New York won, 5–3, the following afternoon.

In the National League the Brooklyn Dodgers and the Philadelphia Phillies hooked up for pennant-deciding battles three years running, 1949–1951. In 1949 St. Louis beat the Cubs and would have tied for the pennant if Philadelphia had beaten Brooklyn. During the next season the Philadelphia Whiz Kids frittered away a big lead. In the decisive final game, Richie Ashburn's ninth-inning throw nipped Cal Abrams at the plate, sending the game into the tenth inning and setting the stage for Dick Sisler's pennant-winning home run. Had the Dodgers won the season-ending game, the Phils and the Dodgers would have gone into a playoff series.

Homers Made Difference

Home runs decided consecutive 1–0 games for the Baltimore Orioles in the 1966 World Series. But the hitting hero of the first of the Series' six 1–0 games was better known as manager of the team he beat. Casey Stengel was with the New York Giants when his homer beat the New York Yankees on October 12, 1923.

Royals Rebound

The 1985 Kansas City Royals were the only club to overcome a 3–1 deficit twice in the same postseason. The team trailed the Toronto Blue Jays in the AL Championship Series, then came back to beat the St. Louis Cardinals in the World Series—giving Kansas City its only World Championship.

1–0 Wonder

John Smoltz (Braves) has been in uniform in three of the 25 1–0 games in World Series history. He pitched nine scoreless innings in 1991 Game 7, won by the Minnesota Twins in the 10th; yielded an unearned run while losing 1996 Game 5 to the New York Yankees; and served as cheerleader when teammates Tom Glavine and Mark Wohlers combined for a one-hitter to win the decisive Game 6 against the Cleveland Indians in 1995.

Wild West

The 1995 Colorado Rockies finished with a 77-67 record—one game behind the Los Angeles Dodgers for the championship of the NL West but one game ahead of the Houston Astros for the NL's wild-card slot. The Rox thus became the first wild-card winner in National League history.

Strange Ending

Game 3 of the 1997 ALCS was the first postseason game to end with a stolen base. Cleveland's Marquis Grissom scored when Omar Vizquel missed an attempted suicide squeeze and Baltimore catcher Lenny Webster missed the ball. Grissom was credited with a steal of home, giving Cleveland a 2–1 win.

A Year for Dramatics

Though postseason play often produces dramatic endings, two of the best examples occurred in the same year.

In the AL Championship Series of 1986, the California Angels held a 3–1 advantage in games as they took a 5–2 lead into the ninth inning of Game 5 against the Boston Red Sox. With two outs, Don Baylor and Dave Henderson delivered two-run homers that put Boston up, 6–5, in a game they eventually won, 7–6, in 11 innings. The Red Sox won both remaining games at Fenway Park to take the pennant.

In the World Series, however, the Sox were the victims. They led the New York Mets 3–2 in games as they entered the ninth inning of Game 6 with a 5–3 lead. Boston got two quick outs but three singles and a wild pitch followed, tying the game. Mookie Wilson's slow roller then dribbled through the legs of gimpy first baseman Bill Buckner to tie a Series the Sox could have won on any of 12 different pitches. The revitalized Mets took Game 7 the next day—leaving Buckner with an indelible blemish on a fine career.

Dodger manager Burt Shotton was criticized for not replacing Abrams, a poor baserunner, with fleet Eddie Miksis. Both Shotton and third-base coach Milt Stock, who waved Abrams home, were dropped that winter.

In 1951 the scenario was reversed. Jackie Robinson's extra-inning homer for Brooklyn beat the Phils and sent the Dodgers into the playoffs with the Giants.

Five years later the Dodgers opened the campaign defending their first World Championship crown. But Milwaukee and Cincinnati challenged to the end, leaving only two games between first and third place.

On the final weekend the Braves were up by one with three to play, but lost two of three to the Cardinals while the Dodgers swept the Pirates to win the pennant. After winning the National League title in both 1957 and 1958, the Braves sought to avenge their one-game deficit of 1956 by beating the Dodgers in a best-of-three playoff. After a three-cornered race, also involving the Giants, the Dodgers won the playoff and, in six games, the World Series over the White Sox.

The 1962 playoff finale bore many similarities to the 1951 classic, won by the Giants with a four-run burst in the ninth. After a devastating late-season slide, the Dodgers lost to National League newcomer Billy Pierce, 8–0, in the opener. They came from behind to win the second, 8–7, and took a 4–2 lead into the ninth inning of the deciding game. The Giants' winning run crossed on a bases-loaded walk.

In 1964 the Philadelphia Phillies suffered the worst collapse of any pennant-bound club. That team has since become synonymous with the word *choke*. Leading the NL by 6½ games with 12 to play, the Phils dropped 10 straight, including crucial three-game series to the suddenly-awake Cardinals and Reds.

On October 1 the Cards—with an eight-game winning streak—led the Reds by ½ and the Phillies by 2½. But the hapless Mets knocked off the Cardinals, 1–0 and 15–5, on successive days, while the Phils won one game from the Reds, 4–3. The Cards were now tied with the Reds and one game ahead of the Phils.

Philadelphia beat the Reds again, 10–0, on the final day, but the Cards won. Had they lost, all three teams would have wound up with identical 92–70 marks, forcing the game's first three-way playoff.

The Los Angeles Dodgers were forced to use ace Sandy Koufax on the last day of the 1966 season. The Dodgers had a "magic number" of 1 on the final day. Any combination of Dodger wins and Giant losses adding up to one would give them the National League pennant.

A Giant win over the Pirates, coupled with a Dodger defeat in a doubleheader with the Phillies, would have forced a playoff. But Koufax won.

Three years after the collapse of the Phillies, the Boston Red Sox pulled off their "Impossible Dream" in the tightest pennant race in American League history.

Hank Greenberg's ninth-inning slam on the final day of the 1945 campaign enabled the Tigers to avert a possible playoff with Washington and enter the World Series.

Named for the lead song in the popular musical *Man of La Mancha*, the Red Sox championship was forged against 100-to-1 odds with the leadership of rookie manager Dick Williams and Triple Crown winner Carl Yastrzemski.

Boston, Chicago, Detroit, and Minnesota were still serious contenders as the last week opened. The pitching-rich White Sox, with a team batting average of .225, dropped out of the race, but the Twins held a one-game lead as they came to Boston's Fenway Park for their final two games. The Tigers, tied with the Red Sox for second place, were home for back-to-back doubleheaders against the Angels.

The Red Sox won the Series opener, reaching a first-place tie, while the Tigers split their doubleheader to pull within a half-game of the lead. On Sunday, Jim Lonborg of Boston won his 22nd game, beating 20-game winner Dean Chance of the Twins, as the Tigers won the first game of their doubleheader from the Angels. A Detroit sweep would force a playoff, but the Angels pulled out a come-from-behind 8–5 win in the nightcap, giving Boston the pennant.

In 1974 the Red Sox seemed certain to sew up another flag when they took an eight-game lead into September. Suddenly, the Baltimore Orioles caught fire, posting a 27-6 mark after August 29, while the Sox were 12-21 over the same period. The Yankees wound up second, two games behind, and the Red Sox third, seven games back.

Boston blew yet another pennant in 1978. On July 17 the Red Sox owned a 14-game lead over the New York Yankees, but fortunes quickly changed. A series of injuries slowed the Hub's pennant express to a crawl, while the Yankees regrouped under low-key manager Bob Lemon, who replaced Billy Martin July 25.

After the teams finished tied, the Yankees won a sudden-death playoff game at Boston's Fenway Park.

The Pittsburgh Pirates won the National League pennant the following year but later blew three straight chances to win another.

After landing Frank Robinson from the Reds in a blockbuster deal, the Baltimore Orioles won four pennants in six seasons. They displayed their flags at their Sarasota Spring training stadium.

Oldest Series Player

Jack Quinn was more than 46 years old when he pitched in the 1930 World Series for the Philadelphia Athletics. He had no record in two innings of work.

Willie Mays' Last Hit

The final hit of Willie Mays' career drove in one of four runs in the 12th inning of Game 2 as the New York Mets defeated the Oakland A's, 10–7, in the 1973 World Series.

Southpaw Slugger

Switch-hitting shortstop Ozzie Smith had played in the majors for eight seasons before hitting a home run left-handed. The solo shot in the ninth inning gave the St. Louis Cardinals a 3–2 win over the Los Angeles Dodgers in Game 5 of the 1985 National League Championship Series. A three-run, ninth-inning homer by Jack Clark in Game 6 gave the Cardinals the pennant.

Tiebreakers

Before the advent of divisional play in 1969, pennant races that ended in ties were settled through best-of-three play-offs in the National League and a single, sudden-death game in the American. That happened in 1946, 1951, 1959, and 1962 in the NL and 1948 in the AL.

Unscheduled playoffs to settle divisional ties occurred in 1978, 1980, 1995, 1998, 1999, 2007, 2008, 2009, and 2013. All were one-game showdowns.

The first tie in baseball history actually occurred in 1908, when the New York Giants and Chicago Cubs finished with identical 98-55 records (the Giants had lost a sure win over the Cubs when the "Merkle's boner" game reverted to a 1–1 tie). When the National League ordered the game replayed, the Cubs took a 4–2 win and the pennant. Technically not a playoff that would have extended the season, it was a make-up of a scheduled game.

Ruth Could Steal Too

Babe Ruth stole second and third base in the same inning of a 1921 World Series game for the Yankees against the Giants.

Jim Lonborg won 22 games to spearhead the "Impossible Dream" pennant drive of the 1967 Boston Red Sox.

Oh, So Close

Had they won one more and lost one less in 1971, 1980, 1982, and 1991, the Los Angeles Dodgers could have won four more championships.

Ted Williams Foils the Shift

Red Sox slugger Ted Williams, a notorious left-handed pull hitter, foiled the "Williams shift" by the St. Louis Cardinals when he bunted safely for one of his five hits in the 1946 World Series.

The Pirates dropped a six-game Championship Series to the Cincinnati Reds in 1990 and frustrating seven-game contests to the Atlanta Braves in both 1991 and 1992.

Pittsburgh's 1991 nemesis was 21-year-old left-hander Steve Avery, who capped his first full year in the majors by pitching a record 16⅓ consecutive scoreless innings in the playoffs.

Avery, who twice got ninth-inning help from Alejandro Pena to keep shutouts intact, was named MVP of a tight NLCS that featured a record three 1–0 games. After leading the league in batting and runs scored during the regular season, Pittsburgh did not score in its last 22 innings overall and its final 27 innings at home.

One year later, star Pirate starter Doug Drabek took a 2–0 lead into the bottom of the ninth in Game 7 but couldn't hold it. Drabek, defeated in the first and fourth games, left after Atlanta loaded the bases with nobody out. Ron Gant greeted reliever Stan Belinda with a long sacrifice fly that was nearly his second grand slam of the series. One out later, seldom-used Francisco Cabrera—given just 10 at-bats all season—lined a two-run single to left for a 3–2 Atlanta victory.

It was the most stunning comeback in the 24-year history of the National League Championship Series.

In 1993, the last year before baseball initiated a three-divisional format that featured wild-card winners, the game enjoyed its last pure pennant race. The Braves, powered by the midyear arrival of slugger Fred McGriff, overcame a 10-game deficit to finish with 104 wins. The Giants, last-day losers, went home with 103.

Two years later the AL West went down to the wire when the California Angels lost 27 of their last 39, blowing a 13-game August lead and matching Seattle's 78-66 record. The Mariners won a sudden-death divisional playoff to reach the postseason for the first time.

The National League needed tiebreakers to determine wild-card winners in both 1998 and 1999. With a possible three-way tie looming, the Cubs, the Giants, and the Mets all lost their final games of 1998, forcing a Giants/Cubs playoff. The Cubs won but then dropped three straight to Atlanta in the Division Series.

A year later the Mets entered a crucial September series in Atlanta just one game behind the Braves. But they lost all three, launching a seven-game losing streak that nearly proved fatal.

The team won its last three while Cincinnati dropped two of three to lowly Milwaukee and another tiebreaker was needed. The Mets won it, then upset Arizona in a four-game Division Series—sparking hope of New York's first Subway Series since 1956.

But Atlanta prevailed in a six-game NLCS that ended with a pair of extra-inning games. For the Braves, it was their fifth pennant of the '90s—two more than any other team.

The World Series

Though some players insist the League Championship Series, a product of divisional play, has superseded the World Series in importance, most baseball insiders contend that the best-of-seven classic between league champions retains its traditional role as the highlight of the baseball year.

Stadiums of participating teams are always full—the Dodgers filled more than 92,000 seats at the Los Angeles Coliseum for

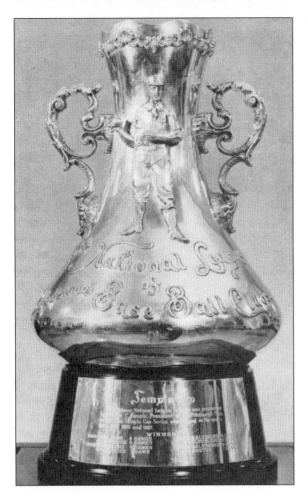

The Temple Cup was given to championship teams before the century changed—and before the World Series began.

Great Collapses

• 1951—Dodgers, 13½ games ahead in August, collapse to tie Giants, who then win best-of-three pennant playoff on Bobby Thomson's ninth-inning homer.

• 1962—Dodgers lose six of last seven, forcing pennant playoff with Giants, who win best-of-three finale with ninth-inning rally.

• 1964—Phillies blow 6½-game lead with 12 left by dropping 10 straight. Cards win on final day, finishing one game ahead of Phils and Reds.

• 1969—Cubs blow 9½-game August lead, finish distant second to Mets in NL East.

• 1978—Red Sox blow 14-game July lead, finish tied with Yankees, then drop sudden-death divisional playoff game.

• 1980—Astros blow three-game lead over Dodgers in three-game, season-ending series in Los Angeles, then win single-game divisional playoff before losing NL Championship Series to Phillies.

• 1978—Red Sox blow 14-game July lead, finish tied with Yankees, then drop sudden-death divisional playoff game.

• 1980—Astros blow three-game lead in season-ending series in Los Angeles, then beat Dodgers in sudden-death NL West playoff before losing NLCS to Phillies.

• 1982—Brewers blow three straight to Orioles on final weekend before winning finale to finish first by one game in AL East, their first division title.

• 1993—Giants blow 10-game July lead to Braves, losing NL West title on final day despite 103 victories.

• 1995—Angels blow 13-game August lead, lose sudden-death divisional playoff game to Mariners.

• 2007—New York Mets, up seven games September 12, lose 12 of last 17, including a 1-6 final homestand.

• 2007—Seeking third straight NL West title, San Diego Padres need one win in a three-game series vs Colorado Rockies but lose whole series plus one-game playoff that went 13 innings.

• 2008—Mets have 82-63 mark and 3½-game lead on September 10 but 89-73 record and three-game deficit 18 days later as Phillies catch them again.

• 2009—Tigers become first team to blow three-game lead with four games left, then lose to Twins in 12-inning tiebreaker for AL Central title.

• 2010—Padres blow August 25 lead of 6½ games with 10-game losing streak, enter final series vs. Giants needing sweep but win only first two.

• 2011—Braves lose last five and 18 of last 26, allowing Cardinals to win NL wild card after trailing by 10½ games on August 25 and by 8½ on September 1.

• 2011—Red Sox squander nine-game September lead, posting 7-20 mark for the month, as Tampa Bay rallies from 7–0, eighth-inning deficit vs. Yankees to win last game and AL wild card.

three games in 1959—and broadcast ratings are high. NBC-TV estimated that 135 million Americans watched at least part of the 1978 World Series.

Interest should be high, because the Series stands as a test of skills between baseball's best teams. Games are played under the glare of the public spotlight, but teams emerging from tight pennant races sometimes tend to let down in the fall classic.

Series history is filled with high drama and bitter disappointment. Don Larsen's perfect game in 1956 was the only no-hitter in the World Series, but Floyd Bevens—another Yankee facing the Brooklyn Dodgers—came within one out of a no-hit game seven years earlier.

Pitcher Ralph Terry of the Yankees pitched a brilliant, 1–0 victory in the seventh game to defeat the Giants in 1962, but two years earlier served a bottom-of-the-ninth home-run ball that gave the World Championship to Bill Mazeroski and the Pittsburgh Pirates.

Babe Ruth starred as a pitcher and a hitter, twice hitting three home runs in one World Series game (Reggie Jackson did it once) and pitching 29⅔ consecutive scoreless innings—a record later shattered by Whitey Ford—for the Boston Red Sox. But even Ruth had his Series disappointment; as a rookie in 1915, after winning 18 of 24 decisions for Boston, he was bypassed in postseason play, appearing only in a single pinch-hitting role.

Errors, strikeouts, shutouts, miracle catches, long hits, and stolen bases are taken for granted during the season, but are so important during a short series that few can be forgotten.

Winning Losers

Bobby Richardson of the 1960 New York Yankees was the only player from a losing team to be named World Series Most Valuable Player.

Dandy Sandy

Sandy Koufax was the lone two-time winner of both competing World Series MVP awards. He swept the Babe Ruth Award and the *Sport Magazine* Award in both 1963 and 1965.

Robinsons Launched 1966 Sweep

Frank and Brooks Robinson hit consecutive home runs against Don Drysdale in the first inning of the 1966 World Series to start the Orioles toward a four-game sweep.

Yanks Win Three

The 1978 New York Yankees were the first team to win three postseason series: a one-game playoff for the divisional title, a best-of-five match for the pennant, and a best-of-seven World Series.

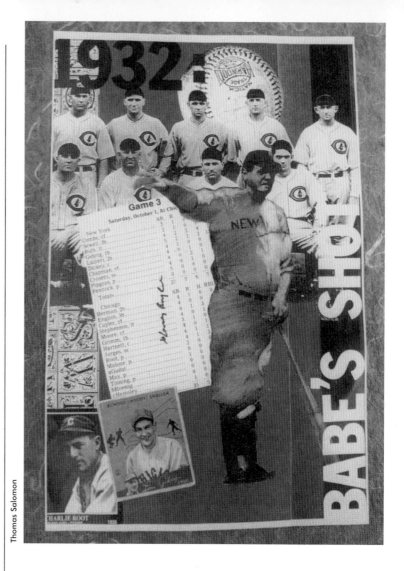

Thomas Salomon

Mantle's Home-Run Mark

Mickey Mantle, the great switch-hitting center fielder of the Yankees, hit a record 18 home runs in the World Series.

How the Series Began

Postseason competition between champions of the major leagues began in 1882, when the American Association joined the six-year-old National League as a bona fide big-league circuit. Chicago (NL) and Cincinnati (AA) split two games before a series of disputes canceled the rest of the match.

The leagues tried again in 1884, with a best-of-five format, and Providence (NL) beat the old New York Mets (AA) three straight. Nothing formal was arranged between leagues, however, and the 1887 "world series" was exactly that. Detroit (NL) challenged St. Louis (AA) to a 15-game tour that started in St. Louis, shifted to Detroit, then went to Pittsburgh, Brooklyn, New York, Philadelphia, Boston, back to Philadelphia, then on to Washington, Baltimore, Brooklyn again, Detroit again, Chicago, and then on to St. Louis for two final games.

The marathon attracted 51,455 fans who paid $42,000 for the privilege of watching two travel-weary teams playing less-than-championship baseball. Since expenses for the series amounted to $18,000, the clubs divided a pot of $24,000—just $3,000 more than the minimum major league salary in 1978!

When the Giants and Browns tried a 10-game series after the 1888 season, receipts for the final two games at St. Louis were so discouraging ($411 and $212) that the marathon concept was scrapped.

The American Association, crippled by the Players League revolt of 1890, dissolved after 1891 and the National League took on four of its teams the following year. In 1894 former Pittsburgh Pirates president William Chase Temple created the Temple Cup series between the National League's two top teams.

Without a divisional format, the first- and second-place clubs had already met as often as any other two teams and the significance of the cup was never established.

The first Temple Cup series carried the best-of-seven format that later would be used in the World Series, but the champion Baltimore Orioles dropped four straight to the second-place New York Giants.

Temple was so unhappy with the result that he sold all his remaining stock in the Pirates. His unhappiness turned to distress when word leaked out that five Orioles had agreed in advance to split their shares with the Giants. The greedy Giant players refused to live up to their agreement, however, and kept their winner's shares of $564 (losers got 30 percent less).

Somehow the Temple Cup survived three more seasons, but it failed to generate enthusiasm among players, fans, or officials.

The first legitimate World Series was played in 1903, two years after the birth of the American League. The Boston Red Sox won a best-of-nine series from the Pittsburgh Pirates, five to three, and 100,000 fans paid double the going rate (50 cents for general admission and $1 for reserved seats) to watch.

There was no World Series in 1904 because John McGraw, manager of the National League champion Giants, refused to acknowledge the major status of the American and shunned its champion. But the Series was renewed to stay in 1905, under the supervision of a three-man National Commission, which then governed the game. Revenue would be divided among players, owners, and the commission.

Except for 1903 and 1919–1921, when a best-of-nine format was used, the World Championship has always been awarded to the first team to win four games.

The Wild Windup of 1960

Though Don Larsen's perfect game for the Yankees against the Dodgers in 1956 stands as the finest—and most unexpected—performance by a pitcher in World Series history, the seven-game classic of 1960 had a twist ending that made it even more memorable.

The Yankees won by scores of 16–3, 10–0, and 12–0, and outscored the Pirates, 55–27, but Pittsburgh won the World Championship.

On October 13 the teams were deadlocked at three games each as play unfolded in Game 7. Vernon Law, winner of two games for the Pirates, opposed Bob Turley, who had won once for the Yankees, but neither lasted six innings. Turley, in fact, left in the second.

The Pirates jumped to a quick 4–0 lead, but the Yankees scored one in the fifth and four in the sixth to forge ahead. When New

Top Series Managers

Joe McCarthy and Casey Stengel each won seven world championships—marks unmatched by any other manager.

Relievers Started Series in '50s

Relief pitchers Jim Konstanty of the Phillies (1950) and Joe Black of the Dodgers (1952) were surprise starters for their teams in World Series openers. Konstanty lost, 1–0, while Black won, 4–2.

Lucky Lonnie

Lonnie Smith is the only man to reach the World Series with four different teams: the 1980 Phillies, the 1982 Cardinals, the 1985 Royals, and the 1991–1992 Braves.

Prolific Pitcher

Randy Johnson (2001 Diamondbacks) and Francisco Rodriguez (2002 Angels) are the only pitchers to win five games in a single postseason. Multiple men have won four times.

Albert's Haul

On October 22, 2011, St. Louis first baseman Albert Pujols became the only man with three home runs, five hits, six runs batted in, and 14 total bases in the same World Series game. Reggie Jackson and Babe Ruth (twice) also hit three homers in a Fall Classic contest while Paul Molitor (Brewers) was the only other man with a five-hit game in the World Series (October 12, 1982).

Fleeting Fame

After winning the first game of the 2006 World Series for St. Louis, Anthony Reyes went 0-10 in his first dozen starts of 2007 and found himself back in the minors.

Lucky Lefty

Mickey Lolich, hero of the 1968 World Series for the Detroit Tigers, threw left-handed because he broke his collarbone in a fall from his tricycle at age three.

After Larsen

Roy Halladay's 4–0 no-hitter for Philadelphia against Cincinnati in the opener of the 2010 NLCS was only the second in the history of postseason play.

The Commissioner's Trophy

World Champions receive a sterling silver Commissioner's Trophy consisting of flags from the major league teams, latitude/longitude lines symbolizing the world, and 24-karat vermeil stitches like those on a baseball. The trophy, which stands 24 inches high and has a diameter of 11 inches, also contains the signature of the commissioner. It takes Tiffany & Co. artisans more than three months and 198.12 troy ounces of sterling silver to create the trophy.

Bill Mazeroski's dramatic last-of-the-ninth homer gave the Pirates a 10–9 victory in Game 7 and made them 1960 World Champions after a hard-fought series against the New York Yankees.

York scored two more in the top of the eighth, Yankee prospects looked good—especially since Bobby Shantz had pitched scoreless ball since entering the game in the third inning.

But Pittsburgh struck in the last of the eighth. Gino Cimoli, Bill Virdon, and Dick Groat rapped consecutive singles, knocking out Shantz and cutting the Yankee lead to 7–5. Bob Skinner sacrificed, moving the runners to second and third, but Rocky Nelson flied to right without further damage. Roberto Clemente kept the rally going with an infield single to first, scoring Virdon, and second-string catcher Hal Smith—who had replaced Joe Christopher (who pinch ran for Smoky Burgess) earlier—strode to the plate.

Jim Coates, who had replaced Shantz, served a fat pitch and Smith socked it over the left-field wall for a three-run homer. Pittsburgh led, 9–7. Ralph Terry came on to retire Don Hoak for the third out.

With all Pittsburgh rabid for revenge against the Yankees—who had beaten the 1927 Pirates four straight in the last Series match between the clubs—Bob Friend took the mound in the top of the ninth. An 18-game winner during the National League season, he had lost twice as a starter earlier in the World Series.

Quick singles by Bobby Richardson (who knocked in 26 runs all season but 12 in the Series) and Dale Long chased Friend, and Harvey Haddix—winner of Game 5—came in. Roger Maris fouled to Hal Smith, but Mickey Mantle singled to score Richardson and send Long to third. Gil McDougald, running for Long, scored on an infield out by Yogi Berra and Bill Skowron hit into a force to retire the side.

Bill Mazeroski led off the last of the ninth. He had hit 11 home runs during the regular season (four of his teammates

Philly Fans Booed Prohibition President

During the 1931 World Series between the Cardinals and the A's, Philadelphia fans booed President Herbert Hoover and chanted repeatedly, "We want beer! We want beer!"

Gashouse Gang Played Music Too

The World Champion Cardinals of 1934—better known as the Gashouse Gang—formed an excellent hillbilly band called the Mississippi Mudcats.

How Players Share Profits

Winners get 60 percent of the funds set aside for players when World Series proceeds are divided. Losers get 40 percent.

did better and a fifth did as well) and one in the first game of the World Series. It was a two-run blast that helped the Pirates win, 6–4.

The score was 9–9. A Pittsburgh score would mean the World Championship. Mazeroski studied Terry. On the second pitch from the New York right-hander, he swung and sent the ball over the left-field wall to win the game and the Series.

Series Predictions Impossible

Matchups between baseball's best teams foil the art of forecasting. Though Las Vegas oddsmakers issue "official lines" on game and Series results, wise baseball observers shy away from bettors.

Who would have bet that neither of the two 20-game winners of the 1905 Philadelphia Athletics—Eddie Plank or Rube Waddell—would beat the New York Giants, or that Christy Mathewson and Joe "Iron Man" McGinnity would pitch shutouts for all four victories? Mathewson, with three, was chiefly responsible for New York's record 0.00 team ERA in that classic. The A's plated three unearned runs in Game 2 to win, 3–0, behind Chief Bender.

Mathewson again defied the odds in 1911, when he lost two of three to the Athletics, then powered by the $100,000 infield of Frank "Home Run" Baker, Jack Barry, Eddie Collins, and Stuffy McInnis from third to first. Philadelphia won in six games—its second straight world title—but finished only third the following year.

The new American League champions, the Boston Red Sox, retained the World Championship when the Giants blew a 2–1 lead in the 10th inning by making misplays in the field. With Mathewson on the mound again, Clyde Engle led off with an easy fly to center fielder Fred Snodgrass. He dropped it, allowing Engle to reach second. Harry Hooper lined to Snodgrass—who caught it this time—but Steve Yerkes walked. Tris Speaker popped up wide of first, but Fred Merkle failed to move from his position and catcher Chief Meyers could not reach the foul fly. Given another chance, Speaker singled to score Engle. Yerkes went to third and scored when Larry Gardner hit a sacrifice fly to left. Snodgrass' error was labeled "the $30,000 muff" because he denied his 16 teammates (only 17 players were then eligible for the Series) the difference between the winner's share of $4,025 and the loser's share of $2,566.

Another memorable muff occurred five years later and also involved the Giants, but this time was an error of omission rather than commission. Trailing the White Sox three games to two, New York literally gave away the decisive Game 6.

In the fourth inning, at the Polo Grounds, third baseman Heinie Zimmerman and outfielder Dave Robertson made consecutive errors, putting runners on first and third with nobody out. Happy

Wagner on Mathewson

Honus Wagner, who hit .328 and stole 723 bases in a 20-year career that ended in 1917, handled even the best pitchers with facility. He hit .324 against Christy Mathewson, whose 373 victories made him the biggest winner (tied with Grover Cleveland Alexander) in National League history.

"Mathewson knew more in five minutes about batters than the modern pitcher does in a whole season," said Wagner in 1929. "He had a fastball, slowball, a great curve, a drop, the fadeaway, and the best control I ever saw.

"The only pitcher I ever faced who had the control Mathewson had was Grover Cleveland Alexander when he was with the Phillies. Neither Mathewson nor Alex ever let you have a ball in the spot where they knew you could hit."

Wagner noted that Mathewson had a faulty delivery that allowed Honus to steal bases against Christy with regularity. "When he was throwing his fadeaway, fastball, curve, or floater, he used an easy overarm motion, swinging his arm a little at the top of his pitch.

"But with his drop ball, he used a full overarm motion, bringing his arm close to his body, and twisted on his right foot a little to get the necessary twist. This loss of a 10th of a second in the midst of his delivery was all the start I needed."

Walter Johnson . . . 1924 World Series hero.

Felsch grounded to pitcher Rube Benton, who threw to Zimmerman when baserunner Eddie Collins broke for home. Zimmerman fired to catcher Bill Rariden, pushing Collins back toward third, and the catcher threw to Zimmerman, moving Collins closer to home. Ball in hand, Zimmerman chased Collins past Rariden and across the unprotected plate for the first run of the game. Chick Gandil singled for two more runs—all the Sox needed in the 4–2 victory.

The following year an early-September series was scheduled when the regular season was shortened by the war. Babe Ruth and Carl Mays won two games each to help the Red Sox beat the Cubs, but Ruth's record streak of 29⅔ scoreless innings in the World Series was snapped one day after he hurt the middle finger of his pitching hand fighting with a teammate on the team train.

Events of the 1919 World Series were dictated, in large part, by seven White Sox players who sold out to gamblers in the game's worst scandal. Cincinnati won, five games to three, in an expanded format, and the "Black Sox" conspirators were banned from the game when word leaked out in 1920.

In 1923, with the Black Sox scandal scar merely an unpleasant memory to a game revitalized by Babe Ruth and the lively ball, "The House That Ruth Built" opened and the Yankees did so well there that they captured their third consecutive pennant. Many World Series games would be played in Yankee Stadium, but the first was noteworthy not because the Yankees beat the Giants, 4–2, but because the Giants' Casey Stengel—later manager of 10 Yankee flag-winners—hit the first two World Series homers in the park.

Ruth hit three homers in that Series—all in the Polo Grounds—and did not hit a World Series homer in Yankee Stadium until 1926.

Two sensational pitchers who won fame as starters became World Series heroes in the '20s. In 1924 Washington won its only World Championship when 37-year-old Walter Johnson—twice beaten by the Giants earlier in the Series—came on in the ninth to hurl four scoreless innings.

Sandy's Save

A spectacular catch by little-known outfielder Sandy Amoros in the sixth inning of Game 7 enabled the Brooklyn Dodgers to beat the New York Yankees, 2–0, and win their first World Championship in 1955. Amoros, who had replaced Junior Gilliam in left at the start of the inning, easily doubled baserunner Gil McDougald after the catch. Left-handed pull hitter Yogi Berra had almost foiled the Dodger defense by slicing the ball down the left-field line.

Series Slugger

Duke Snider of the Dodgers is the only player ever to hit four home runs in a World Series twice.

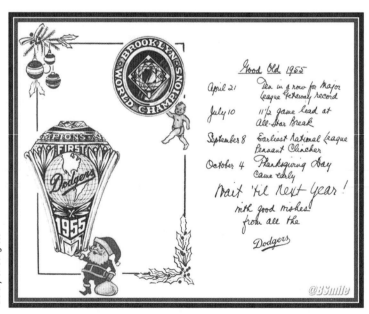

After winning their only world championship in 1955, the Brooklyn Dodgers sent this holiday card to their employees, media members, and season ticket holders.

In the last of the 12th, with the score 3–3, Washington's Muddy Ruel hit a foul pop but Giant catcher Hank Gowdy tripped over his mask and dropped the ball. Able to bat again, Ruel doubled. Johnson followed with a grounder to short, bobbled by Travis Jackson, and rookie Earl McNeely grounded to third baseman Fred Lindstrom.

As Lindstrom reached for the routine grounder, the ball struck a pebble and bounded high over his head into left field. Ruel scored the run that won the World Series.

Two years later Grover Cleveland Alexander pitched the St. Louis Cardinals to a World Championship in their first pennant- winning year. Alexander, 39, came to the Cards from the Cubs in midseason and proved a valuable addition. In the World Series, he pitched complete-game victories in the second and sixth games, winning 6–2 and 10–2, before he was called on again as a reliever in Game 7.

With the Cardinals leading, 3–2 in the seventh, the Yankees loaded the bases with two outs. St. Louis starter Jesse Haines had developed a blister and player/manager Rogers Hornsby decided it was time to put experience on the line. He called for Alexander, who reputedly had been out into the wee hours celebrating his victory of the day before.

Tony Lazzeri—second on the club to Babe Ruth in home runs and runs batted in during the regular season—was the hitter. Alexander went to a 1-1 count, then threw a pitch that Lazzeri laced hard down the left-field line—just foul. After taking a deep sigh of relief, the grizzled veteran fired a third strike to end the rally.

Alexander retired the next five batters, then walked Babe Ruth with two outs in the ninth and the score still 3–2, St. Louis. Bob Meusel, another slugger, came to bat when Ruth suddenly broke for second, trying to steal. Catcher Bob O'Farrell fired a bullet to Hornsby to retire Ruth and bring the World Championship to St. Louis. In two and a third innings, Alexander had yielded no hits, no runs, and one walk.

The 1927 Yankees, perhaps the greatest team of all time, had an easy time with their competition that fall, the Pittsburgh Pirates. New York won four straight but even before the Series began in spacious Forbes Field, Yankee sluggers had terrorized the Pirates with a long-ball display in batting practice. The all-right-handed Pittsburgh pitching staff had to deal with an array of left-handed hitters, including Babe Ruth (.356, 60 HR, 164 RBI that season) and Lou Gehrig (.373, 47, 173). Even the statistics were scary.

Longtime Phillies star Grover Cleveland Alexander was the key man in the first World Championship of the St. Louis Cardinals, in 1926.

Homers That Ended Postseason Series

* 1951—Bobby Thomson (Giants) hits three-run homer vs Ralph Branca (Dodgers) to win best-of-three NL playoff
* 1960—Bill Mazeroski (Pirates) hits 9th-inning leadoff shot to win World Series Game 7
* 1976—Chris Chambliss (Yankees) beats KC with leadoff, 9th-inning shot in LCS Game 5
* 1993—Joe Carter (Jays) homer beats Mitch Williams (Phillies) in decisive Series Game 6
* 1999—Todd Pratt (Mets) hits 10th-inning homer to top D'backs and win four-game NLCS
* 2003—Aaron Boone (Yankees) solves Tim Wakefield in 11th inning of ALCS Game 7
* 2005—Chris Burke (Astros) homers in 18th inning of Game 4 vs Braves to win NLCS
* 2006—Magglio Ordonez (Tigers) hits 9th-inning three-run homer against Oakland to win ALCS
* 2014—Travis Ishikawa (Giants) hits 9th-inning three-run homer against Cardinals in NLCS Game 5
* 2016—Edwin Encarnacion (Jays) hits three-run homer in 11th to win wild-card game vs O's

Cardinal stars Pepper Martin (left) and Chick Hafey helped St. Louis beat the favored Philadelphia A's in the 1931 World Series. Martin, a rookie that year, managed 12 hits in 24 at-bats.

Comparison Costs

Winner's shares in the 1973 World Series between the Oakland A's and the New York Mets were $24,617.57. By 1992, the winning shares for the Toronto Blue Jays were $144,962.16. By comparison, winning shares of the 1903 Boston Pilgrims had been $1,182, but the losing Pirates got $1,316.25 each because Pittsburgh owner Barney Dreyfuss, loyal to his troops, donated his share of the receipts to the players.

Brock's Feet Flew

Lou Brock of the Cardinals twice stole three bases in a single World Series game and seven in an entire Series. The years: 1967 and 1968.

Many experts insist the Philadelphia Athletics of 1929 were even stronger than the 1927 Yankees. Surely the Chicago Cubs would agree; they won the National League pennant by 10½ games but lost the World Series, four games to one.

Enterprising A's manager Connie Mack sent sore-armed pitcher Howard Ehmke to scout the Cubs during the season, then pulled a surprise by naming him the opening-game pitcher. He won, 3–1, fanning 13 in the process.

Game 4 destroyed Chicago's hopes for good. Leading 8–0, going into the home seventh, the Cubs used four pitchers as the A's erupted for 10 runs—the biggest inning of World Series history—and copped the game, 10–8. Part of the scoring resulted from a fly ball lost in the sun by Chicago center fielder Hack Wilson. The misplayed fly became a three-run, inside-the-park homer for Mule Haas.

In 1930 the A's tripped the Cards with two wins each from Lefty Grove and George Earnshaw, but rookie Pepper Martin reversed the results when the same clubs met again the following fall.

In the greatest World Series performance by a freshman, Martin collected 12 hits (including a homer and four doubles) in 24 at-bats, scored five runs, knocked in five, and stole five bases with the leaping, head-first slide that won him the nickname "Wild Horse of the Osage." In Game 4 his single and double were the only hits off A's ace George Earnshaw. Martin also shone afield, gloving a low liner by Max Bishop to save the decisive seventh game for veteran spitballer Burleigh Grimes.

Martin had been moved from center field to third base when the "Gashouse Gang" Cardinals won their only pennant, in 1934, and he pounded 11 hits to share the team lead with Rip Collins and Joe Medwick as the Cards beat the Tigers, 4–3. But the real stars of that Series were the Dean brothers; Dizzy and Paul won two each to account for all the Cardinal victories. Old Diz won Game 7, 11–0, after boasting to the Tiger hitters that he would use only fastballs against them.

Dean wasn't so lucky in 1938, when he lost Game 2 during a four-game sweep of the Cubs by the Yankees. In the second inning, Dean retired two straight after a single by Joe DiMaggio and a walk to Lou Gehrig. Joe Gordon's easy roller went into left field for two bases after Cub infielders Billy Herman and Stan Hack collided, and Dean had to run out to left field to retrieve it. Two runs scored and things never got better for Dean or the Cubs.

In 1939 the Yanks engineered another sweep—this time against the Reds—and the end of the Series was marked by an unusual play. After a walk, a bunt, and an error, Joe DiMaggio singled to right for a run, but Ival Goodman kicked the ball around and Charley "King Kong" Keller tried to score too. He arrived just as burly catcher Ernie Lombardi was taking Goodman's belated throw. Accidentally kicked in the groin, Lombardi lay stunned—the ball beside him—as Keller and DiMaggio plated two insurance runs in the 10th inning of the fourth game.

Another catcher—Mickey Owen—made the most notorious error in World Series history in 1941 when he failed to hold the game-ending third strike for the Dodgers against the Yankees in Game 4 at Brooklyn. Instead of a 3–2 Dodger win, knotting the Series at two games each, the Yankees scored four runs and took a 3–1 lead. They wrapped up the World Championship the next day.

In 1946 Enos Slaughter led the National League with 130 runs batted in, but his legs won the World Series for the Cardinals.

In the seventh game against the Red Sox, he led off the eighth with a single. One out later, with St. Louis needing a run to break a 3–3 deadlock, Slaughter and Harry Walker worked a perfect hit-and-run play.

Slaughter—told to take any risk in an effort to score—broke for second with the pitch and Walker dropped a Texas Leaguer between shortstop Johnny Pesky and substitute center fielder Leon Culberson. Slaughter had reached second while the ball was still in the air and took third easily. Then, remembering Culberson did not have the throwing arm of injured regular Dom DiMaggio, he streaked for home.

Shortstop Pesky, receiving the relay throw, had his back to the infield during Slaughter's dash and was stupefied when he wheeled and saw him approaching the plate.

Pesky hesitated just slightly—giving Slaughter the split-second he needed—before throwing home. Slaughter's run gave the Cardinals a 4–3 victory and the Series crown.

The 1947 World Series had a little of everything. Brooklyn's Al Gionfriddo made a sensational catch to rob Joe DiMaggio of a home run. New York's Yogi Berra hit the first pinch-homer in a World Series. And Cookie Lavagetto ruined Floyd Bevens' no-hitter in the ninth inning.

New York led in games, two to one, as Lavagetto came to bat with two men out, two men on base, and the Yankees leading Game 4 by a 2–1 score. Lavagetto, a utility infielder who had hit .261 during the regular season, found a pitch he liked and rammed a double off the right-field wall. Both runners scored and the Dodgers won, 3–2.

Don Larsen succeeded where Bevens failed. In his 14-year career, Larsen won only 81 games—an average of less than 6 per season—and posted an embarrassing 3-21 record with the 1954 Baltimore Orioles (nee St. Louis Browns). But he thrived with the Yankees, with 45 wins and 24 losses in five Yankee years.

Don Larsen . . . brilliant against Brooklyn.

No Scouting Report for Cuellar

Baltimore Orioles superscout Jim Russo delivered advance reports on the Reds in 1970 and discussed the National League champions with all pitchers except Mike Cuellar. Asked why, Russo responded, "You don't tell Leonard Bernstein how to conduct the New York Philharmonic and we don't tell Mike Cuellar how to pitch. He's an artist."

Bob Gibson pitched eight straight complete games, winning the first seven, in World Series play. The star Cardinal right-hander fanned a record 17 in a game and 35 in a seven-game Series against Detroit in 1968. Previously, Dodgers Sandy Koufax (1963) and Carl Erskine (1953) held one-game strikeout records—recorded against the Yankees—with 15 and 14, respectively.

Sandy Koufax fans Harry Bright for the final out of the 1963 World Series opener at Yankee Stadium. The star Dodger southpaw whiffed 15, topping Carl Erskine's former World Series record, en route to a 5–2 win. He later capped a Dodger sweep by winning Game 4, 2–1. Koufax was later named the World Series and regular-season MVP as well as the Cy Young Award winner.

World Series Slaughter

The Yankees beat the Giants, 18–4, in Game 2 of the 1936 Series.

Mays Made Mighty Catch

His back to the plate, Willie Mays of the Giants hauled down a 460-foot drive by Vic Wertz of the Indians during the 1954 World Series at the Polo Grounds in New York. The play stifled a Cleveland rally in the eighth inning of the opening game.

McNally's Surprise Slam

Baltimore pitcher Dave McNally electrified the baseball world when he hit a grand-slam home run against Cincinnati's Wayne Granger in the sixth inning of Game 3 of the 1970 Series. He won, 9–3.

World Series Workhorse

Reliever Darold Knowles of the Oakland A's appeared in all seven games of the 1973 classic against the New York Mets.

After Dodger bats knocked him out in the second inning of Game 2, Larsen returned in Game 5 on October 8, 1956. He threw only 97 pitches in retiring all 27 batters who faced him. Pinch-hitter Dale Mitchell, batting for Dodger starter Sal Maglie, swung and missed twice, hit a foul into the left-field stands, then took a called third strike to end the game. The score was 2–0.

Larsen said later he was nervous only in the ninth, when Dodger manager Walter Alston hesitated in selecting his pinch-hitter. None of the Yankees—including manager Casey Stengel—talked to Larsen during the game for fear of upsetting him. Jackie Robinson's liner to third, knocked down by Andy Carey and fielded by Gil McDougald, was the most serious threat to the million-to-one gem. Most experts regard Larsen's achievement as the World Series record least likely to fall.

A rookie reliever, Larry Sherry of the Dodgers, was the hero in 1959 when he won two and saved two other World Series victories over the White Sox. Sherry threw hard and slow sliders—perfected in the Venezuelan Winter League—to complement a fastball, curve, and change-up. His 0.71 ERA in 12⅔ World Series innings matched his season-long standard. In relief he was 7-0 with a 0.74 ERA; he lost twice as a starter and had an overall earned run mark of 2.19. Sherry also won one of the Dodgers' two playoff wins against Milwaukee with 7⅔ shutout innings of relief in Game 1.

Seldom-used outfielder Chuck Essegian helped the Dodgers win in six games by slamming two pinch-hit home runs. His emergency heroics recalled the performance of the Giants' Dusty Rhodes during a 1954 sweep of the Cleveland Indians. In addition to two pinch-singles, Rhodes beat Bob Lemon in the opener with one gone in the last of the 10th by hitting a 260-foot fly ball over the short right-field wall.

The Dodgers could have used Dusty Rhodes in 1966, when they were blanked three times in four straight losses to the Baltimore Orioles. Twenty-year-old Jim Palmer became the youngest man to hurl a Series shutout, but the great surprise of the Series was the yeoman work of veteran Moe Drabowsky, a journeyman who pitched the best game of his career as a Game 1 reliever.

After the Dodgers scored their only two runs of the Series against Dave McNally, Drabowsky came out of the bullpen to strike out 11 men and yield only one hit and two walks in 6⅔ innings of shutout relief.

Los Angeles knew the end was near when star center fielder

Yankee southpaw Whitey Ford pitched a record 33⅔ consecutive scoreless innings in the World Series.

Best of Nine

No World Series has ever gone nine games—but it could have. The first Fall Classic, in 1903, and the World Series of 1919, 1920, and 1921 were all played with a best-of-nine format.

Another Series Fix?

The court investigation into the 1919 Black Sox scandal suggested the 1918 World Series might have been fixed too. The highly-favored Chicago Cubs accommodated the Boston Red Sox with errors of omission and commission, including bad baserunning. Three Cubs were picked off, two of them in the decisive sixth game, while a passed ball and wild throw killed the Cubs late in the fourth game. A Max Flack error was the key misplay in the finale, a 2–1 Chicago defeat. Allegations of a 1918 fix remained unsubstantiated because there was no commissioner at the time and no court-delivered indictments. When the Black Sox scandal came to light, the public was so shocked that the questionable behavior of the 1918 Cubs was swept under the rug.

Casey's Clouts

Casey Stengel's home run settled the first 1–0 game in World Series history, on October 10, 1923. Stengel, then with the New York Giants, hit the first two World Series homers at Yankee Stadium; all three Babe Ruth homers in the 1923 World Series came at the Polo Grounds.

Mel Swat

Mel Ott was the first member of the 500 Home Run Club to hit a home run in his first World Series at-bat.

Whitewash Wonder

Lew Burdette of the Milwaukee Braves pitched as many shutouts against the Yankees in the 1957 World Series (2) as the entire American League managed in the 154-game regular season.

Willie Davis made three errors in the fifth inning of Game 2. He dropped two consecutive flies and, seeking to repair the damage, threw the ball over the third baseman's head. The Dodgers also made three other errors that day.

Five years later the Orioles were at Pittsburgh for the first night game in World Series history, on October 13, 1971. The Pirates won, 4–3, and went on to take a seven-game match behind the spirited play of Roberto Clemente, whose .414 mark included a Game 7 homer that made the difference in a 2–1 score.

The Oakland A's won the first of three straight World Championships in 1972 when Dick Williams—guiding hand of the "Impossible Dream" Red Sox of 1967—deployed his pinch-hitters and relief pitchers with uncanny success.

Rollie Fingers won one, saved two, had a 1.74 ERA, and struck out 11 batters in 10⅓ innings over six games. Second-string catcher Gene Tenace, who hit .225 with five homers for the season, became the first man to homer in his first two World Series at-bats, and slammed four during the seven-game set against Cincinnati. And pinch-hitters Gonzalo Marquez, Don Mincher, and Angel Mangual all singled to spark a two-run, last-of-the-ninth rally that won Game 4 by a 3–2 score.

One of the most dramatic fall classics in baseball history

Rare Result

The last game of the 1991 World Series, won by the Twins over the Braves, was the first extra-inning Game 7 since 1924 and the first to end in a 1–0 score since 1962.

Pensive Puckett

Before he hit a game-ending home run in the sixth game of the 1991 World Series, Kirby Puckett had been planning to bunt his way on base. On-deck hitter Chili Davis dissuaded him.

Reversal of Fortune

The 1992 Atlanta Braves were the first team in baseball history to win a decisive playoff game when trailing before the last pitch.

Sudden Awakening

The 1996 Braves were the first National League team to rebound from a 3-1 deficit in the Championship Series. Outscoring the Cardinals 32–1 in the last three games, they set LCS records for hits (22) in Game 5 and runs (15) in Game 7.

Record Score

Before Boston beat Cleveland, 23–7, in Game 4 of the 1999 AL Division Series, the highest-scoring postseason game of all time was Toronto's 15–14 win over Philadelphia in Game 4 of the 1993 World Series.

Almost Perfect

Tom Glavine and Mark Wohlers combined for a one-hitter to win the 1995 World Series finale for Atlanta vs. Cleveland, 1–0. The only Indian hit was a bloop single by Tony Peña leading off the sixth.

Least Likely Homer

The one-out, ninth-inning home run that Scott Podsednik hit to win Game 2 of the 2005 World Series for the White Sox against the Astros might have been the least likely in baseball history. A left-handed hitter who hit 42 career homers in his 11-year career, Podsednik did not deliver any of them during the '05 regular season—despite making 568 plate appearances. He did, however, connect in the Division Series against Boston. His World Series home run was the only walkoff homer ever hit by the journeyman outfielder, who played for seven teams.

occurred when the Cincinnati Reds met the Boston Red Sox in 1975. After the teams split in two games, they cracked six homers in Game 3, but a disputed bunt marred the Reds' 6–5 win.

In the last of the 10th, Cesar Geronimo led with a single for Cincinnati. Pinch-hitter Ed Armbrister dropped a bunt in front of the plate, but Armbrister blocked catcher Carlton Fisk's path; the throw to second sailed into center field. Umpire Larry Barnett refused to heed Boston's charge of interference.

With Geronimo on third and Armbrister on first, and no outs, Pete Rose was intentionally walked to set up a force at home. Merv Rettenmund struck out but Joe Morgan singled over the head of center fielder Fred Lynn to end the game.

Another last-ditch single by Morgan ended the World Series eight days later. Boston manager Darrell Johnson foolishly inserted inexperienced rookie Jim Burton as a ninth-inning reliever with Game 7 tied at 3–3. He immediately walked leadoff hitter Ken Griffey. A sacrifice, infield grounder, and single by Morgan plated the winning run.

The most exciting game of the 1975 classic was the sixth. Boston led, 3–0, through four innings, but the Reds surged ahead, 6–3, in the eighth. Former Red Bernie Carbo then delivered his second pinch-homer of the Series—tying Chuck Essegian's 1959 record—to tie the score. Boston's Dwight Evans leaped to snag a probable home run by Joe Morgan in the 11th, and Carlton Fisk won the game for the Sox with a leadoff homer in the 12th.

Another dramatic homer occurred in Game 1 of the 1988 World Series. Oakland closer Dennis Eckersley, nursing a 4–3 lead in the ninth, issued a rare two-out walk to Mike Davis, bringing injured slugger Kirk Gibson to the plate in a pinch-hit role. Gibson, who could barely walk, took the count to 3-2, ripped several fouls, then connected for a long, game-winning homer—the first come-from-behind, game-winning homer in World Series history. Gibson did not bat again in a World Series won by the underdog Dodgers in five games.

Five years later, Joe Carter hit a three-run, ninth-inning homer vs. Mitch Williams, giving the Blue Jays an 8–6 win that ended the Toronto/Philadelphia World Series with a home run.

In 1996 backup catcher Jim Leyritz became an instant Yankee hero in Game 4 with a three-run, game-tying, eighth-inning homer vs. Atlanta closer Mark Wohlers. Once ahead, 6–0, the Braves lost, 8–6 in 10 innings, to square a series they eventually lost in six games.

After a one-year absence in 1997, the Yankees extended their World Series winning streak to a record-tying 12 games with consecutive sweeps of the San Diego Padres in 1998 and the Braves in 1999. Baseball's first repeat champion since the 1992–1993 Toronto Blue Jays, they were also the first team with successive sweeps since the 1938–1939 Yankees. New York ended the decade with 3 world titles in four years and 25 in the century.

The "Team of the Century" won more World Series games than any other team had even played.

The Bronx Bombers began the new century by winning a five-game Subway Series. The only bright spot for the Mets was a Game 3 win that ended the Yankees' 14-game winning streak in the World Series.

Aaron Boone, an unlikely hero, hit a pennant-winning home run for the New York Yankees on October 16, 2003. Leading off

Arizona Diamondbacks

the bottom of the 11th inning against Boston knuckleballer Tim Wakefield, Boone hit a solo home run to give his team a 6–5 win in LCS Game 7. Mariano Rivera pitched three scoreless innings for the win, giving the Yankees the pennant and a ticket to the World Series against the wild-card Florida Marlins.

Marlins manager Jack McKeon took a calculated gamble in the sixth game. Start Josh Beckett on three days of rest or use him on normal rest in Game 7? McKeon went for the gold and the move paid off: Beckett pitched a five-hit shutout to make the Fish World Champions for the second time in seven seasons.

Watching the wild-card Marlins win twice must have rankled the Red Sox, who had not won a world title since 1918. The drought, called "the Curse of the Bambino" because it coincided with the sale of Babe Ruth to the Yankees in 1920, finally came to a merciful end after 86 years.

After the Sox unraveled in the first three games of the AL Championship Series against the arch-rival Yankees, Boston rebounded to win four straight and take the pennant. No team before or since has recovered from such a deficit in a postseason series.

The Sox were not through; they maintained their momentum, running their winning streak to eight by sweeping the World Series over the St. Louis Cardinals. They never even trailed in a game. Boston also took world titles in 2007 and 2013 but without the drama of 2004.

In the 86 years between Red Sox world titles, there were 15 presidents, 11 Boston mayors, and 7 popes. The price of a World Series ticket changed too, jumping from $3.30 in 1918 to $140 in 2004 for the very same seat.

There was another Series sweep a year later, when the Chicago White Sox smothered the Houston Astros. The only team to get two game-deciding homers in the ninth inning or later in the same postseason series, the Sox also outlasted their opponents in the longest game in World Series history. It consumed 5 hours, 41 minutes, 14 innings, and 43 of the 50 available players, including 17 pitchers.

The 2006 St. Louis Cardinals had the fewest regular-season wins of any World Champion. The Cards lost 10 of their last 14 to finish with 83 wins but revived in time to beat the Padres in four games and the Mets in seven, reaching the World Series for the second time in three years. Then they beat the favored Detroit Tigers, who had swept both preliminary rounds and were well-rested. The Tigers won only one game against the Cards.

After finishing in a last-place tie in the 2006 NL West, both the Arizona Diamondbacks and Colorado Rockies reached the playoffs a year later. In a one-game playoff to decide the wild card, San Diego scored two in the top of the 13th but lost in the bottom half when Trevor Hoffman, then the lifetime leader in saves, yielded three runs. The Rockies won, 9–8, to cap a 14-1 stretch drive that erased a wild-card deficit of five-and-a-half games with two weeks left.

Then they joined the 1976 Reds as the only teams to win their first seven postseason games, sweeping the Phillies in a three-game NLDS and the D'backs in a four-game Championship Series. In fact, the Rockies went into the final round with wins in 20 of their last 21 games.

That momentum evaporated, however, when the red-hot Rockies were idled by an eight-day layoff—the longest ever for a league champion before the World Series. The Red Sox swept up

Arizona power pitchers Randy Johnson (left) and Curt Schilling were co-MVPs of the 2001 World Series after going 4–0 against the Yankees in a seven-game set. Johnson (3–0, 1.04) won the last two, including the finale in relief, while Schilling (1–0, 1.69) started twice on three days' rest. The left/right tandem had 43 wins and a record 665 strikeouts during the season, with Johnson averaging 13.4 Ks per nine innings, also a record.

ALL-STAR GAME SCORES

Year			Year		
1933	AL4	NL2	1974	NL7	AL2
1934	AL9	NL7	1975	NL6	AL3
1935	AL4	NL1	1976	NL7	AL1
1936	NL4	AL3	1977	NL7	AL5
1937	AL8	NL3	1978	NL7	AL3
1938	NL4	AL1	1979	NL7	AL6
1939	AL3	NL1	1980	NL4	AL2
1940	NL4	AL0	1981	NL5	AL4
1941	AL7	NL5	1982	NL4	AL1
1942	AL3	NL1	1983	AL13	NL3
1943	AL5	NL3	1984	NL3	AL1
1944	NL7	AL1	1985	NL6	AL1
1946	AL12	NL0	1986	AL3	NL2
1947	AL2	NL1	1987	NL2	AL0
1948	AL5	NL2	1988	AL2	NL1
1949	AL11	NL7	1989	AL5	NL3
1950	NL4	AL3	1990	AL2	NL0
1951	NL8	AL3	1991	AL4	NL2
1952	NL3	AL2	1992	AL13	NL6
1953	NL5	AL1	1993	AL9	NL3
1954	AL11	NL9	1994	NL8	AL7
1955	NL6	AL5	1995	NL3	AL2
1956	NL7	AL3	1996	NL6	AL0
1957	AL6	NL5	1997	AL3	NL1
1958	AL4	NL3	1998	AL13	NL8
1959	NL5	AL4	1999	AL4	NL1
1959	AL5	NL3	2000	AL6	NL3
1960	NL5	AL3	2001	AL4	NL1
1960	NL6	AL0	2002	AL7	NL7
1961	NL5	AL4	2003	NL6	AL7
1961	NL1	AL1	2004	AL9	NL4
1962	AL9	NL4	2005	NL5	AL7
1963	NL5	AL3	2006	AL3	NL2
1964	NL7	AL4	2007	NL4	AL5
1965	NL6	AL5	2008	AL4	NL3
1966	NL2	AL1	2009	NL3	AL4
1967	NL2	AL1	2010	AL1	NL3
1968	NL1	AL0	2011	NL5	AL1
1969	NL9	AL3	2012	AL0	NL8
1970	NL5	AL4	2013	NL0	AL3
1971	AL6	NL4	2014	AL5	NL3
1972	NL4	AL3	2015	NL3	AL6
1973	NL7	AL1	2016	AL4	NL2

TOTALS

Ties 2 (1961, 2002) | NL—42 | AL—42

1—No game in 1945 due to wartime travel restrictions
2—Two games per year, 1959–1962.

Mighty Mickey

Mickey Owen hit no home runs in 133 games during the 1942 season but produced the only NL run in a 3–1 All-Star Game defeat with a home run.

Sterling Southpaw

Lefty Gomez was the American League's starting pitcher in the first All-Star Game and each of the other four years he made the squad. He pitched the first six innings, an All-Star Game record, in 1935.

Long-Lived Lefty

Warren Spahn was the only pitcher to start All-Star Games in three different decades.

Peaceful Pilots

No manager has ever been ejected from an All-Star Game.

Double D Doubles Up

In 1962 Don Drysdale became the only pitcher to start two All-Star Games in one year. Before the experiment was scrapped, the majors played two All-Star Games from 1959 to 1962.

Ballot Drew Response

In 1976, 8,370,145 All-Star ballots were returned by fans—more than the total number of votes President Abraham Lincoln received in both his victories plus the total population of the United States at the time the Constitution was ratified.

the pieces, winning four straight games to take their second world title in four years.

In 2008, four non-playoff teams in the National League had better won-lost records than the champions of the NL West, the Los Angeles Dodgers (84-78). But divisional play, wild-card winners, extra playoffs, and unbalanced schedules created quirks that could not be avoided.

The American League season, meanwhile, was supposed to end on September 28. But noooooo: the White Sox, one-half game behind the Twins in the AL Central, were forced to make up a game with the Tigers that had been canceled previously. The Sox won, 8–2, forcing a one-game playoff with the Twins. When Chicago took the title with a 1–0 win in the playoff, it marked the first time since 1906 that both Chicago teams had reached the postseason in the same year.

For the third straight year, the regular season had to be extended for a day in 2009. To settle the AL Central, the Minnesota Twins took the Detroit Tigers 12 innings before winning, 6–5. The key play occurred in the top of the 12th when Brandon Inge appeared to be hit by a pitch with the bases loaded. But home-plate umpire Randy Marsh ruled that the ball did not hit the player but his billowing jersey. The win allowed the Twins to make up a seven-game September deficit by going 17-4 when it counted most.

Entering the last weekend of the 2010 campaign, both the Braves and Giants needed to win just once in three-game series in their home parks to reach the playoffs. Instead, they both lost the first two, stretching the drama to the final day. Had the Braves and Giants lost on Sunday, the Giants and Padres would have faced a one-game playoff for the NL West title, with the loser then playing the Braves for the wild card. But the Braves and Giants won, averting the most complicated scenario in postseason history.

Closers couldn't close for the Braves and Red Sox on the last day of the 2011 season. Rookie star Craig Kimbrel blew Atlanta's one-run lead in the ninth, prolonging the agony for a team that

After a seven-week player strike that resulted in a "split-season" format to determine division champions, the 1981 season resumed with a delayed All-Star Game August 9. The 72,000 baseball-hungry fans who filled Cleveland's Municipal Stadium set an All-Star attendance record.

lost in the 13th. And Jonathan Papelbon got within one strike of victory before blowing his third save of the season. Instead of advancing to the playoffs as wild cards, both teams went home for the winter. On August 31, the Red Sox led the AL East by a game and a half over the Yankees and had the second-best record in baseball. But Boston's starting pitching was so bad the rest of the way (7.08 ERA in September) that the team went 7-20 in the final month.

The 2011 World Series proved Yogi Berra right: it ain't over 'til it's over. In Game 6, Rangers closer Neftali Perez had two strikes on Cardinals third baseman David Freese with two on and two outs in the bottom of the ninth inning. Freese hit a two-run triple to tie the game at 7–7. Josh Hamilton's homer in the 10th made it 9–7 but the Cards tied it again after being down to their final strike. Leading off the last of the 11th, Freese froze the Rangers with a walkoff homer, ending a 10–9 game and setting the stage for a 6–2 St. Louis win in the seventh game. His playoff totals included a .397 average, eight doubles, five home runs, 21 runs batted in, 25 hits, 50 total bases, and MVP trophies in both the NLCS and World Series.

Qualifying for the playoffs became more complicated after MLB added a second wild-card team in 2012. Three years later, three NL Central teams posted the league's best records but the Pirates (98-64) had to face the Cubs (97-65) in a sudden-death game to determine the wild-card winner. The teams with the fourth and fifth-best records, the Dodgers and Mets, met in one NLDS while the Cardinals (100-62) had to wait for the Cubs-Pirates winner before starting their series.

Purists screamed when wild-card winners—neither of them champions over the 162-game schedule—met in the World Series twice, in 2002 (Giants vs. Angels) and 2014 (Giants vs. Royals).

The All-Star Game

With Chicago hosting the Century of Progress exposition in 1933, *Chicago Tribune* sports editor Arch Ward decided a baseball game between National League and American League "All-Star" squads would be a worthy added attraction.

Though many club owners opposed a three-day break in midseason for what they considered to be an exhibition game, Ward refused to abandon the thought. He approached Commissioner Kenesaw Mountain Landis who, in turn, contacted National League president John Heydler and his AL counterpart, Will Harridge.

The executives agreed and the idea was born, though its original purpose was strictly to stage a high-caliber contest for the 1933 exposition. There was no thought given to an annual All-Star Game until overwhelming fan reaction mandated continuation of the matchup.

An informal fan poll conducted by the *Tribune* provided "guidelines" for managers Connie Mack of the American League and John McGraw, called out of retirement to manage the National League team. But Mack, the 70-year-old owner/manager of the Philadelphia Athletics, and McGraw, winner of 10 pennants with the Giants, were free to choose their own 18-man squads.

Twenty of the 36 players named eventually found their way to the Hall of Fame gallery at Cooperstown, and the brightest star

Carl Hubbell of the Giants fanned five straight superstars in the 1934 All-Star Game at the Polo Grounds, his home park.

Fancy Fielders

Cleveland's Earl Averill was considered such a strong center fielder that Joe DiMaggio shifted to right the first three times he made the American League All-Star team.

Other Brother

Vince DiMaggio hit a single, a triple, and a homer for the National League in the 1943 All-Star Game. The AL still won, 5–4.

Super Stars

When Cal Ripken Jr. started his 15th straight All-Star Game in 1998, he topped Willie Mays (1957–1966) for the most consecutive All-Star starts.

First Impression

Terry Steinbach was the only man to homer in his first major league at-bat as well as his first All-Star Game at-bat.

of all—Babe Ruth—wasted no time showing that the players took the contest seriously.

Ruth's two-run home run in the third inning paced the American League to a 4–2 triumph on July 6, 1933, at Comiskey Park. Forty-seven thousand fans—all that fire marshals would allow—generated more than $51,000 for the retired players' fund and spread the exciting news about a possible "interleague All-Star series."

Choosing the All-Stars

In 1934, the second year of the All-Star Game, baseball again used the informal fan poll to "suggest" players to managers who were not bound to take any advice. Since both circuits were guided by player/managers that season, NL manager Bill Terry named himself the starting first baseman and AL pilot Joe Cronin doubled as his league's starting shortstop.

Realizing the fan vote was a farce, baseball scrapped the idea, leaving total selection in the hands of the managers. The pilots themselves were the pennant-winners of the previous fall. Blatant favoritism resulted, but AL manager Joe McCarthy countered his critics when he deliberately kept his six Yankee All-Stars on the bench while beating the Nationals without contribution from his powerful club.

From 1947 to 1957, fans were given total control of player selection for the first time. The Associated Press tabulated the results, but AP's crack sportswriters joined in the national protest when Cincinnati fans stuffed the ballot box in 1957 and "elected" seven of the eight Red starters.

Infielders Dick Bartell, Frankie Frisch, and Pepper Martin discuss strategy before the "Game of the Century" at Chicago in 1933. The AL prevailed, 4–2.

Commissioner Ford Frick vetoed the choice of Gus Bell and Wally Post, inserting Willie Mays and Hank Aaron into the National League lineup and ending the fan balloting.

In 1958 a more objective system was introduced when players, coaches, and managers voted only for their own league's representatives. They were barred from voting for teammates—a device that worked to send fairly chosen squads to the All-Star Game.

Though player voting was successful—and respected by fans—new commissioner Bowie Kuhn returned the voting to the fans again in 1970. Problems flared immediately.

A computerized ballot was prepared so early that nominees at each position were frequently traded, injured, or converted to other positions by the time the season opened in April.

That very first year, the "experts" who compiled the listing of 24 National League outfielders did not have the intelligence to include Rico Carty, who had hit .342 the previous season and personally guided the Atlanta Braves to the NL West championship with a sensational September streak.

When Carty opened the 1970 campaign with his bat still smoking, baseball's brass was embarrassed, but the fans saved the day by picking the star outfielder through a difficult write-in process. Only one other write-in—first baseman Steve Garvey of the 1974 Dodgers—won election in the ballot's first four decades.

Instead of promoting All-Star teams made up of the game's best players, the fan voting has degenerated into a popularity contest. Teams urge their fans to vote for hometown favorites. Too often, sentimental choices or well-known names appear instead of true All-Stars.

The Phantom Shortstop

In 1974 Luis Aparicio was listed on the All-Star ballot even though he had been released by the Red Sox before the season opened.

Blue Note

Vida Blue was the first pitcher to start the All-Star Game for both leagues.

Quick Change

During the four years that baseball staged two All-Star Games, the rosters were not identical.

Movers and Shakers

Moises Alou and Gary Sheffield represented five different teams in the All-Star Game.

National League

Braves' Field, Boston, was the setting for the 1936 All-Star Game, won by the National League. Contributing to the victory were (left to right) pitchers Van Lingle Mungo, Dizzy Dean, Lon Warneke, Carl Hubbell, and Curt Davis. All but Mungo pitched.

Paul Molitor

Versatile All-Stars

Paul Molitor duplicated an earlier Pete Rose feat by playing five different positions in All-Star history. But Molitor didn't approach the record of 24 All-Star appearances, shared by Hank Aaron, Willie Mays, and Stan Musial.

All-Star Haymaker

Fred Lynn's grand slam, the only bases-filled home run in All-Star history, allowed the American League to trounce the National, 13–3, in the 50th anniversary All-Star Game at Chicago's Comiskey Park on July 8, 1983. The AL matched its run total, an All-Star record, in 1992 and 1998.

Mighty McGriff

With the American League nursing a 7–5 lead in the ninth inning of the 1994 All-Star Game, National League pinch-hitter Fred McGriff hit a one-out, two-run homer vs. Lee Smith to tie the score. The NL won in the tenth when Tony Gwynn singled and scored on a double by Moises Alou.

Power Plants

Players with two homers in an All-Star Game:

Arky Vaughan, NL, 1941
Ted Williams, AL, 1946
Al Rosen, AL, 1954
Willie McCovey, NL, 1969
Gary Carter, NL, 1981

If fans were prohibited from voting for local players, the balloting would certainly become more objective. Even so, fans are poor selectors because of limited knowledge of the game. They cannot judge the true value of top players because they don't watch baseball daily.

In 1974, 74.2 percent of fans responding to a poll in *The Sporting News* agreed with the idea that players—not fans—should choose the All-Stars.

Perhaps the best way to retain fan interest but guarantee fair elections is to establish a "one-third plan" whereby fan votes would count for one-third; the player/coach/manager vote for one-third; and the media vote for a final third. That way, two-thirds of the ballots would be cast by people who watch baseball every day.

All-Star Highlights

When the best players of both leagues meet in head-to-head competition, unusual feats occur.

Though a starting pitcher is barred from working more than three innings, Carl Hubbell put on the most dazzling pitching exhibition in All-Star history in fewer than three on July 10, 1934.

Working before 48,363 fans in the Polo Grounds, his home park, the crafty southpaw used his screwball to perfection in striking out five straight future Hall-of-Famers—Babe Ruth, Lou Gehrig, Jimmie Foxx, Al Simmons, and Joe Cronin.

Hubbell had given up a single and a walk to start the game but was all business with the American League's big bats. He seemed unruffled even when the two runners pulled a double steal.

The Giants' star nearly had seven straight strikeouts—he had two strikes on Bill Dickey before the Yankee catcher singled—and he whiffed New York pitcher Lefty Gomez. Hubbell held a 4–0 lead when he left after three frames, but the Americans eventually won, 9–7.

Ted Williams of the Boston Red Sox staged the most dramatics by a hitter in 1941. The NL took a 5–3 lead into the last of the ninth at Detroit, but the Americans scored a run when Billy Herman made a bad throw on a double-play grounder that would have ended the game.

With two outs and two on, Williams worked the count to 2-1 against Claude Passeau. Then he smashed a long, game-winning home run against the facade of the third tier in right field. The Williams blast wrested the hero's laurels from NL shortstop Arky Vaughan, who had hit two homers earlier in the game.

Williams hit a pair in 1946—along with two singles—as the Americans coasted to a 12–0 triumph after a one-year hiatus caused by wartime travel restrictions. The Boston left fielder actually batted five times in that game, but received a walk the first time up—from Claude Passeau, his victim in 1941.

The second Williams homer came on a high, arcing blooper pitch thrown by Rip Sewell. "Before the game," Sewell said later, "I'd been talking to Williams and he asked if I would throw that pitch in the game. I said I would. When he came up, he was shaking his head as if to say, 'Don't do it.' I answered back with a nod that said, 'You're going to get it.'

"The first pitch was a blooper. He fouled it off as the crowd roared. They loved it. So I gave him another one. Too high. Then a fastball down the middle. He was surprised and let it go over for a strike. Our eyes met. He grinned because we both knew another blooper would be coming. It was a perfect strike but he timed it and sent it into the bullpen. The crowd went wild."

The pitch, delivered like a fastball, was so deceptive that Sewell led the National League with 21 victories in 1943. He developed it after a gunshot wound to his toe forced him to take an awkward stance on the mound, both feet pointed directly toward the batter. Sewell changed his motion from three-quarters to overhand and released the ball earlier than he released a straight fastball. In 10 years, Williams was the only hitter to bat the blooper over the fence.

There are many cases of timely home runs in All-Star competition. In 1950 a blast by Ralph Kiner tied the AL in the ninth and set the stage for spray-hitting Red Schoendienst to deliver a totally unexpected clout in the 14th.

Stan Musial's shot in the 12th inning won the 1955 classic, 6–5, for the Nationals, and Johnny Callison's three-run homer off fireballer Dick Radatz capped a four-run ninth that brought victory to the NL in 1964. Tony Perez gave the NL a 2–1, 15-inning triumph with a 1967 home run. Al Rosen of the AL in 1954 and Willie McCovey (1969) and Gary Carter (1981) of the NL joined Williams and Vaughan as players with two homers in one All-Star Game.

Enos Slaughter, 37, singled twice, walked once, stole a base, and made a spectacular catch in the outfield to bring victory to the Nationals in 1953, and Willie Mays collected three hits in each of two 1960 games.

Mays, the fourth-ranked home-run hitter in baseball history, ranks as king of the All-Stars. He compiled 23 hits, 20 runs, 40 total bases, and six stolen bases in 24 All-Star Games. He often batted from the unfamiliar leadoff spot

Rival catchers of 1933 All-Stars were Bill Dickey (Yankees) of the American League and Gabby Hartnett (Cubs) of the National League.

in the midsummer classic, as National League managers enjoyed the luxury of overabundant power in the lineup.

Hank Aaron, the career home-run leader, was a mysterious failure in All-Star play until 1971, when he finally hit a home run for the Nationals at Detroit. Aaron saved his most dramatic All-Star show for his hometown Atlanta fans the following year when his sixth-inning blast off old nemesis Gaylord Perry gave the NL a 2–1 lead. It eventually prevailed, 4–3.

Unusual events have marked a number of All-Star contests. In 1961 a stiff wind at San Francisco's Candlestick Park played havoc with fielders and pitchers. National League reliever Stu Miller made the first balk of his career when he was blown off the mound in the middle of his windup. Seven errors marked the fray, won by the Nationals with a two-run burst in the 10th, 5–4. Willie Mays thrilled 44,115 hometown fans when he plated the tying run with a double and scored the winning marker on a single by Roberto Clemente.

In 1942 the only National League run in a 3–1 defeat came on a pinch-hit homer by Mickey Owen, who did not hit another in 133 games that season.

There were two ties—a 1–1 game rained out after nine innings at Boston in 1961 and a 7-7 finish in 2002 after the teams ran out of pitchers—and one game curtailed by rain—a 3–2 win for the Nationals, ended after five innings at Philadelphia in 1952.

The only All-Star Game at Brooklyn's Ebbets Field was noteworthy for the first appearances by black players in All-Star competition. Players included in that 1949 contest were Jackie Robinson, Roy Campanella, Don Newcombe, and Larry Doby.

Chapter 15

Criss-crossing trolley tracks in downtown Brooklyn forced pedestrians to be "Trolley Dodgers." A shortened version of the name stuck to the National League team even after the tracks and the team had been removed.

The Language of Baseball

On Ruth's 60th

Looking back on the growing significance of Babe Ruth's 60th home run in 1927, Washington pitcher Tom Zachary, who threw the pitch, admitted, "If I'd a known it was gonna be a famous record, I'd a stuck it in his ear."

The Necktie Ball

Interviewed with slugger Ernie Banks on the radio, Satchel Paige said, "Know how I'd pitch to you? I'd throw the old necktie ball. You can't hit on your back."

Renderings by Jim Berryman, *The Sporting News*, November 18, 1943.

Baseball Words in American Culture

Baseball's rich heritage is best expressed in its colorful language, which has greatly influenced American culture and speech patterns.

When a businessman fails at a given task, he has *struck out*. When a girl rejects a boy's advances, he *can't get to first base*. When a luncheon speaker can't keep his date, he asks for a *rain check* and tries to find a *pinch-hitter*. A competitor who loses a bid is *shut out*.

Key Phrases and Origins

Ace—The star of any team effort, in or out of sports, is the ace, named for the great Asa Brainard, who pitched every game for the unbeaten Cincinnati Red Stockings of 1869. Whenever a pitcher of that period did especially well, he was called an "asa."

Annie Oakley—Old-timers recall this term as another word for a walk, which is a free base on balls. American League president Ban Johnson saw Annie Oakley perform as a crack rifle shot in Buffalo Bill's Wild West Show, circa 1900, and compared the punched holes in complimentary baseball tickets to Annie Oakley's bullet holes. Ballplayers eventually extended the name to cover anything free.

At bat—A sailor, keeping score at an 1872 game between Boston and the little seaport of Belfast, Maine, coined this phrase and also used the nautical term "on deck" to describe the next hitter.

Bag—In 1857 a newspaper called *Spirit of Times* described a baseball rule this way: "The first, second, and third bases shall be canvas bags, painted white and filled with sand or sawdust."

Baltimore chop—In 1896, as the hard-driving Baltimore Orioles of the National League discovered they could get infield hits on high bouncing ground balls, the *Baltimore News* reported: "A middle-height ball is picked out and is attacked with a terrific swing on the upper side. The ball is made to strike the ground from five to ten feet away from the batsman and, striking the ground with force, bounds high over the head of the third or first baseman."

Baseball—The *New Orleans Picayune*, in 1841, asked, "Who has not played Barn Ball in his boyhood, Base in his youth, and Wicket in his manhood?"

Battery—Describing an 1867 batter, the *Ball Players' Chronicle* reported, "He soon resumed his position, once more facing the battery of Lovett." (At that time, battery referred only to the pitcher rather than the pitcher/catcher tandem.) Explaining how the pitcher/catcher combination took on the name, several experts suggest the term "battery" extends from the military. Since one man provides ammunition for an artillery battery but another fires it, the transition to baseball is logical—the catcher is the "commander" providing ammunition for the pitcher to "fire."

Benchwarmer—A 1912 *Saturday Evening Post* reporter wrote: "A certain rich man offered a manager $10,000 if the manager would carry his son as a combination of mascot and bench-warmer."

Big league—In 1899, when the National was the only major league in operation, this line appeared in the *Chicago Daily News*: "They were telling a story on one of Chicago's crack players now in the Big League."

Bonehead—Phillies manager George Stallings used it for emphasis when describing the inept play of his team in 1898.

Bullpen—The most popular theory, dating back to the turn of the century, indicates that the area where pitchers warm up won its name because almost every ballpark in the country featured a large outfield billboard advertisement for Bull Durham tobacco. Not only did pitchers warm up under the sign—usually in fair territory deep in the outfield—but the company popularized its name by offering $50 to any player who hit the bull when he batted.

The actual word predates baseball. "Bullpen" was once known as a log enclosure used by pioneers attacked by American Indians before they could reach the fort. It was later used to describe any makeshift jail—hence the transition to baseball when Connie Mack began the practice of having his pitchers warm up in a secluded area in 1909.

There are other interpretations:

In bullfighting, the bulls are kept in separate pens. One is led out, bouts with the matador, and eventually dies. The pen opens and another comes out, and so on until the matinee is completed. In baseball, when a pitcher is routed, a gate opens to introduce another.

Some railroad fans insist bullpen was introduced to baseball by Bill Friel, utilityman for the American League's Milwaukee Brewers of 1901 and a former rail employee. There were shanties with benches at intervals along the roadbed and workers would sit and talk there during work breaks. When Friel played, pitchers who weren't working sat on a similar bench, in right field foul territory. He referred to it as the bullpen because the railroad bench had the same name.

Bunt—A derivation of butt, as a goat will do—to push with the head. The 1767 *Boston Gazette*: "The black ram will sometimes . . . give him a paltry bunt at unawares." When Dick Pearce of the Brooklyn Atlantics was unable to connect with his regular swing, he tried the approach for the first time in baseball. His 1866 bunt succeeded.

Bush league—First used in 1910 to describe any baseball league outside the majors, as in an *American Magazine* quote: "The scouts returned from the deepest parts of the bushes proclaiming that the crop was poor." The same magazine, two years later, referred to players from such leagues as "bushers."

Charley horse—This reference to leg injury came into regular usage by 1890, but definitely originated with a lame horse named Charley. Which one is not certain.

On a summer day in Chicago in 1886 the National League's White Stockings (who gave their name to the American League's White Sox but remained a National League franchise as the Cubs) were scheduled to play when heavy morning rains forced a postponement. One of the players reported that the racetrack seven miles south was dry, and the team departed in unison.

Another player reported a "hot tip" on a horse named Charley and his teammates placed their bets on him. The inevitable

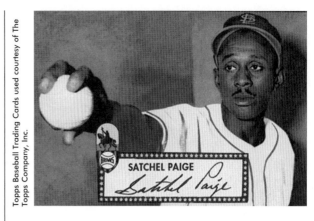

Topps Baseball Trading Cards used courtesy of The Topps Company, Inc.

Satchel Paige's Rules for Staying Young

Satchel Paige was at least 62 years old when he pitched one inning of an exhibition game in Atlanta Stadium and retired Hank Aaron, Ken Boyer, Junior Gilliam, and three other hitters with 12 pitches—only two of them called balls.

Paige, whose career included 2,500 games (153 of them in one season) attributed his longevity to his rules for staying young. "If you're over six years of age, follow these rules closely," he said.

1. Avoid fried meats, which anger up the blood.
2. If your stomach disputes you, lie down and pacify it with cool thoughts.
3. Keep the juices flowing by jangling around gently as you move.
4. Go very light on the vices, such as carrying on in society—the social ramble ain't restful.
5. Avoid running at all times.
6. And don't look back. Something might be gaining on you.

Country Cousins

In baseball, players say that hitters who handle pitchers especially well must be "cousins." George Selkirk was not related to Robert Joyce but he could have been. On May 27, 1939, he hit two home runs for the Yankees against the Philadelphia A's pitcher. Selkirk hit two more home runs when Joyce was used in a relief role the next day. That gave Selkirk four home runs in four at-bats against the same pitcher over a two-day span.

The 10 Commandments
of Pitching

By Carl Hubbell

1. You must have a limber arm.
2. You must have a rugged physique.
3. A good repertoire is a must (fast-ball, breaking ball, change-of-pace, perhaps one other).
4. Control is essential.
5. You must have competitive courage.
6. You must have stamina and endurance.
7. You must be intelligent.
8. Know how to size up a hitter.
9. Be confident.
10. Make sure you can field your position.

The Gashouse Gang

The wild, fun-loving Cardinals of 1934 won the nickname "the Gashouse Gang" when they wore unwashed uniforms during a game in New York. With no clean suits available, and no time to wash the uniforms they wore in a Boston doubleheader on Saturday, the Cards donned the same outfits for their Sunday game against the Giants. Writer Garry Schumacher, referring to the rundown Gashouse area of New York, said, "They look like a gang from the Gashouse district! A real Gashouse gang!"

happened. Charley broke last from the gate, stayed last, and finished far to the rear. After making the appropriate derogatory comments to their bookie/teammate, most of the team left.

The next day, when a Chicago player pulled up lame, one quick-witted companion called him "Charley horse."

Another horse named Charley, overworked from pulling a cab in the days before the automobile, helped drag the infield for the Sioux City club of the Western League in 1889. The aged, tired horse seemed to suffer from arthritis—moving each leg with difficulty. It wasn't long before players started referring to any limp or leg injury as a "charley horse."

Chinese home run—A dated term used primarily to describe the short home runs at New York's Polo Grounds, which was just 258 feet down the line in right field and 280 in left, the term, like many others, is of disputed origin.

New York Tribune sports editor Bill McGeehan used it in the early '20s after noting that the close right-field fence looked thick, low, and not very formidable—like the Great Wall of China.

T. A. Dorgan of the *Journal*, also in the '20s, meant the phrase to mean a home run that wasn't worthy of being a home run. He disliked the Giants in general, and manager John McGraw in particular, and enjoyed deprecating Giant victories.

Diamond—When Alexander Cartwright sketched his first "regulation" baseball field, with bases 90 feet apart, in 1845, it was immediately called a diamond—even though it was actually a square. A true diamond has two acute and two obtuse angles, but the infield has four 90-degree angles. Since the diamond is best viewed from the catcher's perspective, however, the diamond reference is apparent.

Baseball's use of the term also stems from the urban planning of the 19th century. Towns were generally built around a square, featuring public buildings. In the east, that square was called a diamond.

Doubleheader—Two engines on the same train or two games on the same day. No dispute here. The first baseball twin bill was played October 9, 1886, Philadelphia at Detroit.

Eephus—Later used to describe a pitch that had a high arc as it slipped through the strike zone, the term's originator was Lefty Gomez, a zany Yankee star who eventually made the Hall of Fame. He described it as that certain something that marked fine pitching from poor. "Eephus is that little extry you have on your good days," he said.

Fan—During the late 1880s German-born Chris Von der Ahe, owner of the St. Louis Browns in the American Association, was discussing a St. Louis spectator who never missed a game. "Dot feller is a regular FAN-a-tic," he said, accenting the first syllable of the last word. Sportswriter Sam Crane picked up on it.

Foot in the bucket—A hitter who fails to pivot properly when swinging because he's afraid the pitch will come too close to his

body has "his foot in the bucket."

Shirley Povich of *The Washington Post* first used the tag after hearing a sailor, watching such a batsman at the Norfolk Air Base, say, "There's a great hitter for you. He's got his heart and soul in the game and his rear-end in the dugout."

Fungo—Pioneer baseball writer Henry Chadwick referred to it in his *Baseball Reference*, published in 1867: "Fungo is a preliminary practice game in which one player takes the bat and tosses the ball up, hits it as it falls, and if the ball is caught on the fly the player catching it takes the bat. It is useless as practice in batting, but good for taking fly balls."

In modern baseball, coaches use special fungo bats to hit practice balls to fielders before the game. The bat is lighter and thinner than a regular bat, and some historians suggest its resiliency contributed to the term—fungus, fungeous, fungo. Others say the game of hitter and fielder chasing formed the phrase through a combination of "run" and "go."

Hit-and-run—The *Chicago Daily News* of 1899 made reference to this practice of starting the baserunner while ordering the batter to swing at the oncoming pitch, regardless of its location in the strike zone. The result may be (1) a stolen base for the runner if the batter misses the ball, (2) advancement from first to third on a single, or (3) avoidance of a double play if the batter hits a grounder.

Holdout—First used by the *New York Press* (1888) to describe a player who delayed in accepting salary terms, it caught on when Brooklyn pitcher Tommy Lovett held himself out of the game for the entire 1893 season in a salary dispute.

Hot corner—After Reds' third baseman Hick Carpenter caught seven line drives, a Cincinnati writer of 1889 wrote, "The Brooklyns had Old Hick on the hot corner all afternoon and it's a miracle he wasn't murdered."

K—Used to designate a strikeout victim, especially in scoring, the single initial was introduced by *New York Herald* baseball writer M. J. Kelly in 1868. Kelly, who used a system of letters to cover most situations in the game, hit upon *K* because it is the last letter of the word *struck*. He said *S* could not be used because it might be confused with shortstop.

Ladies Day—The tradition of admitting women free when accompanied by male escorts was one of the game's first promotions. It began when executives of the 1889 Cincinnati Reds noticed more females in the stands whenever handsome hurler Tony Mullane worked. The team advertised he would pitch every Monday, which would be Ladies Day. Mullane, who had black, wavy hair and a waved mustache, won 284 games in his career—helped, in part, by his loyal band of female supporters.

Murderers' Row—Great slugging teams, like the 1927 Yankees, are said to have a "Murderers' Row" (hitters who kill pitchers), but the phrase dates back to 1858, when an early baseball writer borrowed it from the isolated Death Row at The Tombs prison in New York.

Night ball—First referred to by name in *Morrison's Chicago Weekly*, 1910, it reached the majors at Cincinnati in 1935 after an earlier trial in the minor leagues.

On deck—A nautical term used to refer to the next hitter, its origin recalls the 1872 Belfast, Maine, sailor who also coined "at bat."

Rain check—Both theories of origination have merit. In pre-1900 baseball, heavy cardboard tickets were sold, but collected

"The Big Train"

Walter "the Big Train" Johnson threw such a lively fastball that its speed was compared to steam locomotives—the fastest form of transportation in the '20s.

Chug Handle

The 1944 Southern Association featured one entry with a historic name: the Chattanooga Choo-Choos. The team wore an artist's rendition of the famous Civil War engine, "The General," on its uniforms that season.

The French Connection

Players with red hair invariably acquire the nickname "Red," as in Red Schoendienst, Red Ruffing, or Red Lucas. Daniel J. "Rusty" Staub, whose hair could stop traffic, was such an immediate hit when traded from Houston to Montreal in 1969 that French-speaking Expos fans came up with the endearing term, "Le Grand Orange."

NICKNAMES

AH, GOOD MORNING, SISTER JONES,... AND WASN'T THE SERMON FINE?

DEACON McKECHNIE REALLY IS ONE....

during each game and used again. When a game was shortened by rain one day in 1889, New Orleans owner Abner Powell saw numerous fence-jumpers and complimentary guests join the paying customers in line for new tickets. He devised the idea of a perforated rain-check stub, and the innovation was so successful it is still in use.

In the majors, the Detroit Baseball Association came up with the first rain checks, circa 1890. They read: "Rain check. In case rain interrupts game of this date before three innings are played, this check will admit bearer to grounds for next league game only."

Rhubarb—Garry Schumacher of *The New York Journal-American* used this word from his boyhood to describe a 1938 Dodger/Giant brawl. He explained that winners of fights in Brooklyn would invariably force the losers to swallow terrible-tasting rhubarb tonic.

Rookie—First mentioned in print by the *Chicago Record-Herald* in 1913, this term for a freshman player may have stemmed from chess, where the rook must wait its turn and is often the last piece to be used as the game opens. In the early days of the game, older players shunned first-year players, who were the last to receive the attention of their teammates.

Scout—The modern baseball scout recommends players for his team, but the original scout—before the Cartwright rules of 1845—was something else. He was a second catcher who played far to the rear of the regular catcher. He grabbed passed balls and wild pitches and fielded "hits" that landed near him. (Fouls were then unknown and batters could run on hits behind the plate as well as in front of it.)

Shutouts—Scoreless games had been called "Chicago's" because a White Stockings pitcher hurled the first one, but a Troy, New York, writer came up with this more appropriate term—borrowed from the world of horse racing—in 1879.

Southpaw—In a world of right handed people, left-handers have always stood out—because they are a small minority. Right-handers seeking to coin an appropriate phrase to describe them derived "southpaw" because most ballparks are laid out in such a way that the afternoon sun is behind the batter and usually in the eyes of the right fielder. Such an alignment makes the home-to-first-base-line run almost directly east and west. Therefore, a lefthander pitches with an arm that faces south.

Texas Leaguer—When Art Sunday, a player with Houston of the Texas League, joined Toledo of the International League in 1889, he immediately proceeded to collect a series of bloop hits that were too far out for the infielders but too far in for the outfielders. Because he had just come from the Texas League, his scratch hits were dubbed "Texas Leaguers."

Former vice president John Nance Garner presented another theory in 1940: he said he himself created the term during his ball-playing days in Texas. Unable to hit the ball hard, Garner concentrated on popping the ball over the infielders' heads. Others followed suit and the practice became known as "hitting Texas Leaguers"—or so Garner said.

Umpire—In its original Middle English form, "noumper" means an extra man, called in when two persons disagreed. The third party was considered not to be an equal or peer of the disagreeing persons. The "n" was eventually dropped, and "umpire"

Minor League Nicknames

Minor league clubs and nicknames undergo constant change, but many minor nicknames are worth remembering for their originality.

Here's a sampling from May 1936:

American Association—Columbus Red Birds, Indianapolis Indians, Kansas City Blues, Louisville Colonels, Milwaukee Brewers, Minneapolis Millers, St. Paul Saints, Toledo Mud Hens

International League—Albany Senators, Baltimore Orioles, Buffalo Bisons, Montreal Royals, Newark Bears, Rochester Red Wings, Syracuse Chiefs, Toronto Maple Leafs

Pacific Coast League—Los Angeles Angels, San Francisco Missions, San Francisco Seals, Oakland Oaks, Portland Beavers, Sacramento Solons, San Diego Padres, Seattle Indians

Southern Association—Atlanta Crackers, Birmingham Barons, Chattanooga Lookouts, Knoxville Smokies, Little Rock Travelers, Memphis Chicks, Nashville Volunteers, New Orleans Pelicans

Texas League—Beaumont Exporters, Dallas Steers, Fort Worth Cats, Galveston Buccaneers, Houston Buffaloes, Oklahoma City Indians, San Antonio Missions, Tulsa Oilers

New York/Pennsylvania League—Allentown Brooks, Binghamton Triplets, Elmira Pioneers, Hazleton Mountaineers, Scranton Miners, Wilkes/Barre Barons, Williamsport Grays, York Roses

Western League—Cedar Rapids Raiders, Davenport Blue Sox, Des Moines Demons, Omaha Robin Hoods, Sioux City Cowboys, Waterloo Hawks

Piedmont League—Asheville Tourists, Durham Bulls, Norfolk Tars, Portsmouth Cubs, Richmond Colts, Rocky Mount Red Sox

South Atlantic League—Augusta Tigers, Columbia Senators, Columbus Red Birds, Jacksonville Tars, Macon Peaches, Savannah Indians

Cotton States League—Clarksdale Ginners, Cleveland Athletics, El Dorado Lions, Greenville Bucks, Greenwood Little Giants, Helena Seaporters, Jackson Senators, Pine Bluff Judges

East Texas League—Gladewater Bears, Henderson Oilers, Jacksonville Jax, Kilgore Braves, Longview Cannibals, Marshall Orphans, Palestine Pals, Tyler Trojans

Middle Atlantic League—Akron Yankees, Charleston Senators, Dayton Ducks, Huntington Red Birds, Canton Terriers, Portsmouth Pirates, Zanesville Greys, Johnstown Jawns

Western Association—Bartlesville Mustangs, Hutchinson Larks, Joplin Miners, Muskogee Seals, Ponca City Angels, Springfield Cardinals

Arkansas/Missouri League—Bentonville Mustangs, Cassville Blues, Fayetteville Bears, Monett Red Birds, Rogers Lions, Siloam Springs Travelers

Evangeline League—Abbeville Athletics, Alexandria Aces, Jeanerette Blues, Lafayette White Sox, Lake Charles Skippers, New Iberia Cardinals, Opelousas Indians, Rayne Rice Birds

Florida State League—Daytona Beach Islanders, DeLand Reds, Gainesville G-Men, Palatka Azaleas, Sanford Lookouts, St. Augustine Saints

Northern League—Crookston Pirates, Duluth Dukes, Eau Claire Bears, Fargo/Moorhead Twins, Jamestown Jimmies, Superior Blues, Wausau Lumberjacks, Winnipeg Maroons

Georgia/Florida League—Albany Travelers, Americus Cardinals, Cordele Reds, Moultrie Packers, Tallahassee Capitals, Thomasville Orioles

Pennsylvania State Association—Monessen Indians, Charleroi Tigers, Greensburg Red Wings, Jeannette Little Pirates, McKeesport Tubers, Butler Yankees

became part of baseball's phraseology when the rules were written for the original Knickerbocker club in 1845.

Whitewash—Its current double meaning includes the old context of a shutout victory. The old *Ball Players' Chronicle* used the term first in 1867 when it reported, "A blank score in Albany, New York, is called a blind; in Connecticut, it is called a whitewash." A white wash, as in laundry, is said to be pure as a pitcher's shutout—because a runless game leaves the pitcher's record untainted.

Quotes

"Nice guys finish last." It came from baseball—from Leo (the Lip) Durocher, longtime player and manager, in 1948. Never at a loss for words, Durocher was talking to a group of Brooklyn writers when he gazed across the field and noticed his contemporary, Giants manager Mel Ott.

"Look at Ott," he told the reporters. "He's such a nice guy and they'll finish eighth for him." Spying Bobby Thomson, Sid Gordon, and other Giant home-run stars, Durocher added, "All nice guys and they'll finish eighth."

The National League had 8 teams until 1962, when expansion swelled the circuit to 10, but it wasn't long after he made the statement that writers had delivered the classic quote to the American public. Since its quick adoption into everyday usage, the substitution from "eighth" to "last" was immediate. But the meaning never changed.

Baseball is a gold mine that could start its own version of *Bartlett's Familiar Quotations*.

Take this one, from writer Grantland Rice: "It's not whether you win or lose, it's how you play the game."

Connie Mack, whose worst season in a 50-year managerial career might have been 1916, when his A's lost 117 games, contributed another classic: "Well, you can't win them all." The 1914 A's had finished first.

And Babe Ruth, after an embarrassing strikeout, summarized the game succinctly: "You're a hero one day and a bum the next."

Not all baseball quotes have found their way into common use, but most make common sense—and are worth recording as part of the game's legacy.

Famous Lines

Executive Branch Rickey, talking about the controversial Leo Durocher, described the fiery manager in no uncertain terms: "He can take a bad situation and make it immediately worse."

O'Rourke Who?

Of the two O'Rourkes who starred in the pre-1900 National League, James Henry won the nickname "Orator" while Timothy Patrick was called "Voiceless."

What's in a Name?

Teams have changed nicknames more than 40 times this century—often returning to monikers used in the past. Here's the complete list:

Year	New Name	Old Name
1901	Cleveland Bluebirds	Cleveland Lake Shores
1901	Detroit Tigers	Detroit Wolverines
1902	Cleveland Broncos	Cleveland Bluebirds
1902	St. Louis Browns	Milwaukee Brewers
1903	Boston Pilgrims	Boston Somersets*
1903	Cleveland Naps	Cleveland Broncos
1903	New York Highlanders	Baltimore Orioles
1905	Washington Senators	Washington Nationals
1907	Boston Doves	Boston Beaneaters
1907	Boston Red Sox	Boston Pilgrims
1911	Boston Rustlers	Boston Doves
1911	Brooklyn Dodgers	Brooklyn Superbas
1912	Boston Braves	Boston Rustlers
1912	Cleveland Molly McGuires	Cleveland Naps
1913	New York Yankees	New York Highlanders
1914	Brooklyn Robins	Brooklyn Dodgers
1915	Cleveland Indians	Cleveland Molly McGuires
1932	Brooklyn Dodgers	Brooklyn Robins
1936	Boston Bees	Boston Braves
1941	Boston Braves	Boston Bees
1943	Philadelphia Blue Jays	Philadelphia Phillies
1944	Cincinnati Red Legs	Cincinnati Reds
1945	Philadelphia Phillies	Philadelphia Blue Jays
1946	Cincinnati Reds	Cincinnati Red Legs
1953	Milwaukee Braves	Boston Braves
1954	Baltimore Orioles	St. Louis Browns
1954	Cincinnati Red Legs	Cincinnati Reds
1955	Kansas City Athletics	Philadelphia Athletics
1958	Los Angeles Dodgers	Brooklyn Dodgers
1958	San Francisco Giants	New York Giants
1961	Cincinnati Reds	Cincinnati Red Legs
1961	Minnesota Twins	Washington Senators
1962	Kansas City A's	Kansas City Athletics
1963	Houston Colt .45s	Houston Colts
1965	California Angels	Los Angeles Angels
1965	Houston Astros	Houston Colt .45s
1966	Atlanta Braves	Milwaukee Braves
1968	Oakland A's	Kansas City A's
1970	Milwaukee Brewers	Seattle Pilots
1972	Texas Rangers	Washington Senators
1987	Oakland Athletics	Oakland A's
1997	Anaheim Angels	California Angels
2005	Washington Nationals	Montreal Expos
2005	Los Angeles Angels of Anaheim	Anaheim Angels
2008	Tampa Bay Rays	Tampa Bay Devil Rays

* The Somersets also were variously known as the Plymouth Rocks, Puritans, and Speedboys.

Managers are eventually fired—scapegoats when their teams go bad—but Birdie Tebbetts put the thought into words: "This is pure insanity. We strive desperately to become managers of big-league clubs, and all the time we're fully aware it's a job from which we have to be fired."

Joe Kuhel, one of many men whose managing could not lift the Washington Senators out of the American League cellar, made a profound pronouncement the day he was axed: "You can't make chicken salad out of chicken feathers."

Solly Hemus, who managed the Cardinals years later, agreed. "I'd say managing makes the difference in about 10 games," he said.

When he ran the Yankees, Joe McCarthy didn't have to do anything, according to rival pilot Jimmie Dykes. "He's just a push-button manager," Dykes declared.

Casey Stengel, who absorbed similar charges years later, said, "I couldn't have done it without my players."

On his deathbed, George Stallings imagined himself still in the dugout, watching his pitcher struggle to throw the ball over the plate. "Oh, those bases on balls," he moaned. Frankie Frisch picked up the cry when he left the Cardinals and went to the Pirates.

Sometimes it's best not to say anything. New York Giants field boss Bill Terry learned that lesson in 1934, when writers asked what he thought of the cross-borough Dodgers. "Oh, is Brooklyn still in the league?" he asked. The Dodgers were nothing more than spoilers that year and the next—but they used the statement as a war cry and helped knock the Giants out of at least one sure pennant.

In the '50s, the Dodgers used double-talk to knock out their own credibility in town—but they didn't need any with a move to Los Angeles in the offing. Owner Walter O'Malley told the press shortly before the shift, "My roots are in Brooklyn, so why should I move?"

Branch Rickey, Dodger executive, inspired a player, Chuck Connors (who traded baseball for television stardom), to talk about his reputation for tight economics: "It was easy to figure out Mr. Rickey's thinking about contracts. He had both players and money and didn't like to see the two of them mix."

Stingy with the dollar, Rickey was quick with the compliment—particularly for one of his own men. Of Eddie Stanky, the scrappy Dodger infielder who later managed several clubs, Rickey said, "He can't hit, he can't run, and he can't throw—all he can do is beat you."

A shrewd trader, Rickey is sometimes credited with saying, "The trades you don't make are your best ones."

Umpire Bill Klem might have been thinking of Rickey when he said, "There are 154 games in a season and you can find 154 reasons why your club should have won every one of them."

Of umpires, American League president Ban Johnson noted, "A good umpire is the umpire you don't even notice. He'll be there all afternoon, but when the game is over, you won't recall his name."

One-time National League president Harry Pulliam had one of sports' classic quotes on a placard he kept on his desk. It read, "Take nothing for granted in baseball." That meant ninth-inning uprisings, surprising pennant races, unusual trades, and classic quotes from colorful characters.

The Things Players Say

Joe Garagiola, player and broadcaster, knew the truth of Pulliam's placard. Here's how he describes the sport: "Baseball is just a boy's game that men play to make a living."

Other players have also contributed to the quote book.

Wee Willie Keeler, whose flood of hits between 1890 and 1910 seemed to have eyes, was ready with a quip when questioned about his proficiency at the plate. "I hit 'em where they ain't," he said.

Ty Cobb, who also began before the century changed, once fought with a roommate over first rights to the hotel bathtub. "I got to be first—all of the time," said Cobb, whose .367 lifetime batting average ranks at the head of the list.

"Shoeless" Joe Jackson, White Sox star, was first in the hearts of Chicago youngsters who supposedly approached him as he emerged from the room where game-fixing charges were being heard in 1920. One of them blurted, "Say it ain't so, Joe."

Yankee pitcher Lefty Gomez was more fortunate. Finding success and a receptive press in the '30s, he announced, "I'd rather be lucky than good."

Not long afterward, a young catching prospect joined the club and received valuable tips from the star who preceded him. Yogi Berra admitted, "Bill Dickey is learning me all his experiences."

Ralph Kiner, who made the Hall of Fame on the strength of his home-run heroics, always maintained, "Home-run hitters drive Cadillacs, singles hitters drive Fords."

Strikeout victims don't last long, umpire Bill Byron told a rookie one day: "You'll have to learn before you're older, you can't hit the ball with the bat on your shoulder."

Roger Maris and Mickey Mantle kept swinging in 1961, and closed with home-run totals of 61 and 54, respectively, the best teammates have done in one season. Talking about his senior partner, Maris said, "It's smarter to give the big man four balls for one base than one ball for four bases."

Maris and Mantle were fine on defense as well as offense, but many major leaguers aren't. Some are good-field, no-hit; others are good-hit, no-field. Mike Gonzales coined this phrase when he looked at a new prospect: "This player—she's good field, no hit."

Feminine references are common in baseball. As a player, Durocher once said, "If I were playing third base and my mother were rounding third with the run that was going to beat us, I'd trip her. Oh, I'd pick her up and brush her off and say, 'Sorry, Mom.' But nobody beats me."

During a 1934 radio interview Detroit pitcher Schoolboy Rowe suddenly thought of his fiancée and casually remarked into the mike, "How'm I doin', Edna?" The media and rival dugouts never let him forget it, and the words live today.

So does Babe Herman's statement about his young son's upcoming birthday. "Buy an encyclopedia for my kid?" he said. "He'll learn to ride a two-wheeler or walk!"

As a broadcaster in wartime, Dizzy Dean was not allowed to give weather conditions. So he said, "I can't tell you why this game is stopped, but if you'll stick your head out the window you'll know what it's all about."

The loquacious Dean closed with this rejoinder: "Don't fail to miss tomorrow's game!"

The Mahatma

Branch Rickey's nickname, "The Mahatma," was a creation of well-known writer Tom Meany. The journalist had been reading *Inside Asia*, wherein John Gunther described Mohandas "Mahatma" Gandhi as "an incredible combination of Jesus Christ, Tammany Hall, and your father." Meany noted that Rickey was part paternal, part political, and part pontifical. He applied the Gandhi moniker, and it stuck.

New Nicknames of Note

Nicknames of recent vintage worth remembering: Orlando "the Baby Bull" Cepeda, Jim "the Toy Cannon" Wynn, Zoilo "Zorro" Versalles, George "the Stork" Theodore, Willie "the Say Hey Kid" Mays, Doug "the Red Rooster" Rader, Larvell "Sugar Bear" Blanks, Greg "the Bull" Luzinski, Roderick Edwin "Hot Rod" Kanehl, Frank "Hondo" Howard, George "the Boomer" Scott, Ralph "the Roadrunner" Garr, Fred "Chicken" Stanley, Tim "Crazy Horse" Foli, Ed "the Glider" Charles, Bob "the Macaroni Pony" Coluccio, Marshall "Sheriff" Bridges, Tom "the Blade" Hall, Al "the Mad Hungarian" Hrabosky, Bob "Hoot" Gibson, Sherman "Roadblock" Jones, Bill "the Spaceman" Lee, Bill "the Singer Throwing Machine" Singer, J. R. "High Rise" Richard, Phil "the Vulture" Regan, and Rick "Buzz" Sawyer.

Shot in the Dark

Outspoken outfielder Jimmy Piersall was once ejected from a game for telling an umpire with the same name as an assassinated president, "They shot the wrong McKinley."

Clever Name

When the original Washington Senators moved to the Twin Cities of Minneapolis/St. Paul in 1961, they became the first team to identify with an entire state. The Minnesota Twins also became the first club whose hat initials were different than their team name. The "TC" on team hats stood for Twin Cities.

Call Me What?

The Angels have changed their name four times without ever leaving Southern California. Created as a 1961 expansion team, they were the Los Angeles Angels from 1961 to 1964, the California Angels from 1965 to 1996, and the Anaheim Angels from 1997 to 2005, when owner Arte Moreno changed the name to Los Angeles Angels of Anaheim. The city of Anaheim lost a four-year court battle against the change.

Time Out

Two-sport star Deion Sanders earned the nickname "Prime Time" for his flamboyant demeanor. When members of the 1997 Cincinnati Reds met his three-year-old son Deion Jr., they called him "Half Time."

How About Costanza?

George is the real first name of Tom Seaver, Sparky Anderson, and Ken Griffey Jr.

After Dean won 30 games in 1934, the next pitcher to reach that almost-insurmountable plateau was Denny McLain, who was 31-6 for the pennant-winning Detroit Tigers of 1968. That spring, the 24-year-old right-hander wondered aloud how many games an above-average pitcher could win in a year. Pitching coach Johnny Sain quoted author Norman Hill: "Anything you can conceive or believe, you can achieve."

Pitcher Mudcat Grant, who won 21 games for the 1965 Twins after some tips from Sain, praised the coach: "That man Sain sure puts biscuits in your pan."

Lefty Gomez also did well financially, but recognized the signs of age late in his career. "I'm throwing twice as hard," he said, "but the ball is getting there half as fast."

Speed was never a problem for Bob Feller, who pitched 12 one-hitters. But recognition was. "Pitching a one-hitter," he said years later, "is like being the second man on the moon. Nobody wants to know you."

Ping Bodie wasn't fast enough; he was thrown out trying to steal second, prompting a remark from witness Bugs Baer: "His head was full of larceny, but his feet were honest."

Mike "King" Kelly of the Chicago White Stockings, who popularized the hit-and-run play, was successful 53 times in 1886 and hit .388 as Chicago beat Detroit in the race for the National League flag. Enchanted by his flamboyance, fans couldn't wait for him to run so they could scream, "Slide, Kelly, slide!"

Kelly never played for Brooklyn, which would have loved to add the slide slogan to its all-star collection of one-liners. About the loud-mouthed but losing Dodgers of the '30s, Eddie Murphy cracked, "If the Dodgers aren't careful, overconfidence might cost them seventh place."

The bumbling Bums of that period developed the famous line—"Wait 'til next year!"—which has been plagiarized hundreds of times.

Baseball Talk

While terms and quotes from the game are widely known, the language of the players themselves is not. Communication on the field is an art, much like discussions among doctors behind closed hospital doors. Moreover, it is constantly changing.

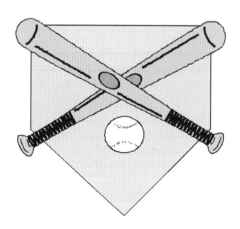

For years, a player who was hit on the hands "pulled a Brenegan," after an obscure third-string catcher who played for the Pirates in 1914. The receiver in question, Sam Brenegan, spent almost all his time in the bullpen, but broke into occasional regular games. Once, when inserted into a close contest, he was hit on the thumb with a pitched ball. Instead of chasing the ball, which rolled back to the screen, he shook his thumb at the plate while a run scored. He was returned to the minors soon afterward.

Likewise, an "Arlie Latham" was a too-hot-to-handle infield smash, named after a pre-1900 infielder who would practice safety first, rather than risk injury on hard shots.

A "Big Bill," named for Bill Bradley of the Indians, was a high infield bounder, later called a Baltimore chop. Bradley specialized in hitting such balls when called upon as a pinch-hitter.

Many phrases have survived the test of time. Walter Johnson's fastball was called "the pneumonia ball" because hitters were said to feel a rush of cold air after the pitch passed them. The modern equivalent would be "Johnson is *bringing it*" or "*throwing aspirins.*"

When a hitter or fielder is *handcuffed*, he is unable to get around on an inside fastball. A *gopher* is a long hit (especially a home run) because batters "go for" four bases.

Good fielders *can pick it* but bad fielders often *kick it*. Fast batters who bunt *lay one down* and weak hitters, unable to hit anything hard, can't even manage a *loud foul*.

In the doghouse means in trouble—in or out of baseball—and one way pitchers can get there in the eyes of rival hitters is to *stick it in their ears*, or throw close to their heads. Such a pitch is commonly called a *beanball* or *duster*. Pitchers who disagree with their catcher's calls *shake them off* in an effort to hang *size 4 collars* on enemy hitters (no hits in four at-bats).

Pull hitters will come around on the ball and hit it to their natural side of the diamond with consistency—right-handed batters to left and left-handed batters to right. But *spray* hitters cannot be classified. Batters who hit for high average generally *go with the pitch* even if it means *hitting to the opposite field* (hitting the ball where it's pitched even though a right-handed hitter may sacrifice power to hit the ball to right field instead of left).

Taking a cut means two things: swinging the bat or finishing on the wrong end of a contract discussion. A *hot dog* or *showboat* is a player with ability who likes to show off, usually a fielder. If he's not talented, he'll probably get little more than a *cup of coffee* (brief trial) in the majors. That's especially true of players who *choke in the clutch* (fold under pressure).

A *bad-ball hitter* reaches for pitches outside the strike zone but may very well be successful (Yogi Berra is a noted example). Curveballs come in good and bad variety—*jughandle* and *nickel*, respectively. Managers play *percentage baseball*, or *go by the book*, if they *platoon* extensively, using only right-handed batters against left-handed pitchers and vice versa. A hitter who refers to a pitcher as his *cousin* means he hits the hurler well; most modern hitters prefer to keep their boasting to a minimum for fear of riling their favorite pitcher.

Baserunners don't take liberties with an outfielder who has a *gun* for an arm, but fast men often outrun infield grounders to

"Baseball's Sad Lexicon"

These are the saddest of possible
words:
   "Tinker to Evers to Chance."
Trio of bear cubs, and fleeter than birds,
   Tinker and Evers and Chance.
Ruthlessly pricking our gonfalon bubble,
   Making a Giant hit into a double—
Words that are heavy with nothing but
   trouble:
"Tinker to Evers to Chance."

                —Franklin P. Adams

"Take Me Out to the Ballgame"

Take me out to the ballgame,
Take me out to the crowd.
Buy me some peanuts and Cracker Jack;
I don't care if I never get back.
So let's root, root, root for the home team,
If they don't win it's a shame.
For it's 1, 2, 3 strikes you're out
At the old ballgame.

                —Jack Norworth

NICKNAMES

PIE TRAYNOR WAS ACTUALLY NUTS ABOUT ... PIE....

SLUP SLUP

The war-shortened season of 1917 ended with the Chicago White Sox wearing this special patriotic logo on their World Series uniforms.

make *leg hits*. Players who prefer privacy are *loners*, while colorful characters are often branded as *flaky*. A *scatter-arm* infielder frequently makes wild throws on balls he reaches but is often victimized by *seeing-eye balls*, or *bleeders*, which find their way through the infield, converting certain outs into hits.

Before air travel became commonplace, leagues that did most of their travel by bus were known as *horse leagues* and a player who complained about the conditions—or anything else—was known as *Alibi Ike*, as in the Ring Lardner story of that name.

Then, as now, athletes were required to *bear down* and play *heads-up baseball* or be accused of *jaking it* (loafing)—the most serious accusation that can be hurled at a player.

Team Nicknames

Nicknames have always been an integral part of baseball—both for teams and persons connected with the game.

Alexander Cartwright's Knickerbocker Baseball Club of New York in 1845 supplied the nickname of New York's National Basketball Association team a century later and paved the way for other early clubs to adopt an appropriate moniker.

Even before the Civil War, newspapers were reporting baseball, with writers referring to teams like the New Yorks, the Brooklyns, or the Bostons. Nicknames were badly needed—especially after professional baseball introduced the concept of placing more than one team in a given city.

In 1864 the Athletic Club of Philadelphia was formed—and the name Athletics remained with the team after it joined the American League in 1901 and through franchise shifts to Kansas City and Oakland. Because the club wore a script "A" on its uniform hat and shirt, writers eventually adopted the abbreviated "A's."

The 1948 World Champion Cleveland Indians wore this patch on their sleeves.

The name Cincinnati Reds also predates the start of organized ball in 1876. The club was known as the Red Stockings two years before it began paying players in 1869, and press box occupants, seeking to save time and space, shortened that to Reds, though Redlegs was used during periods when it was politically dangerous to be identified as "Reds."

Another historic name—and a logical one—is Baltimore Orioles, from the bird. It was applied whenever that city had a big-league club—even though it erased the nickname Browns when St. Louis moved to Baltimore in 1954. Nor could "Orioles" be retained when the original O's shifted to New York after the 1902 campaign.

Team nicknames have long, colorful histories. Of the original 16 clubs that existed before expansion in 1961, only the Pittsburgh Pirates retained their original moniker, though writers sometimes refer to them as Bucs, a shortened version of Buccaneers.

Here's a closer look at club nicknames:

National League

Arizona Diamondbacks—The Phoenix franchise, expected to draw from a vast surrounding region, began play in 1998 after taking the nickname of a dangerous reptile indigenous to the desert.

Atlanta Braves—Braves, also used in Boston and Milwaukee, began in 1912 when owner Jim Gaffney was a Tammany Hall chieftain. Previously, the team was called Doves (after president George B. Dovey) and Beaneaters. After a disastrous 1935 season, management changed the name of the Braves to the Bees, hoping for a fresh start, but it never caught on.

Chicago Cubs—Originally called White Stockings (assumed and shortened by the AL team of 1901), the nickname became Colts after manager Cap Anson appeared on stage in Syracuse, New York, in a play specially written for him in 1896, *A Runaway Colt*. Cowboys and Broncos, natural derivatives, followed, and Rainmakers was used briefly. Sportswriters Fred Hayner and George Rice coined Cubs (and the Little Bears image) when the team had many young players in 1901.

Cincinnati Reds—Red Stockings, Redlegs, Reds.

Colorado Rockies—Like the National Hockey League team that once bore the same name, the 1993 expansion entry sought to represent the entire Rocky Mountain region rather than its host city of Denver.

Miami Marlins—Unlike the venerable Miami Marlins of minor-league vintage, this 1993 expansion team attracts fans from all over the state.

Los Angeles Dodgers—Called Bridegrooms because three 1888 players got married, the team won the 1889 American Association flag and took the title Superbas after a vaudeville troupe, "Hanlon's Superbas." Also called Atlantics, Kings, and Robins—after colorful manager Wilbert Robinson—the name Dodgers is an abbreviated version of Trolley Dodgers, an unkind nickname given turn-of-the-century Brooklynites by New Yorkers.

Milwaukee Brewers—A time-honored name for minor league clubs in Milwaukee, the capital of the brewing industry, the Seattle Pilots assumed it when they transferred to Wisconsin from

DEAR FRIEND:

UNDOUBTEDLY YOU KNOW THAT THE NICKNAME SE-
LECTED FOR NEW YORK'S NEW NATIONAL LEAGUE BASE-
BALL TEAM IS "METS".

AS WE EXPLAINED TO THE PRESS, OUR CHOICE WAS
BASED ON THE FOLLOWING FIVE FACTORS:

1. IT HAS RECEIVED PUBLIC AND PRESS ACCEPTANCE.

2. IT IS CLOSELY RELATED TO OUR CORPORATE NAME—
METROPOLITAN BASEBALL CLUB, INC.

3. IT IS DESCRIPTIVE OF OUR ENTIRE METROPOLITAN
AREA.

4. IT HAS THE DESIRED BREVITY.

5. THE NAME HAS HISTORICAL BASEBALL BACKGROUND.

WE WANT TO THANK YOU FOR YOUR GREAT INTEREST
IN OUR EFFORTS TO FIND A NAME, AND FOR THE SUPPORT
THAT YOU VOICED IN OUR ENDEAVOR TO BRING YOU A
TEAM IN 1962 OF WHICH WE WILL ALL BE PROUD.

METROPOLITAN BASEBALL CLUB, INC.

Charles A. Hurth

GENERAL MANAGER

Washington State in 1970, just one year after their creation. The Pilots had been named for the area's giant aircraft manufacturing industry.

New York Mets—This 1962 addition to the NL, officially called Metropolitan Baseball Club of New York, actually borrowed its abbreviated nickname from the American Association team of the 1880s.

Philadelphia Phillies—Once spelled Fillies, as in horses, the club was called Quakers briefly and is often referred to as Red Quakers—a nickname for a nickname—because of its uniforms. In 1944, exasperated team officials who had heard their club called the "Futile Phillies" for too many years, conducted a name-change contest and renamed the team Blue Jays. The winning entry in a contest that produced 5,064 letters and 634 different suggestions was submitted by a Philadelphia woman who received a $100 war bond as a prize. Mrs. John L. Crooks picked the name, she said, "because it reflects a new team spirit. The blue jay is colorful in personality and plumage. His plumage is a brilliant blue, a color the Phillies could use decoratively and psychologically." One of the more appropriate losing names was "Stinkers." Anyhow, the name Blue Jays failed to stick.

Pittsburgh Pirates—Because management successfully signed a deserting Players League star who rightfully belonged to another club, the moniker took in 1891. Writers also called the team Bucs, derived from Buccaneers. When the team made a surprise pennant march in 1960, broadcaster Bob Prince keyed the fans' war cry of "Beat 'em, Bucs!"

St. Louis Cardinals—Often called Cards or Redbirds, the nickname changed from the original Maroons when the team uniforms changed just before the turn of the century. A female fan, near the press box, noticed the new suits and declared, "What a lovely shade of cardinal!" Writers heard her and the name stuck.

San Diego Padres—This 1969 expansion franchise assumed the name of the old Pacific Coast League team it replaced. The name reflects the region's Spanish heritage.

San Francisco Giants—The nickname traveled west from New York, where its 17 pennants established a tradition that could not be broken by a franchise shift. Manager Jim Mutrie, in 1885, was thrilled with a particular play and jumped to his feet shouting, "My Giants!" The club had previously been called Green Stockings and, after making its National League debut in red-tinged uniforms in 1876, the Mutuals.

Washington Nationals—A 1969 expansion team named after a World's Fair, the Montreal Expos moved to D.C. for the 2005 season and assumed a nickname once applied to the old Washington Senators (an American League team that became the Minnesota Twins in 1961).

American League

Baltimore Orioles—As St. Louis Browns before 1954, the club was named for the brown trimmings on its outfits, but often dubbed "Brownies" because of its inept play.

Boston Red Sox—Once called Pilgrims, then Puritans, then Somersets (after owner Charles Somers), the Red Sox nickname is still one of the oldest in baseball. Bosox is a common abbreviation.

Chicago White Sox—Once the Invaders, the club assumed the discarded nickname of its NL counterpart early in the century but reverted to a shortened form created by sportswriters Carl Green and I. E. Sanborn. They knew headline writers would have a tough time; even now, many newsmen call the club Chisox.

Cleveland Indians—First called Forest Citys, later Molly McGuires (for many Irish players), Blues (for uniforms), Spiders (for players' dexterity), and Naps (for player/manager Napoleon Lajoie) before writers labeled the club Indians in an informal poll. Indians once lived on the shores of Lake Erie.

Detroit Tigers—Because Michigan is the Wolverine State, the Tigers had that nickname before *Detroit Free Press* newsman Phil J. Reid noticed the blue-and-orange striped stockings on the 1901 club. Reminded of the Princeton colors, he gave the team the moniker of the Ivy League college's clubs.

Houston Astros—This 1962 expansion team was first the Colts and then the Colt .45s before moving into the Astrodome three years later. The transition to Astros was a natural, since Houston is the home of the Manned Space Flight Center.

Kansas City Royals—Fans nicknamed the 1969 expansion club.

Los Angeles Angels of Anaheim—The 1961 expansion club took the name of the Los Angeles Angels, the Pacific Coast League team it replaced in the "City of Angels." When it moved down the freeway to Anaheim, it retained the nickname but took a state ID. It took a city ID in 1997 after Disney bought the team. The Angels are sometimes referred to as "Halos" because of a halo decoration on their uniforms.

Minnesota Twins—When the original Washington Senators moved to the twin cities of Minneapolis/St. Paul in 1961, they didn't wish to offend either, nor did they play in either—since their stadium was located in Bloomington. So they incorporated both into their name. In Washington, they had been known variously as the Senators and the Nationals—for obvious reasons. Writers called them "Nats" for short. Some called them "Griffs" after owner Clark Griffith.

New York Yankees—For 11 years after their transfer from Baltimore after the 1902 season, this club was called Highlanders because of the elevation of their park at the entrance to Manhattan Island. They were also called Hilltoppers for a spell before moving from that park into the Polo Grounds, which they shared with the Giants before Yankee Stadium opened in 1923. *New York Press* sports editor Jim Price and *New York Globe* newsman Mark Roth, later a Yankee official, decided either name was too long to fit into a headline and created the name Yankees.

Oakland A's—Merely an abbreviation of the ancient Athletics, the ancestral name from Philadelphia. The A's were called White Elephants for a spell because an elephant balancing a ball was the club's symbol for many years.

Seattle Mariners—The 1977 expansion team honors the nautical tradition of the Pacific Northwest.

Tampa Bay Rays—Another regional team, Tampa Bay plays its home games in St. Petersburg but draws from a wide area. Originally called Devil Rays when the expansion team began play in 1998, the name was often shortened in newspaper headlines. Since it also offended some religious groups, the team changed its

In their last season before moving to Baltimore, the 1953 St. Louis Browns wore an impish patch (above) on their sleeves. Far from the form that produced their only pennant in 1944, St. Louis was belittled for being "first in shoes, first in booze, and last in the American League." More respect was given the eagle insignia patch (below), worn by players returning from wartime service in 1945. It was sometimes called "the ruptured duck."

name and logo before the 2008 season. Its logo now incorporates the sun's rays instead of sea creatures.

Texas Rangers—The modern baseball team, inhabiting the Dallas/Fort Worth area after vacating Washington following the 1971 season, had a similar problem as that faced by the Minnesota Twins, who left Washington 11 years earlier: it did not wish to offend either "host" city but actually played elsewhere (in Arlington). So it took the traditional name of the state's famous lawmen.

Toronto Blue Jays—A fan contest provided the handle for this new 1977 entry, but the name was not new, as the Phils of the mid-'40s used it without much fan enthusiasm before reverting to tradition.

Player Nicknames

Player nicknames come mostly from the animal kingdom. They are too numerous to list in a single chapter, as they merit an entire book of their own, but a sampling of the best should illustrate the point.

Strong players were named after strong animals. Broad-shouldered slugger Jimmie Foxx was not only known as "Double-X" because of his name but also "the Beast" because of his brawn. Charlie "King Kong" Keller and Dave "Kong" Kingman also were strongmen of the batting box.

Jim "Hippo" Vaughn, who weighed 230 and pitched half of the famed double no-hit game of May 2, 1917, was opposed in the classic by 260-pound Fred Toney, the "Man Mountain from Tennessee."

Mike "Bear" Garcia and Fred "Big Bear" Hutchinson were two burly pitchers of note, while Dick "the Monster" Radatz dazzled rivals with a sizzling fastball as a Red Sox reliever of the '60s.

Lou Gehrig, the Yankees' durable slugger of the '30s, was "the Iron Horse," while New York Giants catcher Harry "the Horse" Danning took his name from a Damon Runyon character. Early in the century, Boston Braves pitcher Charley Pittinger was called "Horse Face" and the name became widely known because of its extensive use by Philadelphia writer Horace Fogel, later Phillies president. A female fan objected, writing that she found Pittinger one of the more handsome athletes, but Fogel answered in print, "Lady, can I help it if he looks like a horse?"

Charles "Old Hoss" Radbourn, who won 59 games in 1884, won his name because of his willingness to work, and perform well, whenever asked.

"Iron Man" McGinnity, who pitched for the Orioles and the Giants a decade later, also did yeoman service, pitching three doubleheaders—and winning them all—in August 1903. Few fans knew his name was Joe.

The most famous baseball mule, a close relative of the horse, was George "Mule" Haas, fleet center fielder for the Philadelphia A's and Chicago White Sox. Jimmie Dykes, the veteran manager who pinned the name on him, usually referred to him as "Donkey" or "the Donk." The Mule name fit so well that even Haas' wife used it. An ironic footnote: the name Haas, translated from German, means rabbit.

Frank Thomas, with the Pirates and the Cubs in the '50s, was known as "Donkey" because of his big ears. Ken "Hawk" Harrelson, got his name because of his nose, and "Turkey Mike" Donlin was nicknamed after his walk—or waddle—as was Ron Cey, "the Penguin," more than 50 years later.

Donlin, a star outfielder, missed two seasons when he joined his wife in a vaudeville act in 1909 and 1910, but returned to the New York Giants in 1911, delighting *New York Times* sportswriter Harry Cross. He wrote, "Turkey Mike has been dancing the boards with his wife for two seasons but he still does the turkey trot when he walks on the diamond." Donlin, who hated the moniker, warned Cross not to use it again.

Joe "Ducky" Medwick, a Hall of Fame outfielder who starred with the Gashouse Gang Cardinals, acquired his nickname in the St. Louis farm system when the press overheard an excited Medwick fan scream, "Isn't he a ducky wucky of a ballplayer!"

"Goose" Goslin's nickname seemed to fit his last name better than his given name of Leon Allen, while "Choo-Choo" Coleman, lifetime .197 hitter who chugged after pop fouls as an early-'60s catcher, had a much better calling card than Clarence. Coleman would be entirely forgotten if not for that alliterative nickname.

So would catcher Frank House, if not for his moniker, "the Pig." As a little boy, Frank had a natural lisp but considerable size. When someone would say, "You're big as a house," he would repeat "Pig House."

Tris Speaker, prematurely gray, was "the Gray Eagle" in the press but "Spoke" to teammates. The media referred to Ted Williams as "the Splendid Splinter," to Joe DiMaggio as "The Yankee Clipper," and to Tom Seaver as "the Franchise," but the names did not catch on among ballplayers.

The athletes preferred one or two words: George "Highpockets" Kelly, John "Tight Pants" Titus, Harry "Stinky" Davis, "Gettysburg" Eddie Plank, Fred "Cy" Williams, Hazen "KiKi" Cuyler, Edwin "Duke" Snider, Mike "Pinky" Higgins, Derrel "Bud" Harrelson, Edward "Whitey" Ford, Willie "Stretch" McCovey, Everett Lamar "Rocky" Bridges, Lawrence Peter "Yogi" Berra, and so many more.

Stories Behind the Nicknames

There's always a story behind the name. Charles Arthur "Dazzy" Vance dazzled the opposition with a great curve to go with a great

Larry Wayne Jones Jr. acquired his nickname as a boy when he proved as adept at baseball as his father. The "chip off the old block" soon answered to the nickname Chipper—even though New York fans tried unsuccessfully to rattle him by reciting his real name in derisive tones.

Leroy Paige played for so many different teams during his long career that he was commonly called "Satchel" or "Satch" since he was always schlepping a bag somewhere. Bill Veeck (right) gave the Negro Leagues legend a shot with Cleveland, then brought him to St. Louis when he bought the Browns.

Off Her Rocker

After grandson Len Barker pitched a perfect game in 1981, Tokie Lockhart said, "I'm very proud of him. I hope he does better next time."

Notes on Nicknames

Clarence William "Tilly" Walker, an early American League home-run leader, is one of several players who received nicknames regarded as feminine. William Chester "Baby Doll" Jacobson was another who acquired such a nickname when a fan yelled it out after his home run.

When New York's Italian fans screamed for Tony Lazzeri to hit balls to them in the stands, they yelled, "Poosh 'em up, Tony!" The name stuck.

Luke Daniel "Hot Potato" Hamlin, pitching in the late '30s, developed a juggling routine on the mound.

Ervin "Pete" Fox, Boston outfielder, inherited his nickname from Texas League days, when fans named him "Peter Rabbit" because of his speed. Harold Patrick "Pete" Reiser, later an outfielder for Brooklyn, was named for Two-Gun Pete of the movies.

For no special reasons, players called Babe Ruth "Jidge," a derivation of his given name of George, and Walter Johnson "Barney." Eddie Collins was "Cocky" and Grover Cleveland Alexander "Old Pete" in the dugouts.

Elephants in Baseball

The Oakland A's called Philadelphia home when they acquired their one-of-a-kind logo: a circus elephant balancing on a ball with a bat in its trunk. It happened in 1902, the team's second season, when Giants manager John McGraw gave his opinion of the Philadelphia A's to newsmen. "They're a bunch of white elephants," said the outspoken McGraw, implying that the club and its players were worthless. "B.F. Shibe has a white elephant on his hands." Mack, co-owner of the club with Shibe, responded by adding a white elephant to his team's uniforms. The elephant changed colors over the years but still remains on A's uniforms.

Inappropriate Handle

Spray-hitting Frank (Home Run) Baker acquired his nickname after he hit two home runs in the 1911 World Series.

Cakes?

Hall of Famer Jim Palmer answered to the nickname "Cakes" because he made a habit of eating pancakes before he pitched.

All's Fair

The late, lamented Montreal Expos—an NL expansion team created two years after the city hosted Expo '67—were the only team named for a World's Fair.

Halos Win

The City of Anaheim lost in 2008 its bid to restore the name Anaheim Angels to its resident baseball team. On December 22, the Fourth District Court of Appeal ruled that team owner Arte Moreno did not violate the lease of the city-owned ballpark by calling his club "the Los Angeles Angels of Anaheim."

fastball. Norman Lewis Newsom was known as "Bobo" because he called anyone he met by that Spanish term for fool. Sal Maglie was "the Barber" because he would "shave" hitters with inside pitches. Walter "Boom-Boom" Beck was a pitcher so battered by enemy batters that he won an appropriate nickname. Hollis John "Sloppy" Thurston was an immaculate dresser, William Ellsworth "Dummy" Hoy was a deaf-mute who lasted 14 years.

John Peter Wagner, considered the greatest shortstop of all, was best known as "Honus," the German word for John, but also called "the Flying Dutchman." Harold "Pee Wee" Reese was a whiz with marbles. Charles Leo "Gabby" Hartnett talked a lot; Emil "Dutch" Leonard was one of four Washington knuckleballers on the same staff in the '40s; and Harold Joseph "Pie" Traynor used to run grocery errands for his mother and read a list that invariably ended in "pie."

Perry Werden was called "Peach Pie Perry" because of an amusing incident from the 1880s. Making his rounds of St. Louis on a pie wagon, Werden spotted a game in progress, stopped, and tied up his horse. When a player was injured, Werden got into the game and hit two home runs to help his team win. But a wild throw, just before game's end, struck the horse and the frightened animal bolted, spilling the pies. His bakery job obviously gone, Werden's good performance in the game began his baseball career. He played for the St. Louis club of the Union Association, which folded after the single season of 1884, and then played some in the minors before becoming an umpire.

An umpire of the same era won himself a nickname by arranging a phony presentation in his honor from "appreciative" Cleveland fans. The ump, rookie George Burnham, had taken a beating from abusive Chicagoans and wanted to counteract the bad publicity. He bought a watch, had it inscribed with a "message of appreciation," and arranged for it to be presented to him before a game on July 25, 1883. Word later leaked out and the ump became known as "Watch" Burnham.

Perhaps the best-known nickname, next to Babe Ruth's, was Rabbit Maranville's. His size dictated the name—and the size of his ears didn't hurt. Even his wife used it. Few fans knew his true name was Walter. On a 1931 postseason tour of Japan, Rabbit was the most popular player; Japanese fans wiggled their hands like a rabbit's ears and the impish Rabbit responded to their delight.

Baseball had such felines as Harry "the Cat" Brecheen and Harvey Haddix and Felix Millan, both known as "the Kitten." Millan was named after Felix the Cat, a cartoon character, but was thought too small to be called a cat. "Catfish" Hunter, created by A's owner Charley Finley, added color to an excellent pitcher with the rather ordinary first name of Jim.

Mark "the Bird" Fidrych, who didn't have to worry about cats, was nicknamed both for his abundance of curly hair, which resembled a nest, and for his pecking motions around the pitching mound.

Johnny Murphy, Yankee reliever of the '30s, also had peculiarities as a pitcher; his windup reminded observers of a rocking chair and he took on the nickname "Grandma." Needless to say, he didn't like it.

A later New York relief man, Albert Walker "Sparky" Lyle, was nicknamed because a series of bullpen and clubhouse pranks created the need for a more appropriate first name. The game has seen other Sparkys too—notably former Detroit Tigers manager George "Sparky" Anderson.

NICKNAMES

AN OOM-PAH SERENADE TO THE TIGERS BEFORE HE PITCHED TO THEM IN A WORLD SERIES IS TYPICAL OF WHY *DEAN* WAS TAGGED *DIZZY*....

Jim Berryman

George Robert "Birdie" Tebbetts: The Reds' new manager was the victim of a backfiring nickname. He used to call his older brother Birdie.

Willie "Puddin' Head" Jones: He was nicknamed for a song popular when he was a boy, "Wooden Head, Puddin' Head Jones."

Wilmer "Vinegar Bend" Mizell: That's the name of his home—Vinegar Bend, Alabama.

Harry "Peanuts" Lowrey: When he was three months old, an uncle looked at him and commented, "No bigger than a peanut."

Denton T. "Cy" Young: When Young, an Ohio farm boy, tried out for the Canton, Ohio, team, he repeatedly fired his fastball past a Canton batter. Each time it smashed into the wooden grandstand behind home plate and splintered it.

The batter told his manager later, "Boss, you'd better sign that kid. He did more damage to your grandstand than a cyclone."

He was "Cyclone" Young for a while. Then the name was shortened to "Cy."

Omar "Turk" Lown: Nicknamed not for his nationality, but because he loves that Thanksgiving bird.

NICKNAMES

HAROLD REISER WAS A FAN OF MOVIE-SERIAL DAREDEVIL, TWO-GUN PETE...

Character Builder

"Give a boy a bat, a ball, and a place to play and you'll have a good citizen."
—Manager Joe McCarthy

Sandy Koufax hung the nickname "Bad Henry" on Hank Aaron because he was bad for pitchers. Aaron was one of many players also called strictly by their uniform numbers; in his case "No. 44."

There have been many Mickeys (George Stanley Cochrane and Arnold Malcolm Owen are two notable examples), Rubes (George Edward Waddell and Richard Marquard are best known), and dozens of Docs—medical doctors like Bobby Brown and George Medich, dentists like old White Sox star G. Harry White and Phillies manager James Prothro, and even a relief pitcher—Otis Crandall—who bore the moniker because he took care of sick ballgames.

Elwin Charles "Preacher" Roe was also a pitcher—primarily for the Brooklyn Dodgers of the early '50s—while Lynwood Thomas "Schoolboy" Rowe toiled for the Tigers of the '30s. The former was quiet and serious, the latter a cutup who never seemed to grow up.

Jim "Bad News" Galloway entered baseball from telegraphy, where he acquired the nickname by arranging with a friend in another office a trick to free him for ballgames. The friend would wire Galloway that a relative was sick and, armed with the perfect excuse, he would leave work.

Emil Frederick "Irish" Meusel, who played for Irishman John McGraw with the New York Giants of the early '20s, was Irish only in appearance; in reality, he was of German extraction. McGraw, equipped with an Irish temper to match his savvy as a manager, didn't mind Meusel's nickname, but hated the one stuck to him: Muggsy. The moniker was taken from a Baltimore politician of questionable morals.

The best ever in the nickname department? The vote goes to Bob "Death to Flying Things" Ferguson, who led the National League with 24 walks in 1880. That year a walk was changed from nine to eight called balls.

Chapter 16

Even with war looming, Woodrow Wilson left the White House to throw out the first pitch of the 1916 season in Washington. A presidential first pitch has long been a baseball tradition.

Superstitions and Other Traditions

The Sporting News

LUKE SEWELL LAYS IT DOWN

Superstitions in Baseball

Though 18th-century writer Edmund Burke called superstition "the religion of feeble minds," ballplayers have practiced strange rituals—designed to bring them good luck and ward off evil spirits—since the game began.

The most prominent superstition requires players doing well to wear the same clothes while their hot streaks continue. Some maintain the same daily routine—eating, driving, and even sleeping the same way during hot streaks. Many follow widely accepted routines of not stepping on the foul lines but deliberately touching a base while running out to a defensive position.

Almost all players—and many broadcasters and fans—feel they will "hex" a spectacular achievement by discussing a no-hitter in progress, and "the sophomore jinx" is an imaginary curse stalking second-year players—particularly those who enjoyed fine rookie years.

Baseball is rich in superstition of varied origins and nationalities. Concern over unseen hexes and jinxes blankets the game, extending into every major and minor-league ballpark.

Traditionally, it is good luck in baseball to (1) knock on wood, (2) carry a charm like a rabbit's foot or a four-leaf clover, (3) swing two bats with the regular bat while warming up, (4) see empty barrels, (5) put on the left shoe first, (6) have the pitcher receive the ball from the same man each inning, (7) find a lucky hairpin that is supposed to bring hits, (8) step on third base—or another base—before taking a fielding position, and (9) wear the same clothes, eat the same food, and do the same things while in a hot streak.

Players say it is bad to (1) chew gum instead of tobacco, (2) walk between catcher and umpire when coming to bat, (3) step on the foul lines, (4) put a hat on a hotel bed, (5) open an umbrella in a room, (6) see a black cat, or (7) have anything to do with the number 13.

Pitchers are superstitious sorts. As a group, they don't like to be bothered before a start. They think it is "bad luck" to do anything that will disturb their concentration.

Satchel Paige was one of many players who brought superstition with him to the majors from the Negro Leagues. On July 30, 1949, umpire Bill Summers made Paige remove a lucky string bracelet from his right wrist. But the pitcher wore another under his stocking and beat the Boston Red Sox, 10–6, in 10 innings.

Well-traveled Bobo Newsom, who pitched in the majors for more than 20 years starting in 1929, had a fear of paper on the pitching mound. He always made a show of picking up every scrap he could find, and opposing players took advantage by scattering reams of torn-up sheets as they left the field after each inning.

St. Louis Browns manager Luke Sewell believed that his luck improved when he kept infielders' gloves in the third-base coaching box while the team hit. Current rules prohibit the batting team from leaving equipment in the field.

SUPERSTITIONS

Only the brave wear No. 13, but the Atlanta Braves do not. By executive decree in 1978 the No. 13 was banned throughout their entire major and minor-league systems.

The classic Yankee superstition belongs to veteran pitcher Mel Stottlemyre.

"I will never step on a foul line," Mel said and then proceeded to explain. "We were playing the Twins a few years ago and I was headed for the bullpen to warm up before the start of the game. I avoided the foul line and Jim Hegan [Yankee coach] said I shouldn't be superstitious and that I should step on the line. I did.

"The first batter I faced was Ted Uhlaender and he hit a line drive off my left shin. It went for a hit. Carew, Oliva, and Killebrew followed with extra base hits. The fifth man hit a single and scored and I was charged with five runs. I haven't stepped on a foul line since."

GOOD LUCK CHARMS

Charms	Player	Year
Old time tri-color caps	Chi. White Sox	1880
Wear hat backwards	O.P. Caylor	1887
Yellow dog mascot	Cin. Reds	1887
Spit on horse shoe	Arlie Latham	1887
Close eyes on hit ball	C. Von der Ahe	1890's
Chew on toothpick	Ralph Johnson	1890's
Handful of grass	Curt Welch	1890's
Pebbles in pocket	Jack Glasscock	1890's
Cap	Honus Wagner	1908
Hunchback Charles Faust	NY Giants	1912-13
Wooden horseshoe w/4 leaf clover	Babe Ruth	1920's
Jade monkeys & Totems	Babe Ruth	1920's
Eddie Bennett, batboy	Babe Ruth	1920's
Eddie Bennett, batboy	Herb Pennock	1920's
Gum on button of cap	Waite Hoyt	1928
Home team on 3B side	Dan Howley, Mgr.	1930
Pebbles in pocket	Hughie Critz	1930
Glove face down on field	Goody Rosen	1938
Pennies and rabbits feet	Johnny Hudson	1938
Rub batboys head	Dolf Camili	1938
Religious medals	Hassett, Cuyler Durocher, Lavagetto	1938
Green frog appearance	Lake Charles Team	1939
Double whammy	Harrison Weaver	1942
Stick of gum in back pocket for each win	Ron Bryant	1960's
Pennies worn in athletic supporter for ea. win	Jim Ohms	1960
Stuffed bear in uniform	Ron Bryant	1960
Same seat in dug out	Stan Bahnsen	1960
Colored infield practice ball	Det. Tigers	1968
Mighty Joe Young stuffed ape	Bernie Carbo	1970
Two dimes in back pocket	Vida Blue	1970
Chief Noc-A-Homa	Atl. Braves	1970
Socks	Jim Palmer	1970
2 rubdowns on start day	Jim Hunter	1970
Kukailimoku-war god statue	Milt Wilcox	1975
Hat turned inside out	Chat. Lookouts	1976
Black rabbit	Gaylord Perry	1976
Red rabbit's foot	Frank Tanana	1976
Religious medals	Ginny Ozark	1977
Toupee	Norm Sherry	1977
Same hat since '74	Vida Blue	1978
Old army shirt	Peter Vuckovich	1978
College long johns	Rick Cerone	1979
Batting helmet	Willie Horton	1979
Rubber tree plant	Joe Bodolai	1979
Sock with hole	Keith Hernandez	1980
Same sox since '77	Gorman Thomas	1982
Cap	Mike Caldwell	1982
Two $1 in back pocket	Al Holland	1984
#7 & #17	Wade Boggs	1984
Red sweatshirt from '77	Bake McBride	1984
Hat turned inside out	Texas Rangers	1986

JINXES AND HOODOOS

Superstition	Name	Year
Changing socks	Everyone	Always
Spilt coffee		1880's
Dropped silverware		1880's
Ducks or geese flying		1880's
White horse followed by ringing bell		1880's
Dog on diamond		1880's
Entire team on bench		1880's
Fridays	Terry Larkin	1880's
Davy Force	All Teams	1880's
#6 on scoreboard	Cin. Reds	1887
Cross-eyed negro	Charles Comiskey	1890
Negro carry in basket	Arlie Latham	1890
Brass band	Abner Powell	1890
Funeral procession		1890's
Cross-eyed people		1890's
Join group around injury	3rd basemen	1900's
Shaving cut		1900's
Catcher puts mask upside down		1900's
Socks inside out		1900's
Pick up wrong bat		1900's
Wife in stands	Phil Douglas	1917
Tossing ball to pitcher	Joe Dugan	1920's
Neckties	Bucky Harris	1920's
Touching 3B	Lefty O'Doul	1929
Sign autographs when starting	Van Lingle Mungo	1930's
Someone touching his glove	Van Lingle Mungo	1938
Goat curse	Chi. Cubs	1945-2016
Wife in stands	John Hiller	1968
Scoreboard watching	Bobby Murcer	1972
Walk in front of player	Grant Jackson	1970's
Touching 2B on way to OF	Lou Brock	1970's
Someone touching own bat	Ted Simmons	1970's
Chewing gum in OF	Mickey Stanley	1970's
Walk in front of Ump & catcher	Bud Harrelson	1970's
Step in line	Mel Stottlemyre	1970's
Cutting hair	Al Hrabosky	1977
Interviews when winning	Jim Clancy	1979
His own bat	Willie Stargell	1980
Removal of Noc-A-Homa	Atl. Braves	1982
Changing socks	Duane Walker	1984

HEX BREAKERS

Superstitions	Name	Year
Touch cross-eyed person	C. Von der Ahe	1887
Spit through crossed fingers		1890's
Rub head of black mascot	Cin. Reds	1890's
Bring person to park who has never seen defeat	Cin. Reds	1890's
Enter box from rear	George McGinnis	1890's
Bat lefthanded after letter from home	Player in East. Lg.	1907
Get up from right side of bed	Ernie Koy	1938
Chews tobacco	Heinie Manush	1938
Burning incense	Reggie Smith	1970's
Rubs bat w/magic oil	Rico Carty	1970's
Voodoo enchantress	Cin. Reds	1982
Shaved catcher's moustache	George Stallings	

SAL MAGLIE WOULDN'T SHAVE THE DAY HE PITCHED

MOOSE MORYN TIES A RABBIT-FOOT TO HIS SPIKES.

ERNIE BANKS TWIDDLES HIS RIGHT THUMB,

One for the Books

The Montreal Expos should have stayed home on Friday the 13th of May 1977. They lost, 5–3, at Olympic Stadium to the Chicago Cubs, evening their record at 13-13. The Cubs had 13 hits and left 13 runners on base. The game's winning run was driven in by the Cubs' Larry Biittner, whose No. 26 was 2 x 13. The losing pitcher, Dan Warthen, wore 39, or 3 x 13.

National League

Ralph Branca, who flaunted superstition by wearing No. 13, kids nemesis Bobby Thomson (in uniform) at the 1951 World Series. New York's slugger delivered a pennant-winning homer against Brooklyn's Branca in the last inning of the National League playoff.

Newsom began his day at the ballpark by touching both fair and foul territory, avoiding the dividing foul line, and during the game kept his glove on the ground, face up, with the thumb pointing exactly the same way each time. He also had a water-cooler ritual: he took a sip before he went to the mound each inning—well aware of how he was holding his hands, feet, and head—and returned to drink exactly the same way whenever he retired the side in order.

Another pitcher, Ewell Blackwell of the Reds, alternated red and white sweatshirts. If he won while wearing a certain color, he stuck with it until he lost. Hugh Casey, Vic Raschi, and Chief Bender were among the more adamant of the hurlers who refused to be photographed before a game—and Bender grew so indignant when the ban was broken that he smashed the offender's camera.

Ace Yankee reliever Johnny Murphy always sat in the same spot on the dugout bench while working in a game, and Bob Shawkey wore his "lucky" red sweatshirt no matter what the weather.

A handful of athletes risked wearing No. 13, but one who did— Ralph Branca—threw the most infamous pitch in the history of the game. His last-of-the-ninth pitch to Bobby Thomson with one out and two men on became a three-run homer that erased a 4–2 Dodger lead and gave the New York Giants their miracle pennant of 1951. Branca, then just 25, was crushed. Slowed by a sore arm the next season, he was never again the pitcher he had been before the Thomson home run. He was through before he turned 30.

Sal Maglie, ace of the 1951 Giants, had a superstition that was shared by numerous contemporaries: he didn't shave before he pitched. Maglie was called "the Barber" not only because his pitches passed ominously close to rival hitters' heads but also because he needed one.

Hitters also have their idiosyncrasies. Five of the game's stars—Hal Chase, Eddie Collins, Baby Doll Jacobson, Frank Crosetti, and Phil Rizzuto—regularly removed the gum from their mouths and perched it on their cap buttons for safe-keeping. Collins kept it there until the pitcher had two strikes on him, then replaced the wad in his mouth. With the White Sox, Collins went through this ritual one day when he suddenly discovered—to his chagrin—that playful teammates had placed pepper on the top of his cap. The gum absorbed the pepper in the few seconds it was placed on the button.

Many players had similar "good luck" mannerisms that they did almost without thinking. Frankie Frisch—even as a manager—rubbed his right shoe up and down his left stocking. Babe Ruth knocked the dirt out of his spikes after every strike. Robin Roberts fiddled with the ends of his uniform pants after each pitch. Gil Hodges blew a kiss to his wife whenever he hit a home run in Brooklyn. Tony Taylor crossed himself vigorously each time he stepped into the batter's box. Willie Mays never went to center field without touching second base. Sherm Lollar stuffed his locker with four-leaf clovers. Marty Marion picked up imaginary pebbles.

Two players—Bill Nicholson and Harry Walker—earned nicknames for their well-known routines at the plate. Nicholson, called "Swish," swished his bat several times while waiting for the pitch, and Walker frequently stepped out, putting his hat off and on numerous times. Harry "the Hat" Walker went through three or four caps a year.

Even Ted Williams had a regular ritual. He tucked his bat under his arm and pulled down hard on his cap whenever he had two strikes against him. Jackie Robinson, a fellow Hall of Famer, walked to the plate by passing in front of the catcher; if the catcher was in conference when Robinson's turn came up, Jackie waited until the meeting was over to take his customary stroll.

Minnie Minoso conceived what he thought was the sure cure for anemic achievement; he showered in full uniform—spikes included—during his days as player for the Chicago White Sox.

Old-time players believed that empty beer barrels were a portent of good-hitting days to come—and John McGraw subscribed to the theory while running the Giants. Just before the 1905 World Series he hired a mule team to drag a wagon of barrels past the Polo Grounds, where the Giants were playing the Philadelphia Athletics. New York won the World Series, four games to one.

Stan Hack, former Cubs third baseman, tried to cull good fortune by spending the first inning on the coaching lines at third before managing the rest of the game from the dugout.

George Stallings, like Bobo Newsom, was a paper fanatic who used to frighten Rochester batboy Gabe Paul (later general manager of several major league ballclubs) with shouts to clear paper scraps from the dugout area. "If one little scrap escaped me," Paul said years later, "Mr. Stallings' roar scared the life out of me."

When managing the Browns, Luke Sewell coached at third base full time and kept the gloves of his shortstop and third baseman in the coaching box with him. He then handed each to the rightful owner when the sides changed.

An early Cubs manager, Fred Mitchell (1917–1920), enjoyed a long winning streak after finding a hairpin on a sidewalk near Wrigley Field the day the streak started. Mitchell, honoring the long tradition that a hairpin will bring hits, searched for hairpins every day and found them for 17 more days. On the 19th day, he was unable to locate a hairpin and the Cubs lost.

During the 1924 season Washington Senators manager Bucky

Pitchers Used Voodoo

Philadelphia Athletics pitcher Russ Christopher tried to break a slump by appearing in a straw hat and carrying a big key and other charms on his person. Urban Shocker, ace of the Browns, and Bobo Newsom, who pitched for several clubs, practiced voodoo rites before games.

The Goat Curse

During the last year of World War II, Chicago tavern owner Billy Sianis brought his pet goat to every game at Wrigley Field. After the war's end in August brought most servicemen home, however, the Cubs refused the goat admission to the 1945 World Series. Sianis put a hex on the club, saying it would never reach the World Series again. The curse held for 71 years, making it the longest drought among the original 16 teams, before the 2016 Cubs won the NL pennant and advanced to the Fall Classic.

ROBIN ROBERTS PULLS HIS PANTS DOWN BEFORE EACH PITCH.

Hall of Famer Robin Roberts had a regular routine on the mound.

Harris learned that his team won every time an 11-year-old schoolboy named Bradley Wilson was in the ballpark. During the World Series that fall, Harris arranged for the youngster to attend every game by sending a chauffeured limousine to bring him to the stadium.

St. Christopher's medals, crosses, six-pointed Stars of David, and other religious items were worn by old-time and modern players hoping for good fortune.

General Manager Al Campanis of the Los Angeles Dodgers collected pins in anticipation of hits when he played for Brooklyn and maintained his hobby of collecting Greek charms after his active career ended. Campanis hid the charms in peta (pies) to bring good luck to guests who found them in their portions. When Campanis found them himself, in 1965 and 1966, the Dodgers won pennants.

Traditions

Every aspect of baseball—professional and amateur—has a long tradition. A radical rules change, such as the introduction of the designated hitter by the American League in 1973, may seem the exception, but even that idea was brewing for 45 years (since its conception by National League president John Heydler in 1928).

Intercollegiate baseball predates the turn of the century. As long ago as 1882, the Manhattan College team played under the watchful eye of a coach named Brother Jasper. Before each game, he told the student spectators not to move or leave their seats with the game in progress. One hot afternoon, however, the fans got

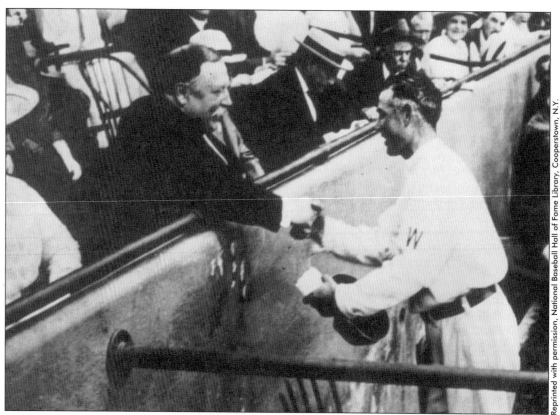

President William Howard Taft, attending the Washington opener in 1910, may have inadvertently started the tradition of the seventh-inning stretch.

restless and, as the team came to bat in the seventh inning, Brother Jasper told them to stand and stretch their legs.

Manhattan College often played in the park of the New York NL club and Giant fans picked up on the "seventh-inning stretch," according to a news release from the school's office in 1958.

Other sources say the seventh-inning stretch began when fans of the Cincinnati Red Stockings, the first professional team in 1869, stood to gain temporary relief from the hard wooden benches of the day.

Some historians insist President William Howard Taft, attending the 1910 opener in Washington, inadvertently started the tradition when he rose to stretch in the seventh inning. Thinking he was leaving, fans stood out of respect for the office. When they saw Taft stretch, they stretched—and continued to do so from that game forward.

There are other traditions associated with fans. Until the home-run era triggered by Babe Ruth in the '20s, fans returned balls hit into the stands. The practice of returning balls was reinstated during the Second World War to benefit the Army Relief Fund.

The "traditional" Sunday doubleheader is a relatively new development. When the American League was founded in 1901, only Chicago played games on Sunday. St. Louis allowed Sunday ball the next year, but Boston didn't approve until 1929 and Philadelphia until 1934.

Like Sunday ball, the tradition of retiring uniform numbers is relatively young. Babe Ruth's No. 3 was not retired until long after the end of his Yankees career in 1934. In the 13 years it remained active, it was worn by George Selkirk, Allie Clark, Bud Metheny, Cliff Mapes, Frank Colman, Eddie Bockman, Roy Weatherly, and (in spring training) Joe Medwick.

Before regular games begin, players sometimes play "pepper," a practice of one man bunting to a row of fielders whose return tosses serve as "pitches." Pepper games were played for Cokes; anyone who made an error was charged a Coke. When Cardinal owner Gussie Busch (of Anheuser-Busch) was playing pepper with his employees during the early '50s, slugger Stan Musial quipped, "What do you play for, breweries?"

The Art of Chewing

Chewing is a well-established baseball tradition. Players chew gum, licorice, tobacco, and a variety of other items because they need constant moisture (especially in the field, where there is no access to a drinking fountain), because constant exercise of the jaw muscle helps athletes concentrate on the game, and because chewing relaxes the nerves.

By far the most widespread "chew" is bubble gum—usually unadulterated but sometimes intertwined with a wad of chewing tobacco. The New York–based Topps Chewing Gum Company even held a national bubble-blowing tournament in 1975, with the finals shown on television. Managers frown on players blowing bubbles during the national anthem, however, and at least one big-league club has imposed a rule against it.

Taft Pleased Both Sides

President William Howard Taft, passing through St. Louis on May 4, 1910—a rare day when both the Cardinals and Browns were at home—did not wish to offend either team. He managed to see parts of both games.

Penny Pincher

Washington Senators first baseman Mickey Vernon picked up pennies he found on the field; he regarded them as omens of base hits to come.

"I can't recall a time that I found a penny and did not get a hit," he said. "Why doesn't the manager throw pennies onto the field near first base? That's the catch. The penny had to be found by accident. You can't fool around with this superstition stuff and get away with it."

How to Change Luck

Some players tried to change bad luck by changing numbers; Roger Craig switched to No. 13 in his second year as a New York Met and lost 22 of 27 decisions after a 10-24 mark the year before. Jake Powell believed hairpins represented hits, collected 241 of them one season, and produced exactly that many hits for his team in the minors. Ron Northey, Pete Reiser, and Al Rosen were among several who made "X" marks at home plate before they batted.

Strange Smell

During their unexpected run to the 2014 World Series, the Royals resorted to superstition—including dousing themselves with perfume normally worn by women. Alcides Escobar tried it late in 2013, got a couple of hits, and believed the ritual would bring good luck. Salvador Perez later subscribed to the same theory.

Ichiro's Secret

Ichiro Suzuki credits his success to an on-deck circle regimen that includes a deep warm-up squat, a twirl of the bat, and a stance that can only be described as decidedly different.

Bill Menzel

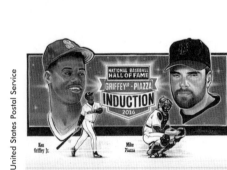

United States Postal Service

The U.S. Post Office celebrated the 2016 Hall of Fame Induction of Mike Piazza and Ken Griffey Jr. with this handsome cachet, postmarked by the Cooperstown post office.

The pitcher is the most obvious gum-chewer, as he frequently makes exaggerated chewing gestures while studying the catcher's signal for the next pitch.

Babe Ruth, Roy Campanella, and Johnny Mize were three of the more prominent former sluggers who enjoyed tobacco almost as much as a home run, but the tradition did not retire with them.

Perennial All-Stars Johnny Bench and Rod Carew chewed, along with pitchers Tug McGraw, Luis Tiant, and Sparky Lyle. Countless other major leaguers also pursued the habit, but few dared to swallow even a drop of the foul-tasting juice.

Although some players insist they prefer chewing tobacco to smoking it, both involve health risks. Throat cancer linked to chewing presumably claimed the lives of Hall of Famers Babe Ruth, just 53, and Tony Gwynn, 54, while fellow users Bill Tuttle and Brett Butler also suffered from throat cancer. Major League Baseball, in concert with the Players Association, issued warnings regarding the use of smokeless tobacco in 2011 but did not ban the product, which contains 28 known carcinogens. Three years later, Gwynn was gone.

The "chaw," a mix of tobacco and bubble gum, fell out of favor as chewing tobacco use declined from a peak of more than 30 percent in the '80s. The warnings helped.

Opening Day

Though each major league team plays 162 games during the regular season, plus two dozen spring exhibitions, and up to 12 more for pennant winners, the highlight of the year for many is Opening Day.

On that festive day in early April, all teams are equal. The worst team and the best team have the same 0-0 records, and the feeling of hope that prevailed through the six-week spring-training period still exists.

For many Americans, Opening Day is the official start of spring, a signal that the miseries of winter are over. Temperatures are still low in many major league cities (and snow is still falling in Canada), but fans, players, and team executives have a special warmth inside on the eve of the season.

Bands play, flags wave, teams are introduced one player at a time, and a celebrity—maybe even a president—throws out the first pitch.

When the Washington Senators were a team, they would always open at home, one day ahead of the other American League teams. Cincinnati enjoys annual advance-opener honors in the National League—a tradition that began in 1876, the league's first season.

The Reds (then the Red Stockings) missed opening at home only once in their long National League tenure (the team was out of the league from 1881 to 1889). The exception occurred in 1877, when rain forced cancellation of the opener for three days and the team boarded a boat for Louisville to open the season there.

Opening Day games have been marked by unusual events on the field. In 1900 the Phillies beat the Braves, 19–17, the highest score ever reported in an NL opener. A year later, in the first

American League game for both clubs, Detroit scored 10 runs in the ninth inning to beat Milwaukee, 14–13.

Leon "Red" Ames of the New York Giants no-hit the Brooklyn Dodgers for the first nine innings in a 1909 opener, but lost in the 13th, 3–0. The next season Walter Johnson won the Washington lid-lifter but lost a no-hitter because right fielder Doc Gessler tripped over a child who was sitting in front of an overflow crowd behind outfield ropes. The ball, which would have been a routine out, dropped for a double.

When Yankee Stadium opened in 1923, a throng of 74,000 swamped the ballpark and more than 25,000 more fans were turned away at the gates. Bob Shawkey beat Boston, thanks to a three-run home run by Babe Ruth, who wasted no time in showing why the park was called "The House That Ruth Built."

In 1925 the Cleveland Indians scored the biggest Opening Day rout, a 21–14 victory over the St. Louis Browns. Cleveland also registered the only no-hitter on Opening Day, a 1–0 triumph pitched by Bob Feller over the Chicago White Sox in 1940. Lefty Grove of the Boston Red Sox nearly upstaged Feller by pitching seven perfect innings at Washington before giving up a one-out single to Cecil Travis in the eighth.

The 1946 openers were marked by the return of the stars from World War II, and 1947 was important because Jackie Robinson's debut in Brooklyn ended the game's color line.

Presidents at the Ballpark

The president of the United States has always had a close association with "America's national pastime," particularly when a club was located in the nation's capital at Washington, D.C.

More than 40 openers were preceded by presidents throwing out the first ball from a box adjacent to the field, and an even dozen presidents took part in the ceremonies.

Former President U. S. Grant smoked cigars while watching New York beat Boston, 7–5, at the Polo Grounds on May 1, 1883, but the

The earliest Opening Day in major league history was played on March 22, 2014, when the Los Angeles Dodgers defeated the Arizona Diamondbacks, 3–1, at Sydney Cricket Ground in Australia.

Gehrig's Last Opener

Lou Gehrig played his last opening game at Yankee Stadium on April 20, 1939. He had no hits and was charged with an error.

Night Sight

The first Opening Day night game was played on April 17, 1950. The Cardinals beat the Pirates, 4–2, at Busch Stadium, St. Louis.

Seaver's Selection

Tom Seaver started a record 16 Opening Day games, one more than fellow Hall of Famer Christy Mathewson.

Huge throngs swamped Yankee Stadium for the 1923 opener. More than 25,000 fans were turned away.

President Herbert Hoover threw out the Opening Day first pitch on April 17, 1929. Cheers turned to jeers a year later, when Hoover risked the wrath of fans six months after a stock market crash triggered The Great Depression.

Presidents Used Real "Body" Guard

Presidents attending baseball games are assigned a "body" guard to protect them from foul balls or bad throws. The guard is usually a utility player from the home team.

Bush Leagues

Presidents George Bush, a left-handed first baseman, and George W. Bush, a right-handed pitcher, played college ball at Yale.

first incumbent president to watch a game was Benjamin Harrison, who watched Cincinnati edge Washington, 7–4 in 11 innings, on June 6, 1892 (Washington was then in the National League).

William Howard Taft, once a standout pitcher at Yale University, was a fan of Walter Johnson in particular and the Washington Senators in general when he threw out the first presidential pitch—on April 14, 1910.

His successor, Woodrow Wilson, not only threw out the first ball three times but also attended games regularly, even after leaving office. Warren Harding, an Ohio sportswriter turned senator, succeeded Wilson in office and maintained an avid interest in the game, but Calvin Coolidge considered the first-ball assignment a task rather than a privilege and once left a game in the second inning.

Herbert Hoover, a Yankee fan, once managed his college baseball team at Stanford. Harry Truman rooted for the St. Louis Browns and—like a good Missouri senator—wished well for the Cardinals too, though Bess Truman developed a definite interest in the Kansas City A's and later the Kansas City Royals, who played near her home in Independence.

Truman probably was the most unorthodox of Opening Day pitchers, as he threw two balls—one with each arm. John F. Kennedy, elected in 1960, knew baseball thoroughly. JFK discussed detailed aspects of the game with George Selkirk, general manager of the "new" Senators, when the baseball executive presented the president with the traditional gold season's pass in 1963. Kennedy attended all three Opening Day games during his short-lived administration.

Jimmy Carter, an excellent softball pitcher, twice threw out the first ball for the Atlanta Braves when he was governor of Georgia, and Senator Henry Jackson—an unsuccessful candidate for the presidential nomination—had the unusual distinction of making the first pitch for the 1969 Seattle Pilots, who lasted only that one season, and the new Seattle Mariners, in 1977.

Ronald Reagan broadcast Chicago Cubs games for Des Moines radio station WHO in the '30s. The team trained on Catalina Island, where actress Joy Hodges heard his voice and offered him a screen test. He passed, became a Hollywood actor and eventually president of the Screen Actors Guild. From there, he made successful runs for governor of California and eventually the presidency.

Lyndon Johnson, Richard Nixon, Gerard Ford, George H.W. and George W. Bush, and Barack Obama were all serious baseball fans, along with Bill and Hillary Clinton.

Before his election in 2000, George W. Bush owned the Texas Rangers and was believed to be more interested in serving as commissioner of baseball than president of the United States. He was the only baseball owner to oppose the introduction of three-divisional play and wild cards.

Farewells

While season openers—especially presidential openers—are festive, happy occasions, farewells are invariably sad, whether the retiring star enjoys a good final season or a bad one.

There was a touch of irony in the final game of Cy Young,

whose 511 pitching victories may never be duplicated. Young, at age 45, pitched a masterful game in his last appearance with the Boston Braves on September 7, 1911, but wound up on the short end of a 1–0 score. The winning pitcher, Philadelphia rookie Grover Cleveland Alexander, not only won 28 games that year but went on to win 373 lifetime, tied with Christy Mathewson for tops in the National League.

Two other all-time pitching stars, Mordecai "Three-Finger" Brown and Mathewson, ended their careers in a specially arranged final duel on September 4, 1916. Brown, 37, was working for the Cubs, while Mathewson, 39, was manager of the Reds, a club he took over after leaving the New York Giants in midseason.

Mathewson beat Brown, 10–8, to register his only decision in a Cincinnati uniform.

Walter Johnson, second to Young with 417 lifetime wins, was 39 when he made his final appearance, but his farewell was unusual for two reasons. First, the great right-hander came up as a pinch-hitter for pitcher Tom Zachary in the ninth inning, and flied out to right fielder Babe Ruth. Second, that was the same game in which Ruth hit his record-smashing 60th home run! The date was September 30, 1927.

Two Hall of Fame hitters, Ted Williams and George Sisler, hit .300 while playing at least 100 games in their final seasons. Williams and Hank Greenberg also hit more than 20 home runs in their last campaigns as active players.

The widely accepted baseball adage, "He knew when to quit," applies most appropriately to Ted Williams. In 1960 he hit .316 with 29 homers in just 310 at-bats—including a home run in his last trip to the plate.

Retiring superstars often receive farewell gifts from respectful rivals. Derek Jeter got a Stetson hat and cowboy boots from the Houston Astros, Todd Helton got a horse from the Colorado Rockies, and Cal Ripken Jr. received a stuffed Oriole from the team mascot, the Oriole Bird.

David Ortiz got seats from the Red Sox spring camps where he trained, Mariano Rivera got a sand sculpture from the Tampa Bay Rays, and Chipper Jones landed a piece of artwork that highlighted his successful career as a Mets rival at Shea Stadium. The Red Sox even gave him his uniform No. 10 from the Green Monster scoreboard at Fenway Park.

A Personal Reaction to
Baseball's Hall of Fame

by Mike Schuman
The Baseball Bulletin

As a kid, after I continually pestered my parents to take me to Cooperstown, they finally relented. My mother was bored, my father was interested but preoccupied, and I was fascinated.

Ten years later, I went back to the Baseball Hall of Fame and was still fascinated.

Sure, kids love the place. But only a true baseball fan realizes that the museum is far more than a place to take the Little Leaguer for the summer. In fact, it's possible that the youngsters may not fully appreciate the history and the tradition of the sport that is preserved in the hall.

Injury Made Koufax Quit

Star pitcher Sandy Koufax of the Los Angles Dodgers took the advice of doctors and retired at age 30 in November 1966. Though he had just won 27, lost nine, and posted a 1.73 earned run average, Koufax revealed that continued pitching could result in permanent disability because of an arthritic left elbow.

Fond Farewell

In 2001, his final season, Cal Ripken Jr. was All-Star Game MVP for the second time. His homer, the second of his All-Star career, paced the AL to a 4–1 win in the Safeco Field game. When he retired at season's end, he was one of seven men with 3,000 hits and 400 homers.

Forgot Something?

Although they played in a city that threw ticker-tape parades for Charles Lindbergh and Douglas MacArthur, the Brooklyn Dodgers never received that honor.

Hockey Tribute

A year after the Montreal Expos became the Washington Nationals, the Montreal Canadiens saluted the lost club by raising a special Expos banner to the rafters of Bell Centre, home of the National Hockey League team. On it were the names and numbers of four players whose numbers had been retired by the Expos but not recognized by the Nationals: Gary Carter (No. 8), Tim Raines (No. 30), and Rusty Staub and Andre Dawson (both No. 10).

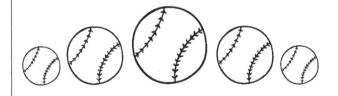

Everything But

These Hall of Fame players never appeared in the World Series:

Luke Appling
Ernie Banks
Jim Bunning
Rod Carew
Jack Chesbro
Andre Dawson
Rick Ferrell
Elmer Flick
Ken Griffey, Jr.
Harry Heilmann
Ferguson Jenkins
Addie Joss
George Kell
Ralph Kiner
Napoleon Lajoie
Ted Lyons
Phil Niekro
Gaylord Perry#
Ryne Sandberg
Ron Santo
George Sisler
Frank Thomas*
Rube Waddell
Bobby Wallace
Billy Williams

#not on 1962 Giants World Series roster
*hurt when 2005 White Sox qualified

Bobby Cox, Miller Huggins, Tony LaRussa, Al Lopez, and Joe Torre were World Series managers who never reached the Fall Classic as players.

Tough Ticket

When he was there in 1993 and 1994, Mike Piazza paid his way into the Baseball Hall of Fame. He figured it was the only way he could get in.

Flag of Excellence

Two weeks after he was admitted to the Baseball Hall of Fame, Ken Griffey Jr. was honored in Seattle, where he started his career. The day before the Mariners retired his No. 24 at Safeco Field, the number flew from a flagpole atop the Space Needle.

"The first scheme for playing baseball, according to the best evidence obtainable to date, was devised by Abner Doubleday at Cooperstown, New York, in 1839." So said the final report of the commission to determine the origin of baseball, which was organized around the turn of the century. This is now generally accepted as fiction rather than fact, but like all such legends, it has stuck. It was the adherence to this finding point that placed America's first museum entirely devoted to a sport in Cooperstown, New York.

Scenic, sleepy, charming, sedate—they're all various epithets used and overused to describe baseball's home. The village was named for the father of James Fenimore Cooper, who lived in that region most of his life and felt justified in naming at least one town after himself. Cooperstown is located halfway between Schenectady and Utica, accessible only through a maze of back roads. To put it bluntly, it's in the middle of nowhere. So when baseball fans drive through the wilds of upstate New York simply to see the Baseball Hall of Fame, there must be something there worth seeing.

The Hall of Fame itself, that is, the special wing which so grandly displays the plaques of the members, takes up only a small portion of the building. The museum occupies the rest—all four floors worth. The displays are such that one can see and enjoy everything in one afternoon, but could discover something new and different every day for a year.

First of all, some displays consist of statistics, which not only take time to sink in, but are constantly changing. The all-time top 10 leaders in major categories are listed smartly on wall displays. The leaders in home runs, RBIs, and runs scored change quite often. Some categories even change from day to day.

Certain exhibits could take a year alone to see wholly. Current and old baseball cards are shown under glass cases, and if I were to examine every card to study its style or to see whose picture was

Dan Schlossberg

Admirers fill the field adjacent to the Clark Sports Center for the annual induction ceremonies, usually held the third Sunday of July. The 2007 induction of Cal Ripken, Jr. and Tony Gwynn drew an estimated 85,000 spectators, a record likely to be short-lived.

The First Hall of Fame Vote

In the first vote for the Hall of Fame, on February 3, 1936, Ty Cobb drew 222 of 226 votes, Babe Ruth and Honus Wagner finished second with 215 each, followed by Christy Mathewson with 205. Walter Johnson, with 189, was the only other man to have the required three-quarters majority for election in the voting, then conducted by players and writers.

Hall of Fame Game

For 68 years, visiting major league teams played an exhibition game at Doubleday Field during Hall of Fame Induction Weekend. That series ended after 2008 and was replaced by a Hall of Fame Classic featuring hand-picked teams of Hall of Famers and other players.

Cooperstown Gallery

The 312 members of the Baseball Hall of Fame before 2017 included 217 former players, 35 Negro Leaguers, 28 executives, 22 managers, and 10 umpires.

Elbow Room

Randy Johnson, the tallest player in the Hall of Fame, and John Smoltz, the only Hall of Famer who had Tommy John surgery, were inducted in the same year, 2015.

Non Starter

Bruce Sutter was the first pitcher to get into the Hall of Fame without ever starting a game.

on it, I'd still be there now. For a fanatic card collector, this single display is worth the trip in itself.

Nostalgia freaks—they'd be right at home, too. In fact, one wouldn't even have to be an avid fan to appreciate the collection of memory bogglers. Even my mother got a kick out of seeing Joe DiMaggio's old uniform. And my father relived the day, many moons ago, when he saw Mickey Owen drop the infamous "third strike." "I was there," he boasted, as he had boasted about it many times before. "I remember that like I remember Pearl Harbor," he recollected, gazing at a last remnant of the Ebbets Field wall.

Younger nostalgia freaks would not be left out. Reading through a list of every no-hitter pitched since 1940, I remembered exactly where I was and what I was doing when Dave Morehead pitched his hitless game for the Red Sox. And I remembered watching on television as Tom Phoebus threw his gem against the Bosox.

Ah, Morehead and Phoebus. Where are they now? Which leads me to another point. Hall of Famers aren't the only ballplayers represented in the museum. A lot of everyday guys are there, too. Of course, there is an entire wing devoted to Babe Ruth, and there is Stan the Man's uniform, along with Ty Cobb's first contract. But there's also a tribute to Harvey Haddix for pitching the most famous of all heartbreakers. And each of the players who endured baseball's longest game are part of the National Baseball Museum, if only in a blown-up box score.

A pocketless baseball glove? Maybe. But a fingerless baseball glove? No way. That's what I would have imagined if I had not seen the thing before my eyes. But there it was—a glove with no fingers, in its little glass-enclosed home, staring me in the face. A most primitive piece of baseball equipment, it was used in the late 1870s. Gloves with no pockets, such as those used by John McGraw and Cy Young, were right there too, keeping their primitive ancestor company.

I also came across a 17-foot bat. But, rest easy. I'm not going to tell you it was used by an original New York Giant. It was a

How the National Baseball Hall of Fame and Museum looked when it was opened in 1939.

The National Baseball Hall of Fame and Museum (above) has expanded greatly since its 1939 opening. Although many of its exhibits rotate, the "Chasing the Dream" salute to Hank Aaron (below) is permanent. Aaron drew 97.83 percent of the vote and huge crowds for his 1982 induction but Ken Griffey, Jr. (right) topped him with a record 99.30 percent in 2016. Griffey's name was left off only three ballots.

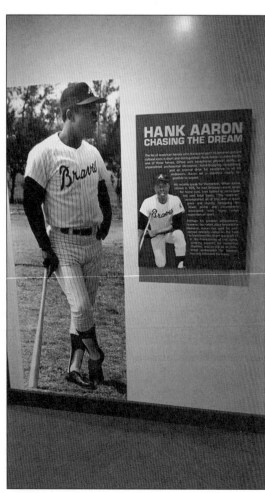

present for Ted Williams made by some admirers. What a potent weapon though, if it ever were to be used. All we'd need is a batter twice the size of Frank Howard.

Mementos of baseball past do not control the building. A room, which did not exist during my first visit, has been set aside to show the goings-on in "Baseball Today." Carpeted in AstroTurf, highlights of this room are 30 displays, one devoted to each team in the majors. Featured here are press guides, uniforms, pictures, and pennants. Also included in this colorful room are special exhibits about current players and recent events.

Walking into the actual Hall of Fame is not unlike entering the Rotunda of the Capitol or Independence Hall. The designers of the hall didn't monkey around when building this shrine to the immortals. Solemnity overtakes the atmosphere as one enters the wing, with its 25-foot-high ceiling and its marble columns. The plaques belonging to each of baseball's greats line the walls to the right and left. On each plaque are the player's greatest accomplishments in nutshell form. Whether it's the facts and figures on the walls, or seeing the names and faces of the best of the best, or simply the monumental architecture of the place, one can't leave the hall without being just somewhat inspired.

I'm looking forward to visiting the epitome of quaintness again and again and again. If for nothing else, simply to see my favorite exhibit in the place: the front page of *The Boston Record* dated October 6, 1967—no headline, no article, just a picture of two big red socks.

The first Hall of Fame class included (clockwise from upper left) Christy Mathewson, Babe Ruth, Honus Wagner, Ty Cobb, and Walter Johnson.

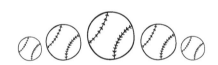

	Rank	Year	Player	Ballots Cast	Votes Rec'd	Omitted	Pct.
Hall of Famers Receiving Highest Percentage of Votes	1	2016	Ken Griffey, Jr.	440	437	3	99.30
	2	1992	Tom Seaver	430	425	5*	98.84
	3	1999	Nolan Ryan	497	491	6	98.79
	4	2007	Cal Ripken, Jr.	545	537	8	98.53
	5	1936	Ty Cobb	226	222	4	98.23
	6	1999	George Brett	497	488	9	98.19
* Seaver was named on 425 of 427 completed ballots, but three voters returned blank ballots to protest the exclusion of the suspended Pete Rose by Hall of Fame directors.	7	1982	Hank Aaron	415	406	9	97.83
	8	2007	Tony Gwynn	545	532	13	97.61
	9	2015	Randy Johnson	549	534	15	97.30
	10	2014	Greg Maddux	571	555	16	97.20
	11	1995	Mike Schmidt	460	444	16	96.52
	12	1989	Johnny Bench	447	431	16	96.42
	13	1994	Steve Carlton	455	436	19	95.82
	14	1936	Babe Ruth	226	215	11	95.13
	15	1936	Honus Wagner	226	215	11	95.13
	16	2009	Rickey Henderson	539	511	28	94.81

Retired Numbers

More than 150 players have had one or more teams retire their numbers as a tribute for their performances. They include the following:

No.	Player & Club	Year Retired
–	Grover Cleveland Alexander, Phillies	
–	Ty Cobb, Tigers	
–	Sam Crawford, Tigers	
–	Rogers Hornsby, Cardinals	
–	Chuck Klein, Phillies	
–	Hughie Jennings, Tigers	
–	Heinie Manush, Tigers	
–	Christy Mathewson, Giants	
–	John McGraw, Giants	
1	Billy Meyer, Pirates	1954
1	Bud Selig, Brewers#	2015
1	Pee Wee Reese, Dodgers	1984
1	Bobby Doerr, Red Sox	1988
1	Fred Hutchinson, Reds	1965
1	Ozzie Smith, Cardinals	1996
1	Rich Ashburn, Phillies	1979
1	Billy Martin, Yankees	1986
2	Red Schoendienst, Cardinals	1996
2	Nellie Fox, White Sox	1976
2	Derek Jeter, Yankees	2016
2	Tom Lasorda, Dodgers	1997
2	Charlie Gehringer, Tigers	1983
3	Babe Ruth, Yankees	1948
3	Earl Averill, Indians	1975
3	Bill Terry, Giants	1984
3	Harmon Killebrew, Twins	1974
3	Dale Murphy, Braves	1994
3	Harold Baines, White Sox	1989
4	Luke Appling, White Sox	1975
4	Earl Weaver, Orioles	1982
4	Duke Snider, Dodgers	1980
4	Ralph Kiner, Pirates	1987
4	Lou Gehrig, Yankees	1939
4	Paul Molitor, Brewers	1999
4	Mel Ott, Giants	1948
4	Joe Cronin, Red Sox	1984
5	Brooks Robinson, Orioles	1978
5	Lou Boudreau, Indians	1970
5	George Brett, Royals	1994
5	Johnny Bench, Reds	1984
5	Hank Greenberg, Tigers	1983
5	Joe DiMaggio, Yankees	1952
5	Jeff Bagwell, Astros	2007
6	Johnny Pesky, Red Sox	2008
6	Steve Garvey, Padres	1988
6	Stan Musial, Cardinals	1963
6	Al Kaline, Tigers	1980
6	Tony Oliva, Twins	1991
6	Bobby Cox, Braves	2011
6	Joe Torre, Yankees	2014
7	Mickey Mantle, Yankees	1969
7	Craig Biggio, Astros	2008
8	Willie Stargell, Pirates	1982
8	Joe Morgan, Reds	1998
8	Yogi Berra, Yankees	1972
8	Bill Dickey, Yankees	1972
8	Carl Yastrzemski, Red Sox	1989
8	Cal Ripken, Jr., Orioles	2001
8	Gary Carter, Expos	1993
9	Ted Williams, Red Sox	1984
9	Reggie Jackson, Athletics	2004
9	Minnie Minoso, White Sox	1983
9	Enos Slaughter, Cardinals	1996
9	Bill Mazeroski, Pirates	1987
9	Roger Maris, Yankees	1984
10	Sparky Anderson, Reds	2005
10	Dick Howser, Royals	1987
10	Phil Rizzuto, Yankees	1985
10	Ron Santo, Cubs	2003
10	Tony LaRussa, Cardinals	2012
10	Tom Kelly, Twins	2012
10	Rusty Staub, Expos	1993
10	Andre Dawson, Expos	1997
10	Chipper Jones, Braves	2013
11	Carl Hubbell, Giants	1944
11	Jim Fregosi, Angels	1998
11	Luis Aparicio, White Sox	1984
11	Paul Waner, Pirates	2007
11	Sparky Anderson, Tigers	2011
11	Barry Larkin, Reds	2012
12	Wade Boggs, Rays	2009
12	Roberto Alomar, Blue Jays	2011
13	Dave Concepcion, Reds	2007
14	Ernie Banks, Cubs	1982
14	Kent Hrbek, Twins	1995
14	Larry Doby, Indians	1994
14	Ken Boyer, Cardinals	1984
14	Gil Hodges, Mets	1973
14	Jim Bunning, Phillies	2001
14	Jim Rice, Red Sox	2009
14	Paul Konerko, White Sox	2015
14	Pete Rose, Reds	2016
15	Thurman Munson, Yankees	1979
16	Ted Lyons, White Sox	1987
16	Whitey Ford, Yankees	1974
16	Hal Newhouser, Tigers	1997
16	Jose Fernandez, Marlins	2016
17	Dizzy Dean, Cardinals	1974
17	Todd Helton, Rockies	2014
18	Ted Kluszewski, Reds	1998
18	Mel Harder, Indians	1990
19	Bob Feller, Indians	1956
19	Billy Pierce, White Sox	1987
19	Junior Gilliam, Dodgers	1978
19	Robin Yount, Brewers	1994
19	Tony Gwynn, Padres	2004
20	Luis Gonzalez, Diamondbacks	2010
20	Monte Irvin, Giants	2010
20	Lou Brock, Cardinals	1979
20	Jorge Posada, Yankees	2015
20	Frank Robinson, Orioles	1972
20	Frank Robinson, Reds	1998
20	Pie Traynor, Pirates	1972
20	Mike Schmidt, Phillies	1990
20	Don Sutton, Dodgers	1998
20	Frank White, Royals	1995
21	Warren Spahn, Braves	1965
21	Roberto Clemente, Pirates	1973
21	Bob Lemon, Indians	1998
22	Jim Palmer, Orioles	1985
23	Don Mattingly, Yankees	1997
23	Ryne Sandberg, Cubs	2005
23	Willie Horton, Tigers	2000
24	Willie Mays, Giants	1972
24	Whitey Herzog, Cardinals	2010
24	Tony Perez, Reds	2000
24	Walter Alston, Dodgers	1977
24	Ken Griffey, Jr., Mariners	2016
24	Rickey Henderson, Athletics	2009
24	Jim Wynn, Astros	2005
25	Jose Cruz, Astros	1992
26	Billy Williams, Cubs	1987
26	Gene Autry, Angels	1982
26	Wade Boggs, Red Sox	2016
26	Johnny Oates, Rangers	2002
27	Carlton Fisk, Red Sox	2000
27	Catfish Hunter, Athletics	1991
27	Juan Marichal, Giants	1983
28	Bert Blyleven, Twins	2011
29	Rod Carew, Twins	1987
29	Rod Carew, Angels	1991
29	John Smoltz, Braves	2012
30	Orlando Cepeda, Giants	1999
30	Nolan Ryan, Angels	1992
30	Tim Raines, Expos	2004
31	Dave Winfield, Padres	2001
31	Ferguson Jenkins, Cubs	2009
31	Greg Maddux, Cubs	2009
31	Greg Maddux, Braves	2009
31	Mike Piazza, Mets	2016
32	Steve Carlton, Phillies	1989
32	Sandy Koufax, Dodgers	1972
32	Elston Howard, Yankees	1984
32	Jim Umbricht, Astros	1965
33	Mike Scott, Astros	1992
33	Eddie Murray, Orioles	1998
33	Honus Wagner, Pirates	1952
34	Rollie Fingers, Brewers	1992
34	Rollie Fingers, Athletics	1993
34	Nolan Ryan, Rangers	1996
34	Nolan Ryan, Astros	1996
34	Kirby Puckett, Twins	1997
34	David Ortiz, Red Sox	2016
35	Phil Niekro, Braves	1984
35	Frank Thomas, White Sox	2010
35	Randy Jones, Padres	1997
36	Gaylord Perry, Giants	2005
36	Robin Roberts, Phillies	1962
37	Casey Stengel, Yankees	1970
37	Casey Stengel, Mets	1965
39	Roy Campanella, Dodgers	1972
40	Danny Murtaugh, Pirates	1977
40	Don Wilson, Astros	1975
41	Eddie Mathews, Braves	1969
41	Tom Seaver, Mets	1988
42	Mariano Rivera, Yankees	2013
42	Jackie Robinson, Dodgers	1972
42	Jackie Robinson's number retired by all teams	1997
42	Bruce Sutter, Cardinals	2006
43	Dennis Eckersley, Athletics	2005
44	Hank Aaron, Braves	1977
44	Hank Aaron, Brewers	1976
44	Willie McCovey, Giants	1980
44	Reggie Jackson, Yankees	1993
45	Bob Gibson, Cardinals	1975
45	Pedro Martinez, Red Sox	2015
46	Andy Pettitte, Yankees	2015
47	Tom Glavine, Braves	2010
49	Larry Dierker, Astros	2002
49	Ron Guidry, Yankees	2003
50	Jimmie Reese, Angels	1995
51	Randy Johnson, Diamondbacks	2015
51	Trevor Hoffman, Padres	2011
51	Bernie Williams, Yankees	2015
53	Don Drysdale, Dodgers	1984
66	Don Zimmer, Rays	2015
72	Carlton Fisk, White Sox	1997
85	Augie Busch, Jr., Cardinals	1984
455	Tribute to Indians fans	2001

Chapter 17

Dan Schlossberg photos

It happens every spring: fans flock to Ed Smith Stadium, Sarasota home of the Baltimore Orioles (top left), and Roger Dean Stadium, the pastel Jupiter park shared by the St. Louis Cardinals and Miami Marlins. Batting cage banter reflects the casual atmosphere of spring training, where Joker Marchant Stadium (bottom right) has been the home of the Detroit Tigers for more than 50 years.

Spring Training

CAP ANSON STARTED IT ALL IN 1886 WHEN HE BOILED THE BEER OUT OF HIS CHICAGO WHITE STOCKINGS AT HOT SPRINGS, ARK.

OOH—ALL THAT LOVELY BREW (CHOKE!) J-JUST EVAPORATIN'!

The "Good" Old Days?

Longtime manager and executive Branch Rickey attended his first training camp in Dallas as a rookie with the 1906 St. Louis Browns. There was no permanent camp—just a traveling road show to Fort Worth and Houston. Three of the twenty players had to be cut by Opening Day; when they were, the team had seven pitchers, three catchers, three outfielders, and four infielders. In camp everyone played except manager Jimmy McAleer, road secretary Lloyd Rickert, and trainer Kirby Samuels. There were no coaches, team doctors, scouts, or newsmen with the ballclub.

An Annual Rite

Spring training is a time when all managers predict pennants, optimism reigns supreme, and autographs are as plentiful as hot dogs.

The atmosphere is so relaxed that established players often get time off and are frequently excused from long bus trips during the 30-game exhibition season.

All fields have natural grass and most games are played in daylight—factors that change when play begins for real in April. Experimentation is everywhere, with players working at new positions, freshmen trying to impress managers, veterans hoping to hang on for one more season, and pitchers loosening up gradually by working only a few innings per start.

Because spring training contests don't count, they're called "exhibition" games, since they are exhibitions of individual and team skills minus the intense pressures of the regular season. Matches are determined primarily by geographic proximity, with games played by the Florida-based clubs listed in newspaper standings as "the Grapefruit League," while games played by the teams in Arizona are grouped under the "Cactus League" heading.

Historic Roots

Spring training traces its roots back to February 1870, when Tom Foley took his newly organized touring club, the Chicago White Stockings, south to New Orleans to train for the task of toppling the undefeated 1869 Cincinnati Red Stockings.

Other teams of the National Association, the loosely organized circuit that began a five-year existence the next season, also trained in New Orleans.

Although the National League was founded in 1876, NL teams trained under the stands of their home parks until A. H. Roden took his Boston Nationals to New Orleans, the first stop of a preseason exhibition swing, in 1884.

Pittsburgh and Louisville of the American Association, then a major league, also staged several spring practices in the warmer climes of the southeast.

But the first journey southward for the specific purpose of entering a period of preseason training did not occur until 1886, when White Stockings manager Cap Anson, concerned about his team's portly condition, decided to force off the suet with sweat under the broiling sun—and in the therapeutic baths—of Hot Springs, Arkansas.

In 1888 the Washington Senators, with Connie Mack as a catcher, went south for the spring with a 15-man contingent. Overnight accommodations

The 1909 Red Sox sweated off a winter of suet at Hot Springs, Arkansas.

were in third-class hotels because the better inns refused ball-players, then considered a rowdy bunch. Two men shared a lower berth when the team traveled during its two weeks of training.

In 1890 Brooklyn's prelude to its first National League season featured a swank boat ride to St. Augustine, Florida, where a game was played against Anson's Chicago club. Brooklyn lost that contest and eight of ten overall but capped the tour with a 28–1 win over a choose-up local nine.

Mack was manager of the Philadelphia A's in 1903, when the team slept on cots in a Jacksonville barracks during the training period and ate at a second-rate establishment named Wolfe's.

Three years later John McGraw's New York Giants became the first team to train in California but the experiment was short-lived. Heavy rains had made fields in the Los Angeles area unplayable, so McGraw headed east in search of suitable surroundings. He finally set up headquarters in San Antonio.

Finding Texas to their liking, the Giants established the first permanent training base in Marlin Springs in 1908. The team received not only an annual subsidy from the town but also the deed to the ballpark. Soon after, the Chicago Cubs pitched camp on Catalina Island, 26 miles from Los Angeles. Theirs was the second regular training site.

Florida was still far from the spring hub of activity it is today, however. In fact, there were only 16 major league teams when Branch Rickey brought the St. Louis Browns to St. Petersburg for a one-night stand in 1914, succeeded by the Phillies the following spring.

Rickey's Florida initiative was the result of a series of letters from former Pittsburgh resident Al Lang, a baseball insider who had gone south for his health in 1911 at age 41. Lang had been a batboy, clubhouse boy, and errand boy for ballplayers in his youth and, as owner of a successful laundry business, retained his ties with people from the game.

His closest friend was Pirate owner Barney Dreyfuss, whose club trained in Hot Springs, Arkansas. When Lang read that snow kept the Pirates out of action three straight days, he wrote Dreyfuss to join him at St. Pete, then a sleepy fishing village of 3,000 residents. Dreyfuss didn't bite.

But Al Lang—and the growing town—struck gold in 1922, when the Boston Braves moved there from Galveston, Texas. At first, few fans turned out for St. Petersburg games. But freezing New Englanders, seeking to cut their winters short, came to see them work out and the city prospered.

In 1927 the Braves were joined by the powerful New York Yankees, shifting sites from New Orleans.

Some spring-training sites were chosen for frivolous reasons. Augusta, for example, was a Detroit spring base because it was the hometown of manager Ty Cobb, the Georgia Peach. When Cobb left Detroit, Detroit left Augusta.

Foreign capitals—Mexico City, Havana, Ciudad Trujillo, and Panama City—also had at least one season as big-league spring-training sites.

Teams could not always afford spring training. In 1919 the St. Louis Cardinals could not pay for the trip south, so Branch Rickey moved them indoors—to the Washington University gymnasium in St. Louis. Out-of-town players tripled up at a nearby hotel, while residents commuted by streetcar. When weather permitted, the Cards practiced on the college's outdoor diamond, which had no outfield fence.

Spring training juggling by third baseman Pinky Higgins (center) and pitchers Al Benton (left) and Bill Dietrich (right) did little to prevent a last-place finish by the 1935 Philadelphia A's.

The Meaning of Spring Training

Hall of Famer Ralph Kiner, home-run king of the Pirates and later a New York broadcaster, on spring training:

"Spring training is made for the owners, managers, and general managers. It's the only time they can really go down and relax, enjoy what's going on, and not worry about whether their team won or lost.

"As a player, I looked on spring training as an experiment—a chance to try things, for maybe 20 or 30 days, to come up with some new theory that I might work on and see if it held up. Sometimes it would be completely different from what I had been doing.

"Probably the biggest thing I ever did in spring training was to go to a much heavier bat. It worked well; I stayed with it and used it the rest of my career. I used a 42-ounce bat and then dropped down to 37, which is extremely heavy compared to what the average player uses (anywhere from 30 to 32 ounces).

"I couldn't have cared less about what I hit during the spring, but I did have to play all the ballgames because I was the so-called 'attraction' of the Pittsburgh Pirates."

Fishing for Tips

When Bucky Harris was running the Washington Senators one spring, he drew special attention from owner Clark Griffith. Standing in the outfield with a young player, Harris appeared to be teaching the art of proper throwing.

"Look at Harris," said Griffith. "He's never too busy to teach a young fellow the right way."

In truth, Harris was getting tips from the rookie, who had been champion flycaster in his home state of Mississippi.

Al Lang's Legacy

The dream of the late Al Lang, who put Florida on the baseball map, lives on in the form of the $3.2 million Al Lang Field in St. Petersburg, spring home of the Tampa Bay Rays.

The field, several blocks east of the National Association of Professional Baseball Leagues (minor-league headquarters), also hosts Florida Instructional League teams in the fall.

Even today, teams don't make money on spring training. Ballparks are too small, schedules too short, and expenses too high to make the six-week training period profitable. But the public relations impact can't be measured: many sports fans swear spring begins the moment pitchers and catchers report in mid-February.

Fans even turn out to watch calisthenics—including stretching, flexibility, and aerobics classes led by female instructors half the size of the players they're coaching.

Though training methods have changed, the basic purpose of spring training has not. For every team, the goal is the same—cutting the roster down to the 25-man limit of Opening Day.

In 1911 the Philadelphia Phillies left spring training with an internal squabble over a rookie pitcher who had been purchased from Syracuse for $500.

Manager Charlie Dooin wanted to return the young player and get his money back, but coach Pat Moran, whose B squad included the man in question, insisted he be kept. The rest is history: Grover Cleveland Alexander went on to win 373 games, as many as Christy Mathewson and more than any other National League pitcher.

According to Clyde King, who pitched for the Brooklyn Dodgers in the '40s and '50s and later managed three major league teams, "I looked forward to spring training. I actually couldn't wait to get there. I was not a great player, so I had to work hard and utilize everything I had to make the ballclub. Some players didn't like training and would make excuses to get there late. On the Brooklyn club, there weren't that many jobs open: we had Gil Hodges, Roy Campanella, Pee Wee Reese, and other stars.

"We went down to Vero Beach and lived together in the barracks. The guys played pool at night, and they had movies some-

American League

Manager Connie Mack, who preferred a business suit to baseball flannels, instructs prospects at the 1949 Philadelphia A's spring camp. From left are pitcher Bobby Shantz (soon to be the club's top star), infielder Todd Davis, catcher Joe Astroth, and pitchers Jim Wilson and Clem Hausman.

times. We ate together in the cafeteria—another one of those togetherness things. If you had your family, you could live out.

"One year we trained in the Dominican Republic. Leo Durocher was our manager and his wife, Laraine Day, was an actress who would bring current movies to our hotel one night a week. There were so many things they did for us that we appreciated—even though we didn't say so."

The tradition of off-the-field entertainment during spring training is almost as old as the game itself. One spring John McGraw offered Ted Sullivan $50 to bring the movies of the 1913–1914 round-the-world baseball tour to the Marlin, Texas, spring-training base of the Giants.

Sullivan came and, with McGraw's approval, hired a piano player to provide background music. The musician was instructed to play "The Marseillaise" when the film showed the group arriving in France and "God Save the King" when it got to England. Rehearsals went perfectly, with Sullivan reading his text to the musical background.

But McGraw managed to bribe the pianist to switch national anthems—playing the German anthem for the arrival in Paris and "The Marseillaise" for England. Sullivan tried to outshout the music as McGraw and company howled.

Yankee management wasn't laughing in 1925, when Babe Ruth nearly ate himself out of the league during spring training. Fined $5,000 by manager Miller Huggins for breaking training rules, Ruth endured a miserable season. Absent for long spells, he lost 88 points from his 1924 batting average, hit 21 fewer home runs, and knocked in 57 fewer runs.

After paying careful attention to his physical condition that winter, Ruth engineered a mighty comeback in 1926, returning the Yankees (seventh in 1925) to the top of the American League.

Ten years later, pitcher Lefty Gomez told writers covering the Yankee camp, "I'm going to stay at 160 pounds. A couple of years ago, Joe McCarthy told me if I could take on 15 pounds, I'd make people forget Lefty Grove. I took 'em on and people almost forgot Lefty Gomez."

Weight is the first thing managers discuss in the spring. When players report, they march to the scales almost before they do anything else. Often they are asked to report at a specific weight and may be fined $100 a pound for every pound exceeding the limit.

Ty Cobb lasted 24 years because he maintained a constant vigil on his physical condition, running 10 miles per day in the winter and wearing weighted shoes during spring training. At Detroit's training camp, he habitually installed steel plates into his shoes when he reported—an effort to strengthen his leg muscles. The plates were removed on Opening Day.

Cobb, Tris Speaker, Honus Wagner, and other Hall of Famers enjoyed long careers because they safeguarded their legs. (Often, when a pitcher retires, he is forced to quit because his legs can no longer take the strain; the arm may still be sound.)

Managers have always emphasized running and nutrition as keys to conditioning, and flexibility has won such recognition from clubs that several have hired special flexibility coaches for spring training. The theory is that flexible athletes—who know how to reach, twist, and even fall—are less likely to suffer serious injuries.

The Sporting News

Out of Steam

The 1916 Philadelphia A's had to shorten their exhibition schedule when the steamboat taking the team to spring training was delayed by bad weather and engine trouble.

Los Angeles Dodgers

Roy Campanella puts on catching gear at Vero Beach, Florida.

WHERE TEAMS TRAIN
American League

Baltimore—Ed Smith Stadium, Sarasota, FL
Boston—jetBlue Park, Fort Myers, FL
Chicago—Camelback Ranch, Glendale, AZ
Cleveland—Goodyear Ballpark, AZ
Detroit—Joker Marchant Stadium, Lakeland, FL
Houston—Ballpark of the Palm Beaches, West Palm Beach, FL
Kansas City—Surprise Stadium, Surprise, AZ
Los Angeles—Tempe Diable Stadium, Tempe, AZ
Minnesota—Hammond Stadium, Fort Myers, FL
New York—George M. Steinbrenner Field, Tampa, FL
Oakland—Hohokam Park, Mesa, AZ
Seattle—Peoria Stadium, Peoria, AZ
Tampa—Charlotte Sports Park, Port Charlotte, FL
Texas—Surprise Recreation Complex, Surprise, AZ
Toronto—Florida Auto Exchange Stadium, Dunedin, FL

National League

Arizona—Salt River Fields at Talking Stick, Scottsdale, AZ
Atlanta—Kissimmee, FL*
Chicago—Sloan Park, Mesa, AZ
Cincinnati—Goodyear Ballpark, Goodyear, AZ
Colorado—Salt River Fields at Talking Stick, Scottsdale, AZ
Los Angeles—Camelback Ranch, Glendale, AZ
Miami—Roger Dean Stadium, Jupiter, FL
Milwaukee—Maryvale Baseball Park, Phoenix, AZ
New York—Tradition Field, Port St. Lucie, FL
Philadelphia—Brought House Field, Clearwater, FL
Pittsburgh Pirates—McKechnie Field, Bradenton, FL
St. Louis—Roger Dean Stadium, Jupiter, FL
San Diego—Peoria Stadium, Peoria, AZ
San Francisco—Scottsdale Stadium, Scottsdale, AZ
Washington—Ballpark of the Palm Beaches, West Palm Beach, FL

(*) new park pending for 2019

Some Comeback

Among the replacement players during 1995 spring training was Jimmy Boudreau, who had last played professionally in 1986. After he struggled during an exhibition game, Pittsburgh broadcaster Steve Blass said, "He should have been better, pitching on 3,195 days' rest."

Since throwing is an unnatural act, pitchers must prepare themselves slowly, building up strength and endurance not only in their arms but also in their legs. When durable Ed Walsh, a 40-game winner for the 1908 White Sox, failed to do that one spring, he began a premature backslide from the pitching heights.

On the first day of training at Paso Robles, California, in 1913, Walsh was on the diamond behind the hotel when he spied fellow pitcher Jim Scott throwing hard to catcher Ray Schalk. Scott had played ball during the winter and was already in prime condition, so he was able to throw at top velocity without any trouble.

Walsh hadn't thrown since the final game of the Chicago City Series the previous fall but a pang of jealousy gave him an urgent desire to throw as hard—or harder—than Scott. Without manager Jim Callahan or coach Kid Gleason around to stop him, Walsh began to throw as hard as he could. The sore arm that followed ruined his career.

Many careers are started or stopped in spring training. The only constant is the fact that spring training provides an annual proving ground—even in wartime.

The Landis Line

To free train transportation vital to the nation's war effort in 1943, Commissioner Kenesaw Mountain Landis ruled that no club could train south of the Ohio or Potomac Rivers nor west of the Mississippi (with the exception of the St. Louis Browns and Cardinals).

Under the mandate of the Landis Line, all but 6 of the 16 teams chose close-to-home sites and trained there all three seasons. The others shifted around—the Braves jumping to Washington, D.C., in 1945 after two springs in Wallingford, Connecticut, and the Phils switching to Hershey, Pennsylvania, the same year from Wilmington, Delaware.

The Philadelphia Athletics, who shared Wilmington in 1943, transferred to Frederick, Maryland, and the Yankees moved from Asbury Park to Atlantic City, New Jersey, at the same time. The Red Sox and White Sox relocated for the final year of training in the north—Boston moving from Medford, Massachusetts, to Atlantic City and Chicago switching from French Lick to Terre Haute, Indiana.

At Lakewood, New Jersey, the New York Giants were sole occupants of a 45-room hotel. The players traveled to practices by horse-and-buggy because it was the most practical means in view of wartime gas rationing and rubber shortages.

The first day of 1943 spring training, the Giants began their journey to the South Jersey pinelands by assembling in the team's New York office on West 42nd Street. They crossed the Hudson by ferry, rode the rails to Lakewood, then boarded the horse-drawn tally-ho to reach the Hotel de Brannick.

New York's other National League entry, the Brooklyn Dodgers, made Bear Mountain, New York, their spring port o' call. The club also had an option to use the West Point fieldhouse for a minimum of three hours per day—and did that when bad weather prevailed.

Asked what players wore, Clyde King remembered, "Everything we had! We wore turtlenecks and more than one sweat-

The concept of spring exercises hasn't changed much since the Philadelphia Athletics worked out in West Palm Beach in 1946.

shirt—sometimes heavy long sweatshirts. I don't remember long johns. I do know there wasn't a whole lot of complaining even though it was cold. And I remember working out on the field at Bear Mountain and seeing Hessian Lake, behind the lodge, frozen over.

"We were ready by the time the season opened—as ready as anyone else because everyone trained in the north. Our site was perfect: we were close to New York and we enjoyed it. Mrs. McKeever, whose husband was a former owner of the Dodgers, used to play the piano in the inn at night. We'd all gather round and sing songs."

Like the Dodgers, the Pittsburgh Pirates learned to cope with unpredictable conditions. The first day at Muncie, Indiana, manager Frankie Frisch told his players, "If you can see your breath when you walk out of the hotel in the morning, don't go to the field. Go to the high school gym. We'll play basketball instead of baseball."

Rostered players were asked how much of their salaries they wanted withheld for the purchase of war bonds, while pitcher Rip Sewell borrowed a potted palm from a local barber shop and brought it to the team's hotel as a reminder of better things to come.

The Yankees and Red Sox, sharing the 112th Field Artillery Armory in Atlantic City on bad-weather days, had to find new quarters after the building was converted into a military hospital. The St. Louis Cardinals also had to move—after their Cairo, Illinois, field was flooded by levee seepage from the swollen Ohio and Mississippi Rivers.

On March 26, 1945, the Cards packed their gear for St. Louis and completed spring training in Sportsman's Park.

A year later, with the war over, every club in the majors returned to the typical tropical climes of spring training—their adventures in the north reduced to an unusual footnote in the long history of the game.

Musial's Views

Hall of Famer Stan Musial, a dud in spring training as a rookie with the 1942 Cardinals, suggests preseason workouts are not accurate indicators of player potential.

"I think there is a tendency to overrate pitchers and underrate hitters down there," he said. "In most of the parks, the background for a hitter is terrible and you really notice the difference when you get home and see those double-decked stands."

Dan Schlossberg

Except for a three-year wartime hiatus, the Detroit Tigers have trained in Lakeland, FL since 1934— longer in one location than any other club. Joker Marchant Stadium opened in 1946.

A month before the sinking of the *Titanic*, the Brooklyn Dodgers ready themselves for the 1912 season in Hot Springs, Arkansas.

Travel restrictions forced the Dodgers to train indoors at Bear Mountain, New York during the Second World War.

Barnstorming Home

The tradition of barnstorming has also become a baseball footnote.

Rising hotel and transportation costs have virtually killed the concept, with current clubs sticking close to their home bases almost to the eve of Opening Day.

Barnstorming began to decline shortly after the Second World War. The 1951 Yankees, training in Phoenix that year, played dates in Los Angeles and San Francisco, minor-league cities at the time, on an 11-game jaunt to the west but made only a $4,000 profit after packing parks at every stop. Smaller crowds had produced larger profits—encouraging such tours—during the Babe Ruth era.

Small towns had small diamonds—with stands seating 3,000 or less—but an appearance by Ruth (whose fame spread through the print media) guaranteed an overflow. Fans stood behind roped-off sections of outfield and daredevil youngsters clung to trees beyond the outfield fence—if indeed there was a fence.

In one southern park, Ruth homered into an imposing oak tree just beyond the right-field barrier. The tree was crammed with young fans yearning for a look at the living legend of the Yankees, but Ruth's blast—hit like a shot—cleared the branches in record time.

The touring Yankees of 1928, sweeping through Texas and Oklahoma after leaving St. Petersburg, compiled a total spring attendance of 128,000 and made a handsome haul of $60,000—big bucks in those days. Ruth received 10 percent of the gate receipts, an arrangement unique in baseball history.

The first whistle-stop spring trip undertaken by special arrangement between major league clubs occurred in 1918, when the Giants and Tigers trained in Texas.

John McGraw's Giants had agreed to barnstorm with Ty Cobb's Tigers, but Detroit's temperamental star scrapped with his rivals, left the tour, and completed his training with the Cincinnati Reds. Cobb's departure, coupled with attendance already hindered by the First World War, posed financial problems for McGraw.

The two-team tour of the longest duration involved the post-McGraw Giants, then based in Miami, and the Cleveland Indians, based in New Orleans when the clubs began their annual spring barnstorming ritual in 1934.

When the clubs became the first to invade Arizona in the late '40s, their barnstorming became even more practical and continued for more than 25 years.

Barnstorming did have advantages: welcoming crowds at every depot, hero-worshipping fans packed into every park, and enough attention and affection in town to cover not only the players but the entire traveling party—even the writers.

Fun in the Sun

Spring training is still fun. It is more sport than business—a game as gentle as the ocean breeze, a pageant whose participants are unhurried, unhassled, and often uninhibited. The late Frankie Frisch wasn't far off the mark when he referred to training camps as "country clubs without dues."

Sun Belt sites from Scottsdale to Fort Lauderdale host cozy ballparks with compact stands close to the action; players pose willingly for cameras; managers disguised in sunglasses sit on folding chairs next to the stands; and teams emphasize conditioning rather than competition. Public-address announcers add to the atmosphere when they give both the local temperature and the latest report from the host team's home city.

For players, spring training is a time for rounding into shape, shedding excess poundage, and sharpening reflexes required for the rigorous 162-game regular season.

For fans, it's a chance to cut winter short, rub elbows with their idols, and catch a sneak preview of their favorite teams and players.

Spring Games Draw Well

Major league teams drew 2,754,300 fans during their 1992 spring-training exhibition season.

A record total of 986,897 fans attended games at regular training sites, while 215,380 more passed through the gates for games at other sites, including major league parks.

Five teams reported new spring-training records.

Although the San Francisco Giants drew the biggest average crowds (8,571 per game), the Chicago Cubs, with one more home date, led the majors with total attendance of 123,920. The Cubs played 15 games at their spring base in Mesa, Arizona.

Milwaukee Blooms in Spring

The city of Milwaukee has twice won teams during spring training. On March 18, 1953, the Boston Braves announced their franchise would become the Milwaukee Braves that season—the first change in the baseball map since 1903. The Braves moved again, to Atlanta, after the 1965 season but in March 1970, with little more than a week before opening day, the Seattle Pilots, a 1969 expansion team with financial woes, became the Milwaukee Brewers.

Willing to try anything that might get players into shape, John McGraw (far left) even resorted to donkeys—and hoped his players wouldn't make asses of themselves.

Pitchers Ahead of Hitters

Early in the baseball season, pitchers have the edge on hitters. Some hurlers have rounded into midseason form long before the hitters have sharpened their batting eyes.

In 1944 Chicago Cubs' manager Jimmie Wilson explained why:

"Any manager can get his pitchers into condition to start off the season at an effective clip, regardless of whether his club trains in the south or in the north. The manager can make the pitchers do the right amount of running and throwing to be ready to hurl at top speed when the bell rings.

"But the manager cannot train his hitters. They must train themselves. He can see to it that they get lots of running and also lots of hitting practice, but he cannot do a single thing about perfecting their timing. That must come from actual competition and even in a long southern training season many hitters do not get enough of this sort of preparation to match the pitchers in being ready to play for keeps. So the pitchers annually start with an edge."

Training Camp Trade

One of the most unusual trades in baseball history occurred in 1951, when the New York Yankees and the New York Giants swapped training camps for one year only. The Giants trained in St. Petersburg, Florida, and the Yankees in Phoenix, Arizona, in 1951, met in the World Series that fall, then reverted to their original sites in 1952.

The Cactus League

That's especially true in Arizona, where most members of the 15-team Cactus League are almost close enough for a home-run ball to travel from one ballpark to another. Teams even share ballparks in Surprise, Peoria, and Glendale.

As a result, the longest "road trip" during Cactus League spring training takes less than half the time of the longest ride between Grapefruit League cities in Florida.

With virtually all of the teams clustered around Phoenix and Scottsdale, fans flock east from California, south from Colorado, and west from Chicago for Cactus League baseball. All the West Coast clubs, both Chicago teams, and teams from Milwaukee, Colorado, and Texas train under the high sky of the desert southwest.

1945 Spring Training Map

Where Clubs Will Kindle Camp-Fires

NATIONAL LEAGUE
(Figures in black circles)
1—Cardinals, Cairo, Ill.
2—Reds, Bloomington, Ind.
3—Dodgers, Bear M'tain, N. Y.
4—Pirates, Muncie, Ind.
5—Cubs, French Lick, Ind.
6—Braves, Washington, D. C.
7—Phils, Wilmington, Del.
8—Giants, Lakewood, N. J.

AMERICAN LEAGUE
(Figures in outlined circles)
1—Yankees, Atlantic City, N. J.
2—Senators, College Park, Md.
3—Indians, Lafayette, Ind.
4—White Sox, Terre Haute, Ind.
5—Tigers, Evansville, Ind.
6—Red Sox, Pleasantville, N. J.
7—Browns, Cape Girardeau, Mo.
8—Athletics, Frederick, Md.

The Sporting News

Baseball is different in Arizona for both players and fans. The state has dry heat, with cacti more prevalent than palm trees and a desert climate known for low humidity and infrequent spring precipitation.

With a large resident community of snowbirds who eschew the bitter winters of Chicago, the Cubs often lead the majors in spring attendance. It helps that their stadium, Sloan Park, is the largest of the spring training facilities in either state (capacity 15,000). No matter how poorly the Cubs perform during the regular season, they always draw a crowd.

The Grapefruit League

A spring training hub for more than a century, Florida plays host to 15 teams—just one less than the combined membership of the National and American Leagues in 1960, the last season before expansion.

Winter-weary fans come in droves from the frozen north, joining dozens of part-time Floridians who come south to avoid the snow, ice, and cold that grips the mainland for months. To them, the first day of spring is the day pitchers and catchers report.

Although the map of spring training sites changes often, clubs are based in clusters to facilitate exhibition game scheduling. The three main hubs are Fort Myers, a southwestern town on the Gulf of Mexico; Tampa-St. Petersburg, also on the gulf; and the Palm Beaches, where four clubs share two stadiums.

There's considerable common ground: all fields have natural grass, most games are played in daylight, and nobody cares who wins or loses once the 30-game exhibition season starts in March.

As in Arizona, cozy ballparks breed a casual, informal atmosphere that almost allows fans to reach out and touch their heroes

Fans love to take in the sun as well as the game during baseball spring training. There are 15 clubs in both the Arizona-based Cactus League and the Florida-based Grapefruit League.

Hollywood History

The Hollywood, California site where the Pittsburgh Pirates trained from 1939 to 1957 is now occupied by CBS Television City.

Marlins Moves

The Marlins, the only team to go north for spring training, traded spring sites with the Montreal Expos in 2003 when that team was owned and operated by Major League Baseball. The Expos went to Space Coast Stadium in Viera, while Florida got closer to its South Florida fan base by moving from Viera to Jupiter.

Vero Veto

The 60-year tenure of the Los Angeles Dodgers in Vero Beach, Florida ended in 2008 when the team decided to accommodate its California fan base by moving to Glendale, Arizona. The last spring games in Vero were managed by the retired Tommy Lasorda while active manager Joe Torre took half the squad to China for two exhibition games against the San Diego Padres.

Bright Idea

McKechnie Field, the last stadium to add lights, hosted its first night game on March 19, 2008. The visiting Yankees defeated the Pirates, 12–9. The oldest of the spring training ballparks was built in 1923.

Coliseum Comeback

To mark the 60th anniversary of their move from Brooklyn to Los Angeles, the Dodgers reactivated the Los Angeles Memorial Coliseum—their first home in California—for an exhibition game against the Boston Red Sox on March 29, 2008. Although the Dodgers lost, 7–4, they drew a record crowd of 115,300.

Cozy Cactus Clubs

Proximity is a plus in the Cactus League: the Texas Rangers are so close to the Peoria facility shared by the Seattle Mariners and San Diego Padres that the Rangers often take batting practice at home in Surprise before playing exhibition games in Peoria.

Cactus Kingpin

Sloan Park in Mesa cost $84 million and seats 15,000—the largest capacity in the Cactus League. Ninety percent of the seats are in the shade. The stadium, which opened in 2014, is the largest spring training park in Arizona.

Hooter Problems

When a great horned owl nested atop the right field lights at Space Coast Stadium, longtime home of the Miami Marlins, the creature couldn't be moved because it was protected by federal law.

Los Angeles Dodgers

Holman Stadium, longtime spring home of the Los Angeles Dodgers in Vero Beach, Florida, had no dugouts. Players sat on long benches in front of the stands while protecting themselves from the sun with towels on their heads.

The resemblance is deliberate: jetBlue Park at Fenway South, spring home of the Red Sox since 2012, looks like a miniature version of the fabled Boston ballpark. Tickets are tough to get at the stadium, which has 9,900 seats and sells out quickly.

at a fraction of the regular-season price. In fact, the only park that holds as many as 10,000 fans is George M. Steinbrenner Field, the Tampa home of the New York Yankees. Its official capacity is 11,076.

Getting tickets without advance planning, however, is no easy matter.

Ducats for Yankees games, especially on their home turf, are always at a premium. But they're not as tough to find as tickets for JetBlue Park, the mini-Fenway Park where the Red Sox train, or for Roger Dean Stadium, where fans of the Cardinals make the stands a sea of red for St. Louis home games.

There's always a game in Jupiter, one of two Florida communities (along with West Palm Beach) where teams share ballparks. Both Roger Dean Stadium and the newer Ballpark of the Palm Beaches are within a stone's throw of both I-95 and the popular Palm Beaches.

Fort Myers has two teams too (Red Sox and Twins) but they don't play in the same place.

Before they moved to Port Charlotte, the Tampa Bay Rays were the first team in modern baseball history to train at home. They played spring games at Al Lang Field, a facility renowned for soaring pelicans, harmonica-playing vendors, and white sails in the bay beyond the outfield fences.

At many parks, fans think they—and not baseball—are the real exhibition. The parade of bikinis and halter tops occasionally detracts from the action between the white lines. Binoculars salesmen would do as well as the card-carrying kids seeking celebrity signatures.

One facility that was once a fan favorite for spring training now stands unused by a major league team. Dodgertown, the Vero Beach site the Dodgers used for 60 years, was left vacant when new team ownership decided an Arizona location would be a better fit for its fan base.

In its heyday, the 450-acre site had a 70-acre orange grove, 27-hole golf course, country club, restaurant, two-and-a-half practice fields, and a well-groomed, 110-acre baseball facility. For most of its tenure, Holman Stadium lacked dugouts and outfield fences—forcing outfielders to rely on an embankment that sloped just in front of a ring of palm trees.

Hope Springs Eternal

Spring is a time of hope—especially among young players seeking permanent jobs in the big leagues. Sometimes, deserving players don't make it because veteran incumbents block the way.

Former Cleveland slugger Al Rosen remembers, "I was sent out three years in a row. I was really down. I had been Most Valuable Player in every league I played in. There wasn't much more that I could prove."

In 1950 things changed. Ken Keltner, starting to deteriorate in the field, couldn't play regularly anymore. "Lou Boudreau, the manager, didn't want to let him go," Rosen said. "He had strong feelings of loyalty to his old players. But Hank Greenberg, the general manager, wanted me."

Barnstormers Babe Ruth and Lou Gehrig (left), here advancing the cause of a world championship rodeo in 1928, enabled the Yankees to rake in huge crowds en route home from spring camp.

Fans in Vero Beach had the best access to athletes since players had to walk from the clubhouse to the diamond on sidewalks shared with spectators.

As the song says, those were the days! Former Dodger manager Tommy Lasorda, a spring-training instructor, often watches exhibition games from the stands while still wearing his uniform.

Clubhouses in Jupiter, home of the Cardinals and the Expos, are also not connected to dugouts. Instead, they're located beyond the center-field fence of Roger Dean Stadium.

Several Grapefruit and Cactus League facilities, including Roger Dean Stadium in Jupiter, host two teams.

The Atlanta Braves trained at Disney's Wide World of Sports for 20 years starting in 1998. The facility, which features a 9,500-seat stadium, includes venues for multiple sports.

Chapter 18

Ronnie Joyner

Dan Schlossberg

Library of Congress

Jackie Mitchell was 17 when she struck out Babe Ruth and Lou Gehrig but Organized Baseball nullified her Chattanooga Lookouts contract, saying the game was too rough for girls.

Library of Congress

Even 100 years ago, baseball owners were interested in expanding the influence of their game. White Sox owner Charles Comiskey organized a 1913 postseason world tour that barnstormed through the southwest and Pacific Coast, then devoid of big-league teams, and eventually stopped in British Columbia, Japan, Ceylon, India, Egypt, and England—where King George V came to watch. The teams, consisting primarily of players from Comiskey's White Sox and John McGraw's National League champion New York Giants, arrived in New York aboard the *Lusitania*, a liner sunk by a German torpedo two years later. Participants included Christy Mathewson, Sam Crawford, Jim Thorpe, Buck Weaver, Fred Merkle, and celebrated umpire Bill Klem.

Other Leagues and Other Lands

The National Association

The minor leagues, widely known as the training ground for the majors, provide a place for talented players to polish their skills and garner valuable experience that might eventually enable them to compete against the best ballplayers in the world.

The National Association of Professional Baseball Leagues has been representing minor-league baseball since September 1901, when it was created to protect minor-league operators against wanton raids of their players by major league teams.

With rare exceptions (Sandy Koufax is one) every big-league player reaches the majors only after spending time in the minors. Ty Cobb, Rogers Hornsby, and Babe Ruth were among the superstars who began their professional careers in the minor leagues.

The first minor league, the International Association, was organized in Pittsburgh on February 20, 1877.

Other leagues sprang up quickly. In 1887 three of them merged to form the International League, but an unwieldy 10-club structure was plagued by numerous franchise shifts and all but extinguished during the Players League revolt of the majors in 1890 (the only year since its founding that the International failed to finish a season).

In 1902 the league launched an 11-year period of stability thanks in part to construction of new ballparks by prosperous streetcar companies. The lines hoped to make money from fans riding trolleys to the parks.

The Winter Series of 1893

Portland (Pacific Northwest) and San Jose (California) played an unusual 19-game playoff series in January 1893. San Jose won.

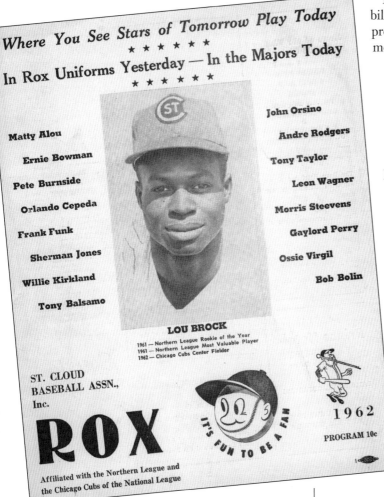

Where You See Stars of Tomorrow Play Today
★ ★ ★ ★ ★
In Rox Uniforms Yesterday — In the Majors Today
★ ★ ★ ★ ★ ★

Matty Alou
Ernie Bowman
Pete Burnside
Orlando Cepeda
Frank Funk
Sherman Jones
Willie Kirkland
Tony Balsamo

John Orsino
Andre Rodgers
Tony Taylor
Leon Wagner
Morris Steevens
Gaylord Perry
Ossie Virgil
Bob Bolin

LOU BROCK
1961 — Northern League Rookie of the Year
1961 — Northern League Most Valuable Player
1962 — Chicago Cubs Center Fielder

ST. CLOUD
BASEBALL ASSN.,
Inc.

ROX

IT'S FUN TO BE A FAN

1962
PROGRAM 10c

Affiliated with the Northern League and
the Chicago Cubs of the National League

Challenges to the Minors

The Federal League, an attempted third major league in 1914 and 1915, weakened the International League by invading many of its cities, and World War I so affected the minors in 1918 that only the IL finished its season.

Since that time the International League has prospered despite much shifting of clubs, usually in proportion to growth or decline of cities along the eastern seaboard.

Along with the other minor leagues, the IL survived raids from the majors by enforcing the National Agreement, originally a 10-year pact that promised to punish players and clubs who violated contracts, established salary limits, fixed a reserve rule that bound each player to his club, and classified leagues according to levels of play.

Top circuits were classified as Double-A, then A, B, C, and D in declining order of ability. Later, the top three categories were changed to AAA, AA, and A. In 1963 all bottom categories were dropped and leagues were changed to AAA, AA, or A with the sole exception of the Rookie Leagues, the modern equivalent of Class D.

Minor leagues are often called "bush leagues," because of the long bus rides, or "hamburger leagues," because players don't receive enough meal money to buy more expensive meat.

With rare exceptions, travel and hotel accommodations are well below major league standards, ballparks have poor lighting systems, and opportunity for recognition is nonexistent.

After escaping the minors, some players often laugh at conditions they left behind: showerheads that came up only waist high in Leesburg, a four-headed shower stall that flooded the clubhouse in Statesville, a movie theater with rocking chairs in the same town, a community washroom in the hotel at Dubuque, and steamy, deteriorating hotels that invariably were in worse condition than the ballparks.

The Tight Economy

Money, always hard to come by in minor-league baseball, was especially scarce during the Depression years. Members of the Los Angeles Angels were happy to get winners' shares of $210 per man for beating the Pacific Coast League All-Stars after the 1934 season. Losing shares were worth $122.

Things became so tight that the Northern League allowed its clubs the use of only one ball per game. One team conserved so well that it had two-dozen balls left to sell to the local school system when the season ended.

In the heyday of the independent operator, Chattanooga owner Joe Engel was trying to sign a player. The athlete sent him a message: "Double your offer or count me out." Engel wired back, "1, 2, 3, 4, 5, 6, 7, 8, 9, 10."

As late as 1972, minor-leaguers in the Class A Midwest League got only $3.50 per day for meal money, as opposed to $18 given major leaguers. The average minor-league salary was little more than $1,000 per month.

In 1926 the St. Louis Cardinals, with Branch Rickey at the controls, sought to purchase a player from the Joplin, Missouri, club. Their interest became known and a small bidding war ensued. The Cardinals, already operating on a shoestring, were knocked out quickly.

"If we can't buy the contracts of players," Rickey told team owner Sam Breadon, "we'll have to raise our own."

When Cardinal scouts started signing large numbers of players, other teams jumped into the act. But baseball commissioner Kenesaw Mountain Landis never liked the idea, called it "slavery," and predicted the farm system would ruin the independence of the minors.

Development of the farms did not hurt the minors, since major league organizations poured their own resources into player development, hired the managers, and maintained the ballparks of their minor-league teams. Many of the major/minor links were by "working agreement," giving the minor-league team the chance to retain local ownership while having a big-league affiliation.

Rickey cultivated his farm system concept so thoroughly that by 1946, when he was running the Brooklyn Dodgers, the club had the amazing total of 20 farm teams, including two each at the Triple-A and Double-A levels.

The Ned Hanlon Cup was presented to the International League's Baltimore Orioles in 1944, the 50th anniversary of the first of three straight National League championships won by Hanlon's original Orioles of 1894. The Orioles returned to the majors in 1954, when the St. Louis Browns relocated there.

Workhorse

In 1878 Buffalo Bisons pitcher Jim Galvin had a record of 75 wins, 25 defeats, and three ties. He completed 96 of 101 games, threw 17 shutouts, and had a 10-5 mark in exhibition play against the National League. He started and finished his club's first 23 games and relieved in the 24th. Buffalo then belonged to the International Association.

First Spitballer

The minor leagues produced the first spitball pitcher—Elmer Stricklett of Sacramento (California League), circa 1900.

Hollywood Players Wore Shorts

The old Hollywood Stars (Pacific Coast) pioneered the concept of short pants for players, but sliding burns ended the experiment. The 1977 Chicago White Sox also tried shorts briefly.

Minor-league life brings fans closer to the players. Tight budgets forced countless promotions, including this Ball Day giveaway by the old Toronto Maple Leafs. Future major league managers Sparky Anderson (right foreground) and Jackie Moore (No. 29) were the key attractions.

High-Scoring Series

From June 9 to 11, 1978, the Reno Silver Sox and Visalia Oaks of the Class A California League combined for 101 runs. The games, played at Reno, Nevada, set several league records for offensive production. Reno won the opener, 24–12. Then Visalia won by consecutive scores of 27–17 and 14–7.

High Score Causes Confusion

When Corsicana swamped Texarkana, 51–3, at Ennis, Texas, on June 15, 1902, disbelieving telegraph operators reported the score as 5–3.

Three years later there were 448 teams in 59 minor leagues—the National Association's largest roll call. Independents and farms thrived; minor-league attendance was 26 million, while major league attendance was 10 million.

By 1963 the minors were reduced to 130 teams in 18 leagues. The farm system idea had taken over and external factors forced reductions in the minor leagues. An agreement between majors and minors stipulated that every major league club must own or have an affiliation with at least one team at each of the three classifications in the minors, AAA, AA, and A.

"What killed the minors? The answer is simple," said Bobby Bragan, president of the National Association in 1978. "Television and air-conditioning were the big things. A fan can sit home and watch a big-league game in the comfort of his living room on a hot summer night instead of spending $1 or $2 to come out to the ballpark."

Bragan said that minor-league teams can counteract such drawbacks by promoting heavily. "Three things are essential for a successful team," he insisted. "Geography, a good operator, and a facility."

The largest crowd ever to attend a minor-league game turned out in Denver for Fireworks Night, an Independence Day celebration, in 1982. A total of 65,555 fans passed through the turnstiles of Mile High Stadium. Denver held the previous minor-league mark with more than 59,000 for Fireworks Night 1981.

Jersey City sold 65,391 tickets to the 1940 opener at Roosevelt Stadium (capacity 40,000), thanks in large measure to the extensive footwork of men working for Mayor Frank Hague. In 1948 and 1949 opening games in the city reported ticket sales of 52,000.

There were 52,833 fans in Baltimore Memorial Stadium for a Little World Series game against Louisville on October 9, 1944. Of the many top teams in minor-league history, the 1937 Newark Bears, an affiliate of the New York Yankees, were probably the strongest. Sixteen of seventeen Newark players made the majors—nine of them in 1938. The club's record for 1937 was 109 wins and 43 losses.

Jack Dunn's Baltimore Orioles, also an International League team, ranks second to Newark. From 1919 to 1925 they won seven straight pennants. The 1920 race was especially exciting when Baltimore and Toronto went into the final month separated by only one game, the Maple Leafs on top. Toronto won 20 of its last 22 but Baltimore won 25 in a row to win the pennant.

The best of the Pacific Coast League's clubs was the Los Angeles Angels of 1934, which recorded a league-record .733 winning percentage with 137 wins and 50 defeats. Among the circuit's top stars was Joe DiMaggio, who put together a 61-game hitting streak for San Francisco in 1933.

The Baseball Hall of Fame is very much aware of the contributions that minor-league baseball has made to the game. At the original dedication of the museum on July 9, 1939, each of 41 existing minor leagues sent one star player to participate in a minor-league all-star game. The "Doubledays" beat the "Cartwrights," 9–6.

Baseball owes a debt to the Western League for introducing runs batted in (1911) and earned run average (1913) as regular statistics. It also owes a debt to the minors for providing the stage for stars to make their final farewells.

Lefty O'Doul, 1929 National League batting champion, went to bat as a pinch-hitter for Vancouver (Pacific Coast) at age 59 in 1956 and belted a triple! He was followed by 51-year-old coach Eddie Taylor, who singled him home.

Warren Spahn, the most successful southpaw in National League history, made token appearances for Tulsa and Mexico City after leaving the NL at age 44 in 1965. Those games came back to haunt Spahn; they delayed his candidacy for the Hall of Fame. Rules stipulate that eligible players must have been retired five years from professional baseball—minor as well as major.

Among perennial minor leaguers of the past were Ox Eckhardt of the San Francisco Seals, Nick Cullop and Tom Winston of Columbus, slugger Joe Bauman, and Smead Jolley, who led six different leagues in hitting.

Steve Bilko, hefty first baseman of the Los Angeles Angels in the mid-'50s, twice hit more than 50 home runs in a season at tiny Wrigley Field, the team's home park, and seemed disappointed when the Reds finally called him to the majors.

Bauman, the only man to hit more than 70 home runs in a minor-league season (he hit 72) never got the call. Gene Rye, who hit three homers in an inning on August 6, 1930, did—and hit .179 with no homers in a quick cup of coffee with the 1931 Red Sox.

Babe Ruth hit exactly one home run in the minors—a three-run blast for Providence (International) on September 5, 1914. Ruth, then a pitcher, also hurled a one-hitter against Toronto that day, winning 9–0.

Billy Martin, scrappy Yankee infielder of the '50s, wasn't a feared hitter in the majors, but he was in the minors. At Phoenix of the Texas League in 1947, the 19-year-old Martin hit .392 with 174 runs batted in, with 230 hits in 130 games. He also made 55 errors at third base; he became a quality second baseman later.

The Modern Major/Minor Relationship

The firm establishment of the farm system has led to certain rules regarding treatment of players owned by one organization.

Each major league player is subject to six options. He may be included on the big-league team's 40-man "protected" list during the off-season and be sent back to that team's minor-league system six times. Once those options expire, the major league team must keep him or risk losing him to another organization through the annual winter draft of minor-leaguers (1) who were not included on their parent team's 40-man "protected list" or (2) whose options have expired, leaving them "frozen" in the minors and ineligible for recall by the parent club.

Should a "frozen" player pass through the draft untouched, he may rejoin the parent team only through purchase—and only after all other clubs have waived their right to claim him.

Draft sessions are conducted in reverse order of the standings, so that the weakest teams will have the chance to obtain the best players in the minor leagues. By the '70s, however, the best minor-

Disease Halted New Orleans

An outbreak of yellow fever in New Orleans in 1905 forced that city's Southern Association club to play all its games on the road.

Numbing Numbers

On May 11, 1923, Pete Schneider of Vernon (Pacific Coast) had five home runs, a double, and 14 runs batted in during a 35–11 victory over Salt Lake City. No major league team of the modern era ever scored that many runs in a game.

Bringing Heat

Tommy Lasorda, the future Hall of Fame manager, fanned 25 men in a 15-inning game while pitching for Schenectady (Canadian-American) against Amsterdam on May 31, 1948.

Competitive Balance

The 1937 St. Louis Cardinals had 37 farm teams as opposed to two affiliated with the Philadelphia Phillies.

Outfield Obstacle

Atlanta's Ponce de Leon Park, home of the powerful Crackers, had a magnolia tree in center field. Though the park was last used in 1964, and subsequently replaced by a shopping center, the magnolia tree was left untouched.

Longest Game

Pawtucket (International) beat Rochester, 3–2, in a 1981 AAA contest that consumed 33 innings, the most in professional baseball history. The game, which took eight hours and 25 minutes to play, began April 18, was suspended, then concluded June 23. The longest previous game, a 29-inning affair in 1969, occurred in the Florida State League.

Early Excitement

When Baltimore made its Federal League debut in April 1914, a crowd of 27,000 stood 15 rows deep in the outfield to watch the Terrapins whip Buffalo, 3–2.

Retreat

When a number of International League clubs moved out of cities invaded by the new Federal League in 1914–1915, the league won the uncomplimentary nickname "the Belgium of Baseball."

An Unorthodox Stolen Base

On June 21, 1917, Ray McKee of San Francisco stole third base with the bases loaded—and was exonerated when the umpire called a balk on the pitcher.

Equal Honors

Each player on the Douglas (Arizona) Copper Kings hit exactly one home run in a game on August 18, 1958.

Brooklyn Bonanza

Brooklyn has had teams in eight different leagues, starting with the Atlantic League in 1861. Brooklyn was in the National Association in 1871, the Interstate League in 1883, the American Association in 1884, the National League and the Players League in 1890, and the Federal League in 1914. The current Brooklyn Cyclones joined the Class A New York-Penn League in 2001 as a farm team of the New York Mets.

Instructional Leagues

To speed the progress of prospects, major league teams sponsor instructional league teams at spring training parks in both Arizona and Florida. The Arizona Fall League features six teams, each with players and coaches from multiple big-league organizations. Each MLB club sends seven players to the league, which operates for six weeks and sometimes conducts experiments. In 2014, after complaints that games were too slow, one game was played with a pitch clock designed to reduce time between pitches.

The Federal League

Though player records from the two-year Federal League are included in major league lifetime statistics, many historians insist the Federal was not a major at all, but a glorified minor circuit that dreamed it had made the big time.

The league began as the financially unstable United States League in 1912, with clubs in such unlikely places as Richmond and Lynchburg, Virginia, and Reading, Pennsylvania. By June the league had folded, but its remains spawned the first Federal League the following year. Superstar pitcher Cy Young managed Pittsburgh, but the 1913 FL was strictly a minor league that received little attention.

Late that year, however, Chicago coal magnate James Gilmore reorganized the league and began to pursue top-caliber players. He and other industrialists built new ballparks in each of the eight FL cities and used the facilities as bait to attract major leaguers. One of the parks, Wrigley Field, remains in use today as home of the Chicago Cubs.

A Cub star of 1912, shortstop Joe Tinker, was the first "name" player to jump from the majors. After he signed as manager of the Chicago Whales, others followed suit: Hal Chase, Danny Murphy, Jack Quinn, and later Chief Bender and Eddie Plank.

But the Federal League failed to attract the quality of talent it sought and was forced to rely primarily on top minor leaguers and second-liners from the majors.

Though Ty Cobb was offered a five-year, $75,000 contract in the Federal League, he didn't want to risk his career on an uncertain venture and chose to retain his $12,000 deal with Detroit. But Chief Bender and Eddie Plank, ace pitchers of the Philadelphia Athletics, jumped after winning 33 games for the champion A's of 1914.

"We lost the World Series because our team was divided into factions," insisted owner/manager Connie Mack. "Half wanted to jump to the Federal League and the other half wanted to stay."

Mack decided to sell his stars before they left him without compensation (the same argument advanced by Oakland A's owner Charley Finley after the advent of free agency in 1976).

Indianapolis won the first FL flag in 1914, but the franchise moved to Newark, New Jersey, the following year. Other Federal teams were located in Chicago, Baltimore, Brooklyn, Buffalo, Kansas City, Pittsburgh, and St. Louis. Robert Ward owned the Brooklyn club and hinted he would name it the Tip-Tops after his well-known bread, but New York writers quickly quashed the idea. The team became the Brookfeds.

Ward's untimely death, coupled with several court actions and failing finances, forced the Federals to fold after the 1915 season.

The National League struck a secret deal to buy out the circuit, but the refusal of American League president Ban Johnson to give a dime to the upstart owners delayed a negotiated peace until December 22.

As part of the deal, Chicago Whales' owner Charles Weeghman took over the Chicago Cubs and Phil Ball of the St. Louis Feds acquired ownership of the St. Louis Browns. Federal contracts were assumed by the league for sale to other teams, with the exception of the Chicago and St. Louis players, who remained with their owners. Players who jumped organized ball were allowed to return immediately.

Unhappy with the sudden sellout, Baltimore of the Federal League filed a million-dollar suit against baseball. It won in the lower courts but lost when the United States Supreme Court handed down its 1922 decision exempting the game from antitrust laws.

The Mexican League

Mexicans took an instant liking to the game after it was introduced with a visit by the Chicago White Sox in 1906. In a country where bullfighting is king and customers eat tacos instead of hot dogs, fans love their "beisbol" as much as their American counterparts do.

Professional baseball began in Mexico in 1925, but the country did not enter the structure of organized ball until 30 years later, when the Mexican League officially became a Double-A circuit.

Mexican interest in the game became most apparent to American fans in 1946, when Jorge Pasquel and four brothers induced several major league stars to play south of the border.

Mickey Owen, Sal Maglie, Max Lanier, and Vern Stephens were among those Giants manager Mel Ott called "jumping beans," but Stephens changed his mind when Commissioner Happy Chandler warned that he would impose a five-year ban from organized ball on anyone who did not return at once.

The Pasquels promised better salaries, newer ballparks, and pennant races guaranteed to be competitive by rules that barred trades but permitted talent to be distributed equally among teams (with the worst served first).

Spicy food, stifling heat, foreign customs, and thin mountain air made life difficult for American imports—and "Montezuma's revenge" and other ills also gave jumpers second thoughts. Most returned within two years. Even after joining organized ball in 1955, Mexican clubs maintained independence from the major leagues; owners were free to sign or sell players at will. Latin stars Rico Carty and Vic Davalillo, thought to be through in the majors, regained their batting eyes in Mexico and were purchased by big-league teams.

Australian Open

The first major league game played in Australia drew 38,266 fans to the Sydney Cricket Ground in 2014. Clayton Kershaw was the starting and winning pitcher for the Los Angeles Dodgers.

Thanks, Mom

Infielder Casey Candaele, who played for several teams in the '90s, is the son of Helen St. Aubin, once a star in the All-American Girls Professional Baseball League.

Corbis photo, reprinted with permission, National Baseball Hall of Fame Library, Cooperstown, N.Y.

Joe DiMaggio had a 61-game hitting streak for the minor-league San Francisco Seals.

Sal Maglie, back from the outlaw Mexican League, helped pitch the New York Giants to the 1951 pennant.

The Cuban Connection

Although baseball is as popular in Cuba as it is in the United States, players who prospered on the island often had difficulty in the mainland.

In addition to the language barrier, black stars who played before Fidel Castro seized control in 1959 often faced discrimination that relegated them to the Negro Leagues in the United States. Only a handful reached the majors—a trickle that Castro stopped.

With professional baseball banned in Cuba and players not allowed to leave the country, dozens decided to defect. Some came during the Mariel boatlift in 1980, others left the Cuban National Team when it played abroad, and a few daring souls drifted across the dangerous Caribbean Sea on rafts or rickety boats that were less than seaworthy.

To avoid the draft system of major league baseball, a number of Cubans defected to countries other than the United States, thus becoming free agents.

The list of those who left Cuba includes Livan Hernandez, whose 1996 debut came a year after he left, and his half-brother Orlando (El Duque) Hernandez, who arrived two years later. Both pitchers helped their teams reach the World Series and lasted a combined 26 years in the majors.

Other prominent players who came from Cuba were Jose Abreu, Danys Baez, Aroldis Chapman, Jose Contreras, Yunel Escobar, Jose Fernandez, Adeiny Hechavarria, Jose Iglesias, Kendrys Morales, Vladimir Nunez, Rey Ordonez, Yasiel Puig, and Alexei Ramirez.

Latin American Ball

By Raquel Barrera Julich
Especially for *The New Baseball Bible*

Baseball came to Latin America in 1866, when a Cuban college student named Nemesio Guillot returned home from the United States with equipment he said was used in a new game called "beisbol."

On October 1, 1868, however, the Spanish governor of the island issued a decree forbidding the sport as "a game that is anti-Spanish, incites insurrection, is contrary to the language, and leads to indifference towards Spain."

That decree was short-lived: on December 27, 1874, Esteban Bellan organized the first recorded baseball game in Cuba, at Palmar de Junco. Havana beat Matanzas, 51–9, in a game shortened to seven innings by darkness.

Bellan, a third baseman, had learned baseball at Fordham University and later played for Troy, New York, of the National Association, the first professional league.

He was not, however, the first Latino to play in the big leagues. That honor belongs to Luis Castro, a Colombian native who joined the Philadelphia Athletics in 1902. Educated at Holy Cross and Manhattan College, Castro was allegedly the son of Venezuelan president Cipriano Castro—a lineage that made him both wealthy and arrogant. Fined after arriving late for a game with the A's, he advised Connie Mack he had enough money to buy the team. Castro took his equipment, went home, and was never heard from again.

A Cuban ballplayer, Emilio Cramer, brought baseball to Venezuela in 1895. The new sport competed with the former national pastime—bullfighting—but got its biggest boost in 1922 after American imports from the Negro Leagues bolstered club rosters.

Funds became available for American players after Royal Dutch Shell and Standard Oil of New Jersey, developing the Venezuelan oil industry, brought new wealth to the country.

With American players playing on Latin soil for the first time, baseball had come full cycle: it began in the eastern United States before being exported to Cuba, the Dominican Republic, Puerto Rico, Mexico, and Venezuela.

In 1939 pitcher Alejandro Aparicio Carrasquel became the first major leaguer from Venezuela.

The first Cubans to reach the majors were Rafael Almeida and Armando Marsans, both with the Cincinnati Red Stockings, in 1911. A later Cuban star, Martin Dihigo, became the first Latin American from the Negro Leagues elected to the Baseball Hall of Fame. He also made the individual Halls of Fame in three Latin countries: Cuba, Mexico, and Venezuela.

Although Fidel Castro's government banished professional sports in 1961, amateur baseball remained a popular, government-sponsored activity. Players in Cuba receive "baseball leaves" from their regular jobs.

To promote greater domestic competition and avoid conflicts with international tournaments, Cuba launched a single-season, 92-game schedule on November 15, 1997. Two eight-team leagues, divided into groups of four, played 52 games within their own league and 40 outside their league. Eight teams, including four wild-cards, reached the playoffs. The Cuban team, loaded with potential big-leaguers, won the gold medal at the 1996 Olympics in Atlanta. But their salaries did little to deter defections.

Livan Hernandez, one of the Marlins' 1997 playoff heroes, was one of several Cuban defectors to star in the major leagues. His half-brother and fellow pitcher Orlando [El Duque] Hernandez later became the first big-leaguer to reach the United States on a raft.

Without government intervention, professional baseball has thrived in the Dominican Republic and Puerto Rico. Baseball has become the No. 1 industry in the Dominican Republic, with an inordinate number of exceptional shortstops from the tiny town of San Pedro de Macoris reaching the major leagues. Big-league teams fund more baseball academies in the Dominican Republic than anywhere else in Latin America.

Ozzie Virgil Sr. became the first Dominican big-leaguer in 1956—13 years after Hiram Bithorn became the first Puerto Rican to reach the majors.

Although local newspapers reported baseball in Puerto Rico as early as 1897, baseball officially began on the island on January 9, 1898, when Amos Iglesias organized the first game. A seat in the shade was 40 centavos, a seat in the sun was 20 centavos, and a bleacher seat cost 10 centavos. Because of rain, the game took three weeks to complete, with Club Borinquen defeating Almendares, 22–11.

Despite widespread warnings that "beisbol" was harmful to young men, the game thrived. Roberto Clemente became the first Puerto Rican—and the first Latino—elected to the Baseball Hall of Fame, in 1973.

The first major leaguer from Mexico was Melo Almada in 1933, but the most famous was Fernando Valenzuela, who was National League Rookie of the Year and Cy Young Award winner in 1981.

For Latin American baseball fans, the highlight of the baseball calendar is the Caribbean World Series. The first winner, Cuba's Team Almendares in 1949, was managed by Philadelphia A's catcher Fermin "Mike" Guerra and powered by big-leaguers Al Gionfriddo, Monte Irvin, Sam Jethroe, and Chuck Connors, later television's *Rifleman*. It swept all six games.

Panama, winner of the second Series del Caribe, dropped out of the annual competition after 1958. Since Cuba was the organizing country, the Caribbean World Series was suspended from 1961 to 1969 in the wake of Fidel Castro's revolution.

Management problems and financial strife halted the 1981 games, while the 1995 competition took on added luster because it occurred during a 232-day major league strike that spanned two seasons.

The winning Puerto Rico club was dubbed "the Dream Team" because of all the big-league players on its roster.

Caribbean winter ball gives Latin stars the chance to play before fans of their native countries and also gives major and minor leaguers an opportunity to improve their game.

Umpires and managers from the United States, like the players, sharpen their skills in the winter leagues. Appearances by major league umpires or managers are rare, but the minors send a steady stream of hopefuls bent on following in the footsteps of Sparky Anderson, Earl Weaver, or Tom Lasorda—who became major league managers after they garnered additional experience in the winter leagues.

BASEBALL ABROAD

An American game with international roots, baseball has developed an international following.

Opening day games have been moved to Mexico, San Juan, Sydney, and Tokyo, and players from the U.S. majors flock to warm-weather winter leagues to hone their skills, learn new positions, or rehabilitate injuries.

The first recorded "away" game occurred in 1874 when Philadelphia and Boston players toured England while teaching baseball and trying their hand at cricket and rounders. Fourteen years later, a world tour crossed many continents—even playing a game in front of the Egyptian pyramids.

Here are some of the countries and regions where baseball has made an impact:

Australia—Just two years after the 1876 advent of The National League in the United States, the first official series was played between the Surry Baseball Club and the New South Wales Cricket Association. Albert Spalding's all-stars visited the Sydney Cricket Ground for three games in 1888 during their world tour and an Australian team—featuring outfielders who did not wear gloves—toured the U.S. seven years later. Various winter and summer leagues came and went, with the first national league established in 1934. A crowd of 104,400 watched a game at the Melbourne Cricket Ground in 1956, the Australian national team won a silver medal at the 2004 Olympics in Athens, and the Los Angeles Dodgers launched their 2014 season in Sydney. Once considered an off-season sport for cricketeers, baseball is now played Down Under year round. Lefthanded relief pitcher Graeme Lloyd was one of several Australians to play in the majors. Dan Quisenberry, nicknamed "the Australian" because his submarine delivery came from Down Under, was not.

Brazil—After American immigrants brought baseball to this huge South American country, the game took hold. An amateur league formed in 1910 and a confederation based in Sao Paulo launched in 1946. Catcher Yan Gomes was the first Brazilian to reach the major leagues.

Caribbean—The first Caribbean World Series, held in 1949, featured teams from Cuba, Panama, Puerto Rico, and Venezuela. Although the Cuban team dominated the first 12 years, the series was scratched when the Communist regime abolished professional baseball. It came back to life in 1970 with clubs from the Dominican, Mexico, Puerto Rico, and Venezuela. The Tigres de Licey, based in Santo Domingo, have dominated since then.

Canada—Long before Canada landed the Montreal Expos (1969) and Toronto Blue Jays (1977), baseball was popular in the dominion. An Ontario-based team called the London Tecumsehs actually belonged to the International Association, an early minor league, and won its 1877 title over the Pittsburgh Alleghenies. The Tecumsehs had hoped to join the new National League because they wanted to keep playing exhibition games against local teams. Even Babe Ruth and Jackie Robinson had Canadian baseball roots; Ruth hit his only minor-league home run for the Providence Grays against the Toronto Maple Leafs on September 5, 1914 and Robinson led the Montreal Royals to the Governors Cup, the International League equivalent of the World Series trophy, in 1946. A native Canadian, Ferguson Jenkins, resides in the Baseball Hall of Fame and two other Hall of Famers, Andre Dawson and Gary Carter, wear Expos caps in the Cooperstown gallery.

Cuba—Baseball has a long history in Cuba. American sailors imported the game during the 1860s and the first team, the Habana Baseball Club, made its debut in 1868. Spanish occupation forces banned the game, forcing Cubans to favor bullfights, but baseball became a token of freedom and survived. A three-team Cuban League started in 1878, integrated in 1900, and provided a winter haven for black stars barred from the major leagues. The Havana Sugar Kings, the top Cincinnati Reds farm team, played in the International League until Fidel Castro nationalized American businesses in 1960. With professional sports abolished, the team moved to Jersey City. Paid just $30 a month, many Cuban stars found their way to the major leagues. That flow should increase in the wake of diplomatic relations restored in 2016 by President Barack Obama. He and baseball commissioner Rob Manfred were among 55,000 spectators who watched the Miami Marlins play a two-game spring exhibition series against Cuba's best players at Estadio Latinoamericano.

Central America—Colombia, Nicaragua, and Panama have also sent players to the American major leagues, including one nicknamed El Presidente (Dennis Martinez). Panama fielded a team in the initial World Baseball Classic in 2006 while Colombia and Nicaragua operate winter leagues.

Dominican Republic—Introduced by Cuban sugar planters fleeing the Ten Years War, baseball thrived on the island because migrant workers from the British West Indies were familiar with cricket. During an American military occupation from 1916 to 1924, U.S. military administrators provided money and equipment. Professional baseball began with teams in Santo Domingo, La Romona, Santiago, and San Pedro de Macoris—a town that developed a reputation as a "shortstop factory" for the major leagues. Ozzie Virgil was the first Dominican to reach the majors but the Alou brothers and Hall of Fame pitchers Juan Marichal and Pedro Martinez followed.

England—There's no professional baseball in the United Kingdom although American games are often televised there. First played on British soil in 1874 during an Albert Spalding visit, the game returned with Spalding's World Tour 14 years later. He and Francis Ley created the National Baseball League of Great Britain, with teams drawing 10,000 per match at games played on soccer fields. Britain beat the U.S. in the inaugural World Cup of Baseball in 1938 and sent a team to the 2013 World Baseball Classic.

Israel—During its single year of existence in 2007, the six-team Israel Baseball League shared three stadiums and employed three former Jewish major-leaguers as managers: Ron Blomberg, Ken Holtzman, and Art Shamsky.

Italy—Baseball interest began right after World War II and never stopped. The Italian national team, combined with the Netherlands all-stars, have gone 25-2 in the recent European Baseball Confederation finals. Americans of Italian descent, including former slugger Mike Piazza, have played for Italy in the World Baseball Classic.

Mexico—A longtime baseball hotbed, Mexico is the home of the Mexican Pacific Winter League and Fernando Valenzuela, the first man to win Rookie of the Year and Cy Young awards in the same season (1981). A two-game exhibition series between the Astros and Padres in March 2016, attended by Commissioner Rob Manfred and Players Association chief Tony Clark, featured multiple fiestas and fan clinics with players.

The Netherlands—An eight-team league called Honkbal Hoofdklasse sends top teams to the Holland Series, a competition created in 1922. Some of the players on the Dutch team actually hail from the Netherlands Antilles, which includes Curacao. One-time World Series hero Andruw Jones is one of them.

New Zealand—More than 100 years after Albert Spalding's World Tour introduced the game, the New Zealand Baseball Federation was founded. The original teams were based in Auckland but Canterbury, Northland, and Manawatu eventually joined them.

South Korea—American missionary P. Gillett taught the game in 1905 but Korea Professional Baseball, a six-team league, did not start until 1982. It now has 10 teams. Korea's team won a gold medal at the 2008 Beijing Olympics and finished second a year later in the World Baseball Classic. The first Korean in the majors was Chan Ho Park, a pitcher, in 1994.

Spain—Immigrants returning from Cuba brought baseball fever with them. But televised soccer matches drew more attention and interest waned.

Taiwan—Introduced by the island's Japanese rulers, baseball was called *yakyu*—the Japanese name for the game. The first official game was played in Taipei City in 1906 but attracted little interest. Only after the Taiwan team won the bronze medal in the 1984 Olympics and the silver in Barcelona eight years later did baseball interest boom. The six-team Taiwan Major League was founded in 1997 and the first native Taiwanese to reach the majors, Chin-Feng Chen, played for the 2002 Los Angeles Dodgers. Four years later, Taiwanese pitcher Chien-Ming Wang broke in with a bang. His 44 wins from 2006 to May 26, 2008 earned him the nickname "Taiwan Glory."

Venezuela—When American oil workers brought baseball to Venezuela, the game caught fire. The national team beat Cuba in the 1941 world championships but then the war intervened. Nothing formal happened until 1945, when the Venezuelan Professional Baseball League began play. Notable Venezuelans who reached the majors were Luis Aparicio and Andres Galarraga.

Puerto Rico native Roberto Clemente leaps to make a catch amid the outfield ivy of Chicago's Wrigley Field in 1960. The rifle-armed right fielder of the Pittsburgh Pirates compiled exactly 3,000 hits before losing his life in a New Year's Eve plane crash while ferrying earthquake relief supplies to Nicaragua. He became the first Latino member of the Baseball Hall of Fame when he was posthumously enshrined in 1973.

The caliber of play in the Caribbean ranks somewhere between Triple-A and the majors, but pitching is erratic and umpiring spotty at best. In Venezuela, for example, all arbiters are natives whose only experience is the winter-league games. The mismatch of major league players with minor-league (and worse) umpires causes constant arguments, many of them justified.

League and team rules, plus regulations of the commissioner of baseball, force the winter-league manager to be a juggler, a mind reader, and often a magician.

At playoff times, gamblers, ticket scalpers, overexcitable fans, and peddlers-turned-vendors swamp the stadiums, causing so many problems that police protection frequently must be provided for visiting teams. Betting, prohibited in organized ball, runs rampant in the Caribbean leagues.

American players and officials look at the leagues as a training ground where young athletes learn new positions, injured regulars test their healing power, and all players perform under conditions that approach major league standards. Fans cheer not only the natives of their country but also their favorite foreigners.

Though some baseball executives insist athletes who play in the winter are too tired to perform well the following season in the majors, veteran Caribbean leagues manager Ozzie Virgil disagrees. "There's no such thing as too much baseball," he said.

The Negro Leagues

Before Jackie Robinson broke baseball's "color line" in 1947, black players displayed their talents in the Negro National League and Negro American League, six-club circuits with uncertain schedules.

Record keeping was difficult because games were played not only against league rivals but also against semipro clubs or any other opposition that would generate enough revenue to keep a Negro League team solvent.

When Monte Irvin first joined Newark in 1937 he made $150 a month plus $1 per day meal money. In certain towns, no hotels would accept blacks and the players were housed in private homes. People renting rooms were glad to get some extra money and enjoyed proximity to players whose devotion to the game was not soured by long bus rides, cold meals at odd hours, or lack of recognition.

Many Negro League stars followed Jackie Robinson to the majors: Satchel Paige, Roy Campanella, Willie Mays, Ernie Banks, and Elston Howard among them. Others, like Josh Gibson, were too old when the gates finally opened.

Pedro Martinez, the best pitcher ever to come out of the Dominican Republic, makes his Red Sox home debut with a two-hitter against Seattle at Fenway Park on April 11, 1998. He won three Cy Young Awards, one of them while pitching for the Montreal Expos, in a four-year span from 1997 to 2000.

Satchel Paige

Satchel Paige, called "the black Matty" after Hall of Famer Christy Mathewson, was probably the most remarkable pitcher in the game's history. The owner of a resilient right arm, which allowed him to work more than 2,500 games and throw at least 100 no-hitters, he first appeared in a Negro League contest in 1926. He ended his active career by pitching three innings in a major league game in 1965—39 years later!

The 6'3", 150-pound pitcher with size 12 shoes pitched 30 straight games in 30 days for the 1941 Kansas City Monarchs. Five years later, he threw 64 consecutive scoreless innings (and yielded two runs in 93 frames) to help that club win the pennant.

Paige first played for the Chattanooga Black Lookouts at $50 a month, then went on to countless other cities. Near the end of his career, he pointed to his face and said, "We seen some sights, it and I."

Paige was the king of the barnstormers. He sometimes grossed $35,000 per year—about $1 per mile—on the barnstorming circuit. He was advertised as "Satchel Paige, World's Greatest Pitcher, Guaranteed to Strike Out the First Nine Men."

He demonstrated his pinpoint control by throwing a strike over the top of a Coke bottle.

In 1934 Paige spent the season pitching for a Bismarck, North Dakota, team that won 104 of its 105 games. That fall he was the starting pitcher in a Hollywood, California, exhibition game against Dizzy Dean, who had just won 30 games for the St. Louis Cardinals. Dean struck out 15 and yielded one run in 13 innings. Paige fanned 17 and pitched a shutout.

The following fall Paige fanned 15 and yielded only three hits to a team of major/minor stars that included Joe DiMaggio. Backed only by a pick-up club, Paige lost, 2–1.

Convinced he had to pitch a shutout to win, the right-hander scored a spectacular 8–0 victory over Bob Feller's All-Stars in Los Angeles in the fall of 1947. Paige, who went up to the majors the next season, struck out 16 members of a squad that included Charlie "King Kong" Keller, Phil Rizzuto, Jeff Heath, Ken Keltner, and Bob Lemon.

As early as 1930, major leaguers knew about Paige. That year Hack Wilson hit an NL record 56 homers and drove home a major league–record 191 runs. But he couldn't handle Paige with an All-Star team headed by Babe Ruth. "That was some pitching," said Wilson. "It looked like you were winding up with a baseball and throwing a pea."

Josh Gibson

Josh Gibson, the Babe Ruth of black baseball, was a catcher who hit more than 70 home runs in a season several times. In his first season, at age 19 in 1930, he hit the only fair ball over the Yankee Stadium roof. His shots were known for distance as well as frequency—and he could hit anyone.

With the Homestead Grays, Gibson faced Kansas City's Satchel Paige in a game at Wrigley Field in Chicago. Gibson hit three home runs and a triple off the top of the fence in right-center field.

Many Negro League Records Lost

Records were not kept in all Negro League games because the media paid little attention to them. Several black newspapers did make an attempt, however. *The Pittsburgh Courier* kept tabs on the Homestead (Pennsylvania) Grays and the *Baltimore Afro-American* and *Chicago Defender* followed other Negro League teams. When *The Courier* went out of business, many of the records—haphazard to begin with—were lost.

Strange Potion Helped Satchel

Satchel Paige maintained that he was able to avoid injury and maintain top condition through application of an ointment called deer oil by the daughter of a Sioux chief he met during his North Dakota days. The Indian's remedy for snakebite did wonders for Paige. "It sent curative sensations vibrating about the muscles," he said.

Oh My Josh

Josh Gibson, reputed to be the Babe Ruth of black baseball, got his start when a team needed a catcher and asked for a volunteer from the stands.

Satchel's Revenge

Willie Mays was 17 when he first hit against Satchel Paige in the Negro Leagues. He doubled, getting the pitcher's attention. The next time they met, Paige whiffed Mays with three straight fastballs. "He threw them right by me," Mays said. "I never saw them. And he must have been 55 then."

Same Old Paige

Satchel Paige was at least 50 years old when he defeated Columbus for Miami in an International League game in the Orange Bowl in 1956. Attendance was 57,000—a minor-league record.

Oldie but Goodie

Satchel Paige made his last major league appearance a good one. Pitching for the Kansas City A's in a 1965 publicity stunt instigated by club owner Charley Finley, the one-time Negro Leagues veteran surrendered just one hit in three innings of play.

Josh Gibson, best hitter in the Negro Leagues, was an exceptional all-around player who consistently won All-Star catching honors over Roy Campanella.

Negro Leagues Museum

The Negro Leagues Baseball Museum features a Field of Legends that honors 10 key figures: Buck Leonard, Pop Lloyd, Judy Johnson, Ray Daniels, Martin Dihigo, Cool Papa Bell, Oscar Charleston, Leon Day, Josh Gibson, and Satchel Paige.

Kiner Had Preview of Jackie

Slugger Ralph Kiner played barnstorming baseball games against Jackie Robinson before Robinson made the majors in 1947. "Actually, baseball was his worst sport," said Kiner, like Robinson a Californian. "He was a fantastic football player and track star who got into baseball as a third sport. I don't think I've ever seen a better competitor than Jackie Robinson."

From 1933 to 1945, Gibson was chosen for the East-West (All-Star) Game every year but 1941, when he played in Mexico. Roy Campanella, the All-Star catcher when Gibson was out of the league, said later, "I couldn't carry Josh's glove. Anything I could do, he could do better."

Gibson hit .457 in 1936 and .440 in 1938, became adept at stealing bases, and worked hard to improve his catching. In the Negro Leagues, freak pitches banned in the majors were legal; many were as hard to catch as they were to hit. Common deliveries included the spitball, emery ball, and shine ball—a pitch smeared so thick with Vaseline it caught the glare of the sun on its flight to the plate.

Other Negro League Stars

Though Satchel Paige and Josh Gibson were the most famous stars of the Negro Leagues, countless others could have been major league standouts had the door been open.

Oscar Charleston, a center fielder who broke in with the Indianapolis ABC's of 1915, was considered the peer of Willie Mays on defense. As player/manager of the Harrisburg Giants in 1925, he led the Eastern Colored League with a .430 average and 14 home runs.

John Beckwith, an outstanding hitter who consistently finished second to Oscar Charleston as batting king of the Negro Leagues, finally won the crown himself by hitting .546 in 1930.

Cool Papa Bell also played center, though he began as a pitcher for the St. Louis Stars in 1922. Bell, who was active for 29 summers and 21 winters of baseball, was compared to Tris Speaker by observers who saw them both. A switch-hitter with exceptional speed, he stole more than 175 bases with the 1933 Pittsburgh Crawfords.

Pitcher Leon Day was the equal of Bob Gibson, and Ray Dandridge the equal of Brooks Robinson, according to Monte Irvin, who spent 10 years in the Negro Leagues before signing with the New York Giants.

Bell, Charleston, Dandridge, Gibson, Irvin, and Paige, plus W. Julius "Judy" Johnson, Marty Dihigo, Buck Leonard, and Pop Lloyd were among those who won enshrinement into the Hall of Fame for their accomplishments in the Negro Leagues. Of the group, only Paige and Irvin played in the majors.

The 1946 Newark Eagles, featuring such sluggers as Monte Irvin (second from left), contended with Satchel Paige and the Kansas City Monarchs for bragging rights in the Negro Leagues.

Barnstorming

Prior to the advent of television, baseball enthusiasts who lived far from major league cities got a chance to see stars in action through the postseason ritual of barnstorming.

Teams of players from various clubs banded together to earn extra money by bringing the game to small towns—usually farming communities—dotted with barns. The invasion of baseball stars became known as "barnstorming."

Both major league and Negro League players regarded barnstorming as an economic necessity. For a little extra money, athletes played under tough lights in county-fair ballparks and lived out of suitcases on trains.

Barnstorming traces its origin to 1888, when the Chicago White Stockings of A. G. Spalding and a team of All-Stars headed by John Montgomery Ward of the New York Nationals headed west on a round-the-world tour. They played in such places as Cedar Rapids, Omaha, St. Paul, Colorado Springs, Salt Lake City, Los Angeles, and San Francisco before boarding a boat for the Kingdom of Hawaii.

After games under the palms in the future 50th state, the Spalding/Ward group played in Sydney and Melbourne, Australia; Cairo, Egypt; Naples and Rome, Italy; Paris, France; and London, England. In Egypt the baseball contingent paraded through the streets with the White Stockings on donkeys, the All-Stars on camels, and their wives in carriages. Games were played with the pyramids as a backdrop.

In 1913 and again in 1924, Giants manager John McGraw participated in similar winter tours. Coupled with Chicago White Sox owner Charles Comiskey on the first trip, McGraw brought the game to Japan and China for the first time. The final game of the 1913 junket was played before 35,000 Britons, including the King of England.

The Game in Japan

Because there is no football, basketball, or hockey to distract the Japanese sports fan, baseball is well established as the national game.

American missionary Horace Wilson taught it to his pupils in 1869 (the same year the Cincinnati Red Stockings became the first professional team) and Hiroshi Hiraoka brought back a translation of American rules in 1877.

Visits by American All-Stars in 1913, 1922, 1931, 1932, and 1934 fanned developing Japanese interest, and the island's first professional league was founded in 1936.

The 1934 All-Star team was overwhelmed by admiring fans when it reached Tokyo by train from the port of Yokohama. They shouted "Banzai Babe Ruth!" and "Banzai Lou Gehrig!" (Long Live Ruth, Long Live Gehrig) until they were hoarse. Police estimated swirling masses in the eight-block Ginza district at one million persons.

Ruth, as popular in Japan as he was at home, poked 13 long home runs to help the 1934 stars win all 16 games from Japanese

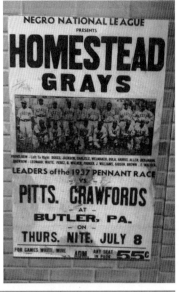

Poster publicizes game between two of the top teams in the Negro Leagues, the Homestead Grays and Pittsburgh Crawfords.

Dan Schlossberg

Reggie's Roots

Reggie Jackson's father Martinez earned $7 a game with the 1933 Newark Eagles, a Negro League team. Thirty-three years later, Reggie signed a five-year, $3 million contract to play for the Yankees.

Say What?

The Negro National League used white umpires during its first two seasons.

How Much?

Two-time MVP Ernie Banks began his baseball career with a black barnstorming team that paid him $15 a game.

Mixed-Gender Clubs

While women had a chance to play pro ball in the All-American Girls Professional Baseball League from 1943 to 1954, no females played on mixed-gender clubs until the Negro Leagues added several as gate attractions in the early '50s. The best was Marcenia "Toni" Stone, a second baseman who played for the Indianapolis Clowns of the Negro American League in 1953.

Second-Class Conditions

Life in the Negro Leagues was not easy. The average salary was $18–$20 per week and the small, cramped, steamy buses broke down frequently. The Newark Eagles became the first team to buy a large, air-conditioned bus, but did not do so until after World War II.

WOMEN IN BASEBALL

The 1992 Geena Davis movie *A League of Their Own* called attention to the fact that women played baseball too. The league, founded in 1943 by Cubs owner P.K. Wrigley to draw new fans while most big-leaguers fought World War II, lasted even after the war ended.

Dottie Schroeder was the only player who appeared in all 12 seasons of AAGPBL action. All but one of the teams in the All-American Girls Professional Baseball League had male managers. The exception was the Kalamazoo Lassies, who hired Mary (Bonnie) Baker to finish the 1950 season after firing their original field pilot.

The Flash had nothing on Sophie Kurys. She stole 166 bases in a season and 1,114 in a career that lasted from 1943 to 1952—all while wearing the skirt mandated by the AAGPBL. Ouch!

Six actresses from the film played in a softball game during the second annual *League of Their Own* reunion sponsored by Davis in Bentonville, Arkansas in 2016.

Also in 2016, the Oakland A's made Justine Siegal the first female coach in the big leagues. The one-time college coach threw batting practice for six major league teams before Oakland hired her. Siegal, a graduate of the MLB Scout Development Program, also has a degree in sports psychology.

As the 2017 season opened, women were working as team and league officials, club owners, writers, broadcasters, and umpires.

Olympic softball star Jennie Finch even became the first female manager in professional baseball. Married to former major-leaguer Casey Daigle, she was the best pitcher in the family. An Olympic gold medalist and celebrity softball star who once fanned Albert Pujols, she made history in 2016 when the Bridgeport Blue Fish of the independent Atlantic League hired her to manage a game against the Southern Maryland Blue Crabs on May 29.

No woman has duplicated the feat of Jackie Mitchell, a teenaged left-handed pitcher. She was just 17 when she struck out Babe Ruth and Lou Gehrig in an exhibition game between the Chattanooga Lookouts and the New York Yankees on May 11, 1931. Although her effort attracted national attention, it also earned the enmity of baseball commissioner Kenesaw Mountain Landis. He canceled her contract, claiming that baseball was too difficult for female players.

Three years later, however, Babe Didrikson Zaharias pitched for several big-league teams during spring training. An all-around athlete whose best sports were golf and basketball, she also toured with the House of David barnstorming team.

Given a chance, Alta Weiss might have proven herself much more than "the Girl Wonder," a title she received while playing with the Vermilion Independents. She even drew 3,182 curious fans to Cleveland's League Park for an exhibition game on Oct. 2, 1907. Her father, a well-to-do doctor, bought the touring team and renamed it the Weiss All-Stars. Alta wore a black uniform while her teammates wore white. Alta Weiss retired in 1922 to become a physician herself.

college opposition, but fans didn't care as long as they could see him play.

A plaque outside Osaka's Koshien Stadium was erected in memory of the visit, which Ruth spiced with such antics as holding a Japanese parasol to fend off the rain while playing first base.

Babe Ruth was the only non-Japanese name on a list of the nation's best-known personalities over a 40-year period. The game was promoted in Japan through an annual Babe Ruth Day, and Japanese soldiers taunted Americans in World War II with the cry, "To hell with Babe Ruth!"

At first glance, Americans might not understand the game in Japan. Spring training is a rigorous two-month training grind that includes eight-hour conditioning sessions of weight-lifting, running, calisthenics, and even wood-chopping.

Pitchers work often (Tadashi Sugiura was 38-4 one season) and don't go to the showers when knocked out; instead, they head for the bullpen and throw until meeting the fans' approval.

During pregame practice, Japanese coaches determine which regulars look rusty and withhold those men from the game. Fans shy away from foul balls in the stands and ushers return them to the umpire.

Beer, peanuts, an import called the "hotto dogu"—plus noodles and seaweed—keep concessions stands busy, and spectators spend more time booing each other than the men on the field. Fans sit in rooting sections for the team of their choice. Average annual attendance is 12 million, but the Yomiuri Giants get close to 25 percent of that total.

Fans pick players for three All-Star Games, which provide one million dollars for the player pension fund—60 percent of the annual input. At age 50, players with 10 years' service (major or minor-league) receive annual stipends of $1,000, about one-eighth of what their American counterparts earn.

An ironclad reserve clause forbids player shifts at will, but most athletes seem satisfied with an average wage of $20,000, though American imports average twice as much. Only two foreigners are permitted on each team's 60-player "control list," which includes an active roster of 28 names. Contracts, by league rule, are for one year only, but bonus clauses are accepted and widely used.

The very best Japanese players are enshrined in an impressive Hall of Fame near Tokyo. The gallery includes artifacts tracing the history of the game in Japan and the prized possessions are photos of the 1934 tour of American stars.

Japanese Baseball in Wartime

World War II had a tremendous impact on the Japanese game. Early in the conflict, the militarist government ordered that only Japanese terms could be used to describe baseball action. Previously, the terms "safe," "out," and "play ball" had been incorporated into the language. American team names (Senators, Tigers, Giants, etc.) were also banned and ordered replaced with

Japanese titles.

Encounters between Americans and Japanese often involved their most common tie: baseball. In December 1941, Dr. Alexander Paul, a missionary in China, was subjected to a search by Japanese soldiers. In his home, they spotted copies of *The Sporting News.* "Baseball!" they shouted, then argued how to divide the captured newspapers.

At Guadalcanal, PFC John Mooney Jr. of Worcester, Massachusetts, recalled taking a Japanese prisoner who asked, in plain English, "Who won the World Series?"

Games in the Central League, then Japan's only major circuit, were suspended from September 1944 to November 1945 as World War II drew to a close.

With the war over, eight teams opened the 1946 Japanese season. Two years later, night ball was introduced at Gehrig Stadium in Yokohama. Warming relations with the Americans allowed a goodwill visit by the San Francisco Seals of the AAA Pacific Coast League in 1949. Japan's second league, the Pacific, began play in 1950.

The Japanese Babe Ruth

In 1959 a left-handed-hitting first baseman named Sadaharu Oh broke into the Japanese leagues with the powerful Yomiuri Giants, one of four clubs in greater Tokyo. In 1977 Oh became the "world" home-run champion when he smashed his 756th ball over the wall.

Oh, whose name means "king" and who wore No. 1, was best known for his Mel Ott batting style: he lifted his front foot high in the air before he swung. A typical year for Oh, whose team played a 130-game schedule, occurred in 1976: 49 home runs, 123 runs batted in, and a .325 batting average.

The six-foot, 174-pound slugger, who unquestionably was the national hero of Japan, helped the Giants win nine straight pen-

Frank Stapleton, Brenner Classic Moments

Sachio Kinugasa, known in Japan as Tetsu jin (The Iron Man), played in 2,215 consecutive games before Cal Ripken Jr. broke his "world record" in 1996. Kinugasa spent his entire 23-year career with the Hiroshima Giants.

Moe Berg . . . athlete, scholar, spy.

Moe Berg's Secret Mission

Though Babe Ruth was the biggest draw on the 1934 tour of Japan, the key man was actually light-hitting catcher Moe Berg. This Princeton graduate, a master of languages, had done little to distinguish himself with two clubs that season, but was added to the "All-Star team" by the United States government.

After learning Japanese in a two-month cram course, Berg presented numerous lectures on the game and became a popular figure. But his mission, which he accomplished with relative ease, was to photograph the Japanese capital. Berg's movies were the principal reference for General Jimmie Doolittle's air raids over the city, which began on April 18, 1942.

Is Baseball a Martial Art?

When baseball was first brought to Japan, sportsmen interpreted the game as an American version of a martial sport—much like judo or karate. The game was played under extremely adverse conditions until the Japanese learned that baseball was primarily a test of skill, not endurance.

All-Nippon Foes

When Shigetoshi Hasegawa (Angels) pitched to Ichiro Suzuki (Mariners) in the ninth inning at Edison International Field on April 13, 2001, it was the first time a native Japanese pitcher and batter faced each other in the U.S. major leagues (Ichiro hit an infield single).

nants, 1965–1973, but lost a televised home-run derby to Hank Aaron, 10–9, late in 1974.

Oh had many advantages over Aaron:

- Japanese stadiums are smaller than those in the United States, with typical dimensions 300 feet to the foul lines and 395 feet to center.
- Pitchers never throw brushback pitches common in the States; when a pitch slips and becomes a duster by accident, they apologize. Thus, Oh could "dig in" and take a comfortable hitting position.
- Because fans support the Giants so heavily, umpires appeared to favor that club, giving Yomiuri pitchers a large strike zone but hitters a small strike zone. Oh got pitches exactly where he wanted them or he didn't swing. He walked 166 times in 1974.
- Fans of both teams preferred an Oh home run to victory by their favorite nine.

A few pitchers from the Japanese leagues have made the majors: left-handed pitcher Masanori Murakami, who went 4–1 with eight saves for the 1965 San Francisco Giants, was the first, but fellow pitcher Hideo Nomo of the Los Angeles Dodgers proved to be the best 30 years later.

Oh, What a Guy

Sadaharu Oh's records stagger the imagination. En route to a career total of 868 home runs, he won 15 home-run titles, 13 RBI crowns, five batting championships, nine Gold Gloves, and nine MVP awards. American observer Clete Boyer said he had the strength of Hank Aaron but the batting eye of Ted Williams.

Williams won six batting crowns, four home-run titles, and four RBI championships, while Aaron led his league in homers and RBIs four times each and batting twice. Babe Ruth led in batting once, RBIs five times, and homers 12 times.

Japanese Customs

In the Japanese major leagues, games—often played on all-dirt infields—can end in ties. Fans use chopsticks to eat noodles and munch on sushi. And special sections of diehards wave banners, pound drums, and bang plastic noisemakers until the game ends.

Dynamic Daisuke

After starring for the Seibu Lions of the Japanese Pacific League for seven seasons, Daisuke Matsuzaka was auctioned to the highest bidder. The Boston Red Sox offered $51.1 million for the rights, then signed the pitcher to a six-year contract for $52 million more. In 2008, his second U.S. campaign, he started the Red Sox opener in the Tokyo Dome and went on to post an 18-3 record and 2.90 ERA.

World View

On May 17, 2008, the Dodgers beat the Angels, 6–3, in an interleague game with an international flavor. The first game featuring pitchers from three different Asian countries involved Chan Ho Park of South Korea, Hong-Chih Kuo of Taiwan, and Takashi Saito of Japan.

Panama Games

The two-game exhibition series between the Yankees and Marlins on March 15-16, 2014 were the first major league games played in Panama since 1947. The games, staged to honor retired Yankees closer Mariano Rivera, were played in Rod Carew Stadium in Panama City.

Across the Dateline

Place	HR	Hits	Wins	Strikeouts
MLB	Barry Bonds 762	Pete Rose 4,256	Cy Young 511	Nolan Ryan 5,714
Japan	Sadaharu Oh 868	Isaa Harimoto 3085	Masaichi Kaneda 400	M. Kaneda 4,490

Chapter 19

Margie Lawrence, reprinted with permission.

Fans

The Master Promoter: Bill Veeck

Bill Veeck was the best of several promotion-minded owners who advanced the theory that helped bad teams prosper without natural fan-drawing power. The theory was "Give 'em a show if you can't give 'em a ballclub."

Veeck, the P. T. Barnum of baseball, believed in both shows and giveaways. And he used his creative genius at every opportunity.

The most outlandish stunt in baseball history involved Veeck's three-foot, seven-inch midget, Eddie Gaedel, age 26. On August 19, 1951, at St. Louis, Gaedel emerged from a birthday cake between games of a doubleheader. He wore a Browns uniform with the numerals ⅛ stitched on the back.

In the last of the first inning in the second game, Gaedel was sent to the plate as a pinch-hitter for leadoff man Frank Saucier. At first umpires Ed Hurley and Art Passarella balked. But when manager Zack Taylor produced the official player's contract Gaedel had signed (for $100 per game), they waved him into the batter's box.

The midget went into the crouch Veeck had taught him in secret session and walked on four pitches. He was immediately replaced by a pinch-runner and never appeared in the majors again. American League president Will Harridge ruled him ineligible and also killed a Veeck plan to employ a nine-foot, three-inch giant from Great Britain.

Five days after the Gaedel caper, more than 1,000 "grandstand managers," selected from applicants who wrote local newspapers, voted on strategy while manager Taylor sat in the stands in street clothes. They split 60-40 on all decisions but the majority was right consistently and the Browns beat the Philadelphia Athletics, 5–3.

In the first inning, when St. Louis ace Ned Garver was hit hard, Veeck groaned when the grandstand managers voted against warming up a new pitcher, but Garver pitched out of trouble and won the game. The night ended with a "skywriting" display in fireworks. It read: "Thank you, G.S. Managers, for a swell job. Zack manages tomorrow."

Veeck considered each individual fan to be very important. He even staged a "day" for night watchman Joe Earley in Cleveland.

In a letter to the *Cleveland Press*, Earley asked why teams were always giving "days" to well-paid stars who really didn't need the money instead of to loyal fans like him, who did. He signed the letter "Good Old Joe Earley."

Veeck, then running the Indians, realized Earley had logic on his side. He called the paper for Earley's address and told him to be at the ballpark.

On the appointed night, gifts were given to fans before Earley took center stage. First he got a series of gag gifts, including an outhouse, a backfiring Model-T, and assorted animals. Then he received a new Ford convertible, a refrigerator, washing machine, luggage, watch, clothes, stereo system, and more. An instant celebrity, he became quite successful from that day on.

Each Veeck promotion was greeted with charges that he was making a travesty of the game. But who could argue with success? In 1948 the Indians smashed previous attendance records with a season's draw of 2,620,627. Against Chicago on August 20, the club drew 78,382.

Manager Zack Taylor with 3'7", 50-pound midget Eddie Gaedel. Wearing number ⅛, Gaedel pinch hit for Bill Veeck's Browns against Detroit. He walked on four pitches, then left the game.

A Veeck Fiasco

Master promoter Bill Veeck was the victim of one of his own gags when fans ran wild during "Disco Demolition Night" festivities at Comiskey Park in 1979. A mass record-burning in the outfield, plus the unruly fans, made the field unplayable for the second half of a scheduled doubleheader. The umpires forfeited the game to the visiting Detroit Tigers.

Nick Altrock and Al Schacht, longtime baseball clowns, stage a pregame boxing match, entertaining a crowd during the '30s.

Grandiose Promotion

Minor-league history is filled with unusual promotions staged by enterprising operators. Chattanooga's Joe Engel, tired of giving away automobiles, hit the jackpot when he auctioned off his popular radio announcer before thousands of cheering women. The winner used him to mow the lawn, wash the dishes, and do other household chores.

The Miami Beach nine gave away orchids, animals, and bicycles on a night that also featured the traditional cow-milking contest. For players with nonfarming backgrounds, the cow contest often ended in *udder* confusion.

With the help of sponsors and local businesses, major league teams took a cue from the minors and planned clever promotions in numbers that increased in direct proportion to the rise of player salaries in the '70s.

Many teams hosted Fan Appreciation Days, with multiple giveaways, at season's end, and most promoted heavily throughout the year. In Philadelphia, team sponsor TastyKake printed its slogan, "All the good things wrapped up in one," on halter tops distributed to female fans by the ballclub.

The 1979 Phillies gave away sweatshirts, batting gloves, gym shorts, pennants, ladies tote bags, wristbands, jackets, tube socks, caps, ponchos, shirts, notebooks, and ski caps—all on different days. Fireworks displays were also part of the promotional calendar.

One Phillies event marked by ingenuity was Music Night. Fans were invited to bring their own instruments (or receive a free kazoo) and play "Take Me Out to the Ball Game" at the seventh-inning stretch. Certificates were awarded to participants stating that they had played with "the world's largest orchestra."

Best Baseball Museums

- National Baseball Hall of Fame and Museum, Cooperstown, NY
- Louisville Slugger Museum and Factory, Louisville, KY
- Negro Leagues Baseball Museum, Kansas City, MO
- National Ballparks Museum, Denver, CO
- Ted Williams Museum and Hitters Hall of Fame, St. Petersburg, FL
- Yogi Berra Museum and Learning Center, Little Falls, NJ
- Babe Ruth Museum, Baltimore, MD
- Bob Feller Museum, Van Meter, IA
- Roger Maris Museum, Fargo, ND
- Shoeless Joe Jackson Museum, Greenville, SC
- Canadian Baseball Hall of Fame, Toronto, ON
- Dizzy Dean Museum, Jackson, MS*

(*) part of Mississippi Sports Hall of Fame

BASEBALL
Ladies' Day
Every Friday
POLO GROUNDS
OR
YANKEE STADIUM
TRAIN "CC" TO BALL PARKS

A 1930 New York City subway sign tells the story about Ladies Day.

Stamp of Greatness

Babe Ruth was featured in the "Decade of the '20s" stamp issued by the U.S. Postal Service in 1998.

A sad Babe Ruth said good-bye during tearful "Babe Ruth Day" ceremony.

Ladies Day

Promotions to swell attendance have long been part of the game. There is dispute about the exact origin of Ladies Day, but the idea of admitting women free—whether accompanied by a paying male escort or not—definitely rates as the oldest promotion in baseball.

New York of the National League used the idea once in 1883, but it was not adopted on a regular basis in the majors until 1889, in Cincinnati. Women gained free admission only with a paid escort.

Two years earlier the New Orleans club had allowed women to enter free, even if unaccompanied, one day per week. The practice violated prevailing social mores and brought waves of protests.

Major league teams eventually discovered the value of admitting females "for a smile." The idea was twofold: to hook women on baseball so that they might become regular paying customers and to lure male fans who would welcome the presence of females who shared their interest in the game.

In 1937 the New York Giants reported the ratio of female guests to paying males was four to ten. The Chicago Cubs did even better business on Ladies Day. After more than 30,000 non-paying females flooded Wrigley Field one day, the team imposed a maximum of 20,000 free tickets for Ladies Day promotions. Those who exceeded the limit were given priority for the following Ladies Day game.

"Days" for Players

"Days" for players are accepted as a common way to honor stars.

Appreciative Tiger fans saluted Charlie Gehringer with "Charlie Gehringer Day" in Detroit on August 14, 1929, and the Mechanical Man responded with a home run, three singles, and a steal of home.

In 1930 "Rabbit Maranville Day" was held at Braves Field, Boston. More than 32,000 fans watched as the city and the ballclub presented the star shortstop with a car, tea set, reading lamp, cigar box, and assorted other gifts—including a gray rabbit that looked very much like the player himself.

While most "days" were happy occasions, the two saddest in the game's history were held at Yankee Stadium. In 1939 Lou Gehrig, wracked by a disease that would kill him two years later, addressed the crowd: "Today, I consider myself the luckiest man on the face of the Earth. I might have been given a bad break, but I've got an awful lot to live for. Thank you."

In 1947 it was Babe Ruth Day. He too was dying. "You know how pained my voice sounds," he said. "Well, it feels just as bad. You know this baseball game of ours . . . the only real game, I think, in the world—baseball."

The Knothole Gang

Though longtime executive Branch Rickey is credited with launching "The Knothole Gang" concept in the majors, the idea was actually the brainchild of minor-league player/manager Abner Powell, who also conceived of the rain check (1887) and the tarpaulin (1889).

When Powell came to Sportsman's Park, New Orleans, during the 1889 campaign, he often encountered a ragged band of boys who loved baseball in general and Powell in particular. They hung around in front of the park, unable to come up with 10 cents for a bleacher seat, and then migrated to the wooden outfield wall when the game started. They punched out a knothole to get a good view of the action inside.

Powell suggested to team owner Toby Hart that he admit the youths free, seating them in a special section of the ballpark. The reluctant owner agreed only after Powell promised he would be responsible for their behavior and pay for any damage. The thoughtful Powell, the team's player/manager, arranged twice-weekly free admissions for the group, but asked them to be neat in appearance and behavior once inside. Beards and tobacco were prohibited.

Old-Timers' Day

When Ruth was playing, the Yankees used the slugger in a typical end-of-season promotion: they let him pitch—twice. In 1930 and again in 1933, the ex-pitcher took to the mound with no preparation on the season's last day and stopped his former Red Sox teammates 9–3 and 6–5, respectively.

With fan interest on the wane for clubs not involved in pennant races, activating an old-time hero helps fill the stands. The practice evolved into the regular once-a-year promotion, Old-Timers' Day.

Before the Yankees introduced the first "official" Old-Timers' Day in 1947, retired players returned to action for fleeting appearances in the final stages of the season.

On September 30, 1934, the St. Louis Browns employed catcher Grover Hartley, 46, and shortstop Charlie O'Leary, 52. Though he had been out of the majors since 1913, O'Leary slammed a pinch-single and scored a run.

St. Louis Cardinals manager Gabby Street, 49, caught three innings on September 20, 1931, when Sylvester Johnson was on the mound. The Johnson/Street battery was supposed to remind fans of the famous tandem of Walter Johnson and Street, Washington Senators stars more than 20 years before.

Jimmy Austin doubled and stole home at age 46 in 1926 and played three innings for the Browns three years later.

The Senators brought back pitcher Nick Altrock, 53, as a right fielder on October 6, 1929, and he managed to get a hit. Minnie Minoso of the Chicago White Sox was 57 when he went 0-for-2 in a Bill Veeck publicity stunt in 1980. But it made Minnie a five-decade performer in the majors.

Johnny Evers, 47, played one inning for the Boston Braves in 1929.

Another old man of September was James (Orator) O'Rourke, who caught a full game for Iron Man McGinnity of the New York Giants on September 22, 1904. O'Rourke had been out of the majors 11 years but got a hit and scored a run; he also made an error.

Fan Collects Songs

Collecting baseball items is a hobby that takes many shapes and forms. Perhaps the most unusual collection ever assembled was the baseball music library put together by J. Francis Driscoll of Brookline, Massachusetts. He obtained the music to more than 50,000 songs, including "Take Me Out to the Ball Game," in a hobby that spanned 40 years.

The Pioneer Promoter

Frank Bancroft, business manager of the Cincinnati Reds from 1892 to 1921, was the first baseball official to promote the game heavily. He staged the first home plate wedding, led major league squads to Cuba, and arranged baseball Olympics, featuring long-distance throwing, races, fungo-hitting, and home-run derbys. A one-time field manager in the early days of the National League, Bancroft had a background as advance man for the circus and vaudeville tours.

Believe It Or Not

Baseball's first collector was sports cartoonist Robert Ripley. A California native who had a tryout as a pitcher for the 1913 New York Giants, Ripley played just once: in a 1939 exhibition game that also included Babe Ruth and Walter Johnson. In between, he created pen-and-ink illustrations of oddities he discovered during his extensive travels. His syndicated "Believe It Or Not" cartoons, which often featured baseball, appeared in 40 countries, and earned him a niche in the Cartoon Art Hall of Fame. The world's first million-dollar cartoonist displayed his collectibles in museums called "Odditoriums" and even appeared at the Louisville Slugger Museum. The "Oddball" exhibition ran through January 8, 2017.

Female fans—and male admirers—flocked to a Farrah Fawcett-Majors look-alike contest in Atlanta Stadium.

Dizzy Dean's Last Game

Colorful Dizzy Dean, Cardinals star of the '30s, had been retired six seasons when the St. Louis Browns reactivated him for one game as a publicity stunt in 1947.

Dean, then a popular St. Louis broadcaster, was not only out of condition but also overweight. But he still had his baseball instincts; he pitched four scoreless innings against the Chicago White Sox, lined a hit to left, and later slid into second while on the base paths.

When the 36-year-old right-hander got up limping at second, his wife Pat leaned over the dugout rail and hailed Browns manager Muddy Ruel. "He's proved his point," she said. "Now get him out of there before he kills himself!"

In the four-inning stint that closed his career, Dean yielded three hits and one walk. He thoroughly enjoyed his unexpected last hurrah as an active player.

Fan Interference

In 1894 Cincinnati ground rules permitted outfielders to pursue batted balls that bounced into the bleachers. Pittsburgh's Elmer Smith, chasing a two-out drive by George "Germany" Smith, was physically assaulted by several fans—one of whom finally made his point by pulling a gun. Not surprisingly, the Reds won, 7–6.

After George Weiss established Old-Timers' Day—the Yankees' lone promotion for years—other clubs quickly followed suit.

Old-Timers' Day has remained as an integral part of the Yankees promotional calendar for more than a half-century. In 2001 the team invited 47 former players to a celebration of the 1961 team led by the late Mickey Mantle and Roger Maris.

Show Biz on the Diamond

Though giveaway days are guaranteed fan favorites, pregame or postgame spectacles have definite pulling power. The Atlanta Braves appealed to a male audience with their Wet T-Shirt Night of 1977, but ran into repercussions when the winner's father turned out to be a Methodist minister.

The Braves countered with such innocent entertainment as ostrich races, bathtub races, fireworks and laser shows, and a look-alike contest for blonde actress Farrah Fawcett-Majors. Wedlock and Headlock Night was something special—mass weddings at home plate before the game and professional wrestling matches afterward.

"What we're trying to do," explained Bob Hope, then Atlanta promotion chief, "is stimulate the feeling that it's fun to come to the ballpark. We want people to say they had a good time even if the home team gets clobbered."

The Browns used a pitcher per inning as a last-game gimmick in 1949; fans entering Brooklyn's Ebbets Field were given candles before the lights were dimmed in birthday tribute to Pee Wee Reese; and John "Hans" Lobert of the Phillies raced a horse around the bases in 1913.

Lobert had been timed at 13⅗ seconds—exceptionally fast by any standard—in circling the bases, but lost his race when the horse violated an agreement to race on the outside of the base paths and crowded him at third base. It won by a nose.

Crowds

Promotions pull fans into ballparks, but other key factors are good weather, an interesting opponent, a reasonable chance the home team will win, and overall interest in baseball by local residents.

Only 17 fans—6 of them paying customers—watched a Pittsburgh Pirate game in 1890, the year of the Players' League revolt, and just 26 saw Baltimore of the International League play a 1914 game; that city had a Federal League team that year.

But the Los Angeles Dodgers drew more than 90,000 spectators four times—three of them during the 1959 World Series against the Chicago White Sox. The team was then in the second of four seasons at the Los Angeles Coliseum, a football bowl that housed the team before Dodger Stadium could be built.

While tenants of the Coliseum, the Dodgers drew the largest crowd ever to watch a game—93,103 for Roy Campanella Night on May 7, 1959. The New York Yankees provided the opposition for an exhibition game that followed pregame tributes to the Dodger catcher whose career was shortened by a winter auto

Ted Turner was such an involved owner in his early years with the Atlanta Braves that he even participated in such zany on-field promotions as pushing a baseball with his nose.

Walter Victor

mishap in New York.

The Coliseum allowed the Dodgers to establish National League standards for day and night crowds, but it was after the move to Dodger Stadium that the club first drew 3,000,000 fans in one year. The Dodgers' day record was 78,672 (vs. the Giants on April 18, 1958) and night mark was 72,140 (vs. the Reds in a twi-night doubleheader on August 16, 1961).

The Colorado Rockies, who spent their first two years in 80,000-seat Mile High Stadium, have since set new marks for regular-season total (4,483,350 in 1993) and single game (80,227 on April 9, 1993, the team's first home opener).

Both the Cleveland Indians and the New York Yankees drew more than 80,000 fans on a single day, with doubleheaders (two games for the price of one) as added incentive. Cleveland had 84,587 paid (86,563 in the park) against the second-place Yankees on September 12, 1954, while New York drew 81,841 on Memorial Day 1938 against the arch-rival Boston Red Sox.

The Indians, then occupants of a ballpark with a capacity of more than 76,000, also established a major league record when they drew 78,382 fans for a night game (against the White Sox on August 20, 1948) and an American League Opening Day mark with 74,420 against the Tigers on April 17, 1973. The Dodgers had drawn 4,000 more for their first game in Los Angeles in 1958.

Rather than turn customers away, many early club executives roped off sections of outfield and allowed fans to stand on the field behind the ropes. This practice made it necessary to set up special ground rules for balls hit into the crowd and also created additional problems for groundskeepers who had to cope with cigarette butts and all kinds of other debris. The Washington Senators were roundly criticized for allowing field crowds in 1941 and 1949, after the practice had gone out of general use in the major leagues.

By drawing more than 64 million fans to ballparks in 1997, Major League Baseball had a greater total attendance than the National Football League, National Hockey League, and National Basketball Association combined.

Early Honor

Expectations were so low for the New York Giants in the 1954 World Series that the city gave them a parade before the Series started.

Great Catch

Red Sox fans once gave a standing ovation to defensively challenged first baseman Dick Stuart after he made a clean catch of a windblown hot dog wrapper.

Who Asked Whom?

John Lennon once asked for Jack Klugman's autograph because he was a fan of *The Odd Couple*. Klugman portrayed sportswriter Oscar Madison in the ABC-TV series and often wore a Mets cap.

Tough Job

Longtime baseball announcer Al Michaels once picked the women for *The Dating Game*.

Do the Chop

As the 1991 season progressed and the Braves looked more like winners, fans responded with a frenzy that rivaled the Beanie Baby craze. They beat tom-toms, waved tomahawks, wore Indian garb, and chanted in unison. The Tomahawk Chant started by spontaneous combustion when David Justice was batting against the Dodgers in a big September series. Even though the organ was silent, the chanting could be heard at Morehouse College, two miles away.

$1 Million Payoff

On June 5, 1997, Seattle fan Pamela Altazan won $1 million when Alex Rodriguez hit for the cycle during a 14–6 win over Detroit. Altazan had entered a contest in which fans were randomly selected. "I don't care if he never gets another hit," she said. "I'm always going to cheer for the man."

Helping Hand

With the Orioles ahead, 4–3, in Game 1 of the 1996 ALCS at Yankee Stadium, New York's Derek Jeter hit a long eighth-inning drive. As Baltimore right fielder Tony Tarasco readied to catch it, 12-year-old Jeffrey Maier reached out and deflected it into the stands. Umpire Rich Garcia, oblivious to the apparent fan interference, ruled it a home run that tied the game. New York won, 5–4, in 11 innings and took the series, four games to one.

Son of Coors

A $2.7 million replica of Coors Field, built especially for youth baseball, opened in the Denver suburb of Lakewood, Colorado, on July 7, 1998, the date the All-Star Game was played at Coors. The youth field, named All-Star Park, was 90 percent the size of the original.

No Bobblehead

The Tampa Bay Rays canceled Manny Ramirez bobblehead day on May 29, 2011 because the outfielder had retired a month earlier.

Bat Factory

Visitors can see bats made for big-leaguers at the Louisville Slugger Museum & Factory, which marked its 20th anniversary in 2016. The museum had a record attendance of 314,149 in 2015.

The Advent of Ushers

Feelings invariably run high in crowds, with the displeasure of the majority vented on the few who dare root against the home team. Intense rivalries between the New York Yankees and the Boston Red Sox of the American League, and the Brooklyn Dodgers and the New York Giants of the National League, frequently flared into confrontations. The practice of using ushers to police the stands began after rowdyism in New York so infuriated Detroit star Ty Cobb in 1912 that he jumped into the stands and attacked a fan.

A suspension resulted and sympathetic teammates pulled a one-day strike that forced the Tigers to recruit a group of semipros as last-minute replacements. The Philadelphia Athletics won, 24–2, and the regular Detroit players, having made their point, then returned.

After Cobb charged the fan, warning posters went up around the majors to remind fans that rowdyism would not be tolerated. Ushers were hired and, where necessary, special police were assigned to stadium duty.

The Season Ticket

The advent of the season ticket proved a lifesaver to numerous teams. The business community pitched in to purchase blocks of seats. With 81 home dates under the 162-game format launched in 1961, clubs could guarantee an attendance of 405,000 simply by selling 5,000 season tickets. Most important of all was the fact that money used to purchase season tickets was immediately available to the team.

Providence, a National League team in 1884, pioneered the season-ticket concept. Its prices were $15 if purchased before March 15, $20 before April 15. Boston charged $15 for a season ticket, but cut $5 off that figure if the tickets were purchased by or for a woman.

To illustrate how times changed, in 1978 a fan could have purchased a seat for himself and his wife in the deluxe loge area of Candlestick Park, San Francisco, for $14.20—just 80 cents less than the price of a season ticket in 1884.

Famous Fans

Fans have watched and listened to and become infatuated with baseball. Songwriter George M. Cohan wrote "Yankee Doodle Dandy" but was an ardent fan of the New York Giants. So were famous New York restaurateurs Toots Shor and Dinty Moore. Jack White of the 18 Club and actress Tallulah Bankhead were known to be distraught when the Giants lost.

Pearl Yount and Dorothy Wolff formed a team of passionate St. Louis Cardinal rooters, attending all weekend and holiday games at Sportsman's Park in the '30s and heading out of town to follow the Redbirds on road trips. The Yount/Wolff tandem became so well known by the Cardinal players and management that an article was written about them in the four-page team house publication.

Another well-known St. Louis fan, Mary Ott, dominated the bleachers of Sportsman's Park during the war years. Her trademark was a piercing laugh that could best be described as a whinny. The rotund Mrs. Ott had a fine arrangement with her second husband; he cooked the meals while she went to the games.

Mrs. Ott looked down upon those who entered free of charge on Ladies Day. "They don't know baseball or how to behave at ballgames," she said.

"The Bell of Ebbets Field"

Brooklyn's Hilda Chester, accompanied by her cowbell, was the head cheerleader of the Ebbets Field faithful at the same time that Ott operated in St. Louis. She was called "The Bell of Ebbets Field" with good reason.

The one-time player for the New York Bloomer Girls developed rheumatism in her arm and received a doctor's advice that she should exercise the arm in the sun. What better way than to ring a four-pound cowbell at the ballpark?

Hilda's act began in batting practice and Dodger players responded with waves as soon as they heard it. She sat in the center-field bleachers, earning money for tickets by selling songsheets at the corner of DeKalb Avenue and Flatbush Extension.

While Hilda Chester was ringing her cowbell, a five-piece band provided a stream of music—or sounds approaching music—from behind the Dodger bench. Broadcaster Red Barber named the group "the Dodger Sym-Phony" and it was so well received that the drummer had the name emblazoned on his instrument.

The Sym-Phony specialized in mocking the actions of rival players with music. When a visiting player approached the water fountain, the band played a chorus of "How Dry I Am." When he returned to his seat on the bench, his act of seating himself was greeted by a clash of the cymbals.

Fans on the Field

As Hilda Chester and the Dodger Sym-Phony illustrated, Brooklyn fans made the most noise and did the craziest things. On July 31, 1935, with the Cardinals in town, a woman named Kitty Burke jumped out of the stands, grabbed a bat, ran to home plate, and took a swing at one of Paul Dean's warm-up pitches. The ball went bounding back to the pitcher, who was speechless for the first time in his career.

Eleven years later a Boston fan decided to try the defensive end of the game. Before 28,000 Fenway Park patrons on August 26, 1946, a midget hopped over the fence, picked up a glove, and took up position at third base. Ted Williams was the hitter and

Morganna Roberts, a former exotic dancer, established a new career as Morganna: the Kissing Bandit—playing the part of a lovesick fan who interrupts games by jumping fences to kiss unsuspecting players. The gimmick, once a publicity stunt for Morganna's act, became a career when she began booking herself as an attraction for minor-league teams.

Library of Congress

Before the advent of radio and television, mechanical devices like this one at Madison Square Garden gave fans instant updates on the progress of important games. Note the lineups of the Boston Red Sox and New York Giants in the 1913 World Series.

Cheap Date

Brooklyn fans in 1920 ate nickel hot dogs and read nickel programs. School-children got bleacher seats for a quarter apiece on Friday afternoons.

Brownout

Only 80,922 fans turned out to watch the last-place St. Louis Browns during the 1935 season.

Flying Objects

Fan safety in baseball has always been a concern to clubs. The only baseball-related fatality occurred in 1970, when a 14-year-old boy was killed by a foul ball at Dodger Stadium. Fans also died after stadium falls in Texas (2011) and Atlanta (2015), while a woman suffered multiple facial fractures when struck by a broken bat of Brett Lawrie at Fenway Park, also in 2015.

Joe D's Bat

A bat used by Joe DiMaggio in the early '40s was sold at auction to the Louisville Slugger Museum for $350,000 in April 2004. The bat was discovered by Patricia Henrich, daughter of former Yankees out-fielder Tommy Henrich, who played with DiMaggio.

Lightning Strikes Twice

The ball Chris Burke hit for the pennant-winning home run in the 18th inning of the last 2005 playoff game in Houston was caught by the same fan who caught Lance Berkman's grand slam in the eighth.

Barry Ball

The ball Barry Bonds hit for his 762nd and last home run was auctioned for $376,612 to an anonymous bidder on April 12, 2008. Twelve days later, a David Ortiz jersey went for $175,100. It had been exhumed from the construction site of the new Yankee Stadium in a hex that went awry.

the entire Cleveland infield, in the Boudreau Shift, had moved to the right side of second base, leaving shortstop and third base wide open. The midget was later identified as vaudevillian Marco Songini.

It wasn't long after Montreal joined the National League in 1969 that Quebec fans found their way into history's footnotes. During an unusual fall fog, a streaker appeared just long enough to be seen before disappearing into the mist. A musically inclined spectator whipped out a violin, jumped on top of the home dugout, and gave Montreal a living *Fiddler on the Roof*. Mrs. Bob Bailey, appearing with other wives in a fashion show, was booed because her husband was in a batting slump. And Expos fans gave umpires crash courses in the off-color words of the French language.

Chicago's Bleacher Bums

The same year the Expos started, the National League's oldest franchise, the Chicago Cubs, appeared headed for the pennant playoffs. Their unexpected achievements of midsummer so excited their fans that they developed an addiction to the game. Bedecked in bright yellow hard hats, they vocally destroyed opponents.

"I would have hated being an opposing player in Wrigley Field at that time," said Randy Hundley, who played for the Cubs then. "They didn't hold anything back. If they knew something personal about a guy, they'd let it rip. They used to get on Willie Davis about his ex-wife. He was ready to go into the stands to fight them."

The team actually had to erect a chicken-wire fence in front of the bleachers because overenthusiastic fans paraded around on a narrow cement walk on top of the outfield wall. The nickname "Bleacher Bums" stuck when Cub fans used it with a certain pride during the abortive pennant chase of 1969.

True Believers

Many fans are as devoted as the man whose letter helped slugger Chuck Klein escape a batting slump in 1935. Klein smashed 17 hits in 50 trips (.340) immediately after receiving the letter from N. L. Silver. The four-paragraph note, written in very humble style, explained a flaw the fan had detected in the slugger's swing.

Jimmie McCullough of Atlantic City, New Jersey, devoted himself not to a player but to an event. In 1926 he began a remarkable streak of watching the World Series in person. He did it for more than 50 years! The streak involved travel of more than 100,000 miles, purchase of $50 tickets from scalpers on occasion, and acquisition of press credentials wherever possible. Since McCullough had a background as publicist and press agent, he sometimes had little trouble joining the huge press corps. An AP dispatch dubbed McCullough "the Babe Ruth of baseball fans."

The "sign man" of the New York Mets, advertising executive Karl Ehrhardt, could also contend for the title. His hand-lettered signs, held aloft at dramatic moments in a game, became such a hit at Shea Stadium that he was even interviewed on Ralph Kiner's postgame television show.

Ehrhardt's signs were direct descendants of the ragged but clever banners that decorated both the Polo Grounds, home of the Mets in 1962 and 1963, and the Flushing ballpark. Zealous young fans displayed their enthusiasm over the new, struggling expansion team by painting bed sheets and parading them around the park.

Mets management realized the promotional potential in the banners and the resulting Banner Day—with prizes awarded in various categories—proved a smashing success.

Collectors

Many fans express their love for baseball by collecting memorabilia ranging from cards to yearbooks, magazines, buttons, photos, press pins, press guides, uniforms, and even broken bats used by big-leaguers.

Collecting mushroomed into a major industry with the nostalgia wave of the '70s. Adults became so adept at the child's game of

This T-206 Honus Wagner card from 1910 sold for $650,500 just days after Eddie Murray's 500th home-run ball brought $500,000.

Wagner Card

Honus Wagner never made much as a player, but his baseball card is worth millions. The T206 Wagner, part of a 1909 American Tobacco set, was pulled because Wagner eschewed tobacco products. Only a half-dozen survived, driving up the price until one of them sold for $2.8 million in a 2007 auction.

Wrigley Collectors

Mark McGwire's prodigious power displays during batting practice at Wrigley Field in 1997 sent dozens of fans onto Waveland Avenue in search of souvenir baseballs. One of them bragged of retrieving 3,000 balls in 40 years—presumably not all of them from McGwire.

Steve Bartman Game

The 2003 Chicago Cubs came within five outs of clinching the pennant. But they collapsed after Steve Bartman, an avowed Cubs fan, prevented Chicago left fielder Moises Alou from reaching into the stands to catch a foul ball in the eighth inning of the sixth game. The Fish scored eight times, setting themselves up to win the finale and the pennant the next day.

Dan Schlossberg

As these fans at Hall of Fame Induction Weekend indicate, interest in baseball memorabilia, from baseball cards to autographed balls, has remained high well into the 21st century.

buying, selling, and trading cards that they established full-time businesses. Publications sprang up strictly to serve this new industry.

By far the most popular collectors items were baseball cards. The Topps Chewing Gum Company of Brooklyn, New York, began to issue complete sets of player cards in 1951, changing the basic design each year.

By the '70s, the Topps name had become synonymous with baseball cards. The company sold more than 250 million each year and gave awards to outstanding players.

Though Topps became the leading manufacturer of baseball cards, it actually borrowed the idea from earlier tobacco, bread, publishing, and even chewing-gum firms.

Old Judge Cigarettes made the first baseball cards in 1886 by photographing players swinging at a ball on a

Mickey Mantle baseball cards are among the game's most coveted collectibles.

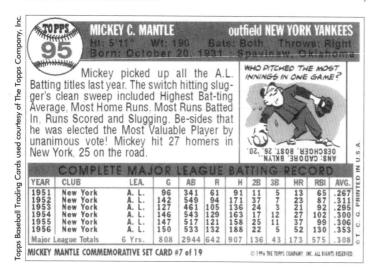

MICKEY MANTLE COMMEMORATIVE SET CARD #7 of 19

string inside a studio. Cracker Jack candy issued a handsome series during the dead-ball era before 1920, and Babe Ruth adorned the face of a Big League Chewing Gum card issued after that date. Three other gum companies—Goudey, DeLong, and National Chicle—were active in the '30s, while Bowman and Fleer were the main competitors when Topps entered the field. As the 21st century began, Topps faced its most serious competition from Fleer and Upper Deck.

The Topps Company, oldest of the current baseball card manufacturers, landed 53 slots in the Top 100 cards of all-time listing published in the February 1998 issue of *Sports Cards* magazine.

The list is headed by the 1952 Mickey Mantle rookie card (No. 311), which has sold for as much as $63,500 in mint condition. The Honus Wagner T-206 card is rated second.

Also in the Top 20 are these Topps issues: the 1954 Ted Williams (No. 6), 1963 Pete Rose rookie (No. 7), 1954 Hank Aaron rookie (No. 9), 1955 Roberto Clemente rookie (No. 11), 1952 Eddie Mathews rookie (No. 16), 1952 Jackie Robinson (No. 18), 1952 Andy Pafko (No. 1), and 1992 Topps Traded rookie Cal Ripken Jr. (No. 20).

In addition to the 53 Topps cards, two O-Pee-Chee cards, produced for Canadian sales, made the magazine's Top 100.

The Babe Ruth of Collectors?

For more than a half-century, Barry Halper was considered the Babe Ruth of collectors. He began as a curious eight-year-old with an after-school habit of hanging around the ballpark of the old Newark Bears, then the top farm club of the New York Yankees.

He had only a few hours at the park each day before his father picked him up at 5:30. "I knew the first ride I missed would be my last," said Halper, who still had more than enough time to befriend the players, run errands, and acquire artifacts.

By the time he reached high school, he had 75 uniforms—not too shabby for a kid whose weekly spending money from his mom was a shiny new quarter.

Years later, as a successful executive in his family's paper products business, Halper had the funds to outbid the donation-dependent Baseball Hall of Fame for many of the most prized possessions in the memorabilia world.

The eight-room basement in his sprawling Livingston, New Jersey home became Cooperstown South, a private baseball mecca open only to those with invitations. Joe DiMaggio became such a frequent visitor that Sharon Halper took lessons in Italian cooking.

To such celebrity guests, and to the parade of reporters and broadcasters lucky enough to tour his compact and colorful baseball fiefdom, Barry Halper was the Babe Ruth of collectors—the man who changed the world of collecting as much as the man who single-handedly converted the game from deadball days to the lively ball.

Eventually, his collection included 1,000,000 cards, 3,000 signed baseballs, and 1,000 uniforms displayed on a rotating rack more commonly used by professional dry cleaners. He even had such one-of-a-kind artifacts as the MVP trophy rejected by Carl Yastrzemski because his name was spelled wrong. Halper's doorbell chimed out the first seven notes of "Take Me Out to the Ballgame" and his New Jersey license plate read YANKS 5—DiMaggio's number.

Halper, who had a physical resemblance to Babe Ruth, was riding high. He owned a small piece of the Yankees, his favorite team, and his collection was featured in *Smithsonian Magazine*.

Late in 1998, however, when plagued with health issues, Halper decided to sell most of his items. Major League Baseball, given first dibs, took 20 percent for $7.5 million and gave it to the Hall of Fame for display in a new exhibit called "Memories of a Lifetime: the Barry Halper Collection." The remaining 80 percent brought $30 million from Sotheby's auction house.

Although a large group of family, friends, and admirers attended his funeral in 2005, Barry Halper would make news again five years later. After investigative reporter Peter J. Nash discovered that Halper's Shoeless Joe Jackson jersey was a forgery, many other items also proved to be misrepresented. *Guerilla Explorer* writer David Meyer wrote that more than $4 million of Halper's collection was erroneous or not authentic.

According to Fay Vincent, a former commissioner of baseball, "Given the evidence that has come to light in the last several years, the Hall of Fame should immediately reconsider the naming of that gallery to honor Barry Halper. I do not think he deserves the honor."

On the other hand, Halper had acquired the memorabilia for his own personal enjoyment with no intent to resell. "My father was not a forensics expert," said Jason Halper. "He never claimed to be an authenticator and may have been gullible when presented with something he thought was an exciting find."

Perhaps the real Babe Ruth of collectors was Jefferson R. Burdick. Born on a Central New York farm in 1900, he was a bachelor whose true love was baseball. His collection of 30,000 cards, estimated to be worth millions, wound up in New York's Metropolitan Museum of Art.

Burdick collected cards not because of their monetary value but because of his interest in history. Like Halper, he loved finding unusual and unorthodox memorabilia.

The Burdick collection included postcards, paper dolls, cigar bands, and even advertisements—anything relating to baseball.

He organized and classified his cards, arranging them by manufacturer and type of illustration. Although he died more than 50 years ago, his system is still used for cards made before 1933.

Unlike current collectors, who preserve their cards in plastic, Burdick pasted them in albums much like stamp collectors do. Those 640 albums are so fragile today that the museum shows them only to serious researchers.

Shaun Clancy, the Irish-born owner of a Manhattan baseball bar called Foley's, created the Irish-American Baseball Hall of Fame to honor major leaguers of Irish descent. Its annual inductions are a major social event for the tavern and its customers.

Foreign Sets

Baseball card sets were popular abroad. They first appeared in Japan in 1898, Cuba in 1909, and Canada in 1912. Production of cards increased dramatically in Japan after World War II.

Mantle Rookie

Because it included the scarce Mickey Mantle rookie card, the 1952 Topps set was the most popular with collectors. Bowman had produced a 1951 Mantle rookie that never had much value.

Strange Places

Baseball cards proved so popular that food companies produced them as part of their packaging. Post Cereals, Hostess, and Kellogg's all produced sets during the early '60s.

Too Many Cards?

A glut of cards, coupled with escalating prices, prompted consolidation in the '90s. The Ted Williams Card Company was the first to fold, followed by Pinnacle and Fleer. Then Donruss lost its license from the Major League Baseball Players Association. By the time the 21st century started, Topps alone was allowed to produce factory sets.

On occasion, however, the museum displays a few dozen Burdick cards in its American Wing.

He explained his fascination with collecting in the 1960 edition of *The American Card Catalog*: "A card collection is like a magic carpet that takes you away from work-a-day cares to relaxing quietude where you can relive the pleasures and adventures of a past day, brought to life in vivid pictures and prose."

He previously published a newsletter called *The Card Collector's Bulletin*.

Many hobby publications followed, including *Baseball Hobby News*, *Sports Collectors Digest*, *Tuff Stuff*, and *Beckett Baseball* and *Baseball Card Price Guide*, both published by Beckett Media.

Inside SABR

The Society for American Baseball Research [SABR] is often described as "the conscience of baseball." Formed in Cooperstown after the 1971 All-Star Game, it has expanded from 16 founders to more than 7,000 members, many of them in professional baseball. Other members are writers, historians, educators, or just rabid fans of baseball. The group holds national and regional conventions and publishes *The Baseball Research Journal* and *The National Pastime: a Review of Baseball History*. It also publishes books and ebooks, holds Negro Leagues and baseball analytics conferences, and embraces the work of committees that research records, biographies, the game's early years, and more. The SABR Defensive Index is considered when Rawlings awards its annual Gold Gloves. Members Bill James, Pete Palmer, Lyle Spatz, and John Thorn are among those who carry on the vision of founder Bob Davids.

Chapter 20

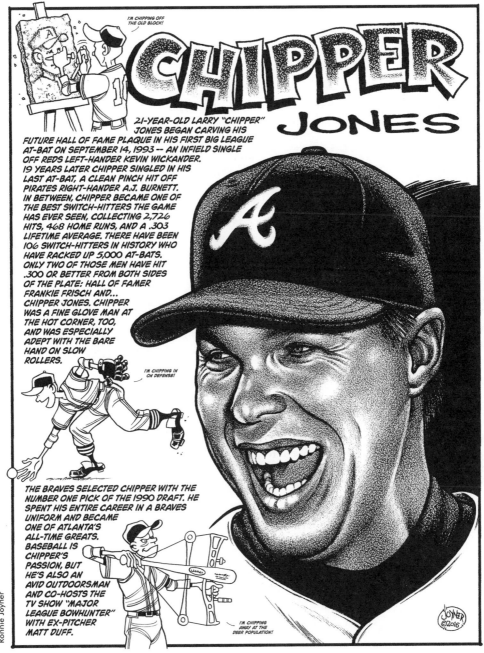

I'M CHIPPING OFF THE OLD BLOCK!

CHIPPER JONES

21-YEAR-OLD LARRY "CHIPPER" JONES BEGAN CARVING HIS FUTURE HALL OF FAME PLAQUE IN HIS FIRST BIG LEAGUE AT-BAT ON SEPTEMBER 14, 1993 -- AN INFIELD SINGLE OFF REDS LEFT-HANDER KEVIN WICKANDER. 19 YEARS LATER CHIPPER SINGLED IN HIS LAST AT-BAT, A CLEAN PINCH HIT OFF PIRATES RIGHT-HANDER A.J. BURNETT. IN BETWEEN, CHIPPER BECAME ONE OF THE BEST SWITCH-HITTERS THE GAME HAS EVER SEEN, COLLECTING 2,726 HITS, 468 HOME RUNS, AND A .303 LIFETIME AVERAGE. THERE HAVE BEEN 106 SWITCH-HITTERS IN HISTORY WHO HAVE RACKED UP 5,000 AT-BATS. ONLY TWO OF THOSE MEN HAVE HIT .300 OR BETTER FROM BOTH SIDES OF THE PLATE: HALL OF FAMER FRANKIE FRISCH AND... CHIPPER JONES. CHIPPER WAS A FINE GLOVE MAN AT THE HOT CORNER, TOO, AND WAS ESPECIALLY ADEPT WITH THE BARE HAND ON SLOW ROLLERS.

I'M CHIPPING IN ON DEFENSE!

THE BRAVES SELECTED CHIPPER WITH THE NUMBER ONE PICK OF THE 1990 DRAFT. HE SPENT HIS ENTIRE CAREER IN A BRAVES UNIFORM AND BECAME ONE OF ATLANTA'S ALL-TIME GREATS. BASEBALL IS CHIPPER'S PASSION, BUT HE'S ALSO AN AVID OUTDOORSMAN AND CO-HOSTS THE TV SHOW "MAJOR LEAGUE BOWHUNTER" WITH EX-PITCHER MATT DUFF.

I'M CHIPPING AWAY AT THE DEER POPULATION!

Ronnie Joyner

JOYNER ©2016

During a 19-year career spent entirely with the Atlanta Braves, Chipper Jones won an MVP, a batting title, and a World Series ring. Able to hit for both average and power, he hit more home runs in a single season (45) than any National League switch hitter and was especially adept at producing in clutch situations.

The Expansion Era

Continental League Forced Expansion

Talk of a third major league, the Continental League, forced reluctant major league owners to expand in 1961–1962. Branch Rickey, president of the proposed Continental, had targeted New York as his key objective. Rickey's circuit collapsed when the majors agreed to add several of its sites, including New York and Houston.

Artificial Turf

Fields with artificial surfaces look prettier, guarantee sure hops for fielders, and reduce rainout prospects because water can be swept off minutes before game time. Ground balls zip through the infield, forcing fielders to play back.

However, artificial turf is a hard surface that causes wear and tear on knees and legs. Over the long term it may shorten careers. The zippered turf also gets unpleasantly hot in the sun. Athletes must wear special shoes to play on it.

Playing Almost Everywhere

The Milwaukee Brewers are the only team to play in four of the six divisions under baseball's 2017 format. They began life as the expansion Seattle Pilots in 1969 (AL West) but moved to Milwaukee after one year. When the Washington Senators became the Texas Rangers in 1972, they moved from the AL East to the AL West, with the Brewers going the other way. Milwaukee was placed in the AL Central in 1994, when the leagues split into three divisions, but jumped to the NL Central in the expansion year of 1998—giving the NL 16 teams and the AL 14.

Heavy Harvey

During their inaugural season in 1993 the Florida Marlins leaned heavily on closer Bryan Harvey. With 45 saves and a win, he figured in a record 70.3 percent of his team's 64 victories.

Historic Hits

Paul Molitor and Ichiro Suzuki were the only men whose 3,000th hit was a triple. Wade Boggs, Derek Jeter, and Alex Rodriguez got number 3,000 with a home run.

The Changing Map

From 1903 to 1953 there were no changes in the baseball map. Both the American and National Leagues contained eight cities each, and five towns (New York, Boston, Philadelphia, St. Louis, and Chicago) had two or more clubs.

The first move that broke up the 50-year status quo in baseball was engineered by Lou Perini, owner of the Boston Braves, on March 18, 1953. Only 281,278 fans visited Braves Field in 1952 and Perini lost $600,000.

With the Braves in Milwaukee, where they immediately drew 1,826,397 fans, the St. Louis Browns began to look elsewhere for a new site. The club was operating on a shoestring budget and realized things would get worse after the Cardinals received fresh financing from Anheuser-Busch, which bought the team in 1953.

The Browns became the Baltimore Orioles in 1954 and the Philadelphia Athletics, under new owner Arnold Johnson, moved to Kansas City in 1955. The three-team situation in New York ended after the 1957 season when the Brooklyn Dodgers moved to Los Angeles and the New York Giants to San Francisco.

After the 1960 campaign the Washington Senators moved to Minneapolis/St. Paul, where they became the Minnesota Twins, and the American League replaced them with an expansion team of the same name. Another new club was established in California as the Los Angeles Angels, now called the Anaheim Angels.

The American League repeated the mistake of placing two teams in one city when its owners OKd the transfer of the Kansas City Athletics to Oakland, across the bay from San Francisco, in 1968. As in the Washington move of 1960, the league replaced the A's with an expansion team, the Kansas City Royals, and added a second new franchise, the Seattle Pilots.

Seattle ran into bad weather and bad financing and gave up after that single season. During spring training of 1970 it became the Milwaukee Brewers, filling a stadium vacated when the National League Braves made their second move—to Atlanta in 1966.

Milwaukee's return to the majors ended that city's pending lawsuit against baseball, but newly abandoned Seattle jumped in where the city fathers of Milwaukee left off. The AL silenced the suit by sending Seattle another team in 1977, when the Mariners and the Toronto Blue Jays swelled the league to 14 members. The Tampa Bay Devil Rays joined the AL in 1998.

One gap remained: Washington. The capital was without a club after the expansion Senators, plagued by bad concessions and broadcast contracts plus falling attendance, switched to Dallas/Fort Worth as the Texas Rangers in 1972.

The National League added New York and Houston in 1962, San Diego and Montreal in 1969, Colorado and Florida in 1993, and the Arizona Diamondbacks in 1998.

After the 2000 season ended, club owners were considering several realignment plans designed to enhance regional rivalries and reduce travel costs.

Expansion

Expansion was a difficult process. When the AL added Washington (replacing the team that moved to Minnesota) and Los Angeles for the 1961 season, the new clubs received players through a special expansion draft from the rosters of established teams.

Each existing team made 15 players available from its 40-man roster and drafting clubs made 28 selections for $75,000 each.

After the 1961 season the National League expansion teams in New York and Houston drafted 20 players each, 16 priced at $75,000 and four at $125,000.

The price of NL draftees was $200,000 in the fall of 1968, as opposed to $175,000 in the American. The AL imposed the same purchase price for the third wave of expansion late in 1976.

After widespread criticism of the "talent" available in the 1961–1962 drafts, the selection system was altered so that existing clubs could protect only 15 players when drafting began.

Drafts were conducted in rounds so that established teams would share the burden of stocking new entries.

In 1992, however, two NL expansion teams drafted players from all 26 existing clubs. The Colorado Rockies and the Florida Marlins paid $95 million each for territorial rights, entry fees, and rosters of 36 draftees each. Another expansion draft, to stock the Arizona Diamondbacks and the Tampa Bay Devil Rays, was held after the 1997 World Series.

Before the Florida Marlins won the World Series in their fifth season, the history of expansion indicated that it takes seven years for a newborn ballclub to win a championship. That was the time span demonstrated by the 1969 World Champion New York Mets.

The first expansion teams finished at, or near, the bottom in their first year. All lost at least 91 games and five lost 100 or more. The best first-year team was the Los Angeles Angels of 1961, which won an expansion-team record 70 games and zoomed from

Quality Quartets

These seven teams hit four consecutive home runs in a game:

1. **Braves vs. Reds,** June 8, 1961. Future Hall of Famers Eddie Mathews and Hank Aaron, followed by Joe Adcock and Frank Thomas, hit four in a row in the seventh inning at Crosley Field. But the Reds still won, 10–8.

2. **Indians vs. Angels,** July 31, 1963. The 8-9-1-2 hitters connected in the sixth inning with two outs, all against Paul Foytack. Woodie Held, Pedro Ramos, Tito Francona, and Larry Brown combined.

3. **Twins vs. A's,** May 2, 1964. Tony Oliva, Bob Allison, Jimmie Hall, and Harmon Killebrew did the honors in the 11th inning at Kansas City Municipal Stadium. Athletics pitchers allowed a record total of 220 home runs that season.

4. **Dodgers vs. Padres,** September 18, 2006. Down 9–5 in the home ninth at Dodger Stadium, Jeff Kent, J.D. Drew, Russell Martin, and Marlon Anderson hit four in a row, setting the stage for a two-run, walk-off shot by Nomar Garciaparra in the 11th. Before that 11–10 victory, the Dodgers had been last in the National League in home runs.

5. **Red Sox vs. Yankees,** April 22, 2007. With two outs in the third inning, Yankees starter Chase Wright threw consecutive gopher balls to Manny Ramirez, J.D. Drew, Mike Lowell, and Jason Varitek. Drew had also been part of the Dodgers quartet who hit four straight seven months earlier.

6. **White Sox vs. Royals,** August 14, 2008. Successive circuit clouts in the sixth inning by Jim Thome, Paul Konerko, Alexei Ramirez, and Juan Uribe power Chicago to a 9–2 victory.

7. **Diamondbacks vs. Brewers,** August 11, 2010. The Snakes strike in the top of the fourth at Miller Park, when Adam LaRoche, Miguel Montero, Mark Reynolds, and Stephen Drew launch Dave Bush pitches over the outfield wall. Arizona wins 8–2 as the Drew brothers become participants in three of the seven four-homer outbursts.

Expansion Records

Year	Team	Won	Lost	Pct.	Pos.	Attendance
1961	Los Angeles Angels*	70	91	.435	8	603,510
1961	Washington Senators**	61	100	.370	9	597,287
1962	Houston Colts***	64	96	.400	8	924,456
1962	New York Mets	40	120	.250	10	922,530
1969	Kansas City Royals	69	93	.426	4W	902,414
1969	Seattle Pilots****	64	98	.395	6W	677,944
1969	Montreal Expos	52	110	.321	6E	1,212,608
1969	San Diego Padres	52	110	.321	6W	512,970
1977	Seattle Mariners	64	98	.395	6W	1,338,511
1977	Toronto Blue Jays	54	107	.335	7E	1,701,052
1993	Colorado Rockies	67	95	.414	6W	4,483,350
1993	Florida Marlins	64	98	.395	6E	3,064,847
1998	Tampa Bay Devil Rays	63	99	.389	5E	2,261,158
1998	Arizona Diamondbacks	65	97	.401	5W	3,600,412

* became California Angels in 1966 and Anaheim Angels in 1997   *** became Houston Astros in 1965
** became Texas Rangers in 1972   **** became Milwaukee Brewers in 1970

After joining the Colorado Rockies for their inaugural 1993 campaign, Andres Galarraga led the National League in each of the three Triple Crown categories, though not in the same season. He had a combined 290 RBI and back-to-back RBI crowns in 1996 and 1997.

Expansion Player Picks

Year	Team	First Draft Choice
1960	Los Angeles Angels	Eli Grba, pitcher, Yankees
	Washington Senators	Bobby Shantz, pitcher, Yankees
1961	Houston Colts	Eddie Bressoud, if, Giants
	New York Mets	Hobie Landrith, catcher, Giants
1968	Kansas City Royals	Roger Nelson, pitcher, Baltimore
	Seattle Pilots	Don Mincher, 1b, California
	Montreal Expos	Manny Mota, of, Pittsburgh
	San Diego Padres	Ollie Brown, of, San Francisco
1976	Seattle Mariners	Ruppert Jones, of, Kansas City
	Toronto Blue Jays	Bob Bailor, ss-of, Baltimore
1992	Colorado Rockies	David Nied, pitcher, Atlanta
	Florida Marlins	Nigel Wilson, of, Toronto
1997	Arizona Diamondbacks	Brian Anderson, pitcher, Cleveland
	Tampa Bay Devil Rays	Tony Saunders, pitcher, Florida

eighth to third in 1962. Good fortune didn't last, however, as the Angels duplicated their initial 70-91 record during a ninth-place season in 1963.

The 1999 Arizona Diamondbacks, reinforced with high-priced free agents, won a division crown in their second year—breaking the rags-to-riches record of the 1995 Colorado Rockies, who reached the playoffs as a wild-card winner in their third season. Two years later, in their fourth season, the Diamondbacks became the fastest expansion team to reach the World Series.

The Amazing Mets

The 1962 Mets, with their 40-120 record, were the most pathetic expansion club, but the return of National League baseball to New York, coupled with the nostalgic appeal of the club's aging stars, generated an amazing emotional response among fans.

With Casey Stengel as manager and former Dodgers Gil Hodges and Roger Craig two of the mainstays, the team substituted memories for hitting, pitching, and fielding.

Positive contributions by Frank Thomas and Richie Ashburn were overshadowed by Marv Throneberry's attempts at fielding, Craig Anderson's 16-game losing streak, Don Zimmer's 0-for-34 batting slump, and the 44 losses suffered by the two "best" starters, Craig and Alvin Jackson.

During a clubhouse birthday party, a cake was carved and Stengel handed the pieces to everyone but Throneberry. "What about me?" the first baseman asked. "We wuz gonna give you a piece," the manager replied, "but we wuz afraid you'd drop it."

The first Mets winning pitcher was Jay Hook, a mechanical engineer who could explain the dynamics of a curveball but couldn't throw one. With an 8-19 record, he was one of the team's better pitchers.

A disappointment to the Mets—but probably a hero to their fans—was Bob Miller, the team's first choice in the premium round ($125,000 purchase price) of the expansion draft. He lost 12 games in succession and seemed headed for a winless season when he won a game just before the season ended. To add to the confusion on the ballclub, the Mets had another pitcher named Bob Miller! Bob G. Miller was left-handed and little more than a journeyman ballplayer. Bob L. Miller, the right-hander whose losing ways drew fans' sympathy, went on to a successful career with the Dodgers, the Twins, and seven other clubs.

Best Picks in Expansion Drafts

Not all expansion clubs suffered the setbacks incurred by the Mets' over-the-hill gang. Many new teams went for youth in expansion drafts and recruited fine prospects.

Pitcher Dean Chance and shortstop Jim Fregosi, selected by the Angels, blossomed into American League All-Stars. Fregosi was so highly regarded by the club that he became manager of the team when his playing career ended in 1978.

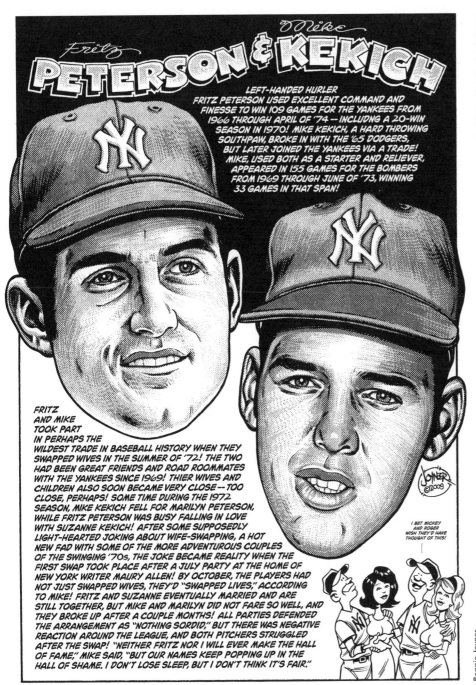

PETERSON & KEKICH
Fritz — Mike

LEFT-HANDED HURLER FRITZ PETERSON USED EXCELLENT COMMAND AND FINESSE TO WIN 109 GAMES FOR THE YANKEES FROM 1966 THROUGH APRIL OF '74 -- INCLUDING A 20-WIN SEASON IN 1970! MIKE KEKICH, A HARD THROWING SOUTHPAW, BROKE IN WITH THE '65 DODGERS, BUT LATER JOINED THE YANKEES VIA A TRADE! MIKE, USED BOTH AS A STARTER AND RELIEVER, APPEARED IN 155 GAMES FOR THE BOMBERS FROM 1969 THROUGH JUNE OF '73, WINNING 33 GAMES IN THAT SPAN!

FRITZ AND MIKE TOOK PART IN PERHAPS THE WILDEST TRADE IN BASEBALL HISTORY WHEN THEY SWAPPED WIVES IN THE SUMMER OF '72! THE TWO HAD BEEN GREAT FRIENDS AND ROAD ROOMMATES WITH THE YANKEES SINCE 1969! THIER WIVES AND CHILDREN ALSO SOON BECAME VERY CLOSE -- TOO CLOSE, PERHAPS! SOME TIME DURING THE 1972 SEASON, MIKE KEKICH FELL FOR MARILYN PETERSON, WHILE FRITZ PETERSON WAS BUSY FALLING IN LOVE WITH SUZANNE KEKICH! AFTER SOME SUPPOSEDLY LIGHT-HEARTED JOKING ABOUT WIFE-SWAPPING, A HOT NEW FAD WITH SOME OF THE MORE ADVENTUROUS COUPLES OF THE SWINGING '70s, THE JOKE BECAME REALITY WHEN THE FIRST SWAP TOOK PLACE AFTER A JULY PARTY AT THE HOME OF NEW YORK WRITER MAURY ALLEN! BY OCTOBER, THE PLAYERS HAD NOT JUST SWAPPED WIVES, THEY'D "SWAPPED LIVES," ACCORDING TO MIKE! FRITZ AND SUZANNE EVENTUALLY MARRIED AND ARE STILL TOGETHER, BUT MIKE AND MARILYN DID NOT FARE SO WELL, AND THEY BROKE UP AFTER A COUPLE MONTHS! ALL PARTIES DEFENDED THE ARRANGEMENT AS "NOTHING SORDID," BUT THERE WAS NEGATIVE REACTION AROUND THE LEAGUE, AND BOTH PITCHERS STRUGGLED AFTER THE SWAP! "NEITHER FRITZ NOR I WILL EVER MAKE THE HALL OF FAME," MIKE SAID, "BUT OUR NAMES KEEP POPPING UP IN THE HALL OF SHAME. I DON'T LOSE SLEEP, BUT I DON'T THINK IT'S FAIR."

I BET MICKEY AND ROGER WISH THEY'D HAVE THOUGHT OF THIS!

Ronnie Joyner

One of the biggest and least expected baseball news stories of the '70s involved an off-the-field trade by Yankee pitchers Fritz Peterson and Mike Kekich. They announced during 1973 spring training that they had traded *families*. It wasn't long before the image-conscious Yankees traded both of *them*.

The Senators scored with versatile Chuck Hinton, twice a .300 hitter, while outfielder Jim Hickman of the Mets and third baseman Bob Aspromonte and pitcher Dave Giusti of the Astros proved to be positive picks in the first National League draft.

The best choices of 1968 were made by the San Diego Padres, who named first baseman Nate Colbert and outfielders Cito Gaston and Downtown Ollie Brown. That same year Montreal selected pitcher Bill Stoneman and outfielders Mack Jones and Manny Mota (Mota and fellow draftee Maury Wills were traded to the Dodgers for Ron Fairly); Kansas City tabbed pitchers Jim Rooker and Dick Drago; and Seattle drafted outfielders Lou Piniella (immediately traded to Kansas City) and Tommy Harper.

Harper stole 73 bases for the Pilots, then became a sudden power hitter and joined the select few players who have hit 30 homers and stolen 30 bases in the same season. He turned the trick after the Pilots became the Milwaukee Brewers in 1970.

Colbert of San Diego became a consistent home-run hitter and All-Star whose biggest day in the majors occurred in Atlanta on August 1, 1972. He hit five home runs and knocked in 13 in a doubleheader against the Braves.

The biggest mistake made by the 1969 expansion teams was Seattle's unloading of pitcher Mike Marshall, who lost 10 games but pitched a shutout for one of his three victories. He stopped in Houston before becoming the game's outstanding relief pitcher with Montreal and later Los Angeles.

Pioneer free agent Andy Messersmith signed with Atlanta after challenging the reserve clause in court.

Mel Bailey

Paltry Turnout

Attendance at the first Mets game was 12,447. Maybe the fans who stayed away from the Polo Grounds knew something.

Hobie's Heroics

Hobie Landrith's lone home run as a member of the Mets was a ninth-inning fly ball that narrowly cleared the Polo Grounds fence, just 257 feet from home plate. It came against future Hall of Famer Warren Spahn, the star pitcher of the Braves, on May 12, 1962 and helped New York top Milwaukee twice that day. The Mets won just 38 other games.

Hoyt Wilhelm on Mike Marshall

After Mike Marshall worked 106 games for the Dodgers in 1974, veteran bullpen star Hoyt Wilhelm said, "If somebody had come along 15 years ago and told me a guy would someday work 100 games while throwing a fair amount of fastballs, I'd have said it was a ridiculous statement. In fact, I'd have said it was about as ridiculous as the breaking of Babe Ruth's lifetime home-run record!"

The second Seattle franchise was more careful when it made its selection in 1976. Its first pick, also the first pick in the draft, was a budding young star named Ruppert Jones, a speedy outfielder.

Selected from Kansas City, Jones slugged 24 homers as a rookie and represented the Mariners in the All-Star Game.

Toronto also chose wisely, naming Baltimore farmhand Bob Bailor, who played both infield and outfield and swung the bat with authority. His .310 rookie average represented the best mark ever recorded by a player on a new expansion club.

Curt Flood vs. the Reserve Clause

Baseball's amateur free-agent draft was created in 1965 to equalize the talent among the teams and cut off the high-priced bidding wars that raised ticket prices and alienated fans. Free agency, created after the fall of the reserve system in 1976, had just the opposite effect.

The beginning of the end for the reserve system can be traced to Curt Flood's suit against baseball, filed after his trade to the Philadelphia Phillies by the St. Louis Cardinals in 1969.

Flood, who had spent 12 years with the Cardinals, refused to accept the deal and did not report in 1970. Instead he challenged baseball's antitrust exemption, which had been upheld by the United States Supreme Court in 1922 and not seriously challenged since.

At that time the court ruled baseball was a sport, not a business, and therefore not subject to laws that governed the business world.

Flood, with his suit to protect, missed the game after his 1970 sit-down strike and signed a traditional contract—with the reserve clause included—with the Washington Senators in 1971. He agreed to play only with the stipulation that such action would not hurt his case. After getting off to a bad start, however, he left the game for good.

The Flood challenge was denied by the Supreme Court in 1972, exactly 50 years after the first baseball decision by the high court, but events were already in motion that would accomplish Flood's objective.

In 1975 pitcher Andy Messersmith "played out his option" by refusing to sign a Dodger contract (the club renewed his 1974 pact under the option clause provided). After the season, he was declared a free agent by arbitrator Peter M. Seitz, the same man who had granted free agency to Oakland A's pitcher Catfish Hunter on a contract technicality the previous year.

The effort by club owners to overturn the Seitz ruling failed in federal court. The old reserve system was dead.

Labor Unrest in Baseball

Before management was forced to hack out the historic 1976 agreement that revamped the reserve system, there were two unpleasant incidents in player/owner relations.

On April 1, 1972, the Major League Baseball Players Association, headed by former steelworkers adviser Marvin Miller, staged a strike over retirement benefits and increased medical premiums. The 12-day strike ended when owners agreed to pay the estimated $1.2 million asked by the players in exchange for cancellation of all games missed to that point. Teams lost up to $200,000 and a player making $75,000 lost more than $1,500 in take-home pay.

Four years later, with another dispute brewing, owners smarting from the Messersmith decision decided they would not open camps and risk another walkout. The Basic Agreement between players and owners had expired and, without resolution in sight, management feared labor would strike to force an unfair agreement under pressure.

Finally, the players agreed not to strike while negotiations continued. A new three-year agreement was reached in July.

The Re-entry System

The terms of the July 1976 agreement replaced the old reserve rule with the re-entry system. Experienced stars could exercise their newly won right to "play out the option year" in their contracts and sell their services to the highest bidder. Such "free agents" hardly deserved that title after 14 of them received $22 million in long-term deals after the 1976 season.

Teams drafted negotiation rights to free-agent stars in the re-entry draft, held several weeks after the World Series. Since more than a dozen clubs could draft rights to a single star, the bidding wars that followed were predictable well in advance.

Critics charged that the re-entry system allowed teams in the best cities, as well as those with the most money, to corner the market on top talent and buy a champion.

Free agency, salary arbitration, and the unchecked escalation of player salaries caused new work stoppages in 1981, 1985, 1990, and 1994–1995. The 1981 walkout sliced seven weeks off the schedule and resulted in a novel "split season" format matching the prestrike and poststrike winners in a special best-of-five series to determine playoff opponents. Although the Cincinnati Reds and the St. Louis Cardinals had the best overall records in their respective National League divisions, neither qualified for the postseason under the artificial format.

The 1994 Walkout

Baseball's most devastating strike was also the longest in the history of professional sports. It lasted from August 12, 1994, through March 31, 1995, when U.S. District Judge Sonia Sotomayor granted the union's request for an injunction that restored 1994 work rules.

Two days later, club owners released the replacement players they had hired, decided to hold an abbreviated spring training, and postponed Opening Day from April 2 to April 26. Umpires, locked out for 120 days, did not return until May 3, after reaching a new agreement with the owners.

Sinkerballer Orel Hershiser, star right-hander of the Los Angeles Dodgers, completed the 1988 season by throwing a record 59 consecutive scoreless innings, one more than the 1968 record of Don Drysdale. He then went on to win MVP honors in both the National League Championship Series and the World Series. In his last 13 outings, including postseason play, Hershiser went 9-0 with three no-decisions, one save, and a 0.59 ERA. He was a unanimous choice for the NL's Cy Young Award.

Bow Wow

Cuban defector Orlando (El Duque) Hernandez got his chance when 1998 Yankees starter David Cone was bitten by a dog and forced to miss a start.

Good Timing

John Olerud, a first baseman not known for his speed, hit for the cycle in 1997 and 2001. Both times, the triples that completed the cycles were the only ones he hit in those years.

Baseball Work Stoppages

1972   Players strike for 13 days (9 in regular season)

1976   Owners lock players out of spring training (17 days)

1980   Players strike for one week during spring training

1981   Players strike for 50 days during season

1985   Players strike for two days during season

1990   Owners lock players out of spring camps (32 days)

1994   Player strike ends season August 12 (232 days)

1995   Continuing strike shortens season to 144 games

Pete Rose posted 10 200-hit seasons, played five different positions in the All-Star Game, tied a National League mark with a 44-game hitting streak, and broke Ty Cobb's record for career hits. But his path to Cooperstown was blocked when Hall of Fame directors ruled suspended players ineligible. Rose, who would have been a certain first-time selection in 1992, was banned for life in 1989 for violating Major League Rule 21. The star player, who spent his first 16 years with Cincinnati and later managed the club, had been under investigation for allegedly betting on baseball games. Less than a year after his suspension he spent five months in jail for income tax evasion.

The strike cost the teams $800 million, the players $600 million, and left the game reeling from fan hostility.

They weren't happy with Acting Commissioner Bud Selig, who canceled the 1994 World Series; Players Association executive director Donald Fehr, a militant Marvin Miller protégé; or the various negotiators who failed to forge a resolution.

Shortly after the walkout ended, angry fans in several cities showered players with bottles, cans, lighters, toilet paper, wooden pennant sticks, beach balls, and other debris.

Three young men wearing GREED T-shirts ran onto the field during New York's Shea Stadium opener and threw dollar bills at the players as fellow fans roared their approval. Two weeks later, the Houston Astros offered free admission to all, drew only 30,828, and listed paid attendance as zero.

Attendance, retail sales of baseball merchandise, TV ratings, and All-Star voting dropped sharply and a Harris Poll revealed 71 percent of fans had less interest in baseball than they did before the strike.

Only the Cleveland Indians and the Colorado Rockies, sudden contenders in new ballparks, were unaffected by the year long malaise. But players and management eventually agreed on a new five-year deal that created revenue sharing and a luxury tax designed to be a drag on inflated player payrolls.

The New Freedom

Free agency and salary arbitration—the underlying causes of every baseball work stoppage—gave players a new freedom of movement. That movement began the minute free agency was established and was directly responsible for ending the five-year championship run of the Oakland Athletics.

Divisional champions from 1971 to 1975 and World Champions from 1972 to 1974, the A's started to disintegrate when Joe Rudi, Rollie Fingers, Gene Tenace, Bert Campaneris, Sal Bando, and Don Baylor played out their options. Two long-term A's who threatened to do so—Reggie Jackson and Ken Holtzman—were traded instead.

Oakland owner Charles O. Finley, seeking compensation for other stars before they became free agents, sold Rudi and Fingers to the Red Sox and Vida Blue to the Yankees in million-dollar deals on June 15, 1976, but was overruled by Commissioner Bowie Kuhn, who said the sales were contrary to "the best interests of baseball."

Finley's worst fears were realized after the season when Rudi and Fingers joined the mass exodus from the A's. Blue was eventually traded twice more by Finley—once in a canceled million-dollar transaction with Cincinnati and finally in a swap that brought seven players and an estimated $400,000 from the Giants.

Other teams also felt the sting of the free-agent revolution. To keep their own stars, teams were forced to dole out huge salary hikes. Wild bidding wars to retain and attract free agents kept club executives scrambling.

The average salary reached seven figures in 1992 and kept climbing. At the 1992 winter meetings, owners spent $258 million in a free-agent signing frenzy. National League MVP Barry Bonds got the biggest prize: a six-year, $42.75 million haul from the Giants. But his status as the game's highest-paid player was short-lived.

How Contracts Have Changed

The seller's market of high-priced free agents in the '70s produced countless cases of salary increases or bonuses equal to the $80,000 Babe Ruth made in 1932.

The figure stood as the top salary for years. Dizzy Dean, one of the game's greatest pitchers, earned just $3,000 per season in both 1932 and 1933, jumped to $7,500 in 1934, and was raised to $18,500 in 1935 after his 30-win season the year before. Dean was paid $27,500 in both 1936 and 1937.

After one of his greatest seasons, Joe DiMaggio asked the Yankees for a raise from $25,000 to $35,000. When they refused, he said, "I insist upon it." The team responded, "If you insist, go home and we'll see you later."

Even Ty Cobb, owner of the highest lifetime batting average, failed to get rich from baseball. He became wealthy after investing in a small soda company in his native Georgia. The name of the firm was Coca-Cola.

A Cobb contemporary, Ed Walsh of the White Sox, won 27 and saved 4 other games in 1911 but took home only $300 per month. Top stars were up to $700 a month by the Depression era.

There were no official minimum salaries until 1947, when the bottom line was established at $5,000. Ten years later, it was $7,000, and 20 years after that it was $19,000. In 1979 the minimum player's salary was $21,000. It had risen to $109,000 by 1992 and $200,000 by the end of the century.

Why Trading Is Tougher Today

Long-term, complex contracts make trading difficult. Unfortunately for the general managers, who make most of the deals, most players are tied up for more than one year. "Before," said Harry Dalton, former Milwaukee Brewers general manager, "all you did was trade a service contract, usually an obligation for one year. There were very few, if any, other restrictions.

"Now you have long-term guaranteed financial commitments, in some cases four or five years, and in many cases millions of dollars. First, it's tough for teams to take on that obligation and second, within the service contract itself, the player has the right to say no. Another general manager might have come up to me and offered a player. "I'd say, 'What's his contract like?' He'd tell me and I'd say, 'I'm not interested.'"

Major Changes

Expansion, free agents, and runaway salaries were three of the many changes baseball encountered following the Second World War.

The electronic era, marked by television and air-conditioning, hurt the minors and forced the majors into widespread promotional

One-time Oakland World Series hero Rollie Fingers, a newcomer to the 1981 Milwaukee Brewers, was the first relief pitcher to win Most Valuable Player and Cy Young Awards in the same season and the second enshrined in Cooperstown (after Hoyt Wilhelm). His record of 341 career saves stood until 1992, when both Jeff Reardon and Lee Smith surpassed it.

Buying a Pennant

Checkbook baseball became a reality in the late '90s. For the second straight season in 1997, the final four teams in baseball's playoff were among the top five in payroll. The Baltimore Orioles (2) played the Cleveland Indians (3) in the AL Championship Series, while the Atlanta Braves (4) met the Florida Marlins (5) in the NLCS. The team with the top payroll, the New York Yankees, lost to the Indians in a best-of-five Division Series that went the limit.

Dick Allen was the game's highest-paid player with the White Sox in the early '70s, but his $225,000 pact was passed by dozens of players with the advent of free agency.

How the 1927 Yankees Were Paid

Ed Barrow, general manager	$25,000
Miller Huggins, manager	37,000
Babe Ruth, outfield	70,000
Herb Pennock, pitcher	17,500
Urban Shocker, pitcher	13,500
Bob Meusel, outfield	13,000
Joe Dugan, third base	12,000
Dutch Ruether, pitcher	11,000
Waite Hoyt, pitcher	11,000
Bob Shawkey, pitcher	10,500
Earle Combs, outfield	10,500
Tony Lazzeri, second base	8,000
Bennie Bengough, catcher	8,000
Lou Gehrig, first base	8,000

Top Ten Salaries: 1950

Ted Williams, Red Sox	$125,000
Joe DiMaggio, Yankees	100,000
Ralph Kiner, Pirates	65,000
Lou Boudreau, Indians	65,000
Hal Newhouser, Tigers	50,000
Stan Musial, Cardinals	50,000
Tommy Henrich, Yankees	45,000
George Kell, Tigers	35,000
Jackie Robinson, Dodgers	35,000
Pee Wee Reese, Dodgers	35,000

Salary Spiral

The highest-paid players of their time:

1947 – Hank Greenberg	$100,000
1977 – Mike Schmidt	500,000
1980 – Nolan Ryan	1,000,000
1982 – George Foster	2,000,000
1990 – Kirby Puckett	3,000,000
1991 – Roger Clemens	5,000,000
1999 – Kevin Brown	15,000,000

Big Payoff

The 1995 New York Yankees were the first team to have an average player salary of more than $2 million per year. Two years later, baseball's average annual salary had reached $1,385,548.

Quick Clinch

The 1998 New York Yankees were the first team in major league history to clinch a postseason berth in August.

Darryl's Odyssey

Darryl Strawberry was the first man to play for all four teams that originated in New York: the Yankees, the Dodgers, the Giants, and the Mets.

campaigns. Night ball, once considered a novelty, became a necessity—though energy shortages of the '70s threatened to curtail excess use of electricity and, in the cases of domed stadiums, giant air-conditioning systems.

Artificial turf replaced grass in many parks (mostly in the National League) and upset the same critics who contended that the designated hitter, first used by the AL in 1973, had destroyed the traditional concept of baseball.

Records established by Babe Ruth and Ty Cobb, the game's greatest stars, were wiped out, and teams in California—out of the majors until 1958—produced the only pitchers to throw at least four no-hitters (Sandy Koufax and Nolan Ryan).

A storm of controversy greeted the entry of the first modern black player in 1947, but Jackie Robinson performed so well for Brooklyn that he won the first Rookie of the Year Award. Pitchers had a hard time winning points in Most Valuable Player voting, but the oversight was corrected when the Cy Young Award was created in 1956 and split into separate awards, one for each league, in 1967; five of its first eight winners won entry to the Hall of Fame.

The cultivation of relief pitching into a highly technical science was definitely a development of the modern age. The Philadelphia "Whiz Kids" of 1950 raised eyebrows all over the majors when they won the pennant primarily because of 33-year-old bullpen ace Jim Konstanty. He worked 74 games—a record that stood more than 10 years—and won 16 while saving 22 others. Konstanty was voted the league's Most Valuable Player.

There have been dozens of top relievers since, including Hoyt Wilhelm—one of 15 to pitch more than 1,000 games in his career—and Mike Marshall—the only man to pitch more than 100 in a season.

Saves—given to relievers who face the tying or winning run but preserve the victory—became an official statistic in 1969.

Divisional play began with the second wave of expansion in 1969, as the majors increased their fan appeal with four title chases instead of two. More mini-races were created in 1994 with the advent of three-divisional play and wild-card champions (runners-up with the best record in each league). Three years later, limited interleague play was introduced.

Doc & Darryl

Doc Gooden was National League Rookie of the Year at 19, a Cy Young Award winner at 20, and a World Series winner at 21. But drug abuse stopped him cold en route to Cooperstown. At age 30, he sat out the 1995 season after he was suspended for using cocaine. With 15 days left on a 60-day drug suspension interrupted by the 1994 player strike that started in August, Gooden was given another 168 days. He later missed the Mets' 1996 World Series parade in Manhattan because he was allegedly snorting cocaine.

Teammate Darryl Strawberry wasn't much better. His third suspension in five years was the longest: Bud Selig banned him for the entire 2000 season after he tested positive for cocaine on January 19. The slugging outfielder was first banned in 1995, sitting out from April 24 to August 4 before Selig relented and let him come back.

Record Breakers

The game's two most talked-about records—Ruth's one-year and career home-run highs—were erased by Roger Maris, with 61 in 1961, and Henry Aaron, who passed Ruth's 714 in 1974 and retired two years later with a final count of 755.

Sixty-one home runs would not have been as surprising if produced by Harmon Killebrew, Rocky Colavito, or Jim Gentile, but Maris never hit more than 39 in any other season. He received a steady diet of good pitches to hit—and was never intentionally walked—because Mickey Mantle, batting directly behind him, was en route to his best home-run year; he ended with 54.

In the National League in 1961, the most noteworthy performance was registered by 40-year-old Warren Spahn, pitcher for the Milwaukee Braves. He led the league with 21 victories, 21 complete games, four shutouts, and a 3.02 earned run average.

Spahn, Early Wynn, Whitey Ford, Don Drysdale, and Sandy Koufax were the Cy Young Award winners, 1956–1963, who advanced to the Hall of Fame. Had he not been forced to retire with arthritis at age 31, Koufax could have challenged Spahn's position as the "winningest" left-hander in National League history (363).

In his last five years, Koufax won 111, lost 34, led NL pitchers in earned run average each year, and struck out 1,444 men. In 1966, pitching in pain, he was 27-9 with 317 strikeouts in 323 innings pitched. He completed 27 of 41 games and recorded a 1.73 earned run average.

Koufax teammate Maury Wills proved the value of speed to managers around the league. The art of base stealing had virtually disappeared in 1950, when Dom DiMaggio led the American League with 15, but Wills revived it and refined it to the point where he could run at will.

In 1962, when the NL pennant was decided in a best-of-three playoff between the Dodgers and the Giants, Wills stole 104 bases, a one-season high that eclipsed Ty Cobb's 96 in 1915.

Lou Brock of the St. Louis Cardinals stole 118 bases, shunting Wills to second place and Ty Cobb to third, in 1974. Brock went on to pass Cobb's lifetime standard of 892 stolen bases. Rickey Henderson later supplanted Brock as the stolen base record holder.

There was the postseason controversy in 1974 when Brock lost the Most Valuable Player designation to Steve Garvey of the champion Dodgers. Wills had won the honor in 1962, and other record breakers had also been voted the MVP: Roger Maris in 1961, Frank Robinson and Carl Yastrzemski for their Triple Crowns in 1966 and 1967, Denny McLain for his 31-6 record, and Bob Gibson for his 1.12 earned run average and 13 shutouts in 1968.

Brock's 1974 season was overshadowed by the yeoman relief pitching of Mike Marshall, right-hander of the Los Angeles Dodgers. He won 15 games, saved 21 others, finished 83 times in 106 appearances, and posted a 2.42 earned run mark for a record 208 relief innings. From June 18 through July 3, Marshall pitched in 13 consecutive games.

Marshall not only owned a rubber arm but knew its stress limitations. He had become an authority on kinesiology, the study of anatomy in relation to human movement. The 31-year-old closer abstained from smoking and drinking, ate only nutritious foods, never wore the traditional sweatshirt, and frequently pitched batting practice to keep his arm in tune.

The Rookie Race of 1975

Teammates Fred Lynn and Jim Rice of the champion Boston Red Sox staged the closest Rookie of the Year race in 1975. Lynn led the league in runs scored, doubles, and slugging percentage; was second in batting; and third in runs batted in. But Rice, his fellow outfielder, almost matched him. Their statistics:

	G	AB	R	H	HR	RBI	SB	BA
Lynn	145	528	103	175	21	105	10	.331
Rice	144	564	92	174	22	102	10	.309

High Prices

In 1997 the average price of a baseball ticket was $11.98 but the Fan Cost Index (FCI) was $106.20—the price of parking, four tickets, two small beers, four small sodas, four hot dogs, two programs, and two caps. Boston had the highest average ticket and Atlanta had the highest FCI while Montreal ranked last in both.

After 12 years as a starter, Dennis Eckersley moved to the bullpen in 1987 and promptly became baseball's most dominating closer. In 1990 he converted 48 of 50 save opportunities, had a 0.61 ERA, and more saves than baserunners allowed (41 hits and four walks in 73⅓ innings). Two years later he won the Cy Young and Most Valuable Player Awards after posting the second 50-save campaign in baseball history (Bobby Thigpen of the White Sox had saved 57 games in 1990).

After the 1974 season Marshall became the first reliever to win the coveted Cy Young Award. Sparky Lyle of the Yankees became the second in 1977.

Unusual Achievements

Changes in baseball came in rapid succession during the '50s. The Boston Braves started a slew of franchise shifts when they moved to Milwaukee in 1953. Within short order, the St. Louis Browns became the Baltimore Orioles, the Athletics moved from Philadelphia to Kansas City, and both the Brooklyn Dodgers and New York Giants relocated to California.

That created a void in New York, which went from three teams to one and had no National League club for four years. When Branch Rickey's Continental League threatened to become a third major league, both the American and National League absorbed several of their proposed cities through expansion. They also placed new teams in New York, filling the NL void, and Washington, allowing the Senators to become the Minnesota Twins.

Both teams and players made many headlines during the turbulent expansion years.

Pennant Races

The 1964 Phillies blew a pennant by losing 10 straight games in September after mounting a six-and-a-half game lead with two weeks left to play.

On the plus side, the 1967 Red Sox and 1969 Mets were "miracle teams" that beat long odds by jumping from ninth place to the pennant.

Perfect Games

With the baseball world still buzzing after the World Series perfect game pitched by Don Larsen for the Yankees against the Dodgers in 1956, Jim Bunning pitched another one in New York.

Unlike Larsen, who notched his gem in Yankee Stadium, Bunning was on the mound at Shea Stadium, facing the third-year New York Mets. The father of nine picked Father's Day to pitch his perfect game for the Philadelphia Phillies in 1964. The losing pitcher in Bunning's game was Tracy Stallard, the same man who had surrendered Roger Maris's 61st home run three years earlier.

The last of the four no-hitters pitched by Dodgers southpaw Sandy Koufax was a perfect game a year after Bunning's gem. More unlikely authors of perfect games before the turn of the century included Len Barker, Mike Witt, Tom Browning, Dennis Martinez, Kenny Rogers. David Wells, and David Cone.

Nine Positions in One Game

Two players—shortstop Bert Campaneris and third baseman Cesar Tovar—proved their versatility by playing nine positions in

After breaking the baseball color line by signing Jackie Robinson, Branch Rickey brought expansion to baseball by threatening to create a third major league. Most of his proposed Continental League cities eventually got major league teams.

Elusive Crown

Twelve of the 30 players who reached 3,000 hits never won a batting crown. They are Craig Biggio, Lou Brock, Eddie Collins, Rickey Henderson, Derek Jeter, Paul Molitor, Eddie Murray, Rafael Palmeiro, Cal Ripken Jr., Alex Rodriguez, Dave Winfield, and Robin Yount.

Sweet 'n' Sour Debuts

Superstar right-hander Juan Marichal of the Giants broke in with a bang by one-hitting the Phillies, 2–0, on July 19, 1960, but teammate Willie Mays had opposite luck in his 1951 debut. Mays went 0-for-5, a dubious debut that Hank Aaron would also suffer—three years later.

The Perry brothers, Gaylord (left) and Jim, created an unusual record in 1970, when both enjoyed 20-victory seasons—the first time brothers had won 20 games each in the same year. One year earlier, the Perrys performed another first when they won three games on the same day, July 20, 1969.

one game. Campy did it for the 1965 Kansas City A's and Tovar three years later for the Minnesota Twins. The former dropped a fly ball in right field and, as a pitcher, walked two and yielded a run-scoring single. But Tovar, starting the game on the mound, not only blanked the opposition but struck out slugger Reggie Jackson. He also induced the first man he faced—Bert Campaneris—to hit a soft foul fly for an out. Scott Sheldon (Rangers) and Shane Halter (Tigers) later played nine positions in a game.

Seven-for-Seven

One of the game's all-time oddities occurred June 21, 1970, when weak-hitting Detroit Tigers shortstop Cesar Gutierrez, wearing No. 7, became the first modern player to get seven hits in seven times at bat (12 innings). The uniform had been temporarily retired after the death of its former wearer, manager Charley Dressen, but the club's equipment man accidentally gave it to Gutierrez when he reported to the team. Gutierrez hit just .243 for the season, his only one as a regular in the major leagues.

Five years later Rennie Stennett of the Pirates went 7-for-7 as Pittsburgh devastated the Chicago Cubs, 22–0, in the regulation nine innings. It was the most lopsided shutout in modern baseball history, erasing 21–0 games of 1901 and 1939.

The record for most hits in a game remained nine—by Cleveland shortstop Johnny Burnett in an 18-inning affair in 1932. Burnett's hits were not consecutive. Like Gutierrez, he was a regular only that one season.

Unwanted Record

Hall of Famer Brooks Robinson holds many records, most of them for his great defense. There is one he doesn't want, however. Robinson hit into four triple plays, more than any other player.

Remarkable Ryan

Nolan Ryan pitched for the Mets, the Angels, the Astros, and the Rangers in a career that stretched a record 27 seasons. At age 44 in 1991, he became the oldest man to pitch a no-hitter when he pitched his seventh (and second in two years). Just one other pitcher—Sandy Koufax—pitched as many as four. Ryan, an 11-time strikeout king, remains the only man to record at least 5,000 career Ks.

The Ryan Express

Nolan Ryan was 12 when he pitched his first no-hitter—in Little League ball in Alvin, Texas.

When he retired in 1993, he held or shared 53 records, including 27 seasons played, 19 low-hit games (one or fewer hits allowed), 5,714 strikeouts, 2,795 walks, and six 300-strikeout seasons. The strikeout king also had the most K's in a season (383) and the most per nine innings by a starting pitcher in a season (11.48) and career (9.55). Randy Johnson now holds the marks for strikeouts per nine innings by a starting pitcher in a season (13.41) and career (10.61).

Ryan was 43 when he won his last strikeout crown and 44 when he pitched the last of his seven no-hitters.

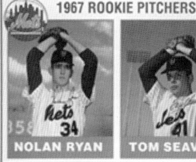

1967 ROOKIE PITCHERS

NOLAN RYAN

TOM SEAVER

Nolan Ryan and Tom Seaver came up with the New York Mets and helped pitch the team to the 1969 world championship. But Ryan's penchant for erratic control convinced management to trade him to the Angels, where he blossomed into a superstar.

Fine Farewell

Joe Pignatano hit into a triple play in his last at-bat in the majors.

Top Dog

Outfielder Rick Monday was the top pick in the first amateur draft in 1965.

Losing No-Hitters

Throwing a no-hitter doesn't always add a "W" to a pitcher's record. Houston's Ken Johnson lost a 1-0 no-hitter to the Reds in 1964 when he made an error in the ninth inning. Boston's Matt Young and the Yankees' Andy Hawkins have also lost complete-game no-hitters. There were even a pair of combined no-hitters that turned up on the wrong end of the score. Baltimore's Steve Barber and Stu Miller no-hit Detroit in 1967 but lost 2-1 because Barber walked 10, hit a batter, and made a wild pitch in 8 2/3 innings. In 2008, Jered Weaver and Jose Arredondo of the Angels did not yield a hit while losing a 1-0, eight-inning no-hitter in an interleague game against the Dodgers at Chavez Ravine. Four years later, Weaver pitched and won a complete-game no-hitter against Minnesota.

Double Trouble

Rival pitchers have twice hurled back-to-back no-hitters in the same series. It happened first on September 17–18, 1968, when Gaylord Perry of the San Francisco Giants no-hit the St. Louis Cardinals the day before Ray Washburn of the Cards no-hit the Giants. On April 30, 1969, Jim Maloney of the Cincinnati Reds pitched a hitless game against the Houston Astros one day before Houston's Don Wilson no-hit the Reds.

Record-Setting Sluggers

The 1977 Los Angeles Dodgers were the first team with four 30-home-run men. Four years earlier, the Atlanta Braves became the first team to have three 40-home-run men.

Interleague Play

Baseball's most radical innovation was the introduction of limited interleague play in 1997. The move, designed to create more regional rivalries, paid off with increased attendance.

For years baseball executives debated the pros and cons of interleague play. Traditionalists complained that the uniqueness of the World Series—previously a meeting of two teams that had not faced each other—would be compromised.

They also said that the hitter who excels against weak interleague pitching could wind up winning a batting title or home-run crown and that long-standing records, including the single-season home-run mark of Roger Maris (61 in 1961), could be unfairly toppled by interleague results.

Skeptics concluded there were few compelling reasons for interleague play aside from a handful of natural rivalries (cities or states with multiple teams).

Despite such objections, club owners were so determined to create fan interest stilled by the 232-day player strike of 1994–1995 that interleague play was approved for 1997, with the consent of the Major League Baseball Players Association.

In its first season, interleague play ended with the National League beating the American League, 117–97, and attendance averaging 20.2 percent higher for interleague games (33,407) than for regular league games (27,800).

The Subway Series in New York (Mets at Yankees) and the Windy City rivalry in Chicago (Cubs at White Sox) set attendance records.

With teams matched geographically (East vs. East, Central vs. Central, and West vs. West), teams in the four-team West divisions played 16 interleague games each (four vs. each opponent), while all others played 15 games (three vs. each opponent). Florida and Montreal finished with the best records, winning 12 times each for an .800 percentage, while Houston and Toronto had the most trouble, posting 4-11 marks (.267).

To boost attendance, interleague games were scheduled around the three summer holiday weekends of Memorial Day, Independence Day, and Labor Day. The interleague schedule consisted of 214 games over 18 days.

In the first interleague game, on June 12, the San Francisco Giants topped the Texas Rangers, 4–3. Darryl Hamilton and Stan Javier, both of the Giants, had the first interleague hit (a single) and home run, respectively, while Glenallen Hill served as the first National League designated hitter in a regular-season game.

AP Photo/Doug Mills, File

Greg Maddux (right) and Tom Glavine (left), born 20 days apart, formed a formidable righty-lefty punch at the top of the Atlanta Braves rotation. During his tenure with the Braves from 1993 to 2003, Maddux went 194-88 for a .688 winning percentage—the best in franchise history. Glavine, with the team from 1987 to 2002 and again in 2008, had a .624 mark (244-147) that was the best by a left-hander, topping Warren Spahn's .609 (356-229). Maddux, Glavine, and John Smoltz (middle) never threw a no-hitter but teammate Kent Mercker, whose career was considerably shorter, was involved in two. He started the first combined no-hit game in National League history on September 11, 1991, working the first six innings and teaming with Mark Wohlers (two innings) and Alejandro Pena (one). Three years later, the lefty pitched a complete-game no-hitter against the Los Angeles Dodgers on April 7.

San Francisco's Mark Gardner was the first winning pitcher in interleague play and Baltimore's Mike Mussina managed to poke a single in his first major league at-bat, against Atlanta at Turner Field June 14 (AL pitchers had to bat in National League parks). Atlanta's Greg Maddux, loser in the decisive Game 6 of the 1996 World Series, extracted a slice of revenge July 2, when he pitched a 2–0 three-hitter for the Braves at Yankee Stadium, where his season had ended the previous fall.

Interleague play made scheduling difficult. After players complained of increased travel and frequent two-game series, both leagues adopted balanced schedules.

Under that arrangement, teams played approximately the same number of games against each opponent. The unbalanced schedule, also tried by both leagues, mandated more games against divisional rivals than against teams from other divisions.

That format returned in 2001.

A New Era

The period from 1978 to 1987 was marked by great competitive balance in baseball. During that span baseball produced 10 different World Champions in as many years. Even divisional winners had a tough time stringing together successive titles.

Benton Faced Ruth and Mantle

Al Benton was the only pitcher to face Babe Ruth and Mickey Mantle in regular-season American League competition.

The Year of Yaz

Red Sox outfielder Carl Yastrzemski had a remarkable year in 1967. Leading his club to a photo-finish pennant against 100-to-1 odds, Yaz won the Triple Crown with a .326 batting average, 44 home runs, and 121 runs batted in. He led in hits, runs, total bases, and slugging average. Down the stretch, he poked 10 hits in his last 13 at-bats, including 4 in the pennant-clinching finale against Minnesota and 3 the previous day.

Big Mac

Mark McGwire broke in with a bang (a rookie-record 49 homers in 1987) and never stopped. The first man with four straight 50-homer seasons won four home-run crowns, two in each league, and hit a record 135 over a two-year span in 1998–1999. Giving hint of things to come, he hit 71 home runs in his first 162 games with the Cardinals.

Pick Me!!

In the initial expansion draft to stock the Kansas City Royals and Seattle Pilots, both teams passed on future Hall of Fame pitcher Jim Palmer, erstwhile Baltimore ace who was left unprotected by the Orioles after shoulder issues. He went on to become baseball's biggest winner during the '70s with 186 wins—all for the O's.

All in the Family

Mookie Wilson is Preston Wilson's uncle and stepfather. Mookie married Preston's mom, who had been Mookie's sister-in-law.

Power Outage

Dodgers shortstop Kevin Elster hit three home runs on Opening Day of the 2000 season, then failed to hit three in any month the rest of the way.

Lucky Ball

Tom House, an obscure left-handed reliever, enjoyed his only strong season after catching Hank Aaron's record-setting 715th home run in the Atlanta bullpen on April 8, 1974.

Base Path Bandits

Montreal speed merchants Ron LeFlore and Rodney Scott stole 160 bases, a two-man record, for the 1980 Expos. Also that season, LeFlore, an ex-con, became the first man to lead both leagues in steals.

Mexican Marvel

Left-handed screwball specialist Fernando Valenzuela, elevated from the Mexican League to the Dodgers in 1981, became the only Cy Young Award winner to win a Rookie of the Year Award in the same season. The first rookie pitcher to start the All-Star Game, he hurled eight shutouts while winning 16 games, three of them in postseason play.

Down to the Wire

From 1978 through 1982, at least one of the divisional races was decided on the last day of the regular season or in a divisional playoff. In 1978 the Yankees beat the Red Sox in a sudden-death playoff for the AL East flag. In 1979 the Pirates needed a win or an Expos loss to clinch the NL East on the final day (they got both). The 1980 NL West race was decided when the Astros rebounded from three straight defeats by the Dodgers to win a one-game playoff. In the East, the Phils avoided a playoff with an 11-inning win over the Expos. The Royals won the second half of the 1981 split season when they won the opener of a makeup doubleheader at Cleveland. In 1982 the Brewers rebounded from three straight losses to beat the Orioles on the last day, finishing first in the AL East by a game. The Braves also kept a one-game margin, winning the NL West when the Dodgers lost to the Giants (the Braves lost to the Padres but still finished first).

When salaries began to reach astronomical levels, however, big-market teams suddenly realized an obvious advantage over clubs based in smaller markets.

There were many outstanding performances, by both teams and individuals, that rewrote the record books.

The 1982 Atlanta Braves and the 1987 Milwaukee Brewers won their first 13 games of the season, while the 1988 Baltimore Orioles lost their first 21; the Kansas City Royals twice recovered from 3–1 game deficits to become World Champions of 1985, the first year that the Championship Series became a best-of-seven event; the Minnesota Twins became 1987 World Champions (vs. St. Louis) when the home team won every World Series game for the first time; and the Chicago Cubs ended their all-daylight menu when they played the Mets in the first official Wrigley Field night game on August 9, 1988.

Pete Rose became the career leader in hits (4,256); Kent Tekulve joined Hoyt Wilhelm as the first men to pitch in 1,000 games; Nolan Ryan zoomed to the top of the career strikeout list; and Cal Ripken Jr. surpassed Lou Gehrig's celebrated record of 2,130 consecutive games played.

Rickey Henderson topped Lou Brock as the single-season and lifetime leader in stolen bases, Darrell Evans became the first player to produce 40-homer seasons in both leagues, and Jeff Reardon became the first with 40-save seasons in both. Lee Smith and John Franco buried Rollie Fingers' former record of 341 career saves.

Roger Clemens fanned 20 hitters in nine-inning games 10 years apart and won seven Cy Young Awards—three more than Steve Carlton and Greg Maddux managed in the National League.

When Clemens led the American League with 21 wins, a 2.05 ERA, and 292 strikeouts in 1997, he became the first American Leaguer to win the Triple Crown of pitching since Hal Newhouser in 1945. Clemens repeated his Triple Crown performance in 1998, then passed the baton to the younger Pedro Martinez, who won the league's third straight pitching trifecta in 1999.

George Brett is the only man to win batting crowns in three different decades. In 1980, his best season, he hit .390 while collecting 118 RBIs in 117 games.

Martinez won another Cy Young, his third, in 2000 after holding hitters to a .167 batting average and .213 on-base percentage, both record lows. The compact Dominican right-hander was one of several pitchers who won the trophy in both leagues.

Doc Gooden, only 20 at the time, was the last National Leaguer to capture the Triple Crown of pitching, winning 24, fanning 268, and posting a 1.53 ERA for the 1985 Mets.

Baseball's most intimidating pitcher of the '90s was Randy Johnson, at 6'10" the tallest player ever to appear in the majors. The flamethrowing southpaw led both leagues in strikeouts six times during the decade and became the third pitcher, after Gaylord Perry and Pedro Martinez, to win Cy Youngs in both leagues (Roger Clemens, Roy Halladay, and Max Scherzer later doubled the size of that elite club).

Although the earth seemed to move when Johnson pitched, participants in the 1989 World Series won't forget the real thing.

At 5:04 P.M. on October 17, less than 30 minutes before Game 3 of the Fall Classic at Candlestick Park, an earthquake measuring 7.1 on the Richter scale struck the Bay Area. When the series resumed 10 days later, Oakland completed its four-game sweep of San Francisco.

Cincinnati's sweep of the favored A's was a big surprise a year later but not as shocking as the presence of the Atlanta Braves and Minnesota Twins in the 1991 World Series. One year after both

Mike Schmidt was the only player in baseball history to hit four consecutive home runs twice. He led the National League in home runs eight times, slugging five times, and RBIs four times while winning 10 Gold Gloves at third base. The three-time MVP was elected to the Hall of Fame in 1995.

Nolan Ryan's seven no-hitters, three more than anyone else, dominate this Hall of Fame exhibit. Ryan was 44 when he pitched his last hitless game.

The Last Brownie

Don Larsen, better known for pitching the only perfect game in World Series history (for the Yankees against the Dodgers in 1956), was also the last active player who performed for the St. Louis Browns. Larsen's career began with the Browns in 1953, their last year, and ended with the Cubs in 1967.

Polo Pong

In 1963, exasperated Mets manager Casey Stengel told pitcher Tracy Stallard, "After this season they're going to tear down this place (the Polo Grounds) but the way you're going, the right-field stands will be gone already."

Don't Blame Me

Bobby Lowe and Bob Horner, Braves who played in different cities a century apart, are the only men to hit four home runs in a game their team lost. Lowe did it for Boston in 1894, Horner for Atlanta in 1986.

Homer Barrage

The Chicago White Sox and the Detroit Tigers combined for a record 12 home runs in a game at Tiger Stadium on May 28, 1995. The 12 homers in that game totaled 4,645 feet—nearly seven times the height of Detroit's 740-foot Renaissance Center, the tallest building in town.

First Blood

Baltimore's Brady Anderson hit a record 12 homers leading off games in 1996. That was one more than the 1973 record held by Bobby Bonds.

Redbird Ripper

On April 23, 1999, Fernando Tatis of the St. Louis Cardinals became the only man in major league history to hit two grand-slam home runs in the same inning. His victim on both occasions was Chan Ho Park of the Los Angeles Dodgers.

When Tony Gwynn won his eighth batting title in 1997 he tied Honus Wagner's mark for the most times leading the National League in that department. The longtime star right fielder of the San Diego Padres also became the first player to win four straight NL batting crowns since Rogers Hornsby won six in a row from 1920 to 1925. Gwynn's .394 average in 1994 was the closest anyone has come to .400 since Ted Williams hit .406 in 1941. He got the ninth five-hit game of his career on April 29, 1998.

teams had finished last in their respective divisions, the Braves and the Twins produced a Series that may have been baseball's most dramatic. There were extra-inning wins in the last two games—including a 10-inning, 1–0 thriller in Game 7—and records for games decided in the club's last at-bat (five), games decided on the last pitch (four), and extra-inning games (three).

The World Series became truly international a year later when the Toronto Blue Jays not only became the first Canadian team to win a pennant but the first to win a World Championship. The Jays repeated in 1993—when Joe Carter joined Bill Mazeroski as the only men to end a World Series with a home run.

His victims were the Philadelphia Phillies, the third team of the '90s to forge a worst-to-first season (the 1997 San Francisco Giants, the 1998 San Diego Padres, and the 1999 Arizona Diamondbacks did it later).

One year later, owners desperate for more revenue created three-divisional formats that included wild-card champions and an extra tier of playoffs before the World Series. Interleague play, another gimmick to boost attendance, was added in 1997. Traditionalists condemned the moves as unnecessary tinkering with a century of tradition.

One tradition that didn't die was the championship march of the New York Yankees.

After rebounding from a 2–0 deficit to win the 1996 World Series, they won 114 games in 1998 to take the AL East by a 22-game margin. Though two wins shy of the major league mark

owned by the 1906 Cubs, the Yankee steamroller buried all opposition—even rolling up an 18-1 postseason mark that included the first successive World Series sweeps since 1938–1939.

The unexpected 1999 sweep over the Atlanta Braves, who had led the majors with 103 wins, gave the Yankees their 25th World Championship. New York also won 36 pennants—far more than any other club—during the 20th century.

Unlike former Yankee teams that bombarded opponents with home-run power, the "new" Yankees relied upon pitching, defense, and a balanced lineup. They even got perfect games from David Wells (in 1998) and David Cone (in 1999).

While the Yankees spent the last two years of the decade proving the value of team play, Mark McGwire and Sammy Sosa showed that individuals could carry some weight too. Both men broke the 37-year-old home-run record of Roger Maris in 1998 and did it again in 1999!

McGwire, in his first full season with the St. Louis Cardinals after a dozen years in Oakland, passed Maris, who hit 61 in 1961, and never looked back. He hit five in his last three games to finish with 70, four more than Sosa, in 1998.

Another fast finish in 1999—six homers in his last seven games—helped McGwire finish with 65, including the 500th of his career, and made him a potential threat to Hank Aaron's career mark of 755. Sosa, after a late slide, wound up with 63.

His effort made McGwire the first man with four straight 50-homer seasons and the first to produce more RBIs (147) than hits (145) in a season.

Portly but perfect, lefty David Wells thrilled a Beanie Baby Day crowd at Yankee Stadium with a 4–0 perfect game against the Minnesota Twins on May 17, 1998. Wells, who fanned 11, got help from second baseman Chuck Knoblauch, who snared a Ron Coomer smash in the eighth.

Stanley Switch Helped '68 Tigers

Manager Mayo Smith, seeking to insert more punch into his lineup, switched outfielder Mickey Stanley to shortstop for the 1968 World Series against the Cardinals. With southpaw Mickey Lolich victorious three times and Stanley playing well at short, the Tigers won in a seven-game contest.

Long-Lived Tigers

Detroit's double-play tandem of Lou Whitaker and Alan Trammell was together 18 years, longer than any other double-play combination. They played second and short, respectively, from 1977 to 1994, a total of 4,459 games.

Death off the Diamond

Two Yankees lost their lives flying their own planes. Thurman Munson, the club's catcher and captain, died on August 2, 1979 while practicing takeoffs and landings in Akron, Ohio. Almost 30 years later, pitcher Cory Lidle lost his life when his plane crashed into a Manhattan high-rise on the Upper East Side.

Valuable Import

Cecil Fielder returned from exile in the Japanese leagues with a huge bang in 1990. Signed as a free agent by the Detroit Tigers, the big first baseman became the first player since 1977 to reach 50 home runs. Fielder finished with 51 homers and 132 RBIs—the first of three straight seasons he led the majors in runs batted in. Only Babe Ruth (1912–1921) had done that previously.

One-Man Show

Boston's Mike Greenwell is the only man in baseball history responsible for all of his team's runs in a nine-run game. He had nine RBI in a 10-inning, 9–8 win vs. Seattle on September 2, 1996. Greenwell had a single, double, and two homers—one of them with the bases loaded.

One for the Mets

Although Tom Seaver, Nolan Ryan, and Doc Gooden did it after they left, no one pitched a no-hitter for the Mets until Johan Santana in 2012.

ROGER CLEMENS

pitcher   **NEW YORK YANKEES®**

Copyright 1999 by Bill Purdom. Reprinted with permission, Bill Goff, Inc./GoodSportsArt.com.

The only active pitcher named to the Team of the Century, Roger Clemens went on to win 354 games and a record seven Cy Young Awards. The first pitcher to start a season with a 20-1 record, he also authored a pair of 20-strikeout games. But allegations about his dependence on performance-enhancing substances—despite his persistent denials—kept him out of the Baseball Hall of Fame.

But National League Most Valuable Player honors went to Atlanta's Chipper Jones, the first player ever to hit .300 with 40 doubles, 40 homers, 100 walks, 100 RBIs, and 20 stolen bases. His 45 homers were 4 more than Todd Hundley's previous mark for an NL switch-hitter but 9 shy of Mickey Mantle's major league record.

Best of the Century

Prior to Game 2 of the 1999 World Series at Atlanta's Turner Field, baseball revealed the names of the 30 players chosen to represent the Team of the Century.

They were selected by a nationwide fan vote, supplemented by a special panel of baseball executives, media members, and historians. Voters were asked to choose two players at each position except for nine outfielders and six pitchers. That created a 25-man roster to which the special panel added five more who were "overlooked."

All living members of the team, along with family members of the deceased, were honored at Turner Field before the Yankees/Braves game of October 24.

The team:
Catcher—Johnny Bench, Yogi Berra
First base—Lou Gehrig, Mark McGwire
Second base—Rogers Hornsby, Jackie Robinson
Shortstop—Ernie Banks, Cal Ripken Jr., Honus Wagner
Third base—Brooks Robinson, Mike Schmidt
Outfield—Hank Aaron, Ty Cobb, Joe DiMaggio, Ken Griffey Jr., Mickey Mantle, Willie Mays, Stan Musial, Pete Rose, Babe Ruth, Ted Williams
Pitcher—Roger Clemens, Bob Gibson, Lefty Grove, Walter Johnson, Sandy Koufax, Christy Mathewson, Nolan Ryan, Warren Spahn, Cy Young

The Team of the Century announcement followed publication of the century's Top 100 players, determined by members of the Society for American Baseball Research (SABR). The group's 865 voters represented a skilled panel of experts, researchers, and hardcore followers of the game. SABR's Top 100, in the order selected:

The Home-Run Kings

Category	Bonds	McGwire	Maris	Ruth
Year	2001	1998	1961	1927
Games	153	155	161	151
HR	73	70	61	60
RBIs	137	147	142	164
Average	.328	.299	.269	.356
Slugging Pct.	.863	.752	.620	.772
Walks	177	162	94	137
At-bats	476	509	590	540
ABs per HR	6.5	7.3	9.7	9.0

Babe Ruth, Lou Gehrig, Ted Williams, Hank Aaron, Stan Musial, Joe DiMaggio, Ty Cobb, Willie Mays, Rogers Hornsby, Honus Wagner.

Walter Johnson, Mickey Mantle, Christy Mathewson, Jimmie Foxx, Warren Spahn, Mike Schmidt, Bob Gibson, Cy Young, Johnny Bench.

Roberto Clemente, Sandy Koufax, Bob Feller, Tris Speaker, Frank Robinson, Grover Alexander, Yogi Berra, Ernie Banks, Tom Seaver, George Brett.

Steve Carlton, Eddie Mathews, Brooks Robinson, Lefty Grove, Roger Clemens, Hank Greenberg, Jackie Robinson, Joe Morgan, Napoleon Lajoie, Tony Gwynn.

Greg Maddux, Carl Hubbell, Mel Ott, Cal Ripken Jr., Nolan Ryan, Carl Yastrzemski, Charlie Gehringer, Roy Campanella, Pete Rose, Eddie Collins.

Mickey Cochrane, Rod Carew, Shoeless Joe Jackson, Ken Griffey Jr., Whitey Ford, George Sisler, Ozzie Smith, Jim Palmer, Juan Marichal, Al Kaline.

Rickey Henderson, Mark McGwire, Willie McCovey, Bill Dickey, Dennis Eckersley, Barry Bonds, Al Simmons, Reggie Jackson, Duke Snider, Harmon Killebrew.

Pie Traynor, Paul Waner, Frankie Frisch, Lou Brock, Dizzy Dean, Three Finger Brown, Rollie Fingers, Hoyt Wilhelm, Bill Terry, Robin Yount.

Wade Boggs, Paul Molitor, Eddie Murray, Robin Roberts, Joe Cronin, Ed Walsh, Luke Appling, Johnny Mize, Luis Aparicio, Ralph Kiner.

Sam Crawford, Harry Heilmann, Carlton Fisk, Willie Stargell, Eddie Plank, Kirby Puckett, Ferguson Jenkins, Rube Waddell, Ryne Sandberg, Addie Joss, Joe Medwick.

Dan Schlossberg

En route to Cooperstown, Johnny Bench joined Yogi Berra as the only catchers named to the Team of the Century in 1999.

Jock-of-All-Trades

Mark Whiten of the Cardinals not only hit four homers in a game vs. the Reds on September 7, 1993, but tied Jim Bottomley's 1924 single-game record of 12 runs batted in.

Ken's Clouts

San Diego slugger Ken Caminiti homered from both sides of the plate in the same game four times—a major league record—in 1996. He later became the first San Diego Padre ever voted Most Valuable Player in the National League.

Jewelry Joust

Seattle reliever Arthur Rhodes was ejected in the ninth inning of a 2001 Safeco Field game after Cleveland shortstop Omar Vizquel complained that the sun glare from the Seattle player's diamond earrings made it difficult to see the pitched ball. Rhodes, who had worn the earrings without incident for two seasons, was tossed by umpire Tim McClelland after a shouting match between the players.

Battering Ballclubs

Three teams had a trio of 40-homer hitters in the same season. The 1973 Atlanta Braves had Hank Aaron, Darrell Evans, and Davey Johnson; the 1996 Colorado Rockies had Ellis Burks, Vinny Castilla, and Andres Galarraga; and the 1997 Rockies had Castilla, Galarraga, and Larry Walker.

Five teams, all in the American League, had seven men with at least 20 homers: the 1996 Orioles, 2000 Blue Jays, 2005 Rangers, 2009 Yankees, and 2010 Blue Jays. In the National League, the Braves twice had six, as the Milwaukee Braves in 1965 and Atlanta Braves in 2003.

Teams that topped 250 homers in a season were the 1997 Seattle Mariners (264), 2005 Texas Rangers (260), 1996 Baltimore Orioles (257), 2010 Toronto Blue Jays (257), and 2016 Baltimore Orioles (253).

The New York Yankees hit a record three grand slams in a game on August 25, 2011. Robinson Cano, Russell Martin, and Curtis Granderson all connected against the Oakland Athletics.

Millennial Ball

As baseball entered the new millennium, it found that the more things change, the more they stay the same. During the 2000 season nobody hit more than 50 home runs, pitched a no-hitter, or fired a manager during the season (the first time that has happened since 1942).

The opening of new ballparks in San Francisco (Pac Bell Park) and Houston (Enron Field) had inconsistent results. The Giants sold every seat, thrived in their new surroundings, and tied the Mets for the NL's best home record. But the Astros ended a string of three straight division titles by finishing 18 games under .500 despite hitting an NL-record 249 home runs (and yielding 234, most in the majors, including an NL-record 48 by Jose Lima).

The other Texas team, the Rangers of the AL West, also had trouble, becoming the fourth team to drop from division winner one year to cellar dweller the next.

When physical problems limited Mark McGwire to 70 starts, Sammy Sosa won his first home-run crown after two straight seasons as runner-up to McGwire. But the Chicago star hit only 50, the lowest total for a leader since 1993.

Todd Helton (Rockies) led the majors with 147 RBIs and a .372414 batting average (narrowly topping Nomar Garciaparra's .372401) but hit 42 home runs, 8 shy of the National League's first Triple Crown since Joe Medwick's in 1937. Helton hit 59 doubles, most in the majors since Medwick had 64 in 1936, and led the NL in slugging (.698), on-base percentage (.463), hits (216), and total bases (405). A year later, he became the first player to produce consecutive seasons with 400 total bases.

Buoyed by Pac Bell and its cozy dimensions, Barry Bonds hit a career-best 49 homers and led the Giants into the playoffs. But the wild-card Mets survived San Francisco and St. Louis series to set up New York's first Subway Series since 1956. The first two games made history: the first because it was the longest in World

CAL RIPKEN

third base **BALTIMORE ORIOLES®**

Cal Ripken Jr. broke Lou Gehrig's 56-year-old record of 2,130 consecutive games on September 6, 1995. Ripken won two MVP awards and two Gold Gloves for his shortstop play during the streak, which started on May 30, 1982, and stretched to 2,632 games before ending on September 20, 1998. When Ripken retired after the 2001 season, he had more than 3,000 hits and 400 home runs.

When Bank One Ballpark opened under the lights on March 31, 1998, few dreamed the World Series would be played there three years later. The Arizona Diamondbacks not only advanced to the Fall Classic in their fourth season, an expansion-team record, but beat the New York Yankees in the 2001 Series.

Series annals and the second because Roger Clemens was fined $50,000 for throwing a jagged bat at Mike Piazza.

Though the Mets won Game 3, ending the Yankees' 14-game World Series winning streak, the Yanks won in five games, giving them three straight world titles. Yankee shortstop Derek Jeter became the first man to be All-Star Game and World Series MVP in the same season.

The Yankees won their 38th flag in 2001, rebounding from an 0–2 deficit in the best-of-five AL Division Series against Oakland and silencing Seattle bats in a five-game Championship Series after the Mariners had won 116 games, tying the single-season mark of the 1906 Cubs.

But the Bronx Bombers struggled in the World Series against the aces of the Arizona Diamondbacks, Randy Johnson and Curt Schilling. The power-pitching pair had combined for 42 wins and 665 strikeouts, a record for a tandem, with Johnson averaging 13.4 Ks per nine innings.

The Johnson/Schilling tandem took three of Arizona's four wins in a five-game NLCS against Atlanta, which won its 10th consecutive division crown—a record for any sport—and swept the heavy-hitting Astros in the first round. Both wild-cards, Oakland and St. Louis, lost in Round 1.

None of the year's big hitters reached the fall classic. In the "walk" year of his six-year Giants deal, Bonds carved a niche in the record book with 73 home runs, walked 177 times, averaged a homer per 6.5 at-bats, and posted an .863 slugging percentage. His .515 on-base percentage was the NL's best since John McGraw's .547 in 1900.

Bonds won his second home-run crown, while Alex Rodriguez won his first, hitting a club-mark 52 for his new team, the Texas Rangers. No shortstop has ever hit more in a season.

Two others, Sammy Sosa (64) and Luis Gonzalez (57), topped 50 homers, giving the majors four at that level for the second time (McGwire, Sosa, Ken Griffey Jr., and Greg Vaughn did it in 1998). Spurred by a trio of three-homer games, Sosa's 160 RBIs were the most in the NL since Hack Wilson's record 190 in 1930, while his 425 total bases were the most in the majors since Stan Musial's 429 in 1948.

Seattle's surge was powered by Ichiro Suzuki, a fleet, left-handed singles hitter who uses only his first name, and retread Bret Boone, who found himself batting fourth for the AL All-Stars en route to an AL RBI title nobody could have predicted. Ichiro not only became the first man since Jackie Robinson in 1949 to lead a league in hitting (.350) and stolen bases (56) but also had 242 hits, most in the majors since Bill Terry's 254 in 1930. The leading vote-getter for the All-Star Game, held at Safeco Field, he later joined Fred Lynn (1974) as the only men to be Rookie of the Year and Most Valuable Player in the same season.

Albert Pujols (Cardinals) also broke in with a bang: he had 88 extra-base hits, 130 RBIs, and 360 total bases, all NL rookie records.

Rickey Henderson (Padres) not only extended his career record for steals (1,395) but became the new leader in runs (2,248) and walks (2,259). He got his 3,000th hit on the last day of the season.

It was also a memorable year for Gary Sheffield (Dodgers), the first man whose homers won three 1–0 games in a season; pitcher Mike Hampton (Rockies), who homered seven times with his new club after hitting none in eight previous campaigns; and Hideo Nomo (Red Sox), who used his first Boston start to become the fourth author of no-hitters in both leagues. A. J. Burnett (Marlins) and rookie Bud Smith (Cardinals) also pitched no-hitters in 2001, though Curt Schilling missed a potential perfect game when San Diego catcher Ben Davis dropped a bunt single with one out in the eighth inning.

Baseball ended on a somber note after terrorists hijacked and crashed four commercial airliners on September 11. Two hit and destroyed New York's World Trade Center, killing nearly 3,000 people, while a third killed 189 at the Pentagon. When play resumed after a six-day mourning period, New York teams wore hats bearing the logos of the police and fire departments.

Sluggers to Remember

* Reggie Jackson was the only player to win league home run crowns with three different teams (A's, Yankees, and Angels).
* Although his 58-homer season in 1997 led the major leagues, Mark McGwire did not win a home run crown that year, which he split between the A's and Cardinals. Since he led neither league, he would have had four straight years as a league leader (1996–1999).
* The only Olympian to hit 50 home runs in a season, McGwire was also the first man to have more runs batted in than hits in a season. During his 70-homer season in 1989, he failed to make contact (walks plus strikeouts) 42.3 percent of the time and never homered with a 3-0 count.
* Before Fernando Tatis became the only man to hit two grand slams in the same inning on April 23, 1999, major leaguers had hit 4,777 slams without ever accomplishing that feat.
* Alex Rodriguez hit more grand slams (25) than any other player.
* Clutch hitter Jim Thome, who starred in both leagues, hit a dozen walk-off home runs, a major league record.
* Seattle's Mike Cameron collected only four RBI with his four-homer game of May 1, 2002. All four shots were solos.
* Shawn Green's 6-for-6 game on May 23, 2002 included four home runs, a double, and a single—good for a record 19 total bases.
* Chipper Jones, the only man to hit two homers in a game against Randy Johnson, did it twice—exactly one year apart—and also was the only switch-hitter to hit .300 with 300 home runs.
* Players with 40 homers and 40 stolen bases in the same season:

Year	Player & Club	HR	SB
1988	Jose Canseco, Athletics	42	40
1996	Barry Bonds, Giants	42	40
1998	Alex Rodriguez, Mariners	42	46
2006	Alfonso Soriano, Nationals	46	41

Chapter 21

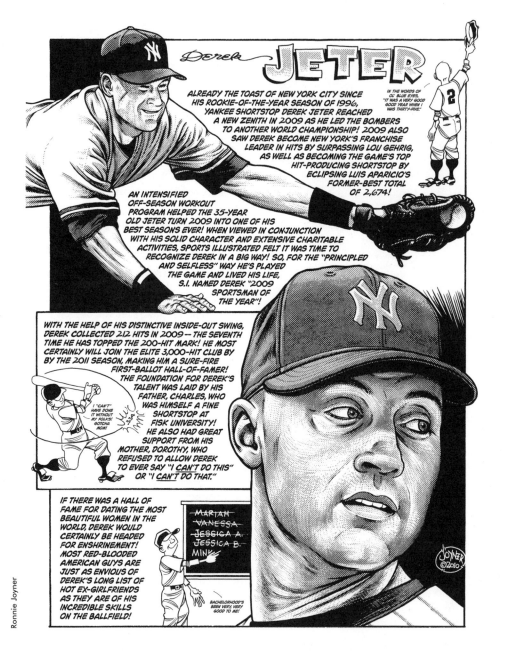

Derek Jeter not only spent his entire career with the Yankees but played more seasons in pinstripes (20) than any other player. A shortstop who compiled more than 3,000 hits, he was a clubhouse leader who helped his team win five world championships.

A New Century

There were many events that took place during the first decade of the 21st century, for better or for worse, which played a part in shaping the history of the great American pastime.

Though some of these events—like the terrorist attacks on American soil on September 11, 2001and the ongoing discussion about performance-enhancing substances—presented changes that were difficult and frustrating, the thrill of competition also presented itself in full force.

There has never been a three-way tie in baseball history. But that doesn't mean teams didn't come close. Heading into the last day of the 2007 season, four teams could have finished with identical 89-73 records—requiring two extra playoff games before the *scheduled* playoffs.

On the final day, the Phillies and Mets were tied for the NL East lead with 88-73 records, while the Padres were perched atop the wild-card race with an 89-72 mark—one game better than the Rockies, Phillies, and Mets. If the Mets, Phils, and Rockies won but the Padres lost, all four would have finished 89-73—forcing a Mets-Phils playoff for the NL East and a Rockies-Padres playoff for the wild card.

As it turned out, the Phillies and Rockies won, the Mets and Padres lost, and Colorado took a 13-inning, 9–8 tiebreaker from San Diego to win the wild card and advance to the NL Division Series against Philadelphia.

In the meantime, scheduling in-season games between teams of opposite leagues was giving officials fits. The American League had 14 teams, with 16 in the National League, and something had to be done to correct the inequity.

Changing Format

Fifty years after they began play as an expansion entry, the Houston Astros moved from the National League to the

What is Sabermetrics?

Sabermetrics was conceived as a novel way to predict baseball performance by players and teams. Combining computer information with theories advanced by the Society for American Baseball Research (SABR), the science got impetus from the 1964 publication of an Earnshaw Cook book called *Percentage Baseball*. Rejected by most clubs, the theories languished before Bill James, a mathematician who loved the game, revived them more than 10 years later. Defined as the empirical analysis of baseball, sabermetrics yielded such new statistics as WAR (wins above replacement) and WHIP (walks plus hits per innings pitched). In addition to James, who began publishing his Baseball Abstracts in 1977, leading advocates of sabermetrics include baseball executives Sandy Alderson and Billy Beane, and Theo Epstein, plus writers Rob Neyer and Joe Posnanski. A 2003 book and movie about Beane's reliance on sabermetrics was called *Moneyball*. SABR holds an annual analytics conference and many of its members subscribe to such sabermetrics publications as *FanGraphs*, *The Hardball Times*, and *Baseball Prospectus*.

AP Photo/Alex Brandon

After signing a lucrative free agent contract with the Washington Nationals, Max Scherzer pitched two no-hitters in his first year and racked up a 20-strikeout game early in his second. He victimized his old team, the Detroit Tigers, in his strikeout frenzy.

Jake Arrieta's 22-win campaign catapulted the Chicago Cubs into the 2015 playoffs and earned him the NL's Cy Young Award in a hotly-contested field.

American, effective in 2013. That created two 15-team leagues, mandating interleague play throughout the year.

To increase interest in more cities—and to raise revenue to meet skyrocketing payrolls—Major League Baseball also revamped the postseason format.

It added a second wild-card team in each league, putting 10 of the 30 teams into playoffs that started with a sudden-death game to determine the wild-card winner. In the first two years of the new format, the Pittsburgh Pirates found their power short-circuited by a pair of pitching studs: Madison Bumgarner (Giants) in 2014 and Jake Arrieta (Cubs) in 2015. Both pitched shutouts, sending the Pirates home for the winter after 162 games of excellence.

Wild-card teams—second-place teams with the highest winning percentages—represented their leagues in the World Series 11 times from 1997 to 2015 and won five world championships (Royals, Red Sox, and Angels once each and the Marlins twice).

New Heroes

In the meantime, young stars were making headlines of their own.

Mike Trout (Angels) became the youngest player in major-league history to reach 100 home runs and 100 stolen bases. He also became the first to win consecutive Most Valuable Player honors in the All-Star Game.

Well before his 30th birthday, Dodgers southpaw Clayton Kershaw sewed up three Cy Young Awards, four ERA crowns, and a 300-strikeout season. His performance stamped him as the best pitcher in the game and conjured up comparisons with Hall of Famer Sandy Koufax.

At age 22, Washington outfielder Bryce Harper was named National League MVP for 2015 after producing a league-best 42 home runs, 118 runs scored, .460 on-base percentage, and .649 slugging percentage.

On the final day of the season, Harper held a narrow lead in the race for the batting title. His .330754 batting average was a smidge better than Dee Gordon's .330606. But the Miami speed merchant led off his game with a double, then followed with consecutive singles to finish with a 3-for-4 game and final mark of .333. Harper went 1-for-4 to close at .330.

The first player since Jackie Robinson in 1949 to lead the league in both hits (205) and stolen bases (58), Gordon got a hefty contract extension from the Fish. Shortly thereafter, however, he was suspended for 80 games after he failed a drug test.

Pete Rose, anxious to overturn his lifetime ban for gambling, had applied for reinstatement in 1997 and 2002 but Selig never ruled on his case. Rose, who admitted in his 2004 biography that he bet on baseball while managing the Reds, hoped that the new commissioner would consider his case. Manfred met with Rose, the career hits leader, at the end of the 2015 regular season, but declined to grant his wish.

Nor was Rose pleased in 2016 when Ichiro Suzuki was dubbed the new hits king by sportswriters who added his Japanese and American totals.

After winning seven straight batting crowns and three MVP awards in Japan's major leagues, Ichiro became the only player to start his US career with six straight 200-hit seasons. He broke in with a bang, collecting both the MVP and Rookie of the Year trophies as a 2001 rookie with Seattle. He later had a 262-hit season, topping George Sisler's mark by five, and hit the only inside-the-park home run in the All-Star Game. He later collected his 3,000th hit in the US.

Ichiro's performance was made more intriguing by the quality of opposing pitchers.

Max Scherzer marked his first year with the Washington Nationals in 2015 by throwing a pair of no-hitters—the fifth man in major league history and first since Nolan Ryan in 1973 to do that. He followed a year later by striking out 20 men in a nine-inning game, a feat performed previously by Kerry Wood, Randy Johnson, and Rogers Clemens (twice).

Scherzer, who signed a seven-year, $210 million contract with the Nats as a free agent, was the first pitcher ever to throw two no-hitters without giving up a walk in either.

Jake Arrieta threw two no-hitters within 10 starts over two seasons, neutralizing the Los Angeles Dodgers for his first on August 30, 2015. Despite an inflated payroll that pushed past $298 million, the Dodgers were no-hit twice in nine days, starting with Milwaukee's Mike Fiers August 21.

Throwing a no-hitter does not necessarily help, though: Cole Hamels pitched one against the Cubs at Wrigley Field in his last start for the Phillies, who thanked him by trading the powerful southpaw to the contending Texas Rangers after he had spent his entire career with the Phils.

Clayton Kershaw, author of a no-hitter himself, crafted a run of four straight ERA titles before Dodgers teammate Zack Greinke ended it by posting a 1.66 mark in 2015. Grienke then said goodbye and jumped to the Arizona Diamondbacks on the strength of a quirky "out" clause in his contract. His new deal paid him an average $1 million per start.

No Miami Miracle

Although the advent of a new ballpark prompted the Miami Marlins to substitute their host city for their host state, the Fish remained a franchise in flux.

After starting the 2006 season with a $15 million payroll, lowest in the majors, owner Jeffrey Loria got into a shouting match with manager Joe Girardi during a game in August. Loria's loud commentary from the stands had irritated the home-plate umpire and Girardi told his boss to stifle it. A 90-minute clubhouse meeting after the game did not clear the air and Girardi was fired after the season. He was quickly hired to succeed Joe Torre, who left the Yankees after a salary dispute with owner George Steinbrenner.

Four years later, after the team started June with 19 losses in 20 games, Loria recycled former manager Jack McKeon, the octogenarian who had guided the Fish to victory in the 2003 Fall Classic. Unable to work his magic again, the fatherly McKeon yielded to the fiery Ozzie Guillen, acquired from the White Sox for a pair of prospects. It didn't help.

Nor did Loria's winter shopping spree that added a slew of free agents.

The idea was to draw fans to the team's new retractable-roof ballpark in the spring of 2012, but Guillen poisoned the well early with remarks sympathetic to Cuban dictator Fidel Castro. He was suspended for five games and eventually fired, while the team retooled by swapping the stars it had signed as free agents. The Fish flopped, losing 93 games and finishing last.

Doubt vs. Clout

Barry Bonds, with seven MVPs of his own, broke Hank Aaron's career record when he smashed No. 756 on August 7, 2007, then finally retired after a career crowded with controversy. Suspected but never charged with using performance-enhancing substances, he hit 762 home runs but failed to earn a niche in the Baseball Hall of Fame or recognition by many as the legitimate home run king.

Sammy Sosa, the only man to hit at least 60 in three different seasons, was also relegated to a back seat in the Cooperstown voting. A similar fate befell fellow sluggers Rafael Palmeiro and Mark McGwire, who had denied knowledge of the steroids epidemic during congressional hearings in 2005. McGwire, the first man to hit 70 homers in a season,

This is the helmet San Franciso's Barry Bonds wore when he hit his 756th home run, most in baseball history. Because he was hounded by accusations of substance abuse, many historians refused to recognize him over Hank Aaron as the new home run king.

The Stench of Steroids

After Major League Baseball mandated its initial drug-testing program in 2005, Commissioner Bud Selig appointed former U.S. Senate Majority Leader George Mitchell, a member of the Red Sox board of directors, to investigate. After a separate two-year investigation, the authors of *A Game of Shadows* alleged that Barry Bonds had used steroids, HGH, insulin, and other performance-enhancing drugs since 1998.

A San Francisco firm named BALCO (Bay Area Laboratory Cooperative) distributed banned performance-enhancing drugs to major league players before it was exposed by the United States government. The firm, founded by Victor Conte, claimed its products were nutritional substances but the U.S. Anti-Doping Agency disagreed. Major League Baseball responded, enacting a new policy that stipulated a 50-game ban for the first offense, 100-game ban for the second, and lifetime suspension for the third. Those penalties were later tightened to 80 games, 162 games, and life.

said he didn't want to talk about the past, while Palmeiro waved his finger at lawmakers and denied juicing. Five months later, he failed a drug test to earn a suspension.

Just before 2008 spring training, pitcher Roger Clemens testified under oath that he had never used performance-enhancing drugs. Although he won a record seven Cy Young Awards en route to 354 career wins (second in victories only to Greg Maddux among living pitchers), Clemens lost his credibility with Hall of Fame electors.

A cloud also hung over Alex Rodriguez, who admitted during 2009 spring training that he had used steroids in his first three seasons with the Texas Rangers after receiving a 10-year, $252 million contract that was then the largest in professional sports history.

A-Rod's admission followed a *Sports Illustrated* report that his name was on a list of 104 players who had tested positive for banned substances in 2003. After federal investigators seized the records and samples, the players union tried to get them back—citing a promise by the commissioner's office that test results would be kept confidential.

Instead, the steroids scandal started to strike some of the game's biggest stars. Manny Ramirez lost more than $7 million of his $25

Alex Rodriguez was a superstar shortstop with the Seattle Mariners when the Texas Rangers landed him through free agency in 2001 with a 10-year, $252 million contract. He was later traded to the New York Yankees, where he moved to third in deference to incumbent shortstop Derek Jeter. He won five home run crowns, three MVP awards, and a batting title but missed a season while suspended for using performance-enhancing substances.

In his first eight seasons with Detroit, Miguel Cabrera collected four batting crowns, two home run crowns, two RBI titles, and the first American League Triple Crown since 1967. The right-handed slugger from Venezuela thrived after the Tigers moved him from third base to first.

Worst-to-First

These teams leaped from last place one season to first place the next:
1. Atlanta Braves and Minnesota Twins, 1991
2. Philadelphia Phillies, 1993
3. San Francisco Giants, 1997
4. San Diego Padres, 1998
5. Arizona Diamondbacks, 1999
6. Arizona Diamondbacks and Chicago Cubs, 2007
7. Tampa Bay Rays, 2008
8. Arizona Diamondbacks, 2011
9. Boston Red Sox, 2013
10. Texas Rangers, 2015
11. Boston Red Sox, 2016

million salary before he returned on July 3, 2009. Ryan Braun, the reigning National League MVP, tested positive for elevated testosterone and initially got a 50-game suspension overturned upon appeal.

A contrite Melky Cabrera even gave up a batting title after his drug abuse was exposed. At the time of his 2012 suspension, he was leading the National League in hits and was a close second in batting. But he was also one plate appearance shy of the minimum number needed to qualify.

Since his .346 average would not have changed if that missing at-bat were added, Cabrera would have won the batting title. But he asked the Players Association to ignore Rule 10.22 (a) and thus gave the title to Giants teammate Buster Posey, who hit 10 points less. It is interesting to note, however, that Cabrera did not return the All-Star Game MVP award he won that summer.

With increasing numbers of players pestering their union to clean up the game, the Players Association and Major League Baseball tightened penalties for performance-enhancing substances and added new ones for domestic abuse.

MLB clamped down on steroids users in 2014 by adopting a test that could not only find a drug but markers of the drug even after it is metabolized. That eliminated the chance of juicing players masking their testosterone levels.

The new rules, coupled with the discretionary powers of the commissioner's office to act "in the best interests of baseball," made multiple impacts immediately.

Rodriguez received a 211-game ban, shortened to 162 games, for falsehoods and cover-ups. Marlon Byrd also was suspended for a full season. And Jenrry Mejia, the erstwhile Mets closer, was banned for life after a third offense.

Suspensions were also issued to players guilty of violating a new domestic violence policy that went into effect late in 2015. The first recipients were Jose Reyes, Aroldis Chapman, and Hector Olivera.

Model Citizens

On the field, however, the game and its appeal continued to grow.

Derek Jeter, the poster boy for clean living, helped the Yankees win division titles, seven pennants, and five World Series. In his final game at Yankee Stadium in 2014, he stroked an opposite-field single to right field in the bottom of the ninth inning to drive in the winning run in a 6–5 win over Baltimore.

Like Jeter, Mariano Rivera spent his entire career with the Yankees. The soft-spoken Panamanian inherited the closer's job from John Wetteland in 1997 and saved a record 652 games before retiring after the 2013 campaign. Although his arsenal was limited to a single pitch, Rivera's cutter allowed him to hold rival clubs to 2.21 earned runs per game. The right-handed Rivera, an American League All-Star 13 times, won five World Series rings during his 19-year career.

One of Rivera's toughest opponents was Detroit first baseman Miguel Cabrera, whose 2012 Triple Crown was the first in either league since Carl Yastrzemski's in 1967. Mike Trout, who reached the majors that same year, won both Rookie of the Year and Major League Player of the Year honors from Baseball America, but Cabrera captured the first of consecutive American League Most Valuable Player awards.

Of the 30 teams, two had never been to a World Series—the Washington Nationals and the Seattle Mariners— but seemed to be making progress in that direction.

Thanks to the annual amateur draft, which gives first picks to the teams with the worst records, the Nationals chose first in the nation two years in a row. Their choices, Stephen Strasburg in 2010 and Bryce Harper in 2011, surfaced quickly and soon blossomed into All-Stars.

As for Seattle, ace Felix Hernandez, like Carl Hubbell years earlier, became known as "King" Felix for his pitching prowess. Although he often lacked support, he took matters into his own hands with a perfect game and perfectly miserly pitching. He even won his second ERA title when Joe Torre, the former catcher and manager in charge of baseball operations for the commissioner's office, changed a hit to an error and allowed four earned runs to become unearned. He was removed from that season-ending game when his ERA reached 2.14, a hair better than Chris Sale's 2.17.

Tim Lincecum, then with the Giants, became the first man to pitch two no-hitters against the same team (San Diego) while Jordan Zimmermann of the Nationals no-hit the Marlins on the last day of the 2014 campaign. The losing pitcher that day was Henderson Alvarez, who had no-hit the Tigers in the final game exactly one year earlier.

Foreign Affairs

New stars of every size, shape, and nationality also made their mark.

After starring for Cuba in the 2013 World Baseball Classic, Jose Abreu signed a six-year, $68 million White Sox pact that was a record for a Cuban player. He then went out and won the American League's Rookie of the Year award with a 36-homer, 107-RBI campaign.

Yoenis Cespedes, another Cuban slugger, won the Home Run Derby at the All-Star Game two years in a row and continued to showcase his power for several clubs before finding a home with the power-hungry New York Mets at the trade deadline in 2015.

Jose Altuve, a diminutive second baseman, won the first batting crown by a member of the Houston Astros by waiting until the last day of the 2014 season. Entering with a three-point lead on Detroit DH Victor Martinez, he went 2-for-4 to finish at .341. His rival went 0-for-3 to close at .335.

The New York Yankees snatched Masahiro Tanaka, a solid starting pitcher, out of the Japanese major leagues after signing him to a seven-year contract worth $155 million, starting in 2014. They were hoping he would follow in the footsteps of Daisuke Matsuzaka, who pitched well for the Boston Red Sox after crossing the ocean to the American major leagues.

Wright or Wrong?

Ron Wright's whole career consisted of three at-bats in which he made six outs: strikeout, double-play, and triple-play.

Not Perfect

When a Hanley Ramirez throwing error permitted a baserunner during Clayton Kershaw's 2014 no-hitter, it was the seventh time a miscue ruined a potential perfect game.

Fallen Felix

Felix Hernandez was disabled by the Seattle Mariners after he strained his right calf muscle while celebrating a home run—in a league where pitchers don't bat.

Might as Well

Kansas City outfielder Lorenzo Cain, Most Valuable Player in the 2014 AL Championship Series, turned to baseball only after he was cut from his high school basketball team. He began his baseball career with a plastic glove, football cleats, and cross-handed batting style.

That Toddlin' Town

Thanks to divisional play, baseball history was made on May 5, 2016 when four first-place teams played in the same city on the same day. The Cubs hosted the Nationals while the White Sox hosted the Red Sox.

Seasons of Surprises

The 2010 season was full of surprises.

On May 7, Phillies junkballer Jamie Moyer became the oldest man to pitch a shutout. A day later, Brewers outfielder Jody Gerut hit for the cycle after entering the game with a .133 average and four hits for the entire season. Arguably an even less likely cycle was completed on July 16, when Bengie Molina, then a Ranger, did it in Boston. Needing a triple in his last at-bat, the slow-moving catcher got one, thus becoming the first backstop to turn the trick in the game's modern era.

Little-known Athletics pitcher Dallas Braden found 15 minutes of fame by pitching a perfect game on Mother's Day and dedicating it to his mother, who had died of cancer nine years earlier.

Rookie outfielder Jason Heyward, 20, homered for the Braves on Opening Day and had 10 by Memorial Day before a head-first slide injured his thumb and forced him to miss the All-Star Game after fans had voted him a starter.

Toronto's surprise slugger was Jose Bautista, whose 54 home runs led runner-up Paul Konerko of the White Sox by 15. Helped by his hitter-friendly home park, the Rogers Centre, Bautista, a 30-year-old journeyman outfielder, had never hit more than 16 home runs in a season while playing for four other clubs.

The Minnesota Twins, meanwhile, found paradise in their new outdoor environs. The team went 53-28, the American League's best home record, at Target Field and drew 3,223,640 fans, the most in franchise history.

While new names were coming in, old ones were going out.

Bobby Cox finished a 30-year managing career that included a record 16 trips to the postseason while star center fielder Ken Griffey Jr., a 13-time All-Star, concluded his playing career without ever reaching the World Series. He did manage to win MVP awards for both the regular season and the All-Star Game—12 years after his father had won the same trophy.

The Yankees lost owner George Steinbrenner and public address announcer Bob Sheppard within a few days of each other. The latter was so beloved by players and fans at Yankee Stadium that team captain Derek Jeter insisted a tape of Sheppard's introduction be used as his introductory announcement every time he came to bat after his demise.

When Jeter needed two hits to join the 3000 Club, he wasted no time. On July 9, 2011, his 5-for-5 effort included a home run for his 3000th hit. The only previous player to do that had been Wade Boggs.

Also in 2011, Pitching prevailed in Philadelphia, where free agent Cliff Lee joined Roy Halladay and Roy Oswalt in a powerful Big Three that led the rotation. Halladay and Lee formed a potent right-left punch that helped the staff post a league-best 3.02 earned run average. Both ranked among the top five pitchers in innings, wins, strikeouts, ERA, and complete games.

Justin Verlander was even better; the Detroit ace parlayed a 24-5 record and 2.40 ERA into Most Valuable Player and Cy Young trophies.

San Francisco's ability to defend its world title ended when star catcher Buster Posey, the 2010 NL Rookie of the Year, suffered a broken leg in a home-plate collision with Scott Cousins of the Marlins on May 25, ending his season. Giants manager Bruce

Mixed Results

May 6, 2012 was a day of good news and bad news for Baltimore Orioles DH Chris Davis. He went 0-for-8 in a 17-inning marathon against the Boston Red Sox but picked up the win in relief after pitching two scoreless innings. The losing pitcher was Boston outfielder Darnell McDonald—making that game the first since October 4, 1925 to involve position players as winning and losing pitchers. On the earlier date, Ty Cobb (Tigers) and George Sisler (Browns) faced each other in the nightcap of a doubleheader on the last game of the season.

King for a Day

The 2012 perfect game by Philip Humber was his first complete game in the major leagues.

Strasburg's Limit

Washington made waves in 2012 by placing a limit of 160 innings on pitcher Stephen Strasburg, a one-time No. 1 draft pick then recuperating from Tommy John surgery. Without their ace starter in the playoffs, the Nationals missed a golden opportunity to reach the World Series for the first time in franchise history.

Great Record

The 2012 Baltimore Orioles went 29-9 in one-run games and finished the season with a record 16 consecutive wins in extra-inning contests.

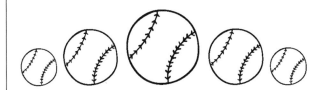

Bochy, a former catcher, successfully suggested a rules change that would protect receivers from taking such hits.

The 2011 season closed with a record surge by the St. Louis Cardinals. Trailing Atlanta in the wild-card race by 10½ games on August 25, they rallied to forge a tie, beat the Braves in the new wild-card playoff, and overpowered the Phillies in the NLDS, the Brewers in the NLCS, and the Rangers in the World Series. In 106 previous World Series, only the 1986 Mets had rallied to win after coming within one pitch of elimination.

Manager Tony La Russa then stunned the baseball world by retiring after 16 years as St. Louis manager. Also departing were manager Terry Francona and general manager Theo Epstein of the Boston Red Sox, a team that blew a nine-game September lead to Tampa Bay in the wild-card race. Both found success elsewhere, with Francona at the helm of the Cleveland Indians and Epstein in the front office of the Chicago Cubs. La Russa also returned to baseball as chief executive of the Arizona Diamondbacks.

Hot pitchers were a hot topic early in the 2012 campaign. Six Mariners combined to hold the Dodgers hitless, duplicating a previous feat by the Houston Astros, and three pitchers were perfect: Matt Cain, Felix Hernandez, and Philip Humber. The White Sox never got much else from Humber, whose April 21 gem was long-forgotten by August. He finished with a 6.44 ERA in 26 games, including 10 out of the bullpen.

Johan Santana pitched the first no-hitter in the history of the Mets, blanking the Cardinals, while Washington welcomed back Stephen Strasburg, who missed most of 2011 recuperating from Tommy John surgery. Still worried about Strasburg's elbow, general manager Mike Rizzo enforced an innings limit on the star pitcher, who finished 15-6 with a 3.16 ERA but did not pitch after reaching the limit of 160 innings.

Thanks to Strasburg and 19-year-old rookie outfielder Bryce Harper, the Nats still led the majors with 98 wins en route to their first NL East title but did not reach the World Series.

Another freshman find was Mike Trout, a New Jersey native who thrived when placed in the outfield of the Los Angeles Angels. The first player with 30 home runs, 45 stolen bases, and 125 runs scored in a season, he was also the first named Rookie of the Year and Major League Player of the Year by *Baseball America*. He finished second in voting for American League MVP, won by Tigers slugger Miguel Cabrera in the wake of his Triple Crown performance—the first since 1967.

Financial Foibles

Hoping for similar results from Albert Pujols, the lifetime Cardinal who signed a 10-year, $240 million contract, the Angels were bitterly disappointed. The 32-year-old first baseman, obviously pressing, did not hit his first home run of the 2012 season until May 6. Owner Arte Moreno, desperate to keep his sinking ship afloat, landed star pitcher Zack Greinke from Milwaukee in a deadline deal for three prospects but failed to salvage his season.

The Los Angeles Dodgers, meanwhile, made negative headlines of their own. The nasty divorce of owners Frank and Jamie McCourt forced the team to file for bankruptcy and Major League Baseball to assume operations, as it had done previously with the

High Octane

Craig Kimbrel (2012) and Aroldis Chapman (2014) are the only pitchers to strike out at least half the batters they faced in a season.

Revere's Rarity

Ben Revere's home run on May 27, 2014 was his first after 1,466 lifetime at-bats. It was the longest home run drought since Frank Taveras finally connected in his 1,594th at-bat in 1977.

Pirate Revival

The 2015 Pittsburgh Pirates reached the playoffs for the third straight season after posting 20 consecutive losing seasons, a professional sports record.

Montreal Expos. The McCourt reign of error officially ended when a group headed by basketball legend Magic Johnson and longtime baseball executive Stan Kasten bought the team, the surrounding land, and the parking lots for $2.15 billion in 2012.

The Boston Red Sox, failing to realize their investment in manager Bobby Valentine, replaced him after the season with Toronto manager John Farrell, whom they obtained in an October trade that also involved several players. The former Boston pitching coach had one more year on his contract with the Blue Jays.

The Sox also lopped $260 million off their bloated payroll by sending Adrian Gonzalez, Carl Crawford, and Josh Beckett to the Dodgers in an August waiver deal that involved nine players.

A low-budget team, the Oakland Athletics proved determination trumped payroll when it rallied in the final week to top the Texas Rangers for the AL West title. Five games behind with nine to go, the A's swept a season-ending, three-game series from the Rangers to cap a comeback that started June 30, when they were 13 games behind. Oakland joined the 1951 New York Giants and 2006 Minnesota Twins as the only teams to win a division title or pennant while spending only one day in first place. Texas, settling for a wild-card berth, had held at least a share of the lead on all but three days of the season. Unable to recover from the Oakland sting, the Rangers lost the sudden-death wild-card game to Baltimore and went home for the winter.

The Pittsburgh Pirates went home even earlier; they completed their 20th consecutive losing season, a professional sports record for dubious achievement.

The 2014 season started in Australia, a first for baseball, when the Los Angeles Dodgers hosted the Arizona Diamondbacks at the Sydney Cricket Ground. Although he pitched in the March 22 opener, the earliest in baseball history, Clayton Kershaw injured his back during the long plane flight home and had to spend 41 days on the disabled list. He still finished with a 21-3 record and 1.77 earned run average. The first pitcher to lead the majors in ERA four years in a row, Kershaw received a seven-year, $210 million new contract from the grateful Dodgers.

David Price, another stud left-hander, joined the Tigers in a three-team July trade, giving Detroit three Cy Young winners in the same rotation for several months. Though Price and Max Scherzer would later leave via free agency, the trio paid dividends when Detroit beat Minnesota on the last day of the season to win the AL Central for the fourth straight time.

Dave Stewart had an odyssey of his own; the former Oakland ace under Tony La Russa gave up a career as a player agent to become general manager of the Arizona Diamondbacks, where La Russa was president of baseball operations.

Ron Washington stepped down as Texas manager, citing personal reasons, after taking the team to consecutive World Series appearances—its first—in 2010 and 2011.

It was no surprise, however, when a member of the Colorado Rockies captured the 2014 National League batting crown. Thanks to Denver's mile-high altitude and hitter-friendly Coors Field, Justin Morneau simply picked up the baton previously carried by Andres Galarraga (1994), Larry Walker (1998–99 and 2001), Todd Helton (2000), Matt Holliday (2007), Carlos Gonzalez (2010), and Michael Cuddyer (2013).

Six men, including three managers, were inducted into the Baseball Hall of Fame in July but Greg Maddux could not decide whether his plaque should feature a Braves or Cubs logo. Another inductee, Frank Thomas, became the first Hall of Famer to have played more than half his games as a designated hitter.

Tough Teams

Both participants in the 2014 World Series, the Kansas City Royals and San Francisco Giants, had to survive three rounds of playoffs to reach the final round. It was the second time the Fall Classic was played without a first-place team (see also 2002, Giants vs. Angels).

The Giants won their third world title in five seasons because Madison Bumgarner beat the Royals three times, including the decisive Game 7 after a five-inning relief stint. He not only pitched a postseason record 52 2/3 innings but posted a 1.03 ERA—far better than the 9.35 posted by the other three Giants starters. The only run Bumgarner yielded in the World Series was a solo home run by Salvador Perez.

The 2014 Los Angeles Angels and 1980 New York Yankees remain the only teams to post the best record in the majors during the regular season but fail to win a postseason game.

Teams are only as good as their players—and sometimes one night makes a big difference.

Role Reversal

Anything can happen and often does when position players are pressed into service as pitchers. Washington catcher Wilson

For Giants fans, the best San Francisco treat was staged by the All-Star battery of Madison Bumgarner and Buster Posey. They hit grand slams in the same game and helped their team win three world championships within a five-year span from 2010 to 2014. Posey won a batting crown and Rookie of the Year award while Bumgarner went 4-0 with a 0.25 ERA in five World Series starts. He was MVP in both the NL Championship Series and World Series in 2014.

Generous Providers

By the end of the 2015 season, the payroll of the Los Angeles Dodgers reached a record $310 million.

Old Alex

Immediately after returning from a year-long suspension for violating baseball drug rules, Alex Rodriguez hit 33 home runs in 151 games and became the 29th player with 3000 hits. He also reached 2000 RBI and 2000 runs scored.

Hamilton on Hold

Josh Hamilton, suspended for three full seasons before reaching the majors with the 2007 Reds, admitted to a drug relapse before 2015 spring training. The Angels traded him back to the Rangers, for whom he had starred in 2008, and included $77 million in the deal to defray his salary. Hamilton, the 2010 American League MVP, agreed to be tested for drugs and alcohol five days a week.

Ramos learned that at Tampa Bay on June 16, 2015, when he became the only man in baseball history to hit two home runs against non-pitchers in the same game.

When strong-armed outfielder Jeff Francoeur took the mound in a mop-up relief role for the Philadelphia Phillies during a game in 2015, he threw 48 pitches—22 more than starter Jerome Williams.

Madison Bumgarner, a regular on the mound, also proved adept at the plate. One of the five home runs he hit in 2015 came against Dodgers ace Clayton Kershaw.

After years of futility, the Chicago Cubs rode the bat of Kris Bryant and the arm of Jake Arrieta into the postseason. Another heavy-hitting pitcher, Arrieta posted a record 0.75 earned run average from the All-Star Game to the end of the season en route to 22 wins, topping both leagues. During his last 20 starts of 2015, Arrieta hit as many home runs as he allowed (2) as the Cubs bid for their first World Series berth since 1945. But the Mets, with potent pitching of their own, held the powerful Cubs to eight runs while sweeping the four-game National League Championship Series.

It helped that Daniel Murphy, better known for collecting singles than home runs, became a sudden slugger, connecting in all four games and the first two games of the World Series against the Kansas City Royals. No other player had ever homered in six straight postseason games.

As they did in 1985, the resilient Royals parlayed pitching and speed into an upset victory over a favored opponent. Kansas City won when Lorenzo Cain scored from first base on a single by Eric Hosmer—duplicating the "Mad Dash" of Enos Slaughter in 1946.

New Ideas

Rob Manfred, the lead negotiator for the owners in talks with the players union, succeeded aging commissioner Bud Selig in 2015 and promised to provide a more youthful perspective. One of his early accomplishments was organizing a two-game spring exhibition series for the Tampa Bay Rays in Havana. Among the 55,000 fans who attended were presidents Barack Obama of the United States and Raul Castro of Cuba.

Although a steady stream of Cuban stars had reached the big leagues after defecting from the island dictatorship, no US team had played there since the Baltimore Orioles did so in 1999.

When the 2016 season started, the minimum salary was $507,500—more than twice the highest salary Hank Aaron ever earned. But the average game-time was much longer: just six seconds short of three hours.

Cubs ace Jake Arrieta pitched no-hitters 10 starts apart: on August 30, 2015 against the Dodgers and April 21, 2016 against the Reds. It was a strong start in his bid to retain the National League's Cy Young Award, although three-time winner Clayton Kershaw of the Dodgers gave him strong competition.

In the NL West, Colorado Rockies rookie Trevor Story made the most of his unexpected opportunity when veteran shortstop Jose Reyes received a 59-game suspension for alleged domestic violence.

2015: A Year of Oddities

- Even the best pitcher has a bad day once in awhile: Felix Hernandez allowed 10 runs on August 15, 2015—three years to the day after pitching a perfect game.
- Gordon Beckham won games on Mother's Day and Father's Day 2015 with walk-off hits—the only ones he got in the 100 games he played that season.
- Five of the first seven hits recorded by 2015 Royals rookie Paulo Orlando, a fleet Brazilian whose playing time was limited, were triples.
- In his first year with the Houston Astros, Evan Gattis hit 11 triples but never stole a base—a pro-and-con statistic that had not occurred in 75 years of major-league play.
- In August, the Dodgers had to pay a $40 million payroll tax for players no longer with the organization.
- On September 19, Detroit second baseman Ian Kinsler scored the winning run twice in one game! The run he scored in the ninth inning was nixed after a video review. Given another chance, he hit a home run in the bottom of the 11th.
- En route to 3,000 career hits, outfielder Ichiro Suzuki pitched the ninth inning for the Miami Marlins against the Philadelphia Phillies on October 4, 2015. He allowed two hits and one run as the Phillies won, 7–2.
- Houston southpaw Dallas Keuchel finished the year 15-0 in 18 starts at Minute Maid Park, making him the first pitcher with at least 14 wins to go undefeated at home in a single season.
- The string of strong pitching even extended to the contenders; the 2015 NLDS playoff opponents, the New York Mets and Los Angeles Dodgers, were no-hit twice during the regular season.
- San Francisco's success at winning world titles in three straight even-numbered years stymied forecasters at the start of the 2015 campaign. Both the New York Mets and Chicago Cubs combined pitching plus power to dominate the National League for most of the season.

Story hit six spring training home runs plus six more *in his first four major league games*. In April alone, he hit 10, a record for a National League rookie, and had twice as many before the All-Star Game. But he was not voted into the starting lineup because overzealous Cubs fans elected their team's entire infield.

Mets fans got a surprise when rotund right-hander Bartolo Colon, just short of his 43rd birthday, became the oldest player to hit his first home run.

New York's top rivals in the NL East, the Washington Nationals, brought veteran manager Dusty Baker out of retirement, snatched Daniel Murphy from the Mets via free agency, and got powerful performances from the pitching tandem of Max Scherzer and Stephen Strasburg.

After pitching a pair of no-hitters for the Nats in 2015, Scherzer crafted a 20-strikeout game on May 11 against the Detroit Tigers, with whom he had started his career. Strasburg started the season with a 13-0 record during the first half while Murphy led the league in hitting. Bryce Harper, the league's most dangerous hitter, drew six walks in one game, duplicating a feat done previously by Jimmie Foxx (1938), Andre Thornton (1984), and Jeff Bagwell (1999).

Harper and Mike Trout were often compared in an unending debate over the game's best player. The Angels outfielder, with more experience, went into 2016 with consecutive MVP awards in the All-Star Game, something no one else had ever done, and first or second spots in the league MVP voting in all four of his previous seasons.

Giancarlo Stanton, another young slugger, also punished opponents with persistent power. His 13-year, $325 million Marlins contract was the largest in the history of professional sports.

Navajo Heritage

Jacoby Ellsbury, a 2007 Red Sox World Series hero who later played for the Yankees, was the first Navajo Indian in the major leagues.

Fleet Sluggers

The father-and-son tandem of Bobby and Barry Bonds were 30/30 men five different times. The only other man to do it at least four times was Alfonso Soriano.

Bondsfolds

Fans convinced that steroids helped Barry Bonds break Hank Aaron's career home run record during the 2007 season set up a website called Boycottbarry.com. They also passed out Bondsfolds—blindfolds for fans who didn't want to watch Barry bat.

Hitless and Wondering

When Jered Weaver and Jose Arredondo no-hit the Dodgers for the Angels on June 28, 2008, their team still lost, 1–0. Since the advent of the modern era in 1900, only four other teams won a game without a hit.

Video vs. Venom

The advent of video replays in the 21st century effectively ended on-the-field arguments between managers and umpires. "Arguing is something you used to work on," lamented Baltimore manager Buck Showalter. "It's a skill set that is slowly being phased out." Before he went to work for the commissioner's office, Joe Torre agreed: "Sometimes you're out there for the sake of the *next* call."

Seattle Strategy

During his first year as manager of the Seattle Mariners in 2016, Scott Servais told writers why he seldom deployed bunt plays. "I'm not a big fan of the sacrifice bunt," he said. "I don't really think it increases your odds (of scoring) when you're giving up an out. Outs are precious."

Timely Gesture

Attempting to speed up the pace of games in 2015, MLB installed clocks on outfield scoreboards and behind home plate. Any breaks counted down from 2:25 for local games and to 2:45 for nationally televised games. Pitchers had to complete their warmup pitches before :30 remained on the clock.

Stupid Injury

White Sox catcher Toby Hall missed playing time in 2008 after injuring his shoulder while trying to hit teammate Jermaine Dye in the face with a shaving-cream pie.

Awful Ending

Just hours after pitching six scoreless innings in his first start, Angels rookie Nick Adenhart was killed in a car crash on April 9, 2009.

Strange Bedfellows

David Ross hit his first home run against a first baseman—Mark Grace was mopping up for the Arizona Diamondbacks in a 19–1 loss.

Home runs flew in 2016, with several clubs getting more than half their runs by batting balls over fences with more regularity than Old Faithful. Entering the season, however, only the 2010 Toronto Blue Jays had scored more than half their runs with home runs.

On the other hand, a power vacuum buried the Atlanta Braves into the basement of the National League East basement. After winning a record 14 straight division crowns from 1991 to 2005, the once-invincible Braves found themselves unable to reap the fruits of their farm system and decided to rebuild by trading veterans for prospects. Among those dealt during a two-year span were Evan Gattis, Jason Grilli, Jason Heyward, Chris Johnson, Kelly Johnson, Craig Kimbrel, Cameron Maybin, Shelby Miller, Bud Norris, Andrelton Simmons, Justin Upton, Melvin Upton Jr., and Alex Wood.

In their final season at Turner Field in 2016, the Braves lost 16 of their first 17—the worst home start since the 1913 Yankees lost their first 17 home games.

The Braves still attracted national attention on July 3 when they hosted the Miami Marlins at Fort Bragg, where a 12,500-seat stadium was specially built for the patriotic holiday celebration. It was the first time any professional sport played a game on a military installation.

Baseball's language barrier finally fell in 2016, when the commissioner's office required all 30 teams to hire Spanish-speaking translators for players.

Ironically, Havana native Fredi Gonzalez was fired as Atlanta manager a few months later.

Although executives are rarely suspended, San Diego Padres general manager A.J. Preller proved an exception during the last month of the 2016 season. He received a 30-day ban without pay from Major League Baseball for his handling of player medical records. The primary complaint against Preller was lodged by the Boston Red Sox after the Padres peddled pitcher Drew Pomeranz to Boston in July.

Dan Schlossberg

The 19-year tenure of Turner Field as home of the Atlanta Braves ended on Oct. 2, 2016, the last day of the season. Named for former owner Ted Turner, the television magnate who owned the team for 20 years, the ballpark opened for the Olympics in 1996 and for baseball the following spring.

Walk in the Park

Mets history includes more stadiums than world championships.

Baseball Hacker

The age of the Internet opened a Pandora's Box. Chris Correa was sentenced to 46 months in prison and ordered to pay $279,037 in restitution for hacking into a Houston Astros personnel database in 2004 while he was scouting director for the St. Louis Cardinals.

Hefty Fine

Yankees closer Aroldis Chapman lost $1,856,557 when he was suspended for 30 days in 2016 after violating baseball's domestic violence policy. The first man penalized under the new rule, he was not the last. Jose Reyes lost $6.25 million of his $22 million salary during his 59-game suspension.

Good Coaching

Stephen Strasburg's college coach at San Diego State was Hall of Famer Tony Gwynn.

Way to Win

The Atlanta Braves won their 14 straight division titles by an aggregate 116½ games.

Birds of a Feather

Bird brains: during the 2006 season, Kansas City's Paul Byrd pursued Doug Bird's club record for most innings pitched without a walk. He chirped about it for weeks.

Roger That

When 44-year-old Roger Clemens started for the Yankees on Old-Timers' Day at Yankee Stadium in 2007, he was older than five of the old-timers.

Tough Name

The Cincinnati Reds actually had a pitcher named Homer Bailey. It wasn't a nickname.

Beating the Shift

Shifting the infielders to defend against opposing hitters does not necessarily help. In the 2015 Red Sox home opener, Mookie Betts took advantage of Nationals fielders by stealing second and third on the same pitch. Washington protested safe calls at both bases but was overruled twice.

Triple Trouble

The Minnesota Twins once got three triples in an inning but scored only one run. Shane Robinson, author of the second triple, got picked off third in the June 14, 2015 game in Texas.

Clayton the K

Clayton Kershaw's no-hitter against the Rockies at Dodger Stadium was the first with no walks and at least 15 strikeouts.

Little Big Man

Height was never a handicap for Jose Altuve. At age 16, the future batting champion was sent home from an Astros tryout camp in the Dominican because scouts thought he had lied about his age. A day later, he returned with his birth certificate, got a trial, and signed a contract.

Whiff Master

A.J. Burnett was the only man to pitch 12-strikeout games for five different teams.

Giant Gesture

A plaque in the home dugout of the San Francisco Giants at AT&T Park honors the memory of Alexis Busch, the first full-time bat girl in the major leagues. A lifelong baseball enthusiast who played baseball in California and Australia, she also earned a degree from the University of San Francisco's Graduate School of Sports Management. An active athlete, Alex was 27 when she and four others drowned when large waves swamped their vessel during a 2012 yacht race. The plaque was placed next to the bat rack in the dugout on August 14, 2016.

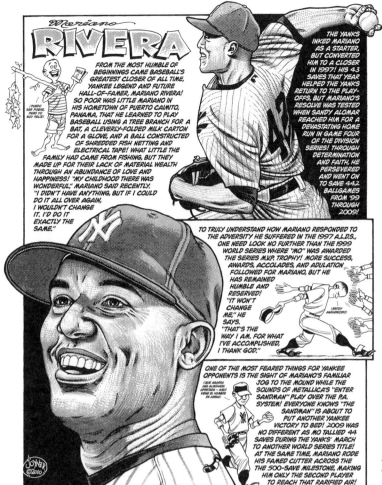

Mariano Rivera saved more games than any closer in baseball history. The Panamanian right-hander, who spent his entire career with the New York Yankees, was instrumental in five of the team's world championships.

Epilogue

2016: A Year to Remember

In baseball, the only sure thing is that there is no sure thing. Never was that statement more apropos than in 2016, a year marked by the advent of new champions but the departure of old heroes.

The Chicago Cubs not only won their first World Series since 1908, beating the Cleveland Indians, but overcame a deficit of three games to one. It wasn't easy, with a rain-interrupted Game 7 requiring 10 innings before Chicago prevailed, 8-7. Ben Zobrist, signed as a free agent after playing for the World Champion Kansas City Royals in 2015, was named World Series MVP after hitting the game-winning double.

Cleveland pitchers combined for a record five shutouts during the playoffs, including two against the Cubs early in the Series, but could not short-circuit Chicago's power, which produced eight home runs in the final four games of the best-of-seven series.

Even before the postseason started, the game produced plenty of individual heroes.

David Ortiz, the 40-year-old designated hitter of the Boston Red Sox, enjoyed the finest farewell season in baseball history, sharing the American League's regular-season RBI title with Toronto's Edwin Encarnacion while joining Hank Aaron and Barry Bonds as the only players ever to produce 500 home runs and 600 doubles.

Prince Fielder was one of several sluggers who retired after the 2016 season.

Turner's Last Stand

Atlanta's Julio Teheran out-dueled Detroit's Justin Verlander, 1–0, in the last game at Turner Field on October 2, 2016.

Chicago Laugher

When Cubs pitcher Jake Arrieta threw a no-hitter against the Reds on April 21, 2016, the 16–0 score represented the most runs ever scored in a hitless game.

Baltimore Bombers

Baltimore batters hammered a record four home runs before the first out of a game against the Houston Astros on August 19, 2016.

Last Hurrah

When the 2016 season ended for the Philadelphia Phillies, the only player remaining from their 2008 world championship team was first baseman Ryan Howard.

Rocky Mountain High

Colorado third baseman Nolan Arenado pushed his way into 2016 MVP consideration by leading the majors with 133 runs batted in and tying Chris Carter for the NL home run crown with 41.

Remember Me?

In his first year with the Washington Nationals after leaving the New York Mets via free agency, Daniel Murphy hit .413 with seven home runs and 21 RBI against his old club. Murphy, the runner-up for the National League's batting crown, had 31 hits in 75 at-bats.

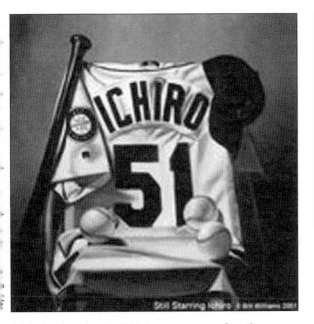

After beginning the 2016 season as a fourth outfielder with the Marlins, Ichiro Suzuki proved advancing athletic age was no handicap. He hit .291 and became the 30th man with 3,000 hits.

Ortiz led both leagues in doubles, extra-base hits, slugging percentage, and OPS (on-base plus slugging) during the 2016 regular season.

Fellow sluggers Prince Fielder, Adam LaRoche, Alex Rodriguez, and Mark Teixeira also retired, for various reasons. LaRoche resented a Chicago White Sox ban on bringing his 14-year-old son into the clubhouse, while Fielder suffered a neck injury that forced him into retirement August 10. The Fielders remain the only father-and-son team with separate 50-homer seasons.

Two days after Prince abdicated, A-Rod left the 25-man roster of the suddenly youth-oriented New York Yankees with 696 home runs—four short of joining Babe Ruth, Hank Aaron, and Barry Bonds in the 700 club. Like Ortiz, he was 40 years old.

The switch-hitting Teixeira, who lasted until the end of the season, had a last hurrah with a ninth-inning Yankee Stadium grand slam that beat the Boston Red Sox just days before the season ended. Plagued by bad knees, he finished his career with 409 home runs.

Also in 2016, two venerable broadcasters hung up their headsets. Dick Enberg walked away from the San Diego Padres while Vin Scully, Voice of the Dodgers since 1950, left the Los Angeles booth at age 89.

On the field, one player proved age to be a matter of mind: if you don't mind, it doesn't matter.

In a year when injuries felled most members of the Mets' rotation, the seemingly ageless New York Mets pitcher Bartolo Colon led the team in victories (15) and innings pitched (191 2/3).

San Francisco shortstop Brandon Crawford tied a National League mark with seven hits in a game on August 8, five weeks after Chicago Cubs slugger Kris Bryant intensified his claim on the league's MVP award with three home runs and two doubles in one game. He was the first man to perform that feat in modern major league history.

Although the Los Angeles Angels suffered through a season sabotaged by injuries, Albert Pujols produced his 14th 30-homer season, joining Hank Aaron, Barry Bonds, and Alex Rodriguez.

As a team, the Baltimore Orioles belted 253 home runs—28 more than any other club—and had the league's most prolific slugger for the third straight year. Mark Trumbo had 47, plus another in the wild-card playoff game the O's lost to the Toronto Blue Jays. Both the Orioles and Jays feathered their nests with power, producing a half-dozen players each with at least 20 home runs.

In a wild finish to the regular season, both leagues mulled the scheduling nightmare that might have been produced by ties in the wild-card races.

Never has baseball experienced any three-way tie, but that possibility existed in both leagues as the final weekend opened. The American League race was so close, in fact, that the Jays, Orioles, Tigers, and Mariners might have finished in a four-way deadlock

Oriole Park at Camden Yards again proved to be a bandbox in 2016. Baltimore belted 253 home runs, easily the most in the majors, and produced its third different home run king in as many years.

Youth Is Served

When he saved 47 games for the 2016 Toronto Blue Jays, Roberto Osuna became the first pitcher under age 22 to record that many.

Record Whitewash

The 15–0 Dodgers win over the Padres on 2016 Opening Day was the most lopsided first-day shutout in baseball history. San Diego suffered two more consecutive shutouts, thus becoming the first team to be blanked in its first three games.

Chris the Ripper

Star White Sox pitcher Chris Sale was suspended five games by his own team after cutting up throwback uniforms he didn't like. The lefty had a 14-3 record at the top of the suspension in July but went 3-7 over the final two months of the 2016 season.

Short But Sweet

Houston second baseman Jose Altuve, at 5'6" the shortest player in the American League during the 2016 campaign, had the most hits in the AL (216) for the third straight year, plus the league's best batting average (.338) for the second time in three seasons.

Starter Dahl

Colorado outfielder David Dahl tied a major league record in 2016 by beginning his career with a 17-game hitting streak.

Stingy Starter

Although he finished the 2016 campaign with an ordinary 9-9 record, Toronto pitcher Marco Estrada allowed five or fewer hits in 11 straight starts—a major league record.

Ragged Relievers

The Cincinnati relief corps allowed at least one run in 23 straight games, a record for futility, in 2016.

Bill Menzel

Noah Syndergaard matched zeroes with Madison Bumgarner in the NL wild-card game, but the Giants won in the ninth inning against Mets relief ace Jeurys Familia.

until a Seattle loss on the next-to-last day of the season silenced that scenario.

Baltimore and Toronto finished 89-73, setting up a wild-card showdown north of the border, while Detroit was 86-75 (a rainout was not rescheduled) and Seattle 86-76.

At the same time, in the National League wild-card race, three teams tangled for two spots, with the Giants, Mets, and Cardinals all alive entering the last day. San Francisco and New York finished with identical 87-75 records, leaving St. Louis out in the cold with an 86-76 mark.

This came about after the late-rushing New York Mets stood 60-62 in mid-August before winning 27 of their last 40.

As a result, the Mets and Giants played each other in a pitching duel that will live in postseason lore. Mets starter Noah Syndergaard, a flame-throwing right-hander completing his first full season, fired seven scoreless innings, yielding only two hits, but San Francisco southpaw Madison Bumgarner, MVP of the 2014 World Series, went the distance on a four-hitter to fashion a 3–0 victory.

The scoreless battle ended in the ninth when Mets closer Jeurys Familia, whose 51 regular-season saves had led the major leagues, yielded two walks and an unlikely home run from backup infielder Conor Gillaspie.

After the game, Syndergaard sent out a Tweet that said, "Baseball has a way of ripping your (heart) out, stabbing it, putting it back in your chest, then healing itself just in time for Spring Training."

The Texas Rangers could relate; after leading the American League with a 95-67 record and winning their second straight AL West title, they lost the Division Series to Toronto for the second year in a row. A cold September by star southpaw Cole Hamels carried over into Game 1 and the Rangers—who thrived all year on late comebacks—never recovered.

Toronto parlayed power and pitching into a path that pointed to the team's first World Series since 1993. Thanks to 20-game winner J.A. Happ and ERA king Aaron Sanchez, the Jays led the league with a 3.78 earned run average. They also got timely home runs from prospective free agents Edwin Encarnacion and Jose Bautista.

Arguably the biggest surprise in the playoff picture was the performance of the Cleveland Indians. En route to their first division title since 2007, the Tribe led the league with 132 stolen bases and an 81 percent success ratio but stood just 17th in home runs. Although they ranked second in runs scored by an American League team, they faced a Division Series opponent with 101 more. Add the fact that two starting pitchers suffered untimely September injuries and an Indians massacre looked likely.

But Cleveland manager Terry Francona, a two-time world champion when he managed the Red Sox, relied on a strong defense and a stingy relief corps headed by Cody Allen and Andrew Miller, a tall left-hander acquired from the Yankees at the trade deadline.

The latter appeared in all four Indians wins over the Blue Jays in the AL Championship Series, retiring 23 of the 25 men he faced and fanning 14 of them. The almost-untouchable Miller, who yielded a hit and a walk but no runs, was named Most Valuable Player of the five-game series.

The battle against Boston was even easier for the Tribe, which won all but one of its playoff games before winning its sixth pennant and reaching the World Series for the first time since 1997. At one point, Cleveland won nine games in a row, six of them in the postseason. The team began by turning the tables on Boston sinkerballer Rick Porcello, a 22-game winner who couldn't sink his sinker.

The Sox unraveled early, losing the first two games in Cleveland when their Killer Bees lost their sting. MVP candidates Mookie Betts and Jackie Bradley Jr., along with Xander Bogaerts and rookie Andrew Benintendi, didn't seem the same once the postseason opened.

Rabid Red Sox rooters, on a roller-coaster ride for four years, watched their team rebound from consecutive last-place finishes to the top of the AL East standings—matching the worst-to-first season of 2013 that ended in a world championship. Thanks to newcomers David Price and Craig Kimbrel, the Bosox became the first team to go from last place to first place twice.

But the team tended to be streaky, winning 11 straight in September before dropping five of six against the Jays and Yankees and three straight to Francona's Indians in the Division Series.

Like the Red Sox, the Orioles had a habit of out-hitting their opponents. Plagued by porous starting pitching, Baltimore manager Buck Showalter banked on a bullpen anchored by Zach Britton. A failed starter, Britton blossomed into a Cy Young candidate by going 47-for-47 in save opportunities and posting a 0.54 earned run average in 69 games. He also had more strikeouts than innings pitched.

But he sat in the bullpen, uncalled, when the tied wild-card game at Toronto went into extra innings. With starter Ubaldo Jimenez on the mound, Bautista delivered a walkoff three-run homer, capping a 5–2 victory.

Most experts insisted the best team in baseball was the Chicago Cubs. It not only won 103 games, most in the majors, but finished 17 games ahead of the St. Louis Cardinals, defending champions of the NL Central. The Cubs clinched the title September 15 with 17 games left to play, reducing the rest of their season to a tune-up for the playoffs.

A potent mix of offense, pitching, and defense, the Cubs had nine hitters reach double digits in home runs and two pitchers finish first and second in the major leagues in earned run average. The team led both leagues with a 3.15 ERA, ranked third in the majors with 808 runs scored, and placed fifth in home runs within the National League. Chicago allowed 3.43 runs per game but scored an average of 4.99, both among the best in the game.

Kyle Hendricks (2.13) and Jon Lester (2.44) were the ERA leaders, while trade deadline arrival Aroldis Chapman cemented the bullpen, yielding three runs in 34 innings before the playoffs. Jake Arrieta, who had won 22 games and the Cy Young Award one year earlier, showed some mortality during the second half but made a mark with his second no-hitter early in the season. He capped his campaign with a three-run homer against postseason superstar Madison Bumgarner in Game 3 of the NL Division Series.

Even the left-right punch of Bumgarner and Johnny Cueto couldn't keep San Francisco from finishing 12 games under .500 after the All-Star Game—after posting the best record in baseball over the first half.

San Francisco went into the postseason seeking its fourth consecutive world championship in an even-numbered year. Although Giants hitters were the toughest to fan in the major leagues, their relief pitchers required federal aid far too frequently. The bullpen blew 29 save opportunities, contributing to the .379 "winning" percentage the team compiled over its last 66 games.

The bullpen even blew a two-run, ninth-inning lead in the third game of the NL Division Series against the Cubs. Playing at home, San Francisco eventually won a nail-biter, 7–6 in 13 innings.

The Los Angeles Dodgers, on the other hand, had the best bullpen ERA in the league. That made rookie manager Dave Roberts look like a genius because 28 players—many of them pitchers—spent time on the disabled list in 2016. Clayton Kershaw, the league leader in earned run average four times, missed several months with a bad back, but the ballclub still finished four games ahead of San Francisco in the NL West.

One reason was the arrival of slugging shortstop Corey Seager, who bid to become the first National Leaguer to win Rookie of the Year and Most Valuable Player honors in the same season. Although the team struggled against left-handed pitching, hitting a league-worst .215, the Dodgers won their fourth straight divisional title—a club record—and sixth in nine years. But a trip to the World Series, which Los Angeles last reached in 1988, remained elusive.

The Washington Nationals, runaway winners in the NL East, went into the Division Series against the Dodgers without two of their best players, catcher Wilson Ramos (knee) and starting pitcher Stephen Strasburg (elbow). Even with 2015 MVP Bryce Harper underachieving, the Nats made maximum mileage from free agent signee Daniel Murphy—whose .347 mark fell a point shy of batting leader DJ LeMahieu—and Trea Turner, who hit .342 with 33 stolen bases and 13 home runs while playing both infield and outfield positions for new manager Dusty Baker, a three-time NL Manager of the Year amazingly unemployed for the two previous seasons.

It helped that Max Scherzer led the National League with 20 wins, 284 strikeouts, and 228 1/3 innings pitched. He also became the fourth pitcher to fan 20 men in a nine-inning game.

Although Scherzer's season made him the top contender for the National League's Cy Young Award, he couldn't add a World Series ring. One of two teams (along with the Seattle Mariners) never to reach the Fall Classic, the Nationals have yet to win a postseason series. Though heavily favored to defeat the Dodgers, they lost the Division Series in five games.

The Cubs, who needed just four to send San Francisco back to the West Coast for the winter, suffered consecutive shutouts against Dodger pitching in the NLCS but scored 10 runs in Game 4 as they sought their first pennant since 1945, the longest drought of any of the original 16 teams.

Several powerful playoff teams from the previous season didn't come close in 2016. The St. Louis Cardinals, seeking their sixth straight postseason appearance and fourth consecutive NL Central crown, led the National League with 225 home runs but went home for the winter at the end of the 162-game schedule. The Pittsburgh Pirates, paralyzed by the poor play of former MVP Andrew McCutchen, finished with an 11-22 slide that left them five games under .500. And injuries idled the defending world

Guillermo of Jimmy Kimmel Live evokes guffaws from towering Cubs outfielder Jason Heyward before a Championship Series game in Los Angeles.

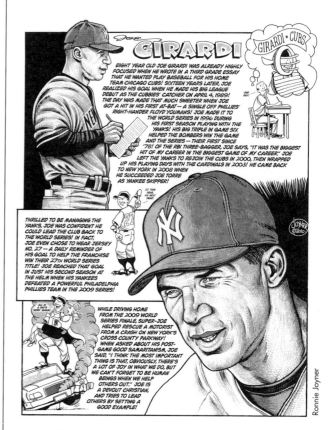

During his 10-season tenure as manager of the Yankees, Joe Girardi reached the postseason six times and won a world championship. Although he pushed a young ballclub within a win of a 2017 World Series berth, Girardi was criticized for lacking communications skills and replaced by the inexperienced Aaron Boone.

New Position

Dodgers closer Kenley Jansen was the catcher for the Netherlands team in the 2009 World Baseball Classic.

Relief Rarity

When he got the last two outs of the final NLDS game for the Dodgers against the Giants, Clayton Kershaw joined Madison Bumgarner and Randy Johnson as the only pitchers to earn a save in the playoffs one or fewer days after a start.

Timely Poke

Proving that playoffs produce unlikely heroes, Cubs catcher Miguel Montero won Game 1 of the NLCS against the Dodgers at Wrigley Field with a two-out, pinch-hit grand-slam on an 0-2 count.

Double Whitewash

Their 6-0 shutout of the Cubs in NLCS Game 3 gave the Dodgers their first back-to-back postseason shutouts in franchise history.

Three for the Record

When Cubs shortstop Addison Russell knocked in six runs during Chicago's 9-3 win over Cleveland in Game 6 of the 2016 World Series, he tied a Series record shared by Bobby Richardson (1960), Hideki Matsui (2009), and Albert Pujols (2011).

Eight Men In

Eight different players—a World Series record for the final game—drove in runs for the Chicago Cubs during their 8-7 Game 7 win over the Cleveland Indians.

Better Late Than Never

Though unable to play defense because of a knee injury that kept him sidelined for the season, Kyle Schwarber of the 2016 Chicago Cubs became the first man ever to get his first hit of the year in the World Series. He hit .412 (7-for-17) as a pinch-hitter and DH.

champion Kansas City Royals, who went 81-81 after two straight AL pennants.

The New York Yankees, defeated by the Houston Astros in the 2015 American League wild-card game, competed for the wild card again but failed to advance to the playoffs. The team did make a conscious effort to get younger, however, when it traded Carlos Beltran, Aroldis Chapman, and Andrew Miller for prospects at the August 1 trade deadline. It also enjoyed the sensational debut of catcher Gary Sanchez, who reached 19 home runs more quickly than any previous player (45 games). Fellow freshmen Aaron Judge and Tyler Austin also became the first teammates to hit their first major league home runs in consecutive at-bats.

The 2016 season will also be remembered by the Cincinnati Reds, whose bullpen yielded a record 103 home runs; the Arizona Diamondbacks, who watched Zack Greinke post a 4.81 home ERA after signing him for $206.6 million; and by the Chicago White Sox, who tied an ignominious mark by hitting seven home runs in a game they lost.

The Cleveland Indians, the visiting team in Toronto on Dominion Day July 1, marked the occasion by wearing Canadian flags on their sleeves. All teams wore red, white, and blue uniforms on July 4. And the Cincinnati Reds let fans know they were halfway to St. Patrick's Day when they donned green uniforms with shamrocks on their sleeves September 18.

Every member of the Miami Marlins wore a uniform emblazoned with the surname and number of star pitcher Jose Fernandez September 26, two days after he and two friends were killed in a nighttime speedboat crash. The 24-year-old Fernandez, one of the most outgoing and popular players in the major leagues, had come to the United States at age 15 after succeeding on his fourth attempt to defect from Cuba.

Among the managers and coaches fired after the season was Barry Bonds, the single-season and career leader in home runs but universally suspected of inflating his production by juicing. Hired by the Marlins as hitting coach, he lasted only one season.

Future seasons could be shorter, perhaps even returning to the original 154-game format, if owners and players agree on compensation for the eight games that would be removed from the schedule. Major League Baseball, also hoping to shorten game times, had earlier enacted rules limiting mound visits to 30 seconds and between-innings breaks to 20. September expansion of rosters to 40 players—many of them pitchers—was also under review by the same study group.

On a lighter note, the FOX television network added *Pitch*, an hour-long drama series about the first female ballplayer, to its regular fall schedule. Cameos by FOX broadcasters were included.

Bibliography

BOOKS

Appel, Marty: *Pinstripe Empire* (Bloomsbury USA, 2014)
Bjarkman, Peter C.: *Cuba's Baseball Defectors ~ The Inside Story* (Rowman & Littlefield, 2016)
Bodley, Hal: *How Baseball Explains America* (Triumph Books, 2014)
Boyle, Timm: *The Most Valuable Players in Baseball* (McFarland, 2003)
Castle, George: *Throwbacks ~ Old School Baseball Players in Today's Game* (Brassey's Inc., 2003)
Chuck, Bill and Kaplan, Jim: *Walkoffs, Last Licks, and Final Outs* (ACTA Sports, 2008)
Cohen, Richard M.; Neft, Davis S.; and Neft, Michael L.: *The Sports Encyclopedia Baseball 2007* (St. Martin's Griffin, 2007)
Decatur, Doug: *Traded ~ Inside the Most Lopsided Trades in Baseball History* (ACTA Sports, 2009)
Dewey, Donald and Acocella, Nicholas: *Total Ballclubs ~ the Ultimate Book of Baseball Teams* (SPORT Media Publishing, 2005)
Krabbenhoft, Herbert O.: *Leadoff Batters of Major League Baseball* (McFarland, 2006)
Kuenster, John: *Heartbreakers ~ Baseball's Most Agonizing Defeats* (Ivan R. Dee, 2001)
Leventhal, Josh, editor: *Baseball America 2015 Almanac* (Baseball America, 2014)
Light, Jonathan Fraser: *The Cultural Encyclopedia of Baseball, 2d ed.* (McFarland & Co., 2005)
Lingo, Will, editor: *Baseball America Almanacs 2007-14* (Baseball America, 2014)
Lingo, Will, editor: *The Baseball Hall of Fame Almanac* (Baseball America, 2016)
Lyons, Douglas: *100 Years of Who's Who in Baseball* (Lyons Press, 2015)
Muller, Donald, editor: *The 86th All-Star Game Media Guide* (Major League Baseball, 2015)
Muller, Donald, editor: *2015 World Series Media Guide* (Major League Baseball, 2015)
Purdy, Dennis: *The Team by Team Encyclopedia of Major League Baseball* (Workman, 2006)
Schlossberg, Dan: *Baseball Bits ~ The Best Stories, Facts, and Trivia from the Dugout to the Outfield* (Alpha Books, 2008)
Schlossberg, Dan: *Baseball Gold ~ Mining Nuggets from Our National Pastime* (Triumph, 2007)
Schlossberg, Dan: *The 300 Club ~ Have We Seen the Last of Baseball's 300-Game Winners?* (Ascend Books, 2010)
Schlossberg, Dan: *When the Braves Ruled the Diamond ~ Fourteen Flags Over Atlanta* (Sports Publishing, 2016)
Stark, Jason: *Wild Pitches ~ Rumblings, Grumblings, and Reflections on the Game I Love* (Triumph, 2014)
Weiss, Peter: *Longshots ~ The Most Unlikely Championship Teams in Baseball History* (Bob Adams, 1992)
Wendel, Tim: *Down to the Last Pitch: How the 1991 Minnesota Twins and Atlanta Braves Gave Us the Best World Series of All Time* (Da Capo, 2014)
Westcott, Rich: *Great Stuff ~ Baseball's Most Amazing Pitching Feats* (Sports Publishing, 2014)

BROADCASTS

BRAVES BANTER [iTunes and BlogTalkRadio.com]

PERIODICALS

The Baseball Bulletin
The New York News
The New York Post
The New York Times
The Sporting News
Sports Illustrated
USA TODAY Sports Weekly
USA TODAY

WEBSITES

Baseball-Almanac.com
Baseball-Reference.com
MLB.com
SABR.org

Index